Econometric Modeling and Inference

The goal of this book is to present the main statistical tools of econometrics, focusing specifically on modern econometric methodology. The authors unify the approach by using a small number of estimation techniques, mainly generalized method of moments (GMM) estimation and kernel smoothing. The choice of GMM is explained by its relevance in structural econometrics and its prominent position in econometrics overall. The book is in four parts. Part I explains general methods. Part II studies statistical models that are best suited for microeconomic data. Part III deals with dynamic models that are designed for macroeconomic and financial applications. In Part IV the authors synthesize a set of problems that are specific to statistical methods in structural econometrics, namely identification and over-identification, simultaneity, and unobservability. Many theoretical examples illustrate the discussion and can be treated as application exercises. Nobel Laureate James J. Heckman offers a foreword to the work.

Jean-Pierre Florens is Professor of Mathematics at the University of Toulouse I, where he holds the Chair in Statistics and Econometrics, and a senior member of the Institut Universitaire de France. He is also a member of the IDEI and GREMAQ research groups. Professor Florens's research interests include statistics and econometrics methods, applied econometrics, and applied statistics. He is coauthor of *Elements of Bayesian Statistics* with Michel Mouchart and Jean-Marie Rolin (1990). The editor or co-editor of several econometrics and statistics books, he has also published numerous articles in major econometric journals, such as *Econometrica*, *Journal of Econometrics*, and *Econometric Theory*.

Vêlayoudom Marimoutou is Professor of Economics at the University of Aix-Marseille 2 and a member of GREQAM. His research fields include time series analysis, non-stationary processes, long-range dependence, and applied econometrics of exchange rates, finance, macroeconometrics, convergence, and international trade. His articles have appeared in publications such as the *Journal of International Money and Finance*, *Oxford Bulletin of Economics and Statistics*, and the *Journal of Applied Probability*.

Anne Péguin-Feissolle is Research Director of the National Center of Scientific Research (CNRS) and a member of GREQAM. She conducts research on econometric modeling, especially nonlinear econometrics, applications to macroeconomics, finance, spatial economics, artificial neural network modeling, and long memory problems. Doctor Péguin-Feissolle's published research has appeared in *Economics Letters*, *Economic Modelling*, *European Economic Review*, *Applied Economics*, and the *Annales d'Economie et de Statistique*, among other publications.

Themes in Modern Econometrics

Managing editor

PETER C. B. PHILLIPS, *Yale University*

Series editors

ERIC GHYSELS, *University of North Carolina, Chapel Hill*
RICHARD J. SMITH, *University of Warwick*

Themes in Modern Econometrics is designed to service the large and growing need for explicit teaching tools in econometrics. It will provide an organized sequence of textbooks in econometrics aimed squarely at the student population, and will be the first series in the discipline to have this as its express aim. Written at a level accessible to students with an introductory course in econometrics behind them, each book will address topics or themes that students and researchers encounter daily. While each book will be designed to stand alone as an authoritative survey in its own right, the distinct emphasis throughout will be on pedagogic excellence.

Titles in series

Statistics and Econometric Models: Volumes 1 and 2
CHRISTIAN GOURIÉROUX *and* ALAIN MONFORT
Translated by QUANG VUONG

Time Series and Dynamic Models
CHRISTIAN GOURIÉROUX *and* ALAIN MONFORT
Translated and edited by GIAMPIERO GALLO

Unit Roots, Cointegration, and Structural Change
G.S. MADDALA *and* IN-MOO KIM

Generalized Method of Moments Estimation
Edited by LÁSZLÓ MÁTYÁS

Nonparametric Econometrics
ADRIAN PAGAN *and* AMAN ULLAH

Econometrics of Qualitative Dependent Variables
CHRISTIAN GOURIÉROUX
Translated by PAUL B. KLASSEN

The Econometric Analysis of Seasonal Time Series
ERIC GHYSELS *and* DENISE R. OSBORN

Semiparametric Regression for the Applied Econometrician
ADONIS YATCHEW

Applied Time Series Econometrics
HELMUT LÜTKEPOHL *and* MARKUS KRÄTZIG

Introduction to the Mathematical and Statistical Foundations of Econometrics
HERMAN J. BIERENS

ECONOMETRIC MODELING AND INFERENCE

JEAN-PIERRE FLORENS
University of Toulouse

VÊLAYOUDOM MARIMOUTOU
GREQAM, University of Aix-Marseille 2

ANNE PÉGUIN-FEISSOLLE
CNRS and GREQAM, France

Translated by Josef Perktold and Marine Carrasco

Foreword by James J. Heckman

CAMBRIDGE
UNIVERSITY PRESS

CAMBRIDGE UNIVERSITY PRESS
Cambridge, New York, Melbourne, Madrid, Cape Town, Singapore, São Paulo, Delhi

Cambridge University Press
32 Avenue of the Americas, New York, NY 10013-2473, USA

www.cambridge.org
Information on this title: www.cambridge.org/9780521876407

First published 2007

Printed in the United States of America

A catalog record for this publication is available from the British Library.

Library of Congress Cataloging in Publication Data

Florens, J. P.
[Économétrie, English]
Econometric modeling and inference = Économétrie : modélisation et
inférence / Jean-Pierre Florens, Vêlayoudom Marimoutou, Anne
Péguin-Feissolle ; translators, Josef Perktold and Marine Carrasco.
    p.   cm.
Includes bibliographical references and index.
ISBN-13: 978-0-521-87640-7 (hardback)
ISBN-10: 0-521-87640-0 (hardback)
ISBN-13: 978-0-521-70006-1 (pbk.)
ISBN-10: 0-521-70006-X (pbk.)
1. Econometric models.   2. Econometrics.   3. Economics–Mathematical models.
I. Marimoutou, Vêlayoudom, 1957–   II. Péguin-Feissolle, Anne, 1954–   III. Title.
HB141.F5913   2007
330.01'5195–dc22   2006101125

ISBN   978-0-521-87640-7 hardback
ISBN   978-0-521-70006-1 paperback

To Nicole
To Cathy
To Denis

Contents

Contents

IV   Structural Modeling   393

Foreword

Jean-Pierre Florens, Vêlayoudom Marimoutou, and Anne Péguin-Feissolle have done economics a great service by writing this basic contribution to the teaching of econometrics. Econometrics is a major research tool for empirical economics. It unites economics with statistics and extends statistical methods to apply to economic problems and economic data.

Many introductory econometrics textbooks for graduate students have a cookbook quality. They summarize existing knowledge useful for particular problems without laying the foundations for extending existing knowledge. Rules are given without reasons and general principles. Readers who do not know the basic principles have trouble adapting existing knowledge to fit their application.

This book provides an introduction to current econometric knowledge that focuses on teaching the reader foundational statistical principles. It exposits the basic statistical principles underlying modern econometrics. This keeps alive and rejuvenates the tradition of Haavelmo (1944), who, in his Nobel Prize–winning contribution, first synthesized economic statistics with rigorous probability theory. It surveys a large array of econometric models and gives the reader the foundations required to adapt and extend those models to fit their applications. This book is wide ranging in that it covers classical econometric methods associated with linear regression and modern semiparametric cross-section and time series methods. It provides the reader with a useful introduction to a powerful set of tools and a guide to where to go to read the more advanced literature on a variety of topics useful in many fields of economics. Rigorous probability foundations are given and problems of inference and estimation are also discussed.

Readers of this book, be they graduate students or professional economists, will benefit from its depth and range. There is much value in learning modern empirical methods unified by rigorous statistical principles.

James J. Heckman
Nobel Laureate in Economic Science
Chicago, USA
July 2004

Preface

The objective of econometrics is to study economic phenomena using statistical observations. Econometrics formalizes the economic theory in the form of relationships (models) whose unknown elements are determined by the available data. Econometrics quantifies and tests economic theories and makes those theories operational through forecasting or simulation of the impact of political or economic decisions.

Historically, econometricians studied first the macroeconomic relationships between large aggregates that describe economic activity at the national level. They then analyzed individual behaviors of consumers and producers. The domain of application later extended to finance, the study of developing countries, education, game theory, and so on.

The aim of econometric research is to discover regular features within the set of variables generated by mechanisms that involve economic components. Hence, it is by nature an applied field, and an econometrics book should provide reliable information on the values of the essential parameters of the economic laws. Reaching this goal is difficult: social phenomena contain few universal laws and each result is limited by the specific conditions in which the phenomenon occurred. Thus, econometrics is essentially a means for the systematic analysis of economic facts and may then be used for forecasting.

The econometric methodology rests on two elements: first, the economic theory that allows us to select the variables, to define the relevant magnitudes to estimate, and to limit the class of models that may be used; second, the statistical techniques for estimating, testing, and forecasting.

The statistical methods used in econometrics have become more and more diverse. Econometrics is built on the analysis of linear regression by the least squares method, but it has developed a larger range of tools for its usage. Because it poses specific questions, it has required original statistical developments. Econometrics draws its specificity from the nature of economic data. On one hand, it is essentially a nonexperimental field that analyzes facts that are unique, nonreproducible, and where the observation conditions are not controlled by the econometrician. It seeks to extract some stable relationships between variables. On the other hand, econometrics adopts a structural approach based on economic theory. The observed magnitudes are considered as the equilibrium values resulting from the interaction between several phenomena, and the econometrician strives to recover from the observation of these equilibria the elementary behavior that generated them. This approach poses an identification problem and leads the econometrician to take an interest in parameters that are not natural for a statistician but are relevant for economic theory. Another important characteristic of econometrics is the unobservability of some important magnitudes (unobserved heterogeneity of individuals, hidden characteristics of the business cycle), which, if not taken into account, induce a bias in the estimation of the structural parameters.

The goal of this book is to present the main statistical tools of econometrics, while focusing on the specificity of the econometric methodology.

Part I of the book explains general methods. Two chapters describe the basic cross-sectional and dynamic models (Chapters 1 and 2), while the usual parametric statistics and tests are the subject of Chapters 3 and 4. The chosen point of view now dominating in econometrics is that of the Generalized Method of Moments (GMM), whereas maximum likelihood is considered only as a special case of this method. The choice of GMM is explained by its relevance in structural econometrics. Chapter 5 on nonparametric methods and Chapter 6 on simulation methods complete this statistical overview.

Parts II and III consider classes of models. Part II studies statistical models that are best suited for microeconomic data and mainly focuses on the study of the conditional expectation that is defined from a probabilistic point of view in Chapter 7. Then, Chapters 8 and 9 examine the estimation by ordinary and generalized least squares, respectively. Chapter 10 studies the nonparametric regression and Chapter 11 considers the case of partially observed data from a parametric and a nonparametric perspective.

Part III deals with dynamic models that are designed for macroeconomic and financial applications. Chapter 12 examines univariate and multivariate stationary linear models and Chapter 13 covers nonstationarity and cointegration. This part is completed by Chapter 14, on the models involving conditional heteroskedasticity, and Chapter 15, on nonlinear dynamic models including switching regressions.

We tried the difficult exercise of synthesizing in the fourth part a set of problems specific to the statistical approach in structural econometrics. Thus, three chapters deal with identification and overidentification (Chapter 16), simultaneity (Chapter 17), and unobservability (Chapter 18).

This quick overview shows that we have tried to reach the ambitious objective of covering almost all the econometric methodology. However, we tried to unify the approach by choosing a small number of estimation techniques, mainly GMM and kernel smoothing. This choice led us to sacrifice the Bayesian approach, sieves estimator, extreme values, efficiency frontiers, and other methods. Although the bootstrap is mentioned, its place is certainly insufficient in regard to the importance of this method.

This book is not an applied econometrics book, as it contains no economic or even numerical examples. In contrast, many theoretical examples illustrate our discussion and can be considered as application exercises.

The three authors of this text have taught econometrics at the undergraduate and graduate levels for many years, mainly at the French universities of Aix-Marseille, Bordeaux, and Toulouse. Hence, their thanks go first to their students who helped them improve the presentation of this book.

A special thought goes to Louis-André Gérard-Varet and to Jean-Jacques Laffont, whose disappearances are still felt with much sorrow; these exceptional personalities have deeply marked the authors in their scientific approach.

We are also particularly grateful to Marine Carrasco and Josef Perktold; indeed, they not only translated this book into English but also, by their always relevant remarks, largely contributed to correct its multiple errors and thus to improve its quality and readability.

We thank P. C. B. Phillips and E. Ghysels, editors of this series, for encouraging the publication of this book.

In addition, this book owes a lot to our professors, coauthors, and friends, who include F. Aprahamian, O. Armantier, S. Bazen, M. Boutahar, M. Carrasco, C. Cazals, H. Chevrou, S. Darolles, R. Davidson, C. de Peretti, J. Drèze, F. Droesbeke, P. Duchemin, G. Dufrenot, F. Fève, P. Fève, D. Fougère, É. Girardin, C. Gouriéroux, J. Heckman, D. Hendry, M. Ivaldi, J. Johannes, X. Joutard, R. Joyeux, T. Kamionka, A. Kurpiel, F. Laisney, S. Lardic, H.W. Lai Tong, S. Larribeau, C. Levevre, M. Lubrano, S. Luchini, E. Malinvaud, S. Marcy, A. Mathis, C. Maurel, C. Meghir, V. Mignon, M. Mouchart, C. Protopopescu, J. P. Raoult, É. Renault, J. F. Richard, J. M. Rolin, T. Roncalli, S. Scotto, L. Simar, A. F. M. Smith, T. Teräsvirta, N. Touzi, S. Van Bellegem, A. Vanhems, J. Voranger, and P. Werquin.

Of course, it would be totally ungrateful not to thank here, for their permanent encouragement and their patient attention, those who might have rejoiced the most at the completion of this book: Nicole, Clémentine, and Vincent Florens (without forgetting Julien and Hélène); Cathy, Mathieu, Guilhem, and Benoît Marimoutou; and Denis, Adrien, and Grégoire Péguin. Finally, we thank Frédéric Aprahamian, Pierre-Henri Bono, Marie-Hélène Dufour, and Denis Péguin for their priceless help with typing and putting the French version of this work into final form. We thank the Région Provence-Alpes-Côte d'Azur for partly financing the translation of this book.

Part I

Statistical Methods

1. Statistical Models

1.1 Introduction

In this chapter, we review the usual statistical terminology that introduces the fundamental notions of sample, parameters, statistical model, and likelihood function. Our presentation avoids all technical developments of probability theory, which are not strictly necessary in this book. For example, σ-fields (or σ-algebras) are not introduced, nor are measurability conditions. The mathematical rigor of the exposition is necessarily weakened by this choice, but our aim is to focus the interest of the reader on purely statistical concepts.

It is expected that the reader knows the usual concepts of probability as well as the most common probability distributions and we refer to various reference books on this theme in the bibliographic notes.

At the end of this chapter, we emphasize conditional models, whose importance is fundamental in econometrics, and we introduce important concepts such as identification and exogeneity.

1.2 Sample, Parameters, and Sampling Probability Distributions

A *statistical model* is usually defined as a triplet consisting of a sample space, a parametric space and a family of sampling probability distributions.

We denote by x the *realization* of a sample. It is always assumed that x is equal to a finite sequence $(x_i)_{i=1,...,n}$ where n is the sample size and x_i is the ith observation. We limit ourselves to the case where x_i is a vector of m real numbers (possibly integers) belonging to a subset X of $\mathbb{R}^m$. Hence, the *sample space* is $X^n \subset \mathbb{R}^{mn}$. The index i of the observations may have various meanings:

- i may index a set of individuals (households, firms, areas...) observed at a given instant. These data are referred to as *cross-sectional data*.
- i may describe a set of periods. Then, the observations x_i form a *time series* (multidimensional if $m > 1$).

- i may belong to a more complex set and be, for instance, equal to a pair (ℓ, t) where ℓ represents an individual and t an observation time. Then, the observations $x_i = x_{\ell t}$ are double indexed and are called *panel data* or longitudinal data.

As the sample space X^n is always assumed to belong to $\mathbb{R}^{nm}$, it is associated with a Borel field, on which some probability will be defined.

The *parameter space* is denoted as Θ and an element of this space is usually denoted θ. The parameters are unknown elements of the statistical problem, the observations provide information about these elements. Two kinds of statistical models can be defined depending on the dimension of Θ:

- If $\Theta \subset \mathbb{R}^k$ where k is a finite integer, the statistical model is said to be *parametric* or a model with vector parameters.
- If Θ is not finite dimensional but contains a function space, the model is said to be *nonparametric* or a model with functional parameters. In some examples, although Θ is infinite dimensional, there exists a function λ of θ which is finite dimensional. Then, the model is called *semiparametric*.

In the following, a parameter will be an element of Θ, whether the dimension of this space is finite or infinite.

The third building block of a statistical model is the family of *sampling probability distributions*. They will be denoted P_n^θ and therefore, for all $\theta \in \Theta$, P_n^θ is the probability distribution on the sample space X^n. If the model is correctly specified, we assume that the available observations $(x_1, \ldots, x_n)$ are generated by a random process described by one of the sampling probability distributions.

We summarize these concepts in the following definition.

Definition 1.1   *A statistical model $\mathcal{M}_n$ is defined by the triplet*

$$\mathcal{M}_n = \left\{ X^n, \Theta, P_n^\theta \right\}$$

where $X^n \subset \mathbb{R}^{nm}$ is the sample space of dimension n, Θ is a parameter space and P_n^θ is the family of sampling probability distributions.   ∎

We use the notation

$$x | \theta \sim P_n^\theta \tag{1.1}$$

to summarize "x is distributed according to the distribution P_n^θ if the parameter value equals θ". Equivalently, we say that x follows the distribution P_n^θ conditionally on θ. Hence, we incorporate the dependence on a parameter in a probabilistic conditioning (which would necessitate, to be rigorous, regularity assumptions not examined here).

Example 1.1 *(Unidimensional normal model) Suppose that $m = 1$ and $x \in \mathbb{R}^n$. Here, the parameter vector is $\theta = (\mu, \sigma^2) \in \Theta = \mathbb{R} \times (0, +\infty)$. Moreover,*

$$x \mid \mu, \sigma^2 \sim N_n \left(\mu \mathbf{1}_n, \sigma^2 I_n \right)$$

where $\mathbf{1}_n$ is a vector of $\mathbb{R}^n$ whose elements are all equal to 1 and I_n is the identity matrix of size n. The notation N_n represents the multidimensional normal distribution of dimension n, but often we will drop the subscript n. □

Example 1.2 *(Binomial model) Let $m = 1$ and $x \in \mathbb{R}^n$ with $x_i \in \{0, 1\} \subset \mathbb{R}$ for all $i = 1, \ldots, n$. The parameter θ is now an element of $\Theta = [0, 1]$. The probability of a vector x given θ is then:*

$$P_n^\theta (\{x\}) = \prod_{i=1}^n \theta^{x_i} (1 - \theta)^{1-x_i} .$$

It follows from this expression that, if $k = \sum_{i=1}^n x_i$,

$$P_n^\theta (k) = C_n^k \theta^k (1 - \theta)^{n-k} .$$ □

The aim of statistical inference is essentially the acquisition of knowledge on the distribution that generates the data or on the parameter θ that characterizes this distribution. In order to relate these two notions, we suppose that the statistical model is identified. This property is defined below.

Definition 1.2 *The model $\mathcal{M}_n$ is identified if, for any pair of (vectorial or functional) parameters θ_1 and θ_2 of Θ, the equality $P_n^{\theta_1} = P_n^{\theta_2}$ implies $\theta_1 = \theta_2$. In other words, the model is identified if the sampling probability distributions define an injective mapping of the elements of Θ.* ■

We will spend more time on this concept in the sequel, in particular in Chapter 16. Examples 1.1 and 1.2 define two identified models. The following model illustrates the lack of identification.

Example 1.3 *Suppose $m = 1$ and $x \in \mathbb{R}^n$ with $\theta = (\alpha, \beta) \in \mathbb{R}^2 = \Theta$. The sampling probability distributions satisfy*

$$x \mid \theta \sim N_n ((\alpha + \beta) \mathbf{1}_n, I_n) .$$

The model is not identified because $\theta_1 = (\alpha_1, \beta_1)$ and $\theta_2 = (\alpha_2, \beta_2)$ define the same distribution as long as $\alpha_1 + \beta_1 = \alpha_2 + \beta_2$, which does not imply $\theta_1 = \theta_2$. □

Given a realization x of a sample of size n, the econometrician will try to estimate θ, that is, to associate with x a value $\hat{\theta}(x)$ (or $\hat{\theta}_n(x)$) of θ, or to perform hypothesis testing, that is, to answer positively or negatively to the question whether θ belongs to a given subset of Θ. The estimation of θ can then serve to forecast new realizations of the sampling process.

In a stylized way, the statistical model empirically translates an economic theory by maintaining some assumptions through the choice of the family of sampling probability distributions. The observations do not lead to reconsidering the choice of the parameter space; instead they permit us to determine the parameter value. This vision is a bit simplistic because recent procedures have been developed to reject or validate a model as a whole, to choose between models, and to determine a model from observations.

The statistical models described here pertain to so-called *reduced forms*. The economic theory describes the complex behaviors of agents, the equilibrium relationship between these behaviors, and the link between relevant economic measures and the observable measures. It is assumed that this set of relationships is solved in order to describe the law of the data. The last part of this book, in particular Chapters 16 and 17, will detail the essential elements of this construction, whereas the first parts suppose that this task of statistical translation of the economic theory has been done.

The vector x is alternatively called *data*, *observations*, or *sample*. The two last terms refer implicitly to different learning schemes; the first one evokes a process of passive acquisition of data (macroeconomic data), whereas the second one refers to a partial or total control of the data collection procedure (poll, stratified survey, experiments). Again, these distinctions will not be exploited until the last part of this book.

Similarly, we will not discuss the choice of random formalization, which is now standard. The stochastic nature of the way observations are generated can be interpreted in various manners, either as a measurement error or an error resulting from missing variables, for instance. Moreover, the economic theory has recently provided constructions that are random per se (for instance, models describing the solution of games with imperfect information) and which we will discuss in the presentation of structural models.

1.3   Independent and Identically Distributed Models

Independent and identically distributed models (*i.i.d.*) constitute the basic structure of statistical inference. Basically, they describe the arrival of a sequence of observations that are generated by the same probability distribution, independently from each other. These models do not provide a sufficient tool for the econometrician who exploits individual observations (and hence generated by different distributions dependent on the individual characteristics) or time series (and hence generally dependent from one another), but they play a fundamental role in the study of statistical procedures.

Definition 1.3 *The model* $\mathcal{M}_n = \{X^n, \Theta, P_n^\theta\}$ *is i.i.d. if*

    a) *The observations* $x_1, \ldots, x_n$ *are independent in terms of the distribution* P_n^θ *for all* θ *(denoted* $\perp\!\!\!\perp_{i=1}^n x_i | \theta$*).*
    b) *The observations* $x_1, \ldots, x_n$ *have the same distribution denoted* Q^θ*, so that* $P_n^\theta = [Q^\theta]^{\otimes n}$. ∎

Example 1.4 *The model defined in Example 1.1 is i.i.d. and* Q^θ *is the normal distribution with mean* μ *and variance* σ^2*. This example permits us to define a new notation:*

$$\left.\begin{array}{l} \perp\!\!\!\perp_{i-1}^n x_i | \theta \\[4pt] x_i | \theta \sim N\left(\mu, \sigma^2\right) \quad \forall i \\[4pt] \theta = \left(\mu, \sigma^2\right) \end{array}\right\} \iff x_i | \theta \sim i.i.N.\left(\mu, \sigma^2\right).$$

□

Example 1.5 *Example 1.2 is again an i.i.d. model satisfying:*

$$\perp\!\!\!\perp_{i=1}^n x_i | \theta \quad and \quad x_i | \theta \sim B\left(\theta\right) \quad \forall i,$$

where $B\left(\theta\right)$ *denotes the Bernoulli random variable, which equals 1 and 0 with probabilities* θ *and* $(1 - \theta)$ *respectively.* □

Consider now some counterexamples of i.i.d. models.

Example 1.6 *Suppose that* $\theta \in \mathbb{R}^n$ *and* $x_i \in \mathbb{R}$ *with*

$$\perp\!\!\!\perp_{i=1}^n x_i | \theta \quad and \quad x_i | \theta \sim N\left(\theta_i, 1\right).$$

The random variables x_i *are independent but their distributions differ.* □

Example 1.7 *Suppose that* $\lambda = (a, \xi, \sigma^2) \in \mathbb{R}^2 \times \mathbb{R}_*^+$ *and that the sample is i.i.d. conditionally on* λ *such that*

$$\perp\!\!\!\perp_{i=1}^n x_i | \lambda \quad and \quad x_i | \lambda \sim N\left(a + \xi, \sigma^2\right).$$

Now, suppose ξ *is an unobservable random variable generated by a normal distribution with mean 0 and variance 1. Then, the parameter of interest is* $\theta = (a, \sigma^2)$*. We integrate out* ξ *to obtain the distribution of the sample conditional on* θ*. It follows that*

$$x | \theta \sim N\left(a, V\right) \quad with \quad V = \sigma^2 I_n + \mathbf{1}_n \mathbf{1}_n'.$$

Then, the observations x_i have the same marginal distributions but are not independent. Moreover, the distribution of x is not modified if one permutes the order of the x_i. In this case, the distribution is said to be exchangeable.   □

This example, based on the presence of an unobservable variable, will also be detailed in the last part of this book.

An important example of an i.i.d. model is provided by the following nonparametric model.

Example 1.8   *The sample $x = (x_1, \ldots, x_n)$, $x_i \in \mathbb{R}^m$, is i.i.d. and each x_i is generated by an unknown distribution Q. This model is denoted as*

$$\amalg_{i=1}^{n} x_i | Q \quad and \quad x_i | Q \sim Q.$$

Here, the parameter θ is equal to Q. It is a functional parameter belonging to the family $\mathcal{P}_m$ of distributions on $\mathbb{R}^m$. We could modify this example by restricting Q (for example, Q could have zero mean or could satisfy some symmetry condition resulting in zero third moment).   □

1.4   Dominated Models, Likelihood Function

The statistical model $\mathcal{M}_n = \{X^n, \Theta, P_n^\theta\}$ is *dominated* if the sampling probability distributions can be characterized by their density functions with respect to the same dominating measure. In a large number of cases, this dominating measure is Lebesgue measure on X^n (included in $\mathbb{R}^{nm}$) and the dominance property means that there exists a function $\ell(x|\theta)$ such that

$$P_n^\theta(S) = \int_S \ell(x|\theta)dx \quad S \subset X^n.$$

Example 1.9   *Return to Example 1.1. The model is dominated and we have*

$$\ell_n(x|\theta) = (2\pi)^{-\frac{n}{2}} \sigma^{-n} \exp - \frac{1}{2\sigma^2}(x - \mu \mathbf{1}_n)'(x - \mu \mathbf{1}_n).$$ □

The definition of dominance by Lebesgue measure is insufficient because it does not cover in particular the models with discrete sampling space. In such cases, we usually refer to the dominance by the counting measure. If X is discrete (for example $X = \{0, 1\}$), the counting measure associates all sets of X with the number of their elements. A probability distribution on X is characterized by the probability of the points x; these probabilities can be considered as the density function with respect to the counting measure.

Example 1.10 *In Example 1.2, we have*

$$P_n^\theta(\{x\}) = \ell_n(x|\theta) = \prod_{i=1}^{n} \theta^{x_i}(1-\theta)^{1-x_i}.$$ $\square$

Definition 1.4 *A model $\mathcal{M}_n = \{X^n, \Theta, P_n^\theta\}$ is said to be dominated if there exists a measure v on X (independent of θ) such that there exists $\ell(x|\theta)$ satisfying*

$$\forall \theta \in \Theta \quad P_n^\theta(S) = \int_S \ell_n(x|\theta)v(dx).$$ (1.2)

The function ℓ_n of $X \times \Theta$ in $\mathbb{R}^+$ is called density (function) of the observations or likelihood function depending on whether it is considered as a function of x for a fixed θ or as a function of θ for a fixed x. ∎

The dominance property is actually related to the dimension of the statistical model. If the family P_n^θ is finite, that is if Θ is finite in the identified case, the model is always dominated by the probability $\frac{1}{n}\sum_{\theta \in \Theta} P_n^\theta$. This property is not true if Θ is infinite dimensional: the nonparametric model of Example 1.8 is not dominated. A parametric model (in the sense of a finite dimensional Θ) is not always dominated as shown by the following example.

Example 1.11 *Let $n = 1$, $X = [0, 1]$ and $\Theta = [0, 1]$. Let*

$$P_1^\theta = \delta_\theta$$

where δ_θ is the Dirac measure at θ defined by the property

$$\delta_\theta(S) = \begin{vmatrix} 1 & \text{if } \theta \in S \\ 0 & \text{if } \theta \notin S. \end{vmatrix}$$

We also use the notation

$$\delta_\theta(S) = I\!I(\theta \in S),$$

where the function $I\!I(.)$ equals 1 if the condition in parentheses is true and 0 otherwise. This model is not dominated but the proof of this result requires more advanced measure theory than we wish to use here. $\square$

The dominance property is particularly useful in i.i.d. models. Suppose that $\mathcal{M}_n = \{X^n, \Theta, P_n^\theta\}$ is i.i.d. and that each observation is generated by the probability distribution, Q^θ. If Q^θ is dominated and admits a density $f(x_i|\theta)$, the independence and the identity of distributions imply that $\mathcal{M}_n$ is dominated and that the density of the observations can be written as

$$\ell_n(x|\theta) = \prod_{i=1}^{n} f(x_i|\theta). \tag{1.3}$$

The logarithm of the likelihood function plays an important role, it is also called *log-likelihood* and is defined as

$$L_n(x, \theta) = \ln \ell_n(x|\theta). \tag{1.4}$$

In the i.i.d. case, it satisfies the property:

$$L_n(x, \theta) = \sum_{i=1}^{n} \ln f(x_i|\theta). \tag{1.5}$$

Example 1.12 *(Multidimensional normal model) Let* $\theta = (\mu, \Sigma)$ *where* $\mu \in \mathbb{R}^m$ *and* Σ *is a symmetric positive definite matrix of dimension* $m \times m$. *Hence,* $\Theta = \mathbb{R}^m \times \mathcal{C}_m$ *where* $\mathcal{C}_m$ *is the cone of symmetric positive definite matrices of size* $m \times m$. *Moreover,* $X = \mathbb{R}^{nm}$ *and the model is i.i.d. with*

$$x_i|\theta \sim N_n(\mu, \Sigma) \quad x_i \in \mathbb{R}^n.$$

Therefore, the model is dominated. We have

$$\ell_n(x|\theta) = \prod_{i=1}^{n} (2\pi)^{-\frac{m}{2}} |\Sigma|^{-\frac{1}{2}} \exp -\frac{1}{2}(x_i - \mu)'\Sigma^{-1}(x_i - \mu)$$

$$= (2\pi)^{-\frac{nm}{2}} |\Sigma|^{-\frac{n}{2}} \exp -\frac{1}{2} \sum_{i=1}^{n} (x_i - \mu)'\Sigma^{-1}(x_i - \mu). \qquad \square$$

1.5 Marginal and Conditional Models

From a statistical model, one can build other models through the usual operations of probability calculus which are marginalization and conditioning. The concept of a conditional model is particularly fundamental in econometrics and allows us to build a first extension of the i.i.d. model which is too restrictive to model economic phenomena. First, we will derive the conditional model as a byproduct of the joint model, but in practice the conditional model is often directly specified and the underlying joint model is not explicitly defined.

Let $x = (x_i)_{i=1,\dots,n}$ be the sample. It is assumed that, for each observation i, x_i can be partitioned into (y_i, z_i) with respective dimensions p and q (with $p + q = m$). Let us denote $y = (y_i)_{i=1,\dots,n}$ and $z = (z_i)_{i=1,\dots,n}$. Moreover, the space X is factorized into $Y \times Z$ with $y_i \in Y$ and $z_i \in Z$. This splitting of x facilitates the presentation, but in some examples, y_i and z_i are two functions of x_i defining a bijective (one-to-one and onto) mapping between x_i and the pair (y_i, z_i). By a relabelling of x_i, one can get back to the current presentation.

Definition 1.5   *From the model $\mathcal{M}_n = \{X^n, \Theta, P_n^\theta\}$, one obtains:*

- *the marginal model on Z^n, denoted $\mathcal{M}_{nz} = \{Z^n, \Theta, P_{nz}^\theta\}$, with sample space Z^n, parameter space Θ, and sampling probability distribution P_{nz}^θ which is the marginal probability of P_n^θ on Z.*
- *the conditional model given Z, denoted $\mathcal{M}_{ny}^z = \{Y^n \times Z^n, \Theta, P_{ny}^{\theta z}\}$, with sample space $Y^n \times Z^n$, parameter space Θ, but which sampling probability distribution is the conditional distribution of Y^n given $z \in Z^n$.*
  In a dominated model (by Lebesgue measure to simplify) with the density of observations denoted $\ell_n(x|\theta)$, the marginal and conditional models are dominated and their densities satisfy:

$$\begin{cases} \ell_{n\ marg}(z|\theta) & = \int \ell_n(y, z|\theta)dy \\ \ell_{n\ cond}(y|z, \theta) = \frac{\ell_n(y,z|\theta)}{\ell_{n\ marg}(z|\theta)}. \end{cases} \tag{1.6}$$

■

Example 1.13   *Consider an i.i.d. model with sample $x_i \in \mathbb{R}^2$ that satisfies*

$$x_i|\theta \sim i.i.N. \left(\binom{\eta}{\zeta}, \Sigma \right)$$

with

$$\theta = (\eta, \zeta, \Sigma) \quad and \quad \Sigma = \begin{pmatrix} \sigma_{yy} & \sigma_{yz} \\ \sigma_{yz} & \sigma_{zz} \end{pmatrix}.$$

Then, $\theta \in \Theta = \mathbb{R}^2 \times \mathcal{C}_2$. We can decompose this model into a marginal model of Z which remains i.i.d. and satisfies

$$\perp\!\!\!\perp_{i=1}^n z_i|\theta \quad and \quad z_i|\theta \sim N(\zeta, \sigma_{zz})$$

and a conditional model characterized by

$$y_i|z_i, \theta \sim N(\alpha + \beta z_i, \sigma^2)$$

with

$$\beta = \frac{\sigma_{yz}}{\sigma_{zz}}, \quad \alpha = \eta - \frac{\sigma_{yz}}{\sigma_{zz}}\zeta \quad and \quad \sigma^2 = \sigma_{yy} - \frac{\sigma_{yz}^2}{\sigma_{zz}}. \qquad \square$$

This example has the property that the parameter θ of the original model can be decomposed into two functions of θ,

$$\theta_{marg} = (\zeta, \sigma_{zz}) \quad and \quad \theta_{cond} = (\alpha, \beta, \sigma^2),$$

whose values can be assigned independently from each other because the mapping

$$\theta \rightarrow (\theta_{marg}, \theta_{cond})$$

from $\mathbb{R}^2 \times \mathcal{C}_2$ into $(\mathbb{R} \times \mathbb{R}_*^+) \times (\mathbb{R}^2 \times \mathbb{R}_*^+)$ is bijective. Let us introduce, in this slightly abstract setting, a definition of exogeneity which we will extend later to dynamic models.

Definition 1.6   *The decomposition of a statistical model into a marginal model and a conditional model operates a cut if the parameter θ can be transformed in a bijective manner into $(\theta_{marg}, \theta_{cond}) \in \Theta_m \times \Theta_c$ such that:*

* θ_{marg} *and θ_{cond} respectively parametrize the marginal and conditional models,*
* θ_{marg} *and θ_{cond} are variation free, that is, no restriction links the two parameters.*

In such case, the observations z are said to be exogenous for the parameter θ_{cond}.   ∎

Marginal and conditional models are useful for various reasons.

1. A motivation for marginal models is the incomplete observation of a phenomenon. One builds a model relative to the generation of x_i which is relevant with respect to the economic theory, but unfortunately only the function z_i of x_i is available. Let us illustrate this absence of information by a few examples.

    Example 1.14   *Let x_i be the unemployment duration of individual i (measured in days). This duration is observed if it is less than two years (730 days); beyond this point the only available information is that x_i is greater than 730. Hence, the observations are given by*

    $$z_i = \begin{vmatrix} x_i & if \ x_i \leq 730 \\ 730 & if \ x_i > 730 \end{vmatrix}$$

    which can be rewritten as

    $$z_i = x_i \, \mathbb{I}(x_i \leq 730) + 730 \ \mathbb{I}(x_i > 730).$$

    In this case, x_i is said to be (right) censored and we denote

    $$\delta_i = \mathbb{I}(x_i \leq 730)$$

    as the censoring indicator.   □

Example 1.15 *The information is further reduced if we observe only the position of a variable with respect to a threshold. If x_i is the willingness to pay price p for a good by individual i and if we only know whether the individual has bought that good or not, then we observe only*

$$z_i = \begin{vmatrix} 1 & \text{if } x_i \geq p \\ 0 & \text{if } x_i < p \end{vmatrix}$$

or alternatively

$$z_i = I\!I\,(x_i \geq p).$$ □

Example 1.16 *The temporal discretization enters into this framework. Let x_i be the function $x_i(t)$, $t \in [0, T]$, describing in continuous time the stock market price of share i at time t between 0 and T. However, we observe this price at times $0, t_1, t_2, \ldots, t_r = T$ (at the end of each day or month...). In this case, z_i is the vector $(x_i(0), x_i(t_1), \ldots, x_i(t_r))$.* □

Example 1.17 *In a rationed market, x_i may be the vector (O_i, D_i) of supply and demand of a given good in year i but only $z_i = \min(O_i, D_i)$ is observable.* □

Example 1.18 *We often develop individual models describing the arrival process of x_{it}, a set of measures associated with individual i in year t but, because only the macroeconomic information is available, we observe only $z_t = \sum_i x_{it}$. Aggregation problems, which are fundamental in economics, are therefore marginalization problems from a statistical point of view.* □

Example 1.19 *Recent microeconomic models introduce more and more frequently unobservable individual characteristics. The model is written in terms of measures $x_i = (z_i, \zeta_i)$, but when it comes to its statistical treatment, only the marginal model on the observable variable z_i is examined and the variable ζ_i is integrated out.* □

2. Another justification of marginal models stems from the possible complexity of the initial joint model. It happens that the generating model of x_i is complex and nonstandard and we look systematically for functions z_i whose marginal models are more standard. The most frequent example in the econometrics of the past ten years is given by cointegration which will be treated later on. Intuitively, the modeling starts by the analysis of a "nonstandard" vector x_i, because it is nonstationary, and proceeds

to extract stationary linear combinations z_i, whose distributions have a certain temporal stability.

3. The conditional modeling obeys a rationale of limited modeling. We generally consider a large set of variables x_i whose generating process may be complex, and we focus on the distribution of a variable given the others, assuming that the conditional distribution is sufficiently stable (across individuals and through time) to be studied statistically. For example, a model of individual consumption considers besides this variable, household income, prices, as well as socio-demographic characteristics (size of the family, type and localization of the housing, socio-professional category). These last variables result from mechanisms that the economist may not wish to explore. Income and prices can be assumed to be generated from mechanisms that are sufficiently independent from the consumption choice so that they do not need to be explicitly introduced. However, it is important to notice that introducing a variable as a conditioning variable prevents us from analyzing the phenomenon of simultaneous determination and the interdependence of this variable on the conditioned variables.

4. Studying and estimating a model of y_i conditional on z_i enables us to forecast y_j for a given z_j (where j belongs to an index set of future observations) but prevents us from forecasting jointly y_j and z_j.

5. Let us stress that, for any model and any partition of x into y and z, it is always mathematically possible to derive the conditional and marginal models, but it may not be economically meaningful. One needs to examine the reparameterization of these two models and make sure that the new parameters are those that the economist wishes to estimate or whether they allow us to recover the parameters of interest for economic theory.

6. As the usual practice of econometrics consists in specifying conditional models, one must wonder whether this approach of not assuming anything on the conditioning variables is sustainable. It can be sustained only to some extent (for example, study of the conditional properties of estimators in small samples) but some assumptions on the generating process of z_i are needed to analyze the asymptotic properties of the estimators and tests. This will appear clearly in the following chapters. In fact, the conditional model is a joint model for which the conditional distribution is subject to precise assumptions (linearity condition, stability of the variance), whereas the generating process of z_i remains vague (z_i i.i.d. for instance, without assuming a specific distribution). We will see later that when the conditional model is wrong (meaning that the true data-generating process does not belong to the model), then it is necessary, in order to study its behavior, to explore the generating process of z_i.

7. In old-fashioned econometrics, drawn from the experimental sciences, the conditioning variables were considered as nonrandom (this required tedious detours to analyze the asymptotic properties of estimators). Clearly when the explanatory variable of a dynamic model is a trend (equal to 1 for the first year, 2 for the second, 3 for the third, etc.), it is difficult to interpret it as a random variable although these are Dirac random variables degenerated at one point. Except for this special case, all conditioning variables are now assumed to be random even if their distributions are not necessarily simple.

8. The cut assumption defined earlier formalizes the fact that to estimate the parameters of one of the two models (θ_{marg} or θ_{cond}), the specification of the auxiliary model is useless because its parameters are not related to the first ones. We will show in subsequent chapters that the parameters of the marginal and conditional models can be estimated separately under the cut assumption.

We complete these remarks by reviewing some useful factorizations of the likelihood function in i.i.d. models. Consider two ways to decompose the likelihood either as

$$\ell_n(x|\theta) = \ell_n(y, z|\theta)$$
$$= \ell_{n\ marg}(z|\theta)\ell_{n\ cond}(y|z, \theta) \tag{1.7}$$

or

$$\ell_n(x|\theta) = \prod_{i=1}^{n} f(x_i|\theta)$$
$$= \prod_{i=1}^{n} f_{marg}(z_i|\theta) \prod_{i=1}^{n} f_{cond}(y_i|z_i, \theta). \tag{1.8}$$

In the representation (1.7), the factorization operates globally, whereas in (1.8) the decomposition marginal/conditional is applied to each observation. This representation (1.8) is not always possible: we can imagine that the generating process of z_i is i.i.d. but that y_i depends on all the z_i, as in dynamic models, for instance. The representation (1.8) contains implicitly the assumption that y_i depends only on z_i, but not on z_j for j different from i. If, moreover, the cut condition is satisfied, we have

$$\ell_n(x|\theta) = \prod_{i=1}^{n} f_{marg}(z_i|\theta_{marg}) \prod_{i=1}^{n} f_{cond}(y_i|z_i, \theta_{cond}). \tag{1.9}$$

The estimation problems will be introduced systematically in Chapter 3, but we can already notice that in presence of a cut, $L_n(x, \theta)$ defined in (1.4) factorizes as

$$L_n(x, \theta) = L_{n\ marg}\left(z, \theta_{marg}\right) + L_{n\ cond}\left(y, z, \theta_{cond}\right). \tag{1.10}$$

The variation free assumption enables us to maximize independently $L_{n\ marg}$ and $L_{n\ cond}$ with respect to θ_{marg} and θ_{cond} respectively.

Notes

The definitions in this chapter constitute the basis of mathematical statistics and therefore appear in numerous books. We can recommend to the reader wishing to go into detail the books by Barra (1981), Dacunha-Castelle and Dufflo (1982 and 1983), DeGroot (2004), Mood and Graybill (1963), and Raoult (1975). These concepts are also recalled and extended in the Bayesian framework by Florens, Mouchart, and Rolin (1990); their presentation in relation with econometrics is detailed in the book by Hendry (1995).

An excellent and concise overview of the principal probability distributions can be found in the book by Monfort (1980) and a deeper study is presented in the various volumes of Johnson and Kotz (1970). One can also refer to Devroye (1986).

The decomposition of statistical models into marginal and conditional models has been initially justified by the study of sufficiency and partial ancillarity properties. In addition, the concept of exogenous variable goes back to the origins of econometrics (see the works by the Cowles Commission and in particular the article by Koopmans (1950)). The relationship between the decompositions of models and exogeneity was most likely introduced by Florens, Mouchart, and Richard (1979) and was later published in Engle, Hendry, and Richard (1983) and Florens and Mouchart (1985b).

2. Sequential Models and Asymptotics

2.1 Introduction

This chapter reviews probability theory and in particular the usual modes of convergence of sequences of random variables and the two foundations for asymptotic statistics, namely the law of large numbers and the central limit theorems. In order to keep the statistics in this book homogeneous, we present these results in parametric models. The advantage of this presentation will be in the presentation of the concept of *uniform convergence in* θ which is indispensable for the general statistical results in the following chapter.

Our exposition is not restricted to i.i.d. models, which evidently do not cover the analysis of dynamic models, but is extended to stationary models in which the temporal dependence between observations decreases fast enough for the basic results of i.i.d. models to hold: properties of convergence (in probability or "almost sure") of sample means to their expectations and $\sqrt{n}$ rate of convergence to the normal distribution.

Recent econometrics is not satisfied with these results but exploits faster convergence rates to more complex distributions in the case of nonstationary processes. These results, however, will only be introduced in Part III of the book.

2.2 Sequential Stochastic Models and Asymptotics

In Chapter 1, we considered a statistical model $\{X^n, \Theta, P_n^\theta\}$ for which the sample size n was fixed. We now move to the case when the sample size n goes to infinity. A compatibility condition is obviously necessary: if $n < n'$, then P_n^θ must be the marginal probability of X^n derived from $P_{n'}^\theta$ defined on $X^{n'}$. Under this condition, there exists only one probability P_∞^θ for $X^\infty = \prod_{i=1}^\infty X_i$ whose marginal probabilities on X^n are P_n^θ.

We already introduced i.i.d. models in Chapter 1. These models assume that for all θ, the random variables x_i are independent and have the same distribution Q^θ.

This assumption will be weakened when we define statistical models that are more complex but maintain a common set of asymptotic properties.

Definition 2.1   *If $n \in \mathbb{N}$, then the sequence of models*

$$\{X^n, \Theta, P_n^\theta\}$$

satisfying the compatibility condition above is called a sequential model and the model

$$\{X^\infty, \Theta, P_\infty^\theta\}$$

is called the asymptotic model. ∎

Definition 2.2   *An asymptotic model is called stationary if, for all θ and for all n, the probability distribution for $x_1, \ldots, x_n$ is identical to the probability distribution of $x_{1+\tau}, \ldots, x_{n+\tau}$ for all values of τ.* ∎

In particular, in a stationary model, the distribution of each observation x_i does not depend on i.

We will return to this question more extensively in Chapter 12 where we will distinguish, for example, between strong stationarity (which we just defined) and weak stationarity.

The construction of a sequential model is often performed in the following way:

- First, the distribution of x_1 given θ is established or, more generally, the distribution of a vector $x_1, \ldots, x_r$ of observations called the *initial conditions* of the process given θ.
- Second, the distribution of x_2 given x_1 and θ is established, then x_3 given x_2, x_1 and θ. More generally, the distribution of x_i is established given $x_1, \ldots, x_{i-1}$ and θ.

In the case of dominated models, the density function of observations is written as:

$$\ell_n(x_1, \ldots, x_n | \theta) = \prod_{i=1}^n f_i(x_i | x_1, \ldots, x_{i-1}, \theta). \qquad (2.1)$$

This expression simplifies if x_i depends on the past only through a finite number of preceding observations $x_{i-1}, \ldots, x_{i-r}$. The statistical model is then said to be *Markov of order r* and we have

$$\ell_n(x_1, \ldots, x_n | \theta) = f_0(x_1, \ldots, x_r | \theta) \prod_{i=r+1}^n f_i(x_i | x_{i-r}, \ldots, x_{i-1}, \theta).$$

$$(2.2)$$

In this expression, f_0 is the density distribution of the initial conditions, and f_i represents the conditional density of x_i given the past summarized by $x_{i-r}, \ldots, x_{i-1}$. We can additionally assume that this conditional probability does not depend on i, which implies that we can suppress the index i in the density f_i in (2.2). The Markovian model is then homogeneous.

The next question asks under which conditions is such a model stationary. Let us consider first the case $r = 1$. One can show easily enough that this model is stationary if and only if the distributions of x_1 and x_2 are identical. This comes down to verifying that f_0 satisfies the equation:

$$f_0(x_2|\theta) = \int f(x_2|x_1, \theta) f_0(x_1|\theta) dx_1 \tag{2.3}$$

where we assume for simplicity that the dominating measure is Lebesgue measure. If Equation (2.3) admits a solution f_0, then the Markovian model has a stationary solution. In this case, if the distribution of x_1 is given by the density f_0, then the model will be stationary. If the distribution of x_1 differs from f_0, then the model is not stationary but becomes stationary as n goes to infinity.

If Equation (2.3) does not admit a solution, then the Markovian model cannot be made stationary by an appropriate choice of the initial conditions and does not converge to a stationary solution.

Example 2.1 *Suppose*

$$\forall i \geq 2 \quad x_i|x_{i-1}, \theta \sim N(\beta x_{i-1}, \sigma^2) \quad \theta = (\beta, \sigma^2)' \in \mathbb{R} \times \mathbb{R}_*^+.$$

The model is, therefore, Markovian of order 1 and homogeneous. If there exists a f_0 such that x_1 and x_2 have the same distribution for all θ, and if the two first moments exist, then we must have:

$$E^\theta(x_2|\theta) = E^\theta(x_1|\theta).$$

But

$$E^\theta(x_2) = E^\theta\left(E^\theta(x_2|x_1)\right) = \beta E^\theta(x_1),$$

and hence $E^\theta(x_1) = 0$ if $\beta \neq 1$. Furthermore:

$$Var^\theta(x_2) = Var^\theta(x_1);$$

but

$$Var^\theta(x_2) = E^\theta\left(Var^\theta(x_2|x_1)\right) + Var^\theta\left(E^\theta(x_2|x_1)\right)$$
$$= \sigma^2 + \beta^2 Var^\theta(x_1),$$

thus

$$Var^\theta(x_1) = \frac{1}{1 - \beta^2}\sigma^2.$$

The last expression, therefore, necessarily assumes $|\beta| < 1$. In this case the initial distribution that assures stationarity is the central normal distribution with variance $\frac{\sigma^2}{1-\beta^2}$ (if $(\beta, \sigma^2) \in (-1, 1) \times \mathbb{R}_*^+$). Otherwise, the Markovian model cannot be rendered stationary. ☐

The method of constructing a stochastic process just illustrated is only an example. Other constructions will be developed more systematically in Part III.

We introduce now the concept of *mixing*. As an introduction, consider the following example.

Example 2.2   *Suppose $(u_i)_{i=1,\dots,n}$ is a series of random variables distributed i.i.d. $N(0, \sigma^2)$ and assume*

$$x_i = u_i + \beta u_{i-1}.$$

The parameters of the model for observation x_i are $\theta = (\beta, \sigma^2)'$. The observations x_i are not independent because x_i and x_{i-1} (or x_{i+1}) are correlated. Nevertheless, x_i and x_{i+r} or x_{i-r} are independent if $r \geq 2$. Two observations sufficiently far apart are therefore independent. ☐

Definition 2.3   *A stationary statistical model is mixing if, for all i, r, and p and for all square integrable functions φ and ψ:*

$$E^\theta \left(\varphi(x_i, \dots, x_{i+r}) \psi(x_{i+\tau}, \dots, x_{i+\tau+p}) \right)$$
$$\longrightarrow E^\theta \left(\varphi(x_i, \dots, x_{i+r}) | \theta \right) E^\theta \left(\psi(x_i, \dots, x_{i+p}) \right)$$

when $\tau \to \infty$. ∎

In other words, two sets of observations of length r and p "become independent" if the gap τ that separates them tends to infinity.

One can show, for example, that under a regularity condition (Doeblin condition), a stationary Markovian model is mixing. This condition is satisfied, in particular, in the case when the distribution of (x_1, x_2) has the same sets of measure zero as Lebesgue measure.

To analyze asymptotic normality, we need mixing conditions that are more restrictive. To define these mixing conditions requires that we introduce the concept of generated σ-algebras. The reader who is not very interested in the mathematical foundations can skip this more theoretical detour. The basic objective of these concepts is in that they allow us to apply the law of large numbers and the central limit theorem to dynamic models; one can simply suppress these mixing conditions and directly assume that these two theorems apply.

Consider a sequence of observations x_i. Even though each x_i belongs to the same set $X \subset \mathbb{R}^n$, we can distinguish by X_i the set to which the ith observation belongs; a sequence $(x_i, \dots, x_j)$ $(j > i)$, hence, belongs to $X_i^j = X_i \times \cdots \times X_j$. We denote by $\mathcal{X}_i^j$ the σ-algebra of sets that are measurable with respect to X_i^j. Consequently, an event of $\mathcal{X}_i^j$ is observed if $(x_i, \dots, x_j)$ is observed.

The measure of dependence is then defined as follows

$$\varphi^\theta \left(\mathcal{X}_i^j, \mathcal{X}_{i'}^{j'} \right) = \sup \left\{ \left| P_\infty^\theta \left(E | F\right) - P_\infty^\theta \left(E\right) \right|, \, E \in \mathcal{X}_i^j, \, F \in \mathcal{X}_{i'}^{j'}, \, P_\infty^\theta \left(F\right) > 0 \right\} \tag{2.4}$$

and we have:

$$\varphi_t^\theta = \sup_i \varphi^\theta \left(\mathcal{X}_1^i, \mathcal{X}_{i+t}^\infty \right). \tag{2.5}$$

Definition 2.4 *A stationary statistical model is φ-mixing (or uniformly mixing) if, for all θ, $\varphi_t^\theta \to 0$ when $t \to \infty$.* ∎

As we will see in the following, this concept of uniform mixing implies that it is possible to use the central limit theorem. Nevertheless, it is much too restrictive for being applied to many econometric models. Specifically, one can verify that the model of Example 2.1 (with $|\beta| < 1$) does not satisfy this condition.

Consequently, a different concept has been recently introduced in the literature, namely *near-epoch dependence* which we denote by "N.E.D." We will not introduce this concept in all its generality but present a version of it in the case of ARMA processes in Chapter 12.

2.3 Convergence in Probability and Almost Sure Convergence – Law of Large Numbers

Consider an asymptotic model $\{X^\infty, \Theta, P_\infty^\theta\}$ and a sequence ξ_n of random vectors defined on X^∞ with values in $\mathbb{R}^k$. In general, ξ_n will be a function of the first n observations of the process, $x_1, \dots x_n$. Probability theory is especially interested in functions which are sample averages of the form

$$\xi_n = \frac{1}{n} \sum_{i=1}^n \varphi(x_i) \quad \text{or} \quad \xi_n = \frac{1}{n} \sum_{i=s+1}^{s+n} \varphi(x_i, \dots, x_{i-s}).$$

Statistical applications use functions that are more complex but most often lead back to these averages. In general, we consider ξ_n as a function of $x \in X^\infty$.

We will use in this section two modes of convergence:

Definition 2.5 *The sequence ξ_n converges to the random vector ξ in P_∞^θ-probability if*

$$\forall \theta \in \Theta, \ \forall j = 1, \ldots, k, \ \forall \varepsilon > 0, \ \forall \alpha > 0,$$

$$\exists N \ s.t. \ n > N \Longrightarrow P_\infty^\theta(|\xi_{jn} - \xi_j| < \alpha) > 1 - \varepsilon$$

where ξ_j and ξ_{jn} are elements of the vectors ξ and ξ_n. ■

We denote this property by $\xi_n \to \xi \ P_\infty^\theta$ -probability.

Definition 2.6 *The sequence ξ_n converges P_∞^θ almost surely to ξ if*

$$\forall \theta \in \Theta, \ \forall j = 1, \ldots, k, \ \exists B \subset X^\infty \ s.t. \ P_\infty^\theta(B) = 0, \forall x \neq B, \ \forall \varepsilon > 0$$

$$\exists N \ s.t. \ n > N \Longrightarrow |\xi_{jn}(x) - \xi_j(x)| < \varepsilon.$$ ■

We denote this property by $\xi_n \to \xi \ P_\infty^\theta$ -a.s.

These two modes of convergence are studied extensively in any book on probability theory. Here, we limit ourselves to reviewing some of their main properties.

1. In each of the previous definitions, coordinate-wise convergence can be replaced by *convergence in norm*. We can thus suppress "$\forall j$" and replace absolute values by $\|\xi_n - \xi\|$, for example:

$$\sup_j |\xi_{jn} - \xi_j|$$

or

$$\left(\sum_j (\xi_{jn} - \xi_j)^p \right)^{\frac{1}{p}}, \quad p \geq 1.$$

2. Almost sure convergence implies convergence in probability, but the converse is false.

3. If $\xi_n \to \xi$ in one of the previous modes and if g is a continuous mapping from $\mathbb{R}^k$ to $\mathbb{R}^k$, then we also have: $g(\xi_n) \to g(\xi)$ in the corresponding mode of convergence.

The previous modes of convergence do not involve the moments of random vectors. Nevertheless, other modes of convergence are available which are based on the existence of moments.

Definition 2.7 *Suppose the components of ξ_n and ξ are integrable to the power p (that is $\int |\xi_{jn}|^p dP_\infty^\theta$ and $\int |\xi_j|^p dP_\infty^\theta$ are finite). We say that ξ_n converges to ξ in $p-$norm if*

$$\forall j, \ \forall \varepsilon > 0, \ \exists N \ s.t. \ n > N \Rightarrow \int |\xi_{jn} - \xi_j|^p dP_\infty^\theta < \varepsilon. \qquad \blacksquare$$

This mode of convergence leads us to the following remarks:

1. Convergence in $p-$norm implies convergence of moments up to order p, that is:

$$E^\theta \left(\prod_j \xi_{jn}^{r_j} \right) \rightarrow E^\theta \left(\prod_j \xi_j^{r_j} \right)$$

   with $\sum_j r_j \leq p$.
2. Convergence in $p-$norm implies convergence in $p'-$norm if $p' < p$, and implies convergence in probability. It does not imply almost sure convergence.

We will list a number of results that are known under the name of law of large numbers. We are, first of all, interested in the limit of expressions of the following form:

$$\xi_n = \frac{1}{n} \sum_{i=1}^n \varphi(x_i) \qquad (2.6)$$

where φ is a random vector defined on X with values in $\mathbb{R}^k$. We distinguish two types of *Laws of Large Numbers*: *weak* laws where convergence in probability is assured, and *strong* laws where almost sure convergence is assured. In addition, we are interested in the case where the x_i are i.i.d., or not i.i.d. and either the assumption of independence or of identical distribution is dropped.

In the i.i.d. case, the *weak Law of Large Numbers* is of only limited interest and we will only present the *strong Law of Large Numbers*

Theorem 2.1 *Given an i.i.d. statistical model and an integrable mapping φ, i.e. such that $E^\theta(\varphi(x))$ is finite for all θ, then*

$$\frac{1}{n} \sum_{i=1}^n \varphi(x_i) \rightarrow E^\theta \left(\varphi(x_i) \right) \qquad P_\infty^\theta - a.s.$$

The converse is true in the following sense: if $\frac{1}{n} \sum_{i=1}^n \varphi(x_i)$ converges to a vector $\mu(\theta)$ in $\mathbb{R}^k$, then φ is integrable and

$$E^\theta(\varphi) = \mu(\theta). \qquad \blacksquare$$

We provide a first extension of the strong law of large numbers to the case when the random variables are independently but not identically distributed.

Theorem 2.2   *Given a statistical model for which the observations are independent with means $\mu_1, \mu_2, \ldots$ and variances $\sigma_1^2, \sigma_2^2, \ldots$. If the series $\sum_{i=1}^{\infty} \frac{\sigma_i^2}{i^2}$ converges, then*

$$\frac{1}{n} \sum_{i=1}^{n} x_i - \frac{1}{n} \sum_{i=1}^{n} \mu_i \to 0 \quad P^\theta - a.s. \; \forall \theta.$$ ∎

In econometrics, it is particularly relevant to analyze the law of large numbers in the case of stationary processes.

Theorem 2.3   *Given a stationary statistical model and a random vector φ defined on $X_1 \times X_2 \times \cdots \times X_s$. Consider the expression:*

$$\frac{1}{n} \sum_{i=1}^{n} \varphi(x_{i+1}, \ldots x_{i+s}).$$

1. *If φ is integrable, then this expression converges P^θ-a.s. to a random vector $\xi(\theta)$.*
2. *A stationary statistical model is said to be ergodic if this limit $\xi(\theta)$ is not random and is equal to $E^\theta(\varphi)$.*
3. *A mixing stationary statistical model is ergodic.*   ∎

When studying statistical problems, notably estimation, we are interested in the convergence of functions that depend on parameters, for example, sums of the type $\frac{1}{n} \sum_{i=1}^{n} \varphi(x_i, \theta)$.

This sum converges, in general, to $E^\theta(\varphi(x_i, \theta))$ which is a function of θ. It is useful that this convergence occurs uniformly in θ. We will analyze this extension for the case of almost sure convergence, but a comparable analysis can be done for other modes of convergence.

Definition 2.8   *The sequence $\xi_n(x, \theta)$ converges locally uniformly to $\xi(x, \theta)$ if $\forall \theta_0$, $\exists$ a closed ball V_{θ_0} centered at θ_0 such that $\exists B \subset X^\infty$ satisfying*

$$P_\infty^\theta(B) = 0, \; \forall \theta \in V_{\theta_0}$$

and such that:

$$\forall x \notin B, \; \forall \varepsilon > 0, \; \forall j = 1, \ldots, k$$

$$\exists N \text{ such that } n > N \Longrightarrow |\xi_{jn}(x, \theta) - \xi_j(x, \theta)| < \varepsilon, \; \forall \theta \in V_{\theta_0}.$$ ∎

Intuitively, in Definition 2.6, the set B and the integer N depend on θ (and on x and ε) while in definition 2.8, B and N do not depend on θ as long as the latter remains in a neighborhood of a given value θ_0.

Consider now an *i.i.d.* sample and a sequence of functions $\frac{1}{n}\sum_{i=1}^{n}\varphi(x_i,\theta)$. We know that this expression converges to $E^{\theta}(\varphi)$ according to the strong law of large numbers. The question whether this convergence is uniform is much more delicate.

2.4 Convergence in Distribution and Central Limit Theorem

Consider a statistical model and a sequence ξ_n of random vectors which are functions of the sample and possibly of parameters. Each of these random vectors has a distribution function F_n defined by

$$\forall t \in \mathbb{R}^k \quad F_n(t) = P_n^{\theta}(\xi_{1n} \leq t_1, \ldots, \xi_{kn} \leq t_k).$$

If ξ is a random vector of dimension k with distribution function F, we define *convergence in distribution* by one of the following equivalent properties.

Definition 2.9 *The sequence ξ_n converges to ξ in distribution (this will be denoted by $\xi_n \to \xi$ P_{∞}^{θ}-distribution or $\xi_n \Rightarrow \xi$) if one of the following equivalent conditions is satisfied:*

1. *$F_n(t) \to F(t)$, for all continuity points t of F.*
2. *$\forall B \subset \mathbb{R}^k$ with boundary that ∂B satisfies $P_{\infty}^{\theta}(\xi \in \partial B) = 0$, we have*

$$P_n^{\theta}(\xi_n \in B) \to P_{\infty}^{\theta}(\xi \in B). \qquad \blacksquare$$

The second condition expresses the fact that the probability that ξ_n belongs to a set B can be approximated by the distribution of ξ. If the limiting law is normal (or more generally admits a density with respect to Lebesgue measure), then the condition that the boundary has probability zero is always satisfied.

In contrast to the previous modes of convergence, the limit cannot be considered component by component. However, we can return to univariate convergence in the case where the limiting distribution is the normal distribution, as the following theorem shows.

Theorem 2.4 *The sequence ξ_n of random vectors converges in distribution to the normal distribution with mean μ and variance Σ if and only if, for any vector a in $\mathbb{R}^k$, the linear combination $a'\xi_n = \sum_j a_j \xi_{jn}$ converges in distribution to the normal distribution with mean $a'\mu$ and variance $a'\Sigma a$. $\qquad \blacksquare$*

Let us recall some useful properties of convergence in distribution:

1. If the random variables satisfy $\xi_n \to \xi$ in distribution and if $\eta_n \to c$ in probability (c constant), then $\xi_n + \eta_n \to \xi + c$, $\xi_n \eta_n \to c\xi$ and $\xi_n/\eta_n \to \xi/c$ ($c \neq 0$) in distribution. This result, obviously, admits a vectorial extension, which is known as *Slutsky's theorem*.
2. Convergence ξ_n to ξ in probability implies convergence in distribution. The converse is true if ξ is a constant.
3. If g is a continuous mapping and if $\xi_n \to \xi$ in distribution, then $g(\xi_n) \to g(\xi)$ in distribution.

The *central limit theorems* ensure the asymptotic normality of empirical means. We will state first the most common theorem that is valid in i.i.d. models.

Theorem 2.5   *Given an i.i.d. model $\{X^\infty, \Theta, P_\infty^\theta\}$ and $\varphi : X \to \mathbb{R}^k$ (or $X \times \Theta \to \mathbb{R}^k$) such that $E^\theta(\varphi) = \mu$ and $Var^\theta(\varphi) = \Sigma$. Then*

$$\sqrt{n}\left(\frac{1}{n}\sum_{i=1}^{n}\varphi(x_i) - \mu\right) \to N(0, \Sigma) \quad \text{in } P_\infty^\theta\text{-distribution.} \qquad \blacksquare$$

This theorem is called the Lindeberg-Levy theorem. One can extend this theorem by keeping independence but dropping the condition of identical distributions. We then obtain the Lindeberg-Feller theorem or its extensions which we will not present here. We will present only one central limit theorem that is useful for mixing stationary models.

Theorem 2.6   *Given a stationary model such that the sequence of observations $(x_i)_i$ is uniformly mixing and satisfies $\sum_t (\varphi_t^\theta)^{\frac{1}{2}} < \infty$. If, moreover, $E^\theta(x_i) = \mu$ and $Cov^\theta(x_i, x_{i+l}) = \Sigma_l$, then we have convergence*

$$\sqrt{n}\left(\frac{1}{n}\sum_{i=1}^{n}x_i - \mu\right) \to N(0, V^\theta) \quad \text{in } P_\infty^\theta\text{-distribution}$$

with $V^\theta = \sum_{l=-\infty}^{+\infty}\Sigma_l$. $\qquad \blacksquare$

In the scalar case, $\Sigma_l = \Sigma_{-l}$ and the expression above is reduced to:

$$V^\theta = \Sigma_0 + 2\sum_{l=1}^{\infty}\Sigma_l. \qquad (2.7)$$

This equality is false in the vector case where the relationship is $\Sigma_l = \Sigma'_{-l}$. One can, moreover, verify that, if x_i is uniformly mixing, then any sequence of random vectors of the form

$$y_i = f(x_i, x_{i-1}, \ldots, x_{i-q})$$

is uniformly mixing for all finite q. Furthermore, if the condition

$$\sum_t \left(\varphi_t^\theta\right)^{\frac{1}{2}} < \infty$$

is satisfied for x_i, then it is also satisfied for y_i. Theorem 2.6 thus applies to y_i for any f. We point out that this result is in general false if q is infinite.

Example 2.3 *Let u_i be an i.i.d. sequence of random variables, normally distributed with mean zero and variance σ^2. This sequence is uniformly mixing because of independence. Let $y_i = (u_i + \beta u_{i-1})^2$. This new process is uniformly mixing and satisfies the conditions of Theorem 2.6. We have then:*

$$\sqrt{n}\left(\frac{1}{n}\sum_{i=1}^{n} y_i - \lambda\right) \to N(0, V)$$

with

$$\lambda = E(y_i) = \left(1 + \beta^2\right)\sigma^2$$

and

$$
\begin{aligned}
V &= Var(y_i) + 2\sum_{l=1}^{\infty} Cov(y_i, y_{i+l}) \\
&= Var(y_i) + 2\,Cov(y_i, y_{i+1}) \\
&= 3\sigma^4\left[2 + 8\beta^2 + 5\beta^4\right].
\end{aligned}
$$
□

Although the assumptions of Theorem 2.6 are not satisfied in an Autoregressive (AR) or Autoregressive Moving Average (ARMA) process, we will see in Chapter 12 that the conclusion of this theorem remains valid for this class of models. Indeed, the theorem can be extended to processes that have the near epoch dependent (NED) property, which is the case of AR and ARMA.

2.5 Noncausality and Exogeneity in Dynamic Models

Let us partition observations $x_i \in \mathbb{R}^m$ into $(y_i, z_i) \in \mathbb{R}^p \times \mathbb{R}^q$. In the same manner as in the static case evoked in Chapter 1, we can decompose the distribution of x_i in marginal and conditional distributions. In the dynamic case, two decompositions are overlaid: sequential decomposition (distribution of x_i given the past $x_{i-1}, \dots$) and decomposition into marginal distribution of z process and conditional distribution of the y process given the z process. The interaction of these two decompositions gives rise to diverse concepts of exogeneity. Before analyzing those, we will present a related concept, namely noncausality.

2.5.1   Wiener-Granger Causality

First, we will present the concept of *noncausality* in an intuitive way by using terms that have been precisely defined; we will show that several definitions of noncausality emerge when a precise mathematical meaning is selected to characterize these notions.

Hence, let us consider a stochastic process y_i (scalar or vectorial) and denote by W_j and X_j two *information sets* such that $W_j \subset X_j$ (the information contained in W_j is also contained in X_j). We say that X_j does not cause y_i given W_j (or that the complement of W_j in X_j does not cause y_i) if the predictions for y_i based on X_j and based on W_j are identical.

The first way of making this notion more precise concerns the nature of information sets and the nature of prediction. Suppose, for simplicity, that we have two processes $(z_i)_i$ and $(w_i)_i$. Still intuitively, X_j describes the set of information contained in the observations of z_l, w_l, and y_l for all $l \leq j$. A very strong concept of prediction is based on conditional distributions. Thus, the prediction of y_i knowing X_j will be the conditional distribution of y_i given

$$(z_j, y_j, w_j, z_{j-1}, y_{j-1}, w_{j-1}, \ldots);$$

the prediction of y_i knowing W_j will be characterized by the distribution of y_i conditional only on

$$(y_j, w_j, y_{j-1}, w_{j-1}, \ldots).$$

In this case, the information set X_j is implicitly given by the σ-algebra generated by the observations of the three processes before j, whereas W_j is the σ-algebra only of the processes y and w, hence,

$$y_i \mid X_j \sim y_i \mid W_j \iff y_i \perp\!\!\!\perp_{i=1}^{n} (z_\ell)_{\ell=1,\ldots,j} \mid (y_\ell, w_\ell)_{\ell=1,\ldots,j}. \qquad (2.8)$$

This concept can be weakened by defining prediction in terms of conditional expectations only. The property of noncausality is, in this case, defined by

$$E^\theta \left(y_i \mid X_j \right) = E^\theta \left(y_i \mid W_j \right) \qquad (2.9)$$

where X_j and W_j are σ-algebras as previously defined. This property is weaker than the preceding one, because, in the second case, it is possible that the variance of y_i conditional on X_j depends on W_j.

Finally, one can be interested in only linear conditional expectations (denoted EL), and predict y_i by its projection (in the sense of L^2) on the closed vector space generated by $z_j, y_j, w_j, z_{j-1}, y_{j-1}, w_{j-1}, \ldots$ (precise definitions of conditional expectation and linear conditional expectation will be given in Chapter 7). In this case, the information sets are closed vector spaces and noncausality becomes

$$EL(y_i \mid X_j) = EL(y_i \mid W_j). \qquad (2.10)$$

Another definition has to be presented that is based on the choice of i and j. It is obvious that the problem is non-trivial only if $i > j$, because if $i \leq j$, the preceding properties are always satisfied.

In discrete time, one can be interested in the case where $i - j = 1$ (for all i, j) and analyze noncausality that is either instantaneous or one period in the future. One can also consider arbitrary i and j, which yields noncausality $i - j$ periods in the future. Possibly, one is interested in noncausality of X_j given W_j on $(y_{j+1}, y_{j+2}, \ldots, y_{j+\tau})$, and one can analyze here the case where τ goes to infinity. In continuous time, instantaneous noncausality becomes noncausality at an "infinitesimal" forecast horizon (between t and $t + dt$).

We can see, therefore, that numerous rigorous definitions of noncausality can be introduced, and one of the natural questions that arise lies in their relationship and possibly their equivalence.

Another type of question consists of the transformation of these general concepts into properties that can be expressed as restrictions on parameters, which in turn can be tested. At this moment, we are required to stay with a stationary specification in order to guarantee the limiting distribution of estimators and of tests. As an example, we will present an equivalence result between two definitions of *strong noncausality*.

Definition 2.10 *We say that* $(z_i)_i$ *does not* GRANGER *-cause* $(y_i)_i$ *if*

$$y_i \mid z_{-\infty}^{i-1}, y_{-\infty}^{i-1} \sim y_i \mid y_{-\infty}^i \text{ where } z_{-\infty}^{i-1} = (z_{i-1}, z_{i-2}, \ldots),$$

or, by using the notation of conditional independence, if

$$y_i \perp\!\!\!\perp_{i=1}^n z_{-\infty}^{i-1} \mid y_{-\infty}^{i-1}. \qquad \blacksquare$$

This defines an "instantaneous" property, but implies a prediction described by the entire conditional distribution.

Definition 2.11 *We say that* $(z_i)_i$ *does not cause* $(y_i)_i$ *in the sense of* SIMS *if*

$$y_i \mid z_{-\infty}^{+\infty}, y_{-\infty}^{i-1} \sim y_i \mid z_{-\infty}^i, y_{-\infty}^{i-1}.$$

This condition written in terms of conditional independence is the following:

$$y_i \perp\!\!\!\perp_{i=1}^n z_{-\infty}^{+\infty} \mid \left(z_{-\infty}^i, y_{-\infty}^{i-1} \right). \qquad \blacksquare$$

This also constitutes a condition on the conditional distribution of y_i. We have then:

Theorem 2.7 *Under the condition*

$$z_{-\infty} \mid y_{-\infty}^{+\infty} \sim z_{-\infty} \mid y_{-\infty} \qquad \left(z_{-\infty} \perp\!\!\!\perp y_{-\infty}^{+\infty} \mid y_{-\infty} \right),$$

the two definitions are equivalent. $\qquad \blacksquare$

Proof: We initially restrict the path of the process to the interval between k and n, and we will reason in terms of densities to keep the presentation simple. Letting "l" denote the density of a random vector, we can write

$$l\left(y_k^n, z_k^n\right) = l(y_k, z_k) \prod_{i=k+1}^{n} l\left(y_i, z_i \mid y_k^{i-1}, z_k^{i-1}\right)$$

$$= l(y_k)l(z_k \mid y_k) \prod_i l\left(y_i \mid y_k^{i-1}, z_k^{i-1}\right) \prod_i l\left(z_i \mid y_k^i, z_k^{i-1}\right).$$

Additionally,

$$l\left(y_k^n, z_k^n\right) = l\left(y_k^n\right) l\left(z_k^n \mid y_k^n\right)$$

$$= l(y_k)l\left(z_k \mid y_k^n\right) \left\{ \prod_i l\left(y_i \mid y_k^{i-1}\right) \right\} \left\{ \prod_i l\left(z_i \mid y_k^n, z_k^{i-1}\right) \right\}.$$

So, we see that, if

$$l(z_k \mid y_k) = l\left(z_k \mid y_k^n\right),$$

we obtain

$$\prod_i l\left(y_i \mid y_k^{i-1}, z_k^{i-1}\right) = \prod_i l\left(y_i \mid y_k^{i-1}\right)$$

$$\Longleftrightarrow \prod_i l\left(z_i \mid y_k^i, z_k^{i-1}\right) = \prod_i l\left(z_i \mid y_k^n, z_k^{i-1}\right).$$

Therefore, as this argument is valid for all n, the two definitions are equivalent when restricted to $k, \ldots, n$. This result remains valid as we let k go to $-\infty$ and n to $+\infty$. ∎

2.5.2 Exogeneity

The concept of exogeneity formalizes the idea that the generating mechanism of the exogenous variables does not contain any relevant information about the parameters of interest, which only appear in the model conditional on these exogenous variables. In dynamic models, we can consider the two decompositions of the likelihood function that we introduced in the proof of Theorem 2.7, but here we use a different decomposition of the parameters.

We say that the decomposition of x_i into (y_i, z_i) forms a sequential cut (or that z_i is weakly exogenous) if θ can be partitioned into $(\theta_{marg}^s, \theta_{cond}^s)$ where the components θ_{marg}^s and θ_{cond}^s are variation free such that

$$l_n \left(z_0^n, y_0^n | \theta \right) = f_0 \left(z_0 | \theta_{marg}^s \right) f_0 \left(y_0 | z_0, \theta_{cond}^s \right) \tag{2.11}$$

$$\times \prod_{i=1}^n f_i \left(z_i | y_0^{i-1}, z_0^{i-1}, \theta_{marg}^s \right) f_i \left(y_i | y_0^{i-1}, z_0^i, \theta_{cond}^s \right).$$

Here, zero is taken as the starting point, which can be replaced by $-\infty$ as in the previous paragraph.

Intuitively, the generating process of z_i does not contain any information about the parameter of interest θ_{cond}^s of the process conditional on the entire past.

On the other hand, the decomposition of x_i in (y_i, z_i) forms a global cut if θ can be partitioned into $\left(\theta_{marg}^g, \theta_{cond}^g \right)$ such that

$$l_n \left(z_0^n, y_0^n | \theta \right) = f_0 \left(z_0 | \theta_{marg}^g \right) f_0 \left(y_0 | z_0, \theta_{cond}^g \right) \tag{2.12}$$

$$\times \prod_{i=1}^n f_i \left(z_i | z_0^{i-1}, \theta_{marg}^g \right) \prod_{i=1}^n f_i \left(y_i | y_0^{i-1}, z_0^n, \theta_{cond}^g \right),$$

hence,

$$l_n \left(z_0^n, y_0^n | \theta \right) = l_n \left(z_0^n | \theta_{marg}^g \right) l_n \left(y_0^n | z_0^n, \theta_{cond}^g \right). \tag{2.13}$$

In this case, the decomposition relates to the entire path of the process and, in particular, z_0^n can be replaced by z_0^∞ in the right-hand side of the last equation. It is valuable that these two concepts merge and that noncausality makes it possible that we obtain equivalence of these definitions.

Under the assumptions of Theorem 2.7, we have the following result.

Theorem 2.8 *If y_i does not Granger-cause z_i, then the sequential and global cuts are equivalent with*

$$\theta_{marg}^s = \theta_{marg}^g \quad and \quad \theta_{cond}^s = \theta_{cond}^g.$$

We say in this case that z is strongly exogenous. ∎

Proof: Take, for example, the sequential cut and consider Inequality (2.12). The assumption of noncausality allows us to write

$$f_i \left(z_i | y_0^{i-1}, z_0^{i-1}, \theta_{marg}^s \right) = f_i \left(z_i | z_0^{i-1}, \theta_{marg}^s \right)$$

and

$$f_i \left(y_i | y_0^{i-1}, z_0^i, \theta_{cond}^s \right) = f_i \left(y_i | y_0^{i-1}, z_0^n, \theta_{cond}^s \right),$$

which makes it possible to immediately obtain Equation (2.13). ∎

Example 2.4	*Suppose that, conditionally on the past, $x_i = (y_i, z_i) \in \mathbb{R}^2$ are generated by the distribution*

$$N \left(\begin{pmatrix} ay_{i-1} + bz_{i-1} \\ cy_{i-1} + dz_{i-1} \end{pmatrix}, \begin{pmatrix} \sigma_{yy} & \sigma_{yz} \\ \sigma_{yz} & \sigma_{zz} \end{pmatrix} \right).$$

y does not cause z if $c = 0$ and z_i is weakly exogenous after the decomposition

$$\theta^s_{cond} = \left(a, b, \sigma_{yy.z} \right) \quad and \quad \theta^s_{marg} = (c, d, \sigma_{zz})$$

(with $\sigma_{yy.z} = \sigma_{yy} - \frac{\sigma^2_{yz}}{\sigma_{zz}}$) if $\sigma_{yz} = 0$. The equivalence between the two definitions of exogeneity is immediate if $c = 0$.	□

Notes

Our presentation refers to the construction of stochastic processes and their fundamental properties which for example are treated by Cox and Miller (1965), Doob (1953), or Karlin (1950). Statements about the modes of convergence and their properties can be found in numerous books on probability theory (see for example Foata and Fachs (1996) or Métivier (1972)) or on statistics (Davidson (1994), Serfling (1980)).

The analysis of the mixing process or NED is, for example, treated in Davidson (1994), as well as the concept of uniform convergence in relation to equicontinuity (see also Newey and McFadden (1994) or Andrews (1994)).

The concepts of noncausality were introduced into econometrics by Granger (1969) and Sims (1972). A rigorous treatment of the equivalence of these concepts is found in Florens and Mouchart (1982) for the general case, and Florens and Mouchart (1985a) for the linear case. The extension to the case of continuous time is in Florens and Fougère (1996). For the dynamic analysis of exogeneity and noncausality, refer to Engle, Hendry, and Richard (1983) and Florens and Mouchart (1985b), where one will find in particular a more precise analysis of Theorem 2.8.

3. Estimation by Maximization and by the Method of Moments

3.1 Introduction

This chapter presents the main statistical tools that enable us to estimate a vector of parameters in an econometric model. We chose a rather general style for our presentation in which the estimator is obtained by either solving a system of equations or by optimization of a criterion. This presentation has the advantage that we can cover maximum likelihood, least squares, or traditional methods based on moments as special cases. This allows us to define a theoretical framework that makes it possible to analyze these statistical methods in the context of misspecification.

The counterpart of this choice of generality is a high level of "abstraction" in our presentation. We tried to avoid this by including examples some of which are extremely elementary. The following chapters will provide many other, more pertinent examples. We also decided to provide only intuitive proofs while trying to motivate the essential assumptions that are introduced.

This chapter begins with a review of the notion of an estimator and its properties. We will then introduce moment conditions and maximization, and the computation of estimators that are associated with them. Finally, the properties of these estimators are examined.

3.2 Estimation

Let us consider a statistical model $\{X^n, \Theta, P_n^\theta\}$. In many examples, the parameter space will be, intuitively speaking, very "large" and the statistician can only hope to estimate a function of θ which, in general, may include functional parameters. This chapter concentrates on the estimation of a parameter vector of interest. We will analyze the estimation of some functional parameters in other chapters.

In this chapter, $\lambda(\theta)$ will be a mapping from θ to a subset of Λ in $\mathbb{R}^k$ and represents the parameters of interest.

Several questions then arise naturally:

- How can the functions $\lambda(\theta)$ be constructed such that the values of the parameters can be interpreted in relation to the statistical model but also in relation to the theory that it represents? The relevant functions $\lambda(\theta)$ will be those that make λ depend on θ through probability distribution P_n^θ.
- How can estimators of $\lambda(\theta)$ be constructed, i.e., mappings $\hat{\lambda}_n(x_1, \ldots, x_n)$, which summarize the information about the values of $\lambda(\theta)$ that is contained in the sample?
- What are the properties of such estimators, and are some estimators preferable to others?

Besides these problems of estimation, problems of testing arise, whether they are tests of a particular value of the parameters or, more generally, tests of the relevance of the selected model. We will consider these tests in Chapter 4.

The most common question with which we will start is that of the properties of an estimator. Thus, let us suppose that $\lambda(\theta)$ is given and consider a mapping

$$\hat{\lambda}_n : X^n \to \Lambda$$

which is called an estimator of $\lambda(\theta)$. Usually, we consider two types of properties of $\hat{\lambda}_n$, finite sample properties and asymptotic properties.

Small sample properties involve either sampling moments or the entire probability distribution of the estimator.

Definition 3.1   *The estimator $\hat{\lambda}_n$ is said to be an unbiased estimator of $\lambda(\theta)$ if the sampling expectation of $\hat{\lambda}_n$ exists and is equal to $\lambda(\theta)$. In other terms,*

$$E^\theta(\hat{\lambda}_n) = \int \hat{\lambda}_n dP_n^\theta = \lambda(\theta). \tag{3.1}$$

If this equality does not hold, then the difference between $E^\theta(\hat{\lambda}_n)$ and $\lambda(\theta)$ is called the bias of the estimator.   ■

Let us provide an elementary example.

Example 3.1   *Suppose the sample x_i $(i = 1, \ldots, n)$ is i.i.d. with $x_i \in \mathbb{R}$ and that $x_i = \mu + u_i$. The residuals u_i are distributed according to an unknown probability distribution Q with mean zero.*

The parameter θ is here the pair $(\mu, Q) \in \mathbb{R} \times \mathcal{P}_0$ ($\mathcal{P}_0$ = set of probability distributions with mean zero). Set $\lambda(\theta) = \mu$ and let $\hat{\lambda}_n$ be defined by

$$\hat{\lambda}_n = \sum_{i=1}^n a_i x_i.$$

The sampling expectation of $\hat{\lambda}_n$ is then $\mu \sum_{i=1}^{n} a_i$ and the estimator is unbiased if $\sum_{i=1}^{n} a_i = 1$. □

Note that, if the sampling expectation of $\hat{\lambda}_n$ exists and if $\hat{\lambda}_n$ is a biased estimator of $\lambda(\theta)$, then there always exists another function $\mu(\theta)$ of the sample such that $\hat{\lambda}_n$ is an unbiased estimator of $\mu(\theta)$. It is obviously sufficient to take $\mu(\theta) = E^\theta(\hat{\lambda}_n)$. Therefore, an estimator is in general an unbiased estimator of something, however, this is not necessarily what we are interested in.

To evaluate the precision of an estimator, the sampling variance is often calculated:

$$Var^\theta(\hat{\lambda}_n) = \int \left(\hat{\lambda}_n - E^\theta(\hat{\lambda}_n)\right)\left(\hat{\lambda}_n - E^\theta(\hat{\lambda}_n)\right)' dP_n^\theta \tag{3.2}$$

which, in the case of an unbiased estimator, is equal to:

$$Var^\theta(\hat{\lambda}_n) = \int \left(\hat{\lambda}_n - \lambda(\theta)\right)\left(\hat{\lambda}_n - \lambda(\theta)\right)' dP_n^\theta. \tag{3.3}$$

In the general case, one calculates the *Mean Squared Error* (MSE) of the estimator, defined by:

$$\begin{aligned}
MSE^\theta(\hat{\lambda}_n) &= \int \left(\hat{\lambda}_n - \lambda(\theta)\right)\left(\hat{\lambda}_n - \lambda(\theta)\right)' dP_n^\theta \\
&= \int \left(\hat{\lambda}_n - E^\theta(\hat{\lambda}_n)\right)\left(\hat{\lambda}_n - E^\theta(\hat{\lambda}_n)\right)' dP_n^\theta \\
&\quad + \left(E^\theta(\hat{\lambda}_n) - \lambda(\theta)\right)\left(E^\theta(\hat{\lambda}_n) - \lambda(\theta)\right)'.
\end{aligned} \tag{3.4}$$

The mean squared error is thus equal to the variance plus a matrix whose elements are squares or products of the bias components of the estimator.

Two estimators of the same function are compared according to their MSE. If $\hat{\lambda}_n$ and $\hat{\mu}_n$ are two unbiased estimators of $\lambda(\theta)$, then we say that $\hat{\lambda}_n$ is more *efficient* than $\hat{\mu}_n$ if the variance of the former is smaller than that of the latter. Recall that a symmetric matrix A is smaller than a symmetric matrix B if $B - A$ is symmetric positive definite (i.e., $\forall x, x'(B - A)x \geq 0$).

Example 3.2   *Let us return to Example 3.1 and assume that the variance of x_i is finite and equal to σ^2 for all i. Then*

$$Var^\theta(\hat{\lambda}_n) = \sigma^2 \sum_{i=1}^{n} a_i^2.$$

Finding a_i such that $\hat{\lambda}_n$ is unbiased and of minimal variance leads to the minimization of $\sum_{i=1}^{n} a_i^2$ subject to the constraint $\sum_{i=1}^{n} a_i = 1$. This is obtained by setting $a_i = 1/n$ for all i. Thus, we have

$$Var^{\theta}(\hat{\lambda}_n) = \frac{\sigma^2}{n}.$$ □

Our interest has focused on the first two sampling moments of $\hat{\lambda}_n$, but it can be useful to analyze the probability distribution of $\hat{\lambda}_n$ conditional on θ.

This analysis is particularly important whenever the statistical model contains distributional assumptions.

Example 3.3   *Let us continue with Examples 3.1 and 3.2. If we assume that x_i are normally distributed with mean zero, then*

$$\hat{\lambda}_n|\theta \sim N\left(\mu \sum_{i=1}^{n} a_i, \sigma^2 \sum_{i=1}^{n} a_i^2\right)$$

or, if $a_i = 1/n$,

$$\hat{\lambda}_n|\theta \sim N\left(\mu, \frac{\sigma^2}{n}\right).$$ □

Example 3.4   *Consider the model where x_i are i.i.d. exponential with parameter $\theta > 0$. Recall that the density of the exponential distribution satisfies:*

$$f(x_i|\theta) = \begin{vmatrix} \theta e^{-\theta x_i} & \text{if } x_i \geq 0 \\ 0 & \text{otherwise.} \end{vmatrix}$$

We set $\lambda(\theta) = \theta$ and study the estimator

$$\hat{\lambda}_n = \frac{n}{\sum_{i=1}^{n} x_i}.$$

One can show that the expectation of $\hat{\lambda}_n$ is equal to $\frac{n}{n-1}\lambda$ (thus, the bias is $-\frac{1}{n-1}\lambda$) and that its sampling distribution is an inverse gamma distribution with density:

$$g(u) = (n\lambda)^n \Gamma(n)^{-1} u^{-(n+1)} e^{-\frac{n\lambda}{u}} \, I\!I(u \geq 0).$$ □

Knowing the *sampling distribution of an estimator* is mainly useful for finding confidence intervals or exact small sample tests.

Unfortunately, with the exception of a small number of cases, the small sample properties do not have an analytical representation. This difficulty is the motivation for the asymptotic analysis, which permits us to use simplifications, such as linearization and approximation by the normal distribution. The development in the use of computers has renewed the interest in finite sample properties, which can be analyzed by simulation. This approach will be presented in Chapter 6.

Let us recall now the main *asymptotic properties* that are relevant for our approach. For this, we consider a sequence $\hat{\lambda}_n$ of estimators and an asymptotic model $\{X^\infty, \Theta, P_\infty^\theta\}$ with respect to which we analyze the behavior of $\hat{\lambda}_n$. We emphasize that $\hat{\lambda}_n$ can be considered as a function defined on X^∞ which, however, only depends on the first n observations.

Definition 3.2

1.   *The sequence $\hat{\lambda}_n$ is a consistent sequence of estimators of $\lambda(\theta)$ P_∞^θ-a.s.
   (P_∞^θ-prob) if*

$$\lim \hat{\lambda}_n = \lambda(\theta) \quad P_\infty^\theta - a.s. \quad \left(P_\infty^\theta - prob\right).$$

2.   *The sequence $\hat{\lambda}_n$ converging in probability is asymptotically normal with
   rate of convergence $\sqrt{n}$ if there exists a matrix Σ_θ as function of θ such
   that*

$$\sqrt{n}(\hat{\lambda}_n - \lambda(\theta)) \to N(0, \Sigma_\theta) \quad P_\infty^\theta - distribution. \quad \blacksquare$$

Example 3.5   *We continue with Example 3.1 and consider now a sample whose
size goes to infinity. Suppose that $a_i = 1/n$ for all i and n, and, thus, $\hat{\lambda}_n = \bar{x}$,
is the sample average. An immediate application of the strong law of large
numbers implies that $\hat{\lambda}_n \to \mu$ P^θ-a.s. and the central limit theorem implies
that*

$$\sqrt{n}(\hat{\lambda}_n - \mu) \to N(0, \sigma^2)$$

in distribution, if we assume that the variance σ^2 of x_i exists. $\square$

The same remark we made earlier with respect to the expectation of an estimator, applies to its *consistency*. A sequence of estimators $\hat{\lambda}_n$ may not be consistent, but in many cases, it may converge towards a limit that is different from the function of the parameters that we wish to estimate. It can be extremely interesting to compare the difference between these two functions, and this is the foundation of numerous tests, in particular of specification tests.

We conclude this section by pointing out two results that will be very useful later. The first is related to quadratic forms associated with estimators that are asymptotically normal, and the second, known under the name of Delta theorem, characterizes the asymptotic distribution of nonlinear transformations of estimators.

Theorem 3.1   *Let $\hat{\lambda}_n$ and $\hat{\Sigma}_n$ be two estimators that satisfy:*

1. $\sqrt{n}(\hat{\lambda}_n - \lambda(\theta)) \to N(0, \Sigma_\theta)$ *in P_∞^θ-distribution*
2. $\hat{\Sigma}_n \to \Sigma_\theta$ P^θ *-prob and $\hat{\Sigma}_n$ and Σ_θ are invertible.*

Then,

$$\sqrt{n}\ \hat{\Sigma}_n^{-\frac{1}{2}} \left(\hat{\lambda}_n - \lambda(\theta)\right) \to N(0, I)$$

and

$$n \left(\hat{\lambda}_n - \lambda(\theta)\right)' \hat{\Sigma}_n^{-1} \left(\hat{\lambda}_n - \lambda(\theta)\right) \to \chi_k^2$$

in distribution where k is the dimension of $\lambda(\theta)$. ∎

Proof: Recall that $\hat{\Sigma}_n$ is symmetric positive definite, and so is $\hat{\Sigma}_n^{-1}$ which can thus be factorized into

$$\hat{\Sigma}_n^{-1} = \hat{\Sigma}_n^{-\frac{1}{2}} \hat{\Sigma}_n^{-\frac{1}{2}}$$

(the notation $\hat{\Sigma}_n^{-\frac{1}{2}}$ is, of course, a convention). We can choose $\hat{\Sigma}_n^{-\frac{1}{2}}$ such that

$$\hat{\Sigma}_n^{-\frac{1}{2}} \to \Sigma_\theta^{-\frac{1}{2}}$$

and the first part of the theorem follows from the properties of convergence in distribution (Section 2.4).

$$\sqrt{n}\hat{\Sigma}_n^{-\frac{1}{2}} \left(\hat{\lambda}_n - \lambda(\theta)\right) \to N \left(0, \Sigma_\theta^{-\frac{1}{2}} \Sigma_\theta \Sigma_\theta^{-\frac{1}{2}'}\right) = N(0, I).$$

Recall, furthermore, that, if $\varepsilon \sim N(\mu, \Omega)$, then $(\varepsilon - \mu)'\Omega^{-1}(\varepsilon - \mu)$ is distributed according to a χ^2 with degrees of freedom equal to the dimension of ε. Still using the properties of Section 2.4, we can verify that

$$n \left(\hat{\lambda}_n - \lambda(\theta)\right)' \Sigma_\theta^{-1} \left(\hat{\lambda}_n - \lambda(\theta)\right)$$

converges in distribution to a χ_k^2. This result remains unchanged if we replace Σ_θ by $\hat{\Sigma}_n$ since

$$\left(\sqrt{n}(\hat{\lambda}_n - \lambda(\theta))\right)' \left(\hat{\Sigma}_n^{-1} - \Sigma_\theta^{-1}\right) \left(\sqrt{n}(\hat{\lambda}_n - \lambda(\theta))\right)$$

goes to zero in probability. In fact, the central term goes to zero, and the two terms on the left and on the right possess a limit in distribution. ∎

Theorem 3.2 *Suppose* $\hat{\lambda}_n$ *is a consistent estimator and* φ *satisfies:*

1. $\sqrt{n}(\hat{\lambda}_n - \lambda(\theta)) \to N(0, \Sigma_\theta)$ *in* P_∞^θ *-distribution*
2. $\varphi : \Lambda \to \Delta \subset \mathbb{R}^r$ *is continuously differentiable.*

Then $\varphi(\hat{\lambda}_n)$ *is a consistent estimator of* $\varphi(\lambda(\theta))$ *in the same sense as* $\hat{\lambda}_n$ *and*

$$\sqrt{n}(\varphi(\hat{\lambda}_n) - \varphi(\lambda(\theta))) \to N(0, \Omega_\theta) \quad P_\infty^\theta - distribution$$

with

$$\Omega_\theta = \left(\frac{\partial\varphi}{\partial\lambda'}\,|_{\lambda=\lambda(\theta)}\right)\Sigma_\theta\left(\frac{\partial\varphi'}{\partial\lambda}\,|_{\lambda=\lambda(\theta)}\right)$$

where $\frac{\partial\varphi}{\partial\lambda'}$ is the $r \times k$ matrix of partial derivatives $\frac{\partial\varphi_l}{\partial\lambda_j}$ ($l = 1,\ldots,r$ and $j = 1,\ldots,k$) and $\frac{\partial\varphi'}{\partial\lambda}$ is the transposed matrix. ∎

This result follows immediately using a first order expansion of φ:

$$\sqrt{n}\left(\varphi\left(\hat{\lambda}_n\right) - \varphi\left(|\lambda\left(\theta\right)\right)\right) \simeq \frac{\partial\varphi}{\partial\lambda'}\lambda\left(\theta\right)\left\{\sqrt{\left(\hat{\lambda}_n - \lambda\left(\theta\right)\right)}\right\}.$$

In the following, we will often use the notation $\frac{\partial\varphi}{\partial\lambda'}(\lambda(\theta))$ instead of $\frac{\partial\varphi}{\partial\lambda'}|_{\lambda=\lambda(\theta)}$.

3.3   Moment Conditions and Maximization

In order to simplify the presentation, we will at first assume that the statistical reference model is *i.i.d.* The observations $x_i \in X \subset \mathbb{R}^m$ are thus independent with distribution Q^θ, $\theta \in \Theta$. Our objective is to describe a class of functions $\lambda(\theta)$ which can be, at the same time, interpreted and readily estimated.

These functions are in fact functions of Q^θ and their dependence on θ is, therefore, determined by the dependence of Q and θ.

Let us introduce the following elements:

- $\Lambda \subset \mathbb{R}^k$ and $\lambda \in \Lambda$.
- $\psi : X \times \Lambda \to \mathbb{R}^r$ is a mapping such that $\psi(x_i, \lambda)$ is Q^θ integrable for all $\lambda \in \Lambda$.

Then, we are interested in the system of equations:

$$E^\theta(\psi(x_i, \lambda)) = 0. \tag{3.5}$$

This equation system will be called the *system of moment equations*. This defines a set of r relations between θ and λ from which the x_i obviously disappear when taking expectations. We are interested in the solution to this system for λ, which is a vector of dimension k. The value of i does not play a role because the model is *i.i.d.* We can assume, in particular, that $i = 1$ without changing the condition. It is thus advisable to investigate existence and uniqueness of the solution to this system. We will always be interested in systems of moment equations such that, if a solution exists, then it is necessarily unique. Indeed, we want to define a function $\lambda(\theta)$ as the solution to this system of equations, and nonuniqueness does not allow such a definition. Although the system (3.5) will be in general nonlinear, an intuitive condition for uniqueness is the existence of a sufficient number of equations, i.e., that $r \geq k$. We will reconsider these conditions at greater length in Chapter 17.

Two cases will be explicitly analyzed:

1. The number of moment conditions is equal to the dimension of λ and the system (3.5) is sufficiently regular such that, for all $\theta \in \Theta$, it admits a (unique) solution $\lambda(\theta)$. We talk therefore of a *simple system of moment equations.*

Let us consider a function φ of $X \times \Lambda$ in $\mathbb{R}$ such that $\varphi(x_i, \lambda)$ is integrable for all λ and examine the problem

$$\max_{\lambda \in \Lambda} E^\theta(\varphi(x_i, \lambda)). \tag{3.6}$$

The case of minimization is obviously equivalent as it suffices to change the sign. Here again, the existence and uniqueness of the solution to (3.6) are not guaranteed. In general, one introduces assumptions that satisfy the following conditions: $E^\theta(\varphi(x_i, \lambda))$ is injective in λ, which implies uniqueness, and the existence of a maximum is implied, for example, by assuming compactness of Λ and continuity of the function φ. Assuming differentiability of φ with respect to λ and the possibility to commute integration and differentiation, solving (3.6) is achieved by solving

$$E^\theta\left(\frac{\partial}{\partial \lambda}\varphi(x_i, \lambda)\right) = 0. \tag{3.7}$$

This procedure of defining $\lambda(\theta)$ leads naturally to a simple system of moment equations. The situation can be a more complicated because the first order conditions (3.7) characterize only a local maximum while a global maximum is required. The relationship between these two approaches is simple only when the system (3.7) admits a unique solution which is the maximum.

2. The number of moment conditions is larger than k and the system, therefore, does not necessarily have a solution. We then define Θ_*, a subset of Θ, such that for any $\theta \in \Theta_*$ the system $E^\theta(\psi(x_i, \lambda)) = 0$ admits a unique solution $\lambda(\theta)$.

It is obviously assumed that Θ_* is nonempty, and this system is called *system of generalized moment equations*

In this case, we see that the system (3.5) defines a function $\lambda(\theta)$ provided that the initial statistical model is restricted to the sub-family of sampling probabilities indexed by Θ_*. The question naturally arises of empirically verifying whether θ belongs to Θ_* by means of a hypothesis test and furthermore to estimate $\lambda(\theta)$. In practice, the estimation method provides a natural test, that we will present.

Example 3.6 *Suppose the x_i are i.i.d. with probability distribution Q and, thus, in this case $\theta = Q$ (see Example 1.8, in Chapter 1) and Θ is the subset of probabilities $\mathcal{P}_m$ such that the expectation of x_i exists. We consider $\psi(x_i, \lambda) = x_i - \lambda$ and $\lambda(Q)$ is then the function that relates Q with the expectation $E^Q(x_i)$.*

More generally, we can take a vector of functions $\psi_0(x_i)$ and limit the parameter space of the model to the set Q such that ψ_0 is integrable. Consider the function $\psi(x_i, \lambda) = \psi_0(x_i) - \lambda$. The solution to the system of moment equations is then

$$\lambda(Q) = E^Q(\psi_0(x_i)).$$

Let us return to $\psi(x_i) = x_i$ and define $\varphi(x_i, \lambda) = (x_i - \lambda)'(x_i - \lambda)$ which constraints Q to admit second order moments. The solution of the minimization problem

$$\min_{\lambda} E^Q \left[(x_i - \lambda)'(x_i - \lambda) \right] = 0$$

is equivalent to solving $E^Q(x_i - \lambda) = 0$ and leads in this case to $\lambda(Q) = E^Q(x_i)$.   □

Example 3.7   *Suppose $x_i \in \mathbb{R}$ and the model is i.i.d. with probability distribution Q, satisfying the integrability of x_i and x_i^2. The generalized system of moment equations is the following*

$$\lambda \in \mathbb{R} \quad and \quad \begin{cases} E^Q(x_i - \lambda) = 0 \\ E^Q((x_i - \lambda)^2 - \lambda^2) = 0 \end{cases}$$

The preceding system imposes on the initial model the restriction that the square of the mean and the variance of x_i are equal and defines $\lambda(Q)$ as the common value. Therefore, the set Θ_* is the set of all probability distributions on $\mathbb{R}$ that satisfy equality of squared mean and variance. It contains for example the exponential distribution.   □

Example 3.8   *Let us introduce linear regression in a simple example. Suppose the $x_i = (y_i, z_i) \in \mathbb{R}^2$ are i.i.d. with probability distribution Q such that second order moments of x_i exist. The following two problems are equivalent:*

$$E^Q \left((y_i - \lambda z_i) z_i \right) = 0$$

and

$$\min_{\lambda \in \mathbb{R}} E^Q \left((y_i - \lambda z_i)^2 \right).$$

They yield a solution

$$\lambda(Q) = \frac{E^Q(y_i z_i)}{E^Q(z_i^2)}$$

which is the coefficient of the linear regression of y_i on z_i.   □

Example 3.9   *The following example is very important and covers an estima-tion method which is used extremely often, namely maximum likelihood method. We are interested in a correctly specified model for which the likelihood func-tion, that is maximized, is correct. Consider the i.i.d. model for the observations x_i and the likelihood function*

$$l_n(x|\theta) = \prod_{i=1}^{n} f(x_i|\theta) \quad \theta \in \Theta \subset \mathbb{R}^k.$$

The dominating measure is the Lebesgue measure for simplicity. We assume additionally that the model is identified (two different values of θ correspond to density functions with different probabilities). Set $\Lambda = \Theta$ and introduce the maximization problem

$$\max_{\lambda \in \Lambda} E^{\theta} (\ln f(x_i|\lambda)) \tag{3.8}$$

for which, under the usual regularity conditions, the first order conditions can be written as

$$E^{\theta} \left(\frac{\partial}{\partial \lambda} \ln f(x_i|\lambda) \right) = 0. \tag{3.9}$$

The above expression is the expectation of the score of the dominated model. We can also verify that the solution $\lambda(\theta)$ of the maximization problem (3.8) is just $\lambda(\theta) = \theta$. Indeed, the problem (3.8) is equivalent to

$$\max_{\lambda \in \Lambda} \left\{ \int \ln f(x_i|\lambda) \, f(x_i|\theta) dx_i - \int \ln f(x_i|\theta) \, f(x_i|\theta) dx_i \right\}$$

$$\Leftrightarrow \min_{\lambda \in \Lambda} \int \ln \frac{f(x_i|\theta)}{f(x_i|\lambda)} \, f(x_i|\theta) dx_i.$$

The quantity in the maximization is the comparison between $f(x_i|\theta)$ and $f(x_i|\lambda)$ called Kullback-Leibler (quantity of) information. Using Jensen's inequality we can immediately verify that

$$\int \ln \frac{f(x_i|\theta)}{f(x_i|\lambda)} f(x_i|\theta) dx_i \geq 0.$$

This value is zero if $f(x_i|\theta)$ and $f(x_i|\lambda)$ are equal, which, under the iden-tification assumption, implies that λ and θ are equal. The minimum of the Kullback-Leibler information is therefore reached at θ.

Therefore, the function $\lambda(\theta)$ that we estimate with maximum likelihood is the identity $\lambda(\theta) = \theta$.   □

In stationary models, the moment or maximization conditions can be more general than presented above and use a sequence $x_i, \ldots, x_{i+s}$ of observations. Thus, we can systematically replace x_i in the preceding presentation by such a sequence; the comments will remain identical. Let us provide an example of moment conditions in a stationary model.

Example 3.10 *Suppose $(x_i)_{i=1,\ldots,n}$ are generated by a stationary process whose first two moments exist. We denote by P the probability distribution of this process and in this statistical model θ is equal to P. Consider the equations*

$$\begin{cases} E^P\left[(x_i - \lambda_1 x_{i-1} - \lambda_2 x_{i-2})x_{i-1}\right] = 0 \\ E^P\left[(x_i - \lambda_1 x_{i-1} - \lambda_2 x_{i-2})x_{i-2}\right] = 0. \end{cases}$$

The solution of this system

$$\begin{pmatrix} \lambda_1(P) \\ \lambda_2(P) \end{pmatrix} = \begin{pmatrix} E^P\left(x_{i-1}^2\right) & E^P\left(x_{i-1}x_{i-2}\right) \\ E^P\left(x_{i-1}x_{i-2}\right) & E^P\left(x_{i-2}^2\right) \end{pmatrix}^{-1} \begin{pmatrix} E^P\left(x_i x_{i-1}\right) \\ E^P\left(x_i x_{i-2}\right) \end{pmatrix}$$

is interpreted as the coefficient of the linear regression of x_i on x_{i-1} and x_{i-2} (see Chapter 7). □

Remark to Moments and Conditional Moments

As we explained in Chapter 1, econometrics primarily analyzes conditional moments explaining the generation of variables y_i given some variables z_i. In terms of moments, this viewpoint translates into the consideration of conditional moment equations. The parameter λ is then defined as the solution of the equation

$$E^\theta\left(\widetilde{\psi}(x_i, \lambda)\big| z_i\right) = 0,$$

where $\widetilde{\psi}$ is a mapping of values in $\mathbb{R}^{\widetilde{r}}$ where $\widetilde{r}$ is not necessarily larger than k, the dimension of λ. Indeed, this condition comes down to assuming an infinite number of moment conditions because we have one condition for each value of the random variable z_i. Insofar as λ is of finite size, we can reduce this infinity of conditions to a finite number.

Let us suppose for simplicity that $\widetilde{r} = 1$. We can then introduce a sequence $h_j, j = 1, \ldots, r$, of functions of z_i (and possibly of λ) by setting

$$h(z_i, \lambda) = \left(h_j(z_i, \lambda)\right)_{j=1,\ldots,r},$$

we have obviously

$$h(z_i, \lambda)\, E^\theta\left(\widetilde{\psi}(x_i, \lambda)\big| z_i\right) = 0,$$

thus

$$E^\theta \left[h\left(z_i, \lambda\right) E^\theta \left(\widetilde{\psi}\left(x_i, \lambda\right) \middle| z_i \right) \right] = E^\theta \left[h\left(z_i, \lambda\right) \widetilde{\psi}\left(x_i, \lambda\right) \right]$$

$$= E^\theta \left[\psi\left(x_i, \lambda\right) \right] \qquad (3.10)$$

$$= 0$$

with

$$\psi\left(x_i, \lambda\right) = h\left(z_i, \lambda\right) \widetilde{\psi}\left(x_i, \lambda\right).$$

We thus pass from a conditional moment condition to a condition where the expectation is taken with respect to the joint probability as in (3.5). The dimension of the moment condition is thus r which is arbitrary but must be larger than k for Equation (3.10) to have a unique solution. The functions h are called instruments, and we can ask what is the optimal choice of these functions and whether there exists an optimal choice with exactly k functions ($r = k$). This question will be studied at the end of this chapter and in Chapters 15 and 17. $\qquad \square$

3.4   Estimation by the Method of Moments and Generalized Moments

In the preceding section, we gave various definitions of the function $\lambda(\theta)$. In each of these definitions, the value of this function depends on θ through the sampling probability which is used to calculate an expectation. The general estimation principle consists in replacing the sampling probability by the empirical probability. The moment condition then becomes a relationship between the sample and λ whose solution yields the estimator $\hat{\lambda}_n$.

First, we limit ourselves to i.i.d. samples for which the observations are the $(x_i)_{i=1,\dots,n}$ with $x_i \in X \subset \mathbb{R}^m$. Recall that the empirical probability distribution associated with this sample is defined by

$$\hat{Q}_n = \frac{1}{n} \sum_{i=1}^n \delta_{x_i}$$

where δ_{x_i} is the Dirac measure on x_i. This is equivalent to defining $\hat{Q}_n(S)$ as the number of observations that belong to S divided by n; if φ is a function of the sample, then its expectation with respect to the empirical probability distribution is equal to

$$\hat{E}_n(\varphi) = \int \varphi d\hat{Q}_n(S) = \frac{1}{n} \sum_{i=1}^n \varphi(x_i). \qquad (3.11)$$

The properties of the empirical probability distribution are treated in more detail in Chapter 5. We will successively consider estimating λ with a simple system of moment conditions, and through maximization. Finally, we will consider the estimation of λ with a generalized system of moment equations.

Consider the simple system

$$E^{\theta}(\psi(x_i, \lambda)) = 0.$$

The estimator $\hat{\lambda}_n$ is defined as the solution to the system

$$\frac{1}{n} \sum_{i=1}^{n} \psi(x_i, \lambda) = 0 \tag{3.12}$$

obtained through the substitution of the expectation with respect to the sampling distribution by that of the empirical distribution.

If the maximization of $E^{\theta}(\varphi(x_i, \lambda))$ (see (3.6)) is the problem that defines $\lambda(\theta)$, then we construct the estimator $\hat{\lambda}_n$ by

$$\hat{\lambda}_n = \arg\max_{\lambda \in \Lambda} \frac{1}{n} \sum_{i=1}^{n} \varphi(x_i, \lambda) \tag{3.13}$$

or by solving

$$\frac{1}{n} \sum_{i=1}^{n} \frac{\partial}{\partial \lambda} \varphi(x_i, \lambda) = 0. \tag{3.14}$$

In these two cases, the solution $\hat{\lambda}_n$ of the empirical moment equations, or of the maximization, exists and is unique under regularity conditions that are not very restrictive in practice. In contrast, if we consider a generalized system of moment equations, then the system of equations

$$\frac{1}{n} \sum_{i=1}^{n} \psi(x_i, \lambda) = 0 \tag{3.15}$$

does not admit a solution in general, even if the true distribution that generated the data satisfies the theoretical equation

$$E^{\theta}(\psi(x_i, \lambda)) = 0, \quad \theta \in \Theta_*.$$

Note in particular that (3.15) is a system that contains more equations than unknowns.

The generalized method of moments is based on the minimization of a norm of the left-hand term in (3.15). We take a symmetric positive definite matrix H_n (possibly a function of the sample), and $\hat{\lambda}_n$ is calculated by

$$\hat{\lambda}_n = \arg\min_{\lambda \in \Lambda} \left(\frac{1}{n} \sum_{i=1}^{n} \psi(x_i, \lambda) \right)' H_n \left(\frac{1}{n} \sum_{i=1}^{n} \psi(x_i, \lambda) \right). \tag{3.16}$$

Studying the asymptotic properties of the estimator will suggest an optimal choice of the sequence of matrices H_n.

Remark. This approach can be interpreted as a change in the function of parameters. Indeed, set

$$\hat{\lambda}(\theta) = \arg\min E^{\theta} \left(\psi(x_i, \lambda) \right)' H E^{\theta} \left(\psi(x_i, \lambda) \right).$$

This function is, in general, defined for all θ and is identical to the solution $\lambda(\theta)$ of (3.5) if $\theta \in \Theta_*$. Therefore, the function $\hat{\lambda}(\theta)$ extends $\lambda(\theta)$ outside of Θ_*. The estimator $\hat{\lambda}_n$ (3.16) is constructed like an estimator of $\hat{\lambda}(\theta)$ obtained by replacing the expectation with sample averages and H by a matrix H_n. $\quad\square$

Before we consider the asymptotic results derived for this estimator, we illustrate their implementation in the examples that we previously introduced.

Example 3.11   *Continuation of Example 3.6. If $\psi(x_i, \lambda) = x_i - \lambda$, the estimator $\hat{\lambda}_n$ of λ is then the sample average*

$$\bar{x} = \frac{1}{n} \sum_{i=1}^{n} x_i.$$

More generally, if $\psi(x_i, \lambda) = \psi_0(x_i) - \lambda$, the estimator of λ will be the sample average of ψ_0, i.e.,

$$\hat{\lambda}_n = \frac{1}{n} \sum_{i=1}^{n} \psi_0(x_i).$$

$\quad\square$

Example 3.12   *Continuation of Example 3.7. Suppose $H_n = I_2$, the unit matrix of dimension 2. The generalized method of moment estimator of λ will then be the solution to the minimization of*

$$\left(\frac{1}{n} \sum_{i=1}^{n} x_i - \lambda \right)^2 + \left(\frac{1}{n} \sum_{i=1}^{n} (x_i - \lambda)^2 - \lambda^2 \right)^2$$

and satisfies, therefore:

$$\hat{\lambda}_n = \frac{\bar{x} \left(1 + 2 \left(\frac{1}{n} \sum_{i=1}^{n} x_i^2 \right) \right)}{1 + 2\bar{x}^2}.$$

$\quad\square$

Example 3.13   *Using the notation of Example 3.5 we can immediately verify the maximization of*

$$\frac{1}{n} \sum_{i=1}^{n} (x_i - \lambda)'(x_i - \lambda)$$

leads to the estimator $\hat{\lambda}_n = \bar{x}$.

$\quad\square$

Example 3.14 *The moment equations of Example 3.8 lead to the estimator*

$$\hat{\lambda}_n = \frac{\sum\limits_{i=1}^{n} y_i z_i}{\sum\limits_{i=1}^{n} z_i^2}$$

which is the coefficient of the linear regression of y_i on z_i. □

Example 3.15 *The example of maximum likelihood that we started to explain in Example 3.9 is extremely important. The estimator $\hat{\lambda}_n$ derived from Equation (3.9) is equal to*

$$\hat{\lambda}_n = \arg\max_{\lambda \in \Lambda} \frac{1}{n} \sum_{i=1}^{n} \ln f(x_i | \lambda)$$

and is the maximum likelihood estimator. Under regularity conditions, this implies that $\hat{\lambda}_n$ satisfies the first order condition

$$\frac{1}{n} \sum_{i=1}^{n} \frac{\partial \ln f(x_i | \hat{\lambda}_n)}{\partial \lambda} = 0.$$
□

Extending the above presentation to stationary processes does not pose any difficulties. Suppose that the moment condition involves the sequence of observations $x_i, \ldots, x_{i+s}$ and can be written as

$$E^\theta (\psi (x_i, \ldots, x_{i+s}, \lambda)) = 0. \tag{3.17}$$

We then replace in this expression the expectation by the sample average

$$\frac{1}{n-s} \sum_{i=1}^{n-s} \psi (x_i, \ldots, x_{i+s}, \lambda) = 0. \tag{3.18}$$

If the dimension of ψ is equal to that of λ, we solve (3.17), and if the number of moment conditions is larger than the dimension of λ, we proceed in an identical way to the one presented for (3.15).

Example 3.16 *Continuation of Example 3.10. We then obtain as an estimator*

$$\begin{pmatrix} \hat{\lambda}_{1n} \\ \hat{\lambda}_{2n} \end{pmatrix} = \begin{pmatrix} \sum\limits_{i=3}^{n} x_{i-1}^2 & \sum\limits_{i=3}^{n} x_{i-1}x_{i-2} \\ \sum\limits_{i=3}^{n} x_{i-1}x_{i-2} & \sum\limits_{i=3}^{n} x_{i-2}^2 \end{pmatrix}^{-1} \begin{pmatrix} \sum\limits_{i=3}^{n} x_i x_{i-1} \\ \sum\limits_{i=3}^{n} x_i x_{i-2} \end{pmatrix}.$$
□

3.5   Asymptotic Properties of Estimators

We will essentially examine two types of results: the almost sure convergence of $\hat{\lambda}_n$ to $\lambda(\theta)$ and the asymptotic normality of $\sqrt{n}(\hat{\lambda}_n - \lambda(\theta))$. Precise proofs of these results are difficult, but we will try, in this section, to outline the main arguments and assumptions treating simultaneously the various estimators that we previously presented. We will start by commenting on the main assumptions.

1. The first set of assumptions is fundamental, it is the most "statistical." We have to assume that the data generating mechanism satisfies the strong law of large numbers. We saw in the previous chapter that these conditions are satisfied if the process is i.i.d. or, more generally, stationary ergodic. In particular, we then have

$$\frac{1}{n} \sum_{i=1}^{n} \psi(x_i, \lambda) \to E^\theta \left(\psi(x_i, \lambda) \right) \quad P^\theta - a.s., \tag{3.19}$$

$$\frac{1}{n} \sum_{i=1}^{n} \varphi(x_i, \lambda) \to E^\theta \left(\varphi(x_i, \lambda) \right) \quad P^\theta - a.s. \tag{3.20}$$

and

$$\left(\frac{1}{n} \sum_{i=1}^{n} \psi(x_i, \lambda) \right)' H_n \left(\frac{1}{n} \sum_{i=1}^{n} \psi(x_i, \lambda) \right)$$
$$\to E^\theta \left(\psi(x_i, \lambda) \right)' H E^\theta \left(\psi(x_i, \lambda) \right) \quad P^\theta - a.s. \tag{3.21}$$

by using the notation of (3.12), (3.15), and (3.16).

Convergence (3.21) requires the additional assumption:

$$H_n \to H \; P^\theta - a.s. \tag{3.22}$$

2. We have to assume additionally that $\hat{\lambda}_n$ and $\lambda(\theta)$ exist and are unique. These assumptions are in particular satisfied if Λ is compact and if ψ (or φ) and its expectation are continuous. The compactness assumption is not very satisfying (because it is not satisfied in the majority of models) and we prefer to assume directly the existence and uniqueness of the estimators and of the functions $\lambda(\theta)$.

3. Finally, we have to assume that the convergence in (3.19), (3.20), and (3.21) is sufficiently regular in λ.

The usual assumption, in addition to the continuity of φ, ψ, and their expectation, is the uniformity of convergence in λ as it was defined in Chapter 2. This uniformity is difficult to verify and sufficient conditions are available in some cases. The necessary condition of uniformity is a local condition (uniform in a compact neighborhood) which can be used when Λ is open. When Λ is compact, we can consider global uniformity.

Under these conditions, the intuitive result is that it is possible to interchange the solution (or maximization) and the passage to the limit.

We thus obtain in the case of a simple moment equation:

$$\lim \hat{\lambda}_n = \lim \text{solution} \left\{ \frac{1}{n} \sum_{i=1}^{n} \psi(x_i, \lambda) = 0 \right\}$$

$$= \text{solution of} \left\{ \lim \frac{1}{n} \sum_{i=1}^{n} \psi(x_i, \lambda) = 0 \right\} \quad (3.23)$$

$$= \text{solution of} \left\{ E^{\theta}(\psi(x_i, \lambda) = 0 \right\}$$

$$= \lambda(\theta) \; P^{\theta} - a.s$$

The argument is the same for estimators based on maximization:

$$\lim \hat{\lambda}_n = \lim \arg \max_{\lambda \in \Lambda} \frac{1}{n} \sum_{i=1}^{n} \varphi(x_i, \lambda)$$

$$= \arg \max_{\lambda \in \Lambda} \lim \frac{1}{n} \sum_{i=1}^{n} \varphi(x, \lambda) \quad (3.24)$$

$$= \arg \max_{\lambda \in \Lambda} E^{\theta} (\varphi(x_i, \lambda))$$

$$= \lambda(\theta) \quad P^{\theta} - a.s.$$

Finally, the same argument applied to a generalized system of moment equations leads to

$$\lim \hat{\lambda}_n = \lim \arg \min \left(\frac{1}{n} \sum_{i=1}^{n} \psi(x_i, \lambda) \right)' H_n \left(\frac{1}{n} \sum_{i=1}^{n} \psi(x_i, \lambda) \right)$$

$$= \arg \min E^{\theta} (\psi(x_i, \lambda))' H E^{\theta} (\psi(x_i, \lambda)) \quad P^{\theta} - a.s. \quad (3.25)$$

If it is furthermore assumed that the condition

$$E^{\theta} (\psi(x_i, \lambda)) = 0$$

holds, i.e., that $\theta \in \Theta_*$, we then have additionally

$$\lim \hat{\lambda}_n = \arg sol\{E^{\theta}(\psi(x_i, \lambda) = 0\} \quad P^{\theta} - a.s. \quad \theta \in \Theta_*$$

$$= \lambda(\theta). \quad (3.26)$$

Now let us analyze the asymptotic normality of these estimators assuming that the conditions for almost sure convergence are satisfied. The additional assumptions are of two types:

4. The data-generating process must satisfy the central limit theorem. We saw in the previous chapter that this assumption is satisfied for i.i.d. processes

and requires a mixing condition that is stronger than the one required by the law of large numbers in the case of stationary processes. Of course we assume that the necessary moments (for example the variance of ψ) exist.

5. The proof of asymptotic normality is essentially based on linear approximations and will therefore require the differentiability of the estimation criterions and their limits. In particular, it requires that $\lambda(\theta)$ is in the interior of Λ and not located on the boundary. We must furthermore assume that it is possible to interchange expectation and derivatives (conditions for "differentiation under the summation sign"). Finally, we require conditions that allow us to neglect the remainder in the linear approximations; these conditions are essentially conditions of bounds on the derivatives of order higher than 1.

Let us show, under these assumptions, the asymptotic normality of an estimator drawn from a simple set of moment conditions.

Consider the linear approximation

$$\psi(x_i, \hat{\lambda}_n) \simeq \psi(x_i, \lambda(\theta)) + \frac{\partial \psi}{\partial \lambda'}(x_i, \lambda(\theta))\left(\hat{\lambda}_n - \lambda(\theta)\right). \qquad (3.27)$$

Then, by summation

$$\frac{1}{n}\sum_{i=1}^{n}\psi(x_i, \hat{\lambda}_n) \simeq \frac{1}{n}\sum_{i=1}^{n}\psi(x_i, \lambda(\theta))$$

$$+ \left(\frac{1}{n}\sum_{i=1}^{n}\frac{\partial \psi}{\partial \lambda'}(x_i, \lambda(\theta))\right)\left(\hat{\lambda}_n - \lambda(\theta)\right). \qquad (3.28)$$

In the following, we use for notational simplicity

$$\frac{\partial \psi}{\partial \lambda'}(x_i, \lambda(\theta)) = \frac{\partial \psi}{\partial \lambda'}.$$

Because the left-hand term is zero by the definition of $\hat{\lambda}_n$, we obtain the approximation

$$\sqrt{n}(\hat{\lambda}_n - \lambda) \simeq -\left(\frac{1}{n}\sum_{i=1}^{n}\frac{\partial \psi}{\partial \lambda'}\right)^{-1}\left(\frac{\sqrt{n}}{n}\sum_{i=1}^{n}\psi(x_i, \lambda(\theta))\right). \qquad (3.29)$$

By the strong law of large numbers,

$$\frac{1}{n}\sum_{i=1}^{n}\frac{\partial \psi}{\partial \lambda'}$$

converges to

$$E^{\theta}\left(\frac{\partial \psi}{\partial \lambda'}\right)$$

which is a matrix that is invertible in a neighborhood of $\lambda(\theta)$ because $\lambda(\theta)$ is the unique solution of $E^\theta(\psi) = 0$ and because of

$$E^\theta\left(\frac{\partial \psi}{\partial \lambda'}\right) = \frac{\partial}{\partial \lambda'} E^\theta(\psi).$$

By the central limit theorem, we see that

$$\frac{\sqrt{n}}{n} \sum_{i=1}^{n} \psi(x_i, \lambda(\theta)) \to N(0, V_\theta) \quad \text{in } P^\theta - \text{distribution}.$$

Indeed ψ has zero expectation at $\lambda(\theta)$.

If the data-generating process is *i.i.d.*, then

$$V_\theta = Var^\theta(\psi). \tag{3.30}$$

In the mixing stationary case, V_θ is given by Theorem 2.6 of Chapter 2 and satisfies the following expression

$$V_\theta = \sum_{j=-\infty}^{+\infty} Cov^\theta\left(\psi(x_i, \theta), \psi(x_{i+j}, \theta)\right). \tag{3.31}$$

Multiplying by $E^\theta(\frac{\partial \psi}{\partial \lambda'})^{-1}$ and using the properties from Section 2.4, we obtain

$$\sqrt{n}\left(\hat{\lambda}_n - \lambda(\theta)\right) \to N(0, \Sigma_\theta) \text{ in } P^\theta - \text{distribution}$$

with

$$\Sigma_\theta = \left[E^\theta\left(\frac{\partial \psi}{\partial \lambda'}\right)\right]^{-1} V_\theta \left[E^\theta\left(\frac{\partial \psi'}{\partial \lambda}\right)\right]^{-1}. \tag{3.32}$$

This proof naturally extends to the case of maximization estimators using the relationship

$$\psi(x_i, \lambda) = \frac{\partial \varphi}{\partial \lambda}(x_i, \lambda) \tag{3.33}$$

and

$$\frac{\partial \psi}{\partial \lambda'}(x_i, \lambda) = \frac{\partial^2 \varphi}{\partial \lambda \partial \lambda'}(x_i, \lambda). \tag{3.34}$$

We summarize the preceding set of results with the following theorem.

Theorem 3.3 *Under Assumptions 1 to 5, the estimator $\hat{\lambda}_n$ given as the solution of $\frac{1}{n}\sum_{i=1}^{n}\psi(x_i, \lambda) = 0$ (or respectively as the argument of the maximum of $\frac{1}{n}\sum_{i=1}^{n}\varphi(x_i, \lambda))$ has the following asymptotic properties:*

1. *$\hat{\lambda}_n \to \lambda(\theta) \ P^\theta - a.s.$ where $\lambda(\theta)$ is the solution of $E^\theta(\psi(x_i, \lambda)) = 0$ (resp. argument of the maximum of $E^\theta(\varphi(x_i, \lambda)))$.*

2. $\sqrt{n}(\hat{\lambda}_n - \lambda(\theta)) \to N(0, \Sigma_\theta)$ in P^θ-distribution.
    with

$$\Sigma_\theta = E^\theta \left(\frac{\partial \psi}{\partial \lambda'} \right)^{-1} V_\theta E^\theta \left(\frac{\partial \psi'}{\partial \lambda} \right)^{-1}$$

$$\left(resp. \ \Sigma_\theta = E^\theta \left(\frac{\partial^2 \varphi}{\partial \lambda \partial \lambda'} \right)^{-1} V_\theta E^\theta \left(\frac{\partial^2 \varphi'}{\partial \lambda \partial \lambda'} \right)^{-1} \right).$$

where V_θ is defined in (3.30) or in (3.31).   ■

Let us consider the extension of this approach to estimators that are defined by the generalized method of moments. The solution $\hat{\lambda}_n$ of the minimization problem (3.16) satisfies the first order conditions

$$\left(\frac{1}{n} \sum_{i=1}^n \frac{\partial \psi'}{\partial \lambda}(x_i, \hat{\lambda}_n) \right) H_n \left(\frac{1}{n} \sum_{i=1}^n \psi(x_i, \hat{\lambda}_n) \right) = 0.$$

Using approximation (3.28), we obtain

$$\left(\frac{1}{n} \sum_{i=1}^n \frac{\partial \psi'}{\partial \lambda}(x_i, \hat{\lambda}_n) \right) H_n \left[\left(\frac{\sqrt{n}}{n} \sum_{i=1}^n \psi(x_i, \lambda(\theta)) \right) \right.$$

$$\left. + \left(\frac{1}{n} \sum_{i=1}^n \frac{\partial \psi}{\partial \lambda'}(x_i, \lambda(\theta)) \right) \sqrt{n} \left(\hat{\lambda}_n - \lambda(\theta) \right) \right] \simeq 0.$$

Note that

$$\frac{1}{n} \sum_{i=1}^n \frac{\partial \psi'}{\partial \lambda}(x_i, \hat{\lambda}_n)$$

has the same limit as

$$\frac{1}{n} \sum_{i=1}^n \frac{\partial \psi'}{\partial \lambda}(x_i, \lambda(\theta))$$

which is equal to $E^\theta(\frac{\partial \psi}{\partial \lambda})$. The assumption $H_n \to H_0$ and the central limit theorem applied to

$$\frac{\sqrt{n}}{n} \sum_{i=1}^n \psi(x_i, \lambda(\theta))$$

imply the asymptotic normality of

$$\sqrt{n}(\hat{\lambda}_n - \lambda(\theta)).$$

Theorem 3.4 *Under the assumptions of Theorem 3.3, the estimator $\hat{\lambda}_n$ defined in (3.16) satisfies the following asymptotic properties:*

1. $\hat{\lambda}_n \to \lambda(\theta) \quad P^0 - as. \; if \theta \in \Theta_*.$
2. $\sqrt{n}(\hat{\lambda}_n - \lambda(\theta)) \to N(0, \Sigma_\theta)$ *in P^θ-distribution if $\theta \in \Theta_*$ with*

$$\Sigma_\theta = \left(E^\theta \left(\frac{\partial \psi'}{\partial \lambda} \right) H E^\theta \left(\frac{\partial \psi}{\partial \lambda'} \right) \right)^{-1} E^\theta \left(\frac{\partial \psi'}{\partial \lambda} \right)$$

$$H V_\theta H E^\theta \left(\frac{\partial \psi}{\partial \lambda'} \right) \left(E^\theta \left(\frac{\partial \psi'}{\partial \lambda} \right) H E^\theta \left(\frac{\partial \psi}{\partial \lambda'} \right) \right)^{-1}.$$

All expressions are evaluated at $\lambda(\theta)$. ∎

We note that, in the case of generalized moments, the matrix $E^\theta(\frac{\partial \psi'}{\partial \lambda})$ is not invertible (as it is not square), which makes the expression for the asymptotic variance more complicated than in Theorem 3.3. It can be easily verified that, if $E^\theta(\frac{\partial \psi'}{\partial \lambda})$ is square and invertible, i.e., the generalized moments are reduced to simple moments, then the two results are identical.

A possibility to simplify the preceding asymptotic variance becomes immediately apparent, by choosing a suitable sequence H_n in such a way that its limit H is the inverse of V_θ.

Theorem 3.5 *If $H = V_\theta^{-1}$, then the asymptotic variance of $\hat{\lambda}_n$ defined in Theorem 3.4 simplifies to*

$$\Sigma_\theta = \left(E^\theta \left(\frac{\partial \psi'}{\partial \lambda} \right) V_\theta^{-1} E^\theta \left(\frac{\partial \psi}{\partial \lambda'} \right) \right)^{-1}$$

and the asymptotic variance of $\hat{\lambda}_n$ derived from this choice of H_0 is smaller than or equal to (in the matrix sense) the asymptotic variance of $\hat{\lambda}_n$ derived from any H. In this case, we say that the sequence H_n is optimal if it converges to V_θ^{-1}. ∎

Proof: It is sufficient to verify that the difference, called K, between the variances appearing in Theorems 3.4 and 3.5 is positive semidefinite. K is given by

$$K = (E'HE)^{-1} E' H V_\theta H E (E'HE)^{-1} - \left(E' V_\theta^{-1} E \right)^{-1}$$

by setting $E = E^\theta(\frac{\partial \psi}{\partial \lambda'})$. Factorizing K and defining D such that $V_\theta^{-1} = D'D$, we obtain, after some matrix manipulations:

$$K = (E'HE)^{-1} E' H \left[D^{-1} D'^{-1} - E(E'D'DE)^{-1} E' \right] H E (E'HE)^{-1},$$

hence,

$$K = (E'HE)^{-1}E'HD^{-1}\left[I - DE(E'D'DE)^{-1}E'D'\right]D'^{-1}HE(E'HE)^{-1}.$$

It is apparent that this difference is positive semidefinite if and only if

$$I - DE^\theta\left(\frac{\partial\psi}{\partial\lambda}\right)\left[E^\theta\left(\frac{\partial\psi'}{\partial\lambda}\right)D'DE^\theta\left(\frac{\partial\psi'}{\partial\lambda}\right)\right]^{-1}E^\theta\left(\frac{\partial\psi'}{\partial\lambda}\right)D$$

is positive semidefinite. This property is obviously satisfied, because this matrix is an orthogonal projection matrix. ∎

We illustrate these results starting with the examples that we presented previously. In particular, we will see that the preceding expressions for the asymptotic variance often simplifies.

As we will see in example 3.18, the optimal asymptotic matrix depends in general on unknown characteristics of the sampling process which must be consistently estimated in order to determine H_n. In particular, H may depend on $\lambda(\theta)$, and it is sufficient to replace this vector by a preliminary estimate, which, for example, can be obtained by generalized method of moments with a weighting matrix equal to the identity matrix or equal to

$$\begin{pmatrix} I_r & 0 \\ 0 & 0 \end{pmatrix}.$$

Example 3.17 *The preceding theorems are not immediately useful to show that in examples 3.6 and 3.11, $\sqrt{n}(\hat{\lambda}_n - E^\theta(\varphi_0))$ converges to a centered normal distribution with variance $Var^\theta(\psi_0)$. This result follows immediately from the application of the central limit theorem. We can show that in this example*

$$E^\theta\left(\frac{\partial\psi}{\partial\lambda'}\right)^{-1} = 1.$$ □

Example 3.18 *Continuation of Example 1.7 and 3.12. The convergence of $\hat{\lambda}_n$ is directly obtained since $\bar{x} \to \lambda$, $\frac{1}{n}\sum_{i=1}^n x_i^2 \to 2\lambda^2$ and thus $\hat{\lambda}_n \to \lambda\ P^\theta -$ a.s. (here we simplify notation by writing λ for $\lambda(Q)$). We can directly calculate the asymptotic variance of $\hat{\lambda}_n$ and verify the result with Theorem 3.4. Let us calculate instead an estimator that corresponds to the optimal choice of H. We can show that*

$$Var^\theta(\psi) = \begin{pmatrix} \lambda^2 & E^\theta(x_i^3) - 4\lambda^3 \\ E^\theta(x_i^3) - 4\lambda^3 & 8\lambda^4 - 4\lambda E^\theta(x_i^3) + E^\theta(x_i^4) \end{pmatrix}.$$

In order to construct a sequence H_n converging to $(Var^\theta(\psi))^{-1}$, we can proceed in the following manner. The theoretical moments $E^\theta(x_i^3)$ and $E^\theta(x_i^4)$ are consistently estimated by the empirical moments

$$\frac{1}{n}\sum_{i=1}^{n} x_i^3 \quad and \quad \frac{1}{n}\sum_{i=1}^{n} x_i^4.$$

The parameter λ appears in the matrix. It is sufficient to have a consistent estimator λ_n^* of λ available, for example the one constructed with the matrix $H_n = I_2$, thus

$$\lambda_n^* = \frac{\bar{x}\left(1 + 2\frac{1}{n}\sum_{i=1}^{n} x_i^2\right)}{1 + 2\bar{x}^2}.$$

Therefore, we proceed in two stages: estimating λ_n^* in a first stage, constructing H_n by

$$H_n^{-1} = \begin{pmatrix} \lambda_n^{*2} & \frac{1}{n}\sum_{i=1}^{n} x_i^3 - 4\lambda_n^{*3} \\ \frac{1}{n}\sum_{i=1}^{n} x_i^3 - 4\lambda_n^{*3} & 8\lambda_n^{*4} - 4\lambda_n^*\left(\frac{1}{n}\sum_{i=1}^{n} x_i^3\right) + \frac{1}{n}\sum_{i=1}^{n} x_i^4 \end{pmatrix}$$

and then estimating λ by the minimization of

$$\left(\frac{1}{n}\sum_{i=1}^{n} x_i - \lambda, \frac{1}{n}\sum_{i=1}^{n} x_i^2 - 2\lambda\frac{1}{n}\sum_{i=1}^{n} x_i\right) H_n \begin{pmatrix} \frac{1}{n}\sum_{i=1}^{n} x_i - \lambda \\ \frac{1}{n}\sum_{i=1}^{n} x_i^2 - 2\lambda\frac{1}{n}\sum_{i=1}^{n} x_i \end{pmatrix}.$$

We leave the calculation of $\hat{\lambda}_n$ and its asymptotic variance as an exercise. □

Example 3.19 *In this example, the asymptotic distribution of the estimator can be directly calculated, but we use the previous theorems for illustration. The estimator $\hat{\lambda}_n$ converges to the linear regression coefficient $\lambda(Q)$ defined in Example 3.8. Let us calculate the asymptotic variance. We have*

$$\psi(x_i, \lambda) = (y_i - \lambda z_i)z_i \quad and \quad \frac{\partial\psi}{\partial\lambda}(x_i, \lambda) = -z_i^2.$$

Thus

$$E^Q\left(\frac{\partial\psi}{\partial\lambda}\right) = -E^Q\left(z_i^2\right).$$

The calculation of the variance of ψ is more complicated. It only simplifies under assumptions that we do not wish to introduce in this chapter. Thus, we conclude this example with the following result

$$\sqrt{n}\left(\hat{\lambda}_n - \lambda(Q)\right) \to N\left(0, \frac{Var^Q\left[(y_i - \lambda z_i)z_i\right]}{\left[E^Q(z_i^2)\right]^2}\right).$$

□

This example is treated in detail in Chapter 8.

Example 3.20 *Here we continue the analysis of maximum likelihood estimator treated as a moment estimator. The arguments presented in Examples 3.9 and 3.15 allow as to conclude that $\hat{\lambda}_n$ converges almost surely to θ (under appropriate assumptions). We calculate the asymptotic variance matrix using Theorem 3.3. We have*

$$\begin{cases} \varphi(x_i, \lambda) & = \ln f(x_i, \lambda) \\ \dfrac{\partial \varphi(x_i, \lambda)}{\partial \lambda} & = \dfrac{\partial \ln f(x_i, \lambda)}{\partial \lambda} \\ \dfrac{\partial^2 \varphi(x_i, \lambda)}{\partial \lambda \partial \lambda'} & = \dfrac{\partial^2 \ln f(x_i, \lambda)}{\partial \lambda \partial \lambda'}. \end{cases}$$

It is known that

$$-E^\theta \left(\frac{\partial^2 \ln f(x_i, \lambda)}{\partial \lambda \partial \lambda'} \right) = Var^\theta \left(\frac{\partial \ln f(x_i, \lambda)}{\partial \lambda} \right) = \mathcal{J}_\theta;$$

the matrix $\mathcal{J}_\theta$ is called the Fisher information matrix. We then obtain the usual result

$$\sqrt{n} \left(\hat{\lambda}_n - \theta \right) \to N \left(0, \mathcal{J}_\theta^{-1} \right) \quad in \quad P^\theta - distribution. \qquad \square$$

Example 3.21 *Here we treat an important class of examples that generalize the preceding study of the maximum likelihood estimator under misspecification. Consider two i.i.d. models of the same sample $(x_i)_{i=1,\dots,n}$ and different parameter spaces Θ and Λ, both of finite but possibly different dimensions. These models are dominated and characterized by their likelihood functions*

$$l_n (x|\theta) = \prod_{i=1}^n f(x_i|\theta) \text{ and } q_n (x|\lambda) = \prod_{i=1}^n g(x_i|\lambda).$$

Let $\hat{\lambda}_n$ be the maximum likelihood estimator of the second model defined as the solution to the program

$$\hat{\lambda}_n = \arg \max_{\lambda \in \Lambda} \frac{1}{n} \sum_{i=1}^n \ln g(x_i, \lambda)$$

$$= solution \ of \ \left\{ \frac{1}{n} \sum_{i=1}^n \frac{\partial}{\partial \lambda} \ln g(x_i, \lambda) = 0 \right\}.$$

We assume that the true generating probabilities of the observations belong to a family defined by the first model, which amounts to the consideration of the properties of $\hat{\lambda}_n$ relative to the probability distribution $P_\infty^\theta, \theta \in \Theta$. The estimator $\hat{\lambda}_n$ is associated with the moment conditions

$$E^\theta \left(\frac{\partial \ln g(x_i, \lambda)}{\partial \lambda} \right) = 0$$

or equivalently with the maximization condition of $E^\theta (\ln g(x_{i,\lambda}))$. In both conditions, the expectation is taken with respect to P_∞^θ because we have assumed that the data is generated by the first model.

Define $\lambda(\theta)$ as the solution to one of the two preceding problems. We can note a third equivalent form of the definition of $\lambda(\theta)$

$$\lambda(\theta) = \arg\min_\lambda \int \ln \frac{f(x_i|\theta)}{g(x_i|\lambda)} f(x_i|\theta)dx_i$$

$$= \arg\min_\lambda \left\{ E^\theta (\ln f(x_i|\theta)) - E^\theta (\ln g(x_i|\lambda)) \right\}.$$

The value $\lambda(\theta)$ minimizes thus the difference between the true density $f(x_i|\theta)$ and a density of the second model $g(x_i|\lambda)$, this difference is measured by the Kullback-Leibler quantity of information. In this context, this value is called the pseudo-true value of the parameter of the second model.

Using Theorem 3.3, we can then show that

$$\sqrt{n}(\hat{\lambda}_n - \lambda(\theta)) \to N(0, \Sigma_\theta) \quad P_\infty^\theta - distribution$$

and that

$$\Sigma_\theta = E^\theta \left(\frac{\partial^2 \ln g(x_i, \lambda)}{\partial\lambda\partial\lambda'} \right)^{-1} Var^\theta \left(\frac{\partial \ln g(x_i, \lambda)}{\partial\lambda} \right) E^\theta \left(\frac{\partial^2 \ln g(x_i, \lambda)}{\partial\lambda\partial\lambda'} \right)^{-1};$$

in general, this product of three matrices does not simplify.

Let us consider two specific models in this class of examples. Here $x_i = (y_i, z_i)' \in \mathbb{R}^2$, and θ and λ are real.

The first model assumes

$$x_i|\theta \sim N_2 \left(\begin{pmatrix} \theta \\ 0 \end{pmatrix}, V \right) \quad V = \begin{pmatrix} v_{11} & v_{12} \\ v_{12} & v_{22} \end{pmatrix},$$

where V is known. The second model is defined by

$$x_i|\lambda \sim N_2 \left(\begin{pmatrix} 0 \\ \lambda \end{pmatrix}, V \right).$$

It is easy to verify that after some manipulations

$$\hat{\lambda}_n = \bar{z} - \frac{v_{12}}{v_{11}} \bar{y}$$

of which the P^θ-a.s. limit is immediate, because $\bar{z} \to 0$ and $\bar{y} \to \theta$ P_∞^θ-a.s. Therefore,

$$\hat{\lambda}_n \to -\frac{v_{12}}{v_{11}} \theta.$$

We leave it to the reader to verify that

$$\lambda(\theta) = -\frac{v_{12}}{v_{11}} \theta$$

minimizes the Kullback-Leibler information between the two normal densities defined above. The asymptotic variance of $\hat{\lambda}_n$ can be obtained starting with Theorem 3.1 or directly by applying the central limit theorem to

$$\frac{\sqrt{n}}{n} \sum_{i=1}^{n} \left(z_i - \frac{v_{12}}{v_{11}} y_i + \frac{v_{12}}{v_{11}} \theta \right).$$

□

Remark: Conditional Moments and Optimal Marginal Moments

Using the notation of expression (3.10), we can then ask ourselves what the *optimal choice of the function h* is; in this case, h is often referred to as optimal instrument. We limit ourselves to the static case (i.i.d. data). For an arbitrary function h the asymptotic variance of the estimator, obtained with the optimal choice of the weighting matrix, can be written

$$\left[E^\theta \left(\frac{\partial \left(h \widetilde{\psi} \right)'}{\partial \lambda} \right) V^\theta \left(h \widetilde{\psi} \right)^{-1} E^\theta \left(\frac{\partial \left(h \widetilde{\psi} \right)}{\partial \lambda'} \right) \right]^{-1}. \tag{3.35}$$

Note that

$$E^\theta \left(\frac{\partial \left(h \widetilde{\psi} \right)}{\partial \lambda'} \right) = E^\theta \left(\frac{\partial h}{\partial \lambda'} \widetilde{\psi} \right) + E^\theta \left(h \frac{\partial \widetilde{\psi}}{\partial \lambda'} \right)$$

$$= E^\theta \left(h \frac{\partial \widetilde{\psi}}{\partial \lambda'} \right)$$

and that

$$V^\theta \left(h \widetilde{\psi} \right) = E^\theta \left(h V^\theta \left(\widetilde{\psi} \, | z \right) h' \right)$$

because

$$E^\theta \left(\frac{\partial h}{\partial \lambda'} \widetilde{\psi} \right) = E^\theta \left(\frac{\partial h}{\partial \lambda'} E^\theta \left(\widetilde{\psi} \, | z \right) \right) = 0.$$

The variance matrix can thus be simplified to

$$\left[E^\theta \left(\frac{\partial \widetilde{\psi}}{\partial \lambda} h' \right) E^\theta \left(h V^\theta \left(\widetilde{\psi} \, | z \right) h' \right)^{-1} E^\theta \left(h \frac{\partial \widetilde{\psi}}{\partial \lambda'} \right) \right]^{-1}. \tag{3.36}$$

Consider a specific choice of h given by

$$h^0 \left(z, \lambda \right) = E^\theta \left(\frac{\partial \widetilde{\psi}}{\partial \lambda} \, | z \right) V^\theta \left(\widetilde{\psi} \, | z \right)^{-1} \tag{3.37}$$

which is of dimension k and thus does not require the choice of a weighting matrix. We obtain in this case an asymptotic variance of the estimator equal to

$$\left\{ E^\theta \left[E^\theta \left(\frac{\partial \tilde{\psi}}{\partial \lambda} \,|z \right) V^\theta \left(\tilde{\psi} \,|z \right)^{-1} E^\theta \left(\frac{\partial \tilde{\psi}}{\partial \lambda'} \,|z \right) \right] \right\}^{-1}.$$

It is fairly simple to show that this matrix is smaller than that given in (3.36), which shows that the choice of h^0 is optimal. This result is little used in practice, except for this particular case, because the calculation of h requires the knowledge of the distribution conditional on z. One can then use a nonparametric approach to find h^0. □

Remark: Generalized Method of Moments and Efficiency

We showed in Example 3.20 that the asymptotic variance of the parameters estimated by maximum likelihood method is equal to J_θ^{-1}. We also know that this variance is minimal, i.e., any consistent, asymptotically normal estimator has an asymptotic variance larger than or equal to J_θ^{-1}.

In general, an estimator obtained by the generalized method of moments will thus be less efficient than the maximum likelihood estimator, even if the weighting matrix H is chosen in an optimal way. This result does not undermine the interest in this method, which is more robust than maximum likelihood, because in general it does not assume that the distribution of the data is specified. Furthermore, recent work shows that, if the number of moments is very large, then the efficiency of the generalized method of moment estimator can be arbitrarily close to that of the maximum likelihood estimator. □

Remark. In order to use the asymptotic results of this chapter, it is necessary to estimate the matrices that appear in the asymptotic variance in Theorems (3.3), (3.4), and (3.5). These matrices involve expectations and variance which are replaced by their empirical counterparts; for example, $E^\theta(\frac{\partial \psi'}{\partial \lambda})$ must be replaced by $\frac{1}{n} \sum_{i=1}^n \frac{\partial \psi'}{\partial \lambda}(x_i, \hat{\lambda}_n)$. This step is, however, more difficult in the dynamic case where the variance contains the matrix V_θ defined in (3.31). This type of problem is treated in Chapter 15, Section 15.2.4. □

Notes

A large part of the content of this chapter again belongs to the statistical foundation and is studied by numerous authors.

In Serfling (1980), one can find a presentation of the properties of maximum likelihood and of moment estimation, preceded by an exposition of the fundamental asymptotic properties of estimators. The generalized method of moments is due to Hansen (1982). Carrasco and Florens (2000) provide an extension of GMM to a continuum of moment conditions. The study of the properties of the maximum likelihood estimator in a misspecified model possibly started with the work of Huber (1967), and these results have been used in econometrics following the article by White (1982).

Theoretical complements to our exposition can be found in Newey (1993) and in Newey and McFadden (1994) or in Rieder (1994) and Van Der Vaart and Wellner (1996).

4. Asymptotic Tests

4.1 Introduction

The objective of this chapter is to briefly develop the principal elements of the theory of asymptotic tests. We will summarize in the briefest possible way, the "general" theory of testing, before presenting the three main classes of tests, which are the Wald test, the Rao test, and the test based on the comparison of minima (the last one is a generalization of the likelihood ratio test introduced by Neyman and Pearson). In order to quickly outline the procedures to construct these three types of tests, let us consider the estimation of a function λ of a parameter obtained through the optimization of a criterion $C(\lambda)$. A hypothesis is then a restriction on λ. There exist three possibilities to measure the validity of the restriction:

- Estimate λ without constraint and measure the difference between this estimator and the set of λ that satisfy the restriction. We then obtain the tests, called Wald tests.
- Calculate the first order conditions of the optimization problem, i.e.,

$$\frac{\partial}{\partial \lambda} C(\lambda) = 0.$$

We know that, by definition, these conditions are exactly satisfied for the unrestricted estimator, and we ask whether these are approximately satisfied by the restricted estimator. The tests constructed in this way are the Rao tests (or Lagrange multiplier tests).
- Compare the value of the optimization criterion with and without constraint. The difference thus obtained is a measure of the validity of the restriction and leads to a generalization of the likelihood ratio tests, which we call tests of comparison of minima.

These different principles for testing a hypothesis can be applied in various contexts, and we have chosen to present them in a rather detailed manner in the framework of generalized method of moments (GMM) estimation. Following this, we will present them again briefly in the framework of maximum likelihood estimation (MLE) with a correctly specified model and a finite parameter space. We end the chapter with the introduction of Wald-type tests but oriented towards the problem of specification testing. These two types of tests are the Hausman test and encompassing test.

4.2   Tests and Asymptotic Tests

Consider a statistical model with parametric space Θ (whose dimension is not necessarily finite). A so-called *null hypothesis* (denoted H_0) is defined by a subspace Θ_0 of Θ. The complement Θ_1 of Θ_0 is called *alternative hypothesis* of Θ_0 and is denoted H_1. If X^n is the sample space of the model, a hypothesis test is characterized by a subset W_n of X^n called the critical region. If x belongs to W_n, Θ_0 is rejected, whereas if x does not lie in W_n, the null hypothesis is accepted. Denoting the sampling probability distribution by P_n^θ as usual, we are interested in the function

$$\theta \in \Theta \rightarrow P_n^\theta(W_n) \in [0, 1] \tag{4.1}$$

called the *power function* of the test. If θ is in Θ_0, $P_n^\theta(W_n)$ represents the probability of rejecting the null hypothesis when it is true (*type I error*), and if θ is in Θ_1, $1 - P_n^\theta(W_n)$ is the probability of accepting H_0 when it is false (*type II error*).

The general statistical problem of hypothesis testing is the following. Given a probability α, we look for tests of *significance level* (or *level*) α, that is such that $P_n^\theta(W_n) \leq \alpha$ for all θ in Θ_0. Among the tests of level α, we look for the test that minimizes the probability of type II error or maximizes

$$sup_{\theta \in \Theta_1} P_n^\theta(W_n).$$

If the retained test satisfies

$$sup_{\theta \in \Theta_0} P_n^\theta(W_n) = \alpha,$$

then the test is said to be of *size α*.

In this chapter, we examine tests associated with GMM estimation, this leads us to modify the previous general framework in two ways.

First, recall that this method enables us to estimate only functions $\lambda(\theta)$ taking their values in a vector space. Hence, we test only the regions Θ_0 of Θ of the form

$$\Theta_0 = \lambda^{-1}(\Lambda_0)$$

where Λ_0 is a subset of $\Lambda \subset \mathbb{R}^k$. Our presentation simplifies by assuming that Θ_0 can be described in two equivalent manners:

1. By a set of restrictions. We write then

$$\Theta_0 = \{\theta : R(\lambda(\theta)) = 0\} \tag{4.2}$$

where R is a function from $\mathbb{R}^k$ to $\mathbb{R}^l$ satisfying some regularity conditions. Specifically, we assume that R is continuously differentiable and that the matrix of derivatives $\frac{\partial R}{\partial \lambda'}$ (of dimension $l \times k$) has rank l, which in particular requires $l \leq k$.

2. As the image of a parameter with lower dimension. It is assumed that

$$\Theta_0 = \{\theta : \lambda(\theta) = \tilde{\lambda}(\mu(\theta))\}$$

where μ is a mapping from Θ to $\mathbb{R}^{k-l}$ and $\tilde{\lambda}$ is a mapping from $\mathbb{R}^{k-l}$ to $\mathbb{R}^k$, which is continuously differentiable and has rank $k - l$.

Our presentation comes to describing Λ_0 as the inverse image of $\{0\}$ of the mapping R or as the image space of the mapping $\tilde{\lambda}$. This construction is always possible if Λ_0 is an affine subspace of $\mathbb{R}^k$, in this case, R and $\tilde{\lambda}$ are affine. If Λ_0 has a more complex structure, our construction is, strictly speaking, valid only locally. However, we limit ourselves to cases where this double characterization is possible globally.

Example 4.1 *Suppose that $\lambda(\theta) = (\lambda_1(\theta), \lambda_2(\theta))'$, $k = 2$, and we wish to test the hypothesis*

$$\lambda_1(\theta) + \lambda_2(\theta) = 1.$$

Here, the function $R(\lambda_1, \lambda_2)$ is equal to $\lambda_1 + \lambda_2 - 1$. Let for example $\mu(\theta) = \lambda_1(\theta)$. Then, we can write

$$\Theta_0 = \left\{\theta : \lambda(\theta) = (\lambda_1(\theta), 1 - \lambda_1(\theta))'\right\} \quad and \quad \tilde{\lambda}(\mu) = (\mu, 1 - \mu)'.$$

$\square$

We explained in Chapter 3 that the introduction of a system of generalized moments implies, in general, constraints on the sampling distributions, constraints which are satisfied only for the θ that belong to $\Theta_* \subset \Theta$. Except for the test presented in Section 4.5, we always assume that the overidentification constraints are satisfied and we set $\Theta = \Theta_*$ for convenience. The hypotheses that we test are in fact subsets of Θ_*, i.e., they are extra restrictions besides those that are imposed by the system of moments.

Second, because the method of moments leads to estimators for which only the asymptotic properties are known, we study only those properties of the tests that are satisfied when the sample size goes to infinity.

We look for tests defined by functions $\tau_n(x_1, \ldots, x_n)$ with values in $\mathbb{R}^+$ whose critical regions are of the following form:

$$W_{n,\tau_0} = \{x = (x_1, \ldots, x_n) : \tau_n(x_1, \ldots, x_n) \geq \tau_0\} \subset X^n.$$

Such a sequence of functions τ_n is called a *test statistic* and τ_0 is the critical value of the test.

The choice of the test statistic is determined by two desirable properties.

1. The consistency of the test. The test is *consistent* if the probability of type II error goes to zero as $n \to \infty$, in other words, if

$$\forall \theta \in \Theta_1 \quad \lim_{n \to \infty} P_n^\theta(W_{n,\tau_0}) = 1.$$

2. The limiting distribution. The statistic τ_n must have a limiting distribution when $n \to \infty$ and when $\theta \in \Theta_0$. This allows us to calculate the asymptotic probability of a Type I error. A particularly desirable situation is that when the limiting distribution of τ_n does not depend on θ as long as $\theta \in \Theta_0$. Then, the statistic is said to be *asymptotically pivotal* under the null hypothesis. This property implies that $\lim_{n \to \infty} P_n^\theta(W_{n,\tau_0})$ does not depend on θ if $\theta \in \Theta_0$, and hence we can look for τ_0 such that this limit is equal to a given value α. This value is the asymptotic size of the test.

The last general question we are addressing concerns the problem of comparing different tests. Consider two sequences of test functions τ_{1n} and τ_{2n} that satisfy the previous properties. We look for the critical values τ_{10} and τ_{20} such that the probabilities of type I errors are equal to each other:

$$\lim_{n \to \infty} P_n^\theta \{x : \tau_{1n}(x) \geq \tau_{10}\} = \lim_{n \to \infty} P_n^\theta \{x : \tau_{2n}(x) \geq \tau_{20}\} = \alpha \; \theta \in \Theta_0$$

where α is a given size. We can compare these two tests only under the alternative because their behaviors are identical under H_0, at least asymptotically. We also cannot compare the limiting probabilities of the critical regions for a fixed point of Θ_1, because these probabilities will be at the limit equal to one for both tests, because both tests are consistent.

A first solution is to give up the asymptotic point of view and compare

$$P_n^\theta \{x : \tau_{1n}(x_1, \ldots, x_n) \geq \tau_{10}\}$$

and

$$P_n^\theta \{x : \tau_{2n}(x_1, \ldots, x_n) \geq \tau_{20}\}$$

for a fixed n and a value θ in Θ_1. This comparison usually depends on θ and can not be obtained analytically. It requires a simulation procedure that will be discussed in Chapter 6. A second solution is to keep the asymptotic point of view while letting some elements of the problem vary with n. Thus, we need to define different types of asymptotic comparisons of tests. We illustrate this point by an example based on the use of a sequence of local alternatives.

Example 4.2 *Let θ be an element of Θ_0 and θ_n be a sequence of elements of Θ_1 converging to θ with n. Such a sequence always exists if $\Theta_0 = \{\theta : R(\lambda(\theta)) = 0\}$. Then, we study*

$$\lim_{n \to \infty} P_n^{\theta_n}(W_{1\tau_{10}}) \quad and \quad \lim_{n \to \infty} P_n^{\theta_n}(W_{2\tau_{20}}).$$

The sequence θ_n can be chosen so that its rate of convergence implies that these two limits do not lie at the boundaries of the interval $[\alpha, 1]$. Then, we can compare those limits. The better test for the sequence of local alternatives is the one for which the above limit is larger. □

This type of calculation will be done in special cases later in this chapter.

4.3 Wald Tests

The test procedure referred to as *Wald test* is one of the most often used in applied econometrics because it is easy to implement and interpret. It has been recently subject to some criticisms that we will mention in the last example of this section.

Consider the vector $\lambda(\theta)$, which is a function of the parameter θ, and the null hypothesis $H_0 : R(\lambda(\theta)) = 0$. The test we present requires a consistent and asymptotically normal estimator $\hat{\lambda}_n$ of $\lambda(\theta)$. Hence, we assume that $\sqrt{n}(\hat{\lambda}_n - \lambda(\theta))$ follows asymptotically a centered normal distribution with variance Σ_θ. This estimator may be obtained from the method of moments or GMM but $\hat{\lambda}_n$ may also come from a completely different approach. Finally, we need to have a sequence $\hat{\Sigma}_n$ converging (in probability) to Σ_θ. The method of moments provides such a sequence as seen in Chapter 3.

The estimator $\hat{\lambda}_n$ allows us to obtain an estimator $R(\hat{\lambda}_n)$. By continuity, $R(\hat{\lambda}_n)$ converges to $R(\lambda(\theta))$ and, using Theorem 3.2 (Chapter 3), we infer that under H_0,

$$\sqrt{n} R(\hat{\lambda}_n) \to N(0, \Omega_\theta) \quad \text{in } P_\infty^\theta\text{-distribution} \tag{4.3}$$

with

$$\Omega_\theta = \frac{\partial R}{\partial \lambda'}(\lambda(\theta)) \Sigma_\theta \frac{\partial R'}{\partial \lambda}(\lambda(\theta)).$$

The basis of the Wald test is the comparison of $R(\hat{\lambda}_n)$ to 0 in the metric defined by the asymptotic variance. In other words, we have in the case of an invertible variance,

$$n R'(\hat{\lambda}_n) \Omega_\theta^{-1} R(\hat{\lambda}_n) \to \chi_l^2 \quad \text{en } P_\infty^\theta\text{-distribution.} \tag{4.4}$$

Moreover, $\frac{\partial R}{\partial \lambda'}(\hat{\lambda}_n)$ converges to $\frac{\partial R}{\partial \lambda'}(\lambda(\theta))$ and hence

$$\hat{\Omega}_n = \frac{\partial R}{\partial \lambda'}(\hat{\lambda}_n)\hat{\Sigma}_n\frac{\partial R'}{\partial \lambda}(\hat{\lambda}_n)$$

is a consistent (in probability) estimator of Ω_θ.

Therefore, it follows that

$$n R'(\hat{\lambda}_n)\hat{\Omega}_n^{-1}R(\hat{\lambda}_n) \to \chi_l^2 \quad \text{in } P_\infty^\theta\text{-distribution} \tag{4.5}$$

for all $\theta \in \Theta_0$. Thus, the above expression is asymptotically a pivotal function under H_0. We summarize the previous construction by the following theorem.

Theorem 4.1   *Under the usual regularity conditions, the test statistic*

$$Wald_n = n R'(\hat{\lambda}_n)\hat{\Omega}_n^{-1}R(\hat{\lambda}_n)$$

follows asymptotically a chi-square distribution with l degrees of freedom, χ_l^2, under the null hypothesis.   ∎

In the table of the χ_l^2 distribution, we look for the value τ_0 such that the probability that a random variable, distributed accordingly, exceeds τ_0 equals the size α. Then, the critical region of the Wald test is given by

$$W_{n,\tau_0} = \{x : n R'(\hat{\lambda}_n)\hat{\Omega}_n^{-1}R(\hat{\lambda}_n) \geq \tau_0\}. \tag{4.6}$$

Moreover, if $\theta \in \Theta_1$, we have

$$n R'(\hat{\lambda}_n)\hat{\Omega}_n^{-1}R(\hat{\lambda}_n) = n \left(R\left(\hat{\lambda}_n\right) - R(\lambda(\theta))\right)' \hat{\Omega}_n^{-1} \left(R(\hat{\lambda}_n) - R(\lambda(\theta))\right)$$

$$+ n R(\lambda(\theta))' \hat{\Omega}_n^{-1} R(\lambda(\theta)) \tag{4.7}$$

$$+ 2n \left(R\left(\hat{\lambda}_n\right) - R(\lambda(\theta))' \hat{\Omega}_n R(\lambda(\theta))\right).$$

The first term of the right-hand side converges in distribution to a χ_l^2 and the other terms go to infinity. The probability that this expression exceeds any critical value goes to 1 when $n \to \infty$ and the test is indeed consistent.

We briefly study the power of the Wald test under a sequence of local alternatives. Our presentation is largely intuitive because a rigorous treatment would require more complex tools than those used in this book.

We limit our presentation to tests of the hypothesis $H_0 : \lambda(\theta) = 0$ but the generalization to $R(\lambda(\theta)) = 0$ is immediate.

Consider a sequence θ_n of elements of the space Θ satisfying

$$\lambda(\theta_n) = \lambda(\theta) - \frac{1}{\sqrt{n}}\delta$$

with $\delta \in \mathbb{R}^k$ given and where θ is an element of Θ_0. Hence, we have

$$\lambda(\theta_n) = -\frac{\delta}{\sqrt{n}}$$

because $\lambda(\theta) = 0$ under H_0. We state without proof that, if the parameters are equal to the sequence θ_n, then

$$\sqrt{n}\left(\hat{\lambda}_n + \frac{\delta}{\sqrt{n}}\right) = \sqrt{n}\hat{\lambda}_n + \delta \to N(\delta, \Sigma_\theta). \tag{4.8}$$

This result is quite intuitive because it is analogous to that obtained with a fixed parameter. Note that if a random vector x of dimension p is distributed according to the distribution $N(\mu, \Sigma)$, the quadratic form $x'\Sigma^{-1}x$ follows by definition a noncentral χ_p^2 distribution with noncentrality parameter $\mu'\Sigma^{-1}\mu$. It follows from (4.8) that

$$n\left(\hat{\lambda}_n + \frac{\delta}{\sqrt{n}}\right)' \hat{\Sigma}_n^{-1}\left(\hat{\lambda}_n + \frac{\delta}{\sqrt{n}}\right) \to \chi_k^2\left(\delta'\Sigma_\theta^{-1}\delta\right).$$

This result enables us to compare two Wald tests based on two estimators, $\hat{\lambda}_n$ and $\hat{\lambda}_n^*$, both converging to $\lambda(\theta)$ and asymptotically normal with respective variances Σ_θ and Σ_θ^*, estimated by $\hat{\Sigma}_n$ and $\hat{\Sigma}_n^*$. The two Wald statistics

$$Wald_n^1 = n\hat{\lambda}_n'\hat{\Sigma}_n^{-1}\hat{\lambda}_n \quad \text{and} \quad Wald_n^2 = n\widehat{\lambda}_n^*\hat{\Sigma}_n^{*-1}\widehat{\lambda}_n^*$$

are both asymptotically χ_k^2 under H_0 and hence are compared to the same critical value τ_0. The powers of these two tests under the sequence of alternatives $-\frac{\delta}{\sqrt{n}}$ are the probabilities of the half-line $(\tau_0, +\infty)$ for noncentral χ_k^2 with noncentrality parameters

$$\delta'\Sigma_\theta^{-1}\delta \quad \text{and} \quad \delta'\Sigma_\theta^{*-1}\delta.$$

From the properties of the noncentral χ^2, it is easy to verify that the most powerful test is that with the largest noncentrality parameter. This comparison depends on δ in general, that is on the sequence of alternative hypotheses. Hence, some estimators give rise to tests that are more powerful in some specific directions. However, if $\hat{\lambda}_n$ is better than $\hat{\lambda}_n^*$ in the sense Σ_θ is smaller than Σ_θ^* (that is $\Sigma_\theta^* - \Sigma_\theta$ is positive semidefinite), the test based on $\hat{\lambda}_n$ is more powerful than that based on $\hat{\lambda}_n^*$ for all δ, and hence for every sequence of local alternatives. Indeed, the efficiency property of $\hat{\lambda}_n$ is equivalent to

$$\Sigma_\theta^{*-1} \leq \Sigma_\theta^{-1}$$

and hence to the inequality

$$\delta'\Sigma_\theta^{*-1}\delta \leq \delta'\Sigma_\theta^{-1}\delta$$

for all δ.

We conclude this section on Wald tests by a remark illustrating the dangers of this test procedure for some nonlinear hypotheses. We assumed that the rank of $\frac{\partial R}{\partial \lambda'}$ is equal to the number of restrictions l for all values of λ. This assumption may not be satisfied in two types of situation.

1. The rank of $\frac{\partial R}{\partial \lambda'}$ is less than l for all λ. This means that we test a set of redundant restrictions and we can get back to our rank condition by reducing the number of restrictions.
2. The rank of $\frac{\partial R}{\partial \lambda'}$ is less than l for some λ, which implies that Ω_θ is singular for some elements of Θ_0. In this case, the previous results do not apply and the behavior of the test statistic may be very different from that given in Theorem 4.1. We illustrate this point by the following example.

Example 4.3 *Let $x_i = (y_i, z_i)'$, $i = 1, \ldots n$, be an i.i.d. sample generated by a distribution $N\left((\alpha, \beta)', I_2\right)$ and we wish to test $H_0 : \alpha\beta = 0$. Using our notations,*

$$\lambda = \theta = (\alpha, \beta)' \quad and \quad R(\lambda) = \alpha\beta.$$

Hence, we have

$$\frac{\partial R}{\partial \lambda'} = (\beta, \alpha)$$

which has rank $l = 1$ except when $\alpha = \beta = 0$. The parameters α and β are estimated by

$$\hat{\alpha}_n = \bar{y} \quad and \quad \hat{\beta}_n = \bar{z}$$

with distribution $N\left((\alpha, \beta)', \frac{1}{n}I_2\right)$. Then, the estimator $\hat{\alpha}_n\hat{\beta}_n$ satisfies

$$\sqrt{n}\left(\hat{\alpha}_n\hat{\beta}_n - \alpha\beta\right) \to N\left(0, \alpha^2 + \beta^2\right).$$

This result gives indeed a nondegenerate limiting distribution if $\alpha^2 + \beta^2 \neq 0$, i.e. if $(\alpha, \beta) \neq (0, 0)$. Otherwise, this result proves only that $\sqrt{n}\hat{\alpha}_n\hat{\beta}_n$ goes to 0 in probability because the convergence to a degenerate distribution is equivalent to convergence in probability. In fact, $\hat{\alpha}_n\hat{\beta}_n$ converges in distribution at the rate n because $n\hat{\alpha}_n\hat{\beta}_n$ is distributed as the product of two independent $\mathcal{X}^2$.

  The Wald statistic is equal to

$$\frac{n\hat{\alpha}_n^2\hat{\beta}_n^2}{\hat{\alpha}_n^2 + \hat{\beta}_n^2}.$$

It follows asymptotically a $\mathcal{X}_1^2$ if $\alpha^2 + \beta^2 \neq 0$. However, it has a different limiting distribution if $(\alpha, \beta) = (0, 0)$. Indeed, in this case, the numerator and denominator go to zero at the same rate. By multiplying the upper and lower *terms with n, we can verify that the Wald statistic is distributed as the product of two independent X_1^2 divided by their sum. A noninformed user could nevertheless compute the test statistic (because $\hat{\alpha}_n^2 + \hat{\beta}_n^2$ is different from 0 with probability 1 even if $\alpha^2 + \beta^2 = 0$) and may use a false asymptotic distribution if he neglects the rank difference in some region of the null hypothesis.* □

Finally, we note that the study of some special cases shows that the Wald statistic may have a finite sample distribution that is very different from the asymptotic distribution and that, therefore, the true level of the test differs significantly from the asymptotic level. This defect can be remedied by calibrating the test via simulations as we will show in Chapter 6.

4.4 Rao Test

Consider a null hypothesis $H_0 : \lambda(\theta) = \tilde{\lambda}(\mu(\theta))$ and an equation of generalized moments $E^\theta(\psi(x_i, \lambda)) = 0$. In contrast to the Wald test that uses only an unrestricted estimate of λ, we use here only a restricted estimate of λ under H_0. One way to obtain this estimate is to minimize the expression

$$\left(\frac{1}{n} \sum_{i=1}^n \psi\left(x_i, \tilde{\lambda}(\mu)\right) \right)' H_n \left(\frac{1}{n} \sum_{i=1}^n \psi\left(x_i, \tilde{\lambda}(\mu)\right) \right) \tag{4.9}$$

with respect to μ, from which we infer that $\hat{\mu}_n$ converges to $\mu(\theta)$. Hence, we have here a usual GMM problem where the function ψ can be replaced by

$$\psi_0(x_i, \mu) = \psi(x_i, \tilde{\lambda}(\mu)).$$

If H_n converges to

$$H = \left[Var^\theta \left(\psi(x_i, \tilde{\lambda}(\mu(\theta))) \right) \right]^{-1}$$

or more generally, in a dynamic model for instance, to a matrix H such that

$$\frac{\sqrt{n}}{n} \sum_{i=1}^n \psi(x_i, \tilde{\lambda}(\mu(\theta)))$$

converges in distribution to a $N(0, H^{-1})$, then $\sqrt{n}(\hat{\mu}_n - \mu(\theta))$ is asymptotically normal with variance

$$\left[E^\theta \left(\frac{\partial \psi_0'}{\partial \mu} \right) H E^\theta \left(\frac{\partial \psi_0}{\partial \mu'} \right) \right]^{-1}$$

$$= \left[\frac{\partial \tilde{\lambda}'}{\partial \mu} E^\theta \left(\frac{\partial \psi'}{\partial \lambda} \right) H E^\theta \left(\frac{\partial \psi}{\partial \lambda'} \right) \frac{\partial \tilde{\lambda}}{\partial \mu'} \right]^{-1}. \tag{4.10}$$

This result follows from the chain rule for differentiating composite functions which, applied to ψ, yields

$$\frac{\partial \psi_0}{\partial \mu'} = \frac{\partial \psi}{\partial \lambda'} \frac{\partial \tilde{\lambda}}{\partial \mu'}.$$

The basic idea of the Rao test can be presented in the following way. Consider the unrestricted estimation of λ and write its first order condition:

$$\left(\frac{1}{n} \sum_{i=1}^{n} \frac{\partial \psi'}{\partial \lambda}(x_i, \lambda) \right) H_n \left(\frac{1}{n} \sum_{i=1}^{n} \psi(x_i, \lambda) \right) = 0. \tag{4.11}$$

This condition is satisfied at $\hat{\lambda}_n$ by construction. Hence, we compute the left-hand term of the above equality at $\tilde{\lambda}(\hat{\mu}_n)$ and reject the null hypothesis when this term is significantly different from 0.

To be more precise, we need to know the limiting distribution of

$$\left(\frac{1}{n} \sum_{i=1}^{n} \frac{\partial \psi'}{\partial \lambda} (x_i, \tilde{\lambda}(\hat{\mu}_n)) \right) H_n \left(\frac{\sqrt{n}}{n} \sum_{i=1}^{n} \psi \left(x_i, \tilde{\lambda}(\hat{\mu}_n) \right) \right). \tag{4.12}$$

This limiting distribution and its application to the construction of the test are treated in the following theorem.

Theorem 4.2   *Under the usual regularity assumptions, the expression (4.12) is asymptotically normal with mean zero and variance:*

$$E^\theta \left(\frac{\partial \psi'}{\partial \lambda} \right) H E^\theta \left(\frac{\partial \psi}{\partial \lambda'} \right)$$

$$- \left\{ E^\theta \left(\frac{\partial \psi'}{\partial \lambda} \right) H E^\theta \left(\frac{\partial \psi}{\partial \lambda'} \right) \frac{\partial \tilde{\lambda}}{\partial \mu'} \left[\frac{\partial \tilde{\lambda}'}{\partial \mu} E^\theta \left(\frac{\partial \psi'}{\partial \lambda} \right) H E^\theta \left(\frac{\partial \psi}{\partial \lambda'} \right) \frac{\partial \tilde{\lambda}}{\partial \mu'} \right]^{-1} \right.$$

$$\times \left. \frac{\partial \tilde{\lambda}'}{\partial \mu} E^\theta \left(\frac{\partial \psi'}{\partial \lambda} \right) H E^\theta \left(\frac{\partial \psi}{\partial \lambda'} \right) \right\}$$

This variance is singular and its generalized inverse is the matrix

$$B = \left(E^\theta \left(\frac{\partial \psi'}{\partial \lambda} \right) H E^\theta \left(\frac{\partial \psi}{\partial \lambda'} \right) \right)^{-1}$$

$$- \frac{\partial \tilde{\lambda}}{\partial \mu'} \left[\frac{\partial \tilde{\lambda}'}{\partial \mu} E^\theta \left(\frac{\partial \psi'}{\partial \lambda} \right) H E^\theta \left(\frac{\partial \psi}{\partial \lambda'} \right) \frac{\partial \tilde{\lambda}}{\partial \mu'} \right]^{-1} \frac{\partial \tilde{\lambda}'}{\partial \mu}$$

whose rank is l. The Rao statistic can be written as

$$RAO_n = n \left(\frac{1}{n} \sum_{i=1}^n \psi\left(x_i, \tilde{\lambda}(\hat{\mu}_n)\right) \right)' H_n \left(\frac{1}{n} \sum_{i=1}^n \frac{\partial \psi}{\partial \lambda'}\left(x_i, \tilde{\lambda}(\hat{\mu}_n)\right) \right) \hat{B}_n$$

$$\times \left(\frac{1}{n} \sum_{i=1}^n \frac{\partial \psi'}{\partial \lambda}\left(x_i, \tilde{\lambda}(\hat{\mu}_n)\right) \right) H_n \left(\frac{1}{n} \sum_{i=1}^n \psi\left(x_i, \tilde{\lambda}(\hat{\mu}_n)\right) \right),$$

where $\hat{B}_n$ is the estimator of B obtained by replacing $E(\frac{\partial \psi}{\partial \lambda'})$ by $\frac{1}{n} \Sigma \frac{\partial \psi}{\partial \lambda'}(x_i, \tilde{\lambda}(\hat{\mu}_n))$ and H by H_n. RAO_n is asymptotically distributed as a χ^2 with l degrees of freedom under the null hypothesis. ∎

Proof: The first step of the proof consists in analyzing the limiting distribution of $\frac{\sqrt{n}}{n} \sum_{i=1}^n \psi(x_i, \tilde{\lambda}(\hat{\mu}_n))$. A series expansion of order one allows us to write

$$\psi\left(x_i, \tilde{\lambda}(\hat{\mu}_n)\right) \simeq \psi\left(x_i, \tilde{\lambda}(\mu(\theta))\right) + \frac{\partial \psi}{\partial \lambda'} \cdot \frac{\partial \tilde{\lambda}}{\partial \mu'}\left(\hat{\mu}_n - \mu(\theta)\right).$$

Moreover, using the same outline as in the proof of Theorem 3.3 in Chapter 3, we have

$$\sqrt{n}\left(\hat{\mu}_n - \mu(\theta)\right) \simeq -\left[\frac{\partial \tilde{\lambda}'}{\partial \mu} E^\theta \left(\frac{\partial \psi'}{\partial \lambda} \right) H E^\theta \left(\frac{\partial \psi}{\partial \lambda'} \right) \frac{\partial \tilde{\lambda}}{\partial \mu} \right]^{-1}$$

$$\times \frac{\partial \tilde{\lambda}'}{\partial \mu} E^\theta \left(\frac{\partial \psi'}{\partial \lambda} \right) H \left(\frac{\sqrt{n}}{n} \sum_{i=1}^n \psi\left(x_i, \tilde{\lambda}(\mu(\theta))\right) \right).$$

Hence,

$$\frac{\sqrt{n}}{n} \sum_{i=1}^n \psi\left(x_i, \tilde{\lambda}(\hat{\mu}_n)\right) \simeq A \frac{\sqrt{n}}{n} \sum_{i=1}^n \psi\left(x_i, \tilde{\lambda}(\mu(\theta))\right)$$

with

$$A = I_r - E^\theta \left(\frac{\partial \psi}{\partial \lambda'} \right) \frac{\partial \tilde{\lambda}}{\partial \mu'} \left[\frac{\partial \tilde{\lambda}'}{\partial \mu} E^\theta \left(\frac{\partial \psi'}{\partial \lambda} \right) H E^\theta \left(\frac{\partial \psi}{\partial \lambda'} \right) \frac{\partial \tilde{\lambda}}{\partial \mu'} \right]^{-1}$$

$$\times \frac{\partial \tilde{\lambda}'}{\partial \mu} E^\theta \left(\frac{\partial \psi'}{\partial \lambda} \right) H.$$

By the central limit theorem, we obtain

$$\frac{\sqrt{n}}{n} \sum_{i=1}^n \psi\left(x_i, \tilde{\lambda}(\hat{\mu}_n)\right) \to N(0, A H^{-1} A') \quad P_\infty^\theta\text{-distribution.}$$

Note that

$$AH^{-1}A' = H^{-1} - E^\theta \left(\frac{\partial\psi}{\partial\lambda'}\right) \frac{\partial\tilde\lambda}{\partial\mu'} \left[\frac{\partial\tilde\lambda'}{\partial\mu} E^\theta \left(\frac{\partial\psi'}{\partial\lambda}\right) HE^\theta \left(\frac{\partial\psi}{\partial\lambda'}\right) \frac{\partial\tilde\lambda}{\partial\mu'}\right]^{-1}$$
$$\times \frac{\partial\tilde\lambda'}{\partial\mu} E^\theta \left(\frac{\partial\psi'}{\partial\lambda}\right).$$

It follows that

$$\frac{1}{n}\sum_{i=1}^{n} \frac{\partial\psi}{\partial\lambda'}(x_i, \tilde\lambda(\hat\mu_n))' H_n\left(\frac{\sqrt{n}}{n}\sum_{i=1}^{n}\psi(x_i, \tilde\lambda(\hat\mu_n))\right)$$

$$\to N\left(0, E^\theta\left(\frac{\partial\psi}{\partial\lambda'}\right) HAH^{-1}A'HE^\theta\left(\frac{\partial\psi'}{\partial\lambda}\right)\right) P_\infty^\theta\text{-distribution.}$$

The variance of this limiting distribution is equal to the expression in Theorem 4.2.

To show that the matrix B is the generalized inverse of this variance, one can verify that B satisfies the conditions characterizing the Moore-Penrose inverse.

B has the same rank as

$$\left[E^\theta\left(\frac{\partial\psi'}{\partial\lambda}\right) HE^\theta\left(\frac{\partial\psi}{\partial\lambda'}\right)\right]^{\frac{1}{2}} B \left[E^\theta\left(\frac{\partial\psi'}{\partial\lambda}\right) HE^\theta\left(\frac{\partial\psi}{\partial\lambda'}\right)\right]^{\frac{1}{2}}$$

which is a symmetric idempotent matrix whose rank is equal to its trace which is obviously equal to l.

Finally, note that if $x \sim N(0, \Omega)$ where Ω is not necessarily invertible,

$$x'\Omega^+x \sim \chi_l^2.$$

In this expression, Ω^+ is the Moore-Penrose generalized inverse of Ω and l is the rank of Ω. The fact that the asymptotic variance can be replaced by a consistent estimator is a consequence of Theorem 3.1 in Chapter 3. ∎

In our presentation, we assumed that the tested hypothesis

$$R(\lambda(\theta)) = 0$$

was explicitly solved by $\lambda(\theta) = \tilde\lambda(\mu(\theta))$. This enabled us to minimize under H_0 without using Lagrange multipliers. An alternative construction would consist in not solving the tested constraint, but in minimizing under constraint with Lagrange multipliers and in testing the restriction by testing whether the multipliers are equal to zero. It can be shown that the resulting test is exactly identical to that following from (4.12).

4.5   Tests Based on the Comparison of Minima

The last general method we are presenting is the generalization of the *likelihood ratio test* to the method of moments. The idea of this method can be explained in the following manner.

Let Θ_0 be the null hypothesis that can always be represented by the condition $R(\lambda(\theta)) = 0$ or by the equality $\lambda(\theta) = \tilde{\lambda}(\mu(\theta))$. The (possibly generalized) moment condition is

$$E^\theta(\psi(x_i, \theta)) = 0.$$

We proceed with two estimations:

- the unrestricted estimation of $\lambda(\theta)$ by $\hat{\lambda}_n$, by minimizing on Λ the usual expression:

$$\left(\frac{1}{n}\sum_{i=1}^{n}\psi(x_i, \lambda)\right)' H_n\left(\frac{1}{n}\sum_{i=1}^{n}\psi(x_i, \lambda)\right); \qquad (4.13)$$

- the restricted estimation under the null hypothesis. We find $\hat{\mu}_n$ by minimizing:

$$\left(\frac{1}{n}\sum_{i=1}^{n}\psi\left(x_i, \tilde{\lambda}(\mu)\right)\right)' H_n\left(\frac{1}{n}\sum_{i=1}^{n}\psi\left(x_i, \tilde{\lambda}(\mu)\right)\right). \qquad (4.14)$$

This last minimization could of course be performed without solving the constraint and by using the form $R(\lambda) = 0$ and Lagrange multipliers.

We consider only the case where H_n is identical in (4.13) and (4.14), and where this matrix converges to H such that H^{-1} is the asymptotic variance of

$$\frac{\sqrt{n}}{n}\sum_{i=1}^{n}\psi\left(x_i, \lambda\left(\mu\left(\theta\right)\right)\right).$$

The matrix H, and hence the sequence H_n, are defined with respect to the null.

Then, the test statistic considered here is equal to the difference of the restricted and unrestricted minima and is defined by

$$COMP_n = n\left[\left(\frac{1}{n}\sum_{i=1}^{n}\psi\left(x_i, \tilde{\lambda}(\hat{\mu}_n)\right)\right)' H_n\left(\frac{1}{n}\sum_{i=1}^{n}\psi\left(x_i, \tilde{\lambda}(\hat{\mu}_n)\right)\right)\right.$$
$$\left. -\left(\frac{1}{n}\sum_{i=1}^{n}\psi\left(x_i, \hat{\lambda}_n\right)\right)' H_n\left(\frac{1}{n}\sum_{i=1}^{n}\psi\left(x_i, \hat{\lambda}_n\right)\right)\right] \qquad (4.15)$$

We have the following result.

Theorem 4.3   *Under the usual regularity assumptions, the statistic $COMP_n$ converges in distribution under the null to a χ^2 distribution with l degrees of freedom.* ∎

Proof: In the first step of the proof, we study of the joint asymptotic distribution of the vector:

$$\frac{\sqrt{n}}{n} \sum_{i=1}^{n} \begin{pmatrix} \psi(x_i, \hat{\lambda}_n) \\ \psi\left(x_i, \tilde{\lambda}(\hat{\mu}_n)\right) \end{pmatrix}.$$

This study is of course very similar to that in the proof of Theorem 4.2. From the approximations

$$\psi(x_i, \hat{\lambda}_n) \simeq \psi\left(x_i, \tilde{\lambda}\left(\mu(\theta)\right)\right) + \frac{\partial \psi}{\partial \lambda'}\left(x_i, \tilde{\lambda}\left(\mu(\theta)\right)\right)\left(\hat{\lambda}_n - \tilde{\lambda}\left(\mu(\theta)\right)\right),$$

$$\psi\left(x_i, \tilde{\lambda}(\hat{\mu}_n)\right) \simeq \psi\left(x_i, \tilde{\lambda}\left(\mu(\theta)\right)\right)$$
$$+ \frac{\partial \psi}{\partial \lambda'}\left(x_i, \tilde{\lambda}\left(\mu(\theta)\right)\right)\frac{\partial \tilde{\lambda}}{\partial \mu'}\left(\mu(\theta)\right)(\hat{\mu}_n - \mu(\theta)),$$

and the relations

$$\sqrt{n}\left(\hat{\lambda}_n - \tilde{\lambda}\left(\mu(\theta)\right)\right) \simeq -\left[E^\theta\left(\frac{\partial \psi'}{\partial \lambda}\right) H E^\theta\left(\frac{\partial \psi}{\partial \lambda'}\right)\right]^{-1}$$
$$\times E^\theta\left(\frac{\partial \psi'}{\partial \lambda}\right) H \left(\frac{\sqrt{n}}{n} \sum_{i=1}^{n} \psi\left(x_i, \tilde{\lambda}\left(\mu(\theta)\right)\right)\right),$$

$$\sqrt{n}\left(\hat{\mu}_n - \mu(\theta)\right) \simeq -\left[\frac{\partial \tilde{\lambda}'}{\partial \mu} E^\theta\left(\frac{\partial \psi'}{\partial \lambda}\right) H E^\theta\left(\frac{\partial \psi}{\partial \lambda'}\right)\frac{\partial \tilde{\lambda}}{\partial \mu'}\right]$$
$$\times \frac{\partial \tilde{\lambda}'}{\partial \mu} E^\theta\left(\frac{\partial \psi'}{\partial \lambda}\right) H \left(\frac{\sqrt{n}}{n} \sum_{i=1}^{n} \psi\left(x_i, \tilde{\lambda}\left(\mu(\theta)\right)\right)\right),$$

it follows that

$$\frac{\sqrt{n}}{n} \sum_{i=1}^{n} \begin{pmatrix} \psi(x_i, \hat{\lambda}_n) \\ \psi\left(x_i, \tilde{\lambda}(\hat{\mu}_n)\right) \end{pmatrix} \simeq A \frac{\sqrt{n}}{n} \sum_{i=1}^{n} \psi\left(x_i, \tilde{\lambda}\left(\mu(\theta)\right)\right)$$

with

$$A = \begin{bmatrix} I_r - E^\theta\left(\frac{\partial \psi}{\partial \lambda'}\right)\left[E^\theta\left(\frac{\partial \psi'}{\partial \lambda}\right) H E^\theta\left(\frac{\partial \psi}{\partial \lambda'}\right)\right]^{-1} E^\theta\left(\frac{\partial \psi'}{\partial \lambda}\right) H \\ I_r - E^\theta\left(\frac{\partial \psi}{\partial \lambda'}\right)\frac{\partial \tilde{\lambda}}{\partial \mu'}\left[\frac{\partial \tilde{\lambda}'}{\partial \mu} E^\theta\left(\frac{\partial \psi'}{\partial \lambda}\right) H E^\theta\left(\frac{\partial \psi}{\partial \lambda'}\right)\frac{\partial \tilde{\lambda}}{\partial \mu'}\right]^{-1}\frac{\partial \tilde{\lambda}'}{\partial \mu} E^\theta\left(\frac{\partial \psi'}{\partial \lambda}\right) H \end{bmatrix}.$$

The central limit theorem permits us to conclude that

$$\frac{\sqrt{n}}{n} \sum_{i=1}^{n} \begin{pmatrix} \psi(x_i, \hat{\lambda}_n) \\ \psi(x_i, \tilde{\lambda}(\hat{\mu}_n)) \end{pmatrix} \to N(0, A H^{-1} A') \quad P_\infty^\theta\text{-distribution.} \quad (4.16)$$

We have the relation

$$\text{COMP}_n = \left(\frac{\sqrt{n}}{n} \sum_{i=1}^{n} \begin{pmatrix} \psi(x_i, \hat{\lambda}_n) \\ \psi\left(x_i, \tilde{\lambda}(\hat{\mu}_n)\right) \end{pmatrix} \right)' \begin{pmatrix} -H_n & 0 \\ 0 & H_n \end{pmatrix}$$

$$\times \left(\frac{\sqrt{n}}{n} \sum_{i=1}^{n} \begin{pmatrix} \psi(x_i, \hat{\lambda}_n) \\ \psi\left(x_i, \tilde{\lambda}(\hat{\mu}_n)\right) \end{pmatrix} \right),$$

which asymptotically becomes

$$\text{COMP}_n = \left(\frac{\sqrt{n}}{n} \sum_{i=1}^{n} \psi\left(x_i, \tilde{\lambda}\left(\mu(\theta)\right)\right) \right)' B \left(\frac{\sqrt{n}}{n} \sum_{i=1}^{n} \psi\left(x_i, \tilde{\lambda}\left(\mu(\theta)\right)\right) \right) \quad (4.17)$$

with

$$B = A' \begin{pmatrix} -H & 0 \\ 0 & H \end{pmatrix} A.$$

Finally, it can be shown that

$$BH^{-1}B = B$$

and that the rank of B is equal to l, which implies the result. This last part is based on the following property. If a random vector ξ is (asymptotically) $N(0, \Omega)$ and if $B\Omega B = B$, then $\xi' B \xi$ is χ^2 with degrees of freedom given by the rank of B. Indeed

$$x'Bx = x'BB^+Bx$$

where B^+ is the generalized inverse of B. Let $y = Bx$. We have $y \sim N(0, B\Omega B)$, hence $y \sim N(0, B)$ and thus $yB^+y \sim \mathcal{X}^2_{rankB}$. Moreover

$$rankB = rankPBP' = tr\,PBP'$$

with $\Omega = P'P$, because PBP' is symmetric idempotent. ∎

Example 4.4 *Test for overidentification implied by the generalized moment conditions.*

Now, we revisit the maintained assumption of this chapter, namely that the set of overidentifying restrictions imposed by the system of generalized moments is satisfied. We wish to test these restrictions.

Consider a statistical model $\mathcal{M}_n = \{X^n, \Theta, P_n^\theta\}$ and a system of moment conditions

$$E^\theta(\psi(x_i, \lambda)) = 0,$$

$\lambda \in \Lambda \subset \mathbb{R}^k$ *and ψ taking its values in $\mathbb{R}^r$ with $r > k$. As in Chapter 3, we denote by Θ_* the set of $\theta \in \Theta$ such that the system $E^\theta(\psi(x_i, \lambda)) = 0$ has a solution, and we wish to test the null hypothesis $H_0 : \Theta_0 = \Theta_*$.*

A natural test statistic consists of the minimum of the objective function

$$\left(\frac{1}{n}\sum_{i=1}^{n}\psi(x_i,\lambda)\right)' H_n \left(\frac{1}{n}\sum_{i=1}^{n}\psi(x_i,\lambda)\right)$$

and hence is equal to

$$HAN_n = n\left(\frac{1}{n}\sum_{i=1}^{n}\psi\left(x_i,\hat{\lambda}_n\right)\right)' H_n \left(\frac{1}{n}\sum_{i=1}^{n}\psi\left(x_i,\hat{\lambda}_n\right)\right).$$

This naming reminds us that this test was first introduced by Hansen in 1982. We always assume that H_n is such that its limit H is the optimal weighting matrix such that $\frac{\sqrt{n}}{n}\Sigma\psi(x_i,\lambda(\theta))$ converges in distribution to a $N(0, H^{-1})$.

Under H_0, it is clear that HAN_n converges to a χ^2_{r-k}. This result can be obtained from the previous proof using only the distribution of $\frac{\sqrt{n}}{n}\Sigma\psi(x_i,\hat{\lambda}_n)$. We leave the details of this proof to the reader. $\qquad\square$

4.6 Test Based on Maximum Likelihood Estimation

As a special case of the tests previously introduced, we present asymptotic tests based on the maximum likelihood estimation of a parametric model. We use the notations of Chapter 3 (Examples 3.9, 3.15, and 3.20), and restrict ourselves to the case where the model is well specified.

Consider an i.i.d. model with parameter $\theta \in \Theta \subset \mathbb{R}^k$ and likelihood function

$$l_n(x|\theta) = \prod_{i=1}^{n} f(x_i|\theta).$$

The estimator $\hat{\lambda}_n$ is obtained by the maximization of the function

$$L_n(\lambda) = \frac{1}{n}\ln l_n(x|\lambda) = \frac{1}{n}\sum_{i=1}^{n}\ln f(x_i|\lambda).$$

We saw that $\hat{\lambda}_n$ converges to θ and that $\sqrt{n}(\hat{\lambda}_n - \theta)$ is asymptotically normal with variance $\mathcal{J}_\theta^{-1}$ satisfying the equality

$$\mathcal{J}_\theta = Var^\theta\left(\frac{\partial}{\partial\theta}\ln f(x_i|\theta)\right) = -E^\theta\left(\frac{\partial^2}{\partial\theta\partial\theta'}\ln f(x_i|\theta)\right).$$

Suppose first that the null hypothesis is the simple hypothesis $H_0 : \theta = \theta_0$. In other words, Θ_0 is reduced to a singleton $\{\theta_0\}$ where θ_0 is a given element of Θ.

The Wald statistic is given by

$$\text{Wald}_n = n\left(\hat{\lambda}_n - \theta_0\right)'\hat{\Sigma}_n^{-1}\left(\hat{\lambda}_n - \theta_0\right) \qquad (4.18)$$

with

$$\hat{\Sigma}_n = -\frac{1}{n} \sum_{i=1}^{n} \frac{\partial^2}{\partial\theta\partial\theta'} \ln f(x_i|\hat{\lambda}_n).$$

The Wald statistic measures the distance between $\hat{\lambda}_n$ and the null θ_0.

The Rao statistic is based on the fact that the first order conditions must be approximately satisfied at θ_0 under H_0. Hence, we calculate

$$\frac{1}{n} \sum_{i=1}^{n} \frac{\partial}{\partial\theta} \ln f(x_i|\theta_0).$$

Under Θ_0,

$$\frac{\sqrt{n}}{n} \sum_{i=1}^{n} \frac{\partial}{\partial\theta} \ln f(x_i|\theta_0)$$

converges in distribution to a $N(0, \mathcal{J}_{\theta_0})$ and then, we calculate

$$\mathrm{RAO}_n = n \left(\frac{1}{n} \sum_{i=1}^{n} \frac{\partial}{\partial\theta} \ln f(x_i|\theta_0)\right)' \mathcal{J}_{\theta_0}^{-1} \left(\frac{1}{n} \sum_{i=1}^{n} \frac{\partial}{\partial\theta} \ln f(x_i|\theta_0)\right).$$

$$(4.19)$$

Note that in this case, this statistic does not require an estimation of the parameter.

Finally the likelihood ratio statistic is based on the difference between the likelihood function at its maximum $\hat{\lambda}_n$ and at the value of θ_0:

$$\mathrm{COMP}_n = 2n \left(L(\hat{\lambda}_n) - L(\theta_0)\right). \qquad (4.20)$$

The three statistics (4.18), (4.19), and (4.20) are all asymptotically distributed as a χ_1^2 under H_0.

This result is immediate in the first two cases. The last case obtains from a second order expansion of $L_n(\lambda)$ and we leave its proof to the reader. In addition, it constitutes a special case of Theorem 4.3.

These results generalize to a multiple hypothesis in the following manner. Let $\Theta_0 \subset \Theta$ defined by the restriction

$$R(\theta) = 0 \qquad (R : \mathbb{R}^k \to \mathbb{R}^l)$$

or by the condition

$$\theta = \tilde{\theta}(\mu) \qquad (\mu \in \mathbb{R}^{k-l} \text{ and } \tilde{\theta} : \mathbb{R}^{k-l} \to \mathbb{R}^k).$$

The Wald test can be written as

$$\mathrm{WALD}_n = n R(\hat{\lambda}_n)' \hat{\Omega}_n^{-1} R(\hat{\lambda}_n) \qquad (4.21)$$

with

$$\hat{\Omega}_n = \frac{\partial R}{\partial \theta'}(\hat{\lambda}_n)\hat{\Sigma}_n\frac{\partial R'}{\partial \theta}(\hat{\lambda}_n).$$

The Rao test is based on the value of the first order conditions at $\tilde{\theta}(\hat{\mu}_n)$ where $\hat{\mu}_n$ is given by

$$\hat{\mu}_n = \arg\max_{\mu} L_n(\tilde{\theta}(\mu))$$

that is $\hat{\mu}_n$ is the restricted MLE. The Rao test takes the form:

$$\text{RAO}_n = n\left(\frac{1}{n}\sum_{i=1}^{n}\frac{\partial}{\partial\theta}\ln f\left(x_i|\tilde{\theta}(\hat{\mu}_n)\right)\right)'\left(\mathcal{J}_{\tilde{\theta}(\hat{\mu}_n)}^{-1} - \frac{\partial\tilde{\theta}'}{\partial\mu}(\hat{\mu}_n)\mathcal{J}_{\hat{\mu}_n}^{-1}\frac{\partial\tilde{\theta}}{\partial\mu'}(\hat{\mu}_n)\right)$$

$$\times\left(\frac{1}{n}\sum_{i=1}^{n}\frac{\partial}{\partial\theta}\ln f(x_i|\tilde{\theta}(\hat{\mu}_n))\right) \tag{4.22}$$

where $\mathcal{J}_\theta$ and $\mathcal{J}_\mu$ are the information matrices of the unrestricted and restricted models respectively.

Finally, the likelihood ratio test compares the maximum of $L_n(\lambda)$ for $\lambda \in \Theta$ and for Θ_0 :

$$\text{COMP}_n = 2n\left(L_n(\hat{\lambda}_n) - L_n(\tilde{\theta}(\hat{\mu}_n))\right)$$
$$= -2n(\max_{\lambda\in\Theta_0} L_n(\lambda) - \max_{\lambda\in\Theta} L(\lambda)). \tag{4.23}$$

Here again, the three test statistics are asymptotically χ_l^2 under the null. The proofs of these results are identical to those for the case with GMM estimation. For instance, for the Rao test, we use Theorem 4.2 with

$$\psi(x_i, \lambda(\theta)) = \frac{\partial}{\partial\theta}\ln f(x_i|\theta),$$

$$H = -\left[E^\theta\left(\frac{\partial^2}{\partial\theta\partial\theta'}\ln f(x_i|\hat{\theta}(\hat{u}_n))\right)\right]^{-1},$$

$$H_n = \left[-\frac{1}{n}\sum_{i=1}^{n}\left(\frac{\partial^2}{\partial\theta\partial\theta'}\ln f(x_i|\hat{\theta}(\hat{u}_n))\right)\right]^{-1},$$

$$\theta = \lambda(\theta) \quad \text{and} \quad \tilde{\lambda}(u) = \tilde{\theta}(u).$$

4.7   Hausman Tests

The Hausman test was first introduced in econometrics as a specification test, that is as a test for the validation of a model as a whole. This presentation is a bit artificial. It is better to present this test as a usual hypothesis test in the general framework of Wald tests. The most popular application of the Hausman test is the test for exogeneity. This test will be introduced in Chapter 17.

Let $\{X^n, \Theta, P_n^\theta\}$ be a statistical model and $\lambda(\theta) \in \Lambda \subset \mathbb{R}^k$ be a function of the parameter that we partition into $\lambda(\theta) = (\mu(\theta), \rho(\theta))$ with dimensions $k - l$ and l respectively. The null hypothesis Θ_0 is $\rho(\theta) = 0$. The main idea of the Hausman test is based on the comparison of two estimators of $\mu(\theta)$, $\hat{\mu}_n$ and $\tilde{\mu}_n$. The first, $\hat{\mu}_n$, does not use the null hypothesis and hence converges to $\mu(\theta)$ for all θ, whereas the second converges to $\mu(\theta)$ only if $\rho(\theta) = 0$. If the gap between $\hat{\mu}_n$ and $\tilde{\mu}$ is small, $\rho(\theta) = 0$ is accepted, while if the difference is large enough, $\rho(\theta) = 0$ is rejected.

Intuitively, we assume that $\mu(\theta)$ is the parameter function of interest while $\rho(\theta)$ should be interpreted as a nuisance parameter. We test $H_0 : \rho(\theta) = 0$ by its implication on the estimation of $\mu(\theta)$.

This presentation is formalized in the following manner.

Theorem 4.4 *Consider two estimators satisfying*

1. $\hat{\mu}_n \to \mu(0)$ $P_\infty^\theta - prob$ $\forall \theta \in \Theta$.
   $\tilde{\mu}_n \to \mu(\theta)$ $P_\infty^\theta - prob$ $\forall \theta \in \Theta_0 = \{\theta | \rho(\theta) = 0\}$

2. $\forall \theta \in \Theta_0,\ \sqrt{n} \begin{pmatrix} \hat{\mu}_n - \mu(\theta) \\ \tilde{\mu}_n - \mu(\theta) \end{pmatrix} \to N(0, \Omega_\theta)$ P_∞^θ-*distribution*

   with $\Omega_\theta = \begin{pmatrix} W_\theta & C_\theta \\ C_\theta' & V_\theta \end{pmatrix}$.

   Note that we assume here the joint normality of the estimators. Moreover, we assume that there exists an estimator $\hat{\Omega}_n$ which converges in probability to Ω_θ.

3. *If $\theta \in \Theta_0$, then $\tilde{\mu}_n$ is the best consistent asymptotically normal estimator (i.e., with the smallest asymptotic variance).*

Then, we have

$$\sqrt{n}(\hat{\mu}_n - \tilde{\mu}_n) \to N(0, W_\theta - V_\theta).$$

If rank $(W_\theta - V_\theta) = k - l$, the Hausman test statistic takes the form

$$HAUS_n = n(\hat{\mu}_n - \tilde{\mu}_n)' \left(\hat{W}_n - \hat{V}_n\right)^{-1} (\hat{\mu}_n - \tilde{\mu}_n)$$

and converges to a χ_{k-l}^2. ■

Proof: It is easy to show from Assumptions 1 and 2 that, if $\theta \in \Theta_0$, then

$$\sqrt{n}(\hat{\mu}_n - \tilde{\mu}_n) \to N\left(0, W_\theta + V_\theta - C_\theta - C_\theta'\right).$$

The asymptotic variance simplifies under Assumption 3 because it implies in particular $V_\theta = C_\theta = C_\theta'$.

Indeed, consider the estimator

$$\mu_n^* = A\hat{\mu}_n + (I - A)\tilde{\mu}_n$$

where A is an arbitrary matrix. This estimator is consistent and asymptotically normal. Its variance is equal to

$$AW_\theta A' + (I - A)V_\theta (I - A') + AC_\theta (I - A') + (I - A)C_\theta' A'$$

which by assumption, is greater than V for all A. This implies:

$$tr\left[A\left(W_\theta + V_\theta - C_\theta - C_\theta'\right) A'\right] - 2tr\left[\left(V_\theta - C_\theta'\right) A'\right] \geq 0 \quad \forall A. \tag{4.24}$$

Moreover, we know that this expression reaches its minimum at $A = 0$ because in this case, $\mu_n^* = \tilde{\mu}_n$. Minimizing (4.24) with respect to A yields the first order condition:

$$2A\left(W_\theta + V_\theta + C_\theta - C_\theta'\right) - 2\left(V_\theta - C_\theta'\right) = 0.$$

This condition must be satisfied for $A = 0$, which implies $V_\theta = C_\theta'$. ∎

We simplify the presentation of the theorem by assuming that $W_\theta - V_\theta$ is invertible, which implies the invertibility of $\hat{W}_n - \hat{V}_n$, for n sufficiently large. This is a special case that happens, under the usual regularity assumptions, only if $k - l \leq l$. If $k - l$ is greater than l, it is in general possible to reduce the dimension of $\mu(\theta)$ in order to consider only a vector of dimension l and then use the previous theorem. A more general presentation would consist in replacing the inverse by the Moore-Penrose inverse (see Example 4.5). If $k - l < l$, the variance is in general invertible but the test is less efficient than a direct Wald test on $\hat{\rho}_n$. Hence, the best choice that maintains the efficiency and does not pose an invertibility problem is that of $k - l = l$.

Example 4.5   *We are going to construct a Hausman test in the case of a normal model and show that the result is, in this special case, identical to a Wald test. Assume that x_i is i.i.d. $N(\theta, \Sigma)$ and $x_i = (y_i', z_i')' \in \mathbb{R}^{m-l} \times \mathbb{R}^l$. The matrix*

$$\Sigma = \begin{pmatrix} \Sigma_{yy} & \Sigma_{yz} \\ \Sigma_{zy} & \Sigma_{zz} \end{pmatrix}$$

is invertible and known, and θ is partitioned into $\theta = (\mu', \rho')$ where μ and ρ have dimensions $m - l$ and l respectively. Here, $k = m$.

The null hypothesis is $H_0 : \rho = 0$. We consider the unrestricted MLE

$$(\hat{\mu}_n, \hat{\rho}_n) = (\bar{y}_n, \bar{z}_n) = \left(\frac{1}{n}\sum_{i=1}^n y_i, \frac{1}{n}\sum_{i=1}^n z_i\right).$$

The "direct" Wald test statistic is equal to $n \, \hat{\rho}'_n \Sigma_{zz}^{-1} \hat{\rho}_n$ *which is distributed as a* χ_l^2. *The estimator* $\tilde{\mu}_n$ *is defined as the MLE of the restricted model, that is*

$$\tilde{\mu}_n = \arg\max -\frac{1}{2} \sum_{i=1}^{n} \begin{pmatrix} y_i - \mu \\ z_i \end{pmatrix}' \Sigma^{-1} \begin{pmatrix} y_i - \mu \\ z_i \end{pmatrix}.$$

An elementary calculation shows that

$$\tilde{\mu}_n = \bar{y} - \Sigma_{yz} \Sigma_{zz}^{-1} \bar{z}.$$

This estimator satisfies the conditions of Theorem 4.4 and the difference

$$\sqrt{n} \, (\hat{\mu}_n - \tilde{\mu}_n) = \sqrt{n} \Sigma_{yz} \Sigma_{zz}^{-1} \bar{z}$$

follows an exact normal distribution with mean zero and variance $\Sigma_{yz} \Sigma_{zz}^{-1} \Sigma_{yz}$ *under* H_0. *We have indeed*

$$W_\theta = \Sigma_{yy} \quad and \quad V_\theta = \Sigma_{yz} \Sigma_{zz}^{-1} \Sigma_{zy}.$$

If Σ_{yz} *is square and invertible (that is if* $m - l = l$*), then the Hausman test statistic is equal to*

$$n \bar{z}' \, \Sigma_{zz}^{-1} \Sigma_{zy} \left(\Sigma_{yz} \Sigma_{zz}^{-1} \Sigma_{yz} \right)^{-1} \Sigma_{yz} \Sigma_{zz}^{-1} \bar{z}_n = n \, \hat{\rho}'_n \, \Sigma_{zz}^{-1} \, \hat{\rho}_n,$$

i.e., to the Wald statistic (this result holds only in this special case). If $m - l > l$, *this result generalizes since we can use the Moore-Penrose generalized inverse of* $\Sigma_{yz} \Sigma_{zz}^{-1} \Sigma_{yz}$ *and set*

$$\left(\Sigma_{yz} \Sigma_{zz}^{-1} \Sigma_{zy} \right)^{+} = \Sigma_{zy} \left(\Sigma_{zy} \Sigma_{yz} \right)^{-1} \Sigma_{zz} \left(\Sigma_{zy} \Sigma_{yz} \right)^{-1} \Sigma_{zy}$$

(if $\Sigma_{zy} \Sigma_{yz}$ *is invertible), and the Hausman test is again equal to the Wald test. If* $m - l < l$, *the Hausman test differs from and is actually less powerful than the Wald test.* □

Example 4.6 *This example considers the Hausman test in the context of maximum likelihood estimation in an i.i.d. model. We assume that the* $x_i \in \mathbb{R}^m$ *have a density* $f(x_i|\theta)$ *and that* $0 = (\mu, \rho) \in \mathbb{R}^{k-l} \times \mathbb{R}^l$. *The null hypothesis is still* $H_0 : \rho = 0$. *Consider the unrestricted MLE of* θ *(denoted* $\hat{\lambda}_n$ *in Examples 3.9, 3.15 and 3.20 in Chapter 3) that can be partitioned into* $(\hat{\mu}_n, \hat{\rho}_n)$. *We partition the matrix* $\mathcal{J}_\theta$ *defined in Example 3.20 in Chapter 3 as*

$$\mathcal{J}_\theta = \begin{pmatrix} \mathcal{J}_{\theta,\mu\mu} & \mathcal{J}_{\theta,\mu\rho} \\ \mathcal{J}_{\theta,\rho\mu} & \mathcal{J}_{\theta,\rho\rho} \end{pmatrix}.$$

Using the partitioned inverse formula, we verify that the upper-left block of $\mathcal{J}_\theta^{-1}$ *is equal to*

$$\left(\mathcal{J}_{\theta,\mu\mu} - \mathcal{J}_{\theta,\mu\rho}\mathcal{J}_{\theta,\mu\rho}^{-1}\mathcal{J}_{\theta,\rho\mu}\right)^{-1}$$

$$= \mathcal{J}_{\theta,\mu\mu}^{-1} + \mathcal{J}_{\theta,\mu\mu}^{-1}\mathcal{J}_{\theta,\mu\rho}\left(\mathcal{J}_{\theta,\rho\rho}^{-1} - \mathcal{J}_{\theta,\rho\mu}\mathcal{J}_{\theta,\mu\mu}^{-1}\mathcal{J}_{\theta,\mu\rho}\right)_\rho^{-1}\mathcal{J}_{\theta,\rho\mu}\mathcal{J}_{\theta,\mu\mu}^{-1}$$

and is just the matrix W_θ in Theorem 4.4. The estimator $\tilde{\mu}_n$ is equal to the MLE in the restricted model under the null,

$$\tilde{\mu}_n = \arg\max \sum_{i=1}^n \ln f\left(x_i | (\mu, 0)\right),$$

and its asymptotic variance matrix V_θ is equal to $\mathcal{J}_\mu^{-1}$. The matrix $\mathcal{J}_\mu$ is equal to $\mathcal{J}_{\theta,\mu\mu}$ by letting $\rho = 0$. Hence, under H_0, the asymptotic variance of the difference $\sqrt{n}\left(\hat{\mu}_n - \hat{\mu}_n\right)$ is equal to

$$\mathcal{J}_\mu^{-1}\mathcal{J}_{\theta,\mu\rho}\left(\mathcal{J}_{\theta,\rho\rho}^{-1} - \mathcal{J}_{\theta,\rho\mu}\mathcal{J}_\mu^{-1}\mathcal{J}_{\theta,\mu\rho}\right)^{-1}\mathcal{J}_{\theta,\rho\mu}\mathcal{J}_\mu^{-1}. \tag{4.25}$$

In practice, we often estimate this variance by estimating $\mathcal{J}_\theta^{-1}$ in a unrestricted model from which we extract the upper left block of this estimator, $\hat{W}_n$, and we calculate $\hat{V}_n$ by estimating $\mathcal{J}_\mu^{-1}$ in the restricted model. The variance (4.25) is then estimated by $\hat{W}_n - \hat{V}_n$. The previous considerations about the rank apply here: under natural regularity conditions, the matrix (4.25) is full rank if $k - l \leq l$, and has rank l if $k - l \geq l$. $\qquad\square$

4.8   Encompassing Test

An important application of the previous results is the encompassing test, which allows us to test one parametric model against another one. This test has also been referred to as test for nonnested hypotheses.

Consider a model $\mathcal{M}_0 = \{X^n, \Theta, P_n^\theta\}$, such that Θ has finite dimension k and for which we have an estimator $\hat{\theta}_n$ consistent in P_∞^θ−probability and asymptotically normal, i.e.,

$$\sqrt{n}(\hat{\theta}_n - \theta) \to N(0, \Sigma_\theta).$$

Let $\mathcal{M}_1$ be another model with sample space X^n and parameter $\lambda \in \Lambda$ of finite dimension l. The specification of the sampling distribution of $\mathcal{M}_1$ is not necessary, but we consider an estimation method of λ leading to an estimator $\hat{\lambda}_n$.

The test is based on the following principle. If $\mathcal{M}_0$ is true (that is if the data are generated by the distribution P_n^θ for some $\theta \in \Theta$), it is assumed that $\hat{\theta}_n \to \theta$ and $\hat{\lambda}_n$ converges to a function $\lambda(\theta)$ in P_n^θ-probability. Hence, if $\mathcal{M}_0$ is true and if $\lambda(\theta)$ is continuous, $\lambda(\hat{\theta}_n)$ and $\hat{\lambda}_n$ converge both to $\lambda(\theta)$, and their difference $(\lambda(\hat{\theta}_n) - \hat{\lambda}_n)$ goes to zero. Moreover, under the usual assumptions for which the central limit theorem holds, $\sqrt{n}(\lambda(\hat{\theta}_n) - \hat{\lambda}_n)$ is asymptotically normal with mean zero and variance V_θ, which implies that

$$n \left(\lambda \left(\hat{\theta}_n \right) - \hat{\lambda}_n \right)' V_\theta^+ \left(\lambda(\hat{\theta}_n) - \hat{\lambda}_n \right)$$

follows asymptotically a χ^2 distribution with degrees of freedom equal to the rank of V_θ. Finally, if $\hat{V}_n$ is a sequence of matrices with the same rank as V_θ and converging to V_θ, then the statistic

$$\text{ENC}_n = n \left(\lambda(\hat{\theta}_n) - \hat{\lambda}_n \right)' \hat{V}_n^+ \left(\lambda(\hat{\theta}_n) - \hat{\lambda}_n \right) \tag{4.26}$$

is also a χ^2 with degrees of freedom equal to the rank of V_θ. This statistic is called encompassing statistic. It belongs to the general class of Wald tests in the sense that it involves estimators without using the criteria by which we obtained them.

Before explaining the calculation of V_θ, it is suitable to justify the interest in this test statistic. It measures the ability of model $\mathcal{M}_0$ to explain the results of model $\mathcal{M}_1$. More precisely, if model $\mathcal{M}_0$ is true, the statistician, who proceeds in estimating λ in $\mathcal{M}_1$, actually does not estimate the parameters of her model but a function of the parameters of $\mathcal{M}_0$. The function $\lambda(\theta)$ enables us to give a meaning to the estimation of a model even if it is misspecified. Model $\mathcal{M}_0$ provides an estimator $\hat{\theta}_n$, so that the statistician may estimate λ by $\lambda(\hat{\theta}_n)$ without reprocessing the sample. If $\lambda(\hat{\theta}_n)$ and $\hat{\lambda}_n$ are close, model $\mathcal{M}_0$ is said to encompass model $\mathcal{M}_1$. The notion of encompassing formalizes the idea that a correct theory should be able to explain the empirical results of erroneous models.

The exact expression of $\lambda(\theta)$ and the steps to obtain the limiting distribution of (4.26) depend on the estimation procedures employed in each model. In particular, different estimators in $\mathcal{M}_1$, which are consistent if $\mathcal{M}_1$ is true, may converge to different values if $\mathcal{M}_1$ is incorrectly specified.

We limit ourselves to two models that are estimated by maximum likelihood. This presentation completes the presentation given by Examples 3.9 and 3.15 in Chapter 3.

Example 4.7 *Suppose that $\mathcal{M}_0$ is an i.i.d. model with likelihood*

$$\prod_{i=1}^n f(x_i | \theta)$$

and that $\mathcal{M}_1$ is another i.i.d. model with likelihood

$$\prod_{i=1}^n g(x_i | \lambda).$$

The first step of the analysis consists in deriving the joint distribution of the MLE $\hat{\theta}_n$ and $\hat{\lambda}_n$, assuming $\mathcal{M}_0$ is true. We know that $\hat{\theta}_n \to \theta$ and that $\hat{\lambda}_n \to \lambda(\theta)$ under $\mathcal{M}_0$ where $\lambda(\theta)$ is the minimum in λ of

$$\int \ln \frac{f(x_i|\theta)}{g(x_i|\lambda)} f(x_i|\theta) dx_i.$$

We notice immediately that $\hat{\theta}_n$ and $\hat{\lambda}_n$ are jointly obtained as the solutions to the system

$$\frac{1}{n} \sum_{i=1}^{n} \begin{pmatrix} \frac{\partial}{\partial \theta} \ln f(x_i|\theta) \\ \frac{\partial}{\partial \lambda} \ln g(x_i|\lambda) \end{pmatrix} = 0.$$

Hence, we can apply the results of Chapter 3 (Theorem 3.3) and infer that

$$\sqrt{n} \begin{pmatrix} \hat{\theta}_n - \theta \\ \hat{\lambda}_n - \lambda(\theta) \end{pmatrix} \to N(0, \Sigma_\theta)$$

with

$$\Sigma_\theta = \begin{pmatrix} E^\theta \left(\frac{\partial^2}{\partial \theta \partial \theta'} \ln f(x_i|\theta) \right) & 0 \\ 0 & E \left(\frac{\partial^2}{\partial \lambda \partial \lambda'} \ln g(x_i|\lambda(\theta)) \right) \end{pmatrix}^{-1}$$

$$\times \begin{pmatrix} Var^\theta \left(\frac{\partial}{\partial \theta} \ln f(x_i|\theta) \right) & Cov^\theta \left(\frac{\partial}{\partial \theta} \ln f(x_i|\theta), \frac{\partial}{\partial \lambda} \ln g(x_i|\lambda(\theta)) \right) \\ Cov^\theta \left(\frac{\partial}{\partial \lambda} \ln g(x_i|\lambda(\theta)), \frac{\partial}{\partial \theta} \ln f(x_i|\theta) \right) & Var^\theta \left(\frac{\partial}{\partial \lambda} \ln g(x_i|\lambda(\theta)) \right) \end{pmatrix}$$

$$\times \begin{pmatrix} E^\theta \left(\frac{\partial^2}{\partial \theta \partial \theta'} \ln f(x_i|\theta) \right) & 0 \\ 0 & E^\theta \left(\frac{\partial^2}{\partial \lambda \partial \lambda'} \ln g(x_i|\lambda(\theta)) \right) \end{pmatrix}^{-1}.$$

Using the notation

$$\Sigma_\theta = \begin{pmatrix} \Sigma_{\theta 11} & \Sigma_{\theta 12} \\ \Sigma_{\theta 21} & \Sigma_{\theta 22} \end{pmatrix},$$

we have

$$\Sigma_{\theta 11}^{-1} = -E^\theta \left(\frac{\partial^2}{\partial \theta \partial \theta'} \ln f(x_i|\theta) \right)$$

which is equal to the information matrix in $\mathcal{M}_0$. Moreover,

$$\Sigma_{\theta 22} = E^\theta \left(\frac{\partial^2}{\partial \lambda \partial \lambda'} \ln g(x|\lambda(\theta)) \right)^{-1} Var^\theta \left(\frac{\partial}{\partial \theta} \ln g(x_i|\lambda(\theta)) \right)$$
$$E^\theta \left(\frac{\partial^2}{\partial \lambda \partial \lambda'} \ln g(x|\lambda(\theta)) \right)^{-1}$$

and

$$\Sigma_{\theta 12} = E^\theta \left(\frac{\partial^2}{\partial\theta\partial\theta'} \ln f(x_i|\theta) \right)^{-1} Cov^\theta \left(\frac{\partial}{\partial\theta} \ln f(x_i|\theta), \frac{\partial}{\partial\lambda} \ln g\left(x_i|\lambda(\theta)\right) \right)$$
$$E^\theta \left(\frac{\partial^2}{\partial\lambda\partial\lambda'} \ln g\left(x_i|\lambda(\theta)\right) \right)^{-1}.$$

Compared to the results of Chapter 3, this calculation establishes the joint normality of the estimators and makes explicit the asymptotic covariance. Then, it suffices to transform $(\hat\theta_n, \hat\lambda_n)$ into $(\lambda(\hat\theta_n), \hat\lambda_n)$ which remains asymptotically normal

$$\sqrt{n} \begin{pmatrix} \lambda(\hat\theta_n) - \lambda(\theta) \\ \hat\lambda_n - \lambda(\theta) \end{pmatrix} \rightarrow N \left(0, \begin{pmatrix} \frac{\partial\lambda}{\partial\theta'}\Sigma_{\theta 11}\frac{\partial\lambda'}{\partial\theta} & \frac{\partial\lambda}{\partial\theta'}\Sigma_{\theta 12} \\ \Sigma_{\theta 21}\frac{\partial\lambda'}{\partial\theta} & \Sigma_{\theta 22} \end{pmatrix} \right)$$

and to infer the asymptotic distribution of $\lambda(\hat\theta_n) - \hat\lambda_n$:

$$\sqrt{n}(\lambda(\hat\theta_n) - \hat\lambda_n) \rightarrow N(0, \Omega_\theta)$$

with

$$\Omega_\theta = \frac{\partial\lambda}{\partial\theta'}\Sigma_{\theta 11}\frac{\partial\lambda'}{\partial\theta} + \Sigma_{\theta 22} - \frac{\partial\lambda}{\partial\theta'}\Sigma_{\theta 12} - \Sigma_{\theta 21}\frac{\partial\lambda'}{\partial\theta}.$$

It follows that

$$n(\lambda(\hat\theta_n) - \hat\lambda_n)'\Omega_{\hat\theta_n}^+(\lambda(\hat\theta_n) - \hat\lambda_n) \rightarrow \chi_r^2$$

with

$$r = rank\,(\Omega_\theta).$$

To obtain a test statistic, we need to choose a consistent sequence of estimators $\hat\Omega_n$ with the same rank as Ω_θ, and to replace $\Omega_{\hat\theta_n}^+$ by $\hat\Omega_n^+$ in this expression. In practice, if Ω_θ is singular, we look for a subvector of $\lambda(\hat\theta_n) - \hat\lambda_n$ such that its asymptotic variance is invertible (if possible with dimension r in order to preserve the power of the test), and we conduct the test on this subvector. The practical difficulty with implementing the encompassing test is the calculation of $\lambda(\theta)$ and of its derivatives necessary for computing the covariance matrix. Their expressions are generally impossible to obtain analytically but can be estimated using the simulation methods that we will present in Chapter 6. □

Example 4.8 *Consider the following two models.*

In M_0, $x_i = (y_i, z_i)' \in \mathbb{R}^2$ is i.i.d. $N \begin{pmatrix} \theta \\ 0 \end{pmatrix}, \Sigma$,   and

in M_1, x_i is i.i.d. $N \left(\begin{pmatrix} o \\ \lambda \end{pmatrix}, \Sigma \right)$

where θ and $\lambda \in \mathbb{R}$.

It is easy to verify that the MLE are

$$\hat{\theta}_n = \bar{y} - \frac{\sigma_{yz}}{\sigma_{zz}}\bar{z} \quad and \quad \hat{\lambda}_n = \bar{z} - \frac{\sigma_{yz}}{\sigma_{yy}}\bar{y}$$

where $\bar{y}$ and $\bar{z}$ are the sample means of y_i and z_i. The estimator $\hat{\lambda}_n$ converges to

$$\lambda(\theta) = -\frac{\sigma_{yz}}{\sigma_{yy}}\theta$$

under M_0. Hence, the encompassing test compares

$$-\frac{\sigma_{yz}}{\sigma_{yy}}\left(\bar{y} - \frac{\sigma_{yz}}{\sigma_{zz}}\bar{z}\right) \quad and \quad \bar{z} - \frac{\sigma_{yz}}{\sigma_{yy}}\bar{y}.$$

The test statistic is based on $(\rho^2 - 1)\bar{z}$ (where ρ is the correlation coefficient between y_i and z_i) and reduces, in this special case, to the usual test for the expectation of z_i to be zero. $\quad\square$

Notes

Asymptotic tests obviously occupy an important place in the statistical literature. The likelihood ratio test was presented in the seminal paper by Neyman and Pearson (1928), while the two other tests were introduced by Wald (1943) and Rao (1948). Pittman (1949) presented the notion of comparing tests through a sequence of local alternatives and the concept of relative asymptotic efficiency, Serfling (1980) provides a synthesis of various points of view in his Chapter 10. For a Bayesian framework, see Lubrano and Marimoutou (1988). It is impossible to cite all the econometric works on asymptotic testing and we refer to the synthesis by Gouriéroux and Monfort (1996a) and to the books by Davidson and McKinnon (1993 and 2004). Note however the interesting criticism of Wald tests by Dufour (1997) and the article by Davidson and McKinnon (1987) on implicit hypotheses.

Exogeneity tests were introduced by Durbin (1954) and Wu (1973), and have been revisited as specification tests by the paper of Hausman (1978), a paper which has been greatly clarified by Holly (1982) and Holly and Monfort (1986). A comparison of the different versions of these tests is given in Nakamura and Nakamura (1981).

Tests for nonnested models are based mainly on the work by Cox (1964 and 1962) and our presentation is close to those of Gouriéroux, Monfort, and Trognon (1983), Mizon and Richard, (1986), Florens, Richard, and Hendry (1996), and Florens and Mouchart (1993).

5.   Nonparametric Methods

5.1   Introduction

Nonparametric methods have recently taken a prominent position in econometrics. One of the essential reasons for this phenomenon is the increasingly frequent use of survey data and administrative data bases in microeconometrics (analysis of labor market, individual consumption, household saving). These samples are often very large. Although the microeconomic theory is well advanced, it does not provide a precise functional form that could be used for the statistical modeling. It is known that a relationship is decreasing or that a distribution has a decreasing hazard rate, but the economic theory does not specify the parametric form of the relationship or distribution.

Nonparametric methods are actually numerous and we will cover only part of them, we will neglect, for instance, rank analysis to focus mainly on smoothing techniques. These methods can be considered "descriptive." However, this analysis of the observations is essential. Moreover, we will see that nonparametric methods extend to semiparametric methods that have as a purpose the estimation of a parameter vector without imposing restrictive specification assumptions.

Note that the treatment of simulated data (see Chapter 6), for which samples can be made as large as desired, heavily uses nonparametric methods.

We focus our presentation on i.i.d. models. Extensions to dynamic models are obviously possible and are used, for instance, in financial econometrics. We will recall first the essential properties of the empirical distribution before studying the density estimation and introducing semiparametric methods. The nonparametric regression will be studied in Part II of the book.

5.2   Empirical Distribution and Empirical Distribution Function

The basic model of nonparametric statistics is the i.i.d. model with unknown probability distribution.

87

This model has been presented in Example 1.8, and we recall here the notation. The observations $x_1, \ldots, x_n$ are the elements of $\mathbb{R}^m$ generated independently by the unknown probability distribution Q. Therefore, the parameter of this statistical model is $Q \in \mathcal{P}_m$, the family of all probability distributions on $\mathbb{R}^m$.

The "natural" estimator of Q is *the empirical distribution* defined as

$$\hat{Q}_n = \frac{1}{n} \sum_{i=1}^{n} \delta_{x_i} \tag{5.1}$$

where δ_{x_i} is the Dirac measure in x_i. If $E \subset \mathbb{R}^m$, $\delta_{x_i}(E)$ equals 1 if $x_i \in E$ and 0 otherwise. Hence, the definition (5.1) means that $\hat{Q}_n(E)$ is equal to the proportion of points in the sample that belongs to E.

It is useful to represent Q by its (cumulative) distribution function F satisfying

$$F : \mathbb{R}^m \to [0, 1] \quad \text{and} \quad F(t) = Q((-\infty, t_1] \times \cdots \times (-\infty, t_m]) \tag{5.2}$$

with $t = (t_1, \ldots, t_m)$.

The empirical distribution function is obtained by replacing Q by $\hat{Q}_n$ so that

$$\hat{F}_n(t) = \frac{1}{n} \sum_{i=1}^{n} \mathbb{I}(x_{i1} \le t_1, \ldots, x_{im} \le t_m) \tag{5.3}$$

where the function $\mathbb{I}(x_{i1} \le t_1, \ldots, x_{im} \le t_m)$, equal to 1 if each component of x_i is less or equal than the corresponding component of t and 0 otherwise, is the distribution function of the Dirac measure δ_{x_i}.

The following theorem presents some small sample properties of the estimators $\hat{Q}_n$ and $\hat{F}_n$.

Theorem 5.1 *If $x_1, \ldots, x_n$ is an i.i.d. sample of probability distribution Q, we have:*

1. *$\forall E$, the sampling distribution of $n\hat{Q}_n(E)$ is the binomial distribution with parameters n and $Q(E)$. In particular:*

   $$E^Q(\hat{Q}_n(E)) = Q(E) \quad and$$

   $$Var^Q(\hat{Q}_n(E)) = \frac{Q(E)(1 - Q(E))}{n}.$$

2. *If $E_1, \ldots, E_L$ is a partition of $\mathbb{R}^m$, the sampling distribution of $n\hat{Q}_n(E_1), \ldots, n\hat{Q}_n(E_L)$ is the multinomial distribution with parameters $nQ(E_1), \ldots, nQ(E_L)$. In particular,*

   $$Cov^Q(\hat{Q}_n(E_l), \hat{Q}_n(E_j)) = -\frac{1}{n} Q(E_\ell) Q(E_j) \quad (l \ne j)$$

3. If $m = 1$, $n\hat{F}_n(t)$ has a binomial sampling distribution with parameters n and $F(t)$. Moreover,

$$Cov^Q(\hat{F}_n(t), \hat{F}_n(s)) = \frac{1}{n}[F(min(s, t)) - F(s)F(t)] \qquad (5.4)$$

∎

Proof: One can consider $n\hat{Q}_n(E)$ as the number of times an event $x_i \in E$ occurred. Because each event has probability $Q(E)$ and the events corresponding to different i are independent, we have result 1.

The multinomial case is an immediate generalization. For point 3, let $E = (-\infty, t]$. Formula (5.4) follows from the equalities

$$Cov^Q\left(\hat{F}_n(t), \hat{F}_n(s)\right) = \frac{1}{n^2}\sum_{i,j} Cov^Q(\mathbb{I}(x_i \le t), \mathbb{I}(x_j \le s))$$

$$= \frac{1}{n^2}\sum_i Cov^Q(\mathbb{I}(x_i \le t), \mathbb{I}(x_i \le s))$$

$$= \frac{1}{n^2}\sum_i \{E^Q(\mathbb{I}(x_i \le t)\mathbb{I}(x_i \le s))$$

$$- E^Q(\mathbb{I}(x_i \le t))E^Q(\mathbb{I}(x_i \le s))\}$$

$$= \frac{1}{n}[F(min(s, t)) - F(t)F(s)].$$

∎

Now, let us briefly consider the asymptotic properties of the estimator of $F(t)$, restricting ourselves to the scalar case. The following theorem is the immediate consequence of the law of large numbers and the central limit theorem.

Theorem 5.2 *Under the assumptions of Theorem 5.1 and if $m = 1$, we have :*

1. $\hat{F}_n(t) \to F(t)$ *a.s.*
2. $\sqrt{n}(\hat{F}_n(t) - F(t)) \to N(0, F(t)(1 - F(t)))$ *in distribution.*
3. *If $t_1, \dots, t_q \in \mathbb{R}$,*

$$\sqrt{n}\begin{pmatrix} \hat{F}_n(t_1) - F(t_1) \\ \vdots \\ \hat{F}_n(t_q) - F(t_q) \end{pmatrix} \to N_q(0, \Sigma)$$

where the element (j, k) of Σ is equal to $F(min(t_j, t_k)) - F(t_j)F(t_k)$.

∎

This theorem can be much improved upon by considering global properties of convergence. These global properties follow from a functional central limit theorem that examines the convergence of the function

$$\sqrt{n}\left(\hat{F}_n - F\right)$$

to a limiting distribution in the space of functions. This study goes beyond the scope of this book, but we mention some implications of this result to the maximum of the gap between $\hat{F}_n$ and the true distribution F. Let

$$D_n = \sup_{t \in \mathbb{R}} |\hat{F}_n(t) - F(t)|. \tag{5.5}$$

One can show:

1. Dvoretsky-Kiefer-Wolfowitz Inequality:

$$\exists C > 0, \ \forall F, \quad \Pr(D_n > d) \leq C e^{-2nd^2} \tag{5.6}$$

   for all $d > 0$. Note that here we have the product of n probability distributions equal to Q.
2. Glivenko-Cantelli Theorem:

$$D_n \to 0 \quad \text{a.s.} \tag{5.7}$$

To test the hypothesis $F = F_0$ (a given distribution function), one uses the statistic D_n with F replaced by F_0. Thus, one obtains the Kolmogorov-Smirnov statistic, and the rejection region of the hypothesis $F = F_0$ is of the form $D_n > d$. To find d such that the probability of the rejection region is equal to a given value, one uses the limiting distribution of D_n, established by Kolmogorov assuming the continuity of F:

$$\lim_{n \to \infty} \Pr(\sqrt{n} D_n \leq d) = 1 - 2 \sum_{j=1}^{\infty} (-1)^{j+1} e^{-2j^2 d^2} \quad (d > 0). \tag{5.8}$$

This expression serves to construct the tables of the Kolmogorov-Smirnov test.

This presentation is extremely summarized and the empirical distribution analysis can be generalized in multiple directions. For instance, one can analyze the distribution function for an arbitrary m or for mixing stationary models instead of i.i.d. One can be interested in the quantile function $F^{-1}(t)$, or consider alternative distances between $\hat{F}_n$ and F, other than Kolmogorov-Smirnov.

5.3   Density Estimation

In the preceding section, no restrictions were imposed on the probability distribution Q. We will introduce one by assuming that Q admits a density f (with respect to Lebesgue measure), that is

$$Q(E) = \int_E f(u)du. \tag{5.9}$$

The aim now is to estimate f or to choose an estimation of Q that has a density.

It is clear that we need to drop or modify the empirical distribution because it does not admit a density and hence does not satisfy the assumptions of the model.

Various strategies are used to construct an estimator of the density. The simplest method consists in drawing a histogram of the observations, and the most popular method is the kernel method that we are going to present. Other methods include the kth nearest neighbor estimator, orthogonal functions, spline functions, and so on. It is possible to encompass various methods within a more general framework but for the sake of simplicity, we concentrate our exposition on the kernel method.

5.3.1   Construction of the Kernel Estimator of the Density

To explain the construction of the estimator, we first consider the case of scalar observations ($m = 1$). The density $f(t)$ can be considered as the derivative (except maybe at a few points) of the distribution function $F(t)$. Hence, we essentially need to look for a differentiable estimator of F. The empirical distribution function $\hat{F}_n$ is not differentiable, but it can be modified by replacing the indicator $I\!\!I(x_i \leq t)$ by a differentiable approximation.

If $\overline{K}(t)$ is a differentiable approximation of $I\!\!I(0 \leq t)$, then $\overline{K}(t - x_i)$ is a differentiable approximation of $I\!\!I(x_i \leq t)$ (by a change of origin) and hence one obtains a differentiable approximation of $\hat{F}_n$ by considering

$$\widehat{F}_n(t) = \frac{1}{n} \sum_{i=1}^{n} \overline{K}(t - x_i). \tag{5.10}$$

If K is the derivative of $\overline{K}$, one builds an estimator of the density by defining:

$$\hat{f}_n(t) = \frac{1}{n} \sum_{i=1}^{n} K(t - x_i). \tag{5.11}$$

This construction will not provide a consistent estimator of F (or of f). Indeed, it follows from the law of large numbers that $\widehat{F}_n(t)$ converges to $E^Q(\overline{K}(t - x_i))$ which differs from $F(t)$. To obtain a consistent estimator, the quality of the approximation of $I\!\!I(x_i \leq t)$ needs to increase with the sample size.

A way to obtain this result is to replace $\overline{K}$ by $\overline{K}(\frac{t-x_i}{h_n})$ where h_n is a real number dependent on n and going to 0. Different values of n will give rise different approximations which will be better for higher n. Hence, formulas (5.10) and (5.11) are modified to obtain

$$\widehat{F}_n(t) = \frac{1}{n} \sum_{i=1}^n \overline{K} \left(\frac{t - x_i}{h_n} \right) \tag{5.12}$$

and

$$\hat{f}_n(t) = \frac{1}{nh_n} \sum_{i=1}^n K \left(\frac{t - x_i}{h_n} \right). \tag{5.13}$$

It remains to define the way to choose $\overline{K}$. A method, that is easy to interpret, consists of choosing $\overline{K}$ as the distribution function of a given probability distribution on $\mathbb{R}$; it is convenient to assume that this distribution has mean zero and is symmetric. Hence, the function K is the density of this distribution and is called the *kernel* of the estimator.

We complete this construction with two remarks:

1. Consider two independent real random variables $\tilde{x}$ and ε. The first, $\tilde{x}$, is discrete and is distributed according to the empirical distribution $\hat{Q}_n$. In other words, $\tilde{x}$ can take the values of the sample $x_1, \ldots, x_n$ with probability $\frac{1}{n}$. The second, ε, is continuous and its density is $K(t)$. One can verify that

   $$\tilde{x} + h_n \varepsilon$$

   is a continuous random variable with density given by (5.13). Indeed:

   $$\text{Prob}\,(\tilde{x} + h_n \tilde{\varepsilon} \le t) = \sum_{i=1}^n \text{Prob}\,(\tilde{x} + h_n \tilde{\varepsilon} \le t | \tilde{x} = x_i)\,\text{Prob}\,(\tilde{x} = x_i)$$

   $$= \frac{1}{n} \sum_{i=1}^n \text{Prob} \left(\varepsilon \le \frac{t - x_i}{h_n} \right) = \frac{1}{n} \sum_{i=1}^n \overline{K} \left(\frac{t - x_i}{h_n} \right).$$

   One recognizes (5.12) and the density (5.13).

   Hence, kernel smoothing comes down to computing the density of the sum (or equivalently the convolution) of a random variable distributed according to the empirical distribution and an independent error of density K multiplied by the scalar h_n, which goes to zero with n so that more and more weight is given to the sample.

2. Efficiency may be gained by considering kernels that are not necessarily positive. The above interpretation is then lost and in small samples, the estimate of the density may not be nonnegative. This extension is not considered in this introductory chapter.

The preceding method can be generalized to the case with several variables and is summarized in the following definition.

Definition 5.1   *Let $x_1, \ldots, x_n$ be an i.i.d. sample of distribution Q in $\mathbb{R}^m$ with density f with respect to Lebesgue measure. Consider $\overline{K}(t)$ $(t \in \mathbb{R}^m)$, a differentiable distribution function on $\mathbb{R}^m$, and its density*

$$K(t) = \frac{\partial^{(m)} \overline{K}}{\partial t_1 \ldots \partial t_m}(t).$$

Suppose that K is symmetric $(K(-t) = K(t))$, unimodal and that the random vector of density K has a finite mean (zero by symmetry) and variance. The estimator of kernel K and window $h_n > 0$ of the density f is equal to

$$\hat{f}_n(t) = \frac{1}{n h_n^m} \sum_{i=1}^{n} K\left(\frac{t - x_i}{h_n}\right) \tag{5.14}$$

where $\frac{t-x_i}{h_n}$ is the vector

$$\left(\frac{t_j - x_{ij}}{h_n}\right)_{j=1,\ldots,m}. \qquad\blacksquare$$

5.3.2   Small Sample Properties of the Kernel Estimator and Choices of Window and Kernel

The choices of the window and the kernel in the estimation of the density are here based on the study of the small sample properties of $\hat{f}_n$. We will summarize these properties by the computation of the distance between $\hat{f}_n$ and f; this distance is the mean integrated squared error (MISE). This measure generalizes the mean squared error to functions and is defined by the value

$$\text{MISE}\left(\hat{f}_n\right) = E^Q \left\{ \int \left(\hat{f}_n(t) - f_n(t)\right)^2 dt \right\}. \tag{5.15}$$

Hence, the MISE is equal to the squared bias and the variance of the estimator. Note that the MISE is defined only for square integrable f. This calculation is identical to that developed in Chapter 3 in (3.4).

The estimator $\hat{f}_n$ is biased, hence the two terms in the decomposition (5.15) remain and we have the following approximation for a density on $\mathbb{R}$.

Theorem 5.3   *Under the assumptions of the definition 5.1, if $x_i \in \mathbb{R}$ and if f is twice continuously differentiable, we have the approximation:*

$$\text{MISE}\left(\hat{f}_n\right) \simeq \frac{h_n^4}{4} \sigma_K^4 \int \left(\frac{d^2 f}{dt^2}(t)\right)^2 dt + \frac{1}{n h_n} \int K^2(u) \, du \tag{5.16}$$

where σ_K^2 is the variance of the random variable with density K. $\blacksquare$

Proof: First consider the bias. We have

$$E^Q\left(\hat{f}_n(t)\right) - f(t) = \int \frac{1}{h_n} K\left(\frac{t-x_i}{h_n}\right) f(x_i)\, dx_i - f(t)$$

$$= \int K(u)(f(t-h_n u) - f(t))\, du$$

by letting $u = \frac{t-x_i}{h_n}$. By a second order approximation, we obtain

$$f(t-h_n u) - f(t) \simeq -h_n u \frac{df(t)}{dt} + \frac{h_n^2 u^2}{2} \frac{d^2 f(t)}{dt^2}$$

which yields, after multiplying by $K(u)$ and integrating,

$$E^Q\left(\hat{f}_n(t) - f(t)\right) \simeq \frac{h_n^2}{2} \frac{d^2 f(t)}{dt^2} \sigma_K^2.$$

By squaring and integrating with respect to t, the first term of the approximation follows. On the other hand,

$$Var^Q\left(\hat{f}_n(t)\right) = \frac{1}{n} Var^Q\left(\frac{1}{h_n} K\left(\frac{t-x_i}{h_n}\right)\right)$$

$$= \frac{1}{n} \int \frac{1}{h_n^2} K^2\left(\frac{t-x_i}{h_n}\right) f(x_i)\, dx_i$$

$$- \frac{1}{n}\left[\int \frac{1}{h_n} K\left(\frac{t-x_i}{h_n}\right) f(x_i)\right]^2.$$

If n is large and h_n is small, the second term is negligible compared to the first one because of the previous calculation. Hence, we just keep the first term which can be rewritten as

$$Var^Q\left(\hat{f}_n(t)\right) \simeq \frac{1}{nh_n} \int K^2(u) f(t-h_n u)\, du$$

$$\simeq \frac{1}{nh_n} \int K^2(u) f(t)\, du - \frac{1}{n} \int K^2(u) u \frac{df(t)}{dt} du.$$

The second term is again negligible because h_n is small. By integrating this expression with respect to t and using $\int f(t)\, dt = 1$, the second term of the theorem follows. ∎

Notice that choosing h_n very small reduces the bias but increases the variance. From the previous result, we can infer the choice of the optimal window, the window which minimizes the MISE for a given kernel.

A simple calculation shows that the expression (5.16) is minimal in h_n if

$$h_n = Cn^{-\frac{1}{5}} \text{ with } C = \sigma_K^{-\frac{4}{5}} \left[\int K^2(u)\,du \right]^{\frac{1}{5}} \left[\int \left(\frac{d^2 f}{dt^2} \right)^2 dt \right]^{-\frac{1}{5}}.$$

(5.17)

This result is not completely satisfying because the constant C depends precisely on the unknown f. A frequently used method consists in replacing f in the constant by the normal density. One can verify that

$$\int \left(\frac{d^2 f}{dt^2} \right)^2 dt$$

is roughly equal to $0.212\, \sigma^{-5}$ where σ^2 is the variance of x_i. If we choose for K the density of the standard normal, we obtain

$$C \simeq 1.06\sigma.$$

Hence, a popular choice for the window in the estimation of a density on $\mathbb{R}$ consists in using

$$h_n = \hat{\sigma}_n n^{-\frac{1}{5}}$$

where the variance σ^2 of Q is estimated by the empirical variance

$$\hat{\sigma}_n^2 = \frac{1}{n} \sum_{i=1}^n (x_i - \bar{x})^2.$$

Again one can use the MISE to select the optimal kernel. We do not detail the calculation but provide the main outline. If we replace h_n by its optimal value (5.17) in the expression of the MISE (5.16), we obtain an expression which is a function of K and of f. This function of K is actually proportional to

$$\sigma_K^{2/5} \left\{ \int K^2(u)\,du \right\}^{4/5}.$$

If we focus our attention to kernels K, which are densities with mean zero and $\sigma_K = 1$, we actually look for a nonnegative function K, which minimizes $\int K^2$ under the constraints

$$\int K(u)\,du = 1, \quad \int u K(u)\,du = 0 \quad \text{and} \quad \int u^2 K(u)\,du = 1.$$

The solution to this problem is the function

$$K(u) = \begin{vmatrix} \frac{3}{4\sqrt{5}} \left(1 - \frac{1}{5}t^2 \right) & \text{if } -\sqrt{5} \leq t \leq \sqrt{5} \\ 0 & \text{otherwise.} \end{vmatrix}$$

(5.18)

This kernel is known as Epanechnikov's kernel. Other popular kernels are the density of the standard normal, the triangular density

$$K(u) = \begin{vmatrix} 1 - |u| & \text{if } |u| < 1 \\ 0 & \text{otherwise} \end{vmatrix} \tag{5.19}$$

and rectangular density

$$K(u) = \begin{vmatrix} 1/2 & \text{if } -1 \leq u \leq 1 \\ 0 & \text{otherwise.} \end{vmatrix} \tag{5.20}$$

5.3.3 Asymptotic Properties

The asymptotic properties concern first the convergence of the estimator $\hat{f}_n$ to f. First, we can look at the pointwise convergence of $\hat{f}_n(t)$ to $f(t)$ or the convergence of the MISE to 0 in the case where f is square integrable and differentiable. The expression of the MISE given by (5.16) in Theorem 5.3 shows that two conditions are necessary to obtain the convergence of the MISE to 0:

— $h_n \to 0$.
— $nh_n \to \infty$ in the case $x_i \in \mathbb{R}$ or more generally, $nh_n^m \to \infty$ if $x_i \in \mathbb{R}^m$.

These two conditions imply also the pointwise mean square convergence (and hence in probability) of $\hat{f}_n(t)$ to $f(t)$.

A stronger convergence requires of course more assumptions. For instance, it is interesting to consider the convergence of

$$\sup_t \left| \hat{f}_n(t) - f(t) \right|$$

to 0 in probability in order to obtain a uniform convergence of $\hat{f}_n$ to f.

In the scalar case, the convergence is obtained if f is uniformly continuous and the condition

$$nh_n \to \infty$$

is replaced by

$$nh_n (\ln n)^{-1} \to \infty.$$

This condition imposes that nh_n goes to infinity faster than $\ln n$. Many other results on convergence appear in the statistical literature. This literature analyzes also the speed of convergence of $\hat{f}_n$ to f. We will not present these results but nevertheless emphasize that the speed of convergence is slow as soon as m is relatively large, which makes the asymptotic results of limited practical interest, except when the sample size is extremely large.

This effect is even worse when it comes to asymptotic normality. Indeed, it can be shown that under the assumptions $h_n \to 0$ and $nh_n^m \to \infty$, if $t \in \mathbb{R}^m$,

$$\sqrt{nh_n^m} \left(\frac{\hat{f}_n(t) - E\left(\hat{f}_n(t)\right)}{\left[f(t) \int K^2(u)\, du \right]^{\frac{1}{2}}} \right) \to N(0, 1) \quad \text{in distribution.}$$

$$(5.21)$$

Moreover, for given $t_1, \ldots, t_q$ of $\mathbb{R}^m$, the limiting distributions of $\hat{f}_n(t_j)$, $j = 1, \ldots, q$, normalized as above, are asymptotically independent.

This result is not very interesting because it does not allow us to construct confidence intervals for $f(t)$. To do this, it is necessary to be able to replace $E\left(\hat{f}_n(t)\right)$ by $f(t)$ in the previous result. This modification is possible if f is twice differentiable, with bounded and integrable derivatives and if $nh_n^{m+4} \to 0$. In this case, it is also possible to replace f in the denominator by its estimator $\hat{f}_n$. We then obtain

$$\sqrt{nh_n^m} \left(\frac{\hat{f}_n(t) - f(t)}{\left[\hat{f}_n(t) \int K^2(u)\, du \right]^{\frac{1}{2}}} \right) \to N(0, 1), \quad (5.22)$$

and a 95% confidence interval for f is given by

$$\hat{f}_n(t) \pm 1,96 \left(\frac{\hat{f}_n(t) \int K^2(u)\, du}{nh_n^m} \right)^{\frac{1}{2}}.$$

The asymptotic independence for different values of t is maintained.

Simulation studies of the small sample properties of the kernel estimator show that the exact distribution differs largely from the asymptotic distribution when the sample size corresponds to that of most econometric data sets. Hence, we recommend to use these normality results with caution and we prefer results following from bootstrap for instance (see Chapter 6).

Remark. It follows from result (5.22) that $\hat{f}_n$ converges to f with the rate $\sqrt{nh_n^m}$. Let $m = 1$ to simplify. If h_n is selected using the rule (5.17), the rate of convergence becomes $n^{\frac{2}{5}}$. This rate improves if it is assumed that f is more than twice differentiable. However, this rate deteriorates if the dimension m increases. In the general case, it can be shown that a density which is s times differentiable in $\mathbb{R}^m$ can be estimated at the rate $n^{\frac{s}{m+2s}}$.

5.4 Semiparametric Methods

Semiparametric methods refer to statistical procedures where the sampling probabilities are indexed by the elements of an infinite dimensional space, but where the statisticians interest lies in a finite dimensional vector. Using the notation of Chapter 1, we are interested in a function $\lambda(\theta) \in \mathbb{R}^k$ of θ, θ being infinite dimensional. This presentation already appeared several times in previous chapters and will be completed by some comments.

In broad outline, two types of sampling models are considered. Their distinction is based on the presence of overidentification assumptions, that is the restrictions on the sampling probability space. Let us introduce this distinction with the following example.

Example 5.1 *The observations are $(x_1, \ldots, x_n)$ with $x_i = (y_i, z_i) \in \mathbb{R}^2$. A first type of model could suppose that the x_i are i.i.d. with distribution Q. Moreover, we constrain Q to be dominated by Lebesgue measure or to be such that the elements of x_i have finite second moments. Hence, such a model introduces some (weak) constraints on the generation of x_i, and we consider that this model is "weakly overidentified" without giving a rigorous mathematical meaning to this phrase.*

A second type of model could assume that the x_i are again i.i.d. with distribution Q, but Q is dominated by Lebesgue measure and its density is elliptic, that is, it can be written as

$$f(u, v) = kg\left((u - \alpha, v - \beta)' H (u - \alpha, v - \beta)\right)$$

where k is a scaling coefficient depending on g and g is a function from $\mathbb{R} \to \mathbb{R}^+$, $\alpha, \beta \in \mathbb{R}$, and H is a 2×2 positive definite matrix. This model (of which the normal distribution is a special case) is such that the density of the pair (y_i, z_i) depends on the distance between this pair and the point (α, β) according to the H metric. Its parameters are α, β, H, and g and therefore it belongs to the class of nonparametric specifications because it has a functional parameter g. However, it introduces much more structure than the previous one and is really overidentified. The advantage of this model compared to a fully nonparametric model lies in the fact that the estimation of a density of two variables is replaced by the estimation of a density of one single variable (g) and five scalar parameters. In addition, it is more flexible than a totally parametric model (as the normal one) where the function g is completely determined a priori. It is possible to test the assumption that the density of the pair is elliptic.   □

Example 5.2 *We observe i.i.d. vectors $x_i = (y_i, z_i')' \in \mathbb{R} \times \mathbb{R}^q$, and we are interested in the conditional model describing the generation of y_i given z_i. A fully nonparametric approach would consist in estimating the conditional distribution of y_i given z_i which is quite difficult in practice if q is large* *(this point is partially considered in Chapter 10). An alternative strategy consists in constraining the conditional distribution, by assuming for instance that the conditional distribution function satisfies*

$$\Pr(y_i \leq t \,|z_i) = F(t)^{R(\beta, z_i)} \tag{5.23}$$

where F is an unknown distribution function and R is a known positive function depending on unknown parameters β, for example

$$R(\beta, z_i) = e^{\beta' z_i}, \qquad \beta \in \mathbb{R}^q.$$

Hence, the conditional model is semiparametric in the sense that it depends on a vector parameter β and on a functional parameter F. However, it is clear that the specification (5.23) introduces constraints on the conditional distribution, which are however weaker than those of a fully parametric model. □

Consider a weakly overidentified model, where the x_i are i.i.d. with distribution Q. This assumption can be relaxed by assuming that the x_i are stationary ergodic (see Chapter 2) and Q is still the marginal distribution of any realization. We are interested in the parameter vector λ, a function of Q, denoted $\lambda = \lambda(Q)$. We distinguish two cases depending on whether the function λ is defined for the empirical distribution, $\hat{Q}_n$, of x_i or not. The previous sections provide examples of both situations. If λ is defined by the moment condition

$$E^Q(\psi(x_i, \lambda)) = 0,$$

we saw that Q can be replaced by $\hat{Q}_n$, from which we derive the estimator $\hat{\lambda}_n$ of λ. In contrast, if $\lambda(Q)$ is the value of the density of Q with respect to Lebesgue measure at t, this function is not defined at $\hat{Q}_n$.

If the function λ is defined for $\hat{Q}_n$, an estimator is immediately obtained by replacing Q by $\hat{Q}_n$ while, if λ is not defined for $\hat{Q}_n$, it is necessary to first transform $\hat{Q}_n$ into a distribution that belongs to the domain of λ, then take the value of this transformation. This happens in particular if λ depends on the density of Q. We are going to illustrate this remark by various examples.

Example 5.3 *If $x_i \in \mathbb{R}$ and if F is the distribution function of Q, we define*

$$\lambda(Q) = F(t_0)$$

where t_0 is a given value. Then, the parameter λ is the probability of the event "x_i is less than or equal to t_0." This function is well defined for $\hat{F}_n$ and we derive the usual estimator $\hat{\lambda}_n$ equal to the proportion of observations less than or equal to t_0. This estimator belongs to the class of method of moments estimators because

$$\lambda(Q) = E^Q(\mathbb{I}(x_i \leq t_0)).$$ □

Example 5.4 *Let $x_i \in \mathbb{R}$ be i.i.d. with dominated distribution Q, and let f be the density of Q. We are looking for the value of*

$$\lambda(Q) = \int \frac{df(t)}{dt} f(t) \, dt$$

equal to the mean of the derivative of the density. This function is not defined at $\hat{Q}_n$. Therefore, we use a differentiable estimator of the density, for instance, a kernel estimator. This estimator is used for the calculation of $\frac{df}{dt}$, but is unnecessary for computing the expectation. Hence, $\lambda(Q)$ is estimated by

$$\hat{\lambda}_n = \frac{1}{n} \sum_{i=1}^{n} \frac{d\hat{f}_n}{dt}(x_i)$$

rather than by

$$\lambda_n^* = \int \frac{d\hat{f}_n(t)}{dt} \hat{f}_n(t) \, dt. \qquad \square$$

We conclude this chapter by providing a few guidelines for the estimation methods for semiparametric models.

As shown by the previous examples, it is appropriate to distinguish problems where the data distribution depends on two elements, one vectorial and the other functional, from the problems where the object of interest, $\lambda(Q)$, is a function of the distribution of the observations.

In the first case, at least two approaches are possible. The first one is particularly interesting but can be used in special cases only.

For the first approach, let $x = (x_i)_{i=1,\dots,n}$ be the sample, λ the parameter vector, and g the functional parameter. The distribution of x depends on λ and g, but it is possible in some models to extract some statistic $S(x_1, \dots, x_n)$, whose distribution depends only on λ. If this statistic has a dominated distribution, then λ can be estimated by maximum likelihood using only the statistic $S(x)$ from the sample.

Example 5.5 *We modify slightly example 5.2 to bring it closer to traditional microeconometric models. Let us describe our model which is a duration model with so-called proportional hazard. The sample $x_i = (y_i, z_i')'$ is composed of a positive number y_i representing a duration (of unemployment for instance) and of z_i a vector of conditioning variables. The conditional model is defined by the independence of the x_i and the property*

$$\Pr(y_i \geq t | z_i) = S(t)^{R(\beta, z_i)} \qquad (5.24)$$

where $S(t) = 1 - F(t)$ and $F(t)$ is an unknown distribution function. The function S is called survival function and is supposed to be differentiable. The *parameters of this model are S and β and the density of one observation is written as*

$$f(y_i|z_i; S, \beta) = R(\beta, z_i)\frac{dS}{dt}S(t)^{R(\beta, z_i)-1}. \tag{5.25}$$

It follows from (5.24) and (5.25) that the hazard function of y_i conditional on z_i, defined as the ratio of (5.25) and (5.24) equals $R(\beta, z_i)$ times the baseline hazard function (defined as $\frac{-dS/dt}{S(t)}$). We retain from the sample only the statistic

$$C(x_1, \ldots, x_n) = (r_i, z_i)_{i=1,\ldots,n}$$

where

$$r_i = \sum_{j=1}^{n} \mathbb{I}(y_j \leq y_i) \in \{1, \ldots, n\}.$$

In other words, we keep only the rank of the explained variable (that is its position in an increasing ordering) and the explanatory variables. To compute the distribution of C, we introduce a permutation σ of $\{1, \ldots, n\}$ and τ its inverse permutation. We have

$$\Pr(\sigma_1 = \tau_1, \ldots, \sigma_n = \tau_n|z) = \Pr(y_{\tau_1} < \cdots < y_{\tau_n}|z)$$

$$= \int_{u=-\infty}^{+\infty} du_1 \ldots \int_{u_{n-1}=u_{n-2}}^{\infty} \int_{u_n=u_{n-1}}^{\infty} \prod_{i=1}^{n} f(u_i|z_{\tau_i}, S, \beta)du_n$$

which becomes, after elementary manipulations,

$$\prod_{i=1}^{n} \frac{R(\beta, z_{\tau_i})}{\sum_{j \text{ such that } y_{\tau_j} \geq y_{\tau_i}} R(\beta, z_{\tau_j})} = \frac{\prod_{i=1}^{n} R(\beta, z_{\tau_i})}{\prod_{i=1}^{n}\sum_{j=1}^{n} R(\beta, z_{\tau_j})\,\mathbb{I}(y_{\tau_j} \geq y_{\tau_i})}.$$

This probability depends on β only and we estimate this parameter vector by maximizing the logarithm of this expression. This approach is called the Cox marginal likelihood method. It is developed and generalized in books on duration models. □

If the previous approach cannot be used because of the lack of a statistic $C(x)$ that satisfies the desired properties, one may use the second approach to be described now. Assume again that λ is a parameter vector and that g is a functional parameter. Moreover, we assume that if λ is known, we have a natural nonparametric estimator of g (denoted $\hat{g}_n(\lambda)$) and that if g is fixed, the distribution of x_i is defined by the density $f(x_i | \lambda, g)$. We proceed in the following manner:

- estimation of λ by $\hat{\lambda}_n$ by maximizing the likelihood function

$$\prod_{i=1}^{n} f(x_i | \lambda, \hat{g}_n(\lambda)),$$

- estimation of g by $\hat{g}_n(\hat{\lambda}_n)$.

The main difficulty with this approach is to analyze the asymptotic properties of this procedure and particularly to measure the impact on λ of the fact that g is unknown and needs to be estimated.

The last estimation problem we consider is that of a vector function $\lambda = \lambda(Q)$ of a distribution Q generating an i.i.d. sample $(x_i)_{i=1,\ldots,n}$. Of course, one must choose $\hat{Q}_n$ in the domain of λ. If for instance, $\lambda(Q)$ depends on the density of Q, we choose an estimator that admits a density (see section 5.2). Under usual regularity conditions, $\lambda(\hat{Q}_n)$ converges to $\lambda(Q)$ (this result follows from the continuity of λ assuming that $\hat{Q}_n$ converges to Q). At least two methods may be used to analyze the asymptotic normality of $\hat{\lambda}_n$ and its rate of convergence. One can go directly from the convergence properties of $\hat{Q}_n$ to those of $\hat{\lambda}_n$ using the Delta method analogous to that given in Chapter 3, but this type of proof relies on tools that are more sophisticated than those used in this text. One can also, on a case-by-case basis, do a direct proof using the Taylor approximation. Then, one gets expressions termed U statistics.

Notes

We refer the readers to books by Davidson (1994) and Serfling (1980) to complete our presentation of the properties of the empirical distribution as well as to the book by Bosq and Lecoutre (1992) that contains a rigorous presentation of various nonparametric methods, including in particular the density estimation. The book by Silverman (1986) is an excellent detailed presentation of Section 5.3.

The literature on semiparametric estimation has experienced an explosion in the last years but untill now was limited to articles, with the exception, in the econometrics literature, of the books by Stocker (1991) and by Pagan and Ullah (1999). Among the important articles, we cite Gallant and Nychka (1987).

We mentioned an example of proportional hazard model, for which a useful reference is Cox and Oakes (1984) for instance.

6.   Simulation Methods

6.1   Introduction

Simulation methods have in common the use of two random samples: the first is constituted of true observations of the studied phenomenon whereas the second is artificially generated by a computer. The distribution of the first sample is unknown and its size is determined by the available databases. The second sample obeys the will of the statistician, who chooses the generating process and its size depends on the available computing power and time.

There are many different reasons for using simulated data in statistical inference. We restrict our presentation to three uses of simulated data. The first one is motivated by numerical problems in an estimation procedure which we illustrate by providing a method for computing integrals. The other two methods pertain to the analysis of the small sample properties of estimators. On one hand, we may look for the small sample properties of an estimator or a test for a given value of the parameters. On the other hand, we can put forward another distribution of the estimators by the method called *bootstrap* which we will try to justify by various arguments. The three sections about the uses of simulations are preceded by a brief introduction to techniques for generating random scalars and vectors.

6.2   Random Number Generators

Consider a probability distribution on $\mathbb{R}^p$ characterized by its distribution function F. We propose to construct algorithms that allow us to generate sequences of independent vectors with distribution F. This general problem actually encompasses two questions of very different nature:

1.   How to generate sequences of numbers that are independent and uniformly distributed on the interval $[0, 1]$?
2.   How to transform these sequences into i.i.d. vectors with distribution F?

Here, we discuss only the second question and assume that the first problem has been solved. Anyone who has used a computer knows that all statistical softwares contain a command to generate numbers that follow a uniform distribution on [0, 1]. In fact, such sequences of numbers are only "pseudo-random" and not really random. Indeed, these sequences are reproducible (the programs permit the specification of a seed that is the starting value of identical sequences) and periodic. This periodicity is obviously in contradiction with the random and independent nature of the sequence. However, the algorithms used in practice generate sequences with extremely large periods which "look like" sequences of random numbers.

Hence, we assume that we dispose of independent and uniform *random numbers* $(u_1, u_2, \ldots)$. Various methods allow us to transform these numbers into realizations from a specific probability distribution. This question has given rise to important developments and we will only briefly touch on these methods. First, we present two general methods for generating scalars from a given distribution, inversion of the distribution function, and rejection. Next, we present a few results concerning the random vector generation, including a short introduction to the Gibbs sampling method.

6.2.1   Inversion of the Distribution Function

Suppose F is the distribution function of a scalar random variable defining a bijection between the support of the distribution (possibly $\mathbb{R}$ itself) and the interval [0, 1] (except in some cases for the extreme points). This bijection is necessarily strictly increasing. One can verify the following property: if u is generated according to a uniform distribution on [0, 1], then

$$x = F^{-1}(u)$$

is generated according to the distribution with distribution function F. Indeed,

$$\Pr(x \leq t) = \Pr(F^{-1}(u) \leq t) = \Pr(u \leq F(t)) = F(t). \tag{6.1}$$

Hence, if F^{-1} has an easy-to-handle expression, we obtain a tractable generating method.

Example 6.1   *Generation of the realizations of an exponential distribution. Suppose that x follows an exponential distribution with parameter λ. Its distribution function is*

$$F(t) = 1 - e^{-\lambda t} \quad (t \geq 0).$$

The preceding method implies that, if u is uniformly distributed, then

$$x = -\frac{\ln(1 - u)}{\lambda}$$

is exponentially distributed. This expression can be simplified by noting that if u is uniformly distributed, so is $1 - u$ and we can write

$$x = -\frac{\ln u}{\lambda}.$$

☐

This method is interesting only if F^{-1} is "simple." However, we know that in many cases, F does not have a simple analytical expression (for instance in the case of a normal distribution) and hence the inversion method of F is not tractable.

6.2.2 Rejection Method

Suppose F admits a density f, that there exists a probability distribution with density g such that

$$\exists c \geq 1 \quad \text{such that} \quad \forall y \in \mathbb{R} \quad cg(y) \geq f(y),$$

and that we know an algorithm that allows us to generate y with density g. The rejection method proceeds in the following manner:

1. We independently draw y with density g and u with the uniform distribution on $[0, 1]$.
2. If $u \leq \frac{f(y)}{cg(y)}$, we set $x = y$, otherwise we proceed to a new draw of y and u.

Then, x is distributed according to F. Indeed, we have

$$\Pr(x \leq t) = \Pr\left(y \leq t \,\middle|\, u \leq \frac{f(y)}{cg(y)}\right)$$

$$= \frac{\Pr\left[(y \leq t) \cap \left(u \leq \frac{f(y)}{cg(y)}\right)\right]}{\Pr\left(u \leq \frac{f(y)}{cg(y)}\right)}.$$

The denominator is equal to

$$\int \Pr\left(u \leq \frac{f(y)}{cg(y)}\,\middle|\, y\right) g(y)dy = \int \frac{f(y)}{cg(y)} g(y)dy = \frac{1}{c},$$

the numerator is given by

$$\int_{-\infty}^{t} \Pr\left(u \leq \frac{f(y)}{cg(y)}\,\middle|\, y\right) g(y)dy = \frac{1}{c}\int_{-\infty}^{t} f(y)dy = \frac{1}{c}F(t),$$

hence the result.

The rejection method is more efficient if the density g is such that c is close to 1. In general, g is defined piecewise, in order to realize a good approximation of f. This is the way realizations of normal random variables are generated.

6.2.3   Random Vector Generators

Generating random vectors poses specific problems only if the components of these vectors are dependent from each other. Several methods are possible.

In the first method, we generate a vector $y \in \mathbb{R}^p$ with independent components and we transform this vector into a vector x which has the desired distribution.

Example 6.2   *To generate a vector $x \in \mathbb{R}^p$ from a normal distribution with mean $\mu \in \mathbb{R}^p$ and variance Σ, we generate y of $\mathbb{R}^p$ whose components are drawn from independent standard normal distributions and we set*

$$x = Ay + \mu$$

where A is a $p \times p$ matrix satisfying $AA' = \Sigma$. The matrix A can be chosen to be lower triangular.   □

This method can be extended to the case where $y \in \mathbb{R}^q$ with $q > p$ as shown in the following example.

Example 6.3   *Let $y \in \mathbb{R}^q$ have independent components, exponentially distributed with parameter 1. Define*

$$x_j = \frac{y_j}{\sum_{i=1}^{q} y_i} \quad j = 1, \dots, q.$$

The vector x is a simplex vector of $\mathbb{R}^q$. Actually, it is a vector of $p = q - 1$ random elements, the last element x_q satisfying

$$x_q = 1 - \sum_{j=1}^{q-1} x_j.$$

We let the reader verify that x is uniformly distributed on the simplex of dimension $q - 1$ on $\mathbb{R}^q$. One can also obtain realizations of other distributions on the simplex by replacing the exponential distribution by other positive distributions (Gamma, Weibull ...)   □

In the second method, we decompose the distribution of x into the marginal distribution of x_1, the conditional distribution of x_2 given x_1, that of x_3 given x_1 and x_2 ... up to the distribution of x_p given $x_1, \dots, x_{p-1}$ and we use algorithms for one dimensional distribution in order to perform each of these generations. This method is particularly useful to simulate dynamic models.

In the third method, we describe the distribution of x by all its conditional distributions. Suppose to simplify that $p = 2$ and that we dispose of algorithms able to generate x_1 given x_2 and x_2 given x_1. The method known as Gibbs sampling is the following. Fix x_1 to an arbitrary value and draw x_2 given x_1. Then, generate x_1 given x_2, next x_2 given the new value of x_1 and iterate this procedure. After a certain number of draws, the pair (x_1, x_2) is generated by the desired distribution. This result is accepted without proof. The implementation of this method is difficult because it is not known how many iterations are needed to "forget" the arbitrary starting point and obtain the desired distribution. Moreover, if we continue the procedure, the successive pairs (x_1, x_2) are always generated by the desired distribution but they are not mutually independent.

6.3 Utilization in Calculation Procedures

This section contains two parts. First, we show how simulations can be used to calculate integrals, then we show how this method is useful in the estimation by the method of moments when the implementation of this method requires numerical integrations.

6.3.1 Monte Carlo Integration

Let φ be a mapping from $\mathbb{R}^p$ to $\mathbb{R}$ such that $I = \int \varphi(\xi) d\xi$ is finite. Note that the fact that the integral is on $\mathbb{R}^p$ is not restrictive because, if we wish to calculate

$$I = \int_A \psi(\xi) d\xi,$$

we set

$$I = \int \varphi(\xi) d\xi$$

with

$$\varphi(\xi) = I\!I(\xi \in A)\psi(\xi).$$

In the case where p equals 1, deterministic methods can be used to efficiently calculate I. One can, for instance, approach φ by trapezoids or use more efficient methods for approximation (the *gaussian quadrature* for example). These methods theoretically generalize to higher dimensions but become completely intractable as soon as p exceeds 3 or 4 because they require too many calculations. The function φ itself is often difficult to evaluate and the integral often depends on a parameter and needs to be computed many times.

Simulation methods provide an efficient alternative to deterministic methods as soon as the dimension of the integral is large. The idea of the *Monte Carlo integration* is the following.

Let $f(\xi)$ be a density on $\mathbb{R}^p$ satisfying

$$f(\xi) = 0 \Rightarrow \varphi(\xi) = 0.$$

Moreover, it is assumed that f can be simulated, that is, we dispose of an algorithm able to generate an i.i.d. sequence $\xi_1, \ldots \xi_N$ with density f. In this setting, f is called the *importance function*.

We rewrite I under the form

$$I = \int \frac{\varphi(\xi)}{f(\xi)} f(\xi) d\xi = E\left(\frac{\varphi}{f}\right), \tag{6.2}$$

where the expectation is taken with respect to the distribution with density f. Dividing by f does not pose a problem because f can be zero only if φ is zero, and we can restrict the integral to the domain where φ does not vanish. The fact that I is finite is equivalent to the existence of the expectation of φ/f.

Hence, we proceed to draw a i.i.d. sample $\xi_1, \ldots \xi_N$ of size N with density f, and we estimate I by $\hat{I}_N$ satisfying

$$\hat{I}_N = \frac{1}{N} \sum_{e=1}^{N} \frac{\varphi(\xi_e)}{f(\xi_e)}. \tag{6.3}$$

The justification of this estimator is based on the law of large numbers. Indeed, $\hat{I}_N$ converges to

$$E\left(\frac{\varphi}{f}\right) = I.$$

The central limit theorem provides a measure of the approximation.

Suppose that

$$E\left(\frac{\varphi^2}{f^2}\right) = \int \frac{\varphi^2(\xi)}{f(\xi)} d\xi \tag{6.4}$$

is finite and let

$$\sigma^2 = Var\left(\frac{\varphi}{f}\right) = E\left(\frac{\varphi^2}{f^2}\right) - I^2.$$

Then, we have

$$\sqrt{N}(\hat{I}_N - I) \rightarrow N(0, \sigma^2) \text{ in distribution} \tag{6.5}$$

and a 95% confidence interval of I takes the form

$$\hat{I}_N \pm 1,96 \frac{\sigma}{\sqrt{N}}.$$

The construction of this confidence interval requires the knowledge of σ^2 which is also evaluated by Monte Carlo, using the same generated ξ_e, through the formula

$$\hat{\sigma}_N^2 = \frac{1}{N} \sum_{e=1}^{N} \frac{\varphi^2(\xi_e)}{f^2(\xi_e)} - \hat{I}_N^2. \tag{6.6}$$

This analysis suggests that one should look for the function f which minimizes σ^2 in order to make the numerical result as precise as possible. In practice, this optimization of the generator f can be done within a given class whose elements are denoted f_α. The optimization of the generator within a given class often involves integrals that need to be calculated numerically, as shown in the following example.

Example 6.4 *We are looking for f in the class of normal distributions with fixed variance Σ. Thus, the problem is to find the vector α of expectations satisfying*

$$\min_{\alpha \in \mathbb{R}^p} \int \frac{\varphi^2(\xi)}{f(\xi)} d\xi.$$

Differentiating below the integral yields the first order condition

$$\int \frac{\varphi^2(\xi)}{f^2(\xi)} \frac{\partial f}{\partial \alpha}(\xi) d\xi = 0.$$

Using the properties of normal densities

$$\frac{\partial f}{\partial \alpha}(\xi) = \Sigma^{-1}(\xi - \alpha) f(\xi),$$

we obtain the system of equations

$$\int \frac{\xi \varphi^2(\xi)}{f(\xi)} d\xi = \alpha \int \frac{\varphi^2(\xi)}{f(\xi)} d\xi.$$

This suggests that we can first perform a quick evaluation by Monte Carlo of the left and right integrals of this expression using an arbitrary α, then deduce a new value for α, and proceed to a more precise evaluation. $\square$

6.3.2 Simulation-Based Method of Moments

We place ourselves into the framework of Section 3.3 and limit ourselves to an estimation problem using a simple system of moment equations. The sample

x_i $(i = 1, \ldots, n)$ is i.i.d. and each x_i is generated by Q^θ, $\theta \in \Theta$. We estimate a parameter λ by solving

$$\frac{1}{n} \sum_{i=1}^{n} \psi(x_i, \lambda) = 0. \tag{6.7}$$

The resulting estimator $\hat{\lambda}_n$ converges to the function $\lambda(\theta)$ of parameters and its distribution is given by Theorem 3.3 in Chapter 3.

We will show later (see Chapter 18 on unobservable variables) that relevant economic problems lead to examine this equation in the case where ψ satisfies

$$\psi(x_i, \lambda) = \int_{\mathbb{R}^p} \overline{\psi}(x_i, \xi, \lambda) d\xi. \tag{6.8}$$

We intend to estimate this integral by the Monte Carlo method. We will address two kinds of questions, the first concerning the implementation of this method and its numerical difficulties, and the second concerning the properties of the estimator obtained after approximating the integral. Various approaches are possible.

Approach 1. Choose a generator of the density f and generate a single sample $\xi_1, \ldots, \xi_N$. Then, $\psi(x_i, \lambda)$ is estimated by

$$\frac{1}{N} \sum_{e=1}^{N} \frac{\overline{\varphi}(x_i, \xi_e, \lambda)}{f(\xi_e)}.$$

This approach involve so-called *common random numbers*. Indeed, the same sequence ξ_e is used for all x_i and λ.

Approach 2. Choose a generator of the density $f_{x_i, \lambda}$, a function of x_i and λ, then generate a sequence of numbers with this generator. More concretely, the solution of (6.7) uses an algorithm which iterates between different values of λ to reach the solution. To go from the value λ_K to the value λ_{K+1}, one generates a sequence ξ_{ie}, where for each $i = 1, \ldots, n$, ξ_{ie} $(e = 1, \ldots, N)$ is drawn from the distribution with density f_{x_i, λ_K}, and the function

$$\frac{1}{n} \sum_{i=1}^{n} \psi(x_i, \lambda_K)$$

is estimated by

$$\frac{1}{nN} \sum_{i=1}^{n} \sum_{e=1}^{N} \frac{\overline{\psi}(x_i, \xi_{ie}, \lambda_K)}{f_{x_i, \lambda_K}(\xi_{ie})}.$$

Approach 3. The previous procedure does not contain common random numbers because the draws ξ_{ie} are different for each i. However, it is possible to introduce such common numbers in the following manner. Suppose drawing a number ξ_{ie} with density $f_{x_i, \lambda}$ can be performed by drawing a number ε_{ie} from the density f_0 independently of x_i and λ, and by transforming it using a function that depends on x_i and λ, denoted $r(x_i, \lambda, \varepsilon_{ie})$. This is possible if $f_{x_i, \lambda}$ is for example the normal density with mean $m(x_i, \lambda)$ and variance $\sigma^2(x_i, \lambda)$: ξ_{ie} is then equal to

$$\sigma(x_i, \lambda)\varepsilon_{ie} + m(x_i, \lambda)$$

where ε_{ie} is generated by a standard normal. We can use the same generated sequence of ε_e for all i and λ and estimate (6.7) by

$$\frac{1}{nN} \sum_{i=1}^{n} \sum_{e=1}^{N} \overline{\psi}(x_i, r(x_i, \lambda, \varepsilon_e), \lambda).$$

This leads us back to the procedure described in the first approach. The ε_e play the role of common random numbers.

Not using common random numbers preserves the independence (in the sense of simulations) between the estimates of $\psi(x_i, \lambda)$ for different values of x_i which may simplify the study of the properties of this procedure. However, the different estimates of $\psi(x_i, \lambda)$ may be less "regular" in λ and as a result, implementing the numerical solution of the moment equations may be more difficult, at least when N is not very large.

In contrast, using common random numbers has a smoothing effect and hence facilitates the search for a numerical solution of (6.7).

The general theorems concerning the asymptotic behavior of moment estimators apply to the analysis of the properties of the estimator which solves the problem with approximated moments. As usual, we denote by $\hat{\lambda}_n$ the solution of (6.7) and by λ_{nN}^* the solution of the approximated problem. Consider for instance the approach without common random numbers, then λ_{nN}^* is the solution of

$$\frac{1}{nN} \sum_{i=1}^{n} \sum_{e=1}^{N} \frac{\psi(x_i, \xi_{ie}, \lambda)}{f_{x_i, \lambda}(\xi_{ie})} = 0. \tag{6.9}$$

The asymptotic analysis of λ_{nN}^* can be conducted by keeping n fixed and letting N go to infinity, or on the contrary, by keeping N fixed and considering a sample size becoming infinitely large. The first approach is more natural because, in practice, the statistician does not choose n but controls N. Hence he can choose N in order to obtain the desired precision. Surprisingly, the econometrics literature has mainly focused on the second approach by analyzing the asymptotic properties of λ_{nN}^* with N fixed and $n \to \infty$.

Asymptotic analysis when the number of simulations goes to infinity. If $N \to \infty$ with fixed n, the convergence is analyzed with respect to the distribution used to generate the simulations conditional on $(x_i)_{i=1,\dots,n}$ and λ. Then, λ^*_{nN} converges to $\hat{\lambda}_n$ almost surely. Indeed, under the regularity conditions of Theorem 3.3 in Chapter 3, we have

$$\frac{1}{nN} \sum_{i=1}^{n} \sum_{e=1}^{N} \frac{\overline{\psi}(x_i, \xi_{ie}, \lambda)}{f_{x_i, \lambda}(\xi_{ie})}$$

$$\to \frac{1}{n} \sum_{i=1}^{n} \int \frac{\overline{\psi}(x_i, \xi_{ie}, \lambda)}{f_{x_i, \lambda}(\xi_{ie})} f_{x_i, \lambda}(\xi_{ie}) d\xi_{ie} = \frac{1}{n} \sum_i \psi(x_i, \lambda) \qquad (6.10)$$

which is equal to zero at $\hat{\lambda}_n$ by assumption. Moreover, it follows from the same theorem that

$$\sqrt{N}(\lambda^*_{nN} - \hat{\lambda}_n) \to N(0, V_{\hat{\lambda}_n}) \qquad (6.11)$$

with

$$V_{\hat{\lambda}_n} = \left[E^s \left(\frac{1}{n} \sum_i \frac{\partial}{\partial \lambda'} \left(\frac{\overline{\psi}(x_i, \xi_{ie}, \lambda)}{f_{x_i \lambda}(\xi_{ie})} \right) \Big|_{\lambda = \hat{\lambda}_n} \right) \right]^{-1} Var^s \left(\frac{1}{n} \sum_i \frac{\overline{\psi}(x_i, \xi_{ie}, \hat{\lambda}_n)}{f_{x_i \hat{\lambda}_n}(\xi_{ie})} \right)$$

$$\qquad (6.12)$$

$$\times \left[E^s \left(\frac{1}{n} \sum_i \frac{\partial}{\partial \lambda} \left(\frac{\overline{\psi}'(x_i, \xi_{ie}, \lambda)}{f_{x_i \lambda}(\xi_{ie})} \right) \Big|_{\lambda = \hat{\lambda}_n} \right) \right]^{-1}.$$

In this expression, E^s and Var^s are the expectation and variance with respect to the distribution of the simulated data.

Asymptotic analysis when the the sample size goes to infinity. Now consider the case where $n \to \infty$ with fixed N. If $\hat{\lambda}_n$ converges with respect to the sampling probability distribution to $\lambda(\theta)$, the solution of

$$E^\theta(\psi(x_i, \lambda)) = 0,$$

then, it is easy to show that λ^*_{nN} converges to the solution of

$$E^{\theta, s} \left(\frac{1}{N} \sum_{e=1}^{N} \frac{\overline{\psi}(x_i, \xi_{ie}, \lambda)}{f_{x_i, \lambda}(\xi_{ie})} \right) = 0$$

where $E^{\theta,s}$ denotes the expectation with respect to the joint distribution of the sample and the simulations. We have

$$E^{\theta,s}\left(\frac{1}{N}\sum_{e=1}^{N}\frac{\overline{\psi}(x_i,\xi_{ie},\lambda)}{f_{x_i,\lambda}(\xi_{i,e})}\right) = \frac{1}{N}\sum_{e=1}^{N}\int\left\{\int\frac{\overline{\psi}(x_i,\xi_{ie},\lambda)}{f_{x_i,\lambda}(\xi_{i,e})}f_{x_i,\lambda}(\xi_{ie})d\xi_{ie}\right\}P_n^{\theta}(dx_i)$$

$$= \frac{1}{N}\sum_{e=1}^{N}E^{\theta}(\psi(x_i,\lambda)) \qquad (6.13)$$

$$= E^{\theta}(\psi(x_i,\lambda))$$

$$= 0$$

which has the function $\lambda(\theta)$ as the unique solution by assumption. The sample, that is considered here, comprises $(x_i,\xi_{i1},\dots,\xi_{iN})_{i=1,\dots,n}$. Hence, it becomes clear that λ_{nN}^{*} and $\hat{\lambda}_n$ converge to $\lambda(\theta)$ even if N is fixed.

The asymptotic variance of λ_{nN}^{*} is larger than that of $\hat{\lambda}_n$, and the difference of variances depends on a term in $\frac{1}{N}$ which goes to 0 as N grows. Indeed, recall that Theorem 3.3 in Chapter 3 implies

$$\sqrt{n}(\hat{\lambda}_n - \lambda(\theta)) \to N(0, A^{-1}BA'^{-1}) \text{ in distribution} \qquad (6.14)$$

and

$$\sqrt{n}(\lambda_{nN}^{*} - \lambda(\theta)) \to N(0, A^{*-1}B^{*}A^{*'-1}) \text{ in distribution,} \qquad (6.15)$$

with

$$A = E^{\theta}\left(\frac{\partial}{\partial\lambda'}\psi(x_i,\lambda(\theta))\right), \qquad (6.16)$$

$$A^{*} = E^{\theta,s}\left(\frac{\partial}{\partial\lambda'}\frac{1}{N}\sum_{e=1}^{N}\frac{\overline{\psi}(x_i,\xi_{ie},\lambda(\theta))}{f_{x_i,\lambda}(\xi_{i,e})}\right), \qquad (6.17)$$

$$B = Var^{\theta}(\psi(x_i,\lambda(\theta))), \qquad (6.18)$$

$$B^{*} = V^{\theta,s}\left(\frac{1}{N}\sum_{e=1}^{N}\frac{\overline{\psi}(x_i,\xi_{ie},\lambda(\theta))}{f_{x_i,\lambda}(\xi_{ie})}\right). \qquad (6.19)$$

We immediately verify (see (6.11)) that $A = A^{*}$.

Moreover, we have

$$B^{*} = Var^{\theta}E^{s}\left(\frac{1}{N}\sum_{e=1}^{N}\frac{\overline{\psi}(x_i,\xi_{ie},\lambda(\theta))}{f_{x_i,\lambda}(\xi_{ie})}\right)$$

$$+ E^{\theta}Var^{s}\left(\frac{1}{N}\sum_{e=1}^{N}\frac{\overline{\psi}(x_i,\xi_{ie},\lambda(\theta))}{f_{x_i,\lambda}(\xi_{ie})}\right). \qquad (6.20)$$

The first term of this sum is equal to B. Using the independence of the simulations, the second term can be rewritten as

$$\frac{1}{N^2} \sum_{e=1}^{N} E^\theta \, Var^s \left(\frac{\bar{\psi}(x_i, \xi_{ie}, \lambda(\theta))}{f_{x_i, \lambda}(\xi_{ie})} \right) = \frac{1}{N} C \qquad (6.21)$$

where

$$C = E^\theta \, Var^s \left(\frac{\bar{\psi}(x_i, \xi_{ie}, \lambda(\theta))}{f_{x_i, \lambda}(\xi_{ie})} \right).$$

Finally, we have

$$A^{*-1} B^* A^{*'-1} = A^{-1} B A'^{-1} + \frac{1}{N} A^{-1} C A'^{-1}, \qquad (6.22)$$

which satisfies the claimed property. Replacing the exact moment condition (6.7) by an approximated condition (6.9) preserves the consistency of the estimator, even if the number of replications N is fixed. However, the variance of the estimator increases by a matrix multiplied by $\frac{1}{N}$, whose importance therefore decreases with the number of replications.

In the case of common random numbers, the properties of λ_{nN}^* are of course different, at least for fixed N. In the case where n is constant and $N \to \infty$, λ_{nN}^* converges to $\hat{\lambda}_n$ conditionally on the x_i and has an asymptotic normal distribution. In the case where N is fixed, λ_{nN}^* does not converge to $\lambda(\theta)$ any longer but to the solution of the problem

$$\frac{1}{N} \sum_{e=1}^{N} \frac{E^\theta(\psi(x_i, \xi_e, \lambda))}{f(\xi_e)} = 0. \qquad (6.23)$$

We leave to the reader the calculation of the asymptotic variance in this case.

To conclude this section, consider the following example of estimation by the method of moments.

Example 6.5   *Consider a sample x_i ($i = 1, \ldots, n$) such that*

$$x_i \sim f(x_i \,|\, \theta)$$

with $\theta \in \mathbb{R}^k$. Suppose also that

$$E(m(x_i) \,|\, \theta) = g(\theta)$$

where m is a known function. We wish to estimate θ.
If g were known, we could write for n sufficiently large

$$\frac{1}{n} \sum_{i=1}^{n} m(x_i) = g(\theta).$$

It would suffice to solve

$$\frac{1}{n} \sum_{i=1}^{n} \psi(x_i, \theta) = 0$$

with

$$\psi(x_i) = m(x_i) - g(\theta).$$

The resulting estimator $\widehat{\theta}_n$ would converge to θ and its distribution would be given by Theorem 3.3 in Chapter 3, that is

$$\sqrt{n}\left(\widehat{\theta}_n - \theta\right) \to N\left(0, E^\theta \left(\frac{\partial g}{\partial \theta'}\right)^{-1} V_\theta E^\theta \left(\frac{\partial g'}{\partial \theta}\right)^{-1}\right) \text{ in } P^\theta - \text{distribution}$$

with $V_\theta = Var^\theta(\psi)$.

Now, we study the case where g is unknown. We are going to estimate g by simulation. We have a generator H of the distribution characterized by the density f such that

$$x_i = H(\varepsilon_i, \theta)$$

where ε_i is generated from a known distribution h_0 which is independent of θ and can be simulated. The simulation method is the following. For each i, we solve

$$\frac{1}{n} \sum_{i=1}^{n} m(x_i) - \frac{1}{N} \sum_{i=1}^{n} \sum_{e=1}^{E} m(x_e) = \frac{1}{n} \sum_{i=1}^{n} \left(m(x_i) - \frac{1}{E} \sum_{e=1}^{E} m(x_e)\right) = 0$$

with $N = nE$, which is equivalent to solving

$$\frac{1}{n} \sum_{i=1}^{n} \bar{\psi}\left(x_i, \varepsilon_e^i, \theta\right) = 0$$

where

$$\bar{\psi}\left(x_i, \varepsilon_e^i, \theta\right) = m(x_i) - \frac{1}{E} \sum_{e=1}^{E} m\left(H\left(\varepsilon_e^i, \theta\right)\right).$$

Using Theorem 3.3 in Chapter 3, it can be established that the resulting estimator $\widehat{\widehat{\theta}}$ has the following properties:

$$\widehat{\widehat{\theta}} \to \theta \; P^\theta - a.s$$

and

$$\sqrt{n}\left(\widehat{\widehat{\theta}} - \theta\right) \to N(0, \Sigma_\theta) \text{ in } P^\theta - \text{distribution}$$

with

$$\Sigma_\theta = E^\theta \left(\frac{\partial \bar{\bar{\psi}}}{\partial \theta'} \right)^{-1} V(\bar{\bar{\psi}}) E^\theta \left(\frac{\partial \bar{\bar{\psi}}'}{\partial \theta} \right)^{-1}.$$

It is easy to show that

$$V(\bar{\bar{\psi}}) = (1 + v) \, Var(m)$$

with $v = 1/E$. *In addition,*

$$E^\theta \left(\frac{\partial \bar{\bar{\psi}}}{\partial \theta'} \right) = -E^\theta \left(\frac{1}{E} \sum_{e=1}^{E} \frac{\partial m \left(H \left(\varepsilon_e^i, \theta \right) \right)}{\partial \theta'} \right)$$

$$= - \int \frac{1}{E} \sum_{e=1}^{E} \frac{\partial m \left(H \left(\varepsilon_e^i, \theta \right) \right)}{\partial \theta'} d\varepsilon_e^i$$

$$= - \frac{\partial}{\partial \theta'} \int \frac{1}{E} \sum_{e=1}^{E} m \left(H \left(\varepsilon_e^i, \theta \right) \right) h_0 \left(\varepsilon_e^i \right) d\varepsilon_e^i$$

$$= - \frac{\partial}{\partial \theta'} \int g(\theta) h_0 \left(\varepsilon_e^i \right) d\varepsilon_e^i$$

$$= - \frac{\partial g(\theta)}{\partial \theta'}.$$

Hence, we conclude

$$\Sigma_\theta = (1 + v) \left(\frac{\partial g(\theta)}{\partial \theta'} \right)^{-1} Var(m) \left(\frac{\partial g(\theta)'}{\partial \theta} \right)^{-1}. \qquad \square$$

6.4   Simulations and Small Sample Properties of Estimators and Tests

Consider a statistical model with sample $x = (x_1, \dots, x_n)$ and sampling probability distribution $P_n^\theta, \theta \in \Theta$. We have a function $\lambda(\theta)$ of P_n^θ and an estimator $\hat{\lambda}_n$ of $\lambda(\theta)$. The asymptotic theory provides approximations of the distribution of $\hat{\lambda}_n$ when n goes to infinity, but the sampling distribution of $\hat{\lambda}_n$ may be very different from its limiting distribution for a given sample size. In a small number of simple cases (essentially normal linear models), the distribution of $\hat{\lambda}_n$ can be described analytically. However, this is in general not possible for more complex models, and simulation methods can replace analytical methods in the study of the distribution of the estimator.

The principle is simple and is based on the assumption that for any value θ, the distribution P_n^θ can be simulated. Then, we construct an i.i.d. sample $x^e = (x_1^e, \dots, x_n^e)$, for $e = 1, \dots, N$, with distribution P_n^θ from which we obtain N draws of the estimator $\hat{\lambda}_n^e = \hat{\lambda}_n(x^e)$. These N draws constitute an i.i.d simulated sample of size N from the sampling distribution of $\hat{\lambda}_n$. This simulated sample is used to determine the characteristics of this distribution. For example, assuming N large,

$$\frac{1}{N} \sum_{e=1}^{N} \hat{\lambda}_n^e$$

is a very good estimator (in the sense of the simulations) of $E^\theta(\hat{\lambda}_n)$ and consequently, we estimate the bias in θ of $\hat{\lambda}_n$ by the difference

$$\frac{1}{N} \sum_{e=1}^{N} \hat{\lambda}_n^e - \lambda(\theta).$$

If we have two estimators available, we can therefore compare their bias for a given value of θ.

A simulation study is also useful for hypothesis testing.

As presented in Chapter 4, testing a hypothesis defined by a subset Θ_0 of Θ is equivalent to determining a critical region W_n in the sample space. This critical region usually results from an asymptotic analysis: the maximum over all $\theta \in \Theta_0$ of the probabilities of W_n with respect to the asymptotic distribution of the test statistic is equal to the given size of the test. But is it still true if the sample size n is finite? To answer this question, we generate a simulated sample for different values of θ in Θ_0, and if the dimension N is large, the proportion of simulated observations belonging to W_n estimates the finite sample probability of the critical region. Then, we can compare the asymptotic size of the test with its real size in a finite sample. If we generate simulations for values of θ that do not belong to Θ_0, then the evaluation of the probability of W_n by simulation provides an estimate of the power of the test for these values of the parameters.

The implementation of a simulation study of the distribution of an estimator or of the power of a test for a finite sample size poses various questions. According to which distribution should we simulate? Which simulation size should we use? How do we treat the simulation results? And how do we summarize results from many simulations?

The first question concerns the definition of the reference distribution from which the simulations are drawn. Note, that even if we wish to analyze the properties of $\hat{\lambda}_n$ as an estimator of $\lambda(\theta)$, it is in principle necessary to completely fix θ in order to determine P_n^θ and hence to simulate the data. This poses a delicate problem, especially when θ belongs to a "large" space, for example in a nonparametric model. Hence, if the x_i are i.i.d. with distribution Q, the simulation requires that we choose this probability even if we are only interested in the sample mean. In such a case, it is very difficult to study the sensitivity to the choice of Q. In such a nonparametric context, the bootstrap method, that we will present in Section 6.5, is an interesting alternative to the present approach.

In the parametric context, it may be worth choosing the statistic, whose distribution needs to be simulated, so that it does not depend on some of the parameters. In that case, the results obtained for a point of the parameter space are actually valid for a subset.

Example 6.6   *Suppose that the $x_i \in \mathbb{R}$ are i.i.d. and generated by a Student t-distribution of parameters μ, σ^2, and v (i.e., $\frac{x_i - \mu}{\sigma}$ follows the usual Student t-distribution with v degrees of freedom). To analyze the distribution of*

$$\bar{x} = \frac{1}{n} \sum_{i=1}^{n} x_i,$$

by simulation, we need to fix μ, σ^2, and v. In constrast, the statistic $\frac{\bar{x}}{\hat{\sigma}}$ with

$$\hat{\sigma}^2 = \frac{1}{n-1} \sum_{i=1}^{n} (x_i - \bar{x})^2$$

has a distribution that is independent of σ^2. □

The most common approach, called *parametric bootstrap*, consists in esti-mating θ by an estimator $\hat{\theta}_n$, and then simulating data from the distribution $P_n^{\hat{\theta}_n}$. We can make this distribution less dependent on the initial estimate by restarting the procedure with values of θ in the neighborhood of $\hat{\theta}_n$.

An econometric model is often conditional and specifies only the distribution, denoted $P_n^{\theta, z}$ in Chapter 1, of $y_1, \ldots, y_n$ conditional on θ and $z_1, \ldots, z_n$. By nature, this model does not explain the distribution of the z_i and those are fixed in the simulations. By generating data from $P_n^{\theta, z}$, we obtain information on the small sample properties of the estimator $\hat{\lambda}_n$ conditional on fixed z_i and the chosen value of the parameters. Which value should we select for the z_i? Without doubt, they should be the observed values if the model is used to analyze actual data. Otherwise, we choose exogenous values that look like those that might be observed in reality and we try to cover all the possible configurations regarding these exogenous variables. The small sample properties of $\hat{\lambda}_n$ may be extremely sensitive to the value of θ and those of the z_i.

Another approach consists in examining the joint sampling distribution of $\hat{\lambda}_n$, that is, the joint distribution of the y_i and the z_i. If the econometric model includes only a conditional distribution, we expand this model by add-ing a marginal distribution (possibly dependent on extra parameters, in which case, we enlarge θ). We generate a sequence of simulated data $(z_1^e, y_1^e, \ldots, z_n^e, y_n^e)_{e=1,\ldots,N}$ with different values of z_i^e for each iteration. Therefore, the dis-tribution of the estimator does not depend any more on a specific value of z_i but on the distribution of these variables.

Second, an important econometric literature emerged in the 1970s and 1980s that proposed various schemes intended to increase the efficiency of simulations in order to reduce their dimensions. Various methods such as control variables and antithetic variables were proposed. This research was motivated by the limited computer power and the desire to construct simulation schemes that could be run within an acceptable time and for a reasonable cost. The amazing development of computing power reduces the interest in these methods and in many cases, a brute force simulation can be performed within a very short time.

Third, the usual statistical tools can obviously be applied to simulated data. It is even a privileged application because the i.i.d. property of the data and the sample size are controlled by the experimenter. Moreover, as the number of replications is large, the nonparametric analysis of the simulated sample is fully justified and these methods find here particularly important applications.

Suppose for example that we wish to calculate the bias of an estimator $\hat{\lambda}_n$ of the function $\lambda(\theta)$. We simulate a sequence $x^e = (x_1^e, \dots, x_n^e), e = 1, \dots, N$, of i.i.d. samples with distribution P_n^θ and calculate the sequence $\hat{\lambda}_n^e$ of estimators. The bias in θ is equal to

$$b_n(\theta) = E^\theta(\hat{\lambda}_n) - \lambda(\theta)$$

and is estimated by

$$\hat{b}_N = \frac{1}{N} \sum_{e=1}^{N} \hat{\lambda}_n^e - \lambda(\theta).$$

By the law of large numbers applied to the simulated data, $\hat{b}_N \to b_n(\theta)$ a.s. when $N \to \infty$. Note that this consistency result assumes the integrability of $\hat{\lambda}_n^e$ which is not always satisfied. Assuming the existence of the second moment, we have moreover

$$\sqrt{N}(\hat{b}_N - b_n(\theta)) \to N\left(0, Var^\theta(\hat{\lambda}_n)\right) \text{ in distribution.}$$

In this expression, the variance of $\hat{\lambda}_n$ is taken with respect to the distribution P_n^θ, according to which the data were generated. This variance is itself unknown and is estimated by the empirical variance of $\hat{\lambda}_n^e$,

$$\widehat{Var}^\theta\left(\hat{\lambda}_n\right) = \frac{1}{N} \sum_{e=1}^{N} \left(\hat{\lambda}_n^e - \left(\frac{1}{N} \sum_{e=1}^{N} \hat{\lambda}_n^e\right)\right)^2.$$

Then, a simple calculation provides the precision of the bias estimation as a function of the number of iterations.

To determine the sampling distribution of $\hat{\lambda}_n$ given the value θ of the parameters by simulation, we estimate for example the distribution function of $\hat{\lambda}_n$. In the scalar case,

$$\frac{1}{N} \sum_{e=1}^{N} I(\hat{\lambda}_n^e \leq t)$$

is a consistent estimator of the distribution function and Theorem 5.2 in Chapter 5 enables us to derive its asymptotic distribution. The quantiles of this distribution are estimated with a precision that can be easily calculated by applying the asymptotic theorems presented in Chapters 2 and 5.

The density of the sampling distribution of $\hat{\lambda}_n$ can be estimated by smoothing using a kernel estimator

$$\frac{1}{N h_N^k} \sum_{e=1}^N K\left(\frac{t - \hat{\lambda}_n^e}{h_N}\right),$$

whose properties have been presented in Section 5.3.

Fourth, the point we are addressing now concerns the treatment of simulation results as a function of θ (and possibly explanatory variables). Consider the following simple case. To measure the bias of an estimator $\hat{\lambda}_n$ of $\lambda(\theta)$, we draw a set of simulations for different values of θ and different sample sizes n. The bias is an unknown exact function of θ and of n, of which we observe realizations $\hat{b}_N$, which have expectation (in the sense of simulations) $b_n(\theta)$. Hence, this is a usual regression problem such as those presented in the second part of this book. We can use nonparametric techniques to estimate $b_n(\theta)$, and we refer the reader to Chapter 10 where this point will be studied. The use of regression methods to condense simulation results is known in econometrics under the name of *response surface*.

Fifth, one of the recent applications of the simulation methods concerns the *Indirect Inference* methods which essentially consists in correcting the properties of an estimator. Let us consider the following example.

Example 6.7   *Let $\hat{\theta}_n$ be a consistent but biased estimator of θ and let $b_n(\theta)$ be its bias function. Thanks to simulations, $b_n(\theta)$ is approximated by $\hat{b}_{nN}(\theta)$ and hence we can correct $\hat{\theta}_n$ by transforming it into $\hat{\theta}_n - \hat{b}_{nN}(\theta)$. Intuitively, this new estimator should be better in terms of bias. We refer to econometric literature for the study of its properties.*   □

The indirect inference is a method that is more general than this example, and here again we refer the reader to the Notes at the end of the chapter.

6.5   Bootstrap and Distribution of the Moment Estimators and of the Density

The *bootstrap* has become one of the most often used simulation techniques in statistics and its name evokes the absurd idea of "pulling oneself's up by one's own bootstraps." For this method, different interpretations have been proposed and relevant properties have been proven.

We do not review all the aspects of this method but present its use for the method of moments and for the nonparametric estimation that we have previously explained. First, we present the *bootstrap distribution* of an estimator, next we present a justification of this distribution.

First, consider an i.i.d. model with sampling distribution P_n^θ and a function $\lambda(\theta) \in \mathbb{R}^k$ defined by the condition $E^\theta(\psi(x_i, \lambda)) = 0$ (see Section 3.3). In the GMM framework, $\hat{\lambda}_n$ denotes as usual the solution to the problem

$$\min_\lambda \left(\sum_{i=1}^n \psi(x_i, \lambda) \right)' H_n \left(\sum_{i=1}^n \psi(x_i, \lambda) \right).$$

We saw in Chapter 3 that $\hat{\lambda}_n$ can be considered a function of the empirical distribution

$$\hat{Q}_n = \frac{1}{n} \sum_{i=1}^n \delta_{x_i}.$$

Indeed,

$$\frac{1}{n} \sum_{i=1}^n \psi(x_i, \lambda) = \int \psi \, d\hat{Q}_n,$$

and hence, $\hat{\lambda}_n$ is the solution to the minimization of

$$\left(\int \psi \, d\hat{Q}_n \right)' H_n \left(\int \psi \, d\hat{Q}_n \right).$$

In the simple method of moments, $\hat{\lambda}_n$ is the solution to the equation

$$\int \psi \, d\hat{Q}_n = 0$$

and in the maximization method, $\hat{\lambda}_n$ is the argument of the maximization of $\int \varphi \, d\hat{Q}_n$ (see formula (3.11)). Hence, in all cases, we can write

$$\hat{\lambda}_n = L(\hat{Q}_n) \tag{6.24}$$

where L is a mapping that associates a vector of $\mathbb{R}^k$ with the distribution $\hat{Q}_n$.

The intuitive idea of bootstrap is to replace $\hat{Q}_n$ by a random probability distribution Q^b and to consider the random vector $\lambda^b = L(Q^b)$. Hence, this vector has a distribution linked to the choice of Q^b and L and, provided that the distribution of Q^b has been suitably chosen, the distribution of λ^b can be considered as the distribution of $\hat{\lambda}_n$, in a sense that we will make precise.

How should we transform $\widehat{Q}_n$ to a random probability distribution? The natural idea is to define Q^b by

$$Q^b = \sum_{i=1}^{n} w_i \delta_{x_i} \tag{6.25}$$

or alternatively

$$Q^b(S) = \sum_{i/x_i \in S} w_i, \quad S \subset \mathbb{R}^n.$$

Hence, Q^b is a weighted sum of Dirac measures at x_i with weights w_i. We see that, if $w_i = \frac{1}{n}$, then we obtain $\widehat{Q}_n$. However, we are going to consider random weights w_i distributed independently of the x_i. For Q^b to be a probability distribution, the w_i must be positive and sum up to 1. Hence, the vector w is a random vector on the simplex with dimension $n - 1$ in $\mathbb{R}^n$. In an i.i.d. sample, the order of the observations does not matter and we wish to maintain this property by considering only distributions of w that do not change when the indices of the observations are permuted. Such distributions are called *exchangeable*. This property implies in particular that the expectation of w_i does not depend on i and is hence equal to $\frac{1}{n}$.

Thus, we have

$$E^b(Q^b) = \widehat{Q}_n. \tag{6.26}$$

The notation E^b recalls that the expectation is taken with respect to the distribution of Q^b for fixed $x_1, \ldots, x_n$.

Let us provide two important examples of distributional choices for the weights $w_1, \ldots, w_n$.

Example 6.8 *Multinomial bootstrap: we make n draws with replacement in the index set $\{1, \ldots, n\}$ where each index has the same probability $\frac{1}{n}$. Then, w_i is set equal to the number of times the index i is drawn divided by n. Hence, the product nw_i is multinomial with parameters n and $(\frac{1}{n}, \ldots, \frac{1}{n})$.* □

Example 6.9 *Bayesian bootstrap: the vector $(w_1, \ldots, w_n)$ is uniformly distributed on the simplex $\{u \in \mathbb{R}^n : u_i \geq 0, \Sigma u_i = 1\}$. The components $(w_1, \ldots, w_{n-1})$ have a density equal to 1 on the simplex and*

$$w_n = 1 - \sum_{i \neq n} w_i.$$

We noticed in Section 6.2 that this property is equivalent to defining

$$w_i = \frac{\gamma_i}{\sum_{j=1}^{n} \gamma_j}$$

where the γ_i are i.i.d. exponentially distributed with parameter 1. Of course, we can generalize this example by considering arbitrary positive i.i.d. random variables γ_i and by setting

$$w_i = \gamma_i / \sum_{j=1}^{n} \gamma_j.$$

□

Example 6.10   *Let us compute the bootstrap distribution of the sample mean. The moment equation is $\lambda = E^\theta(x_i)$ and the estimator satisfies*

$$\hat{\lambda}_n = \frac{1}{n}\sum_{i=1}^{n} x_i = \int u\, d\hat{Q}_n.$$

Replacing $\hat{Q}_n$ by Q^b yields

$$\lambda^b = \sum_{i=1}^{n} w_i x_i.$$

Given the sample $(x_i, \ldots x_n)$, λ^b is random as a transformation of the w_i. We verify that

$$E^b(\lambda^b) = \sum_{i=1}^{n} E^b(w_i)x_i = \hat{\lambda}_n.$$

Obtaining an analytical expression of the density of λ^b is difficult but estimating it through simulation is simple. We draw $(w_{el})_{e=1,\ldots,N}$ from the chosen distribution (multinomial, uniform, and so on) and obtain the realizations $(\lambda_e^b)_{e=1,\ldots,N}$ of λ^b. We can then graph the histogram of λ_e^b or its density by kernel smoothing as shown in the previous chapter. In this example, x_i can be replaced by any function of the sample.

□

Example 6.11   *Consider the parameters of the linear regression. If $x_i = (y_i, z_i) \in \mathbb{R}^{1+k}$, then the vector $\beta \in \mathbb{R}^k$ satisfies*

$$\beta = E^\theta(z_i z_i')^{-1} E^\theta(z_i y_i)$$

and hence

$$\hat{\beta}_n = \left(\sum_{i=1}^{n} z_i z_i'\right)^{-1} \sum_{i=1}^{n} z_i y_i.$$

Replacing the empirical distribution $\widehat{Q}_n$ of x_i by Q^b yields

$$\beta^b = \left(\sum_{i=1}^{n} w_i z_i z_i'\right)^{-1} \sum_{i=1}^{n} w_i z_i y_i$$

and here again, conditionally on the sample $(x_1, \ldots, x_n)$, β^b *has a distribution induced by that of the vector of the w_i. This transformation is not linear and we can not conclude for instance that*

$$E^b(\beta^b) = \hat{\beta}_n.$$

We analyze the distribution of β^b using simulation by drawing the w_i according to the chosen scheme and thus constructing simulated β^b whose moments or density can be obtained using the usual statistical techniques. Note that in our presentation, the bootstrap is executed on the joint distribution of z_i and y_i and not on the residuals. □

Example 6.12   *To analyze the bootstrap distribution of the GMM estimator, we proceed in the following manner. $\hat{Q}_n$ is replaced by*

$$Q^b = \sum_{i=1}^{n} w_i \delta_{x_i}$$

and we proceed by simulation. For $e = 1, \ldots, N$, we draw a vector of weights $w_1^e, \ldots, w_n^e$ and solve

$$\lambda_{ne}^b = \arg\min \left(\sum_{i=1}^{n} w_i^e \psi(x_i, \lambda) \right)' H_n \left(\sum_{i=1}^{n} w_i^e \psi(x_i, \lambda) \right).$$

The resulting $\left(\lambda_{ne}^b \right)_{e=1,\ldots,N}$ provide a sample of size N from the bootstrap distribution of $\hat{\lambda}_n$. □

The bootstrap extends naturally to nonparametric estimation as illustrated in the following example.

Example 6.13   *Let x_i be i.i.d. with density f and consider the kernel estimator of f at the value t,*

$$\hat{f}_n(t) = \frac{1}{n h_n^m} \sum_{i=1}^{n} K \left(\frac{t - x_i}{h_n} \right) = \int \frac{1}{h_n} K \left(\frac{t - u}{h_n} \right) \hat{Q}_n(du).$$

Replacing $\hat{Q}_n$ by Q^b yields the expression

$$f^b(t) = \frac{1}{h_n^m} \sum_{i=1}^{n} w_i K \left(\frac{t - x_i}{h_n} \right)$$

whose distribution conditional on the x_i can be easily simulated.

We verify by linearity that

$$E^b(f^b(t)) = \hat{f}_n(t).$$

This presentation obviously generalizes to a vector $t_1, \ldots, t_p$ in place of t and to the joint distribution of $(f^b(t_1), \ldots, f^b(t_p))$. □

Second, the justifications of the interest in the bootstrap distribution of a parameter λ are relatively complex and require statistical tools that go beyond the scope of this book. We briefly mention only one to conclude this section.

The justification of this distribution relies on the Bayesian statistical analysis. Recall that in a Bayesian model, the sampling probability distribution P_n^θ is complemented by a *prior distribution* on θ and the inference focuses on calculating the *posterior distribution* of θ. In the case where θ is finite dimensional, the prior probability distribution is in general defined by its density $m(\theta)$ and the sampling distribution by the likelihood function $l(x|\theta)$.

Bayes's theorem allows us to calculate the posterior density of θ which is just the conditional density of θ given x,

$$m(\theta|x) = \frac{m(\theta)l(x|\theta)}{\int m(\theta)l(x|\theta)d\theta}. \tag{6.27}$$

The prior density satisfies $\int m(\theta)d\theta = 1$ but it is possible in some cases to select a *noninformative* prior distribution that does not satisfy this condition. If we are interested in a function $\lambda(\theta)$, then we derive from the posterior distribution of θ the posterior distribution of $\lambda(\theta)$.

This approach applies to a nonparametric i.i.d. model. If the x_i are i.i.d. with distribution Q, we can introduce a prior distribution on Q and calculate the posterior distribution of Q. The complexity of this model stems from the fact that we need to consider (prior and posterior) distributions on the family of distributions Q of $\mathbb{R}^m$. However, we can verify that if no prior information is available, the posterior distribution of Q can be simply described: we obtain draws of Q given the sample by generating the distributions $\sum_{i=1}^n w_i \delta_{x_i}$ where $(w_1, \ldots, w_n)$ is uniform on the simplex. Hence, we see that the Bayesian bootstrap entails drawing random distributions from the posterior distribution. If, moreover, λ is a function of Q, then the previously described draws λ^b become draws from the posterior distribution of λ. Therefore, the Bayesian bootstrap is exactly equivalent to the analysis of the posterior distribution of λ derived from a nonparametric model without prior information.

Notes

The problems posed by the generation of nonuniform random variables is the subject of the extremely complete book by Devroye (1985) which is also an outstanding source of information about the principal probability distributions.

Bayesian econometric papers often provide a good presentation of the Monte Carlo integration method. Let us cite the pioneer articles by Kloek and van Dijk (1978), completed by those of Geweke (1988a, 1988b, and 1989) for instance. We can also refer to the book by Bauwens, Lubrano, and Richard (1999). The analysis of simulation-based method of moments has been presented by McFadden (1989), Pakes and Pollard (1989), and Duffie and Singleton (1993). We can refer to Gouriéroux and Monfort (1996b) for the treatment of simulated maximum likelihood and Richard (1996), Richard and Zhang (1996 and 2000), and Danielson and Richard (1993) for the asymptotic analysis and the problems of common random numbers.

The simulation study of the small sample properties of estimators and tests is extremely common but, to our knowledge, has not generated systematically exposed theories, except for the work by Hendry (1984), by Davidson and McKinnon (1999a, 1999b, 2002a and 2002b), and by Gouriéroux and Monfort (1996b). For indirect inference, see Gouriéroux, Monfort, and Renault (1993). For the method of simulated moments and indirect inference, read also Carrasco and Florens (2002) and Gallant and Tauchen (2003).

Bootstrap methods have fueled many articles. A rigorous exposition of their properties can be found in Hall (1992) and in Barbe and Bertail (1994), among others. The Bayesian interpretation of bootstrap is for instance detailed in Florens and Rolin (1996).

Part II

Regression Models

7.   Conditional Expectation

7.1 Introduction

The concept of conditional expectation is fundamental in econometrics because regression models are statistical models of conditional expectation. We consider here conditional expectation with respect to a random vector, but it would be possible to define it more generally with respect to a σ-algebra.

We place ourselves in the Hilbert space L^2 of square integrable variables relative to a reference probability distribution: if z is a real random variable belonging to this space, then $E(z^2) < \infty$. Recall that L^2 is a normed vector space on $\mathbb{R}$ with the norm defined by $\|z\| = [E(z^2)]^{1/2}$. If z_1 and z_2 are two elements of this space, then we can write their inner product as $E(z_1 z_2)$; these variables are said to be orthogonal in the sense of L^2 if $E(z_1 z_2) = 0$. Moreover, we say that a sequence z_n in this space converges to a random variable z if $\|z_n - z\| \to 0$ when $n \to +\infty$. This notion of orthogonality and of mean square convergence (we also say "in the sense of L^2" or "in quadratic norm") will allow us in the following to use the notions of orthogonal projection and best approximations in terms of least squares.

The usual demand on rigorousness requires to distinguish carefully between equality of random variables and almost sure equality. Here, we will not make this distinction, the mathematical readers can naturally add the necessary $P^\theta - a.s.$

In the second section we define the concept of conditional expectation and enumerate its principal properties, especially as it concerns the notion of best approximation in the sense of the L^2-norm. In the third and last section, we address linear conditional expectation from which linear regression is derived.

7.2 Conditional Expectation

In Part I of the book, we introduced the sample $(x_1, \ldots, x_n)$ generated according to a sequence of sampling probabilities P_n^θ. This space plays the role of the reference probability space, and we consider random variables defined on this space. These variables can possibly be components x_i of the sequence of observations or subvectors of x_i. The reference Hilbert space is that of random variables that depend on the sample and are square integrable with respect to P_∞^θ. Being rigorous, this space depends on θ.

Definition 7.1 *Let $\tilde{y}$ be a random variable in L^2 and $\tilde{z}$ a random vector of $\mathbb{R}^q$ whose components belong to L^2. The conditional expectation of $\tilde{y}$ given $\tilde{z}$, denoted by $E^\theta(\tilde{y}|\tilde{z})$, is defined by*

$$E^\theta(\tilde{y}|\tilde{z}) = g(\tilde{z}),$$

where g is a real function on $\mathbb{R}^q$ satisfying $g(\tilde{z}) \in L^2$, such that, for all functions ψ on $\mathbb{R}^q$, satisfying $\psi(\tilde{z}) \in L^2$, we have

$$E^\theta \left[(\tilde{y} - g(\tilde{z})) \psi(\tilde{z}) \right] = 0. \tag{7.1}$$

■

Sometimes the more rigorous notation $E^\theta(\tilde{y}|\tilde{z} = \zeta) = g(\zeta)$ can be found, which we will not use in order to simplify the writing. We systematically abuse notation by using the same symbol for both the random variables and their values (realizations).

The function $g(\tilde{z})$ always exists and is unique.

We can write the conditional expectation using the density function

$$f(\tilde{x}|\theta) = f(\tilde{y}, \tilde{z}|\theta) = f_{marg}(\tilde{z}|\theta) f_{cond}(\tilde{y}|\tilde{z}, \theta) \tag{7.2}$$

where f is the density of $\tilde{x} = (\tilde{y}, \tilde{z})$, f_{marg} is the marginal density of $\tilde{z}$ and f_{cond} is the density $\tilde{y}$ conditional on $\tilde{z}$. The conditional expectation $E^\theta(\tilde{y}|\tilde{z})$ can then be expressed in the following form

$$E^\theta(\tilde{y}|\tilde{z}) = \int \tilde{y} \frac{f(\tilde{y}, \tilde{z}|\theta)}{f_{marg}(\tilde{z}|\theta)} d\tilde{y} = \int \tilde{y} f_{cond}(\tilde{y}|\tilde{z}, \theta) d\tilde{y}.$$

We can easily regain expression (7.1)

$$E^\theta(\tilde{y}\psi(\tilde{z})) = \int \tilde{y}\psi(\tilde{z}) f(\tilde{y}, \tilde{z}|\theta) d\tilde{y} d\tilde{z}$$

$$= \int \left[\int \tilde{y} \frac{f(\tilde{y}, \tilde{z}|\theta)}{f_m(\tilde{z}|\theta)} d\tilde{y} \right] \psi(\tilde{z}) f_{marg}(\tilde{z}|\theta) d\tilde{z}$$

$$= \int E^\theta(\tilde{y}|\tilde{z}) \psi(\tilde{z}) f_{marg}(\tilde{z}|\theta) d\tilde{z}$$

$$= E^\theta \left(E^\theta(\tilde{y}|\tilde{z}) \psi(\tilde{z}) \right).$$

More generally, for all functions $h(\tilde{y})$ in L^2, we have

$$E^\theta(h(\tilde{y})|\tilde{z}) = \int h(\tilde{y}) f_{cond}(\tilde{y}|\tilde{z}) d\tilde{y}. \tag{7.3}$$

We will later see that

$$E^\theta(h(\tilde{y})|\tilde{z}) = E^\theta(h(\tilde{y})) \tag{7.4}$$

when $\tilde{y}$ and $\tilde{z}$ are independent.

We list now some properties of the conditional expectation and generalize them to a vector $\tilde{y}$ in $\mathbb{R}^p$. Beforehand, let us denote the conditional expectation of a vector $\tilde{y}$ given $\tilde{z}$ by the vector of dimension p defined by

$$E^\theta(\tilde{y}|\tilde{z}) = \begin{pmatrix} E^\theta(\tilde{y}_1|\tilde{z}) \\ \vdots \\ E^\theta(\tilde{y}_p|\tilde{z}) \end{pmatrix}.$$

For all random vectors $\tilde{y}$, $\tilde{y}^{(1)}$, $\tilde{y}^{(2)}$ in $\mathbb{R}^p$, and for all random vectors $\tilde{z}$, $\tilde{z}^{(1)}$, $\tilde{z}^{(2)}$ in $\mathbb{R}^q$, we can list, without proof, the following properties.

The following result follows directly from the definition:

$$E^\theta\left(E^\theta(\tilde{y}|\tilde{z})\right) = E^\theta(\tilde{y}) \tag{7.5}$$

or, more generally,

$$E^\theta\left(E^\theta(h(\tilde{y})|\tilde{z})\right) = E^\theta(h(\tilde{y}))$$

for all functions h;

Linearity. If A, B, and b are constants of appropriate dimension, then

$$E^\theta(A\tilde{y} + b|\tilde{z}) = AE^\theta(\tilde{y}|\tilde{z}) + b,$$

$$E^\theta(\tilde{y}B + b|\tilde{z}) = E^\theta(\tilde{y}|\tilde{z})B + b,$$

$$E^\theta(\tilde{y}^{(1)} + \tilde{y}^{(2)}|\tilde{z}) = E^\theta(\tilde{y}^{(1)}|\tilde{z}) + E^\theta(\tilde{y}^{(2)}|\tilde{z});$$

Positivity. For all $i = 1, \ldots, p$, if $\tilde{y}_i \geq 0$, then

$$E^\theta(\tilde{y}_i|\tilde{z}) \geq 0;$$

Inequality. For all $i = 1, \ldots, p$, if $\tilde{y}_i^{(1)} \geq \tilde{y}_i^{(2)}$, then

$$E^\theta(\tilde{y}_i^{(1)}|\tilde{z}) \geq E^\theta(\tilde{y}_i^{(2)}|\tilde{z});$$

If $L^2(\tilde{z})$ is the space of square integrable functions of $\tilde{z}$, then

$$\tilde{y} \in L^2(\tilde{z}) \Leftrightarrow E^\theta(\tilde{y}|\tilde{z}) = \tilde{y},$$

hence

$$E^\theta(\tilde{y}|\tilde{y}) = \tilde{y};$$

Theorem on three perpendiculars: if $L^2(\tilde{z}^{(1)}) \subset L^2(\tilde{z}^{(2)})$, then

$$E^\theta\left(E^\theta(\tilde{y}|\tilde{z}^{(2)})|\tilde{z}^{(1)}\right) = E^\theta\left(E^\theta(\tilde{y}|\tilde{z}^{(1)})|\tilde{z}^{(2)}\right) = E^\theta(\tilde{y}|\tilde{z}^{(1)});$$

Convexity theorem or Jensen's inequality: for all convex functions h from $\mathbb{R}^p$ into $\mathbb{R}$

$$E^\theta(h(\tilde{y})|\tilde{z}) \geq h(E^\theta(\tilde{y}|\tilde{z})).$$

The concept of conditional expectation is fundamental as it allows us to formalize temporal dependence in stochastic processes, as the definition of a martingale shows.

We temporarily reintroduce indexed notations for the random variables.

Definition 7.2   *Let (y_i) be a sequence of square integrable random variables. y_i is a martingale with respect to a sequence of random variables $x_i = (y_i, z_i)$ if and only if*

$$E^\theta(y_{i+1}|x_i, x_{i-1}, \ldots) = y_i \quad \forall i.$$ ∎

This implies that the expectation is constant in the sense that

$$E^\theta(y_{i+1}) = E^\theta\left(E^\theta(y_{i+1}|x_i, x_{i-1}, \ldots)\right) = E^\theta(y_i) \quad \forall i.$$

Furthermore, we can also infer that

$$E^\theta(y_{i+\tau}|x_i, x_{i-1}, \ldots) = y_i \quad \forall i, \forall \tau \geq 0.$$

Thus, the best predictor for $y_{i+\tau}$, given the past by $x_i, x_{i-1}, \ldots$, is simply y_i.

Example 7.1   *Consider a random variable y_i^* defined by $y_i^* = \sum_{k=1}^i y_k$; we assume that the y_i are independent and that $E^\theta(y_i) = 0$ for all i. Then*

$$E^\theta(y_{i+1}^*|y_i, y_{i-1}, \ldots) = E^\theta(y_{i+1} + y_i^*|y_i, y_{i-1}, \ldots) = y_i^*,$$

since

$$E^\theta(y_i^*|y_i, y_{i-1}, \ldots) = y_i^*$$

and

$$E^\theta(y_{i+1}|y_i, y_{i-1}, \ldots) = 0$$

since by assumption $E^\theta(y_{i+1}) = 0$. Hence, y_i is a martingale with respect to the sequence of variables y_i. □

A martingale difference is defined by

$$E^\theta(y_{i+1}|x_i, x_{i-1}, \ldots) = 0 \quad \forall i.$$

Let us return to the notation from the beginning of this chapter.

We can equally talk about the conditional expectation of a random matrix, which allows us to define the variance-covariance matrix of a random vector $\tilde{y}$ in $\mathbb{R}^p$ conditional on $\tilde{z}$ as the following $p \times p$ square matrix

$$Var^\theta(\tilde{y}|\tilde{z}) = E^\theta\left((\tilde{y} - E^\theta(\tilde{y}|\tilde{z}))(\tilde{y} - E^\theta(\tilde{y}|\tilde{z}))'|\tilde{z}\right)$$

and the conditional covariance between two vectors $\tilde{y}^{(1)}$ and $\tilde{y}^{(2)}$ in $\mathbb{R}^{p_1}$ and $\mathbb{R}^{p_2}$, such as

$$Cov^\theta(\tilde{y}^{(1)}, \tilde{y}^{(2)}|\tilde{z}) = E^\theta\left((\tilde{y}^{(1)} - E^\theta(\tilde{y}^{(1)}|\tilde{z}))(\tilde{y}^{(2)} - E^\theta(\tilde{y}^{(2)}|\tilde{z}))'|\tilde{z}\right).$$

Other properties can also be presented:

$$Var^\theta(\tilde{y}|\tilde{z}) = Cov^\theta(\tilde{y}, \tilde{y}|\tilde{z})$$

and

$$Cov^\theta(\tilde{y}^{(1)}, \tilde{y}^{(2)}|\tilde{z}) = E^\theta(\tilde{y}^{(1)}\tilde{y}^{(2)'}|\tilde{z}) - E^\theta(\tilde{y}^{(1)}|\tilde{z})E^\theta(\tilde{y}^{(2)'}|\tilde{z}),$$

hence

$$Var^\theta(\tilde{y}|\tilde{z}) = E^\theta(\tilde{y}\tilde{y}'|\tilde{z}) - E^\theta(\tilde{y}|\tilde{z})E^\theta(\tilde{y}'|\tilde{z})$$

and

$$Cov^\theta(A\tilde{y}^{(1)} + b, B\tilde{y}^{(2)} + c|\tilde{z}) = ACov^\theta(\tilde{y}^{(1)}, \tilde{y}^{(2)}|\tilde{z})B'$$

where A, B, b, and c are constants of appropriate dimensions. Hence

$$Var^\theta(A\tilde{y} + b|\tilde{z}) = AVar^\theta(\tilde{y}|\tilde{z})A',$$

and finally,

$$Var^\theta(\tilde{y}) = Var^\theta\left(E^\theta(\tilde{y}|\tilde{z})\right) + E^\theta\left(Var^\theta(\tilde{y}|\tilde{z})\right) \tag{7.6}$$

or more generally

$$Cov^\theta(\tilde{y}^{(1)}, \tilde{y}^{(2)}) = Cov^\theta\left(E^\theta(\tilde{y}^{(1)}|\tilde{z}), E^\theta(\tilde{y}^{(2)}|\tilde{z})\right)$$
$$+ E^\theta\left(Cov^\theta(\tilde{y}^{(1)}, \tilde{y}^{(2)}|\tilde{z})\right). \tag{7.7}$$

The relationship (7.6) implies in particular that

$$Var^\theta(\tilde{y}) \geq Var^\theta(E^\theta(\tilde{y}|\tilde{z})).$$

Definition 7.1 of the conditional expectation can be interpreted as the orthogonality of $\tilde{y} - E^\theta(\tilde{y}|\tilde{z})$ with all functions of $\tilde{z}$. We can also present a theorem that characterizes the conditional expectation in terms of orthogonal projections, i.e., in terms of the best approximation in the sense of the L^2-norm.

Theorem 7.1 *For all square integrable functions ψ from $\mathbb{R}^q$ to $\mathbb{R}$, we have*

$$E^\theta(\tilde{y} - E^\theta(\tilde{y}|\tilde{z}))^2 \leq E^\theta(\tilde{y} - \psi(\tilde{z}))^2. \tag{7.8}$$

We say that $E^\theta(\tilde{y}|\tilde{z})$ is the best approximation of $\tilde{y}$ in the sense of the L^2-norm. ∎

Proof: The proof rests on the expansion of the right-hand term of Inequality (7.8)

$$E^\theta(\tilde{y} - \psi(\tilde{z}))^2 = E^\theta(\tilde{y} - E^\theta(\tilde{y}|\tilde{z}) + E^\theta(\tilde{y}|\tilde{z}) - \psi(\tilde{z}))^2$$
$$= E^\theta(\tilde{y} - E^\theta(\tilde{y}|\tilde{z}))^2$$
$$+ 2E^\theta((\tilde{y} - E^\theta(\tilde{y}|\tilde{z}))(E^\theta(\tilde{y}|\tilde{z}) - \psi(\tilde{z}))$$
$$+ E^\theta(E^\theta(\tilde{y}|\tilde{z}) - \psi(\tilde{z}))^2.$$

The second term is zero, because by Definition 7.1,

$$E^\theta((\tilde{y} - E^\theta(\tilde{y}|\tilde{z})\delta(\tilde{z})) = 0$$

with $\delta(\tilde{z}) = E^\theta(\tilde{y}|\tilde{z}) - \psi(\tilde{z})$. Furthermore, the last term is always positive or zero. Hence, Inequality (7.8) follows. ∎

7.3 Linear Conditional Expectation

We just saw that the conditional expectation $E^\theta(\tilde{y}|\tilde{z})$ is the orthogonal projection of the random variable $\tilde{y}$ on the subspace of square integrable functions of $\tilde{z}$ in the sense of the L^2-norm. Now, we focus on the special case in which we consider only linear functions of $\tilde{z}$. We define the linear conditional expectation of $\tilde{y}$ by the orthogonal projection of $\tilde{y}$ on the subspace of linear functions of $\tilde{z}$, which we will denote by $L^{*2}(\tilde{z})$. We have $L^{*2}(\tilde{z}) \subset L^2(\tilde{z})$. We restrict ourselves, for the moment, to the case $p = 1$, where p is the dimension of y_i.

Definition 7.3 *The linear conditional expectation of $\tilde{y}$ given $\tilde{z}$, also called linear regression of $\tilde{y}$ on $\tilde{z}$, is the random variable denoted $EL^\theta(\tilde{y}|\tilde{z})$, which is the orthogonal projection of $\tilde{y}$ on the space $L^{*2}(\tilde{z})$ of linear functions of $\tilde{z}$.* ∎

The linear conditional expectation is written as

$$EL^\theta(\tilde{y}|\tilde{z}) = \sum_{j=1}^{q} \beta_j \tilde{z}_j = \beta'\tilde{z},$$

with $\beta = (\beta_1, \ldots, \beta_q)'$ and $\tilde{z} = (\tilde{z}_1, \ldots, \tilde{z}_q)'$. In order to find the parameters β_j, we start with the orthogonality condition

$$E^\theta\left((\tilde{y} - \beta'\tilde{z})\tilde{z}'\right) = 0.$$

From this we obtain, assuming that the matrix $E^\theta(\tilde{z}\tilde{z}')$ is invertible,

$$\beta = \left[E^\theta(\tilde{z}\tilde{z}')\right]^{-1} E^\theta(\tilde{z}\tilde{y}).$$

Hence,

$$EL^\theta(\tilde{y}|\tilde{z}) = E^\theta(\tilde{y}\tilde{z}')\left[E^\theta(\tilde{z}\tilde{z}')\right]^{-1}\tilde{z}. \tag{7.9}$$

The plane defined by the equation

$$\tilde{y}^* = E^\theta(\tilde{y}\tilde{z}')\left[E^\theta(\tilde{z}\tilde{z}')\right]^{-1}\tilde{z} \tag{7.10}$$

is called linear regression plane of $\tilde{y}$ on $\tilde{z}_1, \ldots, \tilde{z}_q$.

Let us consider the linear conditional expectation of $\tilde{y}$ given a vector $(\tilde{z}_1, \ldots, \tilde{z}_q, 1)'$ where 1 is a constant function equal to the scalar 1. Then, we obtain the affine conditional expectation

$$EL^\theta(\tilde{y}|\tilde{z}, 1) = \beta\tilde{z} + c,$$

where c is a scalar. The resulting regression plane is called the affine regression plane of $\tilde{y}$ on $\tilde{z}_1, \ldots, \tilde{z}_q$. This will be studied more precisely later on, in the general case where $\tilde{y}$ is a vector.

A different way of calculating the parameters $\beta_1, \ldots, \beta_q$ is to find the solution to the minimization problem

$$\min_{\lambda_1, \ldots, \lambda_q} E^\theta\left[\left(\tilde{y} - \sum_{j=1}^{q} \lambda_j \tilde{z}_j\right)^2\right].$$

The following two examples illustrate two simple cases, when we consider the projection of a scalar random variable $\tilde{y}$ on a constant and on a scalar random variable $\tilde{z}$.

Example 7.2 *If $\tilde{y}$ is a random variable, we wish to find a constant a which is the closest possible to $\tilde{y}$ in the sense of the L^2-norm. a is the orthogonal projection of $\tilde{y}$ on the subspace of L^2 spanned by the constant 1,*

$$E^\theta\left((\tilde{y} - a).1\right) = 0,$$

hence,

$$a = E^\theta(\tilde{y}). \qquad \square$$

Example 7.3 *If $\tilde{y}$ and $\tilde{z}$ are random variables, then the linear conditional expectation of $\tilde{y}$ given $\tilde{z}$ of the form $EL^\theta(\tilde{y}|\tilde{z}) = \alpha\tilde{z}$ (where α is a scalar), is obtained by the orthogonality condition $E^\theta\left((\tilde{y} - \alpha\tilde{z})\tilde{z}\right) = 0$. This leads to*

$$\alpha = \frac{E^\theta(\tilde{y}\tilde{z})}{E^\theta(\tilde{z}^2)}.$$

Hence,

$$EL^\theta(\tilde{y}|\tilde{z}) = \frac{E^\theta(\tilde{y}\tilde{z})}{E^\theta(\tilde{z}^2)}\tilde{z}. \qquad \square$$

In general, $E^{\theta}(\tilde{y}|\tilde{z})$ and $EL^{\theta}(\tilde{y}|\tilde{z})$ are not equal, and $E^{\theta}(\tilde{y}|\tilde{z})$ is a better approximation to $\tilde{y}$, except in special cases, as we will see in Examples 7.5 (where $\tilde{y}$ and $\tilde{z}$ are normally distributed) and 7.6 (where they are independent).

$$\varepsilon L = \tilde{y} - EL^{\theta}(\tilde{y}|\tilde{z})$$

is called the residual of the linear regression. It is nothing other than the orthogonal projection of $\tilde{y}$ on the subspace that is orthogonal to $L^{*2}(\tilde{z})$.

These notions can be generalized to the case where $\tilde{y}$ is a vector in $\mathbb{R}^p$. $EL^{\theta}(\tilde{y}|\tilde{z})$ becomes a random vector in $\mathbb{R}^p$ for which the ith coordinate, i.e., $EL^{\theta}(\tilde{y}_i|\tilde{z})$, is the orthogonal projection of $\tilde{y}_i$ on $L^{*2}(\tilde{z})$. Then,

$$EL^{\theta}(\tilde{y}|\tilde{z}) = B\tilde{z}$$

where B is a matrix of dimension $p \times q$ which is the solution to the orthogonality condition

$$E^{\theta}\left((\tilde{y} - B\tilde{z})\tilde{z}'\right) = 0,$$

hence

$$E^{\theta}(\tilde{y}\tilde{z}') - BE^{\theta}(\tilde{z}\tilde{z}') = 0.$$

From this we can derive, assuming that the matrix $E^{\theta}(\tilde{z}\tilde{z}')$ is invertible,

$$B = E^{\theta}(\tilde{y}\tilde{z}')\left[E^{\theta}(\tilde{z}\tilde{z}')\right]^{-1}$$

hence,

$$EL^{\theta}(\tilde{y}|\tilde{z}) = E^{\theta}(\tilde{y}\tilde{z}')\left[E^{\theta}(\tilde{z}\tilde{z}')\right]^{-1}\tilde{z}. \tag{7.11}$$

Let us consider now more precisely the case where the vector $\tilde{y}$ is projected on the subspace of affine functions of $\tilde{z}$. The affine conditional expectation can be written in the form

$$EL^{\theta}(\tilde{y}|\tilde{z}, 1) = A\tilde{z} + b$$

The orthogonality conditions are

$$\begin{cases} E^{\theta}\left[(\tilde{y} - EL^{\theta}(\tilde{y}|\tilde{z}, 1))1\right] = 0 \\ E^{\theta}\left[(\tilde{y} - EL^{\theta}(\tilde{y}|\tilde{z}, 1))\tilde{z}'\right] = 0 \end{cases}$$

$$\Leftrightarrow \begin{cases} E^{\theta}(\tilde{y}) - AE^{\theta}(\tilde{z}) - b = 0 \\ E^{\theta}(\tilde{y}\tilde{z}') - AE^{\theta}(\tilde{z}\tilde{z}') - bE^{\theta}(\tilde{z}') = 0. \end{cases}$$

From the first equation, we solve for $b = E^\theta(\tilde{y}) - AE^\theta(\tilde{z})$, then replace b by this expression in the second equation:

$$E^\theta(\tilde{y}\tilde{z}') - AE^\theta(\tilde{z}\tilde{z}') - E^\theta(\tilde{y})E^\theta(\tilde{z}') + AE^\theta(\tilde{z})E^\theta(\tilde{z}') = 0$$
$$\Leftrightarrow A\left[E^\theta(\tilde{z}\tilde{z}') - E^\theta(\tilde{z})E^\theta(\tilde{z}')\right] = E^\theta(\tilde{y}\tilde{z}') - E^\theta(\tilde{y})E^\theta(\tilde{z}')$$
$$\Leftrightarrow A Var^\theta(\tilde{z}) = Cov^\theta(\tilde{y}, \tilde{z})$$
$$\Leftrightarrow A = Cov^\theta(\tilde{y}, \tilde{z}) \left(Var^\theta(\tilde{z})\right)^{-1}.$$

Assuming that $Var^\theta(\tilde{z})$ is an invertible matrix, we have

$$b = E^\theta(\tilde{y}) - Cov^\theta(\tilde{y}, \tilde{z}) \left(Var^\theta(\tilde{z})\right)^{-1} E^\theta(\tilde{z}).$$

Therefore, the affine conditional expectation is

$$EL^\theta(\tilde{y}|\tilde{z}, 1) = E^\theta(\tilde{y}) + Cov^\theta(\tilde{y}, \tilde{z}) \left(Var^\theta(\tilde{z})\right)^{-1} \left(\tilde{z} - E^\theta(\tilde{z})\right). \quad (7.12)$$

Example 7.4 *Let us use expression (7.12) to find the affine conditional expectation of $\tilde{y}$ given $\tilde{z}$, when $\tilde{y}$ and $\tilde{z}$ are both scalar random variables, and to introduce the linear regression coefficient. We have*

$$EL^\theta(\tilde{y}|\tilde{z}, 1) = E^\theta(\tilde{y}) + \frac{Cov^\theta(\tilde{y}, \tilde{z})}{Var^\theta(\tilde{z})} \left(\tilde{z} - E^\theta(\tilde{z})\right).$$

Define the linear regression coefficient of the pair $(\tilde{y}, \tilde{z})$ by

$$\rho = \frac{Cov^\theta(\tilde{y}, \tilde{z})}{\sqrt{Var^\theta(\tilde{y})}\sqrt{Var^\theta(\tilde{z})}}.$$

The equation of the affine regression line of $\tilde{y}$ on $\tilde{z}$ can be written

$$\tilde{y}^* = E^\theta(\tilde{y}) + \rho\frac{\sqrt{Var^\theta(\tilde{y})}}{\sqrt{Var^\theta(\tilde{z})}} \left(\tilde{z} - E^\theta(\tilde{z})\right)$$

or alternatively

$$\frac{\tilde{y}^* - E^\theta(\tilde{y})}{\sqrt{Var^\theta(\tilde{y})}} = \rho\frac{\tilde{z} - E^\theta(\tilde{z})}{\sqrt{Var^\theta(\tilde{z})}}.$$

The coefficient ρ is always in the interval $[-1, 1]$. In addition, we can show that $|\rho| = 1$ if and only if $\tilde{y}$ is already a affine function of $\tilde{z}$. Furthermore, if $\tilde{y}$ and $\tilde{z}$ are independent, then $\rho = 0$ (but its converse is false) and

$$EL^\theta(\tilde{y}|\tilde{z}) = E^\theta(\tilde{y}|\tilde{z}) = E^\theta(\tilde{y})$$

(which we will see again in Example 7.6). □

The expression for the affine conditional expectation (7.12) allows us to quickly show that $EL^\theta(\tilde{y}|\tilde{z}, 1) = E^\theta(\tilde{y}|\tilde{z})$ when $\tilde{y}$ and $\tilde{z}$ are normally distributed random vectors, as we show in the following example.

Example 7.5   *Assume that*

$$\tilde{x} = \begin{pmatrix} \tilde{y} \\ \tilde{z} \end{pmatrix} \sim N(m, \Sigma)$$

where Σ is assumed to be invertible; m and Σ are partitioned in exactly the same way as the vector $\tilde{x}$

$$m = \begin{pmatrix} m_1 \\ m_2 \end{pmatrix} \quad and \quad \Sigma = \begin{pmatrix} \Sigma_{11} & \Sigma_{12} \\ \Sigma_{21} & \Sigma_{22} \end{pmatrix}.$$

The marginal distribution of $\tilde{z}$ and the distribution of $\tilde{y}$ conditional on $\tilde{z}$ are

$$\begin{cases} \tilde{z} \sim N(m_2, \Sigma_{22}) \\ \tilde{y}|\tilde{z} \sim N(m_1 + \Sigma_{12}\Sigma_{22}^{-1}(\tilde{z} - m_2), \Sigma_{11} - \Sigma_{12}\Sigma_{22}^{-1}\Sigma_{21}). \end{cases}$$

Thus, it follows that

$$E^\theta(\tilde{y}|\tilde{z}) = m_1 + \Sigma_{12}\Sigma_{22}^{-1}(\tilde{z} - m_2).$$

We write now $EL^\theta(\tilde{y}|\tilde{z}, 1)$, given by (7.12) in the notation of this example

$$EL^\theta(\tilde{y}|\tilde{z}, 1) = m_1 + \Sigma_{12}\Sigma_{22}^{-1}(\tilde{z} - m_2).$$

It is, thus, evident that we have in the case of normal variables

$$EL^\theta(\tilde{y}|\tilde{z}, 1) = E^\theta(\tilde{y}|\tilde{z}). \qquad \square$$

The various notions of conditional expectation and linear conditional expectation can be illustrated in the following way. Consider a space $L^2(\tilde{z})$, which represents the space of square integrable functions of $\tilde{z}$ and for which the line $L^{*2}(\tilde{z}, 1)$ represents the space of affine functions of $\tilde{z}$. Then, $E^\theta(\tilde{y}|\tilde{z})$ is the orthogonal projection of $\tilde{y}$ on $L^2(\tilde{z})$, and $EL^\theta(\tilde{y}|\tilde{z}, 1)$ is the orthogonal projection of $\tilde{y}$ on $L^{*2}(\tilde{z}, 1)$. It also becomes clear that

$$EL^\theta(E^\theta(\tilde{y}|\tilde{z})|\tilde{z}, 1) = EL^\theta(\tilde{y}|\tilde{z}, 1)$$

and that $E^\theta(\tilde{y}|\tilde{z})$ provides a better approximation of $\tilde{y}$ than $EL^\theta(\tilde{y}|\tilde{z}, 1)$, in the sense that

$$E^\theta\left(\|\tilde{y} - EL^\theta(\tilde{y}|\tilde{z}, 1)\|^2\right) \geq E^\theta\left(\|\tilde{y} - E^\theta(\tilde{y}|\tilde{z})\|^2\right).$$

Let us note now some properties of the conditional linear expectation:

$$EL^\theta(A\tilde{y} + b|\tilde{z}) = AEL^\theta(\tilde{y}|\tilde{z}) + b;$$

$$EL^\theta(\tilde{y}^{(1)} + \tilde{y}^{(2)}|\tilde{z}) = EL^\theta(\tilde{y}^{(1)}|\tilde{z}) + EL^\theta(\tilde{y}^{(2)}|\tilde{z});$$

if $\tilde{y}_i \in L^{*2}(\tilde{z})$, then

$$EL^{\theta}(\tilde{y}_i|\tilde{z}) = \tilde{y}_i;$$

finally,

$$EL^{\theta}(EL^{\theta}(\tilde{y}|\tilde{z}^{(1)})|\tilde{z}^{(2)})) = EL^{\theta}(EL^{\theta}(\tilde{y}|\tilde{z}^{(2)})|\tilde{z}^{(1)})) = EL^{\theta}(\tilde{y}|\tilde{z}^{(1)})$$

if $L^{*2}(\tilde{z}^{(1)}) \subset L^{*2}(\tilde{z}^{(2)})$ (theorem on three perpendiculars).

The following example illustrates the consequences of the independence between $\tilde{y}$ and $\tilde{z}$ on conditional expectation and linear conditional expectation.

Example 7.6 *Suppose that $\tilde{y}$ and $\tilde{z}$ are two independent vectors, respectively in $\mathbb{R}^p$ and in $\mathbb{R}^q$. This means that in the case of continuous distributions, we have*

$$f(\tilde{y}, \tilde{z}) = f_{marg}(\tilde{y}) f_{marg}(\tilde{z})$$

or

$$f_{cond}(\tilde{y}|\tilde{z}) = f_{marg}(\tilde{y})$$

(in order to simplify the notation, both marginal densities are denoted by f_{marg}, but the systematic use of arguments removes any ambiguity). A first consequence is that, for all square integrable functions h

$$E^{\theta}(h(\tilde{y})|\tilde{z}) = E^{\theta}(h(\tilde{y})),$$

since

$$E^{\theta}(h(\tilde{y})|\tilde{z}) = \int h(\tilde{y}) f_{marg}(\tilde{y}) d\tilde{y}$$
$$= E^{\theta}(h(\tilde{y})).$$

As a special case, we obtain $E^{\theta}(\tilde{y}|\tilde{z}) = E^{\theta}(\tilde{y})$.

Furthermore, we have for all square integrable functions h and ψ

$$E^{\theta}(h(\tilde{y})\psi(\tilde{z})) = \int h(\tilde{y})\psi(\tilde{z}) f(\tilde{y}, \tilde{z}) d\tilde{y} d\tilde{z}$$
$$= \int h(\tilde{y}) f_m(\tilde{y}) d\tilde{y} \int \psi(\tilde{z}) f_{marg}(\tilde{z}) d\tilde{z}$$
$$= E^{\theta}(h(\tilde{y})) E^{\theta}(\psi(\tilde{z})).$$

This implies that $E^{\theta}(\tilde{y}\tilde{z}) = E^{\theta}(\tilde{y})E^{\theta}(\tilde{z})$ and $Cov^{\theta}(\tilde{y}, \tilde{z}) = 0$, since

$$Cov^{\theta}(\tilde{y}, \tilde{z}) = E^{\theta}(\tilde{y}\tilde{z}) - E^{\theta}(\tilde{y})E^{\theta}(\tilde{z})$$
$$= 0.$$

The affine conditional expectation $EL^{\theta}(\tilde{y}|\tilde{z}, 1)$, given by (7.12), is therefore equal to $E^{\theta}(\tilde{y})$. Thus, when $\tilde{y}$ and $\tilde{z}$ are independent, then

$$EL^{\theta}(\tilde{y}|\tilde{z}, 1) = E^{\theta}(\tilde{y}|\tilde{z}) = E^{\theta}(\tilde{y}). \qquad \square$$

Here, we do not address a different notion of independence, which is the conditional independence. Let us just mention that $\tilde{y}^{(1)}$ and $\tilde{y}^{(2)}$ are independent conditional on $\tilde{z}$ if, given any two functions h_1 and h_2 in $\mathbb{R}^p$,

$$E^\theta \left[h_1(\tilde{y}^{(1)}) h_2(\tilde{y}^{(2)}) | \tilde{z} \right] = E^\theta \left[h_1(\tilde{y}^{(1)}) | \tilde{z} \right] E^\theta \left[h_2(\tilde{y}^{(2)}) | \tilde{z} \right].$$

Notes

The general concept of conditional expectation with respect to a σ-algebra, as well as the rigorous proof of the existence of the conditional expectation can be found in numerous treaties on probability theory, for example Neveu (1965), Métivier (1968), or Dellacherie and Meyer (1978). We find in those also the precise proofs of the properties of the conditional expectation. Martingales have been only mentioned in this chapter. Further details are found in Neveu (1975) and Dellacherie and Meyer (1982).

Linear and affine conditional expectations are a more statistical concept, developed, for example, by Gouriéroux and Monfort (1996a).

Independence and conditional independence are extensively studied in Florens, Mouchart, and Rollin (1989).

8.   Univariate Regression

8.1   Introduction

In Chapter 7 we introduced the notions of conditional expectation and of linear conditional expectation – or linear regression – in terms of orthogonal projections in the sense of the L^2-norm, respectively, on the set of integrable functions of a random vector z, denoted by $L^2(z)$, and on the set of linear functions of z, denoted by $L^{*2}(z)$. We now apply the concept of regression and of linear regression to specific models and study the problems of estimation and testing.

Let us recall some notions that we have seen in the previous chapters. Consider a statistical model $M_n = \{X^n, \Theta, P_n^\theta\}$ where $X^n \subset \mathbb{R}^{nm}$ is the sample space of dimension n, Θ is the parameter space, and P_n^θ is the family of sampling distributions. Let $x \in X^n$ be a finite sequence $(x_i)_{i=1,\dots,n}$ with $x_i = (y_i, z_i)'$, where $y_i \in \mathbb{R}$, $z_i \in \mathbb{R}^q$, $q = m - 1$. In this chapter we will only consider the case where the dimension p of y_i is equal to one. We assume that the model is i.i.d., i.e. the observations $x_1, \dots, x_n$ are independent in the sense of the distribution P_n^θ for all θ and distributed according to the same probability distribution Q^θ: $P_n^\theta = [Q^\theta]^{\otimes n}$. Furthermore, we also assume that for all $i = 1, \dots, n$, y_i and z_{ij} for $j = 1, \dots, q$ are square integrable random variables, i.e. they belong to $L^2(z)$.

We are interested in the conditional expectation of the form

$$E^\theta(y_i|z_i) = g(z_i, \beta),$$

for all i, where β is a function of θ which, in this chapter, we assume to be finite. We consider the problem of estimating this parameter vector β, assuming that g is known. Define the random vector u in $\mathbb{R}^n$ by $u = (u_1, \dots, u_n)'$ with for all i

$$u_i = y_i - E^\theta(y_i|z_i). \tag{8.1}$$

We will see in the following its main properties.

This leads to the following model

$$y_i = g(z_i, \beta) + u_i \quad i = 1, \ldots, n. \tag{8.2}$$

The choice of g, or more generally the choice of the conditioning or projection space determines the type of model under study. In this manner, if the space is restricted to the set $L^{*2}(z)$, i.e., the space of linear functions of z, then

$$g(z_i, \beta) = EL^\theta(y_i|z_i) = \beta' z_i.$$

In Section 2, we study the case of a model in which the regression is assumed to be linear. In Section 3, we analyze models for which the regression is assumed to belong to a given nonlinear parametric family. In the last section, we consider misspecification.

8.2   Linear Regression

First, we consider assumptions that allow us to specify what we call linear regression model. Recall that $y_i \in \mathbb{R}$ and $z_i = (z_{i1}, \ldots, z_{iq})'$ for all $i = 1, \ldots, n$ with the property that $z_{i1} = 1$, to which we will return in the following.

8.2.1   The Assumptions of the Linear Regression Model

The first assumption is that of linearity.

Assumption A1   *For all $i = 1, \ldots, n$,*

$$E^\theta(y_i|z_i) = EL^\theta(y_i|z_i) = \beta' z_i = \sum_{j=1}^{q} \beta_j z_{ij}$$

with $\beta = (\beta_1, \ldots, \beta_q)'$, additionally $E^\theta(z_i z_i')$ is invertible.   □

We can deduce from this assumption the general form of the linear regression equation, using the expression for the random term u_i given by (8.1):

$$y_i = \beta' z_i + u_i \quad i = 1, \ldots, n.$$

Define the $n \times 1$ vectors y and u by $y = (y_1, \ldots, y_n)'$ and $u = (u_1, \ldots, u_n)'$, and the $n \times q$ matrix Z by

$$Z = (z_{ij})_{i,j} = (z_1, \ldots, z_n)'.$$

The matrix form of the regression equation is

$$y = Z\beta + u.$$

By construction, the term u_i possesses various properties. For all $i = 1, \ldots, n$, we first have

$$E^\theta(u_i|z_i) = 0.$$

Note that the independence of the x_i implies that $E^\theta(u_i|z_i) = E^\theta(u_i|Z)$ and thus

$$E^\theta(u|Z) = 0.$$

Next, we have

$$E^\theta(u_i z_i|z_i) = z_i E^\theta(u_i|z_i) = 0. \tag{8.3}$$

This second property represents the conditional orthogonality between the u_i and the z_i. Also, these properties remain valid in terms of marginal expectations:

$$E^\theta(u_i) = E^\theta\left[E^\theta(u_i|z_i)\right] = 0$$

and

$$E^\theta(u_i z_i) = 0$$

for all $i = 1, \ldots, n$, which constitutes the fundamental estimation equation.

The following identification assumption is the assumption on no collinearity.

Assumption A2 $Rank(Z) = q \quad (n > q)$. $\qquad\qquad\square$

This can be written in the following equivalent ways $Rank(Z'Z) = q$, $det(Z'Z) \neq 0$ or also $Z'Z$ invertible. This is the equivalent assumption in terms of the sample to the distributional assumption that the variance matrix $E^\theta(z_i z_i')$ is invertible, which does not depend on i by assumption.

The third assumption is the one of homoskedasticity.

Assumption A3 $Var^\theta(y_i|z_i) = \sigma^2$, for all $i = 1, \ldots, n$. $\qquad\qquad\square$

We can immediately infer that $Var^\theta(u_i|z_i) = \sigma^2$, for all $i = 1, \ldots, n$. Furthermore, for all i and j, with $i \neq j$, we also have

$$
\begin{aligned}
Cov^\theta(u_i, u_j|Z) &= E^\theta(u_i u_j|Z) \\
&= E^\theta\left[\left(y_i - E^\theta(y_i|z_i)\right)\left(y_j - E^\theta(y_j|z_j)\right)|Z\right] \\
&= E^\theta\left[\left(y_i - E^\theta(y_i|Z)\right)\left(y_j - E^\theta(y_j|Z)\right)|Z\right] \\
&= E^\theta(y_i y_j|Z) - E^\theta\left[y_i E^\theta(y_j|Z)|Z\right] - E^\theta\left[y_j E^\theta(y_i|Z)|Z\right] \\
&\quad + E^\theta\left[E^\theta(y_i|Z)E^\theta(y_j|Z)|Z\right] \\
&= 0,
\end{aligned}
$$

since y_i and y_j are independent conditionally on Z, hence,

$$E^\theta(u_i u_j | Z) = \begin{vmatrix} \sigma^2 & \text{if } i = j \\ 0 & \text{if } i \neq j. \end{vmatrix}$$

This property of the error term can be written in terms of marginals

$$E^\theta(u_i u_j) = E^\theta\left[E^\theta(u_i u_j | Z)\right] = \begin{vmatrix} \sigma^2 & \text{if } i = j \\ 0 & \text{if } i \neq j \end{vmatrix}.$$

or

$$Var^\theta(u) = E^\theta(uu') = Var^\theta(u|Z) = E^\theta(uu'|Z) = \sigma^2 I_n.$$

The forth and last assumption is the assumption of conditional normality.

Assumption A4 $y_i | z_i$ is normally distributed for all $i = 1, \ldots, n$.   □

Assumptions A1, A3, and A4 can by summarized by

$$y_i | z_i \sim i.i.N(\beta' z_i, \sigma^2),$$

for all $i = 1, \ldots, n$, which implies that

$$u_i | z_i \sim i.i.N(0, \sigma^2)$$

or, more precisely

$$u_i \sim i.i.N(0, \sigma^2).$$

This last property summarizes the principal basic assumptions of the linear regression model in a large number of econometric textbooks which specify the model in this way, starting with the error term and deriving from it specifically the assumptions of orthogonality, linearity and homoskedasticity. In our case, the assumptions are specified in terms of random variables, the properties of the error term are derived from it by construction.

8.2.2   Estimation by Ordinary Least Squares

The estimation problem comes down to estimating the parameter vector β. We will use here results of Chapter 7 on the notion of best approximation in the sense of the L^2-norm. The estimator that we obtain by this method is the *Ordinary Least Squares* (OLS) estimator of β.

The estimator of β is obtained as the solution to the problem of minimizing the following function with respect to λ

$$E^\theta\left[\left(y_i - \sum_{j=1}^q \lambda_j z_{ij}\right)^2\right] = E^\theta\left[(y_i - \lambda' z_i)^2\right], \tag{8.4}$$

which leads to the following simple system of moment equations

$$E^\theta \left[z_i(y_i - \lambda'z_i) \right] = 0. \tag{8.5}$$

Equation (8.4) defines β as the solution to a minimization problem described in Chapter 3 by setting

$$\phi(x_i, \lambda) = (y_i - \lambda'z_i)^2.$$

The first order conditions (8.5) form a simple moment equation by setting

$$\psi(x_i, \lambda) = z_i(y_i - \lambda'z_i).$$

Replacing the expectation with respect to the sampling probability distribution by the one calculated using the empirical distribution translates this to the minimization of

$$D(\lambda_1, \ldots, \lambda_q) = \sum_{i=1}^n \left(y_i - \sum_{j=1}^q \lambda_j z_{ij} \right)^2 = \sum_{i=1}^n (y_i - \lambda'z_i)^2, \tag{8.6}$$

with respect to $\lambda_1, \ldots, \lambda_q$, or, in terms of matrices to the minimization of

$$D(\lambda) = (y - Z\lambda)'(y - Z\lambda).$$

with respect to $\lambda = (\lambda_1, \ldots, \lambda_q)$.

The first order conditions of the minimization problem are

$$\frac{\partial D(\lambda)}{\partial \lambda} = -2Z'y + 2Z'Z\lambda - 0. \tag{8.7}$$

This can be rewritten as

$$Z'(y - Z\lambda) = 0$$

or

$$\sum_{i=1}^n z_i(y_i - \lambda'z_i) = 0,$$

which is the sample equivalent to (8.5). This allows us to obtain the expression for the moment estimator $\widehat{\beta}_n$, here also called the ordinary least squares estimator of β,

$$\widehat{\beta}_n = (Z'Z)^{-1}Z'y = \left[\sum_{i=1}^n z_i z_i' \right]^{-1} \sum_{i=1}^n z_i y_i. \tag{8.8}$$

(recall that, according to Assumption A2, $Z'Z$ is invertible). Following the logic of the notation in the first part, this estimator should be denoted by $\widehat{\lambda}_n$. We use, however, notation $\widehat{\beta}_n$ in order to conform to the tradition.

The second order conditions are satisfied because

$$\frac{\partial^2 D(\lambda)}{\partial \lambda \partial \lambda'} = Z'Z$$

is a positive semidefinite matrix, thus $\widehat{\beta}_n$ is a minimum.

Let us set, for all $i = 1, \dots, n$,

$$\widehat{y}_i = \widehat{\beta}_n' z_i$$

and

$$\widehat{u}_i = y_i - \widehat{y}_i$$

and define the vectors $\widehat{y}$ and $\widehat{u}$, both of dimension $n \times 1$, by

$$\widehat{y} = (\widehat{y}_1, \dots, \widehat{y}_n)' \text{ and } \widehat{u} = (\widehat{u}_1, \dots, \widehat{u}_n)'.$$

Under Assumptions A1, A2, and A3, when σ^2 is unknown, it can be estimated by

$$\widetilde{\sigma}_n^2 = \frac{1}{n} \sum_{i=1}^n \left(y_i - \widehat{\beta}_n' z_i \right)^2 \tag{8.9}$$

since

$$\sigma^2 = E^\theta(u_i^2) = E^\theta \left[(y_i - \beta' z_i)^2 \right].$$

However, we prefer a different estimator which, as we will see, is unbiased

$$\widehat{\sigma}_n^2 = \frac{1}{n-q} \sum_{i=1}^n \left(y_i - \widehat{\beta}_n' z_i \right)^2, \tag{8.10}$$

which can also be written as

$$\widehat{\sigma}_n^2 = \frac{1}{n-q} \sum_{i=1}^n \widehat{u}_i^2 = \frac{1}{n-q}(y - \widehat{y})'(y - \widehat{y}) = \frac{1}{n-q} \widehat{u}' \widehat{u}.$$

$\widehat{\sigma}_n^2$ is also equal to

$$\widehat{\sigma}_n^2 = \frac{1}{n-q}(y - Z\widehat{\beta}_n)'(y - Z\widehat{\beta}_n)$$

$$= \frac{1}{n-q}(y'y - y'Z(Z'Z)^{-1}Z'y)$$

$$= \frac{1}{n-q} y' M_Z y$$

where

$$M_Z = I - Z(Z'Z)^{-1}Z'$$

is idempotent and symmetric and is the projection matrix on the hyperplane that is orthogonal to the hyperplane spanned by the columns of matrix Z.

Example 8.1 *This example is important as it expounds the maximum likelihood method which we studied from a general viewpoint in 3.9, 3.15, and 3.20 in Chapter 3. Under the normality Assumption A3, the conditional density of y_i is*

$$f(y_i|z_i, \beta, \sigma) = \frac{1}{\sigma\sqrt{2\pi}} \exp\left\{-\frac{(y_i - \beta'z_i)^2}{2\sigma^2}\right\}.$$

The maximization problem is

$$\max_{\lambda, \rho} E^\theta \left[\ln f(y_i|z_i, \lambda, \rho)\right].$$

The MLE of β and σ^2, which we denote by $\tilde{\beta}_n$ and $\tilde{\sigma}_n^2$, satisfy

$$(\tilde{\beta}_n', \tilde{\sigma}_n^2) = \arg\max_{\lambda, \rho} \frac{1}{n} \sum_{i=1}^n \ln f(y_i|z_i, \lambda, \rho)$$

$$= \arg\max_{\lambda, \rho} \ln l_n(y|Z, \lambda, \rho)$$

where l_n is the likelihood function given by

$$l_n(y|Z, \lambda, \rho) = \prod_{i=1}^n f(y_i|z_i, \lambda, \rho)$$

$$= \frac{1}{\rho^n(2\pi)^{n/2}} \exp\left\{-\sum_{i=1}^n \frac{(y_i - \lambda'z_i)^2}{2\rho^2}\right\}.$$

The estimators are then derived from the first order conditions

$$\frac{\partial}{\partial\lambda} \ln l_n(y|Z, \lambda, \rho) = 0$$

and

$$\frac{\partial}{\partial\rho} \ln l_n(y|Z, \lambda, \rho) = 0.$$

This is equivalent to

$$\frac{\partial}{\partial\lambda} \sum_{i=1}^n (y_i - \lambda'z_i)^2 = \frac{\partial}{\partial\lambda}(y - Z\lambda)'(y - Z\lambda) = 0 \tag{8.11}$$

and

$$\tilde{\sigma}_n^2 = \frac{1}{n} \sum_{i=1}^n (y_i - \lambda'z_i)^2. \tag{8.12}$$

We recognize that the first order condition (8.11) are the same as those of the minimization, (8.7), of the method of moments, thus the MLE of β is just the OLS estimator $\widetilde{\beta}_n = \widehat{\beta}_n$ (see (8.8)). From the second condition (8.12), we can derive the expression for $\widetilde{\sigma}_n^2$:

$$\widetilde{\sigma}_n^2 = \frac{1}{n} \sum_{i=1}^{n} (y_i - \widetilde{\beta}_n' z_i)^2 = \frac{n}{n-q} \widehat{\sigma}_n^2. \qquad (8.13)$$

$\square$

8.2.3 Small Sample Properties

Let us first consider the finite sample properties of $\widehat{\beta}_n$. First, $\widehat{\beta}_n$ can be written in the form Ay, with $A = (Z'Z)^{-1}Z'$, and is thus linear in y. Furthermore,

$$\widehat{\beta}_n = (Z'Z)^{-1}Z'(Z\beta + u) = \beta + (Z'Z)^{-1}Z'u,$$

hence,

$$E^\theta(\widehat{\beta}_n | Z) = \beta;$$

$\widehat{\beta}_n$ is, therefore, an unbiased estimator of β. Its conditional variance is

$$Var^\theta(\widehat{\beta}_n | Z) = E^\theta((Z'Z)^{-1}Z'u | Z) = \sigma^2(Z'Z)^{-1}.$$

Thus, we arrive at the following theorem, called the Gauss-Markov theorem.

Theorem 8.1 *Under Assumptions A1, A2, and A3, the ordinary least squares estimator $\widehat{\beta}_n$ of β has minimal variance in the family of all unbiased linear estimators of β.* ∎

Proof: Consider a different linear estimator of β, denoted by $\widetilde{\beta}_n$, of the form $\widetilde{\beta}_n = Cy$, where C is the following $q \times n$ matrix

$$C = D + (Z'Z)^{-1}Z'$$

where D also has dimension $q \times n$. Suppose this new estimator is unbiased. It follows that

$$E^\theta(\widetilde{\beta}_n | Z) = E^\theta \left[(D + (Z'Z)^{-1}Z')(Z\beta + u) | Z \right] = DZ\beta + \beta$$

which must be equal to β for all β. This implies that $DZ = 0$. Thus, we have

$$\widetilde{\beta}_n = \beta + (D + (Z'Z)^{-1}Z')u.$$

Calculating the variance of $\tilde{\beta}_n$ using the constraint $DZ = 0$ and the fact that $Var^\theta(u|Z) = \sigma^2 I_n$, we obtain

$$Var^\theta(\tilde{\beta}_n|Z) = Var^\theta((D + (Z'Z)^{-1}Z')u|Z)$$

$$= \sigma^2 DD' + \sigma^2(Z'Z)^{-1}$$

$$= \sigma^2 DD' + Var^\theta(\widehat{\beta}_n|Z)$$

$$\geq Var^\theta(\widehat{\beta}_n|Z)$$

since $D'D$ is a positive semidefinite matrix. ∎

Thus, this theorem shows that in a finite sample, $\widehat{\beta}_n$ is the *best linear unbiased estimator* (BLUE) of β.

Now, let us consider the properties of $\widehat{\sigma}_n^2$. This is also an unbiased estimator. To prove this, write

$$\widehat{u} = y - \widehat{y} = M_Z y = M_Z(Z\beta + u) = M_Z u$$

since $M_Z Z = 0$. Thus

$$\widehat{\sigma}_n^2 = \frac{1}{n-q} u' M_Z u.$$

The calculation of its conditional expectation gives

$$E^\theta(\widehat{\sigma}_n^2|Z) = \frac{1}{n-q} E^\theta(u' M_Z u|Z)$$

$$= \frac{1}{n-q} E^\theta(tr(u' M_Z u)|Z)$$

$$= \frac{1}{n-q} tr\left[M_Z E^\theta(uu'|Z)\right]$$

$$= \frac{\sigma^2}{n-q} tr\, M_Z,$$

hence

$$E^\theta\left(\widehat{\sigma}_n^2|Z\right) = \sigma^2,$$

Here we used the properties of the trace: if a is a scalar, then $tr(a) = a$; if A and B are two matrices of appropriate dimensions, then $tr(AB) = tr(BA)$; furthermore,

$$tr(M_Z) = tr(I_n) - tr(Z(Z'Z)^{-1}Z')$$

$$= n - tr((Z'Z)^{-1}Z'Z)$$

$$= n - q.$$

It can also be shown that

$$Var^\theta \left(\widehat{\sigma}_n^2 | Z \right) = \frac{2\sigma^4}{n-q}.$$

Now, we can note that the maximum likelihood estimator $\widetilde{\sigma}_n^2$ of σ^2 given (8.13) is biased (nonetheless, it is consistent).

In the following example we are interested in estimating a part of the vector β. This example is inspired by the idea by Frisch and Waugh in 1933 who noted that the regression with a detrended variable is the same as introducing the trend (i.e., time) as an additional variable in the basic regression.

Example 8.2   *Consider the regression model*

$$y = Z\beta + u$$
$$= Z^{(1)}\beta^{(1)} + Z^{(2)}\beta^{(2)} + u$$

where $Z = [Z^{(1)}, Z^{(2)}]$ and $\beta = \binom{\beta^{(1)}}{\beta^{(2)}}$ are partitioned in a matching fashion. The OLS estimator of $\beta^{(2)}$ follows from the estimator $\widehat{\beta}_n$ of β,

$$\widehat{\beta}_n = \begin{pmatrix} \widehat{\beta^{(1)}}_n \\ \widehat{\beta^{(2)}}_n \end{pmatrix} = (Z'Z)^{-1} Z'y = \begin{pmatrix} Z^{(1)\prime}Z^{(1)} & Z^{(1)\prime}Z^{(2)} \\ Z^{(2)\prime}Z^{(1)} & Z^{(2)\prime}Z^{(2)} \end{pmatrix}^{-1} \begin{pmatrix} Z^{(1)\prime}y \\ Z^{(2)\prime}y \end{pmatrix}$$

by using the inverse formula of partitioned matrices

$$\widehat{\beta^{(2)}}_n = \left(Z^{(2)\prime}M_1 Z^{(2)} \right)^{-1} Z^{(2)\prime}M_1 y$$

with $M_1 = I - Z^{(1)} \left(Z^{(1)\prime}Z^{(1)} \right)^{-1} Z^{(1)\prime}$. M_1 is the matrix of the projection on the hyperplane that is orthogonal to the one spanned by the columns of $Z^{(1)}$. A different way of obtaining $\widehat{\beta^{(2)}}_n$ consists in the following three stage procedure: in the first stage regress y on $Z^{(1)}$ in order to obtain the residuals $M_1 y$; in the second stage regress each column of $Z^{(2)}$ on $Z^{(1)}$ to obtain the matrix $M_1 Z^{(2)}$ whose columns are the residuals of each regression; the last stage is the regression of $M_1 y$ on $M_1 Z^{(2)}$, which corresponds to the model

$$M_1 y = M_1 Z^{(2)}\beta^{(2)*} + u^*.$$

The OLS estimator of $\beta^{(2)*}$ is given by

$$\widehat{\beta^{(2)*}} = \left(Z^{(2)\prime}M_1' M_1 Z^{(2)} \right)^{-1} Z^{(2)\prime}M_1' M_1 y$$
$$= \left(Z^{(2)\prime}M_1 Z^{(2)} \right)^{-1} Z^{(2)\prime}M_1 y = \widehat{\beta^{(2)}}_n$$

since M_1 is an idempotent matrix.   □

8.2.4 Finite Sample Distribution Under the Normality Assumption

Under Assumptions A1, A2, A3, and A4, we immediately obtain

$$\widehat{\beta}_n | Z \sim N(\beta, \sigma^2 (Z'Z)^{-1}), \tag{8.14}$$

since $\widehat{\beta}_n$ is linear in y. This implies that for all $i = 1, \ldots, q$

$$\widehat{\beta}_{in} | Z \sim N\left(\beta_i, \sigma^2 (Z'Z)_{ii}^{-1}\right),$$

(where $(Z'Z)_{ii}^{-1}$ is the element in the ith row and ith column of $(Z'Z)^{-1}$) and

$$\frac{\widehat{\beta}_{in} - \beta_i}{\sigma \sqrt{(Z'Z)_{ii}^{-1}}} | Z \sim N(0, 1). \tag{8.15}$$

Furthermore, we can derive the following equality from the expression for $\widehat{\sigma}_n^2$

$$(n - q) \frac{\widehat{\sigma}_n^2}{\sigma^2} = \left(\frac{u}{\sigma}\right)' M_Z \left(\frac{u}{\sigma}\right). \tag{8.16}$$

Since this quantity is an idempotent quadratic form of a vector $\frac{u}{\sigma}$ that follows a standard normal distribution, it is distributed according to a χ^2 with $rank(M_Z) = tr(M_Z) = n - q$ degrees of freedom (recall that the rank of an idempotent matrix is equal to its trace). Additionally, it is independent of (8.15). To show this, write

$$\frac{\widehat{\beta}_n - \beta}{\sigma} = (Z'Z)^{-1} Z' \left(\frac{u}{\sigma}\right). \tag{8.17}$$

Thus, this leads to verifying the independence of the expressions given in (8.17) and in (8.16). We know that a sufficient condition for the independence between a linear transformation Ax and an idempotent quadratic form $x'Bx$ where x is $N(0, I)$ is that $AB = 0$. Consequently, it suffices to show that

$$(Z'Z)^{-1} Z' M_Z = 0,$$

which is immediate since $Z' M_Z = 0$.

In addition, it is well known that if x is distributed $N(0, 1)$ and z follows a χ_m^2 distribution and is independent of x, then the ratio $x / \sqrt{z/m}$ follows a (Student) t-distribution with m degrees of freedom. Thus, the variable τ_n, defined as the ratio of the independent expressions of (8.15) and (8.16), i.e.,

$$\tau_n = \frac{\widehat{\beta}_{in} - \beta_i}{\widehat{\sigma}_n \sqrt{(Z'Z)_{ii}^{-1}}},$$

follows a t-distribution with $n - q$ degrees of freedom (denoted t_{n-q}).

These results are summarized in the following theorem.

Theorem 8.2   *Under Assumptions A1, A2, A3, and A4, the OLS estimators of β and σ^2 have the following properties:*
  (i)

$$\widehat{\beta}_n | Z \sim N(\beta, \sigma^2 (Z'Z)^{-1}),$$

  (ii)

$$(n - q) \frac{\widehat{\sigma}_n^2}{\sigma^2} | Z \sim (n - q) \frac{\widehat{\sigma}_n^2}{\sigma^2} \sim \chi_{n-q}^2,$$

  (iii)

$$\widehat{\beta}_n \quad and \quad (n - q) \frac{\widehat{\sigma}_n^2}{\sigma^2}$$

are mutually independent conditionally on Z,
  (iv)

$$\frac{\widehat{\beta}_{in} - \beta_i}{\widehat{\sigma}_n \sqrt{(Z'Z)_{ii}^{-1}}} | Z \sim t_{n-q}.$$ ∎

These statistics can be used to test hypotheses about the parameters of the regression model.

Example 8.3   *Let us consider a simple example of the regression model with $q = 2$ and $z_i = (1, z_{i2})'$*

$$y_i | z_i \sim N(\beta_1 + \beta_2 z_{i2}, \sigma^2)$$

for $i = 1, \dots, n$. For testing the null hypothesis $H_0 : \beta_2 = \beta_2^0$ against the alternative hypothesis $H_1 : \beta_2 \neq \beta_2^0$, where β_2^0 is fixed, the obvious choice of the test statistic is

$$\tau_n = \frac{\widehat{\beta}_{2n} - \beta_2^0}{\sqrt{\widehat{Var}(\widehat{\beta}_{2n})}},$$

by setting

$$\widehat{Var}(\widehat{\beta}_{2n}) = \widehat{\sigma}_n^2 \frac{1}{\sum\limits_{i=1}^{n}(z_{i2} - \overline{z})^2}.$$

Under H_0, τ_n is distributed according to the t-distribution with $n - 2$ degrees of freedom. The test procedure of size α consists in rejecting H_0 if and only if

$$|\tau_n| > t_{1-\alpha/2}(n - 2)$$

(this is equivalent to finding a $(1 - \alpha)$ confidence interval for β_2 and rejecting H_0 if and only if this interval does not contain β_2^0).

The hypothesis that is very often tested in empirical applications is the hypothesis that a parameter is zero, for example $H_0 : \beta_2 = 0$. In this case, we use the ratio

$$\tau_n = \frac{\widehat{\beta}_{2n}}{\sqrt{\widehat{Var}(\widehat{\beta}_{2n})}},$$

which is called the t-ratio or t-statistic. □

Sometimes, we have some prior information about the model before we observe the sample. Suppose that this information can be expressed as linear restrictions of the form

$$R\beta = r \tag{8.18}$$

where r is a $J \times 1$ vector and R is a $J \times q$ matrix with rank $J \leq q$, where both r and R are known. The OLS estimation consists in minimizing

$$\sum_{i=1}^{n} (y_i - z_i'\lambda)^2 = (y - Z\lambda)'(y - Z\lambda)$$

with respect to λ under the restriction $R\lambda - r = 0$. The Lagrangian is

$$S = (y - Z\lambda)'(y - Z\lambda) + 2(r' - \lambda'R')\mu$$

where μ is the $J \times 1$ vector of Lagrange multipliers. The solution of the system of equations given by the first order conditions leads to the restricted OLS estimator of β which we denote by $\widehat{\beta}_n^*$

$$\left.\begin{array}{l} \frac{\partial S}{\partial \lambda} = 0 \\ \frac{\partial S}{\partial \mu} = 0 \end{array}\right\} \iff \left\{\begin{array}{l} Z'Z\widehat{\beta}_n^* = Z'y - R'\mu \\ R\widehat{\beta}_n^* = r. \end{array}\right. \tag{8.19}$$

Knowing that the OLS estimator $\widehat{\beta}_n$ of β satisfies $Z'Z\widehat{\beta}_n = Z'y$, we replace $Z'y$ by $Z'Z\widehat{\beta}_n$ in the first equation of the system (8.19) :

$$\widehat{\beta}_n^* = \widehat{\beta}_n - (Z'Z)^{-1}R'\mu. \tag{8.20}$$

Premultipling this last equality by R yields

$$R\widehat{\beta}_n^* = r = R\widehat{\beta}_n - R(Z'Z)^{-1}R'\mu,$$

hence,

$$\mu = \left[R(Z'Z)^{-1}R'\right]^{-1}(R\widehat{\beta}_n - r).$$

since $R(Z'Z)^{-1}R'$ is a positive definite matrix of rank J and therefore invertible.

Next, substitute this expression for μ in (8.20) in order to obtain the expression for $\widehat{\beta}_n^*$

$$\widehat{\beta}_n^* = \widehat{\beta}_n + (Z'Z)^{-1}R'\left[R(Z'Z)^{-1}R'\right]^{-1}(r - R\widehat{\beta}_n). \qquad (8.21)$$

Note that, if $\widehat{\beta}_n$ satisfies the restriction $R\beta = 0$, then $\widehat{\beta}_n^* = \widehat{\beta}_n$.

Example 8.4 *An example of a standard model with a linear restriction is that of the Cobb-Douglas function under the assumption of constant returns to scale*

$$\ln Y_i = \beta_1 + \beta_2 \ln K_i + \beta_3 \ln L_i + u_i \qquad i = 1, \dots, n$$

with $\beta_2 + \beta_3 = 1$ or $R\beta = r$ with $R = (0, 1, 1)$ and $r = 0$. We must mention that in simple cases such as this one, it is more convenient to transform it into a regression model without constraints. Thus by setting $\beta_3 = 1 - \beta_2$, we regain the unrestricted model

$$\ln \frac{Y_i}{L_i} = \beta_1 + \beta_2 \ln \frac{K_i}{L_i} + u_i \qquad i = 1, \dots, n. \qquad \square$$

Knowing the moments of $\widehat{\beta}_n$, we can derive those of $\widehat{\beta}_n^*$. First of all, $\widehat{\beta}_n^*$ is an unbiased estimator of β. Indeed, from (8.21) it follows

$$E^\theta(\widehat{\beta}_n^*|Z) = \beta + (Z'Z)^{-1}R'\left[R(Z'Z)^{-1}R'\right]^{-1}(r - R\beta) = \beta$$

since the constraint is supposed to be satisfied. Furthermore, from (8.21) we can extract a different expression for $\widehat{\beta}_n^*$

$$\widehat{\beta}_n^* = M^*\widehat{\beta}_n + (Z'Z)^{-1}R'\left[R(Z'Z)^{-1}R'\right]^{-1}r$$

with

$$M^* = I - (Z'Z)^{-1}R'\left[R(Z'Z)^{-1}R'\right]^{-1}R.$$

Hence

$$Var^\theta(\widehat{\beta}_n^*|Z) = \sigma^2 M^*(Z'Z)^{-1}M^{*'}.$$

Additionally, under the normality assumption, since $\widehat{\beta}_n$ is normally distributed by Theorem 8.2, $\widehat{\beta}_n^*$ is also normally distributed, i.e.,

$$\widehat{\beta}_n^*|Z \sim N(\beta, \sigma^2 M^*(Z'Z)^{-1}M^{*'}).$$

We leave it to the reader to show that $\widehat{\beta}_n^*$ is the best linear unbiased estimator of β.

Now suppose that before estimating the restricted model, we want to test the assumption

$$H_0 : R\beta = r \text{ against } H_1 : R\beta \neq r,$$

with R and r known. Two cases are possible.

– if $J = 1$ (there is only one linear combination), then

$$\tau_n = \frac{R\widehat{\beta}_n - r}{\widehat{\sigma}_n \left[R(Z'Z)^{-1}R' \right]^{1/2}} \sim t_{n-q} \tag{8.22}$$

under H_0 since

$$Var^\theta(R\widehat{\beta}_n) = \sigma^2 R(Z'Z)^{-1}R'.$$

Thus, the null hypothesis is rejected if the value of this test statistic is greater than a critical value corresponding to the given significance level.

– if $J \geq 2$, then we know according to Theorem 8.2 that under Assumptions A1, A2, A3, and A4 the OLS estimator $\widehat{\beta}_n$ satisfies

$$\widehat{\beta}_n | Z \sim N(\beta, \sigma^2(Z'Z)^{-1}).$$

From this, we infer that

$$R\widehat{\beta}_n | Z \sim N(R\beta, \sigma^2 R(Z'Z)^{-1}R')$$

or

$$R(\widehat{\beta}_n - \beta) | Z \sim N(0, \sigma^2 R(Z'Z)^{-1}R').$$

Hence,

$$\frac{(\widehat{\beta}_n - \beta)'R' \left[R(Z'Z)^{-1}R' \right]^{-1} R(\widehat{\beta}_n - \beta)}{\sigma^2} \sim \chi_J^2 \tag{8.23}$$

(indeed, if the vector X has distribution $N(\mu, \Sigma)$ then $(X - \mu)'\Sigma^{-1}(X - \mu)$ is χ_m^2 distributed where m is the dimension of X).

Additionally, Theorem 8.2 implies

$$(n - q)\frac{\widehat{\sigma}_n^2}{\sigma^2} \sim \chi_{n-q}^2. \tag{8.24}$$

The expressions in (8.23) and in (8.24) are independent since $\widehat{\beta}_n$ and $\widehat{\sigma}_n^2$ are so (see Theorem 8.2), the ratio of these two expressions divided by their respective degrees of freedom follows a (Fisher) F-distribution

$$\frac{(\widehat{\beta}_n - \beta)'R' \left[R(Z'Z)^{-1}R' \right]^{-1} R(\widehat{\beta}_n - \beta)}{J\widehat{\sigma}_n^2} \sim F(J, n - q);$$

hence, we conclude that under the null hypothesis

$$F_c = \frac{(R\widehat{\beta}_n - r)' \left[R(Z'Z)^{-1}R' \right]^{-1} (R\widehat{\beta}_n - r)}{J\widehat{\sigma}_n^2} \sim F(J, n - q). \tag{8.25}$$

Therefore, we reject the null hypotheses when this statistic is greater than a critical value for a given significance level which is taken from the table of the F-distribution with J and $n - q$ degrees of freedom.

Note that for $J = 1$, this statistic is obviously equal to

$$\frac{(R\hat{\beta}_n - r)^2}{\hat{\sigma}_n^2 \left[R(Z'Z)^{-1}R' \right]^{-1}}$$

which is just the square of the expression given in (8.22) (because indeed $F(1, n - q) = t_{n-q}^2$).

Example 8.5   *Let us briefly look at the likelihood ratio testing procedure under the normality assumption. The test statistic that can be derived from this procedure is*

$$\gamma_R = \frac{\max l_n(y|Z, \beta, \sigma)}{\max l_n(y|Z, R\beta = r, \sigma)}.$$

It can be shown that this ratio is just the ratio of the expressions that appear in (8.23) and (8.24), and thus

$$\gamma_R = F_c.$$ □

8.2.5   Analysis of Variance

If we define SST as the total sum of squares, SSR as the residual sum of squares, and SSE as the explained sum of squares in the following way

$$\begin{cases} SST = \sum_{i=1}^n (y_i - \bar{y})^2 = y'y - n\bar{y}^2 \\ SSR = \hat{u}'\hat{u} = \sum_{i=1}^n \hat{u}_i^2 \\ SSE = \sum_{i=1}^n (\hat{y}_i - \bar{y})^2 = \hat{\beta}_n' Z'y - n\bar{y}^2 = \hat{\beta}_n' Z'\hat{y} - n\bar{y}^2, \end{cases}$$

then the following equality holds

$$SST = SSR + SSE.$$

This is easily proven:

$$y'y = (y - \hat{y} + \hat{y})'(y - \hat{y} + \hat{y})$$
$$= (\hat{u} + \hat{y})'(\hat{u} + \hat{y})$$
$$= \hat{u}'\hat{u} + \hat{y}'\hat{y} + 2\hat{y}'\hat{u}.$$

Now note that the product $\hat{y}'\hat{u}$ is zero according to the first order condition of the minimization (8.7), i.e.,

$$\hat{y}'\hat{u} = \hat{\beta}_n' Z'\hat{u} = \hat{\beta}_n' Z'(y - Z\hat{\beta}_n) = 0.$$

Hence,

$$y'y - n\bar{y}^2 = \hat{u}'\hat{u} + \hat{\bar{y}}'\hat{y} - n\bar{y}^2.$$

Then, we can define the coefficient of determination or the square of the multiple correlation coefficient as

$$R^2 = \frac{SSE}{SST} = 1 - \frac{SSR}{SST} = \frac{\sum_{i=1}^{n}(\hat{y}_i - \bar{y})^2}{\sum_{i=1}^{n}(y_i - \bar{y})^2} = 1 - \frac{\sum_{i=1}^{n}\hat{u}_i^2}{\sum_{i=1}^{n}(y_i - \bar{y})^2}.$$

It measures the part of the variance that is explained by the model and is between 0 and 1, under the assumption that the matrix Z contains a column of 1's. For this and other reasons not listed here, we always assume that this requirement is satisfied. One of the drawbacks of R^2 is that any addition of some explanatory variable increases this coefficient. Therefore, we introduce the adjusted R^2, denoted by R_A^2 or $\bar{R}^2$, which takes the number of parameters into account

$$R_A^2 = 1 - \frac{n-1}{n-q}(1 - R^2) = 1 - \frac{\hat{\sigma}_n^2}{\frac{1}{n-1}\sum_{i=1}^{n}(y_i - \bar{y})^2}.$$

Note that $R_A^2 \leq R^2$.

This leads to the table of the analysis of variance which summarizes the principal quantities that we just defined (Table 1).

Table 1: *Analysis of Variance*

	Source	Degrees of Freedom	Mean Square
Regression	$SSE = R^2 SST$	$q - 1$	$SSE/(q - 1)$
Residual	$SSR = (1 - R^2)SST$	$n - q$	$SSR/(n - q)$
Total	SST	$n - 1$	$SST/(n - 1)$

We propose now to test the hypothesis that all coefficients except the one of the constant are zero, i.e., $H_0 : \beta_2 = \cdots = \beta_q = 0$, against the alternative hypothesis that at least one of those is different from zero. The test statistic, denoted F_R, is defined as the ratio of $SSE/(q - 1)$. and $SSR/(n - q)$, which follow χ^2 distributions with $n - 1$ and $n - q$ degrees of freedom respectively. These terms are independent since they contain terms in $\hat{\beta}_n$ and in $\hat{\sigma}_n^2$ which are independent by Theorem 8.2. Therefore,

$$F_R = \frac{SSE/(q - 1)}{SSR/(n - q)} = \frac{R^2/(q - 1)}{(1 - R^2)/|(n - q)} \qquad (8.26)$$

follows an F-distribution $F(q - 1, n - q)$ under H_0. Thus, if F_R is large then the null hypothesis is rejected.

This expression could have been obtained by starting with the test statistic F_c given by (8.25). Indeed, H_0 can be written as $H_0 : R\beta = r$ with R a $(q - 1) \times q$ matrix and r a $(q - 1) \times 1$ vector given by

$$R = \begin{bmatrix} 0_{(q-1)\times 1} & I_{q-1} \end{bmatrix} \text{ and } r = 0_{(q-1)\times 1}.$$

Thus, we have in this case $J = q - 1$. Let us first consider the vector $\widehat{u}^*$ defined by

$$\widehat{u}^* = y - Z\widehat{\beta}_n^*$$

where $\widehat{\beta}_n^*$ is the estimator of the restricted regression model. We can write

$$\widehat{u}^* = y - Z\widehat{\beta}_n - Z(\widehat{\beta}_n^* - \widehat{\beta}_n)$$
$$= \widehat{u} - Z(\widehat{\beta}_n^* - \widehat{\beta}_n)$$

hence,

$$\widehat{u}^{*\prime}\widehat{u}^* = \widehat{u}'\widehat{u} + (\widehat{\beta}_n^* - \widehat{\beta}_n)' Z' Z(\widehat{\beta}_n^* - \widehat{\beta}_n),$$

the other terms disappear since $Z'\widehat{u} = 0$. Thus,

$$\widehat{u}^{*\prime}\widehat{u}^* - \widehat{u}'\widehat{u} = (\widehat{\beta}_n^* - \widehat{\beta}_n)' Z' Z(\widehat{\beta}_n^* - \widehat{\beta}_n)$$
$$= (R\widehat{\beta}_n - r)' \left[R(Z'Z)^{-1} R' \right]^{-1} (R\widehat{\beta}_n - r)$$

by replacing $(\widehat{\beta}_n^* - \widehat{\beta}_n)$ by the expression given by (8.21). According to (8.25), F_c takes the form

$$F_c = \frac{(\widehat{u}^{*\prime}\widehat{u}^* - \widehat{u}'\widehat{u})/(q - 1)}{\widehat{u}'\widehat{u}/(n - q)}.$$

Dividing numerator and denominator by $\sum_{i=1}^{n} (y_i - \overline{y})^2$ yields

$$F_c = \frac{\left(\dfrac{\widehat{u}^{*\prime}\widehat{u}^*}{\sum_{i=1}^{n}(y_i - \overline{y})^2} - (1 - R^2) \right) /(q - 1)}{(1 - R^2)/(n - q)}.$$

Furthermore, $\widehat{u}^*$ is the residual of the restricted model, i.e. $y_i = \beta_1 + u_i^*$. The OLS estimator of β_1 is $\widehat{\beta}_{1n}^* = \overline{y}$, hence

$$\widehat{u}^{*\prime}\widehat{u}^* = \sum_{i=1}^{n} (y_i - \overline{y})^2.$$

Hence, we recover the expression given in (8.26) for F_c.

8.2.6 Prediction

Consider the linear model under Assumptions A1, A2, A3, and A4. The problem consists in predicting the endogenous variable beyond the observation period. Suppose that z_{n+l} are observable for $l \geq 1$ and that

$$E^\theta(y_{n+l}|z_{n+l}) = \beta'z,$$

then

$$y_{n+l} = \beta'z_{n+l} + u_{n+l}$$

with

$$E^\theta(u_{n+l}|z_{n+l}) = 0$$

by construction. The unobservable variable y_{n+l} ($l \geq 1$) can be predicted by

$$\widehat{y}_{n+l} = \widehat{\beta}'_n z_{n+l} \qquad l = 1, 2, \ldots$$

The forecast error is defined by

$$\widehat{u}_{n+l} = y_{n+l} - \widehat{y}_{n+l} \qquad l = 1, 2, \ldots$$

and can also be written as

$$\widehat{u}_{n+l} = \beta'z_{n+l} + u_{n+l} - \widehat{\beta}'_n z_{n+l} = \left(\beta - \widehat{\beta}_n\right)' z_{n+l} + u_{n+l} \qquad l = 1, 2, \ldots$$

We can show that $\widehat{y}_{n+l}$ is an unbiased prediction for y_{n+l} since

$$E^\theta(y_{n+l} - \widehat{y}_{n+l}|Z^{(l)}) = E^\theta((\beta - \widehat{\beta}_n)'z_{n+l}|Z^{(l)}) + E^\theta(u_{n+l}|Z^{(l)})$$
$$= 0$$

where $Z^{(l)} = \{Z, z_{n+l}\}$. Thus,

$$E^\theta(\widehat{u}_{n+l}|Z^{(l)}) = 0.$$

Additionally, the conditional variance of $\widehat{u}_{n+l}$ is

$$Var^\theta(\widehat{u}_{n+l}|Z^{(l)}) = Var^\theta((\beta - \widehat{\beta}_n)'z_{n+l} + u_{n+l}|Z^{(l)})$$
$$= \sigma^2\left[1 + z'_{n+l}(Z'Z)^{-1}z_{n+l}\right].$$

Because $\widehat{u}_{n+l}$ is a linear function of normally distributed random variables, we have

$$\widehat{u}_{n+l}|Z^{(l)} \sim N(0, \sigma^2\left[1 + z'_{n+l}(Z'Z)^{-1}z_{n+l}\right]) \tag{8.27}$$

for $l \geq 1$. It is possible to show that $\widehat{y}_{n+l}$ is an optimal predictor in the sense that $\widehat{u}_{n+l}$ has the smallest variance among all unbiased linear predictors.

In order to construct a confidence interval for $\widehat{y}_{n+l}$, we use (8.27)

$$\frac{y_{n+l} - \widehat{y}_{n+l}}{\sigma\sqrt{1 + z'_{n+l}(Z'Z)^{-1}z_{n+l}}} \sim N(0, 1)$$

and the fact that

$$(n - q)\frac{\widehat{\sigma}_n^2}{\sigma^2} \sim \chi_{n-q}^2$$

according to Theorem 8.2. These two expressions are independent and their ratio follows a Student t-distribution

$$\frac{y_{n+l} - \widehat{y}_{n+l}}{\widehat{\sigma}_n\sqrt{1 + z'_{n+l}(Z'Z)^{-1}z_{n+l}}} \sim t_{n-q}$$

which can be used to construct the confidence intervals.

Remark. Suppose the regression model is estimated with cross-sectional data (for example of households or of firms), and suppose that we want to predict the impact of a change in the explanatory variables on the explained variable for the units of observations that we consider. In this case, we prefer to use the following predictor

$$\tilde{y}_i = \hat{\beta}'_n \tilde{z}_i + \hat{u}_i$$

where $\tilde{z}_i$ are the new values of the explanatory variables. This result, in which we use the estimated residuals for individual i, seems to contradict the conclusion of the previous analysis that the best predictor is $\hat{\beta}'_n \tilde{z}_i$. Indeed, this approach is justified if we consider the residual as partly determined by unobserved explanatory variables, which remain unchanged when z_i is replaced by $\tilde{z}_i$. In this case, the best predictor of u_i is not zero but $\hat{u}_i$. □

8.2.7 Asymptotic Properties

We study the asymptotic properties of the OLS estimator under Assumptions A1, A2, and A3. Thus, we do not assume normality. We showed that the estimator $\widehat{\beta}_n$ can be considered as a particular moment estimator, and thus we can use the set of results of Chapter 3. We will follow this approach in the nonlinear case in the next section. In the linear case, we can study the asymptotic properties directly.

Recall that we assumed the x_i to be i.i.d. and its components to be square integrable. We thus have

$$\frac{1}{n}\sum_{i=1}^{n} z_i z'_i \to E^\theta(z_i z'_i) \quad P^\theta - a.s.$$

and

$$\frac{1}{n}\sum_{i=1}^{n} z_i y_i \rightarrow E^\theta(z_i y_i) \quad P^\theta - a.s.$$

by the law of large numbers. Hence,

$$\widehat{\beta}_n = \left(\frac{1}{n}\sum_{i=1}^{n} z_i z_i'\right)^{-1} \left(\frac{1}{n}\sum_{i=1}^{n} z_i y_i\right) \rightarrow \beta = \left(E^\theta(z_i z_i')\right)^{-1} E^\theta(z_i y_i) \quad P^\theta - a.s.$$

The last result depends on two assumptions. On one hand, the invertibility of $\frac{1}{n}\sum_{i=1}^{n} z_i z_i'$ (or of $Z'Z$), which is an identification assumption in finite samples and guarantees the existence of a unique estimator for a given sample size. This invertibility requires Assumption A2, i.e.,

$$Rank(Z) = q.$$

On the other hand, the invertibility of $E^\theta(z_i z_i')$, which guarantees asymptotic uniqueness and which is the identification condition for the problem in the limit.

Note moreover that the invertibility of $E^\theta(z_i z_i')$ implies the invertibility of $\frac{1}{n}\sum_{i=1}^{n} z_i z_i'$ for n sufficiently large (the converse is obviously false). The equality

$$\beta = \left(E^\theta(z_i z_i')\right)^{-1} E^\theta(z_i y_i)$$

is studied extensively in Chapter 7.

To show asymptotic normality, we start with the equality

$$\sqrt{n}(\widehat{\beta}_n - \beta) = \sqrt{n} \left(\frac{1}{n}\sum_{i=1}^{n} z_i z_i'\right)^{-1} \left(\frac{1}{n}\sum_{i=1}^{n} z_i u_i\right).$$

We saw that

$$\frac{1}{n}\sum_{i=1}^{n} z_i z_i' \rightarrow E^\theta(z_i z_i'),$$

moreover, using the central limit theorem, we can verify that

$$\sqrt{n} \left(\frac{1}{n}\sum_{i=1}^{n} z_i u_i\right) \rightarrow N\left(0, Var^\theta(z_i u_i)\right) \text{ in } P^\theta\text{-distribution,}$$

where the vector $z_i u_i$ is centered. Thus, we conclude that

$$\sqrt{n}\left(\widehat{\beta}_n - \beta\right) \rightarrow N\left(0, \left[E^\theta(z_i z_i')\right]^{-1} Var^\theta(z_i u_i)\left[E^\theta(z_i z_i')\right]^{-1}\right) \text{ in } P^\theta\text{-distribution.}$$

Now note that

$$Var^\theta(z_i u_i) = E^\theta\left(Var^\theta(z_i u_i | z_i)\right) + Var^\theta\left(E^\theta(z_i u_i | z_i)\right).$$

Moreover, under Assumption A1 and according to (8.3), we have $E^\theta(u_i z_i | z_i) = 0$, hence

$$Var^\theta(z_i u_i) = E^\theta\left(Var^\theta(z_i u_i | z_i)\right) = E^\theta\left(z_i Var^\theta(u_i | z_i) z_i'\right) = \sigma^2 E^\theta(z_i z_i'),$$

since, according to Assumption A3, we have $Var^\theta(u_i | z_i) = \sigma^2$ for all i. Therefore, we obtain

$$\sqrt{n}(\widehat{\beta}_n - \beta) \to N(0, \sigma^2 \left[E^\theta(z_i z_i')\right]^{-1}) \text{ in } P^\theta\text{-distribution.} \qquad (8.28)$$

The theoretical moments $E^\theta(z_i z_i')$ are consistently estimated by the empirical moments $\frac{1}{n}\sum_{i=1}^n z_i z_i' = Z'Z/n$. Similarly, σ^2 is consistently estimated by $\widehat{\sigma}_n^2$, i.e.,

$$\widehat{\sigma}_n^2 \to \sigma^2 \ P^\theta\text{-a.s.}$$

A natural estimator of $\Sigma_\theta = \sigma^2 \left[E^\theta(z_i z_i')\right]^{-1}$, denoted $\widehat{\Sigma}_n$, is then

$$\widehat{\Sigma}_n = \widehat{\sigma}_n^2 \left[\frac{1}{n}\sum_{i=1}^n z_i z_i'\right]^{-1} = \widehat{\sigma}_n^2 \left[\frac{Z'Z}{n}\right]^{-1}.$$

Hence,

$$\sqrt{n}\widehat{\Sigma}_n^{-1/2}(\widehat{\beta}_n - \beta) \to N(0, I_q).$$

Intuitively, $\widehat{\beta}_n$ follows approximately a normal distribution with mean β and variance $\widehat{\sigma}_n^2(Z'Z)^{-1}$. Thus, we find the same distribution as in the finite sample under the normality Assumption A4 (Theorem 8.2).

According to Theorem 3.2 in Chapter 3, this result extends to all continuous functions of β: if we have (8.28) and if g is a continuously differentiable function from $\mathbb{R}^q$ to $\mathbb{R}^J$, then

$$\sqrt{n}(g(\widehat{\beta}_n) - g(\beta)) \to N\left(0, \left(\frac{\partial g(\beta)}{\partial \beta'}\right) \Sigma_\theta \left(\frac{\partial g(\beta)'}{\partial \beta}\right)'\right) \text{ in } P^\theta\text{-distribution.}$$

The following example illustrates this.

Example 8.6   *Consider a log-linear model*

$$Y_i = A Z_i^{\beta_2} e^{u_i} \qquad i = 1, \dots, n.$$

Linearize the model

$$\ln Y_i = \ln A + \beta_2 \ln Z_i + u_i$$

where

$$y_i = \beta_1 + \beta_2 z_i + u_i$$

with $y_i = \ln Y_i$, $\beta_1 = \ln A$, and $z_i = \ln Z_i$. The OLS estimation yields in particular the estimator $\widehat{\beta}_{1n}$ of β_1. This estimator is consistent and

$$\widehat{\beta}_{1n} \to N\left(\beta_1, \sigma^2 \frac{\sum_{i=1}^{n} z_i^2}{\sum_{i=1}^{n}(z_i - \overline{z})^2}\right) \quad \text{in } P^{\theta}\text{-distribution}$$

or

$$\widehat{\beta}_{1n} \to N\left(\beta_1, \sigma^2\left[\frac{1}{n} + \frac{\overline{z}^2}{\sum_{i=1}^{n}(z_i - \overline{z})^2}\right]\right) \quad \text{in } P^{\theta}\text{-distribution.}$$

Let $\widehat{A}_n$ be the estimator of A, given by $\widehat{A}_n = e^{\widehat{\beta}_{1n}}$. g is in this case the exponential function. Then, $\widehat{A}_n = g(\widehat{\beta}_{1n})$ is a consistent estimator of $A = g(\beta_1)$ and its asymptotic distribution is given by

$$\widehat{A}_n \to N\left(A, \sigma^2 e^{2\beta_1}\left[\frac{1}{n} + \frac{\overline{z}^2}{\sum_{i=1}^{n}(z_i - \overline{z})^2}\right]\right) \quad \text{in } P^{\theta} - \text{distribution.}$$

However, note that in small samples and under the assumption that the $\ln Y_i$ are normally distributed, the distribution of $\widehat{A}_n$ is not the normal but the log-normal. $\square$

Next, we relate the asymptotic tests to Chapter 4.

In order to test the null hypothesis $H_0 : \beta_i = 0$ against the alternative hypotheses $H : \beta_i \neq 0$, it is sufficient to use the test statistic

$$\tau_n = \frac{\widehat{\beta}_{in}}{\widehat{\sigma}_n \sqrt{(Z'Z)_{ii}^{-1}}}.$$

This follows a $N(0, 1)$ distribution under H_0. Here, $(Z'Z)_{ii}^{-1}$ is the element in the ith line and ith column of $(Z'Z)^{-1}$.

Example 8.7 *We return to the case in which we consider the MLE as a moment estimator. According to Example 3.20 in Chapter 3, the MLE of β, denoted by $\widehat{\beta}_n$, satisfies the following result, since it is equal to the OLS estimator*

$$\sqrt{n}(\widehat{\beta}_n - \beta) \to N(0, J_{\theta}^{-1}) \text{ in } P^{\theta}\text{-distribution}$$

where J_θ is the Fisher information matrix

$$J_\theta = -E^\theta \left[\frac{\partial^2 \ln f(y_i|z_i, \beta, \sigma)}{\partial \beta \partial \beta'} \right]$$

$$= E^\theta(z_i z_i');$$

and we evidently obtain the asymptotic distribution as in (8.28). If the conditional distribution of $y_i|z_i$ is normal, then this result is of little interest, since we showed normality in a finite sample. However, this result remains correct even if the likelihood function is not normal, we are then in a case of consistent pseudo-maximum likelihood. $\square$

Consider next the test of a set of J linear restrictions represented by the hypothesis $H_0 : R\beta = r$ in the notation of (8.18). We test this hypothesis using the Wald procedure linking the results to Section 4.3. in Chapter 4. Let

$$R^*(\beta) = R\beta - r$$

and consider the null hypothesis $H_0 : R^*(\beta) = 0$. Because the OLS estimator $\widehat{\beta}_n$ follows asymptotically a normal distribution given by (8.28), it follows that

$$\sqrt{n}\left(R^*(\widehat{\beta}_n) - R^*(\beta)\right) \to N(0, \Omega_\theta)$$

with

$$\Omega_\theta = \frac{\partial R^*(\beta)}{\partial \beta'} \sigma^2 \left[E^\theta(z_i z_i') \right]^{-1} \frac{\partial R^*(\beta)'}{\partial \beta}$$

$$= \sigma^2 R \left[E^\theta(z_i z_i') \right]^{-1} R'.$$

Under the null hypothesis, we have

$$\frac{n R^*(\widehat{\beta}_n)' \left[R \left(E^\theta(z_i z_i') \right)^{-1} R' \right]^{-1} R^*(\widehat{\beta}_n)}{\sigma^2} \to \chi_J^2.$$

A consistent estimator $\widehat{\Omega}_n$ of Ω_θ is given by

$$\widehat{\Omega}_n = \widehat{\sigma}_n^2 R \left(\frac{Z'Z}{n} \right)^{-1} R'.$$

This implies that

$$\frac{n R^*(\widehat{\beta}_n)' \left[R \left(\frac{Z'Z}{n} \right)^{-1} R' \right]^{-1} R^*(\widehat{\beta}_n)}{\widehat{\sigma}_n^2} \to \chi_J^2$$

under H_0, or equivalently

$$\frac{(R\widehat{\beta}_n - r)' \left[R(Z'Z)^{-1}R'\right]^{-1}(R\widehat{\beta}_n - r)}{\widehat{\sigma}_n^2} \to \chi_J^2 \qquad (8.29)$$

which is the large sample equivalent to the small sample statistic (8.25) which followed a F−distribution. Thus, the F distribution provides a better approximation in small samples but only under normality of y_i. When $J = 1$, a result equivalent to (8.29) is

$$\frac{R\widehat{\beta}_n - r}{\widehat{\sigma}_n\sqrt{R(Z'Z)^{-1}R'}} \to N(0, 1)$$

which is the large sample analogue of the statistic (8.22) which follows a t distribution under the normality assumption.

8.3 Nonlinear Parametric Regression

Next, we consider the properties of the OLS estimator in a nonlinear parametric regression model. We still consider an *i.i.d.* sequence $x_i = (y_i, z_i)'$ for $i = 1, \ldots, n$, where y_i and the elements z_{ij} of the vector z_i in $\mathbb{R}^k$ are square integrable random variables. We are interested in the conditional expectation of the form

$$E^{\theta}(y_i|z_i) = g(z_i, \beta) \qquad i = 1, \ldots, n. \qquad (8.30)$$

We assume that g is continuous and belongs to a parametric family of measurable functions

$$\left\{g(z_i, \lambda), \ \lambda \in \Lambda \subset \mathbb{R}^k\right\} \subset L^2(z_i)$$

where $L^2(z_i)$ is the space of square integrable functions on z_i. In this case, the dimensions of the vectors z_i and β are not necessarily the same. Furthermore, we assume that g is continuous and differentiable in Λ and that it is identified in the sense of

$$\forall z_i \quad g(z_i, \lambda) = g(z_i, \lambda^*) \Rightarrow \lambda = \lambda^*.$$

The model is also assumed to be correctly specified, i.e.,

$$E^{\theta}(y_i|z_i) \in \left\{g(z_i, \lambda), \ \lambda \in \Lambda \subset \mathbb{R}^k\right\}.$$

We can make several comments on these assumptions. The vector β is the unique element of Λ such that Equation (8.30) holds and, therefore, we can write $\beta = \lambda(\theta)$. We obtain β as the unique solution to the following minimization problem

$$\beta = \arg\min_{\lambda} E^{\theta}\left[(y_i - g(z_i, \lambda))^2\right],$$

hence,

$$E^\theta \left[(y_i - g(z_i, \beta))^2 \right] < E^\theta \left[(y_i - g(z_i, \lambda))^2 \right]$$

$\forall \lambda \in \Lambda$ with $\lambda \neq \beta$. It can be obtained in an equivalent way as the unique solution of

$$E^\theta \left[(y_i - g(z_i, \lambda)) \frac{\partial g(z_i, \lambda)}{\partial \lambda} \right] = 0.$$

Remark. The Assumption (8.30) implies the moment equation

$$E^\theta \left[(y_i - g(z_i, \lambda)) h(z_i, \lambda) \right] = 0$$

for any arbitrary function h of explanatory variables. As we saw at the end of Chapter 3 and as we will show in Chapter 15 for the more general case of nonlinear dynamic models, the choice of

$$h(z_i, \lambda) = \frac{\partial g(z_i, \lambda)}{\partial \lambda}$$

is optimal in the case when the residual

$$u_i = y_i - g(z_i, \lambda)$$

is homoskedastic. ☐

Here, the moment estimator of β can also be called nonlinear least-squares estimator and is given by

$$\widehat{\beta}_n = \arg \min_\lambda \sum_{i=1}^n (y_i - g(z_i, \lambda))^2$$

or as the solution of

$$\sum_{i=1}^n (y_i - g(z_i, \lambda)) \frac{\partial g(z_i, \lambda)}{\partial \lambda} = 0.$$

$\widehat{\beta}_n$ is assumed to exist and to be unique in a finite sample. For the asymptotic properties it is sufficient to return to the results in Chapter 3. To do this, let

$$\phi(x_i, \lambda) = (y_i - g(z_i, \lambda))^2.$$

The derivative of this function with respect to λ is, up to a multiplicative constant, equal to

$$\psi(x_i, \lambda) = (y_i - g(z_i, \lambda)) \frac{\partial g(z_i, \lambda)}{\partial \lambda},$$

which is a $k \times 1$ vector. Following Theorem 3.3 in Chapter 3, we obtain:

Theorem 8.3 *Under the assumptions of Theorem 3.3, the estimator* $\widehat{\beta}_n$ *has the following asymptotic properties:*

1) $\widehat{\beta}_n \to \beta \quad P^\theta - a.s.,$
2) $\sqrt{n}(\widehat{\beta}_n - \beta) \to N(0, \Sigma_\theta)$ *in* $P^\theta -$ *distribution* with

$$\Sigma_\theta = \sigma^2 \left(E^\theta \left[\frac{\partial g(z_i, \beta)}{\partial \beta} \frac{\partial g(z_i, \beta)}{\partial \beta'} \right] \right)^{-1}$$

where $\sigma^2 = Var^\theta (y_i | z_i).$ ∎

Indeed, Theorem 3.3 implies

$$\Sigma_\theta = \left[E^\theta \left(\frac{\partial \psi}{\partial \beta'} \right) \right]^{-1} Var^\theta (\psi) \left[E^\theta \left(\frac{\partial \psi'}{\partial \beta} \right) \right]^{-1}.$$

Here, we have

$$E^\theta \left(\frac{\partial \psi}{\partial \beta'} \right) = E^\theta \left[\frac{\partial}{\partial \beta'} \left((y_i - g(z_i, \beta)) \frac{\partial g(z_i, \beta)}{\partial \beta} \right) \right]$$

$$= E^\theta \left[-\frac{\partial g}{\partial \beta} \frac{\partial g}{\partial \beta'} \right] + E^\theta \left[(y_i - g(z_i, \beta)) \frac{\partial^2 g(z_i, \beta)}{\partial \beta \partial \beta'} \right]$$

$$= -E^\theta \left[\frac{\partial g}{\partial \beta} \frac{\partial g}{\partial \beta'} \right].$$

The second term is zero because

$$E^\theta \left[(y_i - g(z_i, \beta)) \frac{\partial^2 g(z_i, \beta)}{\partial \beta \partial \beta'} \right] = E^\theta \left[E^\theta \left(u_i \frac{\partial^2 g(z_i, \beta)}{\partial \beta \partial \beta'} \middle| z_i \right) \right]$$

$$= E^\theta \left[E^\theta (u_i | z_i) \frac{\partial^2 g(z_i, \beta)}{\partial \beta \partial \beta'} \right]$$

$$= 0$$

given the properties of u_i.

Moreover, the moment conditions imply

$$Var^\theta (\psi) = E^\theta \left[Var^\theta (\psi | z_i) \right] + Var^\theta \left[E^\theta (\psi | z_i) \right]$$
$$= E^\theta \left[Var^\theta (\psi | z_i) \right]$$

hence,

$$Var^\theta (\psi) = E^\theta \left[Var^\theta ((y_i - g(z_i, \beta)) \frac{\partial g(z_i, \beta)}{\partial \beta} \middle| z_i \right]$$

$$= E^\theta \left[\frac{\partial g(z_i, \beta)}{\partial \beta} Var^\theta (y_i | z_i) \frac{\partial g(z_i, \beta)}{\partial \beta'} \right].$$

Thus, we have

$$\Sigma_\theta = \left[E^\theta \left(\frac{\partial g}{\partial \beta} \frac{\partial g}{\partial \beta'} \right) \right]^{-1} E^\theta \left[\frac{\partial g(z_i, \beta)}{\partial \beta} Var^\theta(y_i | z_i) \frac{\partial g(z_i, \beta)}{\partial \beta'} \right]$$

$$\times \left[E^\theta \left(\frac{\partial g}{\partial \beta} \frac{\partial g}{\partial \beta'} \right) \right]^{-1} . \tag{8.31}$$

If we assume homoskedasticity, i.e.,

$$Var^\theta(y_i | z_i) = \sigma^2 \qquad i = 1, \dots, n$$

then

$$Var^\theta(\psi) = \sigma^2 E^\theta \left[\frac{\partial g(z_i, \beta)}{\partial \beta} \frac{\partial g(z_i, \beta)}{\partial \beta'} \right]$$

and the expression for Σ_θ is then

$$\Sigma_\theta = \sigma^2 \left(E^\theta \left[\frac{\partial g(z_i, \beta)}{\partial \beta} \frac{\partial g(z_i, \beta)}{\partial \beta'} \right] \right)^{-1} . \tag{8.32}$$

We have

$$\sqrt{n}(\widehat{\beta}_n - \beta) \rightarrow N \left(0, \sigma^2 \left(E^\theta \left[\frac{\partial g(z_i, \beta)}{\partial \beta} \frac{\partial g(z_i, \beta)}{\partial \beta'} \right] \right)^{-1} \right) \text{ in } P^\theta - \text{distribution,}$$

$$\tag{8.33}$$

which can be used for testing and for confidence intervals. Assuming homoskedasticity from now on, the variance matrix in (8.33) can be consistently estimated by

$$\widehat{\Sigma}_n = \widehat{\sigma}_n^2 \left[\frac{1}{n} \sum_{i=1}^n \frac{\partial g(z_i, \widehat{\beta}_n)}{\partial \beta} \frac{\partial g(z_i, \widehat{\beta}_n)}{\partial \beta'} \right]^{-1}$$

where

$$\widehat{\sigma}_n^2 = \frac{1}{n} \sum_{i=1}^n (y_i - g(z_i, \widehat{\beta}_n))^2 .$$

Uniqueness implies the invertibility of

$$E^\theta \left[\frac{\partial g(z_i, \beta)}{\partial \beta} \frac{\partial g(z_i, \beta)}{\partial \beta'} \right]$$

which implies the invertibility of

$$\frac{1}{n} \sum_{i=1}^n \frac{\partial g(z_i, \widehat{\beta}_n)}{\partial \beta} \frac{\partial g(z_i, \widehat{\beta}_n)}{\partial \beta'}$$

for a sufficiently large sample size. Thus, we use the distribution

$$\sqrt{n}(\widehat{\beta}_n - \beta) \to N(0, \widehat{\Sigma}_n).$$

To finish, consider the test of J nonlinear restrictions on β of the form

$$H_o : \eta(\beta) = 0$$

with $\eta(\beta) = (\eta_1(\beta), \ldots, \eta_J(\beta))'$ and $J \leq k$. The functions η_i are assumed to be continuously differentiable and the $J \times k$ matrix of first derivatives of η_i, i.e.,

$$\Gamma = \frac{\partial \eta(\beta)}{\partial \beta'},$$

is supposed to have rank J. We know that $\eta(\widehat{\beta}_n)$ is a consistent estimator of $\eta(\beta)$ and that, following Theorem 3.2 in Chapter 3,

$$\sqrt{n}(\eta(\widehat{\beta}_n) - \eta(\beta)) \to N(0, \Omega_\theta) \text{ in } P^\theta - \text{distribution}$$

with

$$\Omega_\theta = \Gamma \Sigma_\theta \Gamma'.$$

Hence,

$$n(\eta(\widehat{\beta}_n) - \eta(\beta))' \left[\widehat{\Gamma}_n \widehat{\Sigma}_n \widehat{\Gamma}'_n\right]^{-1} (\eta(\widehat{\beta}_n) - \eta(\beta)) \to \chi^2_J$$

in P^θ−distribution, with

$$\widehat{\Gamma}_n = \frac{\partial \eta(\widehat{\beta}_n)}{\partial \beta'}$$

(the estimator $\widehat{\Gamma}_n$ is assumed to have rank J).

The test statistic for the null hypothesis $H_o : \eta(\beta) = 0$ is then

$$n\eta(\widehat{\beta}_n)' \left[\widehat{\Gamma}_n \widehat{\Sigma}_n \widehat{\Gamma}'_n\right]^{-1} \eta(\widehat{\beta}_n)$$

which is χ^2_J distributed under H_0.

8.4 Misspecified Regression

We assumed in the previous sections that the unknown regression function belongs to the parametric family under consideration. Now, we drop this assumption and examine its consequences.

Consider again an i.i.d. sequence of random vectors

$$x_i = (y_i, z'_i)' \in \mathbb{R} \times \mathbb{R}^q$$

for which the components are square integrable. Assume that

$$E^\theta(y_i | z_i) = g(z_i)$$

and that the parametric model has the form $g(z_i, \lambda)$, $\lambda \in \mathbb{R}^k$, such that the family $\{g(z; \lambda) | \lambda \in \Lambda \subset \mathbb{R}^k\}$ does not necessarily contain $g(z)$. We are using here the same letter g for two types of functions, the true regression $g(z)$, and the family of approximations $g(z, \lambda)$.

In this context, we can address three questions:

1. What are the asymptotic properties of the estimators of the misspecified model?
2. How can one influence the approximation properties by the estimation method or by the choice of the approximation?
3. Can we derive asymptotic results for the specification tests?

8.4.1   Properties of the Least Squares Estimators

An econometrician, after choosing a parametric form $g(z, \lambda)$, estimates λ by

$$\widehat{\beta}_n = \arg \min_{\lambda} \sum_{i=1}^{n} (y_i - g(z_i, \lambda))^2.$$

Using the general results of Chapter 3, we can verify that

$$\widehat{\beta}_n \rightarrow \arg \min_{\lambda} E^\theta \left[(y_i - g(z_i, \lambda))^2 \right]$$

which is supposed to exist uniquely and which we denote by $\beta(\theta)$. In terms of the estimated function, the function $g(z, \widehat{\beta}_n)$ converges to $g(z, \beta(\theta))$ for all z if $g(z, \lambda)$ is continuous in λ. We can refine the relationship between $g(z)$ and $g(z, \beta(\theta))$ by noting that

$$E^\theta \left[(y_i - g(z_i, \lambda))^2 \right] = E^\theta \left[(y_i - g(z_i))^2 \right] + E^\theta \left[(g(z_i) - g(z_i, \lambda))^2 \right]$$

since

$$E^\theta \left[(y_i - g(z_i))(g(z_i) - g(z_i, \lambda)) \right]$$
$$= E^\theta \left[(g(z_i) - g(z_i, \lambda))(E^\theta (y_i | z_i) - g(z_i)) \right]$$
$$= 0$$

and, thus,

$$\beta(\theta) = \arg \min_{\lambda} E^\theta \left[(g(z_i) - g(z_i, \lambda))^2 \right].$$

The above shows that $g(z_i, \beta(\theta))$, which attains this minimum, is the best approximation in the sense of the quadratic norm in $L^2(z)$ of g by a function of the family $g(z, \lambda)$. This approximation depends fundamentally on the distribution of the explanatory variables and not only on the conditional distribution.

Example 8.8 *Suppose $z_i \in \mathbb{R}$ ($q = 1$) and examine a quadratic approximation*

$$g(z, \lambda) = \lambda_0 + \lambda_1 z + \lambda_2 z^2.$$

If the true regression is $g(z)$, then we look for $\beta = (\beta_0, \beta_1, \beta_2)$ which minimizes

$$E^\theta \left[(g(z) - \lambda_0 - \lambda_1 z - \lambda_2 z^2)^2 \right].$$

Then, elementary calculations yield

$$\begin{bmatrix} \beta_0(\theta) \\ \beta_1(\theta) \\ \beta_2(\theta) \end{bmatrix} = \begin{bmatrix} 1 & E^\theta(z_i) & E^\theta(z_i^2) \\ E^\theta(z_i) & E^\theta(z_i^2) & E^\theta(z_i^3) \\ E^\theta(z_i^2) & E^\theta(z_i^3) & E^\theta(z_i^4) \end{bmatrix}^{-1} \begin{bmatrix} E^\theta(g(z_i)) \\ E^\theta(z_i g(z_i)) \\ E^\theta(z_i^2 g(z_i)) \end{bmatrix}.$$

Thus, this vector depends on the distribution of the z_i. If, for example, the z_i are $N(0, \sigma^2)$, then

$$\begin{bmatrix} \beta_0(\theta) \\ \beta_1(0) \\ \beta_2(\theta) \end{bmatrix} = \begin{bmatrix} 1 & 0 & \sigma^2 \\ 0 & \sigma^2 & 0 \\ \sigma^2 & 0 & 3\sigma^4 \end{bmatrix}^{-1} \begin{bmatrix} E^\theta(g(z_i)) \\ E^\theta(z_i g(z_i)) \\ E^\theta(z_i^2 g(z_i)) \end{bmatrix},$$

hence

$$\begin{bmatrix} \beta_0(\theta) \\ \beta_1(\theta) \\ \beta_2(\theta) \end{bmatrix} = \frac{1}{2\sigma^4} \begin{bmatrix} 3\sigma^4 E^\theta(g(z_i)) - \sigma^2 E^\theta(z_i^2 g(z_i)) \\ 2\sigma^2 E^\theta(z_i g(z_i)) \\ -\sigma^2 E^\theta(g(z_i)) + E^\theta(z_i^2 g(z_i)) \end{bmatrix}.$$

This example underlines a mistake that we often find in applied econometrics. This error comes from the following argument. Assuming that the true model is

$$y_i = g(z_i) + u_i.$$

and using a second order Taylor series expansion of g around a point z_0, we obtain

$$y_i = g(z_0) + \frac{\partial g}{\partial z}(z_0)(z_i - z_0) + \frac{\partial^2 g}{\partial z^2}(z_0)(z_i - z_0)^2 + \varepsilon_i$$

where ε_i is a term that combines the approximation error and the residual u_i. Then, the model can be written in the form

$$g(z_i, \lambda) = \lambda_0 + \lambda_1 z_i + \lambda_2 z_i^2,$$

but estimating these parameters by least squares does not provide a consistent estimator of the derivatives of the true function at a given point z_0 even if $z_0 = E^\theta(z_i)$, which would seem to be the most natural choice. $\square$

Now, let us consider the limiting distribution of $\sqrt{n}(\hat{\beta}_n - \beta(\theta))$. It follows from the results in Chapter 3 that this distribution is asymptotically normal but with a more complex variance because of the misspecification error. Theorem 3.3 in Chapter 3 implies that

$$\sqrt{n}(\hat{\beta}_n - \beta(\theta)) \to N(0, \Sigma_\theta)$$

with

$$\Sigma_\theta = B_\theta^{-1} A_\theta B_\theta^{-1},$$

$$A_\theta = Var^\theta \left[\frac{\partial}{\partial \lambda} \left((y_i - g(z_i, \lambda))^2 \right) \right] \Big|_{\lambda = \beta(\theta)}$$

and

$$B_\theta = E^\theta \left[\frac{\partial^2}{\partial \lambda \partial \lambda'} \left((y_i - g(z_i, \lambda))^2 \right) \right] \Big|_{\lambda = \beta(\theta)}.$$

The simplifications that we used in the previous section are no longer possible because $E^\theta(y_i | z_i) \neq g(z_i, \beta)$ (see Equation (8.30)).

8.4.2   Comparing the True Regression with Its Approximation

The following example is purposely very simple in order to illustrate the argument.

Example 8.9   *Consider the case $z_i \in \mathbb{R}$ and $E^\theta(z_i) = 0$. We are interested in a linear approximation $g(z_i, \lambda) = \lambda z_i$ ($\lambda \in \mathbb{R}$). The least squares estimator converges evidently to*

$$\beta(\theta) = \frac{1}{\sigma^2} E^\theta(z_i g(z_i))$$

where $\sigma^2 = E^\theta(z_i^2)$. We have already seen that $\beta(\theta)$ is not equal to the derivative of $g(z)$ at a given point z_0 but we may wonder whether the following holds:

$$\beta(\theta) = E^\theta \left(\frac{\partial g}{\partial z}(z_i) \right).$$

This property means that $\hat{\beta}_n$ consistently estimates the expectation of the derivative of g where the expectation is with respect to the distribution of the explanatory variable. This property is equivalent to

$$\beta(\theta) = \int \frac{\partial g}{\partial z}(z) f_m(z) dz = g(z) f_m(z) \Big|_{-\infty}^{+\infty} - \int g(z) \frac{\partial f_m}{\partial z}(z) dz, \quad (8.34)$$

*where f_m denotes the density of z. We know that f_m goes to 0 at infinity and we
assume this is also the case for $g(z)f_m(z)$. The condition (8.34) becomes then*

$$\beta(\theta) = \frac{1}{\sigma^2} \int zg(z)f_m(z)dz = -\int g(z)\frac{\partial f_m}{\partial z}(z)dz.$$

This condition is satisfied for all functions g if

$$\frac{1}{\sigma^2}zf_m(z) + \frac{\partial f_m}{\partial z}(z) = 0. \tag{8.35}$$

*It can be shown without difficulty that (8.35) is satisfied if and only if f_m is the
density of the centered normal distribution with variance σ^2.* □

This example shows a good compatibility between linear approximation,
least squares, and normality of the explanatory variables. This result can be
generalized: in a polynomial approximation, the expectation (with respect to
the distribution of the explanatory variables) of the partial derivatives of the
regression are consistently estimated if and only if the explanatory variables
are normally distributed.

This result can be extended in the following way. Consider the following
moment conditions

$$E^\theta\left[(y_i - g(z_i, \lambda))\frac{\partial^\alpha \tilde{f}_m(z_i)}{f_m(z_i)}\right] = 0 \tag{8.36}$$

in which f_m is the marginal density of z_i, $\tilde{f}_m$ is another density (possibly
the same) in the space of explanatory variables and $\partial^\alpha \tilde{f}_m$ denotes the partial
derivative of $\tilde{f}_m$ (α is a vector of integers $\alpha_1, \ldots, \alpha_q$ and the derivative is taken
α_1 times with respect to the first component of z_i, α_2 times with respect to the
second, and so on). The condition (8.36) is equivalent to

$$\int (y_i - g(z_i, \lambda))\partial^\alpha \tilde{f}_m(z_i)dz_i = 0$$

$$\Leftrightarrow \int (g(z_i) - g(z_i, \lambda))\partial^\alpha \tilde{f}_m(z_i)dz_i = 0$$

$$\Leftrightarrow (-1)^{\alpha_1 + \cdots + \alpha_m} \int (\partial^\alpha g(z_i) - \partial^\alpha g(z_i, \lambda))\tilde{f}_m(z_i)dz_i = 0$$

$$\Leftrightarrow \tilde{E}^\theta(\partial^\alpha g(z_i)) = \tilde{E}^\theta(\partial^\alpha g(z_i, \lambda)). \tag{8.37}$$

The second to last equivalence is obtained by partial integration assuming that
the terms evaluated at $+\infty$ and $-\infty$ cancel. Thus we see that the moment
condition (8.36) are equivalent to the fact the partial derivatives of g and its
approximation are equal in the sense of the density $\tilde{f}_m$. The moment condition
(8.37) allows us to estimate the parameter λ. We consider a set of k conditions

of equality of the derivatives by choosing k values of α ($\alpha^1, \dots, \alpha^k$). Then, we obtain a system of moment conditions which leads to the estimation of β as the solution of

$$\sum_{i=1}^{n} (y_i - g(z_i, \lambda)) \frac{\partial^{\alpha^j} \widetilde{f}_m(z_i)}{f_m(z_i)} = 0 \qquad \forall j = 1, \dots, k.$$

This system assumes that f_m is known. In practice, f_m is estimated. We can use either a nonparametric regression or a parametric regression if we know a parametric family that includes f_m. We do not provide the detailed results for this case.

8.4.3   Specification Tests

These specification tests are inspired by the idea that the solutions to two minimization problems, one of which corresponds to the least squares approximation, are the same when the model is correctly specified. These tests rely on the asymptotic distribution of the difference between the estimators which are the outcome of the minimization problems. This is illustrated in the following example.

Example 8.10   *Suppose that $E^\theta(y_i | z_i) = g(z_i)$ where $z_i \in \mathbb{R}$ for simplicity. Consider the solutions to two simple systems of moment equations, the first deriving from the OLS, the second corresponding to the weighted least squares*

$$E^\theta \left((y_i - \lambda z_i) z_i \right) = 0$$

and

$$E^\theta \left((y_i - \rho z_i) z_i^3 \right) = 0.$$

Here, we take z_i^3 as an example, but any function of z_i that is different from the identity function, would play the same role. The solutions are respectively given by

$$\lambda(\theta) = \frac{E^\theta(z_i y_i)}{E^\theta(z_i^2)}$$

and

$$\rho(\theta) = \frac{E^\theta(z_i^3 y_i)}{E^\theta(z_i^4)}.$$

If there is no problem of misspecification, i.e., we are in the case where $g(z_i) = \beta z_i$, then the solutions $\lambda(\theta)$ and $\rho(\theta)$ are both equal to the parameter of the true regression

$$\lambda(\theta) = \rho(\theta) = \beta.$$

In contrast, if $g(z_i) \neq \beta z_i$, then $\lambda(\theta) \neq \rho(\theta)$.

Consider the null hypothesis H_0 that is implicitly defined by the family

$$\left\{ g(z_i) : \frac{E^\theta\left(z_i g(z_i)\right)}{E^\theta\left(z_i^2\right)} = \frac{E^\theta\left(z_i^3 g(z_i)\right)}{E^\theta\left(z_i^4\right)} \right\}.$$

If g belongs to this family, then $\lambda(\theta) = \rho(\theta) = \beta$.

The moment estimators of $\lambda(\theta)$ and $\rho(\theta)$ under H_0 are

$$\widehat{\lambda}_n = \frac{\sum_{i=1}^{n} z_i y_i}{\sum_{i=1}^{n} z_i^2} = \frac{\sum_{i=1}^{n} z_i \left(g(z_i) + u_i\right)}{\sum_{i=1}^{n} z_i^2} = \beta + \frac{\sum_{i=1}^{n} z_i u_i}{\sum_{i=1}^{n} z_i^2}$$

and

$$\widehat{\rho}_n = \frac{\sum_{i=1}^{n} z_i^3 y_i}{\sum_{i=1}^{n} z_i^4} = \frac{\sum_{i=1}^{n} z_i^3 \left(g(z_i) + u_i\right)}{\sum_{i=1}^{n} z_i^4} = \beta + \frac{\sum_{i=1}^{n} z_i^3 u_i}{\sum_{i-1}^{n} z_i^4}.$$

Then

$$\sqrt{n}\left(\widehat{\lambda}_n - \widehat{\rho}_n\right) = \sqrt{n}\left(\left(\sum_{i=1}^{n} z_i^2\right)^{-1} \sum_{i=1}^{n} z_i u_i - \left(\sum_{i=1}^{n} z_i^4\right)^{-1} \sum_{i=1}^{n} z_i^3 u_i\right)$$

$$\rightarrow \frac{1}{\sqrt{n}}\left(\left(E^\theta\left(z_i^2\right)\right)^{-1} \sum_{i=1}^{n} z_i u_i - \left(E^\theta\left(z_i^4\right)\right)^{-1} \sum_{i=1}^{n} z_i^3 u_i\right) \quad P^\theta - a.s.$$

$$\rightarrow \frac{1}{\sqrt{n}} \sum_{i=1}^{n} \left(\left(E^\theta\left(z_i^2\right)\right)^{-1} z_i - \left(E^\theta\left(z_i^4\right)\right)^{-1} z_i^3\right) u_i \quad P^\theta - a.s.$$

The central limit theorem implies that, under H_0,

$$\sqrt{n}\left(\widehat{\lambda}_n - \widehat{\rho}_n\right) \rightarrow N(0, \kappa(\theta))$$

with

$$\kappa(\theta) = E^\theta\left(\left[\left(\left(E^\theta\left(z_i^2\right)\right)^{-1} z_i - \left(E^\theta\left(z_i^4\right)\right)^{-1} z_i^3\right) u_i\right]^2\right)$$

$$= \frac{E^\theta\left(z_i^2 u_i^2\right)}{\left[E^\theta\left(z_i^2\right)\right]^2} + \frac{E^\theta\left(z_i^6 u_i^2\right)}{\left[E^\theta\left(z_i^4\right)\right]^2} - 2\frac{E^\theta\left(z_i^4 u_i^2\right)}{E^\theta\left(z_i^2\right) E^\theta\left(z_i^4\right)}.$$

$\kappa(\theta)$ *can be estimated by*

$$\widehat{\kappa}_n = \frac{\frac{1}{n}\sum_{i=1}^{n}z_i^2\widehat{u}_i^2}{\left[\frac{1}{n}\sum_{i=1}^{n}z_i^2\right]^2} + \frac{\frac{1}{n}\sum_{i=1}^{n}z_i^6\widehat{u}_i^2}{\left[\frac{1}{n}\sum_{i=1}^{n}z_i^4\right]^2} - 2\frac{\frac{1}{n}\sum_{i=1}^{n}z_i^4\widehat{u}_i^2}{\left(\frac{1}{n}\sum_{i=1}^{n}z_i^2\right)\left(\frac{1}{n}\sum_{i=1}^{n}z_i^4\right)}$$

where $\widehat{u}_i = y_i - \widehat{\lambda}_n z_i$ *or* $\widehat{u}_i = y_i - \widehat{\rho}_n z_i$. *Let* $E^{\theta}(u_i\,|z_i) = \sigma^2$, *then* $\kappa(\theta)$ *and* $\widehat{\kappa}_n$ *can be rewritten as*

$$\kappa(\theta) = \sigma^2\left(\frac{E^{\theta}\left(z_i^6\right)}{\left[E^{\theta}\left(z_i^4\right)\right]^2} - \frac{1}{E^{\theta}\left(z_i^2\right)}\right)$$

and

$$\widehat{\kappa}_n = \widehat{\sigma}_n^2\left(\frac{\frac{1}{n}\sum_{i=1}^{n}z_i^6}{\left[\frac{1}{n}\sum_{i=1}^{n}z_i^4\right]^2} - \frac{1}{\frac{1}{n}\sum_{i=1}^{n}z_i^2}\right)$$

where $\widehat{\sigma}_n^2 = \frac{1}{n}\sum_{i=1}^{n}(y_i - \widehat{\lambda}_n z_i)^2$ *or* $\widehat{\sigma}_n^2 = \frac{1}{n}\sum_{i=1}^{n}(y_i - \widehat{\rho}_n z_i)^2$.

If the statistic $\sqrt{n}(\widehat{\lambda}_n - \widehat{\rho}_n)$ *is larger than the critical value of a normal distribution* $N(0, \widehat{\kappa}_n)$, *then the null hypothesis of correct specification is rejected.*

Note that if the true specification is $g(z_i) = \beta z_i^2$ *and if the* z_i *are normally distributed, then the solutions are*

$$\lambda(\theta) = \beta\frac{E^{\theta}\left(z_i^3\right)}{E^{\theta}\left(z_i^2\right)} = 0$$

and

$$\rho(\theta) = \beta\frac{E^{\theta}\left(z_i^5\right)}{E^{\theta}\left(z_i^4\right)} = 0.$$

We can see that the idea for the specification test based on the asymptotic distribution of the difference between the estimators $\widehat{\lambda}_n$ *and* $\widehat{\rho}_n$ *is no longer valid. This illustrates the importance of the distribution of the explanatory variables in misspecified models.*

An alternative way to construct the specification test is based on the system of moment equations

$$E^{\theta}(\psi(x_i, \delta)) = 0$$

with

$$\psi(x_i, \delta) = \begin{bmatrix} (y_i - \lambda z_i)z_i \\ (y_i - \rho z_i)z_i^3 \end{bmatrix}$$

and $\delta = (\lambda, \rho)'$. Theorem 3.3 in Chapter 3 implies that

$$\sqrt{n}\begin{pmatrix} \widehat{\lambda}_n - \lambda(\theta) \\ \widehat{\rho}_n - \rho(\theta) \end{pmatrix} \to N(0, \Sigma_\theta)$$

with

$$\Sigma_\theta = B_\theta^{-1} A_\theta B_\theta^{-1}, \quad A_\theta = Var^\theta(\psi) \text{ and } B_\theta = E^\theta\left(\frac{\partial \psi}{\partial \delta'}\right).$$

A quick calculation shows that, under the null hypothesis, where $\lambda(\theta) = \rho(\theta) = \beta$,

$$A_\theta = \begin{pmatrix} E^\theta\left(u_i^2 z_i^2\right) & E^\theta\left(u_i^2 z_i^4\right) \\ E^\theta\left(u_i^2 z_i^4\right) & E^\theta\left(u_i^2 z_i^6\right) \end{pmatrix}$$

and

$$B_\theta = \begin{pmatrix} E^\theta\left(z_i^2\right) & 0 \\ 0 & E^\theta\left(z_i^4\right) \end{pmatrix},$$

from which we infer that

$$\sqrt{n}\left(\widehat{\lambda}_n - \widehat{\rho}_n\right) = \sqrt{n}\begin{pmatrix} 1 \\ -1 \end{pmatrix}'\begin{pmatrix} \widehat{\lambda}_n - \lambda(\theta) \\ \widehat{\rho}_n - \rho(\theta) \end{pmatrix} \to N\left(0, \begin{pmatrix} 1 \\ -1 \end{pmatrix}' \Sigma_\theta \begin{pmatrix} 1 \\ -1 \end{pmatrix}\right)$$

with

$$\begin{pmatrix} 1 \\ -1 \end{pmatrix}' \Sigma_\theta \begin{pmatrix} 1 \\ -1 \end{pmatrix} = \kappa(\theta)$$

where $\kappa(\theta)$ is as defined above. □

Notes

The presentation of the regression model in terms of expectation that was outlined in the introduction is, in the linear case, identical to that of Spanos (1986), who calls it linear regression model in contrast to the linear Gaussian model, defined by the usual equation $y = X\beta + u$. For the latter the exogenous variables seem deterministic. Indeed, the linear regression model is based on general probabilistic arguments and the linear Gaussian model is just a special case. A rather general introduction of the regression model is provided by the same author (1986, Chapter 17).

Concerning Section 8.2 on the linear regression model, a more rigorous proof of the equivalence of OLS and the method of moments can be found in Gouriéroux and Monfort (1996a). The restricted regression model has been studied by numerous authors, in particular Gouriéroux and Monfort (1996a, Volume 2), Greene (1990), Spanos (1986), Judge, Griffiths, Hill, Lutkepohl, and Lee (1985), and Judge, Hill, Griffiths, Lutkepohl, and Lee (1988). To show that $\widehat{\beta}_n^*$ is BLUE, see particularly Judge, Hill, Griffiths, Lutkepohl, and Lee (1988). For prediction refer to Spanos (1986), Greene (1990), and Judge,

Hill, Griffiths, Lutkepohl, and Lee (1988). The example on the log-linear model is taken from Greene (1990). For the proof of the almost sure convergence of $\widehat{\sigma}_n^2$ to σ^2, see Monfort (1982). For a comparison of the Wald, Rao, and LR test procedures for the case when the null hypothesis can be expressed in the form $R\beta = r$, see Judge, Griffiths, Hill, Lutkepohl, and Lee (1985) and Spanos (1986).

For the nonlinear parametric regression, we point to Bierens (1994), Gouriéroux and Monfort (1996a, Volume 1), Greene (1990, Chapter 11), Spanos (1986); for the test of linear restrictions to Bierens (1994).

For the last part concerning misspecified models, see White (1980), Florens, Ivaldi and Larribeau (1996), Gallant and White (1988), and White (1994).

9. Generalized Least Squares Method, Heteroskedasticity, and Multivariate Regression

9.1 Introduction

We saw that the linear regression model can be written in matrix form as

$$y = Z\beta + u,$$

and we imposed the assumptions

$$E^\theta(u|Z) = 0$$

and

$$Var^\theta(u|Z) = Var^\theta(u) = \sigma^2 I_n.$$

The first assumption means that $Z\beta$ is the expectation of y conditional on Z and thus cannot be altered without fundamentally changing the nature of the model. In many economic applications, the second assumption needs to be weakened and can be generalized in two ways, first in an i.i.d. setting, making the conditional variance of the u_i depend on the conditioning variables z_i (heteroskedasticity), and secondly in a non-i.i.d. setting, by not assuming that the covariance between residuals is zero. This can be written in a general framework as

$$Var^\theta(u|Z) = \Omega$$

where Ω is a matrix that depends in general on Z and on unknown parameters ρ. In this model, the parameters of interest are β and ρ.

By distinguishing the case where Ω is known up to a multiplicative factor from the general case where Ω is a function of unknown parameters, the usual treatment of this class of models is the following.

First, if $\Omega = \sigma^2 V$, where σ^2 is unknown and V is a given symmetric positive definite matrix, then we can verify that the unbiased linear estimator with the smallest variance solves the following problem

$$\min_{\beta}(y - Z\beta)' V^{-1}(y - Z\beta)$$

179

and is given by

$$\widehat{\beta}_n = (Z'V^{-1}Z)^{-1}Z'V^{-1}y. \tag{9.1}$$

This estimator is called the *generalized least squares* (GLS) *estimator*.

This immediate extension of the Gauss-Markov theorem (known as Aitken theorem) shows in particular that the variance of β conditional on Z is $\sigma^2(Z'V^{-1}Z)^{-1}$ and is the smallest among all unbiased linear estimators. A simple interpretation of this estimator is obtained by realizing that V^{-1} can be factored in $V^{-1} = P'P$ where P is invertible and that the model

$$y^* = Z^*\beta + u^*$$

with $y^* = Py$, $Z^* = PZ$, and $u^* = Pu$ satisfies the optimality conditions of the linear regression model (see Chapter 8), since in particular

$$Var^\theta(u^*|Z) = \sigma^2 PVP' = \sigma^2 I_n.$$

Thus we can use the usual formula

$$\widehat{\beta}_n = \left(Z^{*\prime}Z^*\right)^{-1}Z^{*\prime}y^*$$

and we recover the estimator (9.1).

Finally, the estimator σ^2 is obtained by

$$\widehat{\sigma}_n^2 = \frac{1}{n-q}(y - Z\widehat{\beta}_n)'V^{-1}(y - Z\widehat{\beta}_n).$$

If we assume moreover that

$$y|Z \sim N(Z\beta, \sigma^2 V),$$

then we can easily verify that $\widehat{\beta}_n$ is the MLE of β, and that $\frac{n-q}{n}\widehat{\sigma}_n^2$ is equal to the MLE of σ^2.

Second, if Ω is unknown and depends on a parameter vector ρ, then the approach consists of two stages:

• obtain a preliminary estimate $\widehat{\rho}_n$ of ρ and thus an estimator $\widehat{\Omega}_n$ of Ω, by replacing ρ by $\widehat{\rho}_n$,
• estimate β using formula (9.1) in which V is replaced by $\widehat{\Omega}_n$

$$\widehat{\beta}_n = \left(Z'\widehat{\Omega}_n^{-1}Z\right)^{-1}Z'\widehat{\Omega}_n^{-1}y.$$

Thus, we obtain the *feasible generalized least squares estimator*. This estimator obviously loses the small sample properties of the GLS estimator when V is known and is studied in general from an asymptotic view point.

This chapter is essentially devoted to this study, but we concentrate on the case of heteroskedasticity and on the extension of the GLS estimators to the multivariate case. Both problems stay within the i.i.d. setting, the interdependence of observations follows more naturally from dynamic modeling and is, therefore, relegated to Part III of this book.

In the following section, we present an extension of the method of moments, before analyzing the heteroskedasticity and multivariate regression models, which will be the object of the last two sections.

9.2 Allowing for Nuisance Parameters in Moment Estimation

Consider a model $\{X^n, \Theta, P_n^\theta\}$ and a function ψ defined on $X \times \Lambda \times R$ ($\Lambda \subset \mathbb{R}^k$, $R \subset \mathbb{R}^l$) with values in $\mathbb{R}^k$. The function $\psi(x_i, \lambda, \rho)$ is assumed to be square integrable for all λ and ρ, and we consider equation

$$E^\theta \left(\psi(x_i, \lambda, \rho) \right) = 0. \tag{9.2}$$

This has the following interpretation: if ρ is fixed at a particular value that will depend in general on θ, $\rho(\theta)$, then the system (9.2) defines a function $\lambda(\theta)$ of the parameters of interest, and the function $\rho(\theta)$ defines a function of nuisance parameters. The estimation of the latter is not a priority for the statistician but their treatment is necessary to analyze the parameters of interest. Note that, in the specific situation that we examine, the system (9.2) contains more unknowns than equations and, therefore, cannot be used by itself to estimate $\rho(\theta)$ and $\lambda(\theta)$.

We analyze then this problem for two situations.

The first case is defined by the assumption that the value of ρ is known. This value depends in general on θ and we then assume that ρ is equal to $\rho(\theta)$. Here, λ can be analyzed using the same methods as in Chapter 3. We have a simple system of moment equations which, under the usual regularity conditions, leads to the estimator $\widetilde{\lambda}_n (\rho(\theta))$, given as the solution of

$$\frac{1}{n} \sum_{i=1}^n \psi(x_i, \lambda, \rho(\theta)) = 0. \tag{9.3}$$

We emphasize that $\widetilde{\lambda}_n (\rho(\theta))$ obviously depends on the particular fixed value of $\rho(\theta)$. We then have, following Theorem 3.3 of Chapter 3

$$\widetilde{\lambda}_n (\rho(\theta)) \to \lambda(\theta) \ P^\theta - a.s., \tag{9.4}$$

where $\lambda(\theta)$ is the solution of $E^\theta \left(\psi(x_i, \lambda, \rho(\theta)) \right) = 0$ and

$$\sqrt{n} \left(\widetilde{\lambda}_n (\rho(\theta)) - \lambda(\theta) \right) \to N(0, \Sigma_\theta) \quad \text{in } P^\theta\text{-distribution} \tag{9.5}$$

with

$$\Sigma_\theta = \left[E^\theta \left(\frac{\partial \psi}{\partial \lambda'} \right) \right]^{-1} Var^\theta (\psi) \left[E^\theta \left(\frac{\partial \psi'}{\partial \lambda} \right) \right]^{-1}. \tag{9.6}$$

A second more relevant case is the one in which $\rho(\theta)$ is unknown but we have an estimator $\widehat{\rho}_n$ available which converges to $\rho(\theta)$. We then solve the system

$$\frac{1}{n} \sum_{i=1}^{n} \psi(x_i, \lambda, \widehat{\rho}_n) = 0, \tag{9.7}$$

from which we obtain the estimator $\widehat{\lambda}_n$. It is then natural to ask whether $\widehat{\lambda}_n$ preserves the same asymptotic properties as $\widetilde{\lambda}_n$ ($\rho(\theta)$), and in particular whether the asymptotic variance of the estimator is the same when $\rho(\theta)$ is known and when $\rho(\theta)$ is estimated. The answer is in general negative, but the following theorem provides a simple criterion for which both asymptotic distributions are equal.

Theorem 9.1   *Suppose that $\widehat{\rho}_n$ converges a.s. to $\rho(\theta)$ and that $\sqrt{n}(\widehat{\rho}_n - \rho(\theta))$ has a limiting distribution. If the usual regularity conditions are satisfied, then $\widehat{\lambda}_n$ converges a.s. to $\lambda(\theta)$. If moreover the condition*

$$E^\theta \left(\frac{\partial \psi}{\partial \rho'}(x_i, \lambda, \rho) \Big|_{\lambda(\theta) \text{ and } \rho(\theta)} \right) = 0 \tag{9.8}$$

is satisfied, then the asymptotic distribution of $\sqrt{n}(\widehat{\lambda}_n - \lambda(\theta))$ is the same as in (9.5) and (9.6).   ∎

Proof:
1) First, write the expansion

$$\psi(x_i, \lambda, \widehat{\rho}_n) \simeq \psi(x_i, \lambda, \rho(\theta)) + \frac{\partial \psi}{\partial \rho'}(x_i, \lambda, \rho(\theta))(\widehat{\rho}_n - \rho(\theta)),$$

which is intuitively justified by the convergence of $\widehat{\rho}_n$ to $\rho(\theta)$. Then we have

$$\frac{1}{n} \sum_{i=1}^{n} \psi(x_i, \lambda, \widehat{\rho}_n) \simeq \frac{1}{n} \sum_{i=1}^{n} \psi(x_i, \lambda, \rho(\theta))$$

$$+ \left(\frac{1}{n} \sum_{i=1}^{n} \frac{\partial \psi}{\partial \rho'}(x_i, \lambda, \rho(\theta)) \right) (\widehat{\rho}_n - \rho(\theta)).$$

The third term of this equality goes to zero and we see intuitively that the solutions to the problems

$$\frac{1}{n} \sum_{i=1}^{n} \psi(x_i, \lambda, \widehat{\rho}_n) = 0$$

and

$$\frac{1}{n} \sum_{i=1}^{n} \psi(x_i, \lambda, \rho(\theta)) = 0$$

are arbitrarily close and converge therefore to the same limit $\lambda(\theta)$.

2) The following expansion

$$\psi(x_i, \widehat{\lambda}_n, \widehat{\rho}_n) \simeq \psi(x_i, \lambda(\theta), \rho(\theta)) + \frac{\partial \psi}{\partial \lambda'}(x_i, \lambda(\theta), \rho(\theta))(\widehat{\lambda}_n - \lambda(\theta))$$

$$+ \frac{\partial \psi}{\partial \rho'}(x_i, \lambda(\theta), \rho(\theta))(\widehat{\rho}_n - \rho(\theta)),$$

yields

$$\frac{\sqrt{n}}{n} \sum_{i=1}^{n} \psi(x_i, \lambda(\theta), \rho(\theta)) + \left(\frac{1}{n} \sum_{i=1}^{n} \frac{\partial \psi}{\partial \lambda'}(x_i, \lambda(\theta), \rho(\theta)) \right) \left(\sqrt{n}(\widehat{\lambda}_n - \lambda(\theta)) \right)$$

$$+ \left(\frac{1}{n} \sum_{i=1}^{n} \frac{\partial \psi}{\partial \rho'}(x_i, \lambda(\theta), \rho(\theta)) \right) \left(\sqrt{n}(\widehat{\rho}_n - \rho(\theta)) \right) \simeq 0.$$

We know that

$$\frac{1}{n} \sum_{i=1}^{n} \frac{\partial \psi}{\partial \rho'}(x_i, \lambda(\theta), \rho(\theta))$$

converges a.s. to

$$E^\theta \left(\frac{\partial \psi}{\partial \rho'}(x_i, \lambda(\theta), \rho(\theta)) \right)$$

which is assumed to be zero and that $\sqrt{n}(\widehat{\rho}_n - \rho(\theta))$ has a limiting distribution. Therefore, the product of these two expressions goes to zero, from which the result follows. ∎

This result leads to several remarks:
1) The condition

$$E^\theta \left(\frac{\partial \psi}{\partial \rho'}(x_i, \lambda(\theta), \rho(\theta)) \right) = 0$$

is not necessary. We can indeed obtain the same result with $\sqrt{n}(\widehat{\rho}_n - \rho(\theta)) \to 0$ and any $E^\theta(\frac{\partial \psi}{\partial \rho'}(x_i, \lambda(\theta), \rho(\theta)))$. This case occurs in particular if $\widehat{\rho}_n$ converges to $\rho(\theta)$ with a rate faster than $\sqrt{n}$ (for example, $n(\widehat{\rho}_n - \rho(\theta))$ has a limiting distribution as the one that we obtain in some nonstationary models or in extreme value estimation).
2) We can write an easily verifiable assumption that implies the condition

$$E^\theta \left(\frac{\partial \psi}{\partial \rho'}(x_i, \lambda(\theta), \rho(\theta)) \right) = 0.$$

Consider the asymptotic problem

$$E^\theta(\psi(x_i, \lambda, \rho)) = 0 \tag{9.9}$$

and assume that $E^\theta(\psi(x_i, \lambda, \rho))$ does not depend on ρ. This indicates that the problem (9.9) can be solved for $\lambda(\theta)$ independently of ρ (although $\psi(x_i, \lambda, \rho)$ depends on ρ) and that the estimator $\tilde{\lambda}_n(\rho(\theta))$ converges to $\lambda(\theta)$ for any fixed value of $\rho(\theta)$. If $E^\theta(\psi(x_i, \lambda, \rho))$ does not depend on ρ, its derivative with respect to ρ is zero; hence, by interchanging expectation and derivatives, we obtain Condition (9.8).

Let us return now to the general case and briefly analyze the limiting distribution of $\sqrt{n}(\widehat{\lambda}_n - \lambda(\theta))$ without the simplifying assumption (9.8). A simple way to examine this question is by obtaining an estimator of ρ; this estimation is in general derived from an extra moment equation

$$E^\theta(\overline{\psi}(x_i, \lambda, \rho)) = 0 \tag{9.10}$$

where $\overline{\psi}$ has values in $\mathbb{R}^l$. We are therefore in a setting with a simple system of moment equations by stacking (9.2) and (9.10), and we calculate the estimators for $\widehat{\lambda}_n$ and $\widehat{\rho}_n$ by jointly solving

$$\frac{1}{n}\sum_{i=1}^n \begin{pmatrix} \psi(x_i, \lambda, \rho) \\ \overline{\psi}(x_i, \lambda, \rho) \end{pmatrix} = 0. \tag{9.11}$$

Thus, we are confronted with the usual system of moment conditions and the results of Chapter 3 apply.

To conclude these general considerations that are illustrated in the remainder of this chapter, we note that the following sequential approach can be applied to the case where Equation (9.10) is available and where $E^\theta(\psi(x_i, \lambda, \rho))$ does not depend on ρ:

- fix ρ at an arbitrary value ρ_0 and use (9.3) to calculate $\tilde{\lambda}_n(\rho_0)$ which converges to $\lambda(\theta)$ for all ρ_0,
- replace λ by $\tilde{\lambda}_n(\rho_0)$ in $\frac{1}{n}\sum_{i=1}^n \overline{\psi}(x_i, \lambda, \rho) = 0$, and then obtain a consistent and asymptotically normal estimator of $\rho(\theta)$,
- return to equation $\frac{1}{n}\sum_{i=1}^n \psi(x_i, \lambda, \rho) = 0$ and replace ρ by the previously obtained estimator.

We leave it to the reader to verify that this procedure leads to a consistent and asymptotically normal estimator $\widehat{\lambda}_n$ of $\lambda(\theta)$ with the same asymptotic variance as (9.6). This three-stage procedure suffices to guarantee asymptotic efficiency without solving system (9.11). If we iterate on this procedure, then we evidently converge to the solution of (9.11).

9.3 Heteroskedasticity

In Chapter 8, the conditional distribution could be analyzed using only its conditional expectation. In heteroskedastic models, two moments are relevant, the conditional mean and the conditional variance.

Consider a finite sequence $(x_i)_{i=1,\ldots,n}$ with $x_i = (y_i, z_i)$ where $y_i \in \mathbb{R}^p$, $z_i \in \mathbb{R}^q$ and $p + q = m$. In the current section, we consider the case where $p = 1$, leaving the multivariate case to the next section. The x_i are i.i.d. with the same distribution Q^θ. Moreover, the conditional moments can be written in the form

$$E^\theta(y_i|z_i) = g(z_i, \beta) \in \{g(z_i, \lambda), \lambda \in \Lambda \subset \mathbb{R}^k\} \subset L^2(z_i) \tag{9.12}$$

and

$$Var^\theta(y_i|z_i) = \sigma^2(z_i, \gamma) \in \{\sigma^2(z_i, \rho), \rho \in R \subset \mathbb{R}^l\} \subset L^2(z_i) \tag{9.13}$$

where σ^2 is a positive scalar valued function. Thus the model is assumed to be well specified. If $g(z_i, \beta) = \beta' z_i$, then this forms a linear heteroskedastic model. Additionally, we assume that g and σ^2 are continuous and differentiable functions on Λ and R respectively, and that they are identified in the sense that

$$\forall z_i \quad g(z_i, \lambda) = g(z_i, \lambda^*) \Rightarrow \lambda = \lambda^*$$

and

$$\forall z_i \quad \sigma^2(z_i, \rho) = \sigma^2(z_i, \rho^*) \Rightarrow \rho = \rho^*.$$

Note that not all elements of the vector z_i need to appear in each equation, but the model is considered conditional on all these elements.

9.3.1 Estimation

We are interested in two possible cases, one when γ is known and the other when it has to be estimated.

The Case When γ is Known

First, consider the case when γ is known. The GLS estimator is the solution to the following problem

$$\min_{\lambda \in \Lambda} E^\theta (\phi(x_i, \lambda)) \tag{9.14}$$

with

$$\phi(x_i, \lambda) = \frac{(y_i - g(z_i, \lambda))^2}{\sigma^2(z_i, \gamma)}, \tag{9.15}$$

which is equivalent to the simple system of moment equations given by

$$E^\theta (\psi(x_i, \lambda)) = 0 \tag{9.16}$$

with

$$\psi(x_i, \lambda) = \frac{(y_i - g(z_i, \lambda))}{\sigma^2(z_i, \gamma)} \frac{\partial g(z_i, \lambda)}{\partial \lambda}.$$

An alternative way to obtain (9.16) is to look at the conditional moment condition

$$E\left(y_i - g\left(z_i, \lambda\right) | z_i\right) = 0$$

and to transform this condition into marginal moments using the optimal instruments given in Formula (3.37),

$$h\left(z_i, \lambda, \gamma\right) = \frac{\dfrac{\partial g\left(z_i, \lambda\right)}{\partial \lambda}}{\sigma^2\left(z_i, \gamma\right)}.$$

The moment estimator, $\widehat{\beta}_n$, is obtained as the solution to

$$\frac{1}{n}\sum_{i=1}^{n}\frac{\left(y_i - g(z_i, \lambda)\right)}{\sigma^2(z_i, \gamma)}\frac{\partial g(z_i, \lambda)}{\partial \lambda} = 0. \tag{9.17}$$

The estimator $\widehat{\beta}_n$ is a function of the known vector γ, $\widehat{\beta}_n = \widehat{\beta}_n(\gamma)$. Intuitively, the denominator $\sigma^2(z_i, \gamma)$ in (9.15) introduces a heteroskedasticity correction since

$$Var^\theta\left(\left.\frac{y_i - g(z_i, \lambda)}{\sigma(z_i, \gamma)}\right| z_i\right) = 1.$$

To obtain the asymptotic properties, it is sufficient to apply here the results of the previous section, given by (9.4), (9.5), and (9.6), which were obtained for the case when the value of ρ is assumed to be known:

$$\widehat{\beta}_n \to \beta \quad P^\theta - a.s.,$$

where β is the solution of (9.16) and

$$\sqrt{n}\left(\widehat{\beta}_n - \beta\right) \to N(0, \Sigma_\theta) \quad \text{in } P^\theta\text{-distribution}$$

with

$$\Sigma_\theta = \left[E^\theta\left(\frac{\partial \psi}{\partial \lambda'}\right)\right]^{-1} Var^\theta(\psi)\left[E^\theta\left(\frac{\partial \psi'}{\partial \lambda}\right)\right]^{-1}.$$

Note that here

$$\frac{\partial \psi}{\partial \lambda'} = \frac{1}{\sigma^2(z_i, \gamma)}\left[-\frac{\partial g(z_i, \lambda)}{\partial \lambda}\frac{\partial g(z_i, \lambda)}{\partial \lambda'} + (y_i - g(z_i, \lambda))\frac{\partial^2 g(z_i, \lambda)}{\partial \lambda \partial \lambda'}\right],$$

hence

$$E^\theta\left(\frac{\partial \psi}{\partial \lambda'}\right) = -E^\theta\left(\frac{1}{\sigma^2(z_i, \gamma)}\frac{\partial g(z_i, \lambda)}{\partial \lambda}\frac{\partial g(z_i, \lambda)}{\partial \lambda'}\right)$$

because

$$E^\theta \left(\frac{(y_i - g(z_i, \lambda))}{\sigma^2(z_i, \gamma)} \frac{\partial^2 g(z_i, \lambda)}{\partial \lambda \partial \lambda'} \right)$$

$$= E^\theta \left(\frac{E^\theta \left((y_i - g(z_i, \lambda)) | z_i \right)}{\sigma^2(z_i, \gamma)} \frac{\partial^2 g(z_i, \lambda)}{\partial \lambda \partial \lambda'} \right) = 0$$

since

$$E^\theta \left((y_i - g(z_i, \lambda)) | z_i \right) = 0$$

following (9.12). Moreover, we can write

$$Var^\theta(\psi) = E^\theta(Var^\theta(\psi | z_i)) + Var^\theta(E^\theta(\psi | z_i)) = E^\theta(Var^\theta(\psi | z_i))$$

since $E^\theta(\psi | z_i) = 0$. Thus

$$Var^\theta(\psi) = E^\theta \left[Var^\theta \left(\frac{(y_i - g(z_i, \lambda))}{\sigma^2(z_i, \gamma)} \frac{\partial g(z_i, \lambda)}{\partial \lambda} \bigg| z_i \right) \right]$$

$$= E^\theta \left[\frac{1}{\sigma^4(z_i, \gamma)} \frac{\partial g(z_i, \lambda)}{\partial \lambda} Var^\theta \left((y_i - g(z_i, \lambda)) | z_i \right) \frac{\partial g(z_i, \lambda)}{\partial \lambda'} \right]$$

$$- E^\theta \left(\frac{1}{\sigma^2(z_i, \gamma)} \frac{\partial g(z_i, \lambda)}{\partial \lambda} \frac{\partial g(z_i, \lambda)}{\partial \lambda'} \right).$$

Finally, the matrix Σ_θ is given by

$$\Sigma_\theta - \left[E^\theta \left(\frac{1}{\sigma^2(z_i, \gamma)} \frac{\partial g(z_i, \beta)}{\partial \lambda} \frac{\partial g(z_i, \beta)}{\partial \lambda'} \right) \right]^{-1} \tag{9.18}$$

and can be consistently estimated by

$$\widehat{\Sigma}_n = \left[\frac{1}{n} \sum_{i=1}^n \frac{1}{\sigma^2(z_i, \gamma)} \frac{\partial g(z_i, \widehat{\beta}_n)}{\partial \lambda} \frac{\partial g(z_i, \widehat{\beta}_n)}{\partial \lambda'} \right]^{-1}.$$

The uniqueness assumption implies the invertibility of

$$E^\theta \left(\frac{1}{\sigma^2(z_i, \gamma)} \frac{\partial g(z_i, \lambda)}{\partial \lambda} \frac{\partial g(z_i, \lambda)}{\partial \lambda'} \right)$$

which in turn implies the invertibility of

$$\frac{1}{n} \sum_{i=1}^n \frac{1}{\sigma^2(z_i, \gamma)} \frac{\partial g(z_i, \widehat{\beta}_n)}{\partial \lambda} \frac{\partial g(z_i, \widehat{\beta}_n)}{\partial \lambda'}$$

for a sufficiently large sample size. Thus, we use the distribution $N(0, \widehat{\Sigma}_n)$ as the approximated distribution of $\sqrt{n}(\widehat{\beta}_n - \beta)$.

The following example illustrates these asymptotic results for the case of linear conditional expectation.

Example 9.1 *Suppose that*

$$E^{\theta}(y_i|z_i) = \beta' z_i$$

and

$$Var^{\theta}(y_i|z_i) = \sigma^2(z_i, \gamma)$$

where γ is a known parameter vector. In this case, we have

$$g(z_i, \lambda) = \lambda' z_i \quad and \quad \frac{\partial g(z_i, \lambda)}{\partial \lambda} = z_i.$$

According to (9.17), the GLS estimator of β is obtained as the solution of

$$\frac{1}{n} \sum_{i=1}^{n} z_i \frac{y_i - z_i'\lambda}{\sigma^2(z_i, \gamma)} = 0, \tag{9.19}$$

hence

$$\widehat{\beta}_n = \left[\sum_{i=1}^{n} \frac{z_i z_i'}{\sigma^2(z_i, \gamma)} \right]^{-1} \left[\sum_{i=1}^{n} \frac{z_i y_i}{\sigma^2(z_i, \gamma)} \right] = (Z'\Omega^{-1}Z)^{-1} Z'\Omega^{-1}y, \tag{9.20}$$

by defining the $n \times q$ matrix $Z = (z_1, \ldots, z_n)'$ and the $n \times n$ matrix Ω whose (i, i) elements are equal to $\sigma^2(z_i, \gamma)$. We also have, according to (9.18),

$$\Sigma_{\theta} = \left[E^{\theta} \left(\frac{z_i z_i'}{\sigma^2(z_i, \gamma)} \right) \right]^{-1},$$

which is naturally estimated by

$$\widehat{\Sigma}_n = \left[\frac{1}{n} \sum_{i=1}^{n} \frac{z_i z_i'}{\sigma^2(z_i, \gamma)} \right]^{-1} = n(Z'\Omega^{-1}Z)^{-1}.$$

We thus use the distribution $N(0, n(Z'\Omega^{-1}Z)^{-1})$ as the approximated distribution of $\sqrt{n}(\widehat{\beta}_n - \beta)$. The estimator $\widehat{\beta}_n$ could equally be obtained by starting with the regression model

$$y_i = \beta' z_i + u_i$$

where, by construction,

$$E^{\theta}(u_i|z_i) = 0 \quad and \quad Var^{\theta}(u_i|z_i) = \sigma^2(z_i, \gamma),$$

and by correcting this model to take account of the heteroskedasticity:

$$\frac{y_i}{\sigma(z_i, \gamma)} = \beta' \frac{z_i}{\sigma(z_i, \gamma)} + \frac{u_i}{\sigma(z_i, \gamma)}. \tag{9.21}$$

The error term $\frac{u_i}{\sigma(z_i, \gamma)}$ satisfies the basic conditions of univariate regression model of the preceding chapter. The application of the OLS method is based on the following minimization:

$$\min_{\lambda} \frac{1}{n} \sum_{i=1}^{n} \left(\frac{y_i}{\sigma(z_i, \gamma)} - \lambda' \frac{z_i}{\sigma(z_i, \gamma)} \right)^2$$

with respect to λ which leads to Condition (9.19). This explains why the estimator $\widehat{\beta}_n$ is also called a weighted least squares estimator, the weights appear in an obvious way in (9.21). □

The following example looks at the small sample properties of the GLS estimator in the case of a linear model and describes the MLE under the normality assumption.

Example 9.2 *Consider a heteroskedastic model with a linear conditional expectation in the form*

$$E^{\theta}(y_i|z_i) = \beta' z_i,$$

and a conditional variance that is more general than in the previous example

$$Var^{\theta}(y_i|z_i) = \sigma^2(z_i, \gamma) = \sigma_0^2 v(z_i, \gamma),$$

where σ_0^2 is an unknown scalar parameter and $v(z_i, \gamma)$ is a function with strictly positive values depending on a known parameter vector γ. The GLS estimator of β is given by (9.20), written as:

$$\widehat{\beta}_n = \left[\sum_{i=1}^{n} \frac{z_i z_i'}{v(z_i, \gamma)} \right]^{-1} \left[\sum_{i=1}^{n} \frac{z_i y_i}{v(z_i, \gamma)} \right] = (Z' V^{-1} Z)^{-1} Z' V^{-1} y,$$

$$(9.22)$$

where V is a $n \times n$ matrix whose (i, i) elements are equal to $v(z_i, \gamma)$. Knowing that

$$E^{\theta} \left(\frac{(y_i - \beta' z_i)^2}{v(z_i, \gamma)} \right) = E^{\theta} \left(\frac{E^{\theta} \left((y_i - \beta' z_i)^2 | z_i \right)}{v(z_i, \gamma)} \right) = \sigma_0^2,$$

σ_0^2 is naturally estimated by

$$\widetilde{\sigma}_{0n}^2 = \frac{1}{n} \sum_{i=1}^{n} \frac{(y_i - \widehat{\beta}_n' z_i)^2}{v(z_i, \gamma)} = \frac{1}{n} (y - Z\widehat{\beta}_n)' V^{-1} (y - Z\widehat{\beta}_n) \qquad (9.23)$$

or by the unbiased estimator

$$\widehat{\sigma}_{0n}^2 = \frac{n}{n - q} \widetilde{\sigma}_{0n}^2. \qquad (9.24)$$

$\widehat{\beta}_n$ is linear with respect to y_i, and a quick calculation shows that

$$E^{\theta}(\widehat{\beta}_n|Z) = \beta \quad and \quad Var^{\theta}(\widehat{\beta}_n|Z) = \sigma_0^2(Z'V^{-1}Z)^{-1}.$$

To prove the Aitken theorem, according to which $\widehat{\beta}_n$ is the best linear unbiased estimator, take any other linear unbiased estimator $\widetilde{\beta}_n = Cy$ of β. Let

$$C = D + (Z'V^{-1}Z)^{-1}Z'V^{-1},$$

then

$$\widetilde{\beta}_n = \left(D + (Z'V^{-1}Z)^{-1}Z'V^{-1}\right)y,$$

where

$$E^{\theta}(\widetilde{\beta}_n|Z) = DZ\beta + \beta = \beta$$

only if $DZ = 0$. We can quickly show that the conditional variance of this new estimator is

$$Var^{\theta}(\widetilde{\beta}_n|Z) = \sigma_0^2 DVD' + Var^{\theta}(\widehat{\beta}_n|Z)$$

where

$$Var^{\theta}(\widetilde{\beta}_n|Z) \geq Var^{\theta}(\widehat{\beta}_n|Z)$$

since DVD' is a positive semidefinite matrix. Thus the Aitken theorem is proven. If we assume now conditional normality in the finite sample, i.e.,

$$y|Z \sim N(Z\beta, \sigma_0^2 V), \tag{9.25}$$

then we can immediately infer that

$$\widehat{\beta}_n|Z \sim N(\beta, \sigma_0^2(Z'V^{-1}Z)^{-1}).$$

Under the normality assumption (9.25), the MLEs of β and σ_0^2 are obtained by maximizing the likelihood function

$$l(y|Z, \beta, \sigma_0^2, V) = \frac{1}{\sigma_0^n(2\pi)^{n/2}}\frac{1}{|V|^{1/2}}\exp\left\{-\frac{1}{2\sigma_0^2}(y - Z\beta)'V^{-1}(y - Z\beta)\right\}.$$

One can easily show that the first order conditions of the maximization lead to the estimators $\widehat{\beta}_n$ and $\widetilde{\sigma}_{0n}^2$ given respectively by (9.22) and (9.23). $\square$

The following example shows that the OLS estimator of β, denoted by $\widehat{\beta}_n^*$, remains unbiased but does not attain minimal variance any more.

Example 9.3 *Continuing with the framework of the previous example, the OLS estimator of β is*

$$\widehat{\beta}_n^* = (Z'Z)^{-1}Z'y.$$

We can infer that this estimator is also unbiased and that its variance is given by

$$Var^\theta (\widehat{\beta}_n^* | Z) = \sigma_0^2 (Z'Z)^{-1} Z' V^{-1} Z (Z'Z)^{-1}.$$

According to the Aitken theorem, the estimator does not have minimal variance. This can be confirmed by considering the difference between the variances of $\widehat{\beta}_n$ and $\widehat{\beta}_n^*$:

$$Var^\theta (\widehat{\beta}_n^* | Z) - Var^\theta (\widehat{\beta}_n | Z)$$
$$= \sigma_0^2 (Z'Z)^{-1} Z' V^{-1} Z (Z'Z)^{-1} - \sigma_0^2 (Z'V^{-1}Z)^{-1}$$
$$= \sigma_0^2 A V^{-1} A'$$

where

$$A = (Z'Z)^{-1} Z' - (Z'V^{-1}Z)^{-1} Z'V^{-1}$$

is a positive semidefinite matrix. ☐

In the general case, in which the conditional expectation is not necessarily linear, the OLS estimator is still consistent and has the limiting distribution

$$\sqrt{n} \left(\widehat{\beta}_n^* - \beta \right) \to N(0, \Sigma_\theta^*)$$

with

$$\Sigma_\theta^* = \left[E^\theta \left(\frac{\partial \psi^*}{\partial \lambda'} \right) \right]^{-1} Var^\theta (\psi^*) \left[E^\theta \left(\frac{\partial \psi^{*'}}{\partial \lambda} \right) \right]^{-1}$$

where

$$\psi^*(x_i, \lambda) = (y_i - g(z_i, \lambda)) \frac{\partial g(z_i, \lambda)}{\partial \lambda}.$$

Here, we have

$$E^\theta \left(\frac{\partial \psi^{*'}}{\partial \lambda} \right) = E^\theta \left(-\frac{\partial g(z_i, \lambda)}{\partial \lambda} \frac{\partial g(z_i, \lambda)}{\partial \lambda'} \right)$$

and

$$Var^\theta (\psi^*) = E^\theta \left(Var^\theta (\psi^* | z_i) \right) + Var^\theta \left(E^\theta (\psi^* | z_i) \right)$$
$$= E^\theta \left(Var^\theta (\psi^* | z_i) \right)$$
$$= E^\theta \left(\frac{\partial g(z_i, \lambda)}{\partial \lambda} \sigma^2 (x_i, \gamma) \frac{\partial g(z_i, \lambda)}{\partial \lambda'} \right),$$

hence

$$\Sigma_\theta^* = \left[E^\theta \left(\frac{\partial g(z_i, \beta)}{\partial \lambda} \frac{\partial g(z_i, \beta)}{\partial \lambda'} \right) \right]^{-1} E^\theta \left(\frac{\partial g(z_i, \beta)}{\partial \lambda} \sigma^2(x_i, \gamma) \frac{\partial g(z_i, \beta)}{\partial \lambda'} \right)$$
$$\times \left[E^\theta \left(\frac{\partial g(z_i, \beta)}{\partial \lambda} \frac{\partial g(z_i, \beta)}{\partial \lambda'} \right) \right]^{-1},$$

which can be estimated in the linear case, using the notation of Example 9.1, by

$$\widehat{\Sigma}_n^* = \left[Z'Z \right]^{-1} \left(\frac{1}{n} Z'\Omega Z \right) \left[Z'Z \right]^{-1}.$$

It can be shown that Σ_θ^* is still larger than or equal to the asymptotic variance of the GLS estimator given by (9.18).

The Case When γ is Unknown

Next we examine the case when γ is unknown. Suppose we have an estimator $\widehat{\gamma}_n$ available which converges to γ such that $\sqrt{n}(\widehat{\gamma}_n - \gamma)$ has a limiting distribution. In accordance with (9.7) of Section 9.2, we solve the system

$$\frac{1}{n} \sum_{i=1}^n \frac{(y_i - g(z_i, \lambda))}{\sigma^2(z_i, \widehat{\gamma}_n)} \frac{\partial g(z_i, \lambda)}{\partial \lambda} = 0$$

to find the estimator $\widehat{\beta}_n$ of β. According to Theorem 9.1, $\widehat{\beta}_n$ converges a.s. to β. Furthermore, one can show that the Condition (9.8) of Theorem 9.1 is satisfied

$$E^\theta \left(\frac{\partial \psi}{\partial \rho'}(x_i, \lambda, \rho) \bigg|_{\lambda(\theta) \text{ and } \rho(\theta)} \right) = 0.$$

Indeed

$$\frac{\partial \psi}{\partial \rho'}(x_i, \lambda, \rho) = -2 \frac{(y_i - g(z_i, \lambda))}{\sigma^3(z_i, \widehat{\gamma}_n)} \frac{\partial g(z_i, \lambda)}{\partial \lambda} \frac{\partial \sigma(z_i, \rho)}{\partial \rho'},$$

which implies

$$E^\theta \left(\frac{\partial \psi}{\partial \rho'}(x_i, \lambda, \rho) \right) = -2 E^\theta \left[\frac{1}{\sigma^3(z_i, \widehat{\gamma}_n)} \frac{\partial g(z_i, \lambda)}{\partial \lambda} \frac{\partial \sigma(z_i, \rho)}{\partial \rho'} \right.$$
$$\left. \times E^\theta \left((y_i - g(z_i, \lambda)) | z_i \right) \right] = 0$$

according to (9.12). By Theorem 9.1, the distribution of $\sqrt{n}(\widehat{\beta}_n - \beta)$ is then identical to the one in the case when γ is known, i.e.,

$$\sqrt{n} \left(\widehat{\beta}_n - \beta \right) \to N(0, \Sigma_\theta)$$

with

$$\Sigma_\theta = \left[E^\theta \left(\frac{1}{\sigma^2(z_i, \gamma)} \frac{\partial g(z_i, \lambda)}{\partial \lambda} \frac{\partial g(z_i, \lambda)}{\partial \lambda'} \right) \right]^{-1}$$

which is consistently estimated by

$$\widehat{\Sigma}_n = \left[\frac{1}{n} \sum_{i=1}^n \frac{1}{\sigma^2(z_i, \widehat{\gamma}_n)} \frac{\partial g(z_i, \widehat{\beta}_n)}{\partial \lambda} \frac{\partial g(z_i, \widehat{\beta}_n)}{\partial \lambda'} \right]^{-1}.$$

In the linear case illustrated by Examples 9.1 and 9.2, we obtain

$$\widehat{\Sigma}_n = \left[\frac{1}{n} Z' \widehat{\Omega}_n^{-1} Z \right]^{-1} \quad \text{and} \quad \widehat{\Sigma}_n = \widehat{\sigma}_{0n}^2 \left[\frac{1}{n} Z' \widehat{V}_n^{-1} Z \right]^{-1}$$

where $\widehat{\Omega}_n$ and $\widehat{V}_n$ are diagonal matrices whose (i, i) elements are $\sigma^2(z_i, \widehat{\gamma}_n)$ and $v(z_i, \widehat{\gamma}_n)$, respectively, and $\widehat{\sigma}_{0n}^2$ is given by (9.24).

Hence, we see that the estimation of the parameter vector of interest β rests on the prior estimation of γ, $\widehat{\gamma}_n$. To obtain such an estimator, which converges to γ and possesses a limiting distribution, the natural approach is the following:

- find an estimator of β by the method of moments, denoted $\widetilde{\beta}_n$, without taking heteroskedasticity into account,
- find the estimator $\widehat{\gamma}_n$ of γ which is the solution to

$$\min_\rho \frac{1}{n} \sum_{i=1}^n \left[(y_i - g(z_i, \widetilde{\beta}_n))^2 - \sigma^2(z_i, \rho) \right]^2 ; \tag{9.26}$$

which intuitively leads back to the least squares method for a regression model of the form

$$\widehat{u}_i^2 = \sigma^2(z_i, \rho) + \eta_i \qquad i = 1, \ldots, n,$$

where $\widehat{u}_i$ are the estimated residuals defined by $\widehat{u}_i = y_i - g(z_i, \widetilde{\beta}_n)$. The following example illustrates this approach for a simple case.

Example 9.4 *Assume that the conditional expectation is linear and the variance can be written in the form*

$$\sigma^2(z_i, \rho) = (\rho' z_i)^2,$$

then the natural procedure consists in the OLS estimation of the model

$$y_i = \beta' z_i + u_i \qquad i = 1, \ldots, n,$$

keeping the estimated residuals $\widehat{u}_i, i = 1, \ldots, n$, then estimating the model

$$\widehat{u}_i^2 = (\rho' z_i)^2 + \eta_i \qquad i = 1, \ldots, n,$$

by least squares which yields an estimator $\widehat{\gamma}_n$ of ρ, and finally setting

$$\sigma^2(z_i, \widehat{\gamma}_n) = (\widehat{\gamma}'_n z_i)^2.$$ □

Before we turn to the main tests for homoskedasticity, some words must be said about the specification of the conditional variance $\sigma^2(z_i, \gamma)$. First, we only considered the case when this function depends on the z_i; in the chapter on conditional heteroskedasticity, we extend this specification since it depends in a dynamic way on past y_i and on the z_i, which leads to different types of ARCH models. Moreover, the specification of $\sigma^2(z_i, \gamma)$ can sometimes be dictated by the formulation of the model, as the following example shows. In other cases, it can take on various forms, such as $\gamma'z_i$, $(\gamma'z_i)^2$ or $\gamma_0 \exp(\gamma'z_i)$.

Example 9.5   *Consider the homoskedastic i.i.d. case where*

$$E^\theta(y_{ik}|z_{ik}) = \beta'z_{ik},$$

and

$$Var^\theta(y_{ik}|z_{ik}) = \sigma_0^2,$$

and suppose that only the following means are observed for all $i = 1, \ldots, n$:

$$\begin{cases} \overline{y}_i = \frac{1}{n_i} \sum_{k=1}^{n_i} y_{ik} \\ \overline{z}_i = \frac{1}{n_i} \sum_{k=1}^{n_i} z_{ik} \end{cases}$$

(the n_i are not all equal). The regression model under study is based on the following moments

$$E^\theta(\overline{y}_i|\overline{z}_i) = \beta'\overline{z}_i,$$

and

$$Var^\theta(\overline{y}_i|\overline{z}_i) = \sigma_0^2/n_i,$$

then the regression equation becomes

$$\overline{y}_i = \beta'\overline{z}_i + \overline{u}_i \qquad i = 1, \ldots, n,$$

where $\overline{u}_i = \frac{1}{n_i} \sum_{k=1}^{n_i} u_{ik}$. In this case, using the notation of the previous examples for the linear case, we have

$$\Omega = \sigma_0^2 V = \sigma_0^2 \begin{bmatrix} 1/n_1 & 0 & \cdots & 0 \\ 0 & 1/n_2 & \cdots & 0 \\ \vdots & \vdots & & \vdots \\ 0 & 0 & \cdots & 1/n_n \end{bmatrix}.$$ □

In the following example, we see how the maximum likelihood method can be used to obtain estimators for β and ρ.

Example 9.6 *Consider the heteroskedastic i.i.d. case which was treated in Example 9.2:*

$$E^\theta(y_i|z_i) = \beta'z_i,$$

and a conditional variance that is more general than in the previous example:

$$Var^\theta(y_i|z_i) = \sigma^2(z_i, \gamma) = \sigma_0^2 v(z_i, \gamma),$$

where σ_0^2 is an unknown scalar parameter and $v(z_i, \gamma)$ is a function with strictly positive values depending on a parameter vector γ which we now assume to be unknown. Assume conditional normality, i.e.,

$$y_i|z_i \sim N(\beta'z_i, \sigma_0^2 v(z_i, \gamma)).$$

Denote by $V = V(\gamma)$ the $n \times n$ diagonal matrix whose (i, i) element is $v(z_i, \gamma)$, and let $y = (y_1, \ldots, y_n)'$ and $Z = (z_1, \ldots, z_n)'$, then the log-likelihood function is

$$\sum_{i=1}^{n} \ln l\left(y_i|z_i, \beta, \sigma_0^2, \gamma\right) = -\frac{n}{2} \ln \sigma_0^2 - \frac{1}{2} \ln |V| \tag{9.27}$$

$$-\frac{1}{2\sigma_0^2}(y - Z\beta)' V^{-1}(y - Z\beta).$$

Conditional on γ, the maximization of this function with respect to β and σ_0^2 yields

$$\tilde{\beta}_n(\gamma) = (Z' V^{-1} Z)^{-1} Z' V^{-1} y$$

and

$$\tilde{\sigma}_{0n}^2(\gamma) = \frac{1}{n}(y - Z\tilde{\beta}_n(\gamma))' V^{-1}(y - Z\tilde{\beta}_n(\gamma)).$$

By substituting these two expressions in (9.27), we obtain the concentrated log-likelihood function, denoted $L(\gamma)$,

$$L(\gamma) = -n \ln \left\{(y - Z\tilde{\beta}_n(\gamma))' V^{-1}(y - Z\tilde{\beta}_n(\gamma))\right\} - \ln |V|.$$

The MLE $\tilde{\gamma}_n$ of γ is the value of γ that maximizes $L(\gamma)$. Let $\tilde{V}_n = V(\tilde{\gamma}_n)$, then the MLE of β and σ_0^2 are

$$\tilde{\beta}_n = \tilde{\beta}_n(\tilde{\gamma}_n) = (Z' \tilde{V}_n^{-1} Z)^{-1} Z' \tilde{V}_n^{-1} y$$

and

$$\tilde{\sigma}_{0n}^2 = \tilde{\sigma}_{0n}^2(\tilde{\gamma}_n) = \frac{1}{n}(y - Z\tilde{\beta}_n)' \tilde{V}_n^{-1}(y - Z\tilde{\beta}_n)$$

and have the same form as the moment estimators. $\tilde{\beta}_n$ is asymptotically efficient and we can obtain the asymptotic distribution of $\tilde{\sigma}_{0n}^2$ and $\tilde{\gamma}_n$,

$$\sqrt{n}\left(\begin{bmatrix} \tilde{\beta}_n \\ \tilde{\sigma}_{0n}^2 \\ \tilde{\gamma}_n \end{bmatrix} - \begin{bmatrix} \beta \\ \sigma_0^2 \\ \gamma \end{bmatrix}\right) \rightarrow N(0, J_n^{-1})$$

with

$$J_n = \begin{bmatrix} \sigma_0^{-2}(Z'V^{-1}Z)^{-1} & 0 & 0 \\ 0 & n\sigma_0^{-4}/2 & \sigma_0^{-2}(vecV^{-1})'A/2 \\ 0 & \sigma_0^{-2}A'(vecV^{-1})/2 & A'(V^{-1} \otimes V^{-1})A/2 \end{bmatrix}$$

and

$$A = \frac{\partial vecV}{\partial \gamma}$$

(vec(.) is the operator that stacks the columns of a matrix).   □

Simple hypothesis tests can be derived from the asymptotic distribution of $\sqrt{n}(\hat{\beta}_n - \beta)$ as previously seen, whether γ is known or estimated, as the following example illustrates.

Example 9.7   *Continuation of Example 9.2. To test a set of J linear restrictions, represented by the hypothesis $H_0 : R\beta = r$, we use the statistic*

$$F_c = \frac{(R\hat{\beta}_n - r)'\left[R(Z'V^{-1}Z)^{-1}R'\right]^{-1}(R\hat{\beta}_n - r)}{\hat{\sigma}_{0n}^2}$$

which follows a χ^2 distribution with J degrees of freedom under H_0. If γ is estimated by $\hat{\gamma}_n$, the same formula remains valid when replacing V by $\hat{V} = V(\hat{\gamma}_n)$.   □

9.3.2   Tests for Homoskedasticity

Tests for homoskedasticity can be considered as conditional moment tests, which differ from each other by the moments that are used, by the treatment of nuisance parameters and by the specific form of heteroskedasticity. We provide two examples, the first is the test of Breusch, Pagan, and Godfrey, the second, for which the form of the heteroskedasticity is not specified, is White's test.

Example 9.8   *Consider the model given by its conditional moments*

$$E^\theta(y_i|z_i) = g(z_i, \beta),$$

and

$$Var^{\theta}(y_i | z_i) = \sigma^2(z_i, \gamma) = h(\gamma' z_i^*),$$

where h is an arbitrary function, z_i^* is a vector in $\mathbb{R}^l$ which contains known transformations of the z_i and for which the first element is 1. Denote $h(\gamma_1) = \sigma_0^2$. The test of Breusch, Pagan, and Godfrey applies the Rao procedure to the specific test where the null hypothesis is the hypothesis of homoskedasticity

$$H_0 : \gamma_2 = \cdots = \gamma_l = 0 \text{ or } H_0 : \gamma^* = 0$$

with $\gamma^* = (\gamma_2, \dots, \gamma_l)'$. Under the conditional normality assumption, the Rao statistic can be estimated by (see Chapter 4):

$$\widehat{RAO}_n = n \left(\frac{1}{n} \sum_{i=1}^{n} \frac{\partial \ln f(x_i | \widehat{\lambda}_n)}{\partial \lambda} \right)' \widehat{J}_n^{-1} \left(\frac{1}{n} \sum_{i=1}^{n} \frac{\partial \ln f(x_i | \widehat{\lambda}_n)}{\partial \lambda} \right)$$

where $\widehat{\lambda}_n$ is the parameter vector estimated under

$$H_0 : \widehat{\lambda}_n = (\widehat{\beta}_n, \widehat{\gamma}_{1n}, 0),$$

$\sum_{i=1}^{n} \ln f(x_i | \lambda)$ is the log-likelihood

$$\sum_{i=1}^{n} \ln f(x_i | \lambda) = -\frac{n}{2} \ln(2\pi) - \frac{1}{2} \sum_{i=1}^{n} \ln \left(h(\gamma' z_i^*) \right)$$

$$-\frac{1}{2} \sum_{i=1}^{n} \frac{(y_i - g(z_i, \beta))^2}{h(\gamma' z_i^*)}$$

and

$$\widehat{J}_n^{-1} = -\frac{1}{n} \sum_{i=1}^{n} \frac{\partial^2 \ln f(x_i | \widehat{\lambda}_n)}{\partial \lambda \partial \lambda'}.$$

Given that the information matrix J is block diagonal (in the sense that $E^{\theta}(\frac{\partial^2 \ln f(x_i | \lambda)}{\partial \beta \partial \gamma'}) = 0$), the statistic can be written in the simpler form

$$\widehat{RAO}_n = \frac{1}{2} \left(\sum_{i=1}^{n} z_i^* l_i \right)' \left(\sum_{i=1}^{n} z_i^* z_i^{*'} \right) \left(\sum_{i=1}^{n} z_i^* l_i \right)$$

where

$$l_i = \frac{(y_i - g(z_i, \widehat{\beta}_n))^2}{\widehat{\sigma}_{0n}^2} - 1$$

and

$$\widehat{\sigma}_{0n}^2 = h(\widehat{\gamma}_{1n}) = \frac{1}{n} \sum_{i=1}^{n} (y_i - g(z_i, \widehat{\beta}_n))^2.$$

This can also be written as

$$\widehat{RAO}_n = \frac{1}{2} l' Z (Z'Z)^{-1} Z' l$$

with $Z = (z_i, \ldots, z_n)'$ and $l = (l_1, \ldots, l_n)'$. One can show that $\widehat{RAO}_n$ is asymptotically χ^2 distributed with $(l-1)$ degrees of freedom. In practice, the stages for the test are the following: estimate β by $\widehat{\beta}_n$ and $h(\gamma_1)$ by $\widehat{\sigma}_{0n}^2$, for example by least squares estimation of the model

$$y_i = g(z_i, \beta) + u_i;$$

then calculate l_i, for all i; next estimate the auxiliary regression

$$l_i = \delta' z_i^* + \eta_i;$$

and finally calculate $\widehat{RAO}_n$. This statistic can be approximated in an asymptotically equivalent way by $n R_u^2$, where R_u^2 is the noncentered R^2 of the auxiliary regression. □

Example 9.9 *This example outlines White's test which does not specify a particular form for the heteroskedasticity. Consider the following model, using the notation of Example 9.1,*

$$E^\theta(y_i | z_i) = \beta' z_i,$$

and

$$Var^\theta(y_i | z_i) = \sigma^2(z_i, \gamma),$$

and continue to denote by Ω the $n \times n$ diagonal matrix whose (i, i) elements are equal to $\sigma^2(z_i, \gamma)$. White proposes not to use an estimator of $\sigma^2(z_i, \gamma)$ for all i, but instead an estimator of the matrix product $(Z'\Omega Z)$ given by

$$\widehat{W}_n = \frac{1}{n} \sum_{i=1}^{n} \widehat{u}_i^2 z_i z_i'$$

where $\widehat{u}_i = (y_i - \widehat{\beta}_n^{*'} z_i)$ and $\widehat{\beta}_n^*$ is the OLS estimator of β. He shows that $\widehat{W}_n$ asymptotically approaches $(Z'\Omega Z)$. Furthermore, he suggests that the difference between the variance of the OLS estimator under the assumption of heteroskedasticity and the assumption of homoskedasticity (characterized by $Var^\theta(y_i | z_i) = \sigma_0^2$ for all i), i.e.,

$$(Z'Z)^{-1} Z' \Omega Z (Z'Z)^{-1} - \sigma_0^2 (Z'Z)^{-1}$$

or the simpler difference

$$Z'\Omega Z - \sigma_0^2(Z'Z) = \sum_{i=1}^{n} \left(E^\theta \left((y_i - \beta' z_i)^2 \right) - \sigma_0^2 \right) z_i z_i',$$

can serve as the base for a test for homoskedasticity. Hence, we are interested in the statistic

$$\frac{1}{n} \sum_{i=1}^{n} \left(\widehat{u}_i^2 - \widehat{\sigma}_0^2 \right) z_i z_i'.$$

Based on this idea, the final form of White's test statistic is

$$\tau_c = \left(\frac{1}{n} \sum_{i=1}^{n} \left(\widehat{u}_i^2 - \widehat{\sigma}_0^2 \right) \xi_i \right)' \widehat{D}_n^{-1} \left(\frac{1}{n} \sum_{i=1}^{n} \left(\widehat{u}_i^2 - \widehat{\sigma}_0^2 \right) \xi_i \right)$$

with $\xi_i = (\xi_{1i}, \dots, \xi_{si})'$, $\xi_{ji} = z_{ki} z_{li}$, $k \geq l$, $l, k = 2, \dots, s$, $s = q(q-1)/2$,

$$\widehat{D}_n = \frac{1}{n} \sum_{i=1}^{n} \left(\widehat{u}_i^2 - \widehat{\sigma}_0^2 \right)^2 \left(\xi_i - \overline{\xi}_n \right) \left(\xi_i - \overline{\xi}_n \right)'$$

and

$$\overline{\xi}_n = \frac{1}{n} \sum_{i=1}^{n} \xi_i.$$

Under the hypothesis of homoskedasticity, the statistic τ_c is χ^2 distributed with s degrees of freedom. One can show that this is asymptotically equivalent to

$$\tau_c' = n R^2$$

in the auxiliary regression

$$\widehat{u}_i^2 = \alpha_0 + \alpha_1 \xi_{1i} + \cdots + \alpha_s \xi_{si} + \varepsilon_i.$$

τ_c' is also χ^2 distributed with s degrees of freedom under the hypothesis of homoskedasticity. □

9.4 Multivariate Regression

We generalize the models of heteroskedasticity of the preceding section to the multivariate case, y_i is now a vector. We consider the finite sequence $(x_i)_{i=1,\dots,n}$ with $x_i = (y_i, z_i)$, $y_i \in \mathbb{R}^p$, $z_i \in \mathbb{R}^q$ and $p + q = m$. The x_i are still i.i.d. with the same distribution Q^θ. The conditional moments are

$$E^\theta(y_i | z_i) = g(z_i, \beta) = \begin{bmatrix} g_1(z_i, \beta) \\ \vdots \\ g_p(z_i, \beta) \end{bmatrix} \tag{9.28}$$

and

$$Var^{\theta}(y_i|z_i) = V(z_i, \gamma) = \begin{bmatrix} \sigma_{11}(z_i, \gamma) & \cdots & \sigma_{1p}(z_i, \gamma) \\ \vdots & & \vdots \\ \sigma_{p1}(z_i, \gamma) & \cdots & \sigma_{pp}(z_i, \gamma) \end{bmatrix} \quad (9.29)$$

with, for all $j = 1, \ldots, p$,

$$g_j(z_i, \beta) \in \left\{ g_j(z_i, \lambda), \lambda \in \Lambda \subset \mathbb{R}^k \right\} \subset L^2(z_i)$$

and, for all $j, s = 1, \ldots, p$,

$$\sigma_{js}(z_i, \gamma) \in \left\{ \sigma_{js}(z_i, \rho), \rho \in R \subset \mathbb{R}^l \right\} \subset L^2(z_i).$$

The matrix V is also assumed to be symmetric positive definite for all z_i and all γ. The functions g_j and σ_{js} are assumed to be continuous, differentiable, and identified on Λ and R. It is important to note that we are only interested in the case where the correlations are contemporaneous and not intertemporal, since we are placing ourselves in an i.i.d. setting.

Two cases are possible, depending on whether γ is known or not.

▶ When γ is know, then we are interested in the problem

$$\min_{\lambda \in \Lambda} E^{\theta}(\phi(x_i, \lambda)) \quad (9.30)$$

with

$$\phi(x_i, \lambda) = (y_i - g(z_i, \lambda))' \, V(z_i, \gamma)^{-1} \, (y_i - g(z_i, \lambda)). \quad (9.31)$$

Intuitively, we can note that this formulation allows for the introduction of a heteroskedasticity correction.

Example 9.10   *Consider the case where $V(z_i, \gamma) = V(\gamma)$ i.e., is composed of constants. Since $V(\gamma)$ is symmetric positive definite, so is its inverse which can be written as $V(\gamma)^{-1} = P'P$, hence we can infer from (9.29) that*

$$Var^{\theta}(Py_i|z_i) = PV(\gamma)P' = I.$$

(9.31) becomes then

$$\phi(x_i, \lambda) = [P(y_i - g(z_i, \lambda))]' \, [P(y_i - g(z_i, \lambda))],$$

which shows that the minimization problem (9.30) corresponds to a minimization problem in a homoskedastic multivariate model. □

Another remark concerning (9.30) and (9.31) is that, in the case where $p = 1$, we get back the representation (9.14) and (9.15) of the preceding univariate section.

The problem (9.30) results in a simple system of moment equations given by

$$E^\theta(\psi(x_i, \lambda)) = 0 \tag{9.32}$$

with

$$\psi(x_i, \lambda) = \frac{\partial g(z_i, \lambda)'}{\partial \lambda} V(z_i, \gamma)^{-1} (y_i - g(z_i, \lambda)). \tag{9.33}$$

The moment estimator $\widehat{\beta}_n$ is thus obtained as the solution to

$$\frac{1}{n} \sum_{i=1}^n \frac{\partial g(z_i, \lambda)'}{\partial \lambda} V(z_i, \gamma)^{-1} (y_i - g(z_i, \lambda)) = 0. \tag{9.34}$$

The asymptotic properties of $\widehat{\beta}_n$ derive from (9.4), (9.5), and (9.6) of Section 9.2, i.e.,

$$\widehat{\beta}_n \to \beta \ P^\theta - a.s., \tag{9.35}$$

where β is the solution of (9.32) and

$$\sqrt{n} \left(\widehat{\beta}_n - \beta\right) \to N(0, \Sigma_\theta) \quad \text{in } P^\theta\text{-distribution} \tag{9.36}$$

with

$$\Sigma_\theta = \left[E^\theta \left(\frac{\partial \psi}{\partial \lambda'}\right)\right]^{-1} Var^0(\psi) \left[E^\theta \left(\frac{\partial \psi'}{\partial \lambda}\right)\right]^{-1}.$$

Here we have

$$E^\theta \left(\frac{\partial \psi}{\partial \lambda'}\right) = E^\theta \left(\frac{\partial^2 g(z_i, \lambda)}{\partial \lambda \partial \lambda'} V(z_i, \gamma)^{-1} (y_i - g(z_i, \lambda))\right)$$

$$- E^\theta \left(\frac{\partial g(z_i, \lambda)'}{\partial \lambda} V(z_i, \gamma)^{-1} \frac{\partial g(z_i, \lambda)}{\partial \lambda'}\right)$$

$$= - E^\theta \left(\frac{\partial g(z_i, \lambda)'}{\partial \lambda} V(z_i, \gamma)^{-1} \frac{\partial g(z_i, \lambda)}{\partial \lambda'}\right)$$

since

$$E^\theta \left(\frac{\partial^2 g(z_i, \lambda)}{\partial \lambda \partial \lambda'} V(z_i, \gamma)^{-1} (y_i - g(z_i, \lambda))\right)$$

$$= E^\theta \left(\frac{\partial^2 g(z_i, \lambda)}{\partial \lambda \partial \lambda'} V(z_i, \gamma)^{-1} E^\theta \left[(y_i - g(z_i, \lambda)) | z_i\right]\right) = 0$$

according to (9.28). Moreover, it also follows from (9.28) that

$$Var^0(\psi) = E^\theta \left(Var^0(\psi | z_i)\right) + Var^\theta \left(E^\theta(\psi | z_i)\right) = E^\theta \left(Var^0(\psi | z_i)\right),$$

hence

$$Var^{\theta}(\psi) = E^{\theta}\left[Var^{\theta}\left(\frac{\partial g(z_i, \lambda)'}{\partial \lambda} V(z_i, \gamma)^{-1} (y_i - g(z_i, \lambda)) | z_i \right) \right]$$

$$= E^{\theta}\left[\frac{\partial g(z_i, \lambda)'}{\partial \lambda} V(z_i, \gamma)^{-1} Var^{\theta}((y_i - g(z_i, \lambda)) | z_i) V(z_i, \gamma)^{-1} \frac{\partial g(z_i, \lambda)}{\partial \lambda'} \right]$$

$$= E^{\theta}\left[\frac{\partial g(z_i, \lambda)'}{\partial \lambda} V(z_i, \gamma)^{-1} \frac{\partial g(z_i, \lambda)}{\partial \lambda'} \right]$$

according to the definition of the conditional variance (9.29). Hence, we obtain the expression for Σ_{θ}

$$\Sigma_{\theta} = \left(E^{\theta}\left[\frac{\partial g(z_i, \beta)'}{\partial \lambda} V(z_i, \gamma)^{-1} \frac{\partial g(z_i, \beta)}{\partial \lambda'} \right] \right)^{-1} \tag{9.37}$$

which is naturally estimated by

$$\widehat{\Sigma}_n = \left(\frac{1}{n} \sum_{i=1}^{n} \frac{\partial g(z_i, \widehat{\beta}_n)'}{\partial \lambda} V(z_i, \gamma)^{-1} \frac{\partial g(z_i, \widehat{\beta}_n)}{\partial \lambda'} \right)^{-1}. \tag{9.38}$$

The uniqueness of β implies the invertibility of the matrix which is inverted in (9.37), which implies, for sufficiently large samples, that using the inverse in (9.38) is possible.

▶ When γ is unknown, we assume that we have an estimator $\widehat{\gamma}_n$ available which converges to γ and is such that $\sqrt{n}(\widehat{\gamma}_n - \gamma)$ possesses a limiting distribution. This leads us to solving the system (9.7) of Section 9.2, which in this case can be written as

$$\frac{1}{n} \sum_{i=1}^{n} \frac{\partial g(z_i, \lambda)'}{\partial \lambda} V(z_i, \widehat{\gamma}_n)^{-1} (y_i - g(z_i, \lambda)) = 0.$$

According to the first part of Theorem 9.1 of Section 9.2, $\widehat{\gamma}_n$ converges a.s. to γ. The second part of the theorem implies that, if Condition (9.8) holds, then the asymptotic distribution of $\sqrt{n}(\widehat{\beta}_n - \beta)$ is equal to (9.36) with Σ_{θ} given by (9.37). Let us verify that Condition (9.8) is satisfied:

$$E^{\theta}\left(\frac{\partial \psi}{\partial \rho'}(x_i, \lambda, \rho) \right) = E^{\theta}\left(\frac{\partial g(z_i, \lambda)'}{\partial \lambda} \frac{\partial \left(V(z_i, \gamma)^{-1} \right)}{\partial \rho'} (y_i - g(z_i, \lambda)) \right)$$

$$= E^{\theta}\left(\frac{\partial g(z_i, \lambda)'}{\partial \lambda} \frac{\partial \left(V(z_i, \gamma)^{-1} \right)}{\partial \rho'} E^{\theta}\left[(y_i - g(z_i, \lambda)) | z_i \right] \right)$$

$$= 0.$$

Thus from Theorem 9.1 of Section 9.2 it follows that

$$\sqrt{n}\left(\widehat{\beta}_n - \beta\right) \to N(0, \Sigma_\theta) \quad \text{in } P^\theta\text{-distribution} \tag{9.39}$$

with

$$\Sigma_\theta = \left(E^\theta \left[\frac{\partial g(z_i, \beta)'}{\partial \lambda} V(z_i, \gamma)^{-1} \frac{\partial g(z_i, \beta)}{\partial \lambda'} \right] \right)^{-1}$$

which is naturally estimated by

$$\widehat{\Sigma}_n = \left(\frac{1}{n} \sum_{i=1}^n \frac{\partial g(z_i, \widehat{\beta}_n)'}{\partial \lambda} V(z_i, \widehat{\gamma}_n)^{-1} \frac{\partial g(z_i, \widehat{\beta}_n)}{\partial \lambda'} \right)^{-1}.$$

In the following example we look at the case of a linear conditional expectation.

Example 9.11 *Write the conditional expectation in the form*

$$E^\theta(y_i | z_i) = z_i^{*\prime} \beta$$

where z_i^* is a $k \times p$ matrix formed from the elements of the vector z_i and β is a $k \times 1$ vector. In this case

$$\frac{\partial g(z_i, \lambda)'}{\partial \lambda} = z_i^*.$$

Suppose in addition, that γ is estimated by $\widehat{\gamma}_n$. Therefore, $\widehat{\beta}_n$ is, according to (9.34), the solution of

$$\frac{1}{n} \sum_{i=1}^n z_i^* V(z_i, \widehat{\gamma}_n)^{-1} \left(y_i - z_i^{*\prime} \lambda \right) = 0,$$

hence

$$\widehat{\beta}_n = \left[\sum_{i=1}^n z_i^* V(z_i, \widehat{\gamma}_n)^{-1} z_i^{*\prime} \right]^{-1} \left[\sum_{i=1}^n z_i^* V(z_i, \widehat{\gamma}_n)^{-1} y_i \right]$$

which is the multivariate generalization of (9.22). (9.36), (9.37), and (9.38), implying that

$$\sqrt{n}\left(\widehat{\beta}_n - \beta\right) \to N(0, \Sigma_\theta) \quad \text{in } P^\theta\text{-distribution}$$

with

$$\Sigma_\theta = \left(E^\theta \left[z_i^* V(z_i, \gamma)^{-1} z_i^{*\prime} \right] \right)^{-1}$$

which is naturally estimated by

$$\widehat{\Sigma}_n = \left(\frac{1}{n} \sum_{i=1}^{n} z_i^* V(z_i, \widehat{\gamma}_n)^{-1} z_i^{*\prime} \right)^{-1}.$$

□

We consider now in more detail the relationship between the preceding approach and the traditional way of studying a particular case of a multivariate model, which is the one of *seemingly unrelated regressions* (SUR).

Example 9.12   *Consider the case where the conditional moments are written in the form:*

$$E^\theta(y_i|z_i) = z_i^{*\prime} \beta \tag{9.40}$$

and

$$Var^\theta(y_i|z_i) = V(\gamma) = \begin{bmatrix} \sigma_{11}(\gamma) & \cdots & \sigma_{1p}(\gamma) \\ \vdots & & \vdots \\ \sigma_{p1}(\gamma) & \cdots & \sigma_{pp}(\gamma) \end{bmatrix},$$

z_i^* *is a* $q \times p$ *matrix formed from the elements of the vector* z_i, β *is* $q \times 1$ *vector and* $V(\gamma)$ *is a* $p \times p$ *matrix which we will denote in the following by* V. *Define the* u_i, *for all* $i = 1, \ldots, n$, *as the* $p \times 1$ *vector*

$$u_i = y_i - E^\theta(y_i|z_i) = y_i - z_i^{*\prime} \beta$$

for which by assumption $E^\theta(u_i|z_i) = 0$ *and* $Var^\theta(u_i|z_i) = V(\gamma)$. *Thus the model becomes*

$$y_i = z_i^{*\prime} \beta + u_i \qquad i = 1, \ldots, n. \tag{9.41}$$

Let us define now more precisely the variables and parameters which enter in the expectation of each element of the vector y_i. *To do this, suppose that* $q^{(j)}$ *elements of the vector* z_i *enter the expression for the conditional expectation of* y_{ij}, *for* $i = 1, \ldots, n$ *and* $j = 1, \ldots, p$:

$$E^\theta(y_{ij}|z_i) = z_{i1}^{(j)}\beta_1^{(j)} + z_{i2}^{(j)}\beta_2^{(j)} + \cdots + z_{iq^{(j)}}^{(j)}\beta_{q^{(j)}}^{(j)}$$

(with $\sum_{j=1}^{n} q^{(j)} = q$), *and partition the vectors* z_i *and* β *in (9.40) in the following manner*

$$z_i = \left(z_i^{(1)\prime}, z_i^{(2)\prime}, \ldots, z_i^{(p)\prime} \right)^{\prime}$$

and

$$\beta = \left(\beta^{(1)\prime}, \beta^{(2)\prime}, \ldots, \beta^{(p)\prime} \right)^{\prime}$$

where $z_i^{(j)}$ and $\beta^{(j)}$ are $q^{(j)} \times 1$ vectors composed from the $z_{is}^{(j)}$ and the $\beta_s^{(j)}$ (for all $s = 1, \ldots, q^{(j)}$) respectively. Define for $j = 1, \ldots, p$, the $n \times 1$ vectors $y^{(j)}$ and $u^{(j)}$ and the $n \times q^{(j)}$ matrix $Z^{(j)}$ by

$$
y^{(j)} = \begin{bmatrix} y_{1j} \\ \vdots \\ y_{nj} \end{bmatrix}, \quad u^{(j)} = \begin{bmatrix} u_{1j} \\ \vdots \\ u_{nj} \end{bmatrix} \quad and \quad Z^{(j)} = \begin{bmatrix} z_1^{(j)\prime} \\ \vdots \\ z_n^{(j)\prime} \end{bmatrix}. \tag{9.42}
$$

The model (9.41) can then be written as

$$
y^{(j)} = Z^{(j)}\beta^{(j)} + u^{(j)} \qquad j = 1, \ldots, p \tag{9.43}
$$

or equivalently

$$
y = Z\beta + u \tag{9.44}
$$

where the $np \times 1$ vectors y and u, the $q \times 1$ vector β, and the $np \times q$ matrix Z are defined by

$$
y = \begin{bmatrix} y^{(1)} \\ \vdots \\ y^{(p)} \end{bmatrix}, \quad u = \begin{bmatrix} u^{(1)} \\ \vdots \\ u^{(p)} \end{bmatrix}, \quad \beta = \begin{bmatrix} \beta^{(1)} \\ \vdots \\ \beta^{(p)} \end{bmatrix} \quad and \quad Z = \begin{bmatrix} Z^{(1)} & \cdots & 0 \\ \vdots & & \vdots \\ 0 & \cdots & Z^{(p)} \end{bmatrix}.
$$

We find here again the vector β as it appeared in (9.40) and (9.41). Consider now the second order moments corresponding to this new notation

$$
Cov^\theta(u_k^{(j)}, u_{k'}^{(j')}) = \begin{vmatrix} \sigma_{jj'} & if\ k = k' \\ 0 & otherwise. \end{vmatrix}
$$

for $j, j' = 1, \ldots, p$. Let V be the $p \times p$ matrix of the σ_{ij}. We have by construction

$$
E^\theta(u|Z) = 0 \tag{9.45}
$$

and

$$
Var^\theta(u|Z) = \begin{bmatrix} \sigma_{11}I_n & \cdots & \sigma_{1p}I_n \\ \vdots & & \vdots \\ \sigma_{p1}I_n & \cdots & \sigma_{pp}I_n \end{bmatrix} = V \otimes I_n \tag{9.46}
$$

(where $\otimes$ represents the Kronecker product). The model consisting of Equations (9.44) and Assumptions (9.45) and (9.46) is commonly called a system of seemingly unrelated equations, since the p equations of the system are only *related through the contemporaneous covariances σ_{ij}. Consider now the moment estimator $\widehat{\beta}_n$. The conditional expectation (9.40) can be rewritten as*

$$E^\theta(y_i|z_i) = \beta'z_i = \begin{bmatrix} \beta^{(1)\prime}z_i^{(1)} \\ \vdots \\ \beta^{(p)\prime}z_i^{(p)} \end{bmatrix},$$

hence

$$\frac{\partial g(z_i, \lambda)'}{\partial \lambda} = \begin{bmatrix} z_i^{(1)} & \cdots & 0 \\ \vdots & & \vdots \\ 0 & \cdots & z_i^{(p)} \end{bmatrix}$$

which is of dimension $q \times p$. The moment equations (9.34) are now

$$\frac{1}{n}\sum_{i=1}^{n} \begin{bmatrix} z_i^{(1)} & \cdots & 0 \\ \vdots & & \vdots \\ 0 & \cdots & z_i^{(p)} \end{bmatrix} \begin{bmatrix} \sigma^{11} & \cdots & \sigma^{1p} \\ \vdots & & \vdots \\ \sigma^{p1} & \cdots & \sigma^{pp} \end{bmatrix} \begin{bmatrix} y_i^{(1)} - \beta^{(1)\prime}z_i^{(1)} \\ \vdots \\ y_i^{(p)} - \beta^{(p)\prime}z_i^{(p)} \end{bmatrix} = 0,$$

by setting $V^{-1} = (\sigma^{ij})$. Hence,

$$\widehat{\beta}_n = \begin{bmatrix} \widehat{\beta}_n^{(1)} \\ \vdots \\ \widehat{\beta}_n^{(M)} \end{bmatrix}$$

$$= \begin{bmatrix} \sigma^{11}Z^{(1)\prime}Z^{(1)} & \cdots & \sigma^{1M}Z^{(1)\prime}Z^{(M)} \\ \vdots & & \vdots \\ \sigma^{1M}Z^{(M)\prime}Z^{(1)} & \cdots & \sigma^{MM}Z^{(M)\prime}Z^{(M)} \end{bmatrix}^{-1} \begin{bmatrix} \sum_{i=1}^{M}\sigma^{1i}Z^{(1)\prime}y^{(i)} \\ \vdots \\ \sum_{i=1}^{M}\sigma^{Mi}Z^{(M)\prime}y^{(i)} \end{bmatrix}.$$

A quick calculation shows that $\widehat{\beta}_n$ can be written as

$$\widehat{\beta}_n = \left[Z'(V^{-1} \otimes I_n)Z\right]^{-1} Z'(V^{-1} \otimes I_n)y \tag{9.47}$$

which is the expression one usually finds in econometrics textbooks. In accordance with the properties proven for the general case, $\widehat{\beta}_n$ converges to β and

$$\sqrt{n}\left(\widehat{\beta}_n - \beta\right) \to N(0, \Sigma_\theta) \quad \text{in } P^\theta\text{-distribution}$$

with

$$\Sigma_\theta = \left(E^\theta \left[\begin{bmatrix} z_i^{(1)} & \cdots & 0 \\ \vdots & & \vdots \\ 0 & \cdots & z_i^{(p)} \end{bmatrix} \begin{bmatrix} \sigma^{11} & \cdots & \sigma^{1p} \\ \vdots & & \vdots \\ \sigma^{p1} & \cdots & \sigma^{pp} \end{bmatrix} \begin{bmatrix} z_i^{(1)\prime} & \cdots & 0 \\ \vdots & & \vdots \\ 0 & \cdots & z_i^{(p)\prime} \end{bmatrix} \right] \right)^{-1}$$

or

$$\Sigma_\theta = \left(E^\theta \left[\begin{matrix} \sigma^{11} z_i^{(1)} z_i^{(1)\prime} & \cdots & \sigma^{1p} z_i^{(1)} z_i^{(p)\prime} \\ \vdots & & \vdots \\ \sigma^{p1} z_i^{(p)} z_i^{(1)\prime} & \cdots & \sigma^{pp} z_i^{(p)} z_i^{(p)\prime} \end{matrix} \right] \right)^{-1}$$

which can be estimated by

$$\widehat{\Sigma}_n = \left(\frac{1}{n} \sum_{i=1}^{n} \left[\begin{matrix} \sigma^{11} z_i^{(1)} z_i^{(1)\prime} & \cdots & \sigma^{1p} z_i^{(1)} z_i^{(p)\prime} \\ \vdots & & \vdots \\ \sigma^{p1} z_i^{(p)} z_i^{(1)\prime} & \cdots & \sigma^{pp} z_i^{(p)} z_i^{(p)\prime} \end{matrix} \right] \right)^{-1} = V^{-1} \otimes I_n$$

$$(9.48)$$

When V is unknown and needs to be estimated by $\widehat{V}_n$, then the formulas (9.47) and (9.48) apply with V replaced by $\widehat{V}_n$. We are compelled to two remarks. First, if the equations are not related, i.e., if $\sigma_{ij} = 0$ for all i and j, $i \neq j$, then estimating by the method of moments is the same as estimating each equation separately and independently by OLS. Finally if the matrices of the explanatory variables are all the same, i.e., if $Z^{(i)} = Z^{(0)}$ for all i, then

$$Z = \begin{bmatrix} Z^{(0)} & \cdots & 0 \\ \vdots & & \vdots \\ 0 & \cdots & Z^{(0)} \end{bmatrix} = I \otimes Z^{(0)}.$$

We then have

$$\widehat{\beta}_n = \left[(I \otimes Z^{(0)})'(V^{-1} \otimes I_n)(I \otimes Z^{(0)}) \right]^{-1} (I \otimes Z^{(0)})'(V^{-1} \otimes I_n) y$$

$$= I \otimes (Z^{(0)\prime} Z^{(0)})^{-1} Z^{(0)\prime} y$$

$$= \begin{bmatrix} (Z^{(0)\prime} Z^{(0)})^{-1} Z^{(0)\prime} & \cdots & 0 \\ \vdots & & \vdots \\ 0 & \cdots & (Z^{(0)\prime} Z^{(0)})^{-1} Z^{(0)\prime} \end{bmatrix} \begin{bmatrix} y^{(1)} \\ \vdots \\ y^{(M)} \end{bmatrix}.$$

Hence, for all $i = 1, \ldots, M$

$$\widehat{\beta}_n^{(i)} = (Z^{(0)\prime} Z^{(0)})^{-1} Z^{(0)\prime} y^{(i)}.$$

Therefore, the method of moments is here again the same as OLS applied equation by equation. $\square$

When the parameter vector γ is unknown, it is necessary to find an estimator $\widehat{\gamma}_n$ of γ. This estimator will depend on the formulation of the model; the following example illustrates this point for the setting of the model introduced in the previous example.

Example 9.13 *Consider the notation of the previous example. When the matrix V is unknown, then the moment estimator of β is obtained by replacing V by a consistent estimator $\widehat{V}_n$*

$$\widehat{\beta}_n = \left[Z'(\widehat{V}_n^{-1} \otimes I_n)Z \right]^{-1} Z'(\widehat{V}_n^{-1} \otimes I_n)y. \tag{9.49}$$

This estimator is called Zellner's seemingly unrelated regression estimator. The matrix $\widehat{V}_n$ may be obtained by separately estimating each equation of the system (9.43) or (9.44) by OLS for obtaining the vector of the estimated residuals $\widehat{u}^{(i)OLS}$ for all $i = 1, \ldots, p$ and by setting

$$\widehat{\sigma}_{ijn} = \frac{\widehat{u}^{(i)OLS\prime}\widehat{u}^{(j)OLS}}{n} \tag{9.50}$$

for all $i, j = 1, \ldots, p$. Other choices can be made for the denominator (for example $\sqrt{(n - q^{(i)})(n - q^{(j)})}$ or $n - \max(q^{(i)}, q^{(j)})$). The various estimators of V that result from these choices can be compared in small samples by Monte-Carlo experiments. However, their asymptotic properties are identical. Indeed, the general results for the method of moments remain valid and show that $\widehat{\beta}_n$ in (9.49) has the same asymptotic properties as $\widehat{\beta}_n$ given by (9.47). A different procedure for estimating β and V is the iterated application of the feasible GLS. The $\widehat{\sigma}_{ijn}$ are calculated according to (9.50), then $\widehat{\beta}_n$ according to (9.49); afterward, at each iteration new estimators for σ_{ij} and β are calculated. □

When the number of observations differs from one equation to the next, this has implications for the estimation of the parameters, as the following example illustrates. We limit ourselves to a system of two equations.

Example 9.14 *Consider the following system*

$$\begin{bmatrix} y^{(1)} \\ y^{(2)} \end{bmatrix} = \begin{bmatrix} Z^{(1)} & 0 \\ 0 & Z^{(2)} \end{bmatrix} \begin{bmatrix} \beta^{(1)} \\ \beta^{(2)} \end{bmatrix} + \begin{bmatrix} u^{(1)} \\ u^{(2)} \end{bmatrix},$$

where we have n observations in the first equation and $n + s$ observations in the second. This can also be written as

$$y = Z\beta + u$$

where y and u are $(2n + s) \times 1$ vectors, Z is a $(2n + s) \times (k^{(1)} + k^{(2)})$ matrix, and β is a $(k^{(1)} + k^{(2)}) \times 1$ vector. Suppose that the $(y_i^{(1)\prime}, y_i^{(2)\prime})\prime$ have expectation zero and variance

$$V = \begin{bmatrix} \sigma_{11} & \sigma_{12} \\ \sigma_{12} & \sigma_{22} \end{bmatrix},$$

then

$$E^\theta(uu'|Z) = \Omega = \begin{bmatrix} \sigma_{11} I_n & \sigma_{12} I_n & 0 \\ \sigma_{12} I_n & \sigma_{22} I_n & 0 \\ 0 & 0 & \sigma_{22} I_s \end{bmatrix} \neq V \otimes I.$$

The estimator of β is

$$\widehat{\beta}_n = (Z'\Omega^{-1}Z)^{-1}Z'\Omega^{-1}y$$

and is thus different from

$$(Z'(V^{-1} \otimes I_n)Z)^{-1}Z'(V^{-1} \otimes I_n)y.$$

Let

$$y^{(2)} = \begin{bmatrix} y^{(2)*} \\ y^{(2)0} \end{bmatrix} \quad and \quad Z^{(2)} = \begin{bmatrix} Z^{(2)*} \\ Z^{(2)0} \end{bmatrix}$$

where $y^{(2)*}$ and $Z^{(2)*}$ contain n observations, and $y^{(2)0}$ and $Z^{(2)0}$ contain s observations. Furthermore, let $V^{-1} = (\sigma^{ij})$. Then $\widehat{\beta}_n$ is

$$\widehat{\beta}_n = \begin{bmatrix} \sigma^{11} Z^{(1)\prime} Z^{(1)} & \sigma^{12} Z^{(1)\prime} Z^{(2)*} \\ \sigma^{12} Z^{(2)*\prime} Z^{(1)} & \sigma^{22} Z^{(2)*\prime} Z^{(2)*} + \frac{1}{\sigma_{22}} Z^{(2)0\prime} Z^{(2)0} \end{bmatrix}^{-1}$$

$$\times \begin{bmatrix} \sigma^{11} Z^{(1)\prime} y^{(1)} + \sigma^{12} Z^{(1)\prime} y^{(2)*} \\ \sigma^{12} Z^{(2)*\prime} y^{(1)} + \sigma^{22} Z^{(2)*\prime} y^{(2)*} + \frac{1}{\sigma_{22}} Z^{(2)0\prime} y^{(2)0} \end{bmatrix}.$$

When V is unknown, then its elements can be estimated in various ways, for example

$$\begin{cases} \widehat{\sigma}_{11n} = \frac{1}{n} \left(y^{(1)} - Z^{(1)}\widehat{\beta}_n^{(1)MCO} \right)' \left(y^{(1)} - Z^{(1)}\widehat{\beta}_n^{(1)MCO} \right) \\ \widehat{\sigma}_{12n} = \frac{1}{n} \left(y^{(1)} - Z^{(1)}\widehat{\beta}_n^{(1)MCO} \right)' \left(y^{(2)*} - Z^{(2)*}\widehat{\beta}_n^{(2)MCO} \right) \\ \widehat{\sigma}_{22n} = \frac{1}{s} \left(y^{(2)} - Z^{(2)}\widehat{\beta}_n^{(2)MCO} \right)' \left(y^{(2)} - Z^{(2)}\widehat{\beta}_n^{(2)MCO} \right). \end{cases}$$

Sometimes the problem arises that $\widehat{V}_n$ is not invertible, therefore other estimator have been suggested in the literature.   □

The following example illustrates the maximum likelihood method applied to a multivariate regression model.

Example 9.15 *Suppose the conditional moments are given by*

$$E^\theta(y_i|z_i) = g(z_i, \beta)$$

and

$$Var^\theta(y_i|z_i) = V$$

where V is a symmetric positive definite $p \times p$ matrix of unknown scalar parameters σ_{ij}. Using Example 9.11 which has linear expectations, we can write the model as follows, after regrouping the terms

$$y^{(j)} = G^{(j)}(Z^{(j)}, \beta) + u^{(j)} \qquad j = 1, \ldots, p$$

where $y^{(j)}$ and $Z^{(j)}$ are given by (9.42),

$$u^{(j)} = y^{(j)} - E^\theta(y^{(j)}|Z^{(j)}),$$

$$G^{(j)}(Z^{(j)}, \beta) = \left(g_{1j}(z_1^{(j)}, \beta), \ldots, g_{nj}(z_n^{(j)}, \beta)\right)',$$

and

$$Var^\theta(u|Z) = V \otimes I_n$$

with

$$u = \left(u^{(1)'}, \ldots, u^{(p)'}\right)'.$$

Assuming the normality assumption holds, we have

$$y^{(j)}|Z \sim N(G^{(j)}(Z^{(j)}, \beta), V),$$

the log-likelihood is

$$\ln l(y|Z, \beta, V) = -\frac{np}{2} \ln(2\pi) - \frac{1}{2} \ln|V \otimes I_n|$$

$$-\frac{1}{2}(y - G(Z, \beta))'(V^{-1} \otimes I_n)(y - G(Z, \beta))$$

where

$$G(Z, \beta) = \left(G^{(1)}(Z^{(1)}, \beta), \ldots, G^{(p)}(Z^{(p)}, \beta)\right)'.$$

By the properties of Kronecker product, we have that $\ln|V \otimes I_n| = n \ln|V|$ and

$$(y - G(Z, \beta))'(V^{-1} \otimes I_n)(y - G(Z, \beta)) = tr\left(SV^{-1}\right)$$

where S is a $p \times p$ matrix whose (i, j) element is $u^{(i)'}u^{(j)}$. The function to maximize then becomes

$$\ln l(y \,|\, Z, \beta, V) = -\frac{np}{2} \ln(2\pi) - \frac{n}{2} \ln|V| - \frac{1}{2} tr\left(SV^{-1}\right).$$

It is possible to obtain a concentrated likelihood function for β. In order to do this, we differentiate the above function with respect to V^{-1}. Knowing that

$$\frac{\partial \ln|V^{-1}|}{\partial V^{-1}} = V \quad \text{and} \quad \frac{\partial tr\left(SV^{-1}\right)}{\partial V^{-1}} = S,$$

taking the derivative of the function with respect to V^{-1} yields

$$\frac{\partial \ln l(y|Z, \beta, V)}{\partial V^{-1}} = \frac{n}{2} V - \frac{1}{2} S.$$

Thus, we obtain as an estimator of V:

$$\widehat{V}_n = S/n.$$

The concentrated likelihood function is

$$\ln l(y|Z, \beta, \widehat{V}_n) = -\frac{n}{2} \ln|S|$$

and the estimator of β is obtained by

$$\widehat{\beta}_n = \arg\min_{\beta} |S|$$

$$= \arg\min_{\beta} \begin{vmatrix} u^{(1)'}u^{(1)} & \cdots & u^{(1)'}u^{(p)} \\ \vdots & & \vdots \\ u^{(p)'}u^{(1)} & \cdots & u^{(p)'}u^{(p)} \end{vmatrix}.$$

Then, we take the expression for S in $\widehat{\beta}_n$ as the estimator of V. Hypothesis tests, when V is unknown, are based on the asymptotic approximated distribution:

$$\sqrt{n}(\widehat{\beta}_n - \beta) \sim N\left(0, \left[\frac{\partial G(Z, \widehat{\beta}_n)'}{\partial \beta}(\widehat{V}_n^{-1} \otimes I_n)\frac{\partial G(Z, \widehat{\beta}_n)}{\partial \beta'}\right]^{-1}\right). \quad \square$$

To illustrate the testing possibilities, we consider the following example.

Example 9.16 *Along the same lines as Example 9.12 concerning the SUR models, consider the hypothesis test $H_0 : R\beta = r$. This test can be used, for example, to test the equality of parameter vectors across equations of the system when the dimensions of these vectors are the same. The test statistic that can be used is*

$$F_c = (R\widehat{\beta}_n - r)'\left[R(Z'(V^{-1} \otimes I_n)Z)^{-1}R'\right]^{-1}(R\widehat{\beta}_n - r)$$

if V is known, or by replacing it by $\widehat{V}_n$ if it is unknown. Under the null hypothesis, this statistic is χ^2 distributed with J degrees of freedom where J is the number of rows of R. We can also note that some authors have proposed goodness-of-fit measures, for example

$$R^{*2} = 1 - \frac{(y - Z\widehat{\beta}_n)'(V^{-1} \otimes I_n)(y - Z\widehat{\beta}_n)}{y'(V^{-1} \otimes D_n)y}$$

where $D_n = I_n - jj'/n$, $j = (1, \ldots, 1)'$. R^{*2} is between 0 and 1 and is related to the F-statistic through

$$F = \frac{R^{*2}}{1 - R^{*2}} \frac{pn - q}{k - p}$$

which is used to test the null hypothesis that all coefficients of the system of equations, except for the constants, are zero.   □

Notes

For a traditional presentation of the GLS method refer, for example, to Judge, Griffiths, Hill, Lütkepohl, and Lee (1985), Judge, Hill, Griffiths, Lütkepohl, and Lee (1988), Greene (1990). See also Davidson and MacKinnon (1993, Chapter 9). For prediction see Judge, Hill, Griffiths, Lütkepohl, and Lee (1988).

Concerning the heteroskedastic model and the tests for homoskedasticity, we refer also to Breusch and Pagan (1979), White (1980), Goldfeld and Quandt (1965), besides the mentioned textbooks.

Multivariate regression has been studied by numerous authors, for example Zellner (1962) and Davidson and MacKinnon (1993, Chapter 9). For the case when the numbers of observations differ across equations, see particularly Judge, Griffiths, Hill, Lütkepohl, and Lee (1985) and Judge, Hill, Griffiths, Lütkepohl, and Lee (1988); for other estimators of Σ, see Judge, Griffiths, Hill, Lütkepohl, and Lee (1985). For multivariate models with first order autoregressive error consult Judge, Griffiths, Hill, Lütkepohl, and Lee (1985). Finally, for nonlinear system of equations see Gallant (1987, Chapter 5).

10. Nonparametric Estimation of the Regression

10.1 Introduction

In contrast to other fields, the economic theory rarely specifies functional forms but usually specifies only a list of relevant variables to explain a phenomenon. The specification of the form of the relationship largely results from the empirical study which yields a "good" model which "works well." A first level of the analysis consists in writing a (linear, loglinear, nonlinear, ...) model and in estimating it without taking the approximating nature of the model into account. This approach was explained in Chapters 7, 8, and 9. A second approach consists in specifying a parametric model whose incorrect specification is explicit. This leads for instance to correct the expression for the variances or to choose robust methods to the misspecification. This methodology was the topic of Chapter 9.

Finally, it is possible to free oneself of all specification constraints by adopting a *nonparametric* approach to the estimation of the regression, an approach in which the data itself chooses the form of the function of interest.

Various estimation methods of the nonparametric regression have been developed and are now commonly employed. We will present here the kernel method (corresponding to what we presented in Chapter 5). This method is simple but is dominated in some cases by other approaches (local polynomial, Fourier series expansion, wavelets ...). For these methods, we refer to specialized books and to articles (Härdle (1990), Fan and Gijbels (1992), and so on).

Nonparametric methods are very appealing but nevertheless pose some problems. They require in practice a large number of observations and are usable only for a relatively small number of explanatory variables. Moreover, the result is sensitive to the choice of the smoothing parameter and to a lesser extent of the kernel. They pose a problem for the presentation of the results which cannot be summarized in a compact formula but can be well described only through graphics. Finally, a nonparametric analysis does not allow for an extrapolation outside the domain of the observations, but from our point of view this is an advantage. To remedy some of these difficulties, semiparametric methods have been developed, whose aim it is to estimate only some characteristics of the regression or to constrain the regression function to satisfy some assumptions. The dimension of the problem is hence reduced and the presentation of the results is facilitated. It is also possible to introduce *structural* assumptions on the model (growth or monotonicity, concavity, heterogeneity, . . .).

We first consider the standard kernel estimation of the regression, then we discuss some of the estimation problems of specific characteristics of the regression or of the estimation under constraint. We quickly discuss these points and refer to the profuse literature about these questions. The estimation of other relationships besides the regression will not be treated here (see section 17.5.4 for the nonparametric treatment of endogeneity).

10.2   Estimation of the Regression Function by Kernel

Consider a sample $x_i = (y_i, z_i) \in \mathbb{R} \times \mathbb{R}^q$, i.i.d. with distribution Q and as in Chapter 7, we set

$$g(z) = E\left(\tilde{y}|\tilde{z} = z\right)$$

where $(\tilde{y}, \tilde{z})$ is a random vector with realizations (y_i, z_i). The distribution Q is assumed to be dominated by Lebesgue measure and hence

$$g(z) = \int y \frac{f(y, z)}{f_{marg}(z)} dy = \int y f_{cond}(y|z) dy \qquad (10.1)$$

$\forall z$ such that $f_{marg}(z) \neq 0$.

In this section, we construct an estimator of g by the kernel method. Various presentations of this construction are possible and we adopt the following approach. Consider the first expression in (10.1) and replace f and f_{marg} by their expressions taken from Chapter 5 (Formula (5.14)):

$$\hat{f}_n(y, z) = \frac{1}{nh_n^{1+q}} \sum_{i=1}^{n} K\left(\frac{y - y_i}{h_n}, \frac{z - z_i}{h_n}\right) \qquad (10.2)$$

and

$$\hat{f}_{marg\, n}(z) = \frac{1}{nh_n^q} \sum_{i=1}^{n} K\left(\frac{z - z_i}{h_n}\right). \qquad (10.3)$$

Moreover, we suppose that K can be written as the product of two independent kernels, also denoted K by abuse of notation. Hence,

$$\hat{f}_n(y, z) = \frac{1}{nh_n^{1+q}} \sum_{i=1}^{n} K\left(\frac{y - y_i}{h_n}\right) K\left(\frac{z - z_i}{h_n}\right).$$

Replacing in (10.1) f and f_{marg} by their estimators yields

$$\widehat{g}_n(z) = \frac{\frac{1}{nh_n^{1+q}} \sum_{i=1}^{n} \left[\int y K \left(\frac{y - y_i}{h_n} \right) dy \right] K \left(\frac{z - z_i}{h_n} \right)}{\frac{1}{nh_n^q} \sum_{i=1}^{n} K \left(\frac{z - z_i}{h_n} \right)}. \tag{10.4}$$

If K has mean zero,

$$\int y \frac{1}{h_n} K \left(\frac{y - y_i}{h_n} \right) dy = y_i$$

and then we obtain

$$\widehat{g}_n(z) = \frac{\sum_{i=1}^{n} y_i K \left(\frac{z - z_i}{h_n} \right)}{\sum_{i=1}^{n} K \left(\frac{z - z_i}{h_n} \right)}. \tag{10.5}$$

Note that this expression can be rewritten as

$$\widehat{g}_n(z) = \sum_{i=1}^{n} y_i \alpha_n(z - z_i) \text{ with } \alpha_n(z - z_i) = \frac{K \left(\frac{z - z_i}{h_n} \right)}{\sum_{i=1}^{n} K \left(\frac{z - z_i}{h_n} \right)}$$

$$\tag{10.6}$$

where the α_n are positive and sum up to 1 if K is a density. Thus, the value of $\widehat{g}_n(z)$ is a weighted sum of y_i, where the weights measure the distance between z and the z_i.

For example, if K is the density of the uniform distribution on the cube $[-1, 1]^q$, $\widehat{g}_n(z)$ is equal to the weighted sum of y_i such that z_i belongs to a cube centered on z with half length of the side equal to h_n.

In addition, note that the bandwidths h_n are specific to each component of the vector z and that $\frac{z - z_i}{h_n}$ actually denotes

$$\left(\frac{z_1 - z_{i1}}{h_{1n}}, \dots, \frac{z_q - z_{iq}}{h_{qn}} \right).$$

The choice of the smoothing kernel has little impact on the estimation of g. In practice, we consider almost always independent kernels that are the densities of symmetric probability distributions. Then, we have

$$\frac{1}{h_n^q} K \left(\frac{z - z_i}{h_n} \right) = \prod_{j=1}^{q} \frac{1}{h_{jn}} K \left(\frac{z_j - z_{ij}}{h_{jn}} \right). \tag{10.7}$$

The essential difficulties with this approach result from the problem of dimensionality and the choice of the bandwidth. Indeed, this method can be implemented only for vectors of explanatory variables whose dimension is "small." This is the consequence of two phenomena:

- the larger q, the slower the rate of convergence of the estimator;
- the regression function is correctly estimated only if we observe many points that fill in the support of the distribution of z_i. Hence, in high dimension, one needs a large number of observations to be able to recover the support.

In addition, the choice of the bandwidth is very important and determines the properties of the resulting estimators.

The properties of the estimator $\widehat{g}_n$ can be analyzed in the same way as the density estimator. Three points are important: the calculation of the mean integrated squared error, the study of convergence, and asymptotic normality.

10.2.1   Calculation of the Asymptotic Mean Integrated Squared Error

The calculation of the *asymptotic mean integrated squared error* (AMISE) proceeds in the following manner.

The first step consists in linearizing the distance $\widehat{g}_n(z) - g(z)$:

$$\widehat{g}_n(z) - g(z) = \frac{\int y \widehat{f}_n(y, z) \, dy}{\widehat{f}_{marg\, n}(z)} - \frac{\int yf(y, z) \, dy}{f_{marg}(z)},$$

hence

$$\widehat{g}_n(z) - g(z) \simeq \frac{1}{f_{marg}(z)} \left[\int y \widehat{f}_n(y, z) \, dy - \int yf(y, z) \, dy \right]$$

$$- \frac{g(z)}{f_{marg}(z)} \left[\widehat{f}_{marg\, n}(z) - f_{marg}(z) \right]. \tag{10.8}$$

This linearization is obtained from the first order Taylor expansion of the ratio $\frac{u}{v}$:

$$\frac{u}{v} - \frac{u_0}{v_0} \simeq \frac{1}{v_0}(u - u_0) - \frac{u_o}{v_o^2}(v - v_o).$$

The bias $E(\widehat{g}_n(z) - g(z))$ is therefore equal to

$$E(\widehat{g}_n(z) - g(z)) = \frac{1}{f_{marg}(z)} \left(\frac{1}{nh_n^q} \sum_{i=1}^n E(y_i - g(z)) K\left(\frac{z - z_i}{h_n}\right) \right),$$

or alternatively

$$E\left(\widehat{g}_n\left(z\right) - g\left(z\right)\right) = \frac{1}{f_{marg}\left(z\right)}\frac{1}{h_n^q}E\left(\left(y_i - g\left(z\right)\right)K\left(\frac{z - z_i}{h_n}\right)\right)$$

$$= \frac{1}{f_{marg}\left(z\right)}\frac{1}{h_n^q}\int\left(g\left(z_i\right) - g\left(z\right)\right)K\left(\frac{z - z_i}{h_n}\right)f_{marg}\left(z_i\right)dz_i,$$

which, after applying a change of variables $u = \frac{z - z_i}{h_n}$, becomes:

$$\frac{1}{f_{marg}\left(z\right)}\int\left(g\left(z - h_n u\right) - g\left(z\right)\right)K\left(u\right)f_{marg}\left(z - h_n u\right)du.$$

A double Taylor expansion yields

$$\begin{cases} g\left(z - h_n u\right)f_{marg}\left(z - h_n u\right) \simeq g\left(z\right)f_{marg}\left(z\right) - h_n\dfrac{\partial\left(gf_{marg}\right)}{\partial z'}u \\ \qquad\qquad + \dfrac{1}{2}h_n^2 u'\dfrac{\partial^2\left(gf_{marg}\right)}{\partial z\partial z'}u \\ f_{marg}\left(z - h_n u\right) \sim f_{marg}\left(z\right) - h_n\dfrac{\partial f_{marg}}{\partial z'}u + \dfrac{1}{2}h_n^2 u'\dfrac{\partial' f_{marg}}{\partial z\partial z'}u \end{cases}$$

and using $\int u K\left(u\right)du = 0$, we obtain

$$E\left(\widehat{g}_n\left(z\right) - g\left(z\right)\right) \simeq \frac{1}{f_{marg}\left(z\right)}\frac{h_n^2}{2}\int u'\left(\frac{\partial^2\left(gf_{marg}\right)}{\partial z\partial z'} - \frac{\partial^2 f_{marg}}{\partial z\partial z'}\right)u K\left(u\right)du$$

$$\simeq \frac{1}{f_{marg}\left(z\right)}\frac{h_n^2}{2}tr\left\{\left[\frac{\partial^2 g}{\partial z\partial z'} + 2\frac{\partial f_{marg}}{\partial z}\frac{\partial g}{\partial z'}\right]V_K\right\}$$

where $V_K = \int uu'K\left(u\right)du$. Now, we derive the variance of $\widehat{g}_n\left(z\right) - g\left(z\right)$. Applying the preceding linearization, we have

$$Var\left(\widehat{g}_n\left(z\right) - g\left(z\right)\right)$$

$$= \frac{1}{f_{marg}^2\left(z\right)}\frac{1}{nh_n^{2q}}Var\left[\left(y_i - g\left(z\right)\right)K\left(\frac{z - z_i}{h_n}\right)\right]. \tag{10.9}$$

Using the same argument as for the calculation of the AMISE of the density (Chapter 5), we verify that the above variance reduces to the expectation of the square because the square of the expectation is negligible. Then, we have

$$Var(\widehat{g}_n(z) - g(z))$$

$$= \frac{1}{nh_n^q} \frac{1}{f_{marg}^2(z)} \int (y_i - g(z))^2 \frac{1}{h_n^q} K^2 \left(\frac{z - z_i}{h_n}\right) f(y_i, z_i) \, dy_i dz_i$$

$$= \frac{\int K^2(u) \, du}{nh_n^q f_{marg}^2(z)} \int (y_i - g(z))^2 \frac{1}{h_n^q} K^* \left(\frac{z - z_i}{h_n}\right) f(y_i, z_i) \, dy_i dz_i$$

with $K^* = \frac{K}{\int K^2}$. By Bochner's theorem, we obtain

$$Var(\widehat{g}_n(z) - g(z))$$

$$= \frac{1}{nh_n^q} \frac{\int K^2(u) \, du}{f_{marg}^2(z)} \int (y_i - g(z))^2 f(y_i, z) \, dy_i dz$$

$$= \frac{1}{nh_n^q} \frac{\int K^2(u) \, du}{f_{marg}(z)} Var(\tilde{y}|\tilde{z} = z).$$

In summary, the asymptotic mean squared error is the sum of the squared bias and the variance, i.e.,

$$\frac{h_n^4}{4} \left[\frac{1}{f_{marg}(z)} tr\left\{\left(\frac{\partial^2 g}{\partial z \partial z'} + 2\frac{\partial g}{\partial z}\frac{\partial f}{\partial z'}\right) V_K\right\}\right]^2$$

$$+ \frac{1}{nh_n^q} \frac{\int K^2(u) \, du}{f_{marg}(z)} Var(\tilde{y}|\tilde{z} = z) \tag{10.10}$$

This proof is intuitive because it neglects the rests of the Taylor expansions and does not list the set of regularity assumptions (see Hardle (1990), Pagan and Ullah (1999) and Bosq and Lecoutre (1992) for a detailed presentation).

AMISE is obtained by integrating (10.10) with respect to z

$$AMISE = \frac{h_n^4}{4} \int \left[\frac{1}{f_{marg}(z)} tr\left\{\left(\frac{\partial^2 g}{\partial z \partial z'} + 2\frac{\partial g}{\partial z}\frac{\partial f}{\partial z'}\right) V_K\right\}\right]^2 dz$$

$$+ \frac{1}{nh_n^q} \int \frac{\int K^2(u) \, du}{f_{marg}(z)} Var(\tilde{y}|\tilde{z} = z) \, dz$$

hence is of the form

$$AMISE = ah_n^4 + \frac{b}{nh_n^q}. \tag{10.11}$$

Remark. As for the density estimation, we see that the bias and variance evolve in opposite directions with respect to h_n: decreasing h_n reduces the bias term ah_n^4 but increases the variance b/nh_n^q. ☐

Remark. In practice, the bandwidths will be very often different for each variable. The preceding expression is then transformed in the following manner. In the variance term, h_n^q becomes $\prod_{j=1}^{q} h_{jn}$ while the squared bias term becomes

$$\frac{1}{4} \int \frac{1}{f_{marg}(z)} tr\, H \left\{ \frac{\partial^2 g}{\partial z \partial z'} + 2\frac{\partial g}{\partial z}\frac{\partial f}{\partial z'} H\, V_K \right\}^2$$

where H is the diagonal matrix of bandwidths

$$H = \begin{pmatrix} h_{1n} & & 0 \\ & \ddots & \\ 0 & & h_{qn} \end{pmatrix}.$$

If moreover $h_{jn} = C_j h_n$, Expression (10.10) becomes

$$\frac{h_n^4}{4} \left[\frac{1}{f_{marg}(z)} tr\, \left\{ C \left(\frac{\partial^2 g}{\partial z \partial z'} + 2\frac{\partial g}{\partial z}\frac{\partial f}{\partial z'} \right) C\, V_K \right\} \right]^2$$

$$+ \frac{1}{nh_n^q} \frac{\int K^2(u)\, du \; Var\,(\tilde{y}|\tilde{z} = z)}{\prod_{j=1}^{q} C_j f_{marg}(z)} \qquad (10.12)$$

where C is the diagonal matrix of the C_j $(j = 1, \ldots, q)$. ☐

In addition, the same argument as for the density can be used to determine the bandwidth and kernel. We can use Expression (10.10) of the asymptotic mean squared error to derive the best bandwidth at fixed z. By an obvious calculation, this minimization gives

$$h_n^*(z) = \left(\frac{q\, Var\,(\tilde{y}|\tilde{z} = \tilde{z})}{nf_{marg}(z)\, tr\, \left\{ \left(\frac{\partial^2 g}{\partial z \partial z'} + 2\frac{\partial g}{\partial z}\frac{\partial f}{\partial z'} \right) V_K \right\}} \right)^{\frac{1}{q+4}} = c(z)n^{-\frac{1}{q+4}}.$$

Of course, this calculation requires the knowledge of g and f. We can proceed by estimating f and g first with some initial value of the bandwidth and then using these estimates to improve the choice of the bandwidth. This procedure is rather delicate because it requires estimating derivatives (which convergeslowly and hence need a large sample) and the conditional variance. This *plug-in* method has also been extended to the choice of a specific bandwidth for each explanatory variable.

After replacing the bandwidth by its optimal value, we can seek the optimal kernel which is again the Epanechnikov kernel (considering product kernels for each explanatory variable) as in the case of the density estimation.

An alternative approach for selecting the optimal bandwidth consists of the so-called *cross-validation method*. For each $i = 1, \ldots, n$, we estimate the function g by (10.4) excluding the observation i:

$$\widehat{g}_n^{(i)}(z) = \frac{\sum_{j \neq i} y_j K\left(\frac{z - z_j}{h_n}\right)}{\sum_{j \neq i} K\left(\frac{z - z_j}{h_n}\right)}. \tag{10.13}$$

Then, the sum of squared errors:

$$\sum_{i=1}^{n} \left(y_i - \widehat{g}_n^{(i)}(z_i)\right)^2.$$

This expression does not depend on h_n and can be numerically minimized with respect to h_n (or the vector of h_{jn}) over a given interval.

Remark.   The calculation of AMISE relies on two assumptions: the fact that

$$\int uK(u)\,du = 0 \text{ but } \int uu'K(u)\,du \neq 0$$

and the twice differentiability of the density of the observations (and hence of the regression). The distance between $\widehat{g}$ and g measured by AMISE can be reduced by assuming a differentiability at a higher order or by choosing K such that (in the scalar case)

$$\int u^j K(u)\,du = 0 \text{ for } j < r.$$

In this case, the smallest r in this formula is called the order of the kernel K. Let us remark that if K is a density of probability measure (K nonnegative), then r is equal to 2. The bias term is then equal to (up to a multiplicative constant)

$$h_n^{2\min(s,r)}$$

where s is the order of differentiability and r is the order of the kernel. The drawback of higher-order kernels with order greater than 2 is that they are no longer densities and the estimated densities may be negative at least in small samples.   □

Remark. If h_n is proportional to its optimal values, i.e.,

$$h_n - cn^{-\frac{1}{q+4}},$$

AMISE takes the form

$$\text{AMISE} = ac^4 n^{-\frac{4}{q+4}} + \frac{b}{ncn^{-\frac{q}{q+4}}} = \alpha n^{-\frac{4}{q+4}}.$$

In the general case (see preceding remark), AMISE is proportional to

$$n^{-\frac{2\min(s,r)}{q+2\min(s,r)}}.$$ $\qquad\qquad\square$

10.2.2 Convergence of AMISE and Asymptotic Normality

The convergence of $\widehat{g}_n$ to g is the most delicate point because various types of convergence may be considered. From the preceding calculation , we see that if $h_n \to 0$ and $nh_n^q \to \infty$, then AMISE(z) given by (10.11) goes to 0 and therefore $\widehat{g}_n(z)$ converges to $g(z)$ in mean square and hence in probability. Convergence of stronger types (almost sure and uniform in z or in L^p norm) can be found but they require extra assumptions on the kernel and on the asymptotic behavior of the bandwidths. We refer to Härdle (1990) or Bosq and Lecoutre (1992) for these results.

Remark. If h_n is proportional to the optimal choice, we see that $h_n \to 0$ and that $nh_n^q \to \infty$, which guarantee the convergence. Moreover, we can show that the convergence of AMISE to 0 is the fastest if we choose h_n proportional to $n^{-\frac{1}{q+4}}$. In this case, the rate of convergence of AMISE to 0 is $n^{-\frac{4}{q+4}}$. $\qquad\square$

The asymptotic normality requires also extra regularity assumptions and a "good" behavior of h_n when $n \to \infty$. Intuitively, this study is based on the following arguments. Using the previous linearization, we have

$$
\widehat{g}_n(z) - E(\widehat{g}_n(z))
$$
$$
= \frac{1}{nh_n^q} \left\{ \sum_{i=1}^{n} \frac{1}{f_{marg}(z)} (y_i - g(z)) K\left(\frac{z-z_i}{h_n}\right) \right.
$$
$$
\left. - \frac{1}{f_{marg}(z)} E\left[(y_i - g(z)) K\left(\frac{z-z_i}{h_n}\right)\right] \right\}. \qquad (10.14)
$$

Suppose h_n does not depend on n. Then, the central limit theorem gives

$$
\sqrt{n}(\widehat{g}_n(z) - E(\widehat{g}_n(z)))
$$
$$
\to N\left(0, Var\left(\frac{1}{h_n^q} \frac{(y_i - g(z))}{f_{marg}(z)}\right) K\left(\frac{z-z_i}{h_n}\right)\right) \text{ in distribution.}
$$

Using the same calculation as for the variance term in AMISE, we verify that the variance is of the form

$$\frac{1}{h_n^q} \frac{Var\,(\tilde{y}|\tilde{z} = z) \int K^2}{f_{marg}\,(z)}.$$

We then eliminate the term in h_n^q by multiplying the above expression by $\sqrt{h_n^q}$. Hence, we get

$$\sqrt{nh_n^q}\,(\widehat{g}_n\,(z) - E\,(\widehat{g}_n\,(z)))$$

$$\rightarrow N\left(0, \frac{Var\,(\tilde{y}|\tilde{z} = z) \int K^2}{f_{marg}\,(z)}\right) \quad \text{in distribution.}$$

Moreover, if

$$nh_n^q\,(E\,(\widehat{g}_n\,(z)) - g\,(z))^2 \rightarrow 0,$$

we have

$$\sqrt{nh_n^q}\,(\widehat{g}_n\,(z) - g\,(z))$$

$$\rightarrow N\left(0, \frac{Var\,(\tilde{y}|\tilde{z} = z) \int K^2}{f_{marg}\,(z)}\right) \quad \text{in distribution.}$$

We saw that the squared bias is proportional to h_n^4 and hence the conditions for the asymptotic normality of $\widehat{g}_n - g$ are

$$nh_n^q \rightarrow \infty \quad \text{and} \quad nh_n^{q+4} \rightarrow 0.$$

In particular, if

$$h_{nj} = C_j n^{\alpha},$$

these conditions require

$$-\frac{1}{q} < \alpha < -\frac{1}{q+4}.$$

Remark.   If h_n is equal to the optimal choice, the rate of convergence $\sqrt{nh_n^q}$ becomes

$$\sqrt{nn^{-\frac{q}{q+4}}} = \sqrt{n^{\frac{4}{q+4}}}.$$

This is the optimal nonparametric rate of convergence with dimension q that can be compared with the usual parametric rate, namely $\sqrt{n}$. We verify that indeed the gap between these two rates grows as q increases. On the other hand, we note that if

$$h_n = cn^{-\frac{1}{q+4}},$$

then the property $nh_n^{q+4} \to 0$ is not satisfied, which implies that

$$\sqrt{nh_n^q} \left(\widehat{g}_n(z) - E\left(\widehat{g}_n(z)\right) \right)$$

converges to a noncentered normal distribution. □

Moreover, we can verify that the distribution of the vector

$$\sqrt{nh_n^q} \left(\widehat{g}_n(z_1) - g(z_1), \ldots, \widehat{g}_n(z_k) - g(z_k) \right)$$

is asymptotically normal and that the asymptotic covariances are equal to zero.

To apply this result in practice, we need to estimate the density and the conditional variance. The density is estimated by kernel, and similarly the conditional variance is nonparametrically estimated by applying the equality

$$Var\left(\tilde{y} | \tilde{z} = z \right) = E\left(\tilde{y}^2 | \tilde{z} = z \right) + g(z)^2.$$

The first term is estimated by Formula (10.5) after replacing y_i by y_i^2 and we use the estimate of $g(z)$ for the second term.

10.3 Estimating a Transformation of the Regression Function

Instead of estimating the regression function, we can analyze a transformation of this function. The choice of this transformation is motivated by the economic analysis that defines *parameters of interest*. Obviously, many transformations may be considered, but we focus on a specific class characterized by the relation

$$\lambda = \int g(z) w(z) \, dz. \tag{10.15}$$

In this formula, $g(z) = E\left(\tilde{y} | \tilde{z} = z \right)$, and $w(z)$ is a weighting function that is either scalar or vectorial and satisfies $w(z) = 0$ if $f_{marg}(z) = 0$, which is natural because $g(z)$ is defined only if $f_{marg}(z) > 0$. The parameter of interest λ is also scalar or vectorial. This class of transformation is justified by the properties of the resulting estimator of λ and also by its relevance regarding many applied econometric problems which are special cases of this analysis.

Before getting into the details, we note that this transformation does not introduce overidentification conditions on the distribution of the variables (except for the implicit integrability condition in the definition of λ).

We illustrate the relevance of (10.15) by two examples.

Example 10.1   *Estimating the mean derivatives of the regression. We saw in Chapter 8 that the parametric estimation of a misspecified regression does not allow us to consistently estimate the derivatives of this function at a point. However in many econometric problems, the derivatives are the parameters of interest (if the variables are transformed by taking their logarithm, these derivatives can be interpreted as elasticities). We do not study here the nonparametric estimation of the derivatives of the regression at a point. This estimation is possible but its rate of the convergence is very slow and hence it requires a very large sample. Nevertheless, it suffices in many applications to estimate the mean of the derivatives of the regression, i.e.,*

$$\lambda = \int \partial^{\alpha} g(z) v(z) dz \tag{10.16}$$

where α is a multi index of differentiation and ∂^{α} is the differentiation defined by this multi-index (see Chapter 8). The function $v(z)$ is a density on the explanatory variables that may be equal to $f_m(z)$, the density of the actually observed explanatory variables. If for example z contains only one variable and if $\alpha = 1$, we integrate by parts

$$\lambda = g(z) v(z) \Big|_{-\infty}^{+\infty} - \int g(z) \frac{dv}{dz}(z) dz.$$

If v is such that the first term vanishes at $+\infty$ and $-\infty$, we have

$$\lambda = - \int g(z) \frac{dv}{dz}(z) dz.$$

In the general case, we assume that integration by parts yields the following expression for λ

$$\lambda = (-1)^{|\alpha|} \int g(z) \partial^{\alpha} v(z) dz \tag{10.17}$$

with

$$|\alpha| = \sum_{j=1}^{q} \alpha_j.$$

The equality between (10.16) and (10.17) is satisfied if for instance $v(z)$ has a compact support and is sufficiently differentiable. The equality (10.17) shows then that the estimation of mean derivatives is a special case of (10.15) with

$$w(z) = (-1)^{|\alpha|} \partial^{\alpha} v(z). \qquad \square$$

Example 10.2   *Test for subadditivity. In order to illustrate this example, suppose that the function C is the cost function which associates an expected cost* *with the quantities of various products z. The economic theory is interested in the subadditivity of C, i.e., the property*

$$C\left(\sum_{j=1}^{p} z_j\right) \leq \sum_{j=1}^{p} C\left(z_j\right) \tag{10.18}$$

which means intuitively that the cost of a firm producing $\sum_{j=1}^{p} z_j$ is lower than the cost of several firms producing each z_j. The property (10.18) must be true for every p and every sequence $(z_1, \ldots, z_p)$. It is easy to show that this property is equivalent to the following property. Let φ be the density of $(z_1, \ldots, z_p)$, $\tilde{\varphi}$ the density of the sum $z_1 + \cdots + z_p$ and φ_j the density of z_j. Then, (10.18) is equivalent to the fact that for each φ, we have

$$\int C\left(u\right) \tilde{\varphi}(u) du \leq \sum_{j=1}^{p} \int C\left(z_j\right) \varphi_j\left(z_j\right) dz_j. \tag{10.19}$$

Indeed, subadditivity implies

$$\int C\left(u\right) \tilde{\varphi}\left(u\right) du = \int C\left(z_1 + \cdots + z_p\right) \tilde{\varphi}\left(z_1, \ldots, z_p\right) dz_1 \ldots dz_p$$

$$\leq \int \left(\sum_{j=1}^{p} C\left(z_j\right)\right) \varphi\left(z_1, \ldots, z_p\right) dz_1 \ldots dz_p$$

$$= \sum_{j=1}^{p} \int C\left(z_j\right) \varphi_j\left(z_j\right) dz_j;$$

the converse is obtained by considering the distributions on $(z_1, \ldots, z_p)$ concentrated at a point. Now, we discuss testing subadditivity. The writing (10.19) suggests to look at λ defined in (10.15) with

$$w\left(z\right) = \tilde{\varphi}\left(z\right) - \sum_{j=1}^{p} \varphi_j\left(z\right)$$

and to test the sign of this parameter. □

The estimation of λ defined in (10.15) can be done in two ways. The first consists in estimating g by (10.5) then calculating $\hat{\lambda}_n$ by

$$\hat{\lambda}_n = \int \frac{\sum_{i=1}^{n} y_i K\left(\dfrac{z - z_i}{h_n}\right)}{\sum_{i=1}^{n} K\left(\dfrac{z - z_i}{h_n}\right)} w\left(z\right) dz$$

or equivalently

$$\hat{\lambda}_n = \sum_{i=1}^{n} y_i \int \frac{K\left(\dfrac{z - z_i}{h_n}\right)}{\displaystyle\sum_{i=1}^{n} K\left(\dfrac{z - z_i}{h_n}\right)} w(z) \, dz.$$ (10.20)

The second approach avoids estimating g and is based on the following remark:

$$\lambda = \int g(z) \frac{w(z)}{f_{marg}(z)} f_{marg}(z) \, dz = E\left(g(z) \frac{w}{f_{marg}}\right)$$

and also

$$\lambda = E\left(E(\tilde{y}|\tilde{z} = z) \frac{w(z)}{f_{marg}(z)}\right) = E\left(y \frac{w(z)}{f_{marg}(z)}\right).$$

If $f_{marg}(z)$ were known, λ could be estimated by

$$\frac{1}{n} \sum_{i=1}^{n} y_i \frac{w(z_i)}{f_{marg}(z_i)}.$$

This assumption is rarely satisfied. But we can replace f_{marg} by a parametric or nonparametric estimate. In the latter case,

$$\hat{\lambda}_n = \frac{1}{n} \sum_{i=1}^{n} \frac{y_i w(z_i)}{\dfrac{1}{nh_n^q} \displaystyle\sum_{j=1}^{n} K\left(\dfrac{z_i - z_j}{h_n}\right)}.$$ (10.21)

We implicitly assumed that w was given. In practice, w may be partially or fully unknown (because it is for instance a function of f_{marg}) and hence w must be replaced by an estimate in (10.20) and (10.21).

Remark. A *trimming* procedure is sometimes introduced which consists in eliminating the data that are at the boundaries of the support of the distribution of the explanatory variables. In our presentation, trimming can be included in the function w under the form of a multiplicative indicator function. $\square$

The main asymptotic result is the "fast" rate of convergence of $\hat{\lambda}_n$ to λ. Indeed, we have

$$\sqrt{n}\left(\hat{\lambda}_n - \lambda\right) \to N(0, V)$$

under some regularity assumptions and provided that the bandwidths have an appropriate asymptotic behavior. We show this result for the first estimator we proposed in (10.20).

We have

$$
\sqrt{n}\left(\hat{\lambda}_n - \lambda\right) = \sqrt{n}\left\{\int\int y\,\frac{\hat{f}_n(y, z)}{\hat{f}_{marg\,n}(z)}\,w(z)\,dy\,dz \right.
$$

$$
\left. - \int y\,\frac{f(y, z)}{f_{marg}(z)}\,w(z)\,dy\,dz\right\}.
$$

Using a Taylor expansion

$$
\frac{\hat{f}_n}{\hat{f}_{marg\,n}} - \frac{f}{f_{marg}} \simeq \frac{1}{f_{marg}}\left\{\left(\hat{f}_n - f\right) - \frac{f}{f_{marg}}\left(\hat{f}_{marg\,n} - f_{marg}\right)\right\},
$$

we obtain

$$
\sqrt{n}\left(\hat{\lambda}_n - \lambda\right) \simeq \frac{\sqrt{n}}{n}\sum_{i=1}^n \frac{1}{h_n^{1+q}}\int \frac{1}{f_{marg}(z)}\,(y - g(z))
$$

$$
w(z)\,K\left(\frac{y - y_i}{h_n}, \frac{z - z_i}{h_n}\right)dy\,dz.
$$

Assuming h_n is well behaved, we can replace in the previous sum the term

$$
\int u(y, z)\,\frac{1}{h_n^{1+q}}\,K\left(\frac{y - y_i}{h_n}, \frac{z - z_i}{h_n}\right)dy\,dz
$$

by simply $u(y_i, z_i)$ with

$$
u(y, z) = \frac{1}{f_{marg}(z)}\,(y - g(z))\,w(z).
$$

Hence,

$$
\sqrt{n}\left(\hat{\lambda}_n - \lambda\right) \simeq \frac{\sqrt{n}}{n}\sum_{i=1}^n \frac{1}{f_{marg}(z_i)}\,(y_i - g(z_i))\,w(z_i), \qquad (10.22)
$$

therefore

$$
\sqrt{n}\left(\hat{\lambda}_n - \lambda\right) \to N\left(0, Var\left(\frac{(y - g(z_i))\,w(z_i)}{f_{marg}(z_i)}\right)\right).
$$

The derivation is more complex if w is unknown and depends on f for example. Consider for simplicity the case where we are interested in the partial derivative with respect to the variable z_j.

$$
\lambda = \int \frac{\partial g(z)}{\partial z_j}\,f_{marg}(z)\,dz = -\int y\,\frac{f(y, z)}{f_{marg}(z)}\,\frac{\partial f_{marg}(z)}{\partial z_j}\,dz \qquad (10.23)
$$

$$
\hat{\lambda}_n = -\int y\,\frac{\hat{f}_n(y, z)}{\hat{f}_{marg\,n}(z)}\,\frac{\partial \widehat{f}_{marg\,n}(z)}{\partial z_j}\,dz. \qquad (10.24)
$$

As before, we use the approximation

$$
\frac{\dfrac{\partial \hat{f}_{marg\, n}}{\partial z_j} \hat{f}_n}{\hat{f}_{marg\, n}} - \frac{\dfrac{\partial f_{marg}}{\partial z_j} f}{f_{marg}} \simeq \frac{f}{f_n} \left(\frac{\partial \hat{f}_{marg\, n}}{\partial z_j} - \frac{\partial f_{marg}}{\partial z_j} \right) + \frac{\dfrac{\partial f_{marg}}{\partial z_j}}{f_{marg}} \left(\hat{f}_n - f \right)
$$

$$
- \frac{\dfrac{\partial f_{marg}}{\partial z_j} f}{f_{marg}^2} \left(\hat{f}_{marg\, n} - f_{marg} \right) \tag{10.25}
$$

and repeating the previous argument, we have

$$
\sqrt{n} \left(\hat{\lambda}_n - \lambda \right) \to N \left(0,\ Var \left[(y_i - g(z_i)) \frac{\dfrac{\partial f_{marg}(z_i)}{\partial z_j}}{f_{marg}(z_i)} + \frac{\partial}{\partial z_j} g(z_i) \right] \right).
$$

$$\tag{10.26}$$

10.4   Restrictions on the Regression Function

To limit the dimensionality problems or to impose some restrictions originating from the economic theory, we often suppose that the conditional expectation $g(z)$, which is a function of q variables, actually depends on functions of a smaller number of variables and possibly on some parameters. In fact, two points of view are possible: either we assume that g is really restricted to this specific form, or we look for the best approximation of g by an element that satisfies the restrictions under consideration. We illustrate this approach by a few examples.

10.4.1   Index Models

The *index model* is characterized by a function of explanatory variables z of the form $\psi(\lambda'z)$ where ψ is a function of $\mathbb{R} \to \mathbb{R}$ and $\lambda'z$ is a linear combination of z_j $(j = 1, \ldots, q)$. We can assume that $E(\tilde{y}|\tilde{z} = z)$ is effectively of the form $\psi(\lambda'z)$ or that we seek the best approximation of $E(\tilde{y}|\tilde{z} = z)$ by a function of this form. This model poses an identification problem. If ψ_* is defined by

$$
\psi_*(u) = \psi(ku)
$$

and

$$
\lambda_* = \frac{1}{k}\lambda,
$$

we have

$$
\psi(\lambda'z) = \psi_*(\lambda_*'z)
$$

for each z and hence the pair (ψ, λ) is not identified. We solve this question by normalizing λ, for instance by setting $\lambda_1 = 1$.

If we assume that the model is exact $(E(\tilde{y}|\tilde{z} = z) = \psi(\lambda' z))$, then this restriction introduces an overidentification constraint (see Chapter 16) which manifests itself for example in the fact that a standard nonparametric estimator of the regression does not satisfy this constraint. Hence, we need to define ψ and λ in such a way that they are associated with a large class of estimators. As always, denote

$$g(z) = E(\tilde{y}|\tilde{z} = z).$$

A first estimator is based on the following remark:

$$\frac{\partial}{\partial z_j} g(z) = \lambda_j \frac{\partial}{\partial u} \psi(u)$$

($\frac{\partial \psi}{\partial u}$ being the derivative of $\psi(u) : \mathbb{R} \to \mathbb{R}$ and $u = \lambda' z$). Hence,

$$E\left(\frac{\partial}{\partial z_j} g(z)\right) = \lambda_j E\left(\frac{\partial}{\partial u} \psi(u)\right)$$

for each $j = 1, \ldots, q$ (the expectation is taken here with respect to the distribution of the vector $\tilde{z}$). It follows that

$$\lambda_j = \frac{E\left(\frac{\partial}{\partial z_j} g(z)\right)}{E\left(\frac{\partial}{\partial z_1} g(z)\right)} \tag{10.27}$$

provided $\lambda_1 = 1$. This property is the basis for an estimator of λ_j. If $\widehat{g}_n$ is an estimator of the function g (obtained for instance by kernel), we estimate λ_j by

$$\hat{\lambda}_{j_n} = \frac{\sum\limits_{i=1}^{n} \frac{\partial}{\partial z_j} \widehat{g}_n(z_i)}{\sum\limits_{i=1}^{n} \frac{\partial}{\partial z_1} \widehat{g}_n(z_i)}. \tag{10.28}$$

Once the λ_j are estimated, we perform a nonparametric regression of $\tilde{y}$ on $\hat{\lambda}'_n z$:

$$\hat{\psi}_n(u) = \frac{\sum\limits_{i} y_i K\left(\frac{u - \hat{\lambda}'_n z_i}{h_n}\right)}{\sum\limits_{i} K\left(\frac{u - \hat{\lambda}'_n z_i}{h_n}\right)}. \tag{10.29}$$

A second approach originates from the idea of the best approximation of the conditional expectation by an index model, i.e., minimizing

$$E\left(g(z) - \psi\left(\lambda'z\right)\right)^2$$

with respect to ψ and λ. We know (see Chapter 3) that this problem is also equivalent to the system

$$E\left(\tilde{y}|\lambda'\tilde{z} = u\right) = \psi(u)$$

and

$$E\left[\left(y - \psi\left(\lambda'z\right)\right)\frac{\partial}{\partial u}\psi(u)z_j\right] = 0 \quad \forall j = 1, \ldots, q.$$

In other words, ψ is the regression of $\tilde{y}$ on $\lambda'\tilde{z}$ and λ minimizes the expectation of the squared distance between y and $\psi(\lambda'z)$. The function ψ can be estimated for instance by

$$\hat{\psi}_{\lambda n}(u) = \frac{\sum_{i=1}^n y_i K\left(\frac{u - \lambda'z_i}{h_n}\right)}{\sum_{i=1}^n K\left(\frac{u - \lambda'z_i}{h_n}\right)}.$$

Replacing ψ by its estimator, we solve

$$\hat{\lambda}_n = \arg\min \sum_{\ell=1}^n \left(y_\ell - \frac{\sum_{i=1}^n y_i K\left(\frac{\lambda'z - \lambda'z_i}{h_n}\right)}{\sum_{i=1}^n K\left(\frac{\lambda'z - \lambda'z_i}{h_n}\right)}\right)^2.$$

We obtain $\hat{\psi}_n$ after replacing λ by $\hat{\lambda}_n$ in $\hat{\psi}_{\lambda n}$.

The main asymptotic result is that, under some appropriate assumptions on the behavior of the bandwidths, $\hat{\lambda}_n$ converges at the $\sqrt{n}$ rate, i.e.,

$$\sqrt{n}\left(\hat{\lambda}_n - \lambda\right) \to N(0, v);$$

$\hat{\psi}_n$ is consistent with the usual rate for the regression on a single variable and its asymptotic distribution is identical to that of the regression $\tilde{y}$ on $\lambda'\tilde{z}$. In the case of an estimation using a ratio of derivatives (10.27), we infer v from Formula (10.26).

The model we presented here is a single-index model, which can be generalized to multiple indices $\psi(\lambda_1'z, \lambda_2'z, \ldots)$ (their number must stay small in comparison to q for the model to have an interest).

An important application of index models is the semiparametric study of discrete choice models which will be presented in Chapter 11.

10.4.2 Additive Models

Assume that z is partitioned into (z_1, z_2) with respective dimensions q_1 and q_2 (with $q_1 + q_2 = q$). An additive model is described by two functions ψ_1 and ψ_2 of $\mathbb{R}^{q_1}$ and $\mathbb{R}^{q_2}$ to $\mathbb{R}$ such that $g(z)$ is equal to $\psi_1(z_1) + \psi_2(z_2)$. This assumption can be interpreted in two ways: we may assume that g is exactly equal to $\psi_1 + \psi_2$ or we can look for the best approximation of g by $\psi_1 + \psi_2$. This model poses an identification problem: if $\psi_1^* = \psi_1 + c$ and $\psi_2^* = \psi_2 - c$, we get obviously $\psi_1 + \psi_2 = \psi_1^* + \psi_2^*$ and we cannot empirically discriminate between these two pairs. To solve this difficulty, it suffices (besides some regularity assumptions not described here) that one of the functions is constrained (for example $E(\psi_2(z_2)) = 0$ or $\psi_2(0) = 0$). This additive specification, if considered as exact, introduces an overidentification condition that manifests itself by the fact that even if the assumption is satisfied, a usual estimator of g cannot be decomposed into $\psi_1 + \psi_2$. As in the preceding example, we must link ψ_1 and ψ_2 to standard estimators. Several methods are possible.

First note that under the assumption that the model is well specified, i.e., $g = \psi_1 + \psi_2$,

$$\frac{\partial}{\partial z_2} g(z) = \frac{\partial \psi_2}{\partial z_2}(z_2). \tag{10.30}$$

If g is arbitrary, $\frac{\partial g}{\partial z_1}$ still depends on z_1, which is eliminated by integration

$$E\left\{ \int \left(\frac{\partial}{\partial z_2} g(z) \right) w(z_1) dz_1 \right\} = \frac{\partial \psi_2}{\partial z_2}(z_2). \tag{10.31}$$

Formula (10.31) can be used for estimation. We estimate g by an unrestricted $\widehat{g}_n$, and $\widehat{\psi}_{1n}$ is a primitive function of

$$\int \left[\frac{\partial}{\partial z_2} \widehat{g}_n(z_1, z_2) \right] w(z_1) dz_1.$$

We apply the same to ψ_2 and we determine the integration constants by the conditions

$$E(g) = E(\psi_1) + E(\psi_2) \quad \text{and} \quad E(\psi_2) = 0.$$

A more elegant approach consists in looking for the best approximation of g by $\psi_1 + \psi_2$, i.e., in minimizing

$$E(g(z) - \psi_1(z_1) - \psi_2(z_2))^2$$

or alternatively

$$E(y - \psi_1(z_1) - \psi_2(z_2))^2.$$

This problem yields the conditions

$$E\left(y|\tilde{z}_1 = z_1\right) = \psi_1\left(z_1\right) + E\left(\psi_2\left(z_2\right)|\tilde{z}_1 = z_1\right) \tag{10.32}$$

and

$$E\left(y|\tilde{z}_2 = z_2\right) = E\left(\psi_1\left(z_1\right)|\tilde{z}_2 = z_2\right) + \psi_2\left(z_2\right). \tag{10.33}$$

(To find the first order conditions in ψ_1, we used

$$\tfrac{\partial}{\partial\alpha}E\left(y - \left(\psi_1\left(z_1\right) + \alpha\tilde{\psi}_1\left(z_1\right) - \psi_2\left(z_2\right)\right)\right)^2\big|_{\alpha=0} = 0 \qquad \forall\tilde{\psi}_1$$

$$\Longleftrightarrow E\left[\left(y - \psi_1(z_1) - \psi_2\left(z_2\right)\right)\tilde{\psi}_1\left(z_1\right)\right] = 0 \qquad \forall\tilde{\psi}_1$$

$$\Longleftrightarrow E\left[\left[E\left(y|\tilde{z}_1 = z_1\right) - \psi_1\left(z_1\right) - E\left(\psi_2\left(z_2\right)|\tilde{z}_1 = z_1\right)\right]\tilde{\psi}_1\left(z_1\right)\right] = 0 \qquad \forall\tilde{\psi}_1$$

$$\Longleftrightarrow E\left(y|\tilde{z}_1 = z_1\right) - \psi_1\left(z_1\right) - E\left(\psi_2\left(z_2\right)|\tilde{z}_1 = z_1\right) = 0.$$

We proceeded the same way for ψ_2).

We can replace the conditional expectations by their estimators and solve the system in ψ_1 and ψ_2. We obtain

$$\frac{\sum y_i K\left(\frac{z_1 - z_{1i}}{h_n}\right)}{\sum K\left(\frac{z_1 - z_{1i}}{h_n}\right)} = \psi_1\left(z_1\right) + \frac{\sum \psi_2\left(z_{2i}\right) K\left(\frac{z_1 - z_{1i}}{h_n}\right)}{\sum K\left(\frac{z_1 - z_{1i}}{h_n}\right)} \tag{10.34}$$

and

$$\frac{\sum y_i K\left(\frac{z_2 - z_{2i}}{h_n}\right)}{\sum K\left(\frac{z_2 - z_{2i}}{h_n}\right)} = \frac{\sum \psi_1\left(z_{1i}\right) K\left(\frac{z_2 - z_{2i}}{h_n}\right)}{\sum K\left(\frac{z_2 - z_{2i}}{h_n}\right)} + \psi_2\left(z_2\right). \tag{10.35}$$

By considering these equations for $z_1 = z_{1\ell}$ $(\ell = 1, \ldots, n)$ and $z_2 = z_{2\ell}$ $(\ell = 1, \ldots, n)$, we obtain the system

$$\begin{cases} A_1\underline{y} = \underline{\psi}_1 + A_1\underline{\psi}_2 \\ A_2\underline{y} = A_2\underline{\psi}_1 + \underline{\psi}_2 \end{cases} \Longleftrightarrow \begin{pmatrix} I & A_1 \\ A_2 & I \end{pmatrix}\begin{pmatrix} \underline{\psi}_1 \\ \underline{\psi}_2 \end{pmatrix} = \begin{pmatrix} A_1 y \\ A_2 y \end{pmatrix} \tag{10.36}$$

where

$$A_1 = \left(\frac{K\left(\frac{z_{1\ell} - z_{1i}}{h_n}\right)}{\sum K\left(\frac{z_{1\ell} - z_{1i}}{h_n}\right)}\right)_{\ell,i=1,\ldots,n} \quad , \quad A_2 = \left(\frac{K\left(\frac{z_{2\ell} - z_{2i}}{h_n}\right)}{\sum K\left(\frac{z_{2\ell} - z_{2i}}{h_n}\right)}\right)_{\ell,i=1,\ldots,n},$$

$$\underline{y} = \begin{pmatrix} y_1 \\ \vdots \\ y_n \end{pmatrix}, \quad \underline{\psi}_1 = \begin{pmatrix} \psi_1\left(z_{11}\right) \\ \vdots \\ \psi_1\left(z_{1n}\right) \end{pmatrix} \quad \text{and} \quad \underline{\psi}_2 = \begin{pmatrix} \psi_2\left(z_{21}\right) \\ \vdots \\ \psi_2\left(z_{2n}\right) \end{pmatrix}.$$

This system has rank equal to $2n - 1$ because the rows of A_1 (or A_2) sum up to 1. We solve it by imposing a specific value (for instance $\psi_2\left(z_{21}\right) = 0$).

Transferring this value in the right-hand side of (10.36), we obtain a system of $2n$ equations with $2n - 1$ unknowns that we solve by least squares:

$$Bx = b \implies x = (B'B)^{-1} Bb.$$

The knowledge of $\psi_1 (z_{1i})$ and $\psi_2 (z_{2i})$ allows us to estimate ψ_1 and ψ_2 for all points through (10.34) and (10.35). We can also replace the constraint $\psi_2 (z_{21}) = 0$ by the constraint $\sum_{i=1}^{n} \psi_2 (z_{2i}) = 0$.

This procedure can be easily implemented. It yields consistent estimators of ψ_1 and ψ_2 with the rates $\sqrt{nh_n^{q_1}}$ and $\sqrt{nh_n^{q_2}}$, i.e. the rates for regressions with q_1 and q_2 explanatory variables. Moreover, it can be shown that, under the normalization condition $E(\psi_2) = 0$, $\hat{\psi}_{1n}$ has the same distribution as the conditional expectation of $y - \psi_2(z_2)$ given $\tilde{z}_1 = z_1$. Likewise, $\tilde{\psi}_{2n}$ has the same distribution as the conditional expectation of $y - \psi_1(z_1)$ given $\tilde{z}_2 = z_2$.

Remark. The constraint $E(\psi_2) = 0$ (which leads to $\sum_{i=1}^{n} \psi_2(z_{2i}) = 0$ in the estimation) yields a simple limiting distribution because it maintains the asymptotic independence of the estimators for different values of the explanatory variables. In contrast, the constraint $\psi(z_{21}) = 0$ implies that the variance of $\hat{\psi}_2(z_{21})$ is zero and that the $\hat{\psi}_2(z_2)$ are asymptotically dependent across values of z_2. $\qquad\square$

Notes

Regarding the nonparametric regression, we refer the reader to the books by Bosq (1996), Tsybakov (2004), Wand and Jones (1995), and Fan and Gijbels (1996). The semiparametric methods are treated in various books, such as those by Pagan and Ullah (1999), Horowitz (1998), and Stocker (1991); see also Carrasco, Florens, and Renault (2004) and Newey and McFadden (1994).

11. Discrete Variables and Partially Observed Models

11.1 Introduction

In econometric models, it is usually assumed that the dependent variable may take any value in $\mathbb{R}$ or $\mathbb{R}^p$. In this chapter, we study some types of models that do not fit in this setting:

- models with discrete dependent variables, called qualitative response models, where the endogenous variable can take only two values (*dichotomous*, binomial, or *binary response* models) or a limited number of values (*polychotomous*, multinomial, or *multiple choice* models);
- partially observed models (or *limited dependent variable models*) where the observations of the dependent variable are reduced to a single value after some threshold; we consider here censored models or *sample selection* models. Those latter models are characterized by a truncation process depending on a latent variable that is different from that describing the observed data.

It is obvious that writing the conditional expectation under the form

$$E^{\theta}(y_i|z_i) = \lambda' z_i$$

is not suitable, since it is impossible to restrict $\lambda' z_i$ to take only some discrete values or to belong to a specific interval for all values of z_i. These models are treated in this chapter under the form of *index models*

$$E^{\theta}(y_i|z_i) = \varphi(z_i) = \psi(\omega(z_i)) \tag{11.1}$$

with $\varphi : \mathbb{R}^q \to \mathbb{R}$ and $\psi : \mathbb{R} \to \mathbb{R}$; the function ω is called *index function* and can take any value on the real line; ω is a *linear index function* if it can be written as

$$\omega(z_i) = \lambda' z_i$$

and hence depends on z_i through a linear combination of the elements of z_i. ψ, called transformation function, has the following properties

$$\psi(-\infty) = 0, \quad \psi(+\infty) = 1, \quad \text{and} \quad \frac{\partial \psi(x)}{\partial x} > 0.$$

Thus, ψ projects the real line on the interval $[0, 1]$ and may be, for instance, the cumulative distribution function of some probability distributions.

In Section 2, we study various types of discrete dependent variable models and partially observed models. In Section 3, we address the problems regarding estimation and tests.

11.2 Various Types of Models

11.2.1 Dichotomous Models

Dichotomous models are characterized by the fact that the endogenous variable y_i may take only two values, 0 or 1. The following example, about utility maximization, illustrates the motivations for this type of model.

Example 11.1 *It is assumed that there are only two choices for the endogenous variable, $y_i = 0$ or $y_i = 1$. The utility of agent i who chooses alternative $y_i = j$ is*

$$\tilde{U}_{ij} = U_{ij}(z_i) + u_{ij} \qquad j = 0, 1$$

where z_i is an observable vector of characteristics. The agent chooses alternative j if her utility is greater for j. So, the choice is as follows

$$y_i = \begin{vmatrix} 1 & \text{if } \tilde{U}_{i1} > \tilde{U}_{i0} \\ 0 & \text{otherwise.} \end{vmatrix}$$

Now

$$\tilde{U}_{i1} - \tilde{U}_{i0} = \omega(z_i) - \varepsilon_i$$

with $\omega(z_i) = U_{i1}(z_i) - U_{i0}(z_i)$ and $\varepsilon_i = u_{i0} - u_{i1}$. Then,

$$y_i = \mathbb{I}(\varepsilon_i < \omega(z_i)).$$

Hence, the conditional expectation of y_i is

$$E^\theta(y_i|z_i) = \Pr(y_i = 1|z_i)$$

$$= \Pr(\varepsilon_i < \omega(z_i))$$

$$= F(\omega(z_i))$$

$$= \psi(\omega(z_i)).$$

Here ψ is simply F, the cumulative distribution function of ε_i. ∎

Another motivation for this model is illustrated by the more general example given below in which the notion of latent variable appears.

Example 11.2 *Suppose that the binary choice depends on a latent variable* y_i^*:

$$y_i^* = \omega(z_i) - \varepsilon_i$$

in the following manner

$$y_i = \begin{vmatrix} 1 & \text{if } y_i^* > 0 \\ 0 & \text{otherwise.} \end{vmatrix}$$

or alternatively

$$y_i = \mathbb{I}(y_i^* > 0) = \mathbb{I}(\varepsilon_i < \omega(z_i)).$$

This example encompasses the preceding example by setting

$$y_i^* = \tilde{U}_{i1} - \tilde{U}_{i0}.$$

Similarly, ψ is equal to F, the distribution function of ε_i and

$$E^\theta(y_i|z_i) = F(\omega(z_i)) = \psi(\omega(z_i)).$$ ∎

More generally, the binary choice model can be written as an index model which we assume to have a linear index

$$E^\theta(y_i|z_i) = \psi(\omega(z_i)) = \psi\left(\lambda' z_i\right). \tag{11.2}$$

The function ψ has the properties of a cumulative distribution function. Two cases arise. If ψ is unknown, we estimate the model nonparametrically (see Chapter 10). If ψ is known, we use traditional methods.

In the latter case, the choice of ψ determines the two main types of dichotomous models studied in the literature. The first is the *probit model*; the function ψ is simply Φ, the distribution function of the standard normal

$$F_N(x) \equiv \int_{-\infty}^{x} \frac{1}{\sqrt{2\pi}} e^{-u^2/2} du. \tag{11.3}$$

The second is the *logit model*, where ψ is the logistic function

$$F_L(x) \equiv \frac{e^x}{1 + e^x}, \tag{11.4}$$

hence

$$E^\theta(y_i|z_i) = \frac{e^{\lambda' z_i}}{1 + e^{\lambda' z_i}}$$

and

$$\ln\left(\frac{E^\theta(y_i|z_i)}{1 - E^\theta(y_i|z_i)}\right) = \lambda' z_i.$$

Probit and logit models give rather similar results. When we compare the curves of the two distribution functions $F_N(x)$ and $F_L(x\sqrt{3}/\pi)$ (that of the logistic being normalized by the inverse of its standard deviation), we observe that they are almost identical, except in the tails.

11.2.2 Multiple Choice Models

We distinguish between models of ordered and unordered multiple choice.

Models of Unordered Multiple Choice

The *models of unordered multiple choice* are a simple generalization of the binary choice models. Indeed suppose that we have $J + 1$ possible alternatives, each characterized by its own utility:

$$\tilde{U}_{ij} = U_{ij}(z_i) + u_{ij} \qquad j = 0, \ldots, J$$

where z_i is an observable vector of characteristics. The alternative j is chosen if $\tilde{U}_{ij} \geq \tilde{U}_{il}$ for all $l = 0, \ldots, J$ with $l \neq j$, or equivalently if

$$U_{ij} + u_{ij} \geq U_{il} + u_{il}, \quad \forall l = 0, \ldots, J, \; l \neq j.$$

Assume that y_{ij} represents the choice of alternative j, that is

$$y_{ij} = \begin{vmatrix} 1 & \text{if } j \text{ is chosen} \\ 0 & \text{otherwise} \end{vmatrix}$$

or equivalently

$$y_{ij} = \mathbb{I}(U_{ij} + u_{ij} \geq U_{il} + u_{il}, \; \forall l = 0, \ldots, J, \; l \neq j).$$

The probability that alternative j is chosen is equal to

$$E^\theta(y_{ij}|z_i) = \Pr\left(U_{ij} + u_{ij} \geq U_{il} + u_{il}, \; \forall l = 0, \ldots, J, \; l \neq j\right)$$

$$= \Pr\left(u_{ij} - u_{il} \geq U_{il} - U_{ij}, \; \forall l = 0, \ldots, J, \; l \neq j\right)$$

$$= F_j\left(U_{i0} - U_{ij}, \ldots, U_{ij-1} - U_{ij}, U_{ij+1} - U_{ij}, \ldots, U_{iJ} - U_{ij}\right)$$

$$= \psi\left(U_{i0} - U_{ij}, \ldots, U_{ij-1} - U_{ij}, U_{ij+1} - U_{ij}, \ldots, U_{iJ} - U_{ij}\right)$$

where F_j, the distribution function of $(u_{ij} - u_{i0}, \ldots, u_{ij} - u_{ij-1}, u_{ij} - u_{ij+1}, \ldots, u_{ij} - u_{iJ})$, is assumed to be exchangeable, i.e., $F_j = \psi$ for all j. Assume moreover that $U_{il} - U_{ij}$ is a linear function of z_i of the form $\lambda'_{jl}z_i$; we obtain a multiple linear index model:

$$E^\theta(y_{ij}|z_i) = \psi\left(\lambda'_{j0}z_i, \ldots, \lambda'_{jj-1}z_i, \lambda'_{jj+1}z_i, \ldots, \lambda'_{jJ}z_i\right).$$

Models of Ordered Multiple Choice

The *models of ordered multiple choice* are based on discrete responses which are ordered, for instance the choice of financial assets with different returns. Consider a continuous latent variable defined by

$$y_i^* = \omega(z_i) + \varepsilon_i$$

with various thresholds, $c_0 = -\infty, c_1, \ldots, c_J, c_{J+1} = +\infty$, such that the observed variable y_i is defined by

$$y_i = \begin{vmatrix} 0 & \text{if } y_i^* \leq c_1 \\ 1 & \text{if } c_1 < y_i^* \leq c_2 \\ \vdots & \\ J & \text{if } c_J < y_i^* \end{vmatrix} \tag{11.5}$$

or equivalently

$$y_i = j \quad \text{if } c_j < \omega(z_i) + \varepsilon_i \leq c_{j+1}.$$

If we define a discrete variable d_{ij} by

$$d_{ij} = 1 \quad \text{if } y_i = j,$$

then the expectation of d_{ij} is

$$E^\theta\left(d_{ij}|z_i\right) = \Pr(y_i = j|z_i)$$
$$= \Pr(c_j - \omega(z_i) < \varepsilon_i \leq c_{j+1} - \omega(z_i))$$

and depends on the distribution of ε_i. It follows that

$$E^\theta\left(y_i|z_i\right) = \sum_{j=0}^J j E^\theta\left(d_{ij}|z_i\right)$$

$$= \sum_{j=0}^J j \Pr\left(c_j - \omega(z_i) < \varepsilon_i < c_{j+1} - \omega(z_i)\right)$$

$$= \psi\left(\omega\left(z_i\right)\right).$$

The distribution function of ε_i may be the logistic function (ordered logit model) or the distribution of a standard normal (ordered probit model).

Moreover, if the index function is linear

$$\omega(z_i) = \lambda'z_i,$$

then

$$E^\theta(y_i|z_i) = \psi(\lambda'z_i).$$

11.2.3 Censored Models

These models, also called *tobit models*, are characterized by the fact that the endogenous variable takes a single value starting from some threshold. For instance, the demand for a specific good is censored because it is studied from the sales which can not exceed the production capacity of the firm. Another example consists of the unemployment durations which are censored because some individuals have not exited unemployment yet and hence are not accounted for. Thus, in this type of models, observations cannot be considered as the realization of a continuous random variable, but rather as of a mixture of discrete and continuous variables.

Consider a very simple model with latent variable

$$y_i^* = \lambda'z_i + \varepsilon_i \tag{11.6}$$

and assume that the endogenous variable y_i is observed only if y_i^* is positive

$$y_i = \begin{vmatrix} y_i^* & \text{if } y_i^* > 0 \\ 0 & \text{otherwise} \end{vmatrix} \tag{11.7}$$

which can be written as

$$y_i = \max(y_i^*, 0) = \max(\lambda'z_i + \varepsilon_i, 0)$$

or

$$y_i = (\lambda'z_i + \varepsilon_i)\, 1\!\!1(\varepsilon_i > -\lambda'z_i).$$

Several types of censoring exist:

We have a *left-censored model* (also called *truncated model*) by a constant δ (say) if

$$y_i = \begin{vmatrix} y_i^* & \text{if } y_i^* > \delta \\ \delta & \text{otherwise} \end{vmatrix}$$

or equivalently

$$y_i = \max(y_i^*, \delta) = \max(\lambda'z_i + \varepsilon_i, \delta).$$

It suffices to set

$$y_i^* - \delta = -\delta + \lambda' z_i + \varepsilon_i = \tilde{\lambda}' \tilde{z}_i + \varepsilon_i$$

with

$$\tilde{\lambda} = \begin{pmatrix} -\delta \\ \lambda \end{pmatrix} \quad \text{and} \quad \tilde{z}_i = \begin{pmatrix} 1 \\ z_i \end{pmatrix}$$

to obtain the representation (11.6) and (11.7).

A *right-censored model* is such that

$$y_i = \begin{vmatrix} y_i^* & \text{if } y_i^* < \delta \\ \delta & \text{otherwise} \end{vmatrix}$$

or equivalently

$$y_i = \min \left(y_i^*, \delta \right) = \min \left(\lambda' z_i + \varepsilon_i, \delta \right).$$

It suffices to write

$$-y_i = \max \left(-y_i^*, -\delta \right) = \max \left(-\lambda' z_i - \varepsilon_i, -\delta \right)$$

to obtain again the above representation.

To return to the formulation (11.6) and (11.7), there are two possibilities.

1. First, we can consider only positive data, i.e., those for which $y_i > 0$. In this case, we have

$$E^\theta(y_i | z_i, y_i > 0) = \lambda' z_i + E^\theta(\varepsilon_i | \varepsilon_i \geq -\lambda' z_i)$$
$$= \psi(\lambda' z_i).$$

2. The second possibility consists in considering all the data. In this case, we have

$$E^\theta(y_i | z_i) = E^\theta \left(y_i^* | z_i, y_i^* > 0 \right) \Pr \left(y_i^* > 0 \right)$$
$$= \left[\lambda' z_i + E^\theta(\varepsilon_i | \varepsilon_i > -\lambda' z_i) \right] (1 - F(-\lambda' z_i))$$
$$= \psi(\lambda' z_i),$$

where F is the distribution function of ε_i.

The following examples illustrate results derived from these two possibilities when normality is assumed. Each example starts with a review of some properties of the normal distribution.

Example 11.3 *We consider here only positive data. If f is the density function of a random variable x and a a constant, called truncation threshold, then the density and expectation of the truncated distribution are given by*

$$f(x|x > a) = \frac{f(x)}{\Pr(x > a)}$$

and

$$E^\theta(x|x > a) = \int\limits_a^{+\infty} xf(x|x > a)dx.$$

Note that $\int_a^{+\infty} f(x|x > a)dx = 1$ and hence the denominator $\Pr(x > a)$ represents the normalization factor. Assume that x follows a normal distribution $N(\mu, \sigma^2)$ and denote by F_N and f_N, respectively, the distribution function and the density of a standard normal. We can write

$$\Pr(x > a) = 1 - \Pr(x < a) = 1 - \Pr\left(\frac{x - \mu}{\sigma} < \frac{a - \mu}{\sigma}\right) \tag{11.8}$$

hence

$$\Pr(x > a) = 1 - F_N(\alpha) \tag{11.9}$$

where $\alpha = \frac{a-\mu}{\sigma}$. Thus

$$f(x|x > a) = \frac{f(x)}{1 - F_N(\alpha)} = \frac{\frac{1}{\sigma}f_N(\frac{x-\mu}{\sigma})}{1 - F_N(\alpha)}. \tag{11.10}$$

It can also be shown that

$$E^\theta(x|x > a) = \mu + \sigma\lambda(\alpha) \tag{11.11}$$

and that

$$Var^\theta(x|x > a) = \sigma^2(1 - \eta(\alpha))$$

with

$$\lambda(\alpha) = \frac{f_N(\alpha)}{1 - F_N(\alpha)} \quad and \quad \eta(\alpha) = \lambda(\alpha)(\lambda(\alpha) - \alpha).$$

If the truncation is given by $x < a$, then $\lambda(\alpha) = \frac{-f_N(\alpha)}{F_N(\alpha)}$. Now assume that the censored regression model takes the form

$$y_i = \lambda'z_i + \varepsilon_i$$

where $\varepsilon_i \sim N(0, \sigma^2)$, or alternatively $y_i|z_i \sim N(\lambda'z_i, \sigma^2)$, and that the data are observed if $y_i > a$. Then,

$$E^\theta(y_i|z_i, y_i > a) = \lambda'z_i + \sigma\frac{f_N(\alpha)}{1 - F_N(\alpha)}$$

with $\alpha = \frac{a-\lambda'z_i}{\sigma}$ (it suffices to set $x = y_i$ and $\mu = \lambda'z_i$ in the preceding expressions). Similarly, it can be shown that

$$Var^\theta(y_i|z_i, y_i > a) = \sigma^2\left[1 - \frac{f_N(\alpha)}{1 - F_N(\alpha)}\left(\frac{f_N(\alpha)}{1 - F_N(\alpha)} - \alpha\right)\right].$$

∎

Example 11.4   *We now take all data into account. We study first the censored normal distribution. Let $x^* \sim N(\mu, \sigma^2)$ and define x as*

$$x = \begin{vmatrix} x^* & \text{if } x^* > 0 \\ 0 & \text{otherwise.} \end{vmatrix}$$

The censoring point is here assumed to be zero. Recall again that F_N and f_N are the distribution function and the density of the standard normal. We have

$$\Pr(x = 0) = \Pr(x^* \leq 0) = \Pr\left(\frac{x^* - \mu}{\sigma} \leq \frac{-\mu}{\sigma}\right)$$

$$= F_N\left(-\frac{\mu}{\sigma}\right) = 1 - F_N\left(\frac{\mu}{\sigma}\right).$$

Moreover, if $x^* > 0$, x has the same density as x^*. The total probability is thus equal to 1 because we report on the censoring point, here 0, the probability of the censored region. We have

$$E^\theta(x) = 0\Pr(x = 0) + E^\theta(x^*|x^* > 0)\Pr(x^* > 0).$$

From (11.11),

$$E^\theta(x^*|x^* > 0) = \mu + \sigma\lambda(\alpha)$$

with

$$\alpha = -\frac{\mu}{\sigma} \quad \text{and} \quad \lambda(\alpha) = \frac{f_N\left(-\frac{\mu}{\sigma}\right)}{1 - F_N\left(-\frac{\mu}{\sigma}\right)}.$$

It follows from the symmetry of the normal density that

$$f_N\left(-\frac{\mu}{\sigma}\right) = f_N\left(\frac{\mu}{\sigma}\right) \quad \text{and} \quad 1 - F_N\left(-\frac{\mu}{\sigma}\right) = F_N\left(\frac{\mu}{\sigma}\right),$$

hence

$$\lambda(\alpha) = \frac{f_N\left(\frac{\mu}{\sigma}\right)}{F_N\left(\frac{\mu}{\sigma}\right)}.$$

Therefore

$$E^\theta(x^*|x^* > 0) = \mu + \sigma \frac{f_N\left(\frac{\mu}{\sigma}\right)}{F_N\left(\frac{\mu}{\sigma}\right)}.$$

Moreover

$$\Pr(x^* > 0) = F_N\left(\frac{\mu}{\sigma}\right).$$

Hence, we can write

$$E^\theta(x) = \left[\mu + \sigma \frac{f_N\left(\frac{\mu}{\sigma}\right)}{F_N\left(\frac{\mu}{\sigma}\right)}\right] F_N\left(\frac{\mu}{\sigma}\right) = \mu F_N\left(\frac{\mu}{\sigma}\right) + \sigma f_N\left(\frac{\mu}{\sigma}\right).$$

$$(11.12)$$

Consider now a censored normal model defined by

$$y_i = \begin{vmatrix} \lambda'z_i + \varepsilon_i & \text{if } \varepsilon_i > -\lambda'z_i \\ 0 & \text{otherwise.} \end{vmatrix}$$

with $\varepsilon_i \sim N(0, \sigma^2)$. *Then, by setting* $x = y_i$ *and* $\mu = \lambda'z_i$ *in (11.12), we obtain*

$$E^\theta(y_i|z_i) = \lambda'z_i F_N\left(\frac{\lambda'z_i}{\sigma}\right) + \sigma f_N\left(\frac{\lambda'z_i}{\sigma}\right).$$ ∎

11.2.4 Disequilibrium Models

These models have been developed to take into account that, in some markets, the traded quantity is not equal at the same time to the supply and the demand, or in other words, that some sellers and buyers are not able to exchange at the market price.

Consider thus the following model

$$\begin{cases} y_t^D = z_t^{D\prime}\lambda^D + z_t^*\lambda^{*D} + u_t^D \\ y_t^S = z_t^{S\prime}\lambda^S + z_t^*\lambda^{*S} + u_t^S \\ y_t = \min\left(y_t^D, y_t^S\right), \end{cases}$$

$$(11.13)$$

where y_t^D and y_t^S are the demand and supply which are unobservable variables, z_t^* is the price, z_t^D and z_t^S are vectors of exogenous variables, and y_t is the traded quantity which is observed. This model is completed by a mechanism of price adjustment which may take the following simple form

$$\Delta z_t^* = \lambda^s \left(y_t^D - y_t^S \right) \tag{11.14}$$

with $\lambda^s \geq 0$, or may be characterized by different adjustment speeds depending on whether there is excess supply or excess demand

$$\Delta z_t^* = \begin{vmatrix} \lambda_1^\Delta \left(y_t^D - y_t^S \right) & \text{if } y_t^D - y_t^S \geq 0 \\ \lambda_2^\Delta \left(y_t^D - y_t^S \right) & \text{if } y_t^D - y_t^S < 0 \end{vmatrix} \tag{11.15}$$

with λ_1^Δ and $\lambda_2^\Delta \geq 0$; Δz_t^* is defined by $z_{t+1}^* - z_t^*$ or $z_t^* - z_{t-1}^*$. Given (11.13) and (11.15), we can write:

$$y_t = \begin{vmatrix} y_t^S = y_t^D - \frac{1}{\lambda_1^\Delta}\Delta z_t^* = z_t^{D\prime}\lambda^D + z_t^*\lambda^{*D} - \frac{1}{\lambda_1^\Delta}\Delta z_t^* + u_t^D & \text{if } \Delta z_t^* \geq 0 \\ y_t^D = y_t^S + \frac{1}{\lambda_2^\Delta}\Delta z_t^* = z_t^{S\prime}\lambda^S + z_t^*\lambda^{*S} + \frac{1}{\lambda_2^\Delta}\Delta z_t^* + u_t^S & \text{if } \Delta z_t^* < 0 \end{vmatrix}$$

or

$$y_t = \begin{vmatrix} z_t^{D\prime}\lambda^D + z_t^*\lambda^{*D} - \frac{1}{\lambda_1^\Delta}D_t + u_t^D & \text{if } \Delta z_t^* \geq 0 \\ z_t^{S\prime}\lambda^S + z_t^*\lambda^{*S} + \frac{1}{\lambda_2^\Delta}S_t + u_t^S & \text{if } \Delta z_t^* < 0 \end{vmatrix} \tag{11.16}$$

with

$$D_t = \begin{vmatrix} \Delta z_t^* & \text{if } \Delta z_t^* \geq 0 \\ 0 & \text{otherwise} \end{vmatrix} \quad \text{and} \quad S_t = \begin{vmatrix} \Delta z_t^* & \text{if } \Delta z_t^* < 0 \\ 0 & \text{otherwise.} \end{vmatrix}$$

11.2.5 Sample Selection Models

These models, also called models with *incidental truncation* or *generalized tobit models*, involve a truncation process based on a latent variable different from the variable that describes the observed data. For instance, the desired number of work hours of an individual which may depend on the wage and characteristics of the household, is observed only if the individual actually works, i.e., receives a wage greater than her reservation wage.

Consider a latent variable defined by

$$y_i^{(0)*} = \lambda^{(0)\prime}z_i^{(0)} + \varepsilon_i. \tag{11.17}$$

Suppose in addition that the observation of the endogenous variable y_i depends on another latent variable

$$y_i^{(1)*} = \delta(z_i^{(1)}) + v_i \tag{11.18}$$

in the following way

$$
y_i = \left|
\begin{array}{ll}
y_i^{(0)*} & \text{if } y_i^{(1)*} > 0 \\
0 & \text{otherwise.}
\end{array}
\right.
\tag{11.19}
$$

If we return to the example mentioned above, $y_i^{(0)*}$ is the desired numbers of work hours and $y_i^{(1)*}$ represents the difference between the wage and reservation wage. Thus

$$
y_i = \left|
\begin{array}{ll}
\lambda^{(0)\prime} z_i^{(0)} + \varepsilon_i & \text{if } v_i > -\delta(z_i^{(1)}) \\
0 & \text{otherwise.}
\end{array}
\right.
$$

Define the discrete variable d_i by

$$
d_i = \left|
\begin{array}{ll}
1 & \text{if } v_i > -\delta(z_i^{(1)}) \\
0 & \text{otherwise.}
\end{array}
\right.
$$

So

$$
\begin{aligned}
y_i &= y_i^{(0)*} d_i \\
&= \left(\lambda^{(0)\prime} z_i^{(0)} + \varepsilon_i \right) 1 \left(v_i > -\delta(z_i^{(1)}) \right).
\end{aligned}
$$

Hence, the regression for positive responses is

$$
E^\theta \left(y_i | z_i^{(0)}, z_i^{(1)}, y_i > 0 \right) = \lambda^{(0)\prime} z_i^{(0)} + E^\theta \left(\varepsilon_i | v_i > -\delta(z_i^{(1)}) \right).
$$

The index model can be written as

$$
\begin{cases}
E^\theta(y_i | z_i) = G^{(0)} \left(\lambda^{(0)\prime} z_i^{(0)}, \delta(z_i^{(1)}) \right) \\
E^\theta(d_i | z_i) = G^{(1)} \left(\delta(z_i^{(1)}) \right).
\end{cases}
$$

where $z_i = (z_i^{(0)\prime}, z_i^{(1)\prime})\prime$ and $G^{(0)}$ and $G^{(1)}$ are some functions of $\lambda^{(0)\prime} z_i^{(0)}$, $\delta(z_i^{(1)})$, and $\delta(z_i^{(1)})$ respectively.

We illustrate this type of model by an example where the pair (ε_i, v_i) follows a bivariate normal distribution.

Example 11.5 *Consider first a bivariate distribution with truncation on one coordinate. If y and z follow such a distribution, the truncated density is written as*

$$
f(y, z | z > a) = \frac{f(y, z)}{\Pr(z > a)}.
$$

Assume that

$$\begin{bmatrix} y \\ z \end{bmatrix} \sim N \left(\begin{bmatrix} \mu_y \\ \mu_z \end{bmatrix}, \begin{bmatrix} \sigma_y^2 & \rho\sigma_y\sigma_z \\ \rho\sigma_y\sigma_z & \sigma_z^2 \end{bmatrix} \right),$$

we state the following results

$$E^\theta(y|z > a) = \mu_y + \rho\sigma_y\lambda(\alpha_z) \tag{11.20}$$

and

$$Var^\theta(y|z > a) = \sigma_y^2(1 - \rho^2\eta(\alpha_z))$$

with

$$\alpha_z = \frac{a - \mu_z}{\sigma_z}, \quad \lambda(\alpha_z) = \frac{f_N(\alpha_z)}{1 - F_N(\alpha_z)}$$

and

$$\eta(\alpha_z) = \lambda(\alpha_z)(\lambda(\alpha_z) - \alpha_z)$$

(if the truncation is given by $z < a$, then $\lambda(\alpha_z) = \frac{-f_N(\alpha_z)}{F_N(\alpha_z)}$). Now, consider the sample selection model

$$y_i = \begin{vmatrix} \lambda^{(0)\prime}z_i^{(0)} + \varepsilon_i & if\ v_i > -\lambda^{(1)\prime}z_i^{(1)} \\ 0 & otherwise. \end{vmatrix}$$

with

$$\begin{bmatrix} \varepsilon_i \\ v_i \end{bmatrix} \sim N \left(\begin{bmatrix} 0 \\ 0 \end{bmatrix}, \begin{bmatrix} \sigma_\varepsilon^2 & \rho\sigma_\varepsilon\sigma_v \\ \rho\sigma_\varepsilon\sigma_v & \sigma_v^2 \end{bmatrix} \right).$$

Then, we have

$$E^\theta\left(y_i|z_i^{(0)}, z_i^{(1)}, y_i > 0\right) = \lambda^{(0)\prime}z_i^{(0)} + E^\theta\left(\varepsilon_i|v_i > -\lambda^{(1)\prime}z_i^{(1)}\right)$$

$$= \lambda^{(0)\prime}z_i^{(0)} + \rho\sigma_\varepsilon\lambda(\alpha_v)$$

with

$$\alpha_v = \frac{\lambda^{(1)\prime}z_i^{(1)}}{\sigma_v}, \quad \lambda(\alpha_v) = \frac{f_N\left(\frac{\lambda^{(1)\prime}z_i^{(1)}}{\sigma_v}\right)}{1 - F_N\left(\frac{\lambda^{(1)\prime}z_i^{(1)}}{\sigma_v}\right)}$$

(it suffices to set $a = 0$ and $\mu_z = \lambda^{(1)\prime}z_i^{(1)}$ in (11.20)). ∎

Other types of sample selection models have been proposed in the literature such as the one described in the example below, where each individual can be in one of two possible states of which only one is observed.

Example 11.6 *This example is a first introduction to the models with counterfactuals that are studied more deeply in Section 18.6 in Chapter 18. Denote by $y_i^{(1)}$ and $y_i^{(0)}$ the two possible outcomes for individual i. For instance, if we study the effect of a medical treatment, $y_i^{(1)}$ and $y_i^{(0)}$ represent two alternative treatment effects, depending on whether the individual is treated or not; but of course we observe one outcome only. This example has been introduced in medical treatment effect models, but it can be extensively applied in econometrics for the evaluation of public policy (for example, employment policy, education policy, and so on). In other words, we observe y_i defined by*

$$y_i = d_i y_i^{(1)} + (1 - d_i) y_i^{(0)}$$

with

$$d_i = \begin{vmatrix} 1 & \text{if } i \text{ is treated} \\ 0 & \text{otherwise.} \end{vmatrix}$$

Let d_i^* be the latent variable defined by a linear index in z_i:

$$d_i^* = \lambda' z_i - \eta_{d_i};$$

then d_i can be written as

$$d_i = \begin{vmatrix} 1 & \text{if } d_i^* \geq 0 \\ 0 & \text{otherwise.} \end{vmatrix}$$

Define the equation of potential income if i participates in the treatment

$$y_i^{(1)*} = w_i \lambda_1 - \eta_i^{(1)}.$$

We observe $y_i^{(1)}$ defined by

$$y_i^{(1)} = \begin{vmatrix} 1 & \text{if } y_i^{(1)*} \geq 0 \\ 0 & \text{otherwise.} \end{vmatrix}$$

The income equation if i does not participate in the treatment is

$$y_i^{(0)*} = w_i \lambda_0 - \eta_i^{(0)}.$$

and we observe $y_i^{(0)}$ defined by

$$y_i^{(0)} = \begin{vmatrix} 1 & \text{if } y_i^{(0)*} \geq 0 \\ 0 & \text{otherwise.} \end{vmatrix}$$

Assume that η_{d_i}, $\eta_i^{(1)}$, and $\eta_i^{(0)}$ are continuous with respect to Lebesgue measure and that $(\eta_{d_i}, \eta_i^{(1)}, \eta_i^{(0)})$ are independent of (z_i, w_i).

Consider the treatment effect on individual i:

$$\Delta_i = y_i^{(1)} - y_i^{(0)}$$

which obviously is not observable.

We can study three different effects:

- *The average treatment effect (ATE):*

$$\Delta^{ATE}(z_i, w_i) = E^\theta(\Delta_i | z_i)$$

$$= E^\theta\left(y_i^{(1)} | z_i\right) - E^\theta\left(y_i^{(0)} | z_i\right)$$

$$= \Pr\left(y_i^{(1)*} \geq 0\right) - \Pr\left(y_i^{(0)*} \geq 0\right)$$

$$= \Pr\left(w_i \lambda_1 \geq \eta_i^{(1)}\right) - \Pr\left(w_i \lambda_0 \geq \eta_i^{(0)}\right)$$

$$= F_{\eta_i^{(1)}}(w_i \lambda_1) - F_{\eta_i^{(0)}}(w_i \lambda_0).$$

- *The expected treatment effect on the treated individual (TT):*

$$\Delta^{TT}(z_i, w_i) = E^\theta(\Delta_i | z_i, w_i, d_i = 1)$$

$$= \frac{1}{F_{\eta_d}(x_i \lambda_d)}\left[F_{\eta_d, \eta_i^{(1)}}(x_i \lambda_d, w_i \lambda_1)\right.$$

$$\left. - F_{\eta_d, \eta_i^{(0)}}(x_i \lambda_d, w_i \lambda_0)\right].$$

- *The local parameter defined by local instrumental variables:*

$$\Delta^{LIV}(z_i, w_i) = \frac{\partial E^\theta(y_i | w_i, \Pr(w_i))}{\partial w_i}. \qquad \blacksquare$$

11.3 Estimation

Various estimation methods may be used. First, we study the nonparametric estimation of models represented by index models without any assumption on the index function. Second we study the semiparametric estimation assuming some form of the index functions. Finally, we discuss the maximum likelihood estimation.

11.3.1 Nonparametric Estimation

The models seen in Section 2 can be written as index models

$$E^\theta(y_i | z_i) = \psi(\lambda' z_i) = \varphi(z_i),$$

where ψ is a function from $\mathbb{R}$ to $\mathbb{R}$ and $\lambda' z_i$ is a linear combination of elements of z_i. We assume that ψ is differentiable and that z_i has a continuous density f. In addition, to solve the problem of non idenfication of the pair (ψ, λ), we normalize λ by setting $\lambda_1 = 1$, in accordance with Section 10.4.1 of Chapter 10 regarding index models. Moreover, we will use some of its other results here.

From the normalization constraint and from the equality

$$
E\left[\frac{\partial \varphi(z)}{\partial z_j}\right] = \lambda_j E\left[\frac{\partial \psi(u)}{\partial u}\right],
$$

for all $j = 1, \dots q$, it follows that

$$
\lambda_j = \frac{E\left[\frac{\partial \varphi(z)}{\partial z_j}\right]}{E\left[\frac{\partial \psi(z)}{\partial z_1}\right]}.
$$

Using this result, the estimation proceeds by the following steps:

1. Estimate φ by the kernel estimator $\widehat{\varphi}_n$.
2. Estimate λ_j by

$$
\widehat{\lambda}_{jn} = \frac{\sum\limits_{i=1}^{n} \frac{\partial \widehat{\varphi}_n(z_i)}{\partial z_j}}{\sum\limits_{i=1}^{n} \frac{\partial \widehat{\varphi}_n(z_i)}{\partial z_1}}.
$$

3. Nonparametrically regress y on $\widehat{\lambda}'_n z$ where $\widehat{\lambda}_n$ is the vector of $\widehat{\lambda}'_{jn}$, which yields

$$
\widehat{\psi}_n(u) = \frac{\sum\limits_{i=1}^{n} y_i K\left(\frac{u - \widehat{\lambda}'_n z_i}{h_n}\right)}{\sum\limits_{i=1}^{n} K\left(\frac{u - \widehat{\lambda}'_n z_i}{h_n}\right)}.
$$

Another estimation procedure also described in Section 10.4.1 of Chapter 10 is based on the minimization of $E[(\varphi(z) - \psi(\lambda' z))^2]$ with respect to ψ and λ. It is described as follows:

1. Find an estimation of ψ

$$
\widehat{\psi}_{\lambda n}(u) = \frac{\sum\limits_{i=1}^{n} y_i K\left(\frac{u - \lambda' z_i}{h_n}\right)}{\sum\limits_{i=1}^{n} K\left(\frac{u - \lambda' z_i}{h_n}\right)}. \tag{11.21}
$$

2. Estimate λ by

$$\widehat{\lambda}_n = \arg\min \sum_{l=1}^{n} \left(y_l - \frac{\sum_{i=1}^{n} K\left(\frac{\lambda'z - \lambda'z_i}{h_n}\right) y_i}{\sum_{i=1}^{n} K\left(\frac{\lambda'z - \lambda'z_i}{h_n}\right)} \right).$$

3. An estimator $\widehat{\psi}_n$ is obtained by replacing λ by $\widehat{\lambda}_n$ in (11.21).

It can be shown that these estimators of λ are consistent with $\sqrt{n}$ rate and asymptotically normal and that tests can be implemented. Thus, to test the null hypothesis $H_0 : R\lambda = r_0$, the Wald statistic

$$W = \left(R\widehat{\lambda}_n - r_0\right)' \left(R\widehat{\Sigma}_{\lambda_n} R'\right)^{-1} \left(R\widehat{\lambda}_n - r_0\right)$$

follows asymptotically a χ^2, where $\widehat{\lambda}_n$ and $\widehat{\Sigma}_{\lambda_n}$ are respectively consistent estimators of λ and the asymptotic covariance matrix Σ_λ.

11.3.2 Semiparametric Estimation by Maximum Likelihood

In some cases, such as the binary choice models, the index model

$$E^\theta \left(y_i \,|z_i\right) = \psi \left(\lambda'z_i\right)$$

is such that the function ψ has the properties of a distribution function. When ψ is known, traditional estimation methods such as maximum likelihood should be used. On the contrary, when ψ is unknown, we turn to specific nonparametric methods which exploit the property that ψ is a distribution function.

We apply this idea to dichotomous models in the following example.

Example 11.7 *Return to the binary choice model (11.2) that takes the form of a linear index model*

$$E^\theta(y_i|z_i) = \psi \left(\lambda'z_i\right) = \Pr(y_i = 1|z_i)$$

where ψ has all the properties of a distribution function. If ψ were known, λ could be estimated by maximizing the log-likelihood

$$L(\lambda) = \sum_{i=1}^{n} \left[y_i \ln \psi \left(\lambda'z_i\right) + (1 - y_i)\ln \left(1 - \psi \left(\lambda'z_i\right)\right)\right].$$

Since ψ is unknown, we replace ψ by a nonparametric estimator $\widehat{\psi}_{ni}$:

$$\widehat{\psi}_{ni} = \frac{\frac{1}{nh_n} \sum\limits_{j \neq i} y_j J_{nj} K\left(\frac{z - \lambda' z_j}{h_n}\right)}{\frac{1}{nh_n} \sum\limits_{j \neq i} J_{nj} K\left(\frac{z - \lambda' z_j}{h_n}\right)}$$

with

$$J_{nj} = \begin{vmatrix} 1 & \text{if } z_j \in A_{nz} \\ 0 & \text{otherwise.} \end{vmatrix}$$

where

$$A_{nz} = \left\{ z_i \big| \|z_i - z_i^*\| < 2h_n, \ z_i^* \in A_z \right\},$$

$$A_z = \left\{ z_i \big| \psi(\lambda' z_i) \geq \eta, \ \lambda \in B \right\},$$

and B is the compact set of all possible λs. Hence, we maximize

$$\sum_{i=1}^{n} \left[y_i \ln \widehat{\psi}_{ni} \left(\lambda' z_i\right) + (1 - y_i) \ln \left(1 - \widehat{\psi}_{ni} \left(\lambda' z_i\right)\right) \right]$$

which yields the estimator $\widehat{\lambda}_n$ of λ. It can be shown that this estimator is consistent and asymptotically normal. ∎

11.3.3   Maximum Likelihood Estimation

Models with discrete variables and partially observed models are usually estimated by the maximum likelihood method. We return to some models presented in the first section of this chapter and use their traditional presentation, i.e., not in the form of a nonparametric index model.

Dichotomous Models

Consider the traditional representation of dichotomous models, where the variable y_i is assumed to take two values ($y_i = 0$ or 1) so that

$$\begin{cases} \Pr(y_i = 1) = \psi(\lambda' z_i) \\ \Pr(y_i = 0) = 1 - \psi(\lambda' z_i) \end{cases}$$

hence

$$E^\theta (y_i \,|z_i) = 0 \left[1 - \psi(\lambda' z_i)\right] + 1 \left[\psi(\lambda' z_i)\right] = \psi(\lambda' z_i).$$

Assuming that the y_i are mutually independent, the likelihood function is

$$L_n(y_1, \ldots, y_n) = \prod_{y_i=1} \left[\psi(\lambda' z_i) \right] \prod_{y_i=0} \left[1 - \psi(\lambda' z_i) \right]$$

$$= \prod_{i=1}^{n} \left[\psi(\lambda' z_i) \right]^{y_i} \left[1 - \psi(\lambda' z_i) \right]^{1-y_i}.$$

Thus, the log-likelihood is given by

$$\ln L_n = \sum_{y_i=1} \ln \psi(\lambda' z_i) + \sum_{y_i=0} \ln \left(1 - \psi(\lambda' z_i) \right) \qquad (11.22)$$

or equivalently

$$\ln L_n = \sum_{i=1}^{n} \left[y_i \ln \psi(\lambda' z_i) + (1 - y_i) \ln \left(1 - \psi(\lambda' z_i) \right) \right]. \qquad (11.23)$$

It can be shown that the global maximum of $\ln L_n$ is unique because this function is concave, whether the model is probit or logit. Indeed, in the latter case, i.e., when $\psi(x)$ is given by (11.4), it is easy to show that for all x

$$\frac{\partial^2 \ln \psi(x)}{\partial x^2} = -\frac{e^x}{(1 + e^x)^2} < 0.$$

Therefore $\ln \psi(x)$ is concave and $\ln (1 - \psi(x))$ is also concave since

$$\ln (1 - \psi(x)) = \ln \frac{e^{-x}}{1 + e^{-x}} = -x + \ln \frac{1}{1 + e^{-x}} = -x + \ln \psi(x).$$

It follows that $\ln L_n$ given by (11.22) is concave.

Under the usual conditions, the maximum likelihood estimator $\widehat{\lambda}_n$ of λ is consistent and asymptotically normal

$$\widehat{\lambda}_n \sim N \left(\lambda, \left[-E^\theta \left(\frac{\partial^2 \ln L_n}{\partial \lambda \partial \lambda'} \right) \right]^{-1} \right).$$

In the context of a logit model, the asymptotic variance matrix is

$$\left[-E^\theta \left(\frac{\partial^2 \ln L_n}{\partial \lambda \partial \lambda'} \right) \right]^{-1} = \left[\sum_{i=1}^{n} \psi(\lambda' z_i) \left(1 - \psi(\lambda' z_i) \right) z_i z_i' \right]^{-1}.$$

Multiple Choice Models

a) Models of Unordered Multiple Choice   Suppose that individual i must choose among $J + 1$ possible alternatives labelled $j = 0, 1, \ldots, J$. The utility of alternative j is

$$U_{ij} = \lambda_j' z_i + \varepsilon_j.$$

Individual i chooses j if $U_{ij} > U_{il}, \forall l \neq j$. Let

$$\Pr(y_i = j) = \frac{e^{\lambda'_j z_i}}{1 + \sum\limits_{k=1}^{J} e^{\lambda'_k z_i}}, \quad j = 1, 2, \ldots, J$$

and

$$\Pr(y_i = 0) = \frac{1}{1 + \sum\limits_{k=1}^{J} e^{\lambda'_k z_i}}$$

(we use here the normalization $\lambda_0 = 0$ to guarantee the identification of the λ_j). This model is called *multinomial logit* model. Using the notation, for $j = 1, \ldots, J+1$,

$$d_{ij} = \begin{vmatrix} 1 & \text{if alternative } j \text{ is chosen} \\ 0 & \text{otherwise,} \end{vmatrix}$$

the log-likelihood is written as

$$\ln I_n = \sum_{i-1}^{n} \sum_{j=0}^{J} d_{ij} \ln \Pr(y_i = j).$$

There are other types of models such as the conditional logit model.

b) Models of Ordered Multiple Choice   Assume that a latent variable is defined by

$$y_i^* = \lambda' z_i + \varepsilon_i$$

and that the observed variable is given by (11.5). If moreover the ε_i are normally distributed, then we have

$$\begin{cases} \Pr(y_i = 0) = \Phi(c_1 - \lambda' z_i) \\ \Pr(y_i = 1) = \Phi(c_2 - \lambda' z_i) - \Phi(c_1 - \lambda' z_i) \\ \vdots \\ \Pr(y_i = J) = 1 - \Phi(c_J - \lambda' z_i). \end{cases}$$

Thus, the log-likelihood is

$$\ln L_n = \sum_{j=0}^{J} j \ln \Pr(y_i = j).$$

Tobit Models

Consider the tobit model defined by (11.6) and (11.7) and assume that the residuals are normally distributed. The log-likelihood is

$$
\ln L_n = \sum_{y_i=0} \ln F_N \left(-\frac{\lambda' z_i}{\sigma} \right) - \frac{1}{2} \sum_{y_i>0} \left[\ln 2\pi\sigma^2 + \frac{(y_i - \lambda' z_i)^2}{\sigma^2} \right]
$$

$$
= \sum_{y_i=0} \ln F_N \left(-\frac{\lambda' z_i}{\sigma} \right) - \frac{n_1}{2} \ln 2\pi\sigma^2 - \frac{1}{2\sigma^2} \sum_{y_i>0} (y_i - \lambda' z_i)^2,
$$

(11.24)

where n_1 is the number of positive y_i. This log-likelihood has a nonstandard form because we have a mixture of a discrete and a continuous distribution, but it can be maximized using a usual iterative method for obtaining the MLE. Usually, a reparametrized version of (11.24) is studied with $\gamma = \frac{\lambda}{\sigma}$ and $\delta = \frac{1}{\sigma}$, i.e.,

$$
\ln L_n = \sum_{y_i=0} \ln F_N \left(-\gamma' z_i \right) - \frac{n_1}{2} \ln 2\pi + n_1 \ln \delta - \frac{1}{2} \sum_{y_i>0} (\delta y_i - \gamma' z_i)^2.
$$

Disequilibrium Model

Return to the disequilibrium model represented by Equation (11.16). Consider for instance the case where the price variation is defined by

$$
\Delta z_t^* = z_{t+1}^* - z_t^*.
$$

Two cases are possible. If $y_t^S > y_t^D$, then $\Delta z_t^* < 0$ from (11.15), and $\Delta z_t^* = \lambda_2^\Delta (y_t - y_t^S)$ (since $y_t = y_t^D$). In this case, assuming the normality of the residuals u_t^D and u_t^S in (11.13), we can write

$$
\Delta z_t^* | y_t \sim N \left(\lambda_2^\Delta \left(y_t - z_t^{S'} \lambda^S - z_t^* \lambda^{*S} \right), \lambda_2^{\Delta 2} \sigma_S^2 \right)
$$

and

$$
y_t \sim N \left(z_t^{D'} \lambda^D + z_t^* \lambda^{*D}, \sigma_D^2 \right).
$$

Similarly, in the case where $y_t^S \leq y_t^D$, we have

$$
\Delta z_t^* | y_t \sim N \left(\lambda_1^\Delta \left(-y_t + z_t^{D'} \lambda^D + z_t^* \lambda^{*D} \right), \lambda_1^{\Delta 2} \sigma_D^2 \right)
$$

and

$$
y_t \sim N \left(z_t^{S'} \lambda^S + z_t^* \lambda^{*S}, \sigma_S^2 \right).
$$

Denote by S_1 the set of the n_1 observations such that $\Delta z_t^* < 0$, and by S_2 the set of the n_2 other observations ($n_1 + n_2 = n$). The log-likelihood is

$$
\ln L_n = -n \ln (2\pi \sigma_S \sigma_D) - n_1 \ln \lambda_2^\Delta - n_2 \ln \lambda_1^\Delta
$$
$$
- \frac{1}{2\sigma_D^2} \sum_{S_1} \left(y_t - z_t^{D\prime} \lambda^D - z_t^* \lambda \right)^2
$$
$$
- \frac{1}{2\sigma_S^2} \sum_{S_2} \left(y_t - z_t^{S\prime} \lambda^S + z_t^* \lambda^{*S} \right)^2
$$
$$
- \frac{1}{2\lambda_2^{\Delta 2} \sigma_S^2} \sum_{S_1} \left(\Delta z_t^* - \lambda_2^\Delta \left(y_t - z_t^{S\prime} \lambda^S - z_t^* \lambda^{*S} \right) \right)^2
$$
$$
- \frac{1}{2\lambda_1^{\Delta 2} \sigma_D^2} \sum_{S_2} \left(\Delta z_t^* + \lambda_1^\Delta \left(y_t - z_t^{D\prime} \lambda^D - z_t^* \lambda^{*D} \right) \right)^2 .
$$

Sample Selection Models

Return to Equations (11.17), (11.18), and (11.19):

$$
y_i = \begin{vmatrix} y_i^{(0)*} & \text{if } y_i^{(1)*} > 0 \\ 0 & \text{otherwise} \end{vmatrix}
$$

with

$$
y_i^{(0)*} = \lambda^{(0)\prime} z_i^{(0)} + \varepsilon_i
$$

and

$$
y_i^{(1)*} = \lambda^{(1)\prime} z_i^{(1)} + v_i .
$$

Moreover, assume that

$$
\begin{pmatrix} \varepsilon_i \\ v_i \end{pmatrix} \sim N \left(\begin{pmatrix} 0 \\ 0 \end{pmatrix}, \begin{pmatrix} \sigma_0^2 & \rho \sigma_0 \sigma_1 \\ \rho \sigma_0 \sigma_1 & \sigma_1^2 \end{pmatrix} \right).
$$

The likelihood function is given by

$$
L_n = \prod_{y_i = 0} F_N \left(-\frac{\lambda^{(1)\prime} z_i^{(1)}}{\sigma_1} \right) \prod_{y_i \neq 0} \frac{1}{\sigma_0} f_N \left(\frac{y_i - \lambda^{(0)\prime} z_i^{(0)}}{\sigma_0} \right)
$$
$$
\times \prod_{y_i \neq 0} F_N \left(\frac{1}{\sqrt{1-\rho^2}} \left(\frac{\lambda^{(1)\prime}}{\sigma_1} z_i^{(1)} + \frac{\rho}{\sigma_0} \left(y_i - \lambda^{(0)\prime} z_i^{(0)} \right) \right) \right).
$$

Since the pair $(\lambda^{(1)}, \sigma_1)$ is not identified, we make the change of parameters

$$\delta_0 = \frac{1}{\sigma_0}, \quad c_0 = \frac{\lambda^{(0)}}{\sigma_0} \quad \text{and} \quad c_1 = \frac{\lambda^{(1)}}{\sigma_1},$$

hence

$$L_n = \prod_{y_i=0} F_N\left(-c_1' z_i^{(1)}\right) \prod_{y_i \neq 0} \delta_0 f_N\left(\delta_0 y_i - c_0' z_i^{(0)}\right)$$

$$\times \prod_{y_i \neq 0} F_N\left(\frac{1}{\sqrt{1-\rho^2}}\left(c_1' z_i^{(1)} + \rho\left(\delta_0 y_i - c_0' z_i^{(0)}\right)\right)\right).$$

This likelihood can be maximized by the usual methods. But notice that it is also possible to use a two-stage estimation procedure:

1. Consider the probit model associated with the preceding model

$$w_i = \begin{vmatrix} 1 & \text{if } y_i^{(1)*} > 0 \\ 0 & \text{otherwise;} \end{vmatrix}$$

then

$$\Pr(w_i = 1) = \Pr\left(y_i^{(1)*} > 0\right) = F_N\left(\frac{\lambda^{(1)\prime}}{\sigma_1} z_i^{(1)}\right) = F_N\left(c_1' z_i^{(1)}\right).$$

Hence, it is possible to estimate c_1 by $\widehat{c}_{1n}$.

2. Now, look at the positive y_i

$$E^\theta\left(y_i | y_i > 0\right) = \lambda^{(0)\prime} z_i^{(0)} + \rho \sigma_0 \frac{f_N\left(\frac{\lambda^{(1)\prime}}{\sigma_1} z_i^{(1)}\right)}{F_N\left(\frac{\lambda^{(1)\prime}}{\sigma_1} z_i^{(1)}\right)}$$

therefore

$$E^\theta\left(y_i | y_i > 0\right) = \lambda^{(0)\prime} z_i^{(0)} + \rho \sigma_0 \frac{f_N\left(c_1' z_i^{(1)}\right)}{F_N\left(c_1' z_i^{(1)}\right)}.$$

Let

$$\widehat{\delta}_{in} = \frac{f_N\left(\widehat{c}_{1n} z_i^{(1)}\right)}{F_N\left(\widehat{c}_{1n} z_i^{(1)}\right)}.$$

Regressing the positive observations of y_i on $z_i^{(0)}$ and $\widehat{\delta}_{in}$ leads to asymptotically unbiased estimators of $\lambda^{(0)}$ and $\rho \sigma_0$, but they are not efficient.

Indeed, it can be shown that the errors in the regression are heteroskedastic.

3. Finally, for estimating σ_0, consider the estimated residuals of the former regression

$$\widehat{\eta}_i = y_i - \widehat{\lambda}^{(0)\prime} z_i^{(0)} - \widehat{\rho\sigma_0} \widehat{\delta}_{in}.$$

Since

$$Var^\theta \left(y_i | y_i \neq 0 \right) = Var^\theta \left(y_i^{(0)} | y_i^{(1)*} > 0 \right)$$

$$= \sigma_0^2 + (\rho\sigma_0)^2 \left[-c_1' z_i^{(1)} \frac{f_N \left(c_1' z_i^{(1)} \right)}{F_N \left(c_1' z_i^{(1)} \right)} - \left(\frac{f_N \left(c_1' z_i^{(1)} \right)}{F_N \left(c_1' z_i^{(1)} \right)} \right)^2 \right],$$

we can estimate σ_0^2 by

$$\widehat{\sigma}_0^2 = \frac{1}{n_1} \sum_{y_i \neq 0} \widehat{\eta}_i^2 + \frac{(\widehat{\rho\sigma_0})^2}{n_1} \sum_{y_i \neq 0} \left[\widehat{\delta}_{in} \widehat{c}_{1n} z_i^{(1)} + \widehat{\delta}_{in}^2 \right]$$

where n_1 is the number of y_i different from zero. Thus we obtain consistent and asymptotically normal estimators.

Notes

The book by Stocker (1991) outlines the treatment of index models. For various examples of models, we refer to Greene (1999).

Example 11.6 of Paragraph 11.2.5. is drawn from Aakvik, Heckman, and Vytlacil (1998) (see also Heckman, Ichimura, Smith, and Todd (1998) and Heckman and Vytlacil (2005)).

Regarding the nonparametric estimation by maximum likelihood that exploits the property of the index function as distribution function, this idea has been developed by Klein and Spady (1993) in the setting of dichotomous models and is illustrated in Example 11.7; it is treated in Horowitz (1998) and has been extended to single-index models by Ai (1997).

The treatment by maximum likelihood of the models studied in this chapter can be found in various books, such as those by Gouriéroux (1989), Fomby, Hill, and Johnson (1984), and Greene (1999). For the disequilibrium models, we also refer to the articles by Fair and Jaffee (1972), Amemiya (1974a), Gouriéroux, Laffont, and Monfort (1980), and Laffont and Garcia (1977).

Part III

Dynamic Models

12. Stationary Dynamic Models

12.1 Introduction

This chapter is dedicated to the study of linear dynamic models, more precisely to the study of the temporal evolution of one or several variables. It is organized in the following way. The first part provides the definitions of stochastic processes in discrete time. Next, we study models that have a particular representation, namely the univariate $ARMA(p, q)$ models. In the last part we extend these models to the multivariate setting.

Generally speaking, a stochastic process is a family of random variables on a common probability space indexed by the elements of an ordered set T which is the time index set. The random variable indexed by an element $i \in T$ describes the state of the process at time i. The stochastic processes considered here are defined in the following way.

Definition 12.1 *A stochastic process is a family of random variables* $\{x_i, i \in T\}$ *where the time index set T is a subset of the real line* $\mathbb{R}$. ∎

We could denote by T the set of all parameters, but to avoid the confusion with the parameters in a statistical sense, we call it the time index set. It is often called the domain of the definition of the stochastic process $\{x_i, i \in T\}$. If T is an interval of the real line, then the process is said to be a continuous-time process. Most often, T may be $\mathbb{N}^*$, $\mathbb{Z}$ or $\mathbb{R}^+ = [0, +\infty)$. Let $\{x_i, i \in T\}$ be a scalar-valued random process and $\{i_1, \ldots, i_n\} \subset T$ where $i_1 < i_2 < \cdots < i_n$, then

$$F_{i_1,\ldots,i_n}(x_1, \ldots, x_n) = \Pr\left\{x_{i_1} \leq x_1, \ldots, x_{i_n} \leq x_n\right\}$$

is the marginal distribution function for finite dimension of the process $\{x_i, i \in T\}$, which constitutes one of the characteristics of the scalar random process. The probability distribution of the process is given by the family of functions F satisfying

$$F_{i_1,\ldots,i_k}(x_1,\ldots,x_k) = F_{i_1,\ldots,i_k,\ldots,i_n}(x_1,\ldots,x_k,\infty,\ldots,\infty).$$

In a statistical model, we do not consider a single distribution but a family of distributions indexed by parameters $\theta \in \Theta$.

12.2   Second Order Processes

Definition 12.2   *A scalar random process $\{x_i,\ i \in T\}$ is said to be second order if, for all $i \in T$, $x_i \in L^2$ or x_i is square integrable for all values of $\theta \in \Theta$.*
∎

In general, the L^2 space depends on θ. The second order processes are often called "Hilbert processes." We often assume in the following that

$$E^\theta(x_i) = 0 \quad \forall i \in T.$$

Definition 12.3   *The covariance function $C_x^\theta(i, j)$ of the process is the second cross-moment, i.e.,*

$$C_x^\theta(i, j) = Cov^\theta(x_i, x_j) = E^\theta\left[\left(x_i - E^\theta(x_i)\right)\left(x_j - E^\theta(x_j)\right)\right],$$
(12.1)

and in particular

$$C_x^\theta(i, i) = Var^\theta(x_i).$$
∎

To simplify the notation, and when it is without ambiguity, we suppress the index x and denote the covariance by $C^\theta(i, j)$. Dividing the terms in (12.1) by $(C^\theta(i, i) \times C^\theta(j, j))^{\frac{1}{2}}$, we obtain the autocorrelation function $\rho^\theta(i, j)$. Moreover, from (12.1), we conclude

$$C^\theta(i, j) = C^\theta(j, i).$$
(12.2)

The covariance function of a second order process always has finite values. This comes from the Schwarz inequality:

$$\left|C^\theta(i, j)\right|^2 \le C^\theta(i, i)C^\theta(j, j),$$
(12.3)

$C^\theta(i, i)$ and $C^\theta(j, j)$ are finite by assumption since x_i and x_j are in L^2. The covariance function has a certain number of properties which we describe next.

1.   The matrix $C^\theta(i, j)_{i,j \in I}$ is symmetric positive semidefinite for a finite set I of time periods
2.   For all symmetric positive semidefinite functions $C^\theta(i, j)$ on $T \times T$, there exists a second order process $\{x_i,\ i \in T\}$ for which the covariance

function is precisely $C^\theta(i, j)$. This process is obviously not unique. When we are interested in the analysis of processes in L^2, we concentrate on the estimation of the covariance function, and we do not distinguish among processes which have the same covariance function.

3. If C_1 and C_2 are two covariance functions with a common time index set T, then linear combinations with strictly positive coefficients, as well as products of two covariance functions are again covariance functions. Moreover, if $(C_n)_{n\in\mathbb{N}}$ is a sequence of covariance functions and $C = \lim_{n\to\infty} C_n$ then C is also a covariance function.

To a large part, the models and methods of time series analysis are constructed starting with the notion of stationarity. Let

$$\{x_i, \ i \in T\} \tag{12.4}$$

be a second order process. The stochastic process is said to be *weakly stationary* if, for all i, j and τ:

$$E^\theta(x_i) = E^\theta(x_{i+\tau}) \tag{12.5}$$

and

$$E^\theta(x_{i+\tau} x_{j+\tau}) = E^\theta(x_i x_j).$$

In this case, $E^\theta(x_i)$ is clearly a constant which we denote by μ, and the covariance function $C^\theta(i, j)$ is a function of $i - j$, i.e.

$$\mu = E^\theta(x_i) \quad \text{and} \quad E^\theta(x_i x_{i+\tau}) = C^\theta(i, i + \tau) = C^\theta(\tau). \tag{12.6}$$

The terms second order stationarity, covariance stationarity, and weak stationarity are used exchangeably. The same letter is used to refer to the covariance function of a stationary process which only depends on the difference τ, i.e., $C^\theta(\tau)$. From (12.6), we conclude that $C^\theta(-\tau) = C^\theta(\tau)$. In the following we assume without loss of generality that

$$\mu = E^\theta(x_i) = 0$$

and

$$C^\theta(i, i) = Var^\theta(x_i) = C^\theta(0).$$

If the process x_i is not centered, then we take the difference from its mean.

The concept of stationarity is important since the majority of the statistical results requires more than the notion of stationarity in the weak sense. The definitions have been provided in Chapter 1. In the following, we consider only processes that are stationary ergodic when we are interested in asymptotic properties.

Definition 12.4   *The process $\{u_i, i \in T\}$ is said to be a weak white noise of mean zero and variance σ^2, where*

$$\{u_i\} \sim WN\left(0, \sigma^2\right),\tag{12.7}$$

if and only if $\{u_i\}$ has mean zero and covariance function

$$C_u^\theta(\tau) = \begin{vmatrix} \sigma^2 & if\,\tau = 0 \\ 0 & if\,\tau \neq 0. \end{vmatrix}$$

Moreover, if the random variables u_i are i.i.d., or

$$\{u_i\} \sim i.i.d.(0, \sigma^2),\tag{12.8}$$

then we have a strong white noise.   ∎

12.3   Gaussian Processes

Definition 12.5   *The stochastic process $\{x_i, \, i \in T\}$ is a Gaussian process if and only if, for each $\{i_1, \ldots, i_n\} \subset T, \, n = 1, 2, \ldots,$*

$$\{x_{i_1}, \ldots, x_{i_n}\}$$

is jointly Gaussian.   ∎

Note that a Gaussian process is evidently a second order process. Recall that if $\{x_1, \ldots, x_n\}$ is a sequence of jointly normal random variables, then these random variables are mutually independent if and only if the covariance matrix of the system is diagonal.

Whatever are the covariance function $C^\theta(i, j)$ and the vector $\mu_i = E^\theta(x_i)$, we can always find a Gaussian process for which the former are the second and first order moments. Thus, the analysis in L^2 essentially comes down to the analysis of Gaussian processes.

Theorem 12.1   *A scalar Gaussian process $\{x_i \, ; i \geq 0\}$ with mean zero and covariance function $C^\theta(i, j)$ is stationary if and only if*

$$C^\theta(i, j) = C^\theta(0, i - j) = C^\theta(i - j) \quad \forall i, j, \, 0 \leq i \leq j.\tag{12.9}$$
  ∎

Corollary 12.1   *For a Gaussian process, weak and strong stationarity are equivalent.*   ∎

12.4 Spectral Representation and Autocovariance Generating Function

Let $C^\theta(\tau)$ be the covariance function of a stationary process. This function is symmetric positive definite. The form of symmetric positive semidefinite functions on $\mathbb{Z}$ or $\mathbb{R}$ is given by the following theorem.

Theorem 12.2 *(Herglotz) Let $C^\theta(\tau)$ be a symmetric positive semidefinite functions from $\mathbb{Z}$ to $\mathbb{R}$. There exists a bounded measure M^θ on $[-\pi, \pi)$ such that, for all $\tau \in \mathbb{Z}$,*

$$C^\theta(\tau) = \int_{-\pi}^{\pi} e^{i\tau\lambda} M^\theta(d\lambda).$$ ∎

Note that here "i" is evidently the imaginary number satisfying $i^2 = -1$.

Definition 12.6 *In the previous statement, the measure M^θ is the spectral measure of x. If M^θ has a density m_θ with respect to Lebesgue measure, then this density is the spectral density of x:*

$$C^\theta(\tau) = \int_{-\pi}^{\pi} e^{i\tau\lambda} m_\theta(\lambda)(d\lambda).$$ ∎

Theorem 12.3 *Let x be a stationary, centered sequence. The following two conditions are equivalent:*

1. *x has a spectral density m_θ .*
2. *There exists a weak white noise (u_i) and a sequence (c_n) satisfying*

$$\sum_{p=-\infty}^{\infty} c_{n-p}^2 < \infty$$

such that

$$x_i = \sum_{p=-\infty}^{\infty} c_{n-p} u_p.$$

In this case, the function m_θ can be written as

$$m_\theta(\lambda) = \frac{1}{2\pi} \sum_{\tau=-\infty}^{\infty} C^\theta(\tau) e^{-i\lambda\tau} = \frac{1}{2\pi} \sum_{\tau=-\infty}^{\infty} C^\theta(\tau) \cos \lambda\tau, \ \forall \lambda \in \mathbb{R}.$$ ∎

The convergence of the sequence used in part 2 of the theorem is assured by Theorem 12.4 of the following section. We note that $C^\theta(\tau)$ and the functions m_θ contain the same information.

Example 12.1   *We return to Example 1 in Chapter 1:*

$$\forall i, \ i \geq 2, \ x_i = \beta \, x_{i-1} + u_i, \quad \text{and} \quad |\beta| < 1.$$

u_i is a Gaussian white noise $(0, \sigma^2)$. The spectral density function is symmetric and thus we only need to consider it on $[0, \pi]$. It satisfies:

$$m_\theta(\lambda) = \frac{2\sigma^2}{1 + \beta^2 - 2\beta \cos 2\pi \lambda}, \quad \lambda \in [-\pi, \pi].$$

The spectral density is increasing if and only if $\beta > 0$, and it admits an inflection point at

$$\lambda = \frac{1}{2\pi} \arccos \left\{ \frac{-(1 + \beta^2) + \sqrt{(1 + \beta^2) + 32\beta^2}}{4\beta} \right\}.$$

Moreover, for this λ,

$$m_\theta(\lambda) = 2\sigma^2 \left\{ 1 + \beta^2 + \frac{1 + \beta^2 - \sqrt{(1 + \beta^2) + 32\beta^2}}{2} \right\}^{-1}.$$

This inflection point is the closer to high frequencies (respectively low frequencies), the closer β is to -1 (respectively to $+1$).   □

Example 12.2   *Consider now a process that satisfies*

$$x_i = u_i - \beta u_{i-1},$$

where

$$u_i \sim WN(0, \sigma^2) \quad \text{and} \quad |\beta| < 1.$$

The spectral density is

$$m_\theta(\lambda) = 2\sigma^2(1 + \beta^2 - 2\beta \cos 2\pi \lambda),$$

$m_\theta(\lambda)$ is strictly increasing (respectively decreasing) if $0 < \beta < 1$ (respectively $-1 < \beta < 0$). The inflection point occurs at a constant point:

$$\lambda = 0.25 \quad \forall \beta$$

and the corresponding value of the spectral density is

$$m(0.25) = 2\sigma^2(1 + \beta^2).$$ □

12.5 Filtering and Forecasting

12.5.1 Filters

Let $\{x_i, \ i \in T\} \subset L^2$ be a weakly stationary process with $E^\theta(x_i) = 0$ which admits a spectral density $m_\theta(\lambda)$. Suppose that the input process x_i (treated as function of time) enters a device and is transformed in such a way that a new process $\{y_i \ ; i \in T\}$ is obtained. The transformation $\Phi : \mathbb{R}^{\mathbb{Z}} \to \mathbb{R}^{\mathbb{Z}}$ that associates $\{y_i\}_{i \in \mathbb{Z}}$ with $\{x_i\}_{i \in \mathbb{Z}}$ is called a *filter*:

$$y_i = \Phi_i \left[x_{i+j}, \ j \in \mathbb{Z} \right].$$

Φ is described by the sequence of $\Phi_i : \mathbb{R}^{\mathbb{Z}} \to \mathbb{R}, \ i \in \mathbb{Z}$. If a linear combination of input functions is associated with the same linear combination of output functions

$$y_i = \Phi_i \lfloor x_{i+j}, \ j \in \mathbb{Z} \rfloor \tag{12.10}$$

then the filter is said to be *linear*. We can express y_i in the following way

$$y_i = \sum_{j=-\infty}^{\infty} \varphi_{ij} x_{i+j}.$$

If a time shift in the input process corresponds to the same time shift at the output, then the transformation is said to be time invariant and

$$y_i = \sum_{j=-\infty}^{\infty} \varphi_j x_{i+j}.$$

More generally, the time invariant filter Φ_i does not depend on i.

If y_i is represented by

$$y_i = \sum_{j=0}^{\infty} \varphi_{ij} x_{i-j},$$

i.e., it does not depend on future values of x, then Φ is a realizable linear filter. Finally, the filter is realizable and time invariant if

$$y_i = \sum_{j=0}^{\infty} \varphi_j x_{i-j}.$$

If the process x_i at the input of the filter Φ admits a spectral representation

$$C_x^\theta (\tau) = \int e^{i\lambda\tau} M^\theta (d\lambda),$$

then the process y_i admits a spectral representation

$$C_y^\theta (\tau) = \int e^{i\lambda\tau} \varphi(\lambda) M^\theta (d\lambda)$$

where

$$\varphi(\cdot) \in L^2.$$

It is said that the process $C_y^\theta (\tau)$ is obtained from $C_x^\theta (\tau)$ by linear transformation.

If x is a stationary process with values in $\mathbb{R}$ and if $\varphi : \mathbb{R}^{k+r+1} \to \mathbb{R}$ is an arbitrary measurable function, then the process $y_i = \varphi(x_{i-k}, \ldots, x_{i+r})$ is also stationary. Starting with a stationary Gaussian process x, one can then construct an infinity of stationary processes, which in general will not be Gaussian. This extends to function φ of $\mathbb{R}^{\mathbb{Z}} \to \mathbb{R}$. The transformation $y = \varphi(x)$ is an example of a nonlinear filter. In contrast, in the absence of time invariance, weak stationarity is in general not preserved by a filter $\varphi(.)$ of the above type unless φ is linear.

Let $\{x_i, i \in T\}$ be a stationary process. Let $L : (x_i)_{i \in T} \longrightarrow (x_{i-1})_{i \in T}$ be the *lag operator*, such that

$$L x_i = x_{i-1}, \quad \forall i \in T \quad \text{and} \quad L^j x_i = x_{i-j}. \tag{12.11}$$

Evidently, $Lx_1 = x_0$. If $T = \mathbb{N}$, then Lx_0 is not defined and $L^j x_i$ only exists for $j \leq i$. If $T = \mathbb{Z}$, then Lx_i is defined for all i.

Let $\alpha(L)$ be a polynomial of degree p in the lag operator L:

$$\alpha(L) = \alpha_0 + \alpha_1 L + \cdots + \alpha_p L^p$$

characterized by $(\alpha_0, \alpha_1, \ldots, \alpha_p)$. Thus, we have

$$\begin{aligned} \alpha(L)x_i &= \left(\alpha_0 + \alpha_1 L + \cdots + \alpha_p L^p\right) x_i \\ &= \alpha_0 x_i + \alpha_1 x_{i-1} + \cdots + \alpha_p x_{i-p}. \end{aligned}$$

Theorem 12.4 *If $\{x_i, i \in T = \mathbb{Z}\}$ is weakly stationary, then $\alpha(L)x_i$ is also weakly stationary:*

$$\begin{cases} y_i = \alpha(L)x_i = \alpha_0 x_i + \alpha_1 x_{i-1} + \cdots + \alpha_p x_{i-p} = \sum_{l=0}^{p} \alpha_l x_{i-l}, \\ E^\theta(y_i) = \mu \sum_{l=0}^{p} \alpha_l, \text{ since } E^\theta(x_i) = \mu, \\ C_y^\theta(i, j) = \sum_{l,r=0}^{p} \alpha_l \alpha_r E^\theta \left(x_i \times x_j\right) = C_y^\theta (i - j) = C_y^\theta (\tau). \end{cases} \quad \blacksquare$$

The set of polynomials forms a ring. We have

$$\deg\left(P(L) + Q(L)\right) = \max(\deg P(L), \deg Q(L))$$

and

$$\deg\left(P(L)Q(L)\right) = \deg P(L) + \deg Q(L),$$

but there is no inverse operation since $P(L)^{-1}$ is not a polynomial. The series $S(L) = P(L)^{-1}$ is then introduced. These series pose a convergence problem, the criteria for convergence are established in Theorem 12.5. The union of these series and the set of polynomials constitutes a field.

Example 12.3 *We show that the inverse of $(1 - \alpha L)$ is necessarily an infinite series:*

$$(1 - \alpha L)^{-1} \left(\beta_0 + \beta_1 L + \beta_2 L^2 + \cdots + \beta_q L^q\right) = 1.$$

Identifying the parameters yields

$$1 \times \beta_0 = 1 \Rightarrow \beta_0 = 1$$

$$-\alpha + \beta_1 = 0 \Rightarrow \beta_1 = \alpha$$

$$\beta_2 - \alpha^2 = 0 \Rightarrow \beta_2 = \alpha^2$$

$$\beta_3 - \alpha^3 = 0 \Rightarrow \beta_3 = \alpha^3.$$

By induction, we obtain $\beta_{p+1} = \alpha^{p+1}$, and hence the result

$$\frac{1}{1 - \alpha L} = \sum_{m=0}^{\infty} \alpha^m L^m.$$

Under the condition $|\alpha| < 1$, the series $\sum_{m=0}^{\infty} \alpha^m L^m$ applied to a stationary process converges. □

Theorem 12.5 *If $\{x_i, \ i \in T\}$ is a weakly stationary process, there exists a φ_j such that $\sum |\varphi_j| < \infty$, then:*

$$\sum_{j=-\infty}^{\infty} \varphi_j x_{i+j}$$

converges in L^2 to y_i, and y_i is a weakly stationary process. ∎

Proof: Using the Cauchy criterion applied to the $|\varphi_j|$, it is necessary to show that $\lim\limits_{n,m} \sum_{j=n}^{m} \varphi_j x_{i+j}$ converges in L^2.

$$\left\| \sum_{j=n}^{m} \varphi_j x_{i+j} \right\| \leq \sum_{j=n}^{m} |\varphi_j| \, \|x_{i+j}\| = \sigma(0) \sum_{j=n}^{m} |\varphi_j|.$$

Now, since by assumption $\sum |\varphi_j| < \infty$, $\sum_{j=n}^{m} |\varphi_j|$ converges to zero. ∎

This theorem is also valid if x_i is a vector and φ_j are matrices. In that case, $|\varphi_j|$ represents the norm of φ_j, i.e., the sum of the absolute values of all components of φ_j.

Corollary 12.2   *If* $\Phi(L) = \alpha(L)^{-1}$ *and if the roots of* $\alpha(L)$ *are outside the unit circle, then* $\sum |\varphi_j| < \infty$, $\alpha(L)^{-1} x_i$ *defines a second order stationary process.*   ∎

Proof: $\alpha(L)^{-1} = \sum \varphi_j L^j$ converges if $\sum |\varphi_j| < \infty$. To show this, consider

$$\alpha(L) = \alpha_0 \prod_{l=1}^{p} \left(1 - \frac{1}{z_l} L\right)$$

$$\alpha(L)^{-1} = \alpha_0^{-1} \prod \left(1 - \frac{1}{z_l} L\right)^{-1}$$

$$\left|\frac{1}{z_l}\right| < 1 \Rightarrow |z_l| > 1.$$

Note that $(1 - \frac{1}{z_l} L)^{-1}$ applied to a stationary process is stationary (see Example 12.3). The result follows from successive applications of $(1 - \frac{1}{z_l} L)^{-1}$, $l = 1, \ldots, p$ to processes that are stationary.   ∎

12.5.2   Linear Forecasting – General Remarks

Let $\{x_i ; i \in T\} \subset L^2$ be a second order stationary centered stochastic process. We denote by H^x the vector subspace spanned by $\{x_i ; i \in T\}$. For any $i \in T$, H_i^x is the closed subspace spanned by the random variables $x_s, s \leq i$ and $s \in T$. The subspace H_i^x represents the past and the present (in a linear sense) of the stochastic process. For all $i_1 \leq i_2$:

$$H_{i_1}^x \subseteq H_{i_2}^x.$$

Note that

$$H_{-\infty}^x = \bigcap_{i \in T} H_i^x,$$

$H_{-\infty}^x$ represents the past at the infinite horizon.

Definition 12.7   *If* $H_{-\infty}^x = H_i^x$ *or, equivalently, if* H_i^x *is the same for all* $i \in T$, *then the stochastic process* x_i *is said to be deterministic. If on the other hand, $H_{-\infty}^x$ is strictly included in H_i^x, then the process is said to be nondeterministic. Finally, if $H_{-\infty}^x = \{0\}$, then x_i is said to be purely random.*   ∎

To make this definition more explicit, we return to the problem of linear prediction. Indeed the optimal linear forecast (or prediction) given the past of x at time i, is obtained by orthogonal projection on H_i^x (see Chapter 7). The problem is to find a predictor for $x_{i+\tau}$ at τ periods in the future and this for all

$\tau > 0$, given the realizations of x_s for $s \leq i$. The best linear predictor of $x_{i+\tau}$ is the orthogonal projection on H_i^x of x_i which we denote by

$$\widehat{x}_{i+\tau|i} = H_i^x x_{i+\tau} = EL(x_{i+\tau} \mid x_i, x_{i-1}, \ldots) = H_i^x(H_{i+u}^x x_{i+\tau})$$

with $i \leq i + u \leq i + \tau$, i.e., $\widehat{x}_{i+\tau|i}$ is the projection of $\widehat{x}_{i+\tau|i+u}$ on H_i^x. The difference $x_{i+\tau} - \widehat{x}_{i+\tau|i}$ is called the forecast error, which by definition satisfies the orthogonality condition

$$(x_{i+\tau} - \widehat{x}_{i+\tau|i}) \perp H_i^x. \tag{12.12}$$

The L^2−norm given by

$$\delta_i(\tau) = \left\| x_{i+\tau} - \widehat{x}_{i+\tau|i} \right\| \tag{12.13}$$

is called the norm of the linear prediction error. It is independent of i if the process is weakly stationary.

Theorem 12.6 *If $\{x_i, i \in T\}$ is a weakly stationary process, then for all τ_1, τ_2 with $0 < \tau_1 \leq \tau_2$:*

$$\delta(\tau_1) \leq \delta(\tau_2) \quad and \quad \delta(\tau) = 0 \ \ for \ \tau \leq 0. \tag{12.14}$$

∎

Proof: Since

$$x_{i+\tau_2} - \widehat{x}_{i+\tau_2|i} = x_{i+\tau_2} - \widehat{x}_{i+\tau_2|i+\tau_1} + \widehat{x}_{i+\tau_2|i+\tau_1} - \widehat{x}_{i+\tau_2|i}.$$

thus:

$$\left\| x_{i+\tau_2} - \widehat{x}_{i+\tau_2|i} \right\| = \left\| x_{i+\tau_2} - \widehat{x}_{i+\tau_2|i+\tau_1} \right\| + \left\| \widehat{x}_{i+\tau_2|i+\tau_1} - \widehat{x}_{i+\tau_2|i} \right\|$$

because

$$x_{i+\tau_2} - \widehat{x}_{i+\tau_2|i+\tau_1} \perp \widehat{x}_{i+\tau_2|i+\tau_1} - \widehat{x}_{i+\tau_2|i}$$

and thus

$$\delta(\tau_2)^2 \geq \delta(\tau_1)^2.$$

∎

If the process $\{x_i \ ; i \in T\}$ is deterministic, then

$$x_{i+\tau} \in H_i^x = H_{-\infty}^x, \quad \forall i, \tau \in \mathbb{Z} \Rightarrow x_i \in H_i^x \Rightarrow x_i = H_{-\infty}^x x_i,$$

which implies that

$$x_{i+\tau} = H_i^x x_{i+\tau} = \widehat{x}_{i+\tau|i}.$$

Conversely, suppose the equality

$$x_{i+\tau} = \widehat{x}_{i+\tau|i} \in H_\tau^x, \quad \forall \tau \leq \tau_0.$$

holds for all $i \in T$. This implies that

$$H_{i+\tau}^x \subset H_i^x, \quad \forall i \in T \text{ and } \tau > 0.$$

As a consequence $H_{i+\tau}^x = H_i^x$.

The computation of the projection on a infinite dimensional vector space is in general complex. We state the following theorem which allows us to approximate this projection on finite dimensional spaces.

Theorem 12.7 *The projection of x_j, $j \geq i$, on H_i^x is the limit in the sense of L^2 of the projection of x_j on the vector space spanned by $\{x_i, x_{i-1}, \ldots, x_{i-\tau}\}$ when $\tau \longrightarrow +\infty$.* ■

Theorem 12.8 *The stochastic process x_i is purely random if and only if $\delta^2(\tau) \to C^\theta(0)$ when $\tau \to +\infty$.* ■

Proof: $\delta(\tau) \to C^\theta(0)$ when $\tau \to +\infty$ since

$$\left\| x_{i+\tau} - \widehat{x}_{i+\tau|i} \right\| = \left\| x_i - \widehat{x}_{i|i-\tau} \right\|. \tag{12.15}$$

Thus

$$\left\| x_i - \widehat{x}_{i|i-\tau} \right\|^2 \to \|x_i\|^2 = C^\theta(0). \qquad ■$$

12.5.3   Wold Decomposition

Let $\{x_i ; i \in T\} \subset L^2$ be a weakly stationary process. The Wold decomposition shows that such a process can be represented as the sum of two orthogonal weakly stationary processes, one purely random and the other purely deterministic.

Theorem 12.9 *(of Wold) Let $\{x_i ; i \in T\}$ be a centered second order weakly stationary process. It can be rewritten in the following way:*

$$x_i = x_{1i} + x_{2i} \tag{12.16}$$

where $\{x_{1i} ; i \in T\}$ is a second order purely random process and $\{x_{2i} ; i \in T\}$ is a purely deterministic process. Moreover,

$$x_{1i} \perp x_{2j} \quad \forall i, j \in T \tag{12.17}$$

and x_{1i} then becomes

$$x_{1i} = \sum_{k=0}^{\infty} \alpha_k \, u_{i-k}.$$

$\{u_i, i \in T\}$ is a sequence of uncorrelated random variables with

$$E^\theta(u_i) = 0, \quad E^\theta(u_i^2) = \sigma^2, \quad \alpha_0 = 1, \quad H_{-\infty}^{x_1} = H_{-\infty}^{u_k}, \quad \forall i$$

and $\{\alpha_k\}_1^\infty$ is a sequence of numbers such that

$$\sum_{k=1}^\infty |\alpha_k|^2 < \infty. \qquad \blacksquare$$

For the proof, see Brockwell and Davis (1987, Theorem 5.7.1).

The sequence $\{u_i\}_{-\infty}^\infty$ is often called the sequence of *innovations* for the process $\{x_i\}_{-\infty}^\infty$, for the reason that the u_{i+1} provide the "new information" that is necessary to obtain $H_{-\infty}^x$. Indeed,

$$u_{i+1} = x_{i+1} - \widehat{x}_{i+1|i}.$$

Corollary 12.3 *A weakly stationary process $\{x_i, i \in T\}$ is purely random if and only if it can be represented by*

$$x_i = \sum_{k=0}^\infty \gamma_k u_{i-k} \qquad (12.18)$$

where $\{u_i, i \in T\}$ is a weak white noise and

$$\sum_{k=0}^\infty |\gamma_k|^2 < \infty. \qquad \blacksquare$$

The process (12.18) is called an infinite moving average process and admits a spectral density. This theorem is popular in econometrics.

12.6 Stationary *ARMA* Processes

12.6.1 Introduction

In this section, we introduce an important class of time series $\{x_i, i \in T\}$ using weak white noise and linear difference equations with constant coefficients. This additional structure defines a parametric family of stationary processes, namely the *Autoregressive Moving Average (ARMA)* processes. This class of models is very useful to describe the dynamics of time series. For every co-variance function $C(.)$ such that $\lim_{\tau \to \infty} C(\tau) = 0$, and for all integers $k > 0$, it is possible to find an *ARMA* process with covariance function $C^\theta(\tau) = C(\tau)$, $\tau = 0, 1, \ldots, k$. The linear structure of the *ARMA* processes leads to a very simple theory of forecasting which we will see later.

Regarding the presentation of random processes in discrete time, two points of views can be adopted:

- The most widespread approach starts with a difference (or recurrence) equation and introduces a noise process that satisfies a set of properties. For example, suppose

$$x_i = \alpha x_{i-1} + u_i + \beta u_{i-1}$$

where u_i is a noise process. A very large number of processes can generally be the solution to this equation, and we can ask if we can characterize a unique solution by adding other properties such as stationarity. We analyze in particular this solution.
- The second point of view that we adopt does not construct the process x_i but takes it as given and assumes typically that it satisfies stationarity (in levels, in differences, in deviations from a time trend). Next, representation assumptions are introduced in the form of stochastic difference equations for which we want to estimate the parameters and which we can use, for example, for forecasting.

12.6.2   Invertible *ARMA* Processes

Definition 12.8   *(ARMA (p, q) processes)   Let $\{x_i, i \in T\}$ be a stationary stochastic process (respectively weakly stationary). We say that $\{x_i, i \in T\}$ is a strong (resp. weak) ARMA (p, q) process if there exists a strong (resp. weak) white noise $\{u_i, i \in T\}$ and real numbers $\alpha_1, \ldots, \alpha_p, \beta_1, \ldots, \beta_q$ such that*

$$x_i - \alpha_1 x_{i-1} - \cdots - \alpha_p x_{i-p} = u_i + \beta_1 u_{i-1} + \cdots + \beta_q u_{i-q}. \quad (12.19)$$

■

The weak white noise is justified in terms of the representation of the process in L^2, but the asymptotic theory is easier to develop in the setting of strong $ARMA(p, q)$ processes.

We can rewrite (12.19) more compactly by using the linear transformation that is given by the lag operator

$$\alpha(L) x_i = \beta(L) u_i, \quad i \in T \qquad (12.20)$$

where $\alpha(L)$ and $\beta(L)$ are polynomials in the lag operator of degrees p and q, i.e.,

$$\alpha(z) = 1 - \alpha_1 z - \cdots - \alpha_p z^p \qquad (12.21)$$

and

$$\beta(z) = 1 + \beta_1 z + \cdots + \beta_q z^q. \qquad (12.22)$$

We can note that in general the linear spaces H^x and H^u do not coincide. In the sequel, we provide regularity conditions on the model that assure the equality of theses two spaces.

Two particular cases are commonly used, those where either q or p is equal to zero.

If $\alpha(z) = 1$, then

$$x_i = \beta(L)u_i \tag{12.23}$$

and the process is called *Moving Average of order q* $(MA(q))$. Recall that $\beta_0 = 1$ and $\beta_j = 0$ for all $j > q$. The moments of the process satisfy

$$E^\theta(x_i) = \sum_{j=0}^q \beta_j \, E^\theta(u_{i-j}) = 0$$

and $\forall \tau \geq 0$

$$C^\theta(\tau) = \begin{vmatrix} \sigma^2 \sum_{j=0}^{q-\tau} \beta_j \beta_{j+\tau} & \text{if } \tau \leq q, \\ 0 & \text{if } \tau > q. \end{vmatrix}$$

If $\beta(z) = 1$, then

$$\alpha(L)x_i = u_i \tag{12.24}$$

and the process is called *Autoregressive of order p* $(AR(p))$.

Consider the $AR(1)$ process

$$x_i = u_i + \alpha_1 x_{i-1} = (1 - \alpha_1 L)^{-1} u_i. \tag{12.25}$$

Iterating (12.25), we obtain

$$x_i = u_i + \alpha_1 u_{i-1} + \alpha_1^2 x_{i-2}$$

$$= \cdots$$

$$= u_i + \alpha_1 u_{i-1} + \cdots + \alpha_1^k u_{i-k} + \alpha_1^{k+1} x_{i-k-1}.$$

Thus, if $|\alpha_1| < 1$,

$$x_i = \sum_{j=0}^\infty \alpha_1^j u_{i-j} \tag{12.26}$$

is well defined, converges, is stationary and is the solution of Equation (12.25). Theorem 12.4 implies

$$E^\theta(x_i) = \sum_{j=0}^\infty \alpha_1^j E^\theta(u_{i-j}) = 0$$

and

$$C^\theta(\tau) = \lim_{n \to \infty} E^\theta \left[\left(\sum_{j=0}^{n} \alpha_1^j u_{i+\tau-j} \right) \left(\sum_{k=0}^{n} \alpha_1^k u_{i-\tau} \right) \right]$$

$$= \sigma^2 \alpha_1^{|\tau|} \sum_{j=0}^{\infty} \alpha_1^{2j}$$

$$= \frac{\sigma^2 \alpha_1^{|\tau|}}{(1 - \alpha_1^2)}.$$

In the case where $|\alpha_1| > 1$, the series (12.26) does not converge in L^2. However, we can rewrite (12.25) in the following way

$$x_i = -\alpha_1^{-1} u_{i+1} + \alpha_1^{-1} x_{i+1}. \tag{12.27}$$

Iterating (12.27), we obtain

$$x_i = -\alpha_1^{-1} u_{i+1} - \alpha_1^{-2} u_{i+2} + \alpha_1^{-2} x_{i+2}$$

$$= \cdots$$

$$= -\alpha_1^{-1} u_{i+1} - \cdots - \alpha_1^{-k-1} u_{i+k+1} + \alpha_1^{-k-1} x_{i+k+1}$$

which shows that

$$x_i = -\sum_{j=1}^{\infty} \alpha_1^{-j} u_{i+j}. \tag{12.28}$$

(12.28) is well defined and is the unique stationary solution of (12.25). In this case, Equation (12.25) does not define the distribution of x_i given the past; in particular the u_i are not the innovations of the process, and the conditional expectation of x_i given the past is not $\alpha_1 x_{i-1}$. Solution (12.28) is a forward solution conditioning on the future. The case where $\alpha_1 = 1$ will be examined later on.

Definition 12.9   *A stationary process admits a canonical ARMA(p, q) representation if it satisfies Definition 12.8 and*

- $\alpha_p \neq 0$, $\beta_q \neq 0$,
- *the polynomials $\alpha(z)$ and $\beta(z)$ have their roots outside the unit circle,*
- *$\alpha(z)$ and $\beta(z)$ do not have any roots in common.*   ■

If $\{x_i, i \in T\}$ is a stationary process with a canonical *ARMA(p, q)* representation

$$\alpha(L) x_i = \beta(L) u_i, \quad i \in T$$

then, using Theorem 12.4 it follows that:

1. $\{x_i, i \in T\}$ admits an $MA(\infty)$ representation

$$x_i = \frac{\beta(L)}{\alpha(L)} u_i = \sum_{j=0}^{\infty} \psi_j L^j u_i = \sum_{j=0}^{\infty} \psi_j u_{i-j}, \ \psi_0 = 1.$$

2. $\{x_i, i \in T\}$ admits a $AR(\infty)$ representation

$$\frac{\alpha(L)}{\beta(L)} x_i = \sum_{j=0}^{\infty} \pi_j L^j x_i = \sum_{j=0}^{\infty} \pi_j x_{i-j}, \ \pi_0 = 1.$$

This property is called invertibility.

3. $\{x_i, i \in T\}$ admits an innovation process $\{u_i, i \in T\}$.

In the following, we only consider $ARMA(p, q)$ processes in their canonical form.

The first property that we can state is $H^u = H^x$. We have $u_j \in H_i^x$, and in particular $H_i^x = H_i^u$, and $x_j \in H_i^u$ for $j \leq i$.

The canonical $ARMA(p, q)$ process is purely random as we show with the decomposition of the $MA(\infty)$ process.

12.6.3 Computing the Covariance Function of an $ARMA(p, q)$ Process

The autocorrelation function provides information about the intertemporal dependence.

Theorem 12.10 *The autocovariance function of a process $\{x_i, i \in T\}$ that has a $ARMA(p, q)$ representation is such that*

$$C^\theta(\tau) + \sum_{j=1}^{p} \alpha_j C^\theta(\tau - j) = 0, \ \forall \tau \geq q + 1. \qquad \blacksquare$$

Proof: Let

$$x_i + \sum_{j=1}^{p} \alpha_j x_{i-j} = u_i + \sum_{j=1}^{q} \beta_j u_{i-j}.$$

Multiplying each side by $x_{i-\tau}$, $\tau \geq q + 1$, and taking expectation, we obtain

$$C^\theta(\tau) + \sum_{j=1}^{p} \alpha_j C^\theta(\tau - j) = Cov^\theta \left(x_{i-\tau}, u_i + \sum_{j=1}^{q} \beta_j u_{i-j} \right) = 0.$$

Thus, the sequence of covariances satisfies a recurrence equation of order p from $q + 1$ on. This relationship does not yet enable us to determine all values

$C(\tau)$, since we still need initial conditions. These first values of the autocovariance function can be determined through the expansion of the infinite moving average:

$$C^\theta(\tau) + \sum_{j=1}^{p} \alpha_j C^\theta(\tau - j) = Cov^\theta \left(u_i + \sum_{j=1}^{q} \beta_j u_{i-j}, \sum_{j=0}^{\infty} u_{\tau-j-h} \right).$$

By using this relationship, the recurrence equation and the fact that $C^\theta(\tau) = C^\theta(-\tau)$, we can obtain all values of the autocovariance function. ∎

Example 12.4 *ARMA$(1, 1)$ model. Consider the representation*

$$x_i + \alpha_1 x_{i-1} = u_i - \beta_1 u_{i-1}, \quad |\alpha_1| < 1, \ |\beta_1| < 1.$$

For $\alpha_1 = \beta_1$, we have $x_i = u_i$. For $\alpha_1 \neq \beta_1$,

$$C_x^\theta(\tau) = \alpha_1 C_x^\theta(\tau - 1) + C_{ux}^\theta(\tau) - \beta_1 C_{ux}^\theta(\tau - 1).$$

Suppose $\tau = 1$, then

$$C_x^\theta(1) = \alpha_1 C_x^\theta(0) + C_{ux}^\theta(1) - \beta_1 C_{ux}^\theta(0)$$
$$= \alpha_1 C_x^\theta(0) - \beta_1 C_{ux}^\theta(0).$$

For $\tau = 0$,

$$C_x^\theta(0) = \alpha_1 C_x^\theta(-1) + C_u^\theta(0) - \beta_1 C_{ux}^\theta(-1)$$

and

$$C_{ux}^\theta(1) = \alpha_1 C_{ux}^\theta(0) - \beta_1 C_u^\theta(0),$$

hence the autocorrelation function

$$\rho(0) = 1$$

$$\rho(1) = \frac{(1 - \alpha_1 \beta_1)(\alpha_1 - \beta_1)}{1 + \alpha_1^2 - 2\alpha_1 \beta_1}$$

$$\vdots$$

$$\rho(\tau) = \alpha_1 \rho(\tau - 1). \qquad \square$$

12.6.4 The Autocovariance Generating Function

If $\{x_i, i \in T\}$ is a stationary process with autocovariance function $C_x^\theta(.)$, then the *autocovariance generating function* is defined by

$$G_x^\theta(z) = \sum_{\tau=-\infty}^{\infty} C_x^\theta(\tau) z^\tau \qquad (12.29)$$

if the series converges for all z. In this case the autocovariance generating function is easy to calculate, the autocovariance at lag τ is determined by identifying the coefficient of z^τ or $z^{-\tau}$. Clearly, $\{x_i\}$ is white noise if and only if the autocovariance generating function $G(z)$ is constant for all z. If

$$x_i = \sum_{j=-\infty}^{\infty} \psi_j u_{i-j}, \quad \{u_i\} \sim WN(0, \sigma^2) \tag{12.30}$$

and if

$$\sum_{j=-\infty}^{\infty} |\psi_j| z^j < \infty, \tag{12.31}$$

then the autocovariance generating function takes on a very simple form. It is easily seen that

$$C_x^\theta(\tau) = C_x^\theta(x_{i+\tau}, x_i) = \sigma^2 \sum_{j=-\infty}^{\infty} \psi_j \psi_{j+|\tau|}$$

and that

$$G_x^\theta(z) = \sigma^2 \sum_{\tau=-\infty}^{\infty} \sum_{j=-\infty}^{\infty} \psi_j \psi_{j+|\tau|} z^\tau$$

$$= \sigma^2 \left[\sum_{j=-\infty}^{\infty} \psi_j^2 + \sum_{\tau=1}^{\infty} \sum_{j=-\infty}^{\infty} \psi_j \psi_{j+\tau} \left(z^\tau + z^{-\tau} \right) \right]$$

$$= \sigma^2 \left(\sum_{j=-\infty}^{\infty} \psi_j z^j \right) \left(\sum_{h=-\infty}^{\infty} \psi_\tau z^{-\tau} \right).$$

Defining

$$\psi(z) = \sum_{j=-\infty}^{\infty} \psi_j z^j,$$

we can write

$$G_x^\theta(z) = \sigma^2 \psi(z) \psi(z^{-1}).$$

Example 12.5 *Consider the following $MA(2)$ process*

$$x_i = u_i + \theta_1 u_{i-1} + \theta_2 u_{i-2}$$

with the usual assumption on the u_i. Then

$$G_x^\theta(z) = \sigma^2 (1 + \theta_1 z + \theta_2 z^2)(1 + \theta_1 z^{-1} + \theta_2 z^{-2})$$

$$= \sigma^2 [(1 + \theta_1^2 + \theta_2^2) + (\theta_1 + \theta_1 \theta_2)(z + z^{-1}) + \theta_2(z^2 + z^{-2})]$$

hence

$$C_x^\theta(0) = \sigma^2(1 + \theta_1^2 + \theta_2^2)$$

$$C_x^\theta(\pm 1) = \sigma^2(\theta_1 + \theta_1\theta_2) = \sigma^2\theta_1(1 + \theta_2)$$

$$C_x^\theta(\pm 2) = \sigma^2\theta_2$$

$$\vdots$$

$$C_x^\theta(\tau) = 0 \quad for \ |\tau| > 2. \qquad \qquad \Box$$

12.6.5   The Partial Autocorrelation Function

Like the autocorrelation function, the partial autocorrelation function (pacf) contains important information about the serial dependence of the stationary process. Like the autocorrelation function, it only depends on the second order properties of the process.

Theorem 12.11   *(Frisch and Waugh)   The partial autocorrelation function* $\kappa^\theta(\tau)$ *of a stationary process is defined by*

$$\kappa^\theta(1) = corr^\theta(x_2, x_1) = \rho^\theta(1)$$

and

$$\kappa^\theta(\tau) = corr^\theta\left(x_i - H_{i-1,\tau-1}^x x_i, \ x_{i-\tau} - H_{i-1,\tau-1}^x x_{i-\tau}\right)$$

where $H_{i-1,\tau}^x$ *is the history of length* τ *up to* $i-1$, *i.e., the finite dimensional vector space spanned by* $\{x_{i-1}, \ldots, x_{i-1-\tau}\}$. *Since the process is stationary, we can write it for* $\tau + 1$ *obtaining*

$$\kappa^\theta(\tau) = corr^\theta\left(x_{\tau+1} - H_{\tau,\tau-1}^x x_{\tau+1}, \ x_1 - H_{\tau,\tau-1}^x x_1\right)$$

where

$$H_{\tau,\tau-1}^x x_{\tau+1} \ and \ H_{\tau,\tau-1}^x x_1$$

are the projections of $x_{i+\tau}$ *and* x_i *on the subspace spanned by* $\{x_{i+1}, \ldots, x_{i+\tau}\}$. *The partial autocorrelation* $\kappa^\theta(\tau)$, $\tau \geq 2$, *is thus the correlation between two residuals that are obtained after regressing* $x_{\tau+1}$ *and* x_1 *on the intermediate observations* $x_2, \ldots, x_\tau$. ∎

Considering the theorem of Frisch and Waugh, we can provide an equivalent definition of the partial autocorrelation function.

Let $\{x_i, i \in T\}$ be a stationary process with covariance function $C(.)$ such that $C(\tau) \to 0$ when $\tau \to \infty$. Suppose that the $\psi_{\tau j}$, $j = 1, \ldots, \tau$, and $\tau = 1, 2, \ldots$, are the coefficients in the following representation

$$x_{\tau+1} = \sum_{j=1}^{k} \psi_{\tau j} x_{\tau+1-j}.$$

Then, from the equations

$$\langle x_{\tau+1} - H_{i,\tau}^x x_{\tau+1}, x_j \rangle = 0, \quad j = \tau, \ldots, 1,$$

we obtain

$$
\begin{bmatrix}
\rho(0) & \rho(1) & \rho(2) & \cdots & \rho(\tau-1) \\
\rho(1) & \rho(0) & & \cdots & \rho(\tau-2) \\
\rho(2) & & \rho(0) & \cdots & \\
\vdots & \vdots & \vdots & & \vdots \\
\rho(\tau-1) & \rho(\tau-2) & & \cdots & \rho(0)
\end{bmatrix}
\begin{bmatrix}
\phi_{\tau 1} \\
\phi_{\tau 2} \\
\phi_{\tau 3} \\
\vdots \\
\phi_{\tau\tau}
\end{bmatrix}
=
\begin{bmatrix}
\rho(1) \\
\rho(2) \\
\rho(3) \\
\vdots \\
\rho(\tau)
\end{bmatrix}, \quad \tau \geq 1
$$

(12.32)

with $\rho(0)$ always equal to 1.

Definition 12.10 *The partial autocorrelation $\kappa^\theta(\tau)$ of $\{x_i\}$ at lag τ is*

$$\kappa^\theta(\tau) = \phi_{\tau\tau}, \quad \tau \geq 1$$

where $\phi_{\tau\tau}$ is uniquely determined by (12.32). ∎

In general, the $\phi_{\tau\tau}$, $\tau \geq 1$ are obtained as the ratio of two determinants, the determinant in the numerator has the same elements as the determinant in the denominator, except that the last column is replaced by the $\rho(\tau)$.

Example 12.6   *For* $\tau = 1, 2, 3 \ldots$, *we have*

$$\phi_{11} = \rho(1)$$

$$\phi_{22} = \frac{\begin{vmatrix} 1 & \rho(1) \\ \rho(1) & \rho(2) \end{vmatrix}}{\begin{vmatrix} 1 & \rho(1) \\ \rho(1) & 1 \end{vmatrix}} = \frac{\rho(2) - \rho(1)^2}{1 - \rho(1)^2}$$

$$\phi_{22} = \frac{\begin{vmatrix} 1 & \rho(1) & \rho(1) \\ \rho(1) & 1 & \rho(2) \\ \rho(2) & \rho(1) & \rho(3) \end{vmatrix}}{\begin{vmatrix} 1 & \rho(1) & \rho(2) \\ \rho(1) & 1 & \rho(1) \\ \rho(2) & \rho(1) & 1 \end{vmatrix}}.$$ □

For an autoregressive process of order p, the $\phi_{\tau\tau}$ are non-zero for $\tau \leq p$ and zero for $\tau > p$, and for a moving average process of order q, the autocorrelation function goes to zero with an exponential decay rate.

12.7   Spectral Representation of an *ARMA(p,q)* Process

Theorem 12.12   *Let* $\{x_i \; ; \; i \in T\}$ *be a centered stationary process such that*

$$x_i = \sum_{j=0}^{\infty} \psi_j \, u_{i-j} \quad where \sum_{j=0}^{\infty} |\psi_j| < \infty,$$

and $| \psi_j |$ *represents the norm of* ψ_j.
Then

$$\{x_i \; ; \; i \in T\}$$

is stationary with spectral distribution function

$$F_x(\lambda) = \left| \sum_{j=0}^{\infty} \psi_j \, e^{-ij\lambda} \right|^2 F_u(\lambda), \quad -\pi \leq \lambda \leq \pi.$$

where $F_u(\lambda)$ *is the spectral distribution function of* $\{u_i \; ; \; i \in T\}$ *(here "i" is evidently the imaginary number satisfying* $i^2 = -1$*).*   ∎

Applying this theorem, we can determine the spectral density of any *ARMA* (p, q) process.

Theorem 12.13 *Let $\{x_i \; ; \; i \in T\}$ be an ARMA(p, q) process satisfying*

$$\alpha (L) \, x_i = \beta (L) \, u_i, \quad u_i \sim WN \left(0, \sigma^2\right).$$

Then, the spectral density of $\{x_i \; ; \; i \in T\}$ is

$$f_x (\lambda) = \frac{\sigma^2 \left|\beta \left(e^{-i\lambda}\right)\right|^2}{2\pi \left|\alpha \left(e^{-i\lambda}\right)\right|^2}, \quad -\pi \leq \lambda \leq \pi,$$

where $||$ represents the modulus of a complex number. ∎

Example 12.7 *(the ARMA$(1, 1)$ process) The spectral density of the ARMA$(1, 1)$ process defined by*

$$(1 - \alpha L)x_i = (1 - \beta L)u_i, \quad u_i \sim WN(0, \sigma^2) \text{ and } |\beta| < 1, \; |\alpha| < 1,$$

is

$$f_x(\lambda) = 2\sigma_u^2 \frac{1 + \alpha^2 - 2\beta \cos 2\pi \lambda}{1 + \beta^2 - 2\alpha \cos 2\pi \lambda}.$$

If $\beta < \alpha$ (respectively $\alpha < \beta$), then the spectral density is decreasing (respectively increasing). □

Since the spectral density of an *ARMA* process is a ratio of trigonometric polynomials, it is a rational function of $e^{-i\lambda}$.

Theorem 12.14 *A stationary process $\{x_i, i \in T\}$ is an ARMA process that admits a spectral density if and only if $\{x_i, i \in T\}$ has a rational spectrum.* ∎

12.8 Estimation of *ARMA* Models

Modeling a stationary time series by an *ARMA*(p, q) requires the resolution of numerous interdependent problems. This includes the choice of p and q, and the estimation of the remaining parameters, i.e., the coefficients

$$\left\{\alpha_i, \beta_j, \quad i = 1, \ldots, p, \; j = 1, \ldots, q\right\}$$

and the variance σ^2, for given values of p and q.

This part is essentially dedicated to the estimation of the parameters $\alpha = (\alpha_1, \ldots, \alpha_p)'$, $\beta = (\beta_1, \ldots, \beta_q)'$ and σ^2 for fixed values of p and q.

12.8.1 Estimation by the Yule-Walker Method

Let $\{x_i\}_{i \in T}$ be a centered strong $AR(p)$ process that thus satisfies

$$x_i - \alpha_1 x_{i-1} - \cdots - \alpha_p x_{i-p} = u_i \text{ with } u_i \sim i.i.d.(0, \sigma^2). \quad (12.33)$$

Multiplying (12.33) by x_{i-j} $(j = 0, \ldots, p)$ and taking the expectation leads to the Yule-Walker equation

$$\Gamma_p^\theta \alpha = C_p^\theta \tag{12.34}$$

where Γ_p^θ is the variance-covariance matrix $(C^\theta(i - j))_{i,j=1,\ldots,p}$ of p realizations of the process x_i and $C_p^\theta = (C^\theta(1), \ldots, C^\theta(p))'$. This is Theorem 12.10 in matrix notation. The intuitive idea for estimation by Yule-Walker consists in replacing $C(\tau)$ by its empirical estimator

$$\widehat{C}(\tau) = \frac{1}{n} \sum_{i=1}^n x_{i-\tau} x_i, \quad 0 \leq \tau \leq p. \tag{12.35}$$

It is assumed that the process is observed between $-p + 1$ and n. We then compute the estimators $\widehat{\Gamma}_{pn}$ and $\widehat{C}_{pn}$ of Γ_p and of C_p. Replacing Γ_p and C_p in (12.34) by these estimators, we obtain the estimator

$$\widehat{\alpha}_n = \widehat{\Gamma}_{pn}^{-1} \widehat{C}_{pn} \tag{12.36}$$

where we assumed the invertibility of the matrix Γ_p (which implies the invertibility of $\widehat{\Gamma}_{pn}$ for n sufficiently large).

This estimator can also be considered as moment estimator. Indeed, let

$$\psi(x_i, \ldots, x_{i-p}, \lambda)$$

$$= \begin{pmatrix} x_{i-1} \\ \vdots \\ x_{i-p} \end{pmatrix} (x_i - \lambda_1 x_{i-1} - \cdots - \lambda_p x_{i-p}) = \begin{pmatrix} x_{i-1} \\ \vdots \\ x_{i-p} \end{pmatrix} u_i$$

and consider the equation

$$E^\theta(\psi(x_i, \ldots, x_{i-p}, \lambda)) = 0 \tag{12.37}$$

with $\lambda = (\lambda_1, \ldots, \lambda_p)'$. The specification assumption for the process x_i ($AR(p)$ with coefficients α) implies that the solution $\lambda(\theta)$ of this equation is the vector α. This moment condition can be understood in the following way: the $AR(p)$ assumption means that

$$x_i - \sum_{j=1}^p \alpha_j x_{i-j}$$

is orthogonal to the elements of the process H_{i-1}^x and thus orthogonal to $x_{i-1}, \ldots, x_{i-p}$. It follows that

$$E^\theta \left(\left[x_i - \sum_j \alpha_j x_{i-j} \right] . x_{i-l} \right) = 0, \quad \text{for all } l = 1, \ldots, p,$$

which implies (12.37). With a finite sample, this condition becomes

$$\frac{1}{n} \sum_{i=1}^{n} \psi(x_i, \ldots, x_{i-p}, \lambda) = 0$$

for which the solution $\widehat{\lambda}_n$ is clearly equal to the estimator $\widehat{\alpha}_n$ that we previously introduced. Thus we have:

Theorem 12.15 *The estimator $\widehat{\alpha}_n$ is consistent (in almost sure sense) and satisfies*

$$\sqrt{n}(\widehat{\alpha}_n - \alpha) \to N(0, \sigma^2 \Gamma_p^{-1})$$

where $\sigma^2 = Var(u_i)$. ∎

Proof: The argument for consistency is based on Theorem 3 in Chapter 2 noting that a strong stationary $AR(p)$ process is ergodic and therefore satisfies the strong law of large numbers. We also note, that under the assumption of correct specification α is the unique solution to the asymptotic moment condition. The normality result rests on the application of the central limit theorem for $AR(p)$ processes. This possibility derives from the fact that these processes satisfy *near epoch dependence* (NED) (see Chapter 1). Indeed, they can be represented in MA form which implies NED. To use Theorem 3 in Chapter 2, we have to calculate the asymptotic variance of

$$\frac{\sqrt{n}}{n} \sum_{i=1}^{n} \psi(x_i, \ldots, x_{i-p}, \alpha),$$

that is

$$\sum_{j=-\infty}^{\infty} Cov^\theta \left(\psi(x_i, \ldots, x_{i-p}, \alpha), \psi(x_{i+j}, \ldots, x_{i+j-p}, \alpha) \right).$$

Even though there is temporal dependence, the covariances are zero for $j \neq 0$. Indeed, for $j > 0$:

$$Cov^\theta (\psi(x_i, \ldots, x_{i-p}, \alpha), \psi(x_{i+j}, \ldots, x_{i+j-p}, \alpha))$$

$$= E^\theta \left[u_i u_{i+j} \begin{pmatrix} x_{i-1} \\ \vdots \\ x_{i-p} \end{pmatrix} \left(x_{i-1} \cdots x_{i-p} \right) \right]$$

$$= E^\theta \left[u_i \begin{pmatrix} x_{i-1} \\ \vdots \\ x_{i-p} \end{pmatrix} \left(x_{i-1} \cdots x_{i-p} \right) E^\theta \left(u_{i+j} \,|\, x_{i+j-1}, x_{i+j-2}, \ldots \right) \right].$$

This last conditional expectation is zero, since by assumption the u_{i+j} is the innovation in x_{i+j}, and thus the covariance is zero. The same argument can be applied to the case when $j < 0$. For $j = 0$, we have

$$Var^{\theta}\left(\psi(x_i, \ldots, x_{i-p}, \alpha)\right)$$

$$= E^{\theta}\left[u_i^2 \begin{pmatrix} x_{i-1} \\ \vdots \\ x_{i-p} \end{pmatrix} \begin{pmatrix} x_{i-1} & \cdots & x_{i-p} \end{pmatrix}\right] = \sigma^2 \Gamma_p.$$

Moreover,

$$E^{\theta}\left(\frac{\partial \psi}{\partial \lambda'}\right) = -\Gamma_p^{-1},$$

hence the result.   ∎

The empirical estimator of Γ_p is consistent because of ergodicity. σ^2 is estimated by

$$\widehat{\sigma}_n^2 = \frac{1}{n}\sum_{i=1}^{n}\left(x_i - \sum_{j=1}^{p}\widehat{\alpha}_{jn}x_{i-j}\right)^2$$

$$= \widehat{C}_n(0)\left[1 - \widehat{\rho}_n(p)\widehat{R}_{pn}^{-1}\widehat{\rho}_n(p)\right]$$

where

$$\widehat{R}_{pn} = \widehat{C}_n^{-1}(0)\widehat{\Gamma}_{pn}$$

and

$$\widehat{\rho}_n(p) = \widehat{C}_n(p)/\widehat{C}_n(0).$$

Consistency of $\widehat{\sigma}_n^2$ can be easily verified. The asymptotic variance of $\widehat{\alpha}_n$ can thus be estimated by $\widehat{\sigma}_n^2 \widehat{\Gamma}_{pn}^{-1}$. This result is the same as the usual variance of the least squares estimator of the coefficients α (minimization of $\sum_{i=1}^{n}(x_i - \sum_{j=1}^{p}\alpha_j x_{i+j})^2$).

There also exist other methods based on the minimization of the sum of squared residuals and on the maximization of the likelihood function. We apply MLE in the multivariate setting in the following section.

12.8.2 Box-Jenkins Method

A process $\{x_i\}$, $i \geq 0$, is said to admit an *ARMA* representation if it satisfies an equation of the type

$$\alpha(L)x_i = \beta(L)u_i, \quad i \in T$$

with

$$\alpha(L) = \alpha_0 + \alpha_1 L + \cdots + \alpha_p L^p, \quad \alpha_0 = I_d, \quad \alpha_p \neq 0$$
$$\beta(L) = \beta_0 + \beta_1 L + \cdots + \beta_p L^p, \quad \beta_0 = I_d, \quad \beta_p \neq 0$$

where the variables $x_{-1}, \ldots, x_{-p}, u_{-1}, \ldots, u_{-p}$ are assumed to be uncorrelated with $u_0, \ldots, u_i$ and where the process $\{u_i\}$, $i \geq 0$, is a white noise with variance Ω.

Among all nonstationary processes that admit an $ARMA$ representation, the most important are *Autoregressive Integrated Moving Average ARIMA*. The $ARIMA(p, d, q)$ processes form a class of models that can represent nonstationary processes or difference stationary processes. This class of models has been extensively used by Box and Jenkins because the nature of the nonstationarity (whether deterministic or random) is not taken into account, stationarity is achieved through application of the difference operator.

Definition 12.11 *A process $\{x_i\}$, $i \geq 0$, admits an ARIMA representation if it satisfies a difference equation of the following type*

$$\alpha(L)x_i = \beta(L)u_i \quad, i \in T$$

and

- *$\alpha(z)$ has all roots outside the unit circle*
- *$\beta(z)$ has all roots outside the unit circle, except for some which are on the unit circle.* ∎

Such processes are used in the following case. Consider the first difference operator

$$\Delta x_i = x_i - x_{i-1}$$

and suppose that the autoregressive polynomial can be written as

$$\alpha(L) = \varphi(L)\Delta^d$$

where the polynomial $\varphi(L)$ is such that $\varphi(L)$ has only roots outside the unit circle. The model becomes

$$\varphi(L)\Delta^d x_i = \beta(L)u_i, \quad i \geq 0$$

If the degree of $\varphi(L)$ is p and the degree of $\beta(L)$ is q, then the process admits an $ARIMA(p, d, q)$ representation.

Theorem 12.16 *If $\{x_i, i \in T\}$ is an ARIMA(p, d, q) process, then the function $\mu = E^\theta(x_i)$ is the solution to the recurrence equation $\alpha(L)E^\theta(x_i) = 0$, $i \geq 0$, with initial values $E^\theta(x_{-\tau})$, $\tau = 1, \ldots, p + d$.* ∎

Since $\alpha(L) = (1 - L)^d \varphi(L)$, the characteristic polynomial of the difference equation that is satisfied by μ is $(1 - z)^d z^p \varphi(z^{-1})$, for which the d roots are equal to 1 and the remaining roots have moduli smaller than 1. Consequently, μ is asymptotically equivalent to a polynomial in i of degree $d - 1$.

Note that we can, of course, put x_i also in a moving average and in an auto-regressive form.

Forecasting with the Box-Jenkins Method

Box and Jenkins (1970) proposed a general approach to forecasting univariate time series. This approach considers $ARIMA$ process in the form

$$\varphi(L)\Delta^d x_i = \mu + \beta(L)u_i$$

under the usual assumption on the lag polynomials and the noise. The regression coefficients depend on the parameters of the model, that need to be estimated. Box and Jenkins distinguish two types of parameters:

- the integer parameters (p, d, q), where p and q represent the order of the lag polynomials and d is the degree of differentiation that is necessary to make the process stationary,
- the parameters φ_i and β_j of the lag polynomials and the variance of the noise.

The Box-Jenkins approach is outlined in the following way:

- An identification stage when we look for plausible values of p, d, and q using the autocorrelation and the partial autocorrelation function. In this phase, M models with possible (p_i, d_i, q_i) are retained.
- For each of these models, we estimate the remaining parameters φ_i, β_j, and σ^2. At the end of this estimation stage, we have several models which we need to validate.
- In the validation stage, we are interested in a number of specification tests on the parameters and the distributions. This stage refers to validation since a number of models will be naturally eliminated.
- The remaining models have in general very similar statistical properties. We will keep one of these models using information criteria with the underlying idea of minimizing the forecast error.
- We then proceed to the forecasting stage, using the theoretical formula for forecasting but replacing the unknown parameters by their estimates.

This approach is summarized in Figure 12.1.

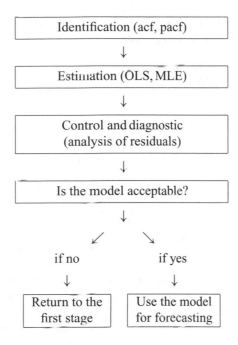

Figure 12.1. Box-Jenkins approach flow chart

12.9 Multivariate Processes

So far we only considered univariate processes, that is the evolution over time of a single random variable. In practice, we generally have simultaneously observations available for several variables, and the interest lies in studying how they evolve over time and especially how and with which lag they interact with each other. We therefore generalize the preceding results for stochastic real scalar processes and extend them to the case of stochastic vector processes. As in the univariate case, we restrict ourselves to time series that admit a linear representation as a function of a white noise.

12.9.1 Some Definitions and General Observations

Definition 12.12 *(Stochastic vector process) A stochastic real vector process $x_i = (x_{1i}, \ldots, x_{mi})'$ in discrete time is a family of real random variables $\{x_i ; i \in T\}$. As in the univariate case, we consider in the following $T \subseteq \mathbb{Z}$.* ∎

This process has m components x_j, $j = 1, \ldots, m$, each of which constitutes a stochastic process in the sense of Definition 12.2. In the following, we assume that these components are weakly stationary.

Definition 12.13   *(Weak stationarity) A vector process with m components $(x_i ; i \in T)$ is said to be weakly stationary if:*

(i) $E^\theta \left(\|x_i\|^2 \right) < \infty,\ \forall i \in \mathbb{Z},\ where\ \|x_i\|^2 = x_i x_i'.$
(ii) $E^\theta(x_i) = \mu,\ \forall i \in \mathbb{Z}\ with\ \mu \in \mathbb{R}^m.$
(iii) $\forall i, \tau \in \mathbb{Z}$

$$C^\theta (i, j) = \Gamma^\theta(i, j) = E^\theta \left[(x_i - E^\theta (x_i)) (x_j - E^\theta (x_j))' \right]$$

$$= \Gamma^\theta(i + \tau, j + \tau) = C^\theta(0, i - j)$$

and we set

$$\Gamma^\theta(\tau) = \left[Cov^\theta \left(x_{g,i}, x_{j,i+\tau} \right) \right]_{i \le g \le m,\, j \le g \le m}$$

where $\Gamma^\theta(\tau)$ is a real $m \times m$ matrix.   ∎

If x_i is a stationary vector process with m components, then each of the m components is also stationary. The converse is obviously not true, stationarity of each of the m components implies that for $j = 1, \ldots, m$, $E^\theta(x_{ji})$, and $Cov^\theta(x_{ji}, x_{ji+\tau})$ are independent of i for any τ, but it does not imply that the covariances between two distinct components g and j, $Cov^\theta(x_{gi}, x_{ji+\tau})$, for $g \ne j$ with $g = 1, \ldots m$ and $j = 1, \ldots, m$, are independent of i.

Analogously to the scalar case, a white noise is defined by:

Definition 12.14   *(Vectorial white noise) A stationary vector process $\{u_i ; i \in T\}$ is called a vectorial weak white noise process with variance-covariance matrix Σ (denoted by $u_i \sim WN(0, \Sigma)$) if:*

(i) $E^\theta(u_i) = 0$
(ii) $\Gamma^\theta(\tau) = \begin{vmatrix} \Sigma & if\ \tau = 0 \\ 0 & if\ \tau \ne 0 \end{vmatrix}$

where Σ is a real symmetric positive definite $m \times m$ matrix.

If u_i is i.i.d., the white noise is said to be a strong white noise.   ∎

Definition 12.15   *(Multivariate ARMA(p, q) process) Similarly to the univariate case, a centered stationary vector process with m components $\{x_i, i \in T\}$ is a ARMA(p, q) process if it is the solution of*

$$x_i - \alpha_1 x_{i-1} - \cdots - \alpha_p x_{i-p} = u_i + \beta_1 u_{i-1} + \cdots + \beta_q u_{i-q} \quad (12.38)$$

where the α_i and β_i are now square matrices of dimension m and $u_i \sim$ i.i.d.$(0, \Sigma)$.   ∎

Definition 12.16 *(Canonical multivariate ARMA(p, q))   The centered stationary vector process $\{x_i, i \in T\}$ is a canonical multivariate ARMA(p, q) process if it is the solution of (12.38) and if*

    (i) $\det \alpha(z) \neq 0$ *for all $z \in \mathbb{C}$ such that $|z| < 1$,*
    (ii) $\det \beta(z) \neq 0$ *for all $z \in \mathbb{C}$ such that $|z| < 1$,*
    (iii) $\alpha(z)$ *and $\beta(z)$ do not have any roots in common,*
    (iv) $\alpha_p \neq 0$ *and $\beta_q \neq 0$.*   ■

Depending on whether u_i is a weak white noise or is i.i.d., the canonical representation is either weak or strong. As in the univariate case, (12.38) can be rewritten in the compact form

$$\alpha(L)x_i = \beta(L)u_i \tag{12.39}$$

where α and β are matrix polynomials of the lag operator L with highest degrees p and q.

As in the univariate case, if the polynomials $\det \alpha(z)$ and $\det \beta(z)$ have roots with modulus larger than 1 then we can write it as

$$x_i = \sum_{j=0}^{+\infty} \psi_j u_{i-j} \text{ with } \psi_0 = I, \sum_{j=1}^{+\infty} \|\psi_j\| < \infty \quad (MA(\infty) \text{ form}) \tag{12.40}$$

and

$$u_i = \sum_{j=0}^{+\infty} \pi_j x_{i-j} \text{ with } \pi_0 = I, \sum_{j=1}^{+\infty} \|\pi_j\| < \infty \quad (AR(\infty) \text{ form}) \tag{12.41}$$

where the ψ_j and the π_j are square matrices of dimension m.

Also as in the scalar case, we note that u_i is the residual of the linear regression of x_i on the past values $x_{i-1}, x_{i-2} \ldots$ The linear regression of x_i is the projection of the components of x_i on the closed vector subspace spanned by the components of x_j, $j \leq i - 1$. The vector u_i is the vector of innovations of the process x_i at date i. Indeed, the closed subspaces of L^2 spanned by the coordinates of $\{u_j\}_{j \leq i}$ and $\{x_j\}_{j \leq i}$ are identical, and the coordinates of u_{i+1} are orthogonal to these subspaces. In the following, except for forecasting, we assume the the vector *ARMA* process is in its canonical form.

If $q = 0$, then the process reduces to a vector autoregressive process of order p (denoted $AR(p)$). Similarly, if $p = 0$, we have a vector moving average process of order q (denoted $MA(q)$). Although the form of a multivariate *ARMA* model closely resembles the form of a univariate *ARMA* model, the multivariate models have a complex structure. Indeed the equation for each component $x_{gi}, g = 1, \ldots, m$, does not include only the lags of x_{gi} (as well as of u_{ji}), but also the lagged values of other components $x_{ji}, j = 1, \ldots, m$, with $j \neq g$.

The representation corresponding to the identification condition $\beta_0 = I$, $\alpha_0 = I$, and unrestricted Σ is called the *reduced form*. If we substitute a constraint $\Sigma = I_m$ on the variance covariance matrix Σ, then we obtain a representation with white noise and orthonormal components. We obtain this by writing $\zeta_t = \eta^{-1} u_i$ where η is a nonsingular matrix that satisfies $\eta \eta' = \Sigma$. Then, we rewrite (12.39) in terms of the new white noise process ζ_t. However the preceding equation does not determine η in a unique way, unless a condition that η is a lower triangular matrix is imposed. The matrix η is the factor in the Cholesky decomposition of Σ. Thus, an alternative to the reduced form is the condition $\Sigma = I_m$ and α_0 is a lower triangular matrix. This representation is sometimes called *structural form*. To find a representation in the form of dynamic simultaneous equations, it is necessary to impose restrictions on $\alpha(L)$, $\beta(L)$, and Σ. We treat this question in more detail in Part 4 of this book.

12.9.2   Underlying Univariate Representation of a Multivariate Process

From a multivariate model, it is possible to extract the univariate models corresponding to each variable.

Theorem 12.17   *Consider a canonical vector ARMA model*

$$\alpha(L) x_i = \beta(L) u_i, \qquad u_i \sim i.i.d. (0, \Sigma). \tag{12.42}$$

This model can be rewritten in the form

$$\det \alpha(L) x_i = \beta^\circ(L) u_i \tag{12.43}$$

with $\beta^\circ(L) = \alpha^*(L) \beta(L)$, where $\alpha^*(L)$ is the adjoint matrix of $\alpha(L)$ (transposed matrix of cofactors). The univariate processes are given by the representation

$$\det \alpha(L) x_i = \widetilde{\beta}(L) \zeta_t \quad with \quad \zeta_t \sim WN(0, \Sigma^0) \tag{12.44}$$

where $\widetilde{\beta}(L)$ is a diagonal matrix of lag polynomials, ζ_t is the vector of univariate innovations and Σ^0 is a positive diagonal matrix.   ■

Proof: Since $\alpha(L) \ x_i = \beta(L) \ u_i$ is assumed to be canonical and thus invertible, we can write it in the form

$$x_i = \alpha(L)^{-1} \beta(L) u_i$$

with $\alpha(L)^{-1} = \frac{\alpha^*(L)}{\det \alpha(L)}$; by setting $\beta^\circ(L) = \alpha^*(L) \beta(L)$, we obtain (12.43).

Starting with the representation (12.43), each element of $\beta^\circ(L) u_i$ is a sum of moving average processes. We can represent this sum by a moving average process and do this for each element of $\beta^\circ(L)u_i$, thus the representation (12.44). ∎

The gth equation of (12.44) is given by

$$\det\alpha(L)\,x_{gi} = \widetilde{\beta}_i(L)\,\zeta_{gi} \tag{12.45}$$

where $\widetilde{\beta}(L)$ is the gth row of $\widetilde{\beta}(L)$.

It can be seen that each univariate representation has an *ARMA* form. This is true even if (12.42) is restricted to be a vector autoregressive process $(\alpha(L) = I_m)$. In contrast, if (12.42) is a moving average process, then the problem requires only the orthogonalization of the white noise vector to obtain the univariate representations (which are then also moving average processes).

The parameters and order of the lag polynomial of the autoregressive part of each univariate representation are in general the same, with the possible exception of common factors in $\det\alpha(L)$ and $\widetilde{\theta}_g(L)$.

$\widetilde{\beta}(L)$ is determined with the following procedure.

Denote by $\overline{\beta}_g$, $g = 1, \ldots, m$, the gth component of the vector $\alpha^*(L)\beta(L)u_i$ (part of the right side of (12.43)). This component $\overline{\beta}_g$ is the sum of moving averages:

$$\overline{\beta}_g = \sum_{j=1}^{m} \overline{\beta}_g^j(L)\,u_{ji}$$

where $\overline{\beta}_g^j$ is the jth moving average, $j = 1, \ldots, m$, of the gth row of $\phi^*(L)\theta(L)u_i$.

To find the finite moving average process that represents this sum, we compute the covariance generating function $G_g(z)$ of $\overline{\beta}_j$.

This function is the sum of the covariance generating functions of the $\overline{\beta}_g^j$, $j = 1, \ldots, m$, and all the cross-covariance generating functions of $\overline{\beta}_g^j\overline{\beta}_k^j$, $j, k = 1, \ldots, m$, $j \neq k$. This can be written in the form

$$G_g(z) = \sum_{j=1}^{m} \overline{\beta}_g^j(z)\overline{\beta}_g^j(z^{-1})\,\sigma_{jj}^2$$

$$+ \sum_{j=1}^{m-1}\sum_{k=j+1}^{m}\left[\overline{\beta}_g^j(z)\overline{\beta}_k^j(z^{-1}) + \overline{\beta}_k^j(z)\overline{\beta}_g^j(z^{-1})\right]\sigma_{jk}^2.$$

Once we know the covariance generating function $G_g(z)$ of Θ_g, we can determine a moving average process, which is an element of the class of processes that has $G_g(z)$ as covariance generating function, by means of the innovation algorithm for example.

12.9.3   Covariance Function

The Yule-Walker equations for a $VAR(p)$ process are obtained by post-multiplying x_i by $x_{i-\tau}$ and taking expectations. For $\tau = 0$, and taking into account that $C^\theta(\tau) = C^\theta(-\tau)'$, we have

$$C^\theta(0) = \alpha_1 C^\theta(-1) + \cdots + \alpha_p C^\theta(-p) + \Sigma_u$$

(12.46)

$$= \alpha_1 C^\theta(1)' + \cdots + \alpha_p C^\theta(p)' + \Sigma_u$$

and for $\tau > 0$

$$C^\theta(\tau) = \alpha_1 C^\theta(\tau - 1) + \cdots + \alpha_p C^\theta(\tau - p).$$ (12.47)

These equations can be obtained by recursively computing the $C^\theta(\tau)$ for $\tau \geq p$ if $\alpha_1, \ldots, \alpha_p$ and $C^\theta(\tau - 1), \ldots, C^\theta(0)$ are known.

Example 12.8   *Consider the VAR(1) representation of the process $\{x_i, i \in T\}$:*

$$x_i = \alpha x_{i-1} + u_i, \quad u_i \sim WN(0, \Sigma).$$

Thus, we have for $\tau = 0$

$$C^\theta(0) = \alpha C^\theta(-1) + \Sigma = \alpha C^\theta(1)' + \Sigma$$

and for $\tau > 0$

$$C^\theta(\tau) = \alpha C^\theta(\tau - 1).$$ (12.48)

These are the Yule-Walker equations. If α and $C^\theta(0)$ are known, then we can recursively calculate $C^\theta(\tau)$ using (12.48). $\square$

In general, the covariances depend on the measurement units of the variables in the system and are sometimes difficult to interpret. The correlation functions are more practical.

12.10   Interpretation of a $VAR(p)$ Model Under Its $MA(\infty)$ Form

12.10.1   Propagation of a Shock on a Component

We are interested in a process with white noise with orthonormal components, as this allows us to analyze the way in which a shock on a variable in the model propagates over time. Consider a representation of the form (12.39) that satisfies $\Sigma = I_m$ and β_0 is lower triangular. Its $MA(\infty)$ form is written as

$$x_i = \sum_{j=0}^{+\infty} \psi_j u_{i-j} \quad \text{with } u_i \sim i.i.d. (0, I_m)$$ (12.49)

where $\psi_j = (\psi_j^{gk})_{g,k=1,\ldots,r}$ are square matrices of dimension m.

The u_i^g, $g = 1, \ldots, m$, are orthogonal to each other, and the gth component of x_i becomes

$$x_{gi} = \sum_{j=0}^{+\infty} \sum_{k=0}^{m} \psi_j^{gk} \, u_{i-j}. \tag{12.50}$$

A unit shock on u_0^k, i.e., on x_{k0}, propagates to the component x_g as shown in (12.50) and changes x_{gi} by ψ_j^{gk}. The sequence of the ψ_j^{gk} represents the impulse response of x_g to a unit shock on x_{k0}. The amount of change in x_i at period n is measured by $\sum_{j=0}^{n} \psi_j^{gk}$.

Generally, the response of the variable j to a unit shock in variable k is usually shown graphically in order to obtain a visual impression of the dynamic relationships in the system. If the variables have different scales, it is sometimes useful to consider innovations equal to one standard deviation instead of a unit shock. An innovation in the variable k has no effect on the other variables if the former variable does not Granger cause the set of remaining variables.

A cumulative shock after several periods can be determined by summing the matrices of the MA coefficients. These are the cumulative response functions or long-term effects.

12.10.2 Variance Decomposition of the Forecast Error

The MA representation

$$x_i = \sum_{j=0}^{\infty} \pi_j P P^{-1} u_{i-j} = \sum_{g=0}^{\tau-1} \beta_g u_{i+\tau-g} \quad \text{with } \Sigma_u = I_m$$

provides another way of interpreting a $VAR(p)$ model. Consider the optimal forecast error at horizon τ:

$$x_{i+\tau} - \widehat{x}_i(\tau) = \sum_{i=0}^{\tau-1} \beta_g u_{i+\tau-g}.$$

Denoting the mjth element of β_i by $\beta_{mj,i}$, the forecast error for the τ periods ahead forecast of the jth component of x_i is

$$x_{j,i+\tau} - \widehat{x}_{j,i}(\tau) = \sum_{i=0}^{\tau-1} (\beta_{j1,g} u_{1,i+\tau-g} + \cdots\cdots\cdots + \beta_{jr,g} u_{r,i+\tau-g})$$

$$= \sum_{k=1}^{r} (\beta_{jk,0} u_{k,i+\tau} + \cdots\cdots\cdots + \beta_{jk,\tau-1} u_{k,i+1}).$$

Thus, it is possible that the forecast error of the jth component also consists of innovations in other components of x_i. Since the $u_{k,i}$ are uncorrelated and have unit variance, the mean squared error of $\widehat{x}_{j,i}(\tau)$ is

$$E^\theta\left((x_{j,i+\tau} - \widehat{x}_{j,i}(\tau))^2\right) = \sum_{k=1}^{r}(\beta_{jk,0}^2 + \cdots\cdots\cdots\cdots + \beta_{jk,\tau-1}^2).$$

Moreover,

$$\beta_{jk,0}^2 + \cdots + \beta_{jk,\tau-1}^2 \tag{12.51}$$

is sometimes interpreted as the contribution of the innovations in the variable k to the variance of the forecast error for the t periods ahead forecast of variable j. Dividing (12.51) by the MSE of $\widehat{x}_{j,i}(\tau)$, we obtain the proportional measure of this contribution to the forecast error. In this way, the variance of the forecast error is decomposed into its components that are accounted for by the innovations of the different variables of the system.

12.11 Estimation of $VAR(p)$ Models

The results of the preceding section for the univariate case can be extended to the multivariate case. There are principally two estimation methods: the direct methods of the Yule-Walker type and maximum likelihood method. In this part, we present the maximum likelihood method. From a statistical viewpoint, the MLE can yield the best results. This is true in particular for short observation sequences or for models that are close to nonstationarity. The use of MLE became more attractive as computing power has increased. The criterion of the log-likelihood is also more appropriate than the one of least squares. It protects against instabilities in the log terms that converge to infinity when the parameters approach the boundaries of the stability region. Several estimators have been proposed that are asymptotically efficient and are based on the maximization of an approximated (multivariate) log-likelihood function. These estimators are equivalent to the MLE if the latter exists. The approximate log-likelihood can be maximized using the Newton-Raphson algorithm. If the initial estimator is appropriately chosen, then the resulting estimator is asymptotically efficient. A large number of algorithms exist for maximizing the likelihood using the exact computation of first derivatives of the log-likelihood. These algorithms use the iterative technique of Fisher to construct the estimator and are quite simple to implement.

Let $\{x_i\}$ be a stochastic process of dimension m. The dynamics of the $\{x_i\}$ is generated by a $VAR(p)$ of the form

$$x_i = \mu + \alpha_1 x_{i-1} + \alpha_2 x_{i-2} + \cdots + \alpha_p x_{i-p} + \varepsilon_i \text{ with}$$

$$\varepsilon_i \sim i.i.d.(0, \Omega).$$

We assume that each of the m variables is observed for $(n + p)$ periods. As in the scalar case, the simplest approach is to condition on the first p observations, denoted by $(x_{-p+1}, x_{-p+2}, \ldots, x_0)$, and to construct the estimation for the last n observations $(x_1, x_2, \ldots, x_n)$. The objective therefore is to construct the conditional likelihood

$$f_{x_n, x_{n-1}, \ldots, x_1 | x_0, x_{-1}, \ldots, x_{-p+1}} \left(x_n, x_{n-1}, \ldots, x_1 \mid x_0, x_{-1}, \ldots, x_{-p+1} \, ; \theta \right),$$

which then is maximized with respect to the parameter vector of interest $\theta = (\mu, \alpha_1, \alpha_2, \ldots, \alpha_p, \Omega)'$. The $VAR(p)$ are generally estimated based on the conditional likelihood function instead of the unconditional. Conditioning on the values of x at $i - 1$, the value of x at period i is equal to

$$\mu + \alpha_1 x_{i-1} + \alpha_2 x_{i-2} + \cdots + \alpha_p x_{i-p}$$

plus a random variable distributed $N(0, \Omega)$. Thus, we have

$$x_i \mid x_{i-1}, x_{i-2}, \ldots, x_{-p+1}$$
$$\sim N \left(\mu + \alpha_1 x_{i-1} + \alpha_2 x_{i-2} + \cdots + \alpha_p x_{i-p}, \, \Omega \right)$$

We can rewrite this in a more compact way as

$$y_i = \begin{pmatrix} 1 \\ x_{i-1} \\ x_{i-2} \\ \vdots \\ x_{i-p} \end{pmatrix}$$

where y_i has dimension $(mp + 1) \times 1$. Let Π be the $m \times (mp + 1)$ matrix given by

$$\Pi = \begin{bmatrix} \alpha_1 & \alpha_2 & \ldots & \alpha_p \end{bmatrix};$$

then the conditional mean is equal to $\Pi' y_i$. The jth row of Π' contains the parameters of the jth equation of $VAR(p)$. Using this notation, we can rewrite the model in the following way

$$x_i \mid x_{i-1}, x_{i-2}, \ldots, x_{-p+1} \sim N \left(\Pi' y_i, \, \Omega \right).$$

The conditional density of the ith observation is then

$$f_{x_i, x_{i-1}, \ldots, x_1 | x_0, x_{-1}, \ldots, x_{-p+1}} \left(x_i \mid x_{i-1}, x_{i-2}, \ldots, x_1, x_0, x_{-1}, \ldots, x_{-p+1} \, ; \theta \right)$$
$$= (2\pi)^{-\frac{n}{2}} \left| \Omega^{-1} \right|^{\frac{1}{2}} \exp \left[\left(-\frac{1}{2} \right) \left(x_i - \Pi' y_i \right)' \Omega^{-1} \left(x_i - \Pi' y_i \right) \right].$$

The joint density of the observations in periods 1 to i, conditional on $x_0, x_{-1}, \ldots,$ x_{-p+1} satisfies

$$f_{x_i, x_{i-1}, \ldots, x_1 | x_0, x_{-1}, \ldots, x_{-p+1}} \left(x_i, x_{i-1}, \ldots, x_1 \mid x_0, x_{-1}, \ldots, x_{-p+1} ; \theta \right)$$

$$= f_{x_{i-1}, \ldots, x_1 | x_0, \ldots, x_{-p+1}} \left(x_{i-1}, \ldots, x_1 \mid x_0, x_{-1}, \ldots, x_{-p+1} ; \theta \right)$$

$$\times f_{x_i | x_{i-1}, x_{i-2}, \ldots, x_{-p+1}} \left(x_i \mid x_{i-1}, x_{i-2}, \ldots, x_{-p+1} ; \theta \right).$$

Applying this recursively, the likelihood for the entire sample conditional on the initial condition is the product of the individual conditional densities:

$$f_{x_i, x_{i-1}, \ldots, x_1 | x_0, x_{-1}, \ldots, x_{-p+1}} \left(x_i, x_{i-1}, \ldots, x_1 \mid x_0, x_{-1}, \ldots, x_{-p+1} ; \theta \right)$$

$$= \prod_{i=1}^{n} f_{x_i | x_{i-1}, x_{i-2}, \ldots, x_{-p+1}} \left(x_i \mid x_{i-1}, x_{i-2}, \ldots, x_{-p+1} ; \theta \right),$$

hence, we obtain the log-likelihood function

$$L(\theta) = \sum_{t=1}^{n} \log f_{x_i | x_{i-1}, x_{i-2}, \ldots, x_{-p+1}} \left(x_i \mid x_{i-1}, x_{i-2}, \ldots, x_{-p+1} ; \theta \right)$$

$$= -\frac{im}{2} \log (2\pi) + \frac{n}{2} \log \left| \Omega^{-1} \right| \tag{12.52}$$

$$- \frac{1}{2} \sum_{i=1}^{n} \left[\left(x_i - \Pi' y_i \right) \Omega^{-1} \left(x_i - \Pi' y_i \right) \right].$$

12.11.1   Maximum Likelihood Estimation of Π

We first consider the estimation of Π. The estimator is given by

$$\widehat{\Pi}' = \left[\sum_{i=1}^{n} x_i y_i' \right] \left[\sum_{i=1}^{n} y_i y_i' \right]^{-1}, \tag{12.53}$$

where $\widehat{\Pi}'$ has $m \times (mp + 1)$ dimension, the gth row of $\widehat{\Pi}'$ is

$$\widehat{\pi}' = \left[\sum_{i=1}^{n} x_{gi} y_i' \right] \left[\sum_{i=1}^{n} y_i y_i' \right]^{-1},$$

which has dimension $1 \times (mp + 1)$ and which is the coefficient vector estimated by a least squares regression of x_{ji} on y_i. Thus, the MLE of the coefficients of the gth equation of a *VAR* are obtained by least squares regression of x_{gi} on a constant and on the p lags of the variables of the system. To verify (12.53), we rewrite the sum that appears in the log-likelihood function as

$$\sum_{i=1}^{n} \left[(x_i - \Pi' y_i)' \, \Omega^{-1} \, (x_i - \Pi' y_i) \right] \tag{12.54}$$

$$= \sum_{i=1}^{n} \left[(x_i - \widehat{\Pi}' y_i + \widehat{\Pi}' y_i - \Pi' y_i)' \, \Omega^{-1} \, (x_i - \widehat{\Pi}' y_i + \widehat{\Pi}' y_i - \Pi' y_i) \right]$$

$$= \sum_{i=1}^{n} \left[\left[\widehat{\varepsilon}_i + (\widehat{\Pi} - \Pi)' \, y_i \right]' \Omega^{-1} \left[\widehat{\varepsilon}_i + (\widehat{\Pi} - \Pi)' \, y_i \right] \right]$$

with

$$\widehat{\varepsilon}_i = x_i - \widehat{\Pi}' y_i.$$

We can expand (12.54) in the following way

$$\sum_{i=1}^{n} \left[(x_i - \Pi' y_i) \, \Omega^{-1} \, (x_i - \Pi' y_i) \right]$$

$$= \sum_{i=1}^{n} \widehat{\varepsilon}_i' \Omega^{-1} \widehat{\varepsilon}_i + 2 \sum_{i=1}^{n} \widehat{\varepsilon}_i' \Omega^{-1} \left(\widehat{\Pi} - \Pi \right)' y_i \tag{12.55}$$

$$+ \sum_{i=1}^{n} y_i' \left(\widehat{\Pi} - \Pi \right) \Omega^{-1} \left(\widehat{\Pi} - \Pi \right)' y_i.$$

Consider the terms in the middle of (12.55). Since it is a scalar, it remains unchanged, when taking the trace:

$$\sum_{i=1}^{n} \widehat{\varepsilon}_i' \Omega^{-1} \left(\widehat{\Pi} - \Pi \right)' y_i = trace \left[\sum_{i=1}^{n} \widehat{\varepsilon}_i' \Omega^{-1} \left(\widehat{\Pi} - \Pi \right)' y_i \right]$$

$$= trace \left[\sum_{i=1}^{n} \Omega^{-1} \left(\widehat{\Pi} - \Pi \right)' y_i \widehat{\varepsilon}_i' \right] \tag{12.56}$$

$$= trace \left[\Omega^{-1} \left(\widehat{\Pi} - \Pi \right)' \sum_{i=1}^{n} y_i \widehat{\varepsilon}_i' \right].$$

Note that $\sum_{i=1}^{n} y_i \widehat{\varepsilon}_{gi} = 0$, $\forall g$, by construction and thus $\sum_{i=1}^{n} y_i \widehat{\varepsilon}_i' = 0$. Thus, (12.56) is zero and (12.55) becomes

$$\sum_{i=1}^{n} \left[(x_i - \Pi' y_i) \, \Omega^{-1} \, (x_i - \Pi' y_i) \right]$$

$$= \sum_{i=1}^{n} \widehat{\varepsilon}_i' \Omega^{-1} \widehat{\varepsilon}_i + \sum_{i=1}^{n} y_i' \left(\widehat{\Pi} - \Pi \right) \Omega^{-1} \left(\widehat{\Pi} - \Pi \right)' y_i. \tag{12.57}$$

Since Ω is positive definite, Ω^{-1} is also positive definite. If we define the $n \times 1$ vector $y_i^* = (\widehat{\Pi} - \Pi)'y_i$, then the last term in (12.57) becomes

$$\sum_{i=1}^{n} y_i' \left(\widehat{\Pi} - \Pi\right) \Omega^{-1} \left(\widehat{\Pi} - \Pi\right)' y_i = \sum_{i=1}^{n} y_i^{*'}\Omega^{-1}y_i^*.$$

This is positive for all sequences $\{y_i^*\}_{i=1}^{n}$ other than $y_i^* = 0$ for each i. Thus, the smallest value of (12.57) is attained at $y_i^* = 0$, or at $\Pi = \widehat{\Pi}$. Since (12.57) is minimized for $\Pi = \widehat{\Pi}$, (12.52) is maximized by setting $\Pi = \widehat{\Pi}$, which establishes that the OLS regression yields the MLE of the coefficients of the multivariate autoregressive model.

12.11.2   Maximum Likelihood Estimation of Ω

After estimating $\widehat{\Pi}$, the log-likelihood (12.52) is

$$L\left(\widehat{\Pi}, \Omega\right) = -\frac{im}{2} \log\left(2\pi\right) + \frac{n}{2} \log\left|\Omega^{-1}\right| - \frac{1}{2} \sum_{i=1}^{n} \widehat{\varepsilon}_i'\Omega^{-1}\widehat{\varepsilon}_i. \qquad (12.58)$$

Our objective is to find a symmetric positive definite matrix such that this function is maximized. First, we maximize (12.58) treating Ω (of dimension $n \times n$) as unrestricted. To do this, we differentiate (12.58) with respect to the elements of Ω^{-1}:

$$\frac{\partial L\left(\widehat{\Pi}, \Omega\right)}{\partial \Omega^{-1}} = \frac{n}{2}\frac{\partial \log\left|\Omega^{-1}\right|}{\partial \Omega^{-1}} - \frac{1}{2}\sum_{i=1}^{n}\frac{\partial \widehat{\varepsilon}_i'\Omega^{-1}\widehat{\varepsilon}_i}{\partial \Omega^{-1}}$$

$$= \frac{n}{2}\Omega' - \frac{1}{2}\sum_{i=1}^{n}\widehat{\varepsilon}_i\widehat{\varepsilon}_i'. \qquad (12.59)$$

The likelihood is maximized if this derivative is zero, i.e., at

$$\widehat{\Omega} = \frac{1}{n}\sum_{i=1}^{n}\widehat{\varepsilon}_i\widehat{\varepsilon}_i'. \qquad (12.60)$$

The (j, j) element of $\widehat{\Omega}$ is given by

$$\widehat{\sigma}_j^2 = \frac{1}{n}\sum_{i=1}^{n}\widehat{\varepsilon}_{ji}^2;$$

the (j, l) element of $\widehat{\Omega}$ is given by

$$\widehat{\sigma}_{jl} = \frac{1}{n}\sum_{i=1}^{n}\widehat{\varepsilon}_{ji}\widehat{\varepsilon}_{li}.$$

Thus, it follows that

$$L\left(\widehat{\Pi}, \widehat{\Omega}\right) = -\frac{im}{2} \log\left(2\pi\right) + \frac{n}{2} \log\left|\widehat{\Omega}^{-1}\right| - \frac{1}{2} \sum_{i=1}^{n} \widehat{\varepsilon}_i' \widehat{\Omega}^{-1} \widehat{\varepsilon}_i \quad (12.61)$$

with $\widehat{\Omega}$ determined by (12.60). The last term in (12.61) is

$$\frac{1}{2} \sum_{i=1}^{n} \widehat{\varepsilon}_i' \widehat{\Omega}^{-1} \widehat{\varepsilon}_i = \frac{1}{2} trace\left[\sum_{i=1}^{n} \widehat{\varepsilon}_i' \widehat{\Omega}^{-1} \widehat{\varepsilon}_i\right]$$

$$= \frac{1}{2} trace\left[\widehat{\Omega}^{-1}\left(n\widehat{\Omega}\right)\right] = \frac{1}{2} trace\left(n I_m\right)$$

$$= \frac{nm}{2}.$$

Substituting this into (12.61), we obtain

$$L\left(\widehat{\Pi}, \widehat{\Omega}\right) = -\frac{im}{2} \log\left(2\pi\right) + \frac{n}{2} \log\left|\widehat{\Omega}^{-1}\right| - \frac{nm}{2}.$$

12.11.3 Asymptotic Distribution of $\widehat{\Pi}$ and of $\widehat{\Omega}$

The MLE of $\widehat{\Pi}$ and of $\widehat{\Omega}$ are consistent even if the true innovations are not Gaussian.

Proposition 12.1 *Let*

$$x_i = \mu + \alpha_1 x_{i-1} + \alpha_2 x_{i-2} + \cdots + \alpha_p x_{i-p} + \varepsilon_i$$

where $\varepsilon_i \sim i.i.d.\,(0, \Omega)$ *and*

$$E\left(\varepsilon_{li}\varepsilon_{mi}\varepsilon_{ni}\varepsilon_{ot}\right) < \infty, \quad \forall l, m, n, o$$

and where the roots of

$$\left|I_m - \alpha_1 z - \alpha_2 z - \cdots - \alpha_p z^p\right| = 0$$

are outside the unit circle. Let $k = mp + 1$ *and let* y_i' *be the* $1 \times k$ *vector*

$$y_i' = \left(1, x_{i-1}', x_{i-2}', \ldots, x_{i-p}'\right).$$

Let $\widehat{\pi}_n = vec\left(\widehat{\Pi}_n\right)$ *be the* $mk \times 1$ *vector of coefficients obtained by least squares regression of each element of* x_i *on* y_i *for a sample of size n:*

$$\widehat{\pi}_n = \begin{pmatrix} \widehat{\pi}_{1,n} \\ \widehat{\pi}_{2,n} \\ \vdots \\ \widehat{\pi}_{r,n} \end{pmatrix}$$

where

$$\widehat{\pi}_{g,n} = \left[\sum_{i=1}^{n} y_i y_i'\right]^{-1} \left[\sum_{i=1}^{n} y_i x_{ji}\right]$$

and let π be the corresponding $(mk + 1)$ vector of coefficients. Finally, let

$$\widehat{\Omega}_n = \frac{1}{n}\sum_{i=1}^{n} \widehat{\varepsilon}_i \widehat{\varepsilon}_i'$$

where

$$\widehat{\varepsilon}_i' = (\widehat{\varepsilon}_{1i}, \widehat{\varepsilon}_{2i}, \ldots, \widehat{\varepsilon}_{mi})$$

$$\widehat{\varepsilon}_{gi} = x_{gi} - y_i'\widehat{\pi}_{g,n}.$$

Then
(a)

$$\frac{1}{n}\sum_{i=1}^{n} y_i y_i' \xrightarrow{P} Q$$

where

$$Q = E\left(y_i y_i'\right)$$

(b)

$$\widehat{\pi}_n \xrightarrow{P} \pi$$

(c)

$$\widehat{\Omega} \xrightarrow{P} \Omega$$

(d)

$$\sqrt{n}\left(\widehat{\pi}_n - \widehat{\pi}\right) \xrightarrow{L} N\left(0, \left(\Omega \otimes Q^{-1}\right)\right). \qquad \blacksquare$$

Proposition 12.2   *Let*

$$x_i = \mu + \alpha_1 x_{i-1} + \alpha_2 x_{i-2} + \cdots + \alpha_p x_{i-p} + \varepsilon_i$$

where $\varepsilon_i \sim i.i.d.(0, \Omega)$ and where the roots of

$$\left|I_r - \alpha_1 z - \alpha_2 z - \cdots - \alpha_p z^p\right| = 0$$

are outside the unit circle. Let $\widehat{\pi}_n$, $\widehat{\Omega}_n$ and Q be as defined in the previous proposition. Then

$$\begin{bmatrix} \sqrt{n}\left(\widehat{\pi}_n - \widehat{\pi}\right) \\ \sqrt{n}\left[vech\left(\widehat{\Omega}_n\right) - vech\left(\Omega\right)\right] \end{bmatrix} \xrightarrow{L} N\left[\begin{pmatrix} 0 \\ 0 \end{pmatrix}, \begin{pmatrix} \left(\Omega \otimes Q^{-1}\right) & 0 \\ 0 & \Sigma_{22} \end{pmatrix}\right]$$

$\blacksquare$

Notes

The book by Box and Jenkins (1976) provides the outline for our treatment of stationary ergodic processes, notably for the ARIMA models. For the multivariate case, we direct the reader to Hamilton (1994), Reinsel (1993), and Lütkepohl (1993). For a more statistical approach, we refer to the work by Brockwell and Davis (1987). Information criteria are developed by Akaike (1970, 1974) and Schwartz (1978). The criteria for identification for multivariate models have been studied by Hannan (1970), and the extraction of the univariate series are described in Zellner and Palm (1974). The asymptotic study of the multivariate models has been the object of an important literature and a number of algorithms have been proposed. We cite Akaike (1973), Nicholls (1976), and Pham (1975) to mention only a few. The analysis of dynamic multipliers and of impulse response functions has been proposed by Sims (1980).

13. Nonstationary Processes and Cointegration

13.1 Introduction

In Chapter 12, we focused on a class of processes in which stationarity, invertibility, and ergodicity were essential conditions. Ergodicity, φ-mixing, and α-mixing are three types of asymptotic independence, implying that two realizations of a time-series become almost independent from each other when the time elapsed between them increases. As we saw in Chapter 1, a process $\{x_i, i \in T\}$ is said to be mixing if

$$\left| F(x_1, \ldots, x_n, x_{h+1}, \ldots, x_{h+p}) - F(x_1, \ldots, x_n) F(x_{h+1}, \ldots, x_{h+p}) \right| \to 0$$

when $h \to \infty$, i.e., the joint distribution function of two subsets of realizations of $\{x_i, i \in T\}$ converges to the product of the distribution function of each subset when the distance between the two subsets increases.

The independence between random variables is only an approximation of reality. We know that performing inference as if the variables were independent, when they are (even weakly) correlated, may have non-negligible effects.

The representations of the $ARMA(p, q)$ type and the stationary homogeneous Markov models (whose spectrums are regular and correlations decrease exponentially fast) allow us to obtain more reliable results than those obtained under the assumption of independence. A stationary series with mean $E^\theta(x_i)$ independent of i and with bounded variance does not vary systematically in time. It tends to return to its mean, and its fluctuations around this mean have a constant amplitude. In contrast, a nonstationary series has moments that vary in time and we can not refer to them without specifying a time period. The simplest example of a nonstationary process is the *random walk* without drift,

$$x_i = x_{i-1} + u_i, \text{ with } u_i \sim i.i.d\,(0, \sigma_u^2)$$

with a fixed initial condition, $x_0 = 0$, so that

$$x_i = \sum_{i=1}^{n} u_i.$$

The variance of x_i is $n\sigma^2$ and goes to infinity when $n \longrightarrow \infty$, although the mean is constant and equal to zero. Whereas a stationary process tends to return to its mean value and fluctuates around it, a nonstationary process has moments that are different for different time points.

Now consider the stochastic process $\{x_i, i \in T\}$ such that

$$E^\theta [x_i \mid X_{i-1}] = x_{i-1}, \quad \forall i \in T,$$

where X_{i-1} represents the information available at time $i - 1$. Define the process

$$\{y_i = x_i - x_{i-1} = (1 - L)x_i = \Delta x_i, i \in T\}.$$

The stochastic process $\{y_i, i \in T\}$ is made stationary by the difference operator Δ. A process is said to be *integrated of order d* (or $I(d)$) if the process $\Delta^d x_i$ is stationary and if $\Delta^{d'} x_i$ is nonstationary for $d' < d$. If $d = 1$ and if u_i is a white noise, the resulting process is called *random walk*; this is the simplest example of an integrated process of order one. Note that if x_i is stationary, then so is $\Delta^d x_i$ for values of $d \in \mathbb{N}$. Hence, the stationarity of $\Delta^d x_i$ alone is not sufficient to guarantee that x_i is integrated of order d ($I(d)$).

Example 13.1 *Consider an $AR(1)$ process*

$$x_i = \alpha_0 + \alpha_1 x_{i-1} + u_i,$$

with $u_i \sim i.i.d(0, \sigma_u^2)$, $x_0 = 0$, $|\alpha_1| < 1$ and $i = 1, \ldots, n$; $\{x_i\}$ is not stationary because

$$E^\theta (x_i) = \alpha_0 (1 - \alpha_1^i)(1 - \alpha_1)^{-1}$$

is not constant over time, although the process is asymptotically stationary. This is a nonstationary series that is not integrated in the sense above. Similarly, consider the following process

$$x_i = \alpha_0 + \alpha_1 x_{i-1} + \gamma i^t + u_i,$$

with $u_i \sim i.i.d(0, \sigma_u^2)$, $x_0 = 0$, $|\alpha_1| < 1$ and $i = 1, \ldots, n$. It is clear that $E^\theta (x_i)$ is not constant over time. □

The chapter is organized in the following manner. First, we analyze the asymptotic properties of the OLS estimators in the context of processes with stochastic trend. Second, we present tests for unit root. Finally, we discuss the transformation of these nonstationary processes and the search for common components in long-term equilibria.

13.2 Asymptotic Properties of Least Squares Estimators of $I(1)$ Processes

Before analyzing the statistical inference of univariate processes with a unit root, we should stress that the convergence criteria and the asymptotic distributions of the estimated coefficients of $I(1)$ processes differ from those of stationary processes. Denote by $W(t)$, $1 \geq t \geq 0$, the standard *Wiener process* (to be defined later). The asymptotic distributions of $I(1)$ processes can be described as functions of $W(.)$. We examine various cases using examples.

We provide a more precise definition of integrated processes than the one given in the introduction in order to use the representations of these processes. First, we limit the class of stationary processes that we use by defining a $I(0)$ process.

Definition 13.1   *A $I(0)$ process is a process $\{u_i, i \in T\}$ that satisfies*

$$u_i = B(L)\varepsilon_i$$

with

$$B(L) = \sum_{j=0}^{\infty} B_j L^j; \ B(1) \neq 0$$

where ε_i is a weak white noise with variance σ_ε^2 and $\sum_{j=1}^{\infty} j \, |B_j|$ is a convergent sequence (where $|B_j|$ is the norm of B_j).   ∎

Note in particular that the process is centered. This restriction in the definition of $I(0)$ is not very strong. It supposes that the process is a priori centered, purely random, and weakly stationary. The above representation follows then from Wold theorem. The only extra assumption concerns the stronger condition of convergence of the series. Now we can define:

1. A process $\{x_i, i \in T\}$ is $I(1)$ if Δx_i is $I(0)$. Note that the restriction $B(1) \neq 0$ prevents x_i to be $I(0)$. Indeed, if x_i were $I(0)$,

   $$x_i = B(L)(1 - L)\varepsilon_i = B^*(L)\varepsilon_i$$

   with

   $$B^*(L) = B(L)(1 - L).$$

   Δx_i is not $I(0)$ because $B^*(1) = 0$. Hence, the class $I(1)$ is composed of nonstationary processes that are stationary in first differences. This result provides an informative interpretation of $I(0)$ and $I(1)$ models in terms of the properties of the long-run forecasts of these series. If x_i is integrated of order 1, its long-run forecast is a martingale, whereas if u_i is integrated of order zero, its long run forecast tends toward its unconditional mean. In this sense, if x_i is integrated of order 1, then x_i has a stochastic trend. Beveridge and Nelson formally established the equivalence between the order of integration of a series and the existence of a stochastic trend.

2. A process $\{x_i, i \in T\}$ is $I(2)$ if Δx_i is $I(1)$ and $\Delta^2 x_i$ is $I(0)$. By the same argument, $I(2)$ comprises only nonstationary processes whose first-difference is also nonstationary. This construction can be iterated for $d \geq 2$, but $I(d)$ processes used in practice belong to $I(1)$ or $I(2)$.

We focus in our presentation on a more detailed description of $I(1)$. Let $\{x_i, i \in T\}$ be a $I(1)$ process. Of course, we can write

$$x_i = x_0 + \sum_{j=1}^{i} u_j \tag{13.1}$$

where $u_j = x_j - x_{j-1}$ is $I(0)$. From this representation, we obtain the following lemma.

Lemma 13.1 *(Beveridge-Nelson decomposition) Let x_i be a $I(1)$ process (i.e., $\Delta x_i = u_i \sim I(0)$, $u_i = B(L)\varepsilon_i$ and $\sum j |B_j| < \infty$, ε_i is a weak white noise). Then*

$$x_i = B(1) \sum_{i=1}^{n} \varepsilon_i + B^*(L)\varepsilon_i + \tilde{u}_0$$

with

$$B^*(L) = \sum B_j^* L^j,$$

$B_j^* = -\sum_{l=j+1}^{\infty} B_l$ *and $B^*(L)\varepsilon_i$ is stationary. $\tilde{u}_0$ defined by*

$$\tilde{u}_0 = x_0 - B^*(L)\varepsilon_0$$

is a random vector. ∎

Proof: First we examine the equation

$$B(L) - B(1) = B^*(L)(1 - L).$$

We can infer that

$$(-B_1 - B_2 - \cdots) + B_1 L + B_2 L^2 + \cdots$$
$$= B_0^* + \left(B_1^* - B_0^*\right) L + \left(B_2^* - B_1^*\right) L^2 + \cdots$$

hence

$$B_0^* = -B_1 - B_2 - \cdots$$

$$B_1^* = -B_2 - B_1 - \cdots$$

and in general

$$B_j^* = - \sum_{p=j+1}^{\infty} B_p.$$

Let us verify that $B^*(L)$ applied to a white noise defines indeed a stationary process. We know that it suffices that $\sum_{i=0}^{\infty} |B_i^*| < \infty$. Now

$$\sum_{j=0}^{\infty} |B_j^*| = \sum_{j=0}^{\infty} \left| \sum_{p=j+1}^{\infty} B_p \right| \leq \sum_{j=0}^{\infty} \sum_{p=j+1}^{\infty} |B_p|$$

$$= \sum_{j=0}^{\infty} j |B_j| < \infty \text{ by assumption.}$$

Finally, we have

$$x_i = x_0 + \sum_{j=1}^{i} u_j = x_0 + B(L) \sum_{j=1}^{i} \varepsilon_j$$

$$= B(1) \sum_{j=1}^{i} \varepsilon_j + (B(L) - B(1)) \sum_{j=1}^{i} \varepsilon_j + x_0$$

$$= B(1) \sum_{j=1}^{i} \varepsilon_j + B^*(L)(1 - L) \sum_{j=1}^{i} \varepsilon_j + x_0$$

$$= B(1) \sum_{j=1}^{i} \varepsilon_j + B^*(L)(\varepsilon_i - \varepsilon_0) + x_0$$

$$= B(1) \sum_{j=1}^{i} \varepsilon_j + B^*(L)\varepsilon_i + x_0 - B^*(L)\varepsilon_0. \qquad \blacksquare$$

These results can be clarified by three comments:

1. Consider the scalar process $\{x_i\}$ that admits an $ARMA$ representation

$$\alpha(L) x_i = \beta(L) \varepsilon_i.$$

In Chapter 12, we used to assume that all the roots of the equation $\alpha(z) = 0$ lay strictly outside the unit circle. Suppose now that 1 is a root of order d of this equation. We can write

$$\alpha(L)x_i = (1 - L)^d \alpha^*(L)x_i = \beta(L)\varepsilon_i.$$

Assuming that all roots of $\alpha^*(L)$ have their modulus greater than one, we have

$$\Delta^d x_i = \frac{\beta(L)}{\alpha^*(L)}\varepsilon_i$$

and we see clearly that x_i is a $I(d)$ process. This remark explains the terminology \unit roots" and \integrated" processes.

2. The lemma shows that any $I(1)$ process can be written as the sum of a random walk $B(1)\sum_{j=0}^{i}\varepsilon_i$ and a stationary component. The random walk term can be interpreted as the long-run forecast of u_i. As $B^*(L)$ is summable, the long-run forecast $u_{i+k|i}$ for a very large k is $B(1)\sum_{s=1}^{i}\varepsilon_s$. This justifies the fact that $I(d)$ processes are often referred to as pro-cesses with *stochastic trend,* by opposition to *deterministic trend,* i.e., processes that can be written under the form $x_i = f(i) + \eta_i$, where $f(i)$ is a function of time and η_i is a stationary component.

3. If x_i satisfies

$$x_i = x_{i-1} + \mu + u_i,$$

we have

$$x_i = \mu i + x_0 + \sum_{j-1}^{i} u_j$$

and we can apply Beveridge-Nelson decomposition to the sum of the two last terms. The process x_i is I(1) with drift.

If u_i is stationary, has sufficiently many moments, and is weakly dependent, then $n^{-1}\sum_{i=1}^{n}u_i^2$ converges in probability and the normalized sums such as $n^{-\frac{1}{2}}\sum_{i=1}^{n}u_i$ satisfy the central limit theorem. By nature, the central limit the-orem does not apply to most statistics that we will study in this chapter. For example, the unit root test statistic depends on components that do not satisfy the standard asymptotics and hence its distribution under the null hypothesis does not have a standard distribution.

Consider the process

$$x_i = \rho x_{i-1} + u_i$$

which, under $H_0 : \rho = 1$, generates the following random walk process:

$$x_i = u_i + u_{i-1} + \cdots + u_0 \text{ with } u_0 = 0 \text{ and } u_i \sim i.i.d. \left(0, \sigma^2\right).$$

Then

$$x_i^2 = (x_{i-1} + u_i)^2 = x_{i-1}^2 + u_i^2 + 2x_{i-1}u_i,$$

which implies

$$x_{i-1}u_i = \frac{1}{2}\left(x_i^2 - x_{i-1}^2 - u_i^2\right),$$

hence

$$\sum_{i=1}^{n} x_{i-1}u_i = \frac{1}{2}\left(x_n^2 - x_0^2\right) - \frac{1}{2}\sum_{i=1}^{n}u_i^2;$$

it follows that for $x_0 = 0$

$$\frac{1}{n}\sum_{i=1}^{n} x_{i-1}u_i = \left(\frac{1}{2}\right)\left(\frac{1}{n}\right)x_n^2 - \left(\frac{1}{2}\right)\left(\frac{1}{n}\right)\sum_{i=1}^{n}u_i^2.$$

Dividing each term by σ^2 yields

$$\left(\frac{1}{n\sigma^2}\right)\sum_{i=1}^{n} x_{i-1}u_i = \left(\frac{1}{2}\right)\left(\frac{x_n}{\sigma\sqrt{n}}\right)^2 - \left(\frac{1}{2\sigma^2}\right)\left(\frac{1}{n}\right)\sum_{i=1}^{n}u_i^2$$

$$= \frac{1}{2}\left[\left(\frac{\sqrt{n}}{n}\sum_{i=1}^{n}\frac{u_i}{\sigma}\right)^2 - \frac{1}{\sigma^2}\frac{1}{n}\sum_{i=1}^{n}u_i^2\right].$$

By the central limit theorem,

$$\frac{\sqrt{n}}{n}\sum_{i=1}^{n}\frac{u_i}{\sigma}$$

is distributed as a $N(0, 1)$ when $n \to \infty$. Hence, $(\frac{x_n}{\sigma\sqrt{n}})^2$ converges in distribution to a χ^2 with one degree of freedom (χ_1^2). $\sum_{i=1}^{n}u_i^2$ is the sum of n i.i.d. random variables, each with mean σ^2 and, by the law of large numbers,

$$\frac{1}{n}\sum_{i=1}^{n}u_i^2 \to \sigma^2.$$

In this chapter, we use the notation "$\to$" instead of "$\to$ in P^θ -distribution." Then, we have

$$\frac{1}{(n\sigma^2)}\sum_{i=1}^{n} x_{i-1}u_i \to \frac{1}{2}(X - 1)$$

with $X \sim \chi_1^2$. The OLS estimator of ρ satisfies

$$\widehat{\rho} - 1 = \frac{\sum_{i=1}^{n} x_{i-1}u_i}{\sum_{i=1}^{n} x_{i-1}^2}.$$

Consider the denominator of

$$n\left(\widehat{\rho}-1\right)=\frac{\frac{1}{n}\sum_{i=1}^{n}x_{i-1}u_{i}}{\frac{1}{n^{2}}\sum_{i=1}^{n}x_{i-1}^{2}}.$$

We will show later that $x_{i-1}\sim N\left(0,\sigma^{2}\left(i-1\right)\right)$ and hence

$$E\left(x_{i-1}^{2}\right)=\sigma^{2}\left(i-1\right).$$

Consider now

$$E\left[\sum_{i=1}^{n}x_{i-1}^{2}\right]=\sigma^{2}\sum_{i=1}^{n}(i-1)=\sigma^{2}\left(n-1\right)\frac{n}{2}.$$

In order to construct a random variable which has a limiting distribution, we see that $\sum_{i=1}^{n}x_{i-1}^{2}$ must be divided by n^{2}.

In summary, if the true process is a random walk, the difference between the OLS estimator of ρ and its true value, namely $(\widehat{\rho}_{n}-1)$, must be multiplied by n instead of $\sqrt{n}$ to obtain a variable with a useful asymptotic distribution. Moreover, this distribution is not the usual normal distribution, but the ratio of two distributions, where the numerator is a χ_{1}^{2} and the denominator is a nonstandard distribution.

We saw above that the asymptotic results derived from nonstationary processes do not follow directly from the central limit theorem. However, we can obtain these results from its functional generalization. The mathematical tools necessary for a rigorous presentation are relatively difficult, thus we adopt here an exposition that is very intuitive and not too technical.

Let $(e_{i})_{i=1,\dots,n}$ be a sequence of i.i.d. centered random variables with variance σ^{2}. Denote, for all $t\in[0,1]$,

$$S_{n}(t)=\begin{vmatrix} 0 & \text{if } 0\le t<\frac{1}{n} \\ \frac{e_{1}+\cdots+e_{i}}{\sigma\sqrt{n}} & \text{if } \frac{i}{n}\le t<\frac{i+1}{n} \\ \frac{e_{1}+\cdots+e_{n}}{\sigma\sqrt{n}} & \text{if } t=1. \end{vmatrix}$$

This function from $[0,1]$ to $\mathbb{R}$ is a step function and is random because it depends on e_{i}. It is actually the path of a random process in continuous time. Consider another random function $W(t)$ ($t\in[0,1]$ and $W(t)\in\mathbb{R}$), called *Wiener process* (or *Brownian motion*). This random process is characterized by the following properties: $W(0)=0$ and for all $t_{1},\dots,t_{k}$, the differences $W_{t_{j}}-W_{t_{j-1}}$ are independent and normally distributed with mean zero and variance $|t_{j}-t_{j-1}|$.

In contrast to $S_{n}(t)$, $W(t)$ is a continuous function and in particular, $W(t)\sim N(0,t)$. $W(t)$ is the continuous time generalization of the random walk. An important theorem of probability calculus states that the random function $S_{n}(t)$ converges in distribution to $W(t)$. This theorem is a form of Donsker's theorem and is called *functional central limit theorem*. We do not verify this result.

Note for instance that if t is fixed to a specific value t_0, we have

$$S_n(t_0) = \frac{1}{\sigma\sqrt{n}}\sum_{i=1}^{[nt_0]}e_i \simeq \sqrt{t_0}\frac{1}{\sigma\sqrt{[nt_0]}}\sum_{i=1}^{[nt_0]}e_i$$
$$\to N(0, t_0)$$

and on the other hand

$$W(t_0) \sim N(0, t_0)$$

because, as $n \to \infty$, $[nt_0] \to nt_0$ and $[nt_0]$ is the integer part of nt_0, i.e., the largest integer smaller than or equal to nt_0. However, the theorem is much stronger than this because it actually states that for all transformations φ of S_n, we have

$$E(\varphi(S_n)) \to E(\varphi(W))$$

(φ must satisfy some regularity assumptions).

Finally, it can be shown that if H is a (continuous) transformation of S_n, $H(S_n)$ converges in distribution to $H(W)$ (*Continuous mapping theorem, invariance principle*, or *Measure preserving theorem*).

As an example, we can take for H the \sup" function. Then, we have

$$\sup_t S_n(t) \to \sup_t W(t).$$

The distribution of $\sup_t W(t)$ is known and gives the asymptotic distribution of the largest of the normalized partial sums

$$\left(\frac{e_1}{\sigma\sqrt{n}}, \frac{e_1 + e_2}{\sigma\sqrt{n}}, \ldots\right).$$

Hence, we have the limiting distribution of $\max_{i<n} S_i$ (with appropriate normalization) if we know the distribution of $\sup_t W(t)$. A technique to determine the latter distribution is to calculate the limiting distribution of $\max_{i<n} S_i$ in each special case.

Example 13.2 *(Unit root process)   Let*

$$x_i = x_{i-1} + u_i, \quad u_i \sim i.i.d. \left(0, \sigma^2\right).$$

We are looking for the distribution of $\sum_{i=1}^n x_i$ appropriately multiplied by a term of the form n^α. Note that

$$\int_0^1 S_n(t)dt = \sum_{i=1}^n \frac{1}{n}\left(\frac{u_1 + \cdots + u_i}{\sigma\sqrt{n}}\right) = \frac{1}{\sigma n^{\frac{3}{2}}}\sum_{i=1}^n x_i.$$

By the functional central limit theorem and continuous mapping theorem, we have

$$\int_0^1 S_n(t)dt \to \int_0^1 W(t)dt$$

and hence

$$n^{-\frac{3}{2}} \sum_{i=1}^n x_i \to \sigma \int_0^1 W(t)dt.$$

The expression $\int_0^1 W(t)dt$ represents a scalar random variable that can be shown to be distributed as a $N(0, \frac{1}{3})$. However, we can directly show this result in the following manner

$$\begin{aligned}
n^{-\frac{3}{2}} \sum_{i=1}^n x_{i-1} &= n^{-\frac{3}{2}} [u_1 + (u_1 + u_2) + (u_1 + u_2 + u_3) + \cdots \\
&\quad + (u_1 + u_2 + \cdots + u_{n-1})] \\
&= n^{-\frac{3}{2}} [(n-1)u_1 + (n-2)u_2 + (n-3)u_3 + \cdots \\
&\quad + [n - (n-1)]u_{i-1}] \\
&= n^{-\frac{3}{2}} \sum_{i=1}^n (n-i)u_i \\
&= n^{-\frac{1}{2}} \sum_{i=1}^n u_i - n^{-\frac{3}{2}} \sum_{i=1}^n i u_i \\
&= \sum_{i=1}^n \left(n^{-\frac{1}{2}} - n^{-\frac{3}{2}}i\right) u_i.
\end{aligned} \tag{13.2}$$

We have here a weighted sum of random variables but where the weights are not equal to the usual value $\frac{1}{\sqrt{n}}$. Hence, we need to use an extension of the central limit theorem (Lindeberg theorem). A necessary condition for the asymptotic normality is that the variance of the sum converges, i.e.,

$$\begin{aligned}
\sigma^2 \sum_{i=1}^n \left(n^{-\frac{1}{2}} - n^{-\frac{3}{2}}i\right)^2 \\
= \sigma^2 \left(n^{-1}n + n^{-3}\sum_{i=1}^n i^2 - 2n^{-2}\sum_{i=1}^n i\right) \\
\to \sigma^2 \left[1 + \frac{1}{3} - 2\frac{1}{2}\right] = \frac{\sigma^2}{3}
\end{aligned}$$

because

$$\frac{1}{n^{\nu+1}} \sum_{i=1}^{n} i^{\nu} \rightarrow \frac{1}{\nu+1}.$$

It follows that $n^{-3/2} \sum_{i=1}^{n} x_{i-1}$ is asymptotically normal with mean zero and variance equal to $\frac{\sigma^2}{3}$. The integral $\sigma \int_0^1 W(t) dt$ describes a random variable with distribution $N(0, \frac{\sigma^2}{3})$. Hence, if x_i is a random walk without drift, $n^{-1} \sum_{i=1}^{n} x_i$ diverges but $n^{-3/2} \sum_{i=1}^{n} x_{i-1}$ converges to a random variable whose distribution can be described as the integral of a Brownian motion with variance σ^2. It follows from (13.2) that the asymptotic distribution of $n^{-3/2} \sum_{i=1}^{n} i u_i$ as a function of a Brownian motion is

$$n^{-3/2} \sum_{i=1}^{n} i u_i = n^{-1/2} \sum_{i=1}^{n} u_i - n^{-3/2} \sum_{i=1}^{n} x_{i-1}$$

$$\rightarrow \sigma W(1) - \sigma \int_0^1 W(t) dt \qquad \qquad \square$$

Example 13.3   *The same argument can be used to describe the asymptotic distribution of the sum of the square of a random walk. The statistic $S_n(t)$ defined by*

$$S_n(t) = n [X_n(t)]^2$$

is described by

$$X_n(t) = \begin{vmatrix} 0 & for\ 0 \leq t < \frac{1}{n} \\ x_1^2/n & for\ \frac{1}{n} \leq t < \frac{2}{n} \\ x_2^2/n & for\ \frac{2}{n} \leq t < \frac{3}{n} \\ \vdots & \\ x_n^2/n & for\ t = 1 \end{vmatrix}.$$

and

$$\int_0^1 S_n(t) dt = \frac{x_1^2}{n^2} + \frac{x_2^2}{n^2} + \cdots + \frac{x_{n-1}^2}{n^2};$$

hence

$$n^{-2} \sum_{i=1}^{n} x_{i-1}^2 \rightarrow \sigma^2 \int_0^1 [W(t)]^2 dt.$$

Two useful results are

$$n^{-5/2} \sum_{i=1}^{n} i x_{i-1} = n^{-3/2} \sum_{i=1}^{n} \left(\frac{i}{n}\right) x_{i-1}$$

$$\rightarrow \sigma \int_0^1 t W(t) dt$$

for $t = \frac{i}{n}$ and

$$n^{-3} \sum_{i=1}^{n} i x_{i-1}^2 = n^{-2} \sum_{i=1}^{n} \frac{i}{n} x_{i-1}^2 \rightarrow \sigma^2 \int_0^1 t [W(t)]^2 dt. \qquad \square$$

We summarize the previous results and some others that can be proven in a similar way in the following proposition.

Proposition 13.3 *Suppose that x_i follows a random walk without drift*

$$x_i = x_{i-1} + u_i \text{ where } x_0 = 0 \text{ and } \{u_i\} \sim i.i.d. \left(0, \sigma^2\right).$$

Then

$$n^{-\frac{1}{2}} \sum_{i=1}^{n} u_i \rightarrow \sigma W(1) \sim N\left(0, \sigma^2\right),$$

$$n^{-1} \sum_{i=1}^{n} x_{i-1} u_i \rightarrow \left(\frac{1}{2}\right) \sigma^2 \left\{[W(1)]^2 - 1\right\},$$

$$n^{-\frac{3}{2}} \sum_{i=1}^{n} i u_i \rightarrow \sigma W(1) - \sigma \int_0^1 W(t) dt,$$

$$n^{-\frac{3}{2}} \sum_{i=1}^{n} x_{i-1} \rightarrow \sigma \int_0^1 W(t) dt,$$

$$n^{-2} \sum_{i=1}^{n} x_{i-1}^2 \rightarrow \sigma^2 \int_0^1 [W(t)]^2 dt,$$

$$n^{-\frac{5}{2}} \sum_{i=1}^{n} i x_{i-1} \rightarrow \sigma \int_0^1 t W(t) dt,$$

$$n^{-3} \sum_{i=1}^{n} i x_{i-1}^2 \rightarrow \sigma^2 \int_0^1 t [W(t)]^2 dt,$$

$$n^{-(v+1)} \sum_{i=1}^{n} i^v \rightarrow \frac{1}{v+1} \text{ for } v = 0, 1, \ldots \qquad \blacksquare$$

The asymptotic distributions of the proposition are all written as functions of a standard Brownian motion denoted $W(t)$. The proposition can be rewritten similarly in the multivariate case by setting $B(1) \neq 0$ (see Hamilton (1994)). We now use the results of this proposition in the following examples, in order to calculate the asymptotic distributions in simple regressions involving unit roots.

Example 13.4 *(Random walk with drift)   Consider the model*

$$x_i = \alpha + \rho x_{i-1} + u_i, \quad i = 1, \ldots, n$$

in which the true values are $\alpha = 0$ and $\rho = 1$. The OLS estimators of $(\alpha, \rho)'$ are

$$\begin{bmatrix} \widehat{\alpha}_n \\ \widehat{\rho}_n \end{bmatrix} = \begin{bmatrix} n & \sum x_{i-1} \\ \sum x_{i-1} & \sum x_{i-1}^2 \end{bmatrix}^{-1} \begin{bmatrix} \sum x_i \\ \sum x_{i-1} x_i \end{bmatrix}$$

or

$$\begin{bmatrix} \widehat{\alpha}_n - 0 \\ \widehat{\rho}_n - 1 \end{bmatrix} = \begin{bmatrix} n & \sum x_{i-1} \\ \sum x_{i-1} & \sum x_{i-1}^2 \end{bmatrix}^{-1} \begin{bmatrix} \sum u_i \\ \sum x_{i-1} u_i \end{bmatrix}.$$

$\widehat{\alpha}_n$ and $\widehat{\rho}_n$ have different rates of convergence. To describe their limiting distributions, we consider

$$\begin{pmatrix} n^{\frac{1}{2}} & 0 \\ 0 & n \end{pmatrix} \begin{bmatrix} \widehat{\alpha}_n \\ \widehat{\rho}_n - 1 \end{bmatrix} = \left\{ \begin{pmatrix} n^{\frac{1}{2}} & 0 \\ 0 & n \end{pmatrix}^{-1} \begin{pmatrix} n & \sum x_{i-1} \\ \sum x_{i-1} & \sum x_{i-1}^2 \end{pmatrix} \begin{pmatrix} n^{\frac{1}{2}} & 0 \\ 0 & n \end{pmatrix}^{-1} \right\}^{-1}$$

$$\times \left\{ \begin{pmatrix} n^{\frac{1}{2}} & 0 \\ 0 & n \end{pmatrix}^{-1} \begin{pmatrix} \sum u_i \\ \sum x_{i-1} u_i \end{pmatrix} \right\}$$

hence

$$\begin{pmatrix} n^{\frac{1}{2}} \widehat{\alpha}_n \\ n (\widehat{\rho}_n - 1) \end{pmatrix} = \begin{bmatrix} 1 & n^{-\frac{3}{2}} \sum x_{i-1} \\ n^{-\frac{3}{2}} \sum x_{i-1} & n^{-2} \sum x_{i-1}^2 \end{bmatrix}^{-1} \begin{bmatrix} n^{-\frac{1}{2}} \sum u_i \\ n^{-1} \sum x_{i-1} u_i \end{bmatrix}.$$

Note that

$$\begin{bmatrix} 1 & n^{-\frac{3}{2}} \sum x_{i-1} \\ n^{-\frac{3}{2}} \sum x_{i-1} & n^{-2} \sum x_{i-1}^2 \end{bmatrix} \rightarrow \begin{bmatrix} 1 & \sigma \int W(t) dt \\ \sigma \int W(t) dt & \sigma^2 \int [W(t)]^2 dt \end{bmatrix}$$

$$= \begin{bmatrix} 1 & 0 \\ 0 & \sigma \end{bmatrix} \begin{bmatrix} 1 & \int W(t) dt \\ \int W(t) dt & \int [W(t)]^2 dt \end{bmatrix} \begin{bmatrix} 1 & 0 \\ 0 & \sigma \end{bmatrix}$$

where the integral sign denotes an integration from 0 to 1 with respect to t. Similarly,

$$\begin{bmatrix} n^{-\frac{1}{2}} \sum u_i \\ n^{-1} \sum x_{i-1} u_i \end{bmatrix} \to \begin{bmatrix} \sigma W(1) \\ \frac{1}{2}\sigma^2 \{[W(1)]^2 - 1\} \end{bmatrix}$$

$$= \sigma \begin{bmatrix} 1 & 0 \\ 0 & \sigma \end{bmatrix} \times \begin{bmatrix} W(1) \\ \frac{1}{2}\{[W(1)]^2 - 1\} \end{bmatrix}.$$

Hence, we have

$$\begin{bmatrix} n^{\frac{1}{2}}\widehat{\alpha}_n \\ n(\widehat{\rho}_n - 1) \end{bmatrix} \to \sigma \begin{bmatrix} 1 & 0 \\ 0 & \sigma \end{bmatrix}^{-1} \begin{bmatrix} 1 & \int W(t)dt \\ \int W(t)dt & \int [W(t)]^2\, dt \end{bmatrix}^{-1}$$

$$\times \begin{bmatrix} 1 & 0 \\ 0 & \sigma \end{bmatrix}^{-1} \begin{bmatrix} 1 & 0 \\ 0 & \sigma \end{bmatrix} \begin{bmatrix} W(1) \\ \frac{1}{2}\{[W(1)]^2 - 1\} \end{bmatrix}$$

$$= \begin{bmatrix} \sigma & 0 \\ 0 & 1 \end{bmatrix} \begin{bmatrix} 1 & \int W(t)dt \\ \int W(t)dt & \int [W(t)]^2\, dt \end{bmatrix}^{-1} \begin{bmatrix} W(1) \\ \frac{1}{2}\{[W(1)]^2 - 1\} \end{bmatrix}.$$

Moreover

$$\begin{bmatrix} 1 & \int W(t)dt \\ \int W(t)dt & \int [W(t)]^2\, dt \end{bmatrix}^{-1}$$

$$= \frac{1}{\int [W(t)]^2\, dt - [\int W(t)dt]^2} \begin{bmatrix} \int [W(t)]^2\, dt & -\int W(t)dt \\ -\int W(t)dt & 1 \end{bmatrix}$$

hence

$$n(\widehat{\rho}_n - 1) \to \frac{\frac{1}{2}\{[W(1)]^2 - 1\} - W(1)\int W(t)dt}{\int [W(t)]^2\, dt - [\int W(t)dt]^2}.$$

Dickey and Fuller (1981) proposed an alternative test based on the Student's t-statistic under the null hypothesis of a unit root

$$t_n = \frac{\widehat{\rho}_n - 1}{\widehat{\sigma}_{\widehat{\rho}_n}}$$

with

$$\widehat{\sigma}^2_{\widehat{\rho}_n} = s_n^2 \begin{bmatrix} 0 & 1 \end{bmatrix} \begin{bmatrix} n & \sum x_{i-1} \\ \sum x_{i-1} & \sum x_{i-1}^2 \end{bmatrix}^{-1} \begin{bmatrix} 0 \\ 1 \end{bmatrix}$$

and

$$s_n^2 = (n - 2)^{-1} \sum_{i=1}^{n} (x_i - \widehat{\alpha}_n - \widehat{\rho}_n x_{i-1})^2 .$$

Hence

$$n^2 \widehat{\sigma}_{\widehat{\rho}_n}^2 = s_n^2 \begin{bmatrix} 0 & n \end{bmatrix} \begin{bmatrix} n & \sum x_{i-1} \\ \sum x_{i-1} & \sum x_{i-1}^2 \end{bmatrix}^{-1} \begin{bmatrix} 0 \\ n \end{bmatrix}$$

$$= s_n^2 \begin{bmatrix} 0 & 1 \end{bmatrix} \begin{bmatrix} n^{\frac{1}{2}} & 0 \\ 0 & n \end{bmatrix} \begin{bmatrix} n & \sum x_{i-1} \\ \sum x_{i-1} & \sum x_{i-1}^2 \end{bmatrix}^{-1} \begin{bmatrix} n^{\frac{1}{2}} & 0 \\ 0 & n \end{bmatrix} \begin{bmatrix} 0 \\ 1 \end{bmatrix} .$$

From

$$\begin{bmatrix} n^{\frac{1}{2}} & 0 \\ 0 & n \end{bmatrix} \begin{bmatrix} n & \sum x_{i-1} \\ \sum x_{i-1} & \sum x_{i-1}^2 \end{bmatrix}^{-1} \begin{bmatrix} n^{\frac{1}{2}} & 0 \\ 0 & n \end{bmatrix}$$

$$= \left\{ \begin{bmatrix} n^{\frac{1}{2}} & 0 \\ 0 & n \end{bmatrix}^{-1} \begin{bmatrix} n & \sum x_{i-1} \\ \sum x_{i-1} & \sum x_{i-1}^2 \end{bmatrix} \begin{bmatrix} n^{\frac{1}{2}} & 0 \\ 0 & n \end{bmatrix}^{-1} \right\}^{-1}$$

$$= \begin{bmatrix} 1 & n^{-\frac{3}{2}} \sum x_{i-1} \\ n^{-\frac{3}{2}} \sum x_{i-1} & n^{-2} \sum x_{i-1}^2 \end{bmatrix}^{-1}$$

$$\rightarrow \begin{bmatrix} 1 & 0 \\ 0 & \sigma \end{bmatrix}^{-1} \begin{bmatrix} 1 & \int W(t)dt \\ \int W(t)dt & \int [W(t)]^2 \, dt \end{bmatrix}^{-1} \begin{bmatrix} 1 & 0 \\ 0 & \sigma \end{bmatrix}^{-1} ,$$

it follows that

$$n^2 \widehat{\sigma}_{\widehat{\rho}_n} \rightarrow s_n^2 \begin{bmatrix} 0 & \sigma^{-1} \end{bmatrix} \begin{bmatrix} 1 & \int W(t)dt \\ \int W(t)dt & \int [W(t)]^2 \, dt \end{bmatrix}^{-1} \begin{bmatrix} 0 \\ \sigma^{-1} \end{bmatrix} .$$

It is easy to show that $s_n^2 \rightarrow \sigma^2$, therefore

$$n^2 \widehat{\sigma}_{\widehat{\rho}_n}^2 \rightarrow \begin{bmatrix} 0 & 1 \end{bmatrix} \begin{bmatrix} 1 & \int W(t)dt \\ \int W(t)dt & \int [W(t)]^2 \, dt \end{bmatrix}^{-1} \begin{bmatrix} 0 \\ 1 \end{bmatrix}$$

$$= \frac{1}{\int [W(t)]^2 \, dt - \left[\int W(t)dt \right]^2} .$$

In summary, we have

$$t_n = \frac{n\left(\widehat{\rho}_n - 1\right)}{\left\{n^2 \widehat{\sigma}_{\widehat{\rho}_n}^2\right\}^{\frac{1}{2}}} \to n\left(\widehat{\rho}_n - 1\right) \times \left\{\int [W(t)]^2 \, dt - \left[\int W(t) dt\right]^2\right\}^{\frac{1}{2}}$$

$$\to \frac{\frac{1}{2}\left\{[W(1)]^2 - 1\right\} - W(1) \int W(t) dt}{\left\{\int [W(t)]^2 \, dt - [\int W(t) dt]^2\right\}^{\frac{1}{2}}}.$$

This distribution, sometimes called Dickey-Fuller distribution, has been tab-ulated by Dickey and Fuller. Tables can be constructed using simulations of functions of a Wiener process. In stationary models, $n^{1/2}$ times the estima-tion error converges in distribution to a random variable and this variable follows a normal distribution with mean zero. In random walk models, the last expression reveals that n (instead of $\sqrt{n}$) times the estimation error con-verges in distribution to a random variable and that this one has a nonstandard distribution. □

Example 13.5 *(continued)   Consider the process*

$$x_i = \alpha + x_{i-1} + u_i$$
$$= x_0 + \alpha i + (u_1 + u_2 + \cdots + u_i)$$
$$= x_0 + \alpha i + \xi_i$$

where α is not restricted to be zero, $\xi_i = u_1 + u_2 + \cdots + u_i$, $i = 1, \ldots, n$ and $\xi_0 = 0$. Consider

$$\sum_{i=1}^{n} x_{i-1} = \sum_{i=1}^{n} [x_0 + \alpha(i-1) + \xi_{i-1}].$$

The first term nx_0 is constant if divided by n. The second term $\sum \alpha(i-1)$ must be divided by n^2 in order to converge

$$n^{-2} \sum_{i=1}^{n} \alpha(i-1) \to \frac{\alpha}{2}.$$

The third term converges if divided by $n^{\frac{3}{2}}$

$$n^{-\frac{3}{2}} \sum_{i=1}^{n} \xi_{i-1} \to \sigma \int_0^1 W(t) dt.$$

Hence in

$$\sum_{i=1}^{n} x_{i-1} = \sum_{i=1}^{n} x_0 + \sum_{i=1}^{n} \alpha(i-1) + \sum_{i=1}^{n} \xi_{i-1},$$

the deterministic trend $\alpha (i - 1)$ *dominates the other two components:*

$$n^{-2} \sum_{i=1}^{n} x_{i-1} = n^{-1}x_0 + n^{-2} \sum_{i=1}^{n} \alpha (i - 1) + n^{-\frac{1}{2}} \left\{ n^{-\frac{3}{2}} \sum_{i=1}^{n} \xi_{i-1} \right\}$$

$$\rightarrow 0 + \frac{\alpha}{2} + 0.$$

Similarly, we have

$$\sum_{i=1}^{n} x_{i-1}^2 = \sum_{i=1}^{n} [x_0 + \alpha (i - 1) + \xi_{i-1}]^2$$

$$= \sum_{i=1}^{n} x_0^2 + \sum_{i=1}^{n} \alpha^2 (i - 1)^2 + \sum_{i=1}^{n} \xi_{i-1}^2 + \sum_{i=1}^{n} 2x_0\alpha (i - 1)$$

$$+ \sum_{i=1}^{n} 2x_0\xi_{i-1} + \sum_{i=1}^{n} 2\alpha (i - 1) \xi_{i-1}.$$

When dividing by n^3, the only term that does not vanish asymptotically is $\alpha^2 (i - 1)^2$:

$$n^{-3} \sum_{i=1}^{n} x_{i-1}^2 \rightarrow \frac{\alpha^2}{3}.$$

Finally, we observe that

$$\sum_{i=1}^{n} x_{i-1}u_i = \sum_{i=1}^{n} [x_0 + \alpha (i - 1) + \xi_{i-1}] u_i$$

$$= x_0 \sum_{i=1}^{n} u_i + \sum_{i=1}^{n} \alpha (i - 1) u_i + \sum_{i=1}^{n} \xi_{i-1}u_i$$

hence

$$n^{-\frac{3}{2}} \sum_{i=1}^{n} x_{i-1}u_i \rightarrow n^{-\frac{3}{2}} \sum_{i=1}^{n} \alpha (i - 1) u_i;$$

Sims, Stock, and Watson (1990) propose to use the scaling matrix:

$$\begin{bmatrix} n^{\frac{1}{2}} & 0 \\ 0 & n^{\frac{3}{2}} \end{bmatrix} \begin{pmatrix} \widehat{\alpha}_n - \alpha \\ \widehat{\rho}_n - 1 \end{pmatrix} = \left\{ \begin{bmatrix} n^{-\frac{1}{2}} & 0 \\ 0 & n^{-\frac{3}{2}} \end{bmatrix} \begin{bmatrix} n & \sum x_{i-1} \\ \sum x_{i-1} & \sum x_{i-1}^2 \end{bmatrix} \begin{bmatrix} n^{-\frac{1}{2}} & 0 \\ 0 & n^{-\frac{3}{2}} \end{bmatrix} \right\}^{-1}$$

$$\times \left\{ \begin{pmatrix} n^{-\frac{1}{2}} & 0 \\ 0 & n^{-\frac{3}{2}} \end{pmatrix} \begin{pmatrix} \sum u_i \\ \sum x_{i-1}u_i \end{pmatrix} \right\}$$

or

$$
\begin{bmatrix} n^{\frac{1}{2}} (\widehat{\alpha}_n - \alpha) \\ n^{\frac{3}{2}} (\widehat{\rho}_n - 1) \end{bmatrix} = \begin{bmatrix} 1 & n^{-2} \sum x_{i-1} \\ n^{-2} \sum x_{i-1} & n^{-3} \sum x_{i-1}^2 \end{bmatrix}^{-1} \begin{bmatrix} n^{-\frac{1}{2}} \sum u_i \\ n^{-\frac{3}{2}} \sum x_{i-1} u_i \end{bmatrix}.
$$

Now

$$
\begin{bmatrix} 1 & n^{-2} \sum x_{i-1} \\ n^{-2} \sum x_{i-1} & n^{-3} \sum x_{i-1}^2 \end{bmatrix} \rightarrow \begin{bmatrix} 1 & \frac{\alpha}{2} \\ \frac{\alpha}{2} & \frac{\alpha^2}{3} \end{bmatrix}
$$

and

$$
\begin{bmatrix} n^{-\frac{1}{2}} \sum u_i \\ n^{-\frac{3}{2}} \sum x_{i-1} u_i \end{bmatrix} \rightarrow \begin{bmatrix} n^{-\frac{1}{2}} \sum u_i \\ n^{-\frac{3}{2}} \sum \alpha (i-1) u_i \end{bmatrix}
$$

$$
\rightarrow N \left[\begin{pmatrix} 0 \\ 0 \end{pmatrix}, \sigma^2 \begin{pmatrix} 1 & \frac{\alpha}{2} \\ \frac{\alpha}{2} & \frac{\alpha^2}{3} \end{pmatrix} = \sigma^2 Q \right].
$$

with $Q = \begin{bmatrix} 1 & \frac{\alpha}{2} \\ \frac{\alpha}{2} & \frac{\alpha^2}{3} \end{bmatrix}$, *hence*

$$
\begin{bmatrix} n^{\frac{1}{2}} (\widehat{\alpha}_n - \alpha) \\ n^{\frac{3}{2}} (\widehat{\rho}_n - 1) \end{bmatrix} \rightarrow N \left[0, \, Q^{-1} \sigma^2 Q Q^{-1} \right] = N \left[0, \, \sigma^2 Q^{-1} \right].
$$

The main conclusion we draw from this example is that the asymptotic distributions of the OLS of α and ρ drastically differ whether there is a drift or not. For $\alpha \neq 0$, their distributions are normal, whereas for $\alpha = 0$, their distributions are some functions of a Wiener process. □

Example 13.6 *(random walk with drift and purely determinist component) Consider the process generated by*

$$
\begin{aligned}
x_i &= \alpha + \rho x_{i-1} + \delta i + u_i \\
&= (1 - \rho) \alpha + \rho [x_{i-1} - \alpha (i-1)] + (\delta + \rho \alpha) i + u_i \\
&= \alpha^* + \rho^* \xi_{i-1} + \delta^* i + u_i
\end{aligned}
$$

for $i = 1, \ldots, n$, with

$$
\alpha^* = (1 - \rho) \alpha, \quad \rho^* = \rho, \quad \delta^* = \delta + \rho \alpha \text{ and } \xi_i = x_i - \alpha i.
$$

The OLS estimators of α^*, ρ^*, and δ^* are

$$
\begin{bmatrix} \widehat{\alpha}_n^* \\ \widehat{\rho}_n^* \\ \widehat{\delta}_n^* \end{bmatrix} = \begin{bmatrix} n & \sum \xi_{i-1} & \sum i \\ \sum \xi_{i-1} & \sum \xi_{i-1}^2 & \sum i\xi_{i-1} \\ \sum i & \sum i\xi_{i-1} & \sum i^2 \end{bmatrix}^{-1} \begin{bmatrix} \sum x_i \\ \sum \xi_{i-1}x_i \\ \sum ix_i \end{bmatrix}.
$$

Under the null hypothesis $H_0 : \rho = 1$ and $\delta = 0$, that is

$$
\alpha = \alpha_0, \ \ \rho = 1 \ and \ \delta = 0, \ \ \alpha^* = 0, \ \ \rho^* = 1 \ and \ \delta^* = \alpha_0,
$$

we have

$$
\begin{bmatrix} \widehat{\alpha}_n^* \\ \widehat{\rho}_n^* - 1 \\ \widehat{\delta}_n^* - \alpha_0 \end{bmatrix} = \begin{bmatrix} n & \sum \xi_{i-1} & \sum i \\ \sum \xi_{i-1} & \sum \xi_{i-1}^2 & \sum i\xi_{i-1} \\ \sum i & \sum i\xi_{i-1} & \sum i^2 \end{bmatrix}^{-1} \begin{bmatrix} \sum u_i \\ \sum \xi_{i-1}u_i \\ \sum iu_i \end{bmatrix}.
$$

As before, we use the scaling matrix $\begin{pmatrix} n^{\frac{1}{2}} & 0 & 0 \\ 0 & n & 0 \\ 0 & 0 & n^{\frac{3}{2}} \end{pmatrix}$,

$$
\begin{bmatrix} n^{\frac{1}{5}} & 0 & 0 \\ 0 & n & 0 \\ 0 & 0 & n^{\frac{3}{2}} \end{bmatrix} \begin{bmatrix} \widehat{\alpha}_n^* \\ \widehat{\rho}_n^* - 1 \\ \widehat{\delta}_n^* - \alpha_0 \end{bmatrix}
$$

$$
= \left\{ \begin{bmatrix} n^{-\frac{1}{2}} & 0 & 0 \\ 0 & n^{-1} & 0 \\ 0 & 0 & n^{-\frac{3}{2}} \end{bmatrix} \begin{bmatrix} n & \sum \xi_{i-1} & \sum i \\ \sum \xi_{i-1} & \sum \xi_{i-1}^2 & \sum i\xi_{i-1} \\ \sum i & \sum i\xi_{i-1} & \sum i^2 \end{bmatrix} \begin{bmatrix} n^{-\frac{1}{2}} & 0 & 0 \\ 0 & n^{-1} & 0 \\ 0 & 0 & n^{-\frac{3}{2}} \end{bmatrix} \right\}^{-1}
$$

$$
\times \left\{ \begin{bmatrix} n^{-\frac{1}{2}} & 0 & 0 \\ 0 & n^{-1} & 0 \\ 0 & 0 & n^{-\frac{3}{2}} \end{bmatrix} \begin{bmatrix} \sum u_i \\ \sum \xi_{i-1}u_i \\ \sum iu_i \end{bmatrix} \right\},
$$

or

$$
\begin{bmatrix} n^{\frac{1}{2}}\widehat{\alpha}_n^* \\ n\left(\widehat{\rho}_n^* - 1\right) \\ n^{\frac{3}{2}}\left(\widehat{\delta}_n^* - \alpha_0\right) \end{bmatrix} = \begin{bmatrix} 1 & n^{-\frac{3}{2}}\sum \xi_{i-1} & n^{-2}\sum i \\ n^{-\frac{3}{2}}\sum \xi_{i-1} & n^{-2}\sum \xi_{i-1}^2 & n^{-\frac{5}{2}}\sum i\xi_i \\ n^{-2}\sum i & n^{-\frac{5}{2}}\sum i\xi_i & n^{-3}\sum i^2 \end{bmatrix}^{-1} \begin{bmatrix} n^{-\frac{1}{2}}\sum u_i \\ n^{-1}\sum \xi_{i-1}u_i \\ n^{-\frac{3}{2}}\sum iu_i \end{bmatrix}
$$

It follows from Proposition 13.1 that the asymptotic distribution is

$$
\begin{bmatrix} n^{\frac{1}{2}}\widehat{\alpha}_n^* \\ n\left(\widehat{\rho}_n^* - 1\right) \\ n^{\frac{3}{2}}\left(\widehat{\delta}_n^* - \alpha_0\right) \end{bmatrix} \rightarrow \begin{bmatrix} 1 & \sigma\int W(t)dt & \frac{1}{2} \\ \sigma\int W(t)dt & \sigma^2\int [W(t)]^2\,dt & \sigma\int tW(t)dt \\ \frac{1}{2} & \sigma\int tW(t)dt & \frac{1}{3} \end{bmatrix}^{-1}
$$

$$
\times \begin{bmatrix} \sigma W(1)\frac{1}{2}\sigma^2\left\{[W(1)]^2 - 1\right\} \\ \sigma W(1) - \int W(t)dt \end{bmatrix}
$$

$$
= \sigma \begin{bmatrix} 1 & 0 & 0 \\ 0 & \sigma & 0 \\ 0 & 0 & 1 \end{bmatrix}^{-1} \begin{bmatrix} 1 & \int W(t)dt & \frac{1}{2} \\ \int W(t)dt & \int [W(t)]^2\,dt & \int tW(t)dt \\ \frac{1}{2} & \int tW(t)dt & \frac{1}{3} \end{bmatrix}
$$

$$
\times \begin{bmatrix} 1 & 0 & 0 \\ 0 & \sigma & 0 \\ 0 & 0 & 1 \end{bmatrix}^{-1} \begin{bmatrix} 1 & 0 & 0 \\ 0 & \sigma & 0 \\ 0 & 0 & 1 \end{bmatrix} \begin{bmatrix} W(1) \\ \frac{1}{2}\left\{[W(1)]^2 - 1\right\} \\ W(1) - \int W(t)dt \end{bmatrix}
$$

$$
= \begin{bmatrix} \sigma & 0 & 0 \\ 0 & 1 & 0 \\ 0 & 0 & \sigma \end{bmatrix} \begin{bmatrix} 1 & \int W(t)dt & \frac{1}{2} \\ \int W(t)dt & \int [W(t)]^2\,dt & \int tW(t)dt \\ \frac{1}{2} & \int tW(t)dt & \frac{1}{3} \end{bmatrix}
$$

$$
\times \begin{bmatrix} W(1) \\ \frac{1}{2}\left\{[W(1)]^2 - 1\right\} \\ W(1) - \int W(t)dt \end{bmatrix}.
$$

Regarding the asymptotic distribution of $\widehat{\sigma}^2_{\widehat{\rho}_n}$:

$$n^2\widehat{\sigma}^2_{\widehat{\rho}_n} = n^2 s_n^2 \begin{bmatrix} 0 & 1 & 0 \end{bmatrix} \begin{bmatrix} n & \sum \xi_{i-1} & \sum i \\ \sum \xi_{i-1} & \sum \xi_{i-1}^2 & \sum i\xi_{i-1} \\ \sum i & \sum i\xi_{i-1} & \sum i^2 \end{bmatrix}^{-1} \begin{bmatrix} 0 \\ 1 \\ 0 \end{bmatrix}$$

$$= s_n^2 \begin{bmatrix} 0 & 1 & 0 \end{bmatrix} \begin{bmatrix} n^{\frac{1}{2}} & 0 & 0 \\ 0 & n & 0 \\ 0 & 0 & n^{\frac{3}{2}} \end{bmatrix} \begin{bmatrix} n & \sum \xi_{i-1} & \sum i \\ \sum \xi_{i-1} & \sum \xi_{i-1}^2 & \sum i\xi_{i-1} \\ \sum i & \sum i\xi_{i-1} & \sum i^2 \end{bmatrix}^{-1}$$

$$\times \begin{bmatrix} n^{\frac{1}{2}} & 0 & 0 \\ 0 & n & 0 \\ 0 & 0 & n^{\frac{3}{2}} \end{bmatrix} \begin{bmatrix} 0 \\ 1 \\ 0 \end{bmatrix}$$

$$= s_n^2 \begin{bmatrix} 0 & 1 & 0 \end{bmatrix} \begin{bmatrix} 1 & n^{-\frac{3}{2}}\sum \xi_{i-1} & n^{-2}\sum i \\ n^{-\frac{3}{2}}\sum \xi_{i-1} & n^{-2}\sum \xi_{i-1}^2 & n^{-\frac{5}{2}}\sum i\xi_{i-1} \\ n^{-2}\sum i & n^{-\frac{5}{2}}\sum i\xi_{i-1} & n^{-3}\sum i^2 \end{bmatrix}^{-1} \begin{bmatrix} 0 \\ 1 \\ 0 \end{bmatrix}$$

$$\to \sigma^2 \begin{bmatrix} 0 & 1 & 0 \end{bmatrix} \begin{bmatrix} 1 & 0 & 0 \\ 0 & \sigma & 0 \\ 0 & 0 & 1 \end{bmatrix}^{-1}$$

$$\times \begin{bmatrix} 1 & \int W(t)dt & \frac{1}{2} \\ \int W(t)dt & \int [W(t)]^2 \, dt & \int tW(t)dt \\ \frac{1}{2} & \int tW(t)dt & \frac{1}{3} \end{bmatrix}^{-1} \begin{bmatrix} 1 & 0 & 0 \\ 0 & \sigma & 0 \\ 0 & 0 & 1 \end{bmatrix}^{-1} \begin{bmatrix} 0 \\ 1 \\ 0 \end{bmatrix}$$

$$= \begin{bmatrix} 0 & 1 & 0 \end{bmatrix} \begin{bmatrix} 1 & \int W(t)dt & \frac{1}{2} \\ \int W(t)dt & \int [W(t)]^2 \, dt & \int tW(t)dt \\ \frac{1}{2} & \int tW(t)dt & \frac{1}{3} \end{bmatrix}^{-1} \begin{bmatrix} 0 \\ 1 \\ 0 \end{bmatrix} \equiv Q$$

hence

$$t_n = \frac{n\,(\widehat{\rho}_n - 1)}{\left(n^2\widehat{\sigma}^2_{\widehat{\rho}_n}\right)^{\frac{1}{2}}} \to \frac{n\,(\widehat{\rho}_n - 1)}{\sqrt{Q}}.$$

Here and in the previous examples, the test statistics have been presented in the absence of autocorrelation of the residuals. These results can be generalized to the case where the residuals are serially correlated. Two approaches are possible: the first approach due to Phillips and Perron estimates the regression the same way as explained above but modify the test statistics in order to take *into account the correlation of the residuals and the potential heteroskedasticity. The second approach proposed by Dickey and Fuller consists in adding lags of x_i as explanatory variables in the regression.* □

13.3   Analysis of Cointegration and Error Correction Mechanism

The intuitive idea of the study of cointegration is to find out whether some linear transformations of a vector nonstationary process are stationary in the sense of their marginal distributions. The starting point of this construction is a $I(1)$ vector process x_i. We do not consider here the case where x_i is integrated to a higher order.

Definition 13.2   *Let (x_i), $x_i \in \mathbb{R}^m$ be a process with fixed initial conditions x_0 and x_i is a $I(1)$ process with drift (i.e. $\Delta x_i - E(\Delta x_i) \sim I(0)$). We call cointegrating vector any vector $C \in \mathbb{R}^m$ such that $C'x_i$ is $I(0)$. More generally, a $m \times r$ matrix C is called cointegrating matrix if $C'x_i \sim I(0)$ (as vectors of $\mathbb{R}^r$).* ∎

In general, we consider only full rank matrices, which eliminates vectors that can be expressed as linear combinations of other vectors.

Example 13.7   *Let the model*

$$y_i = \alpha z_{i-1} + u_i$$

$$z_i = z_{i-1} + v_i$$

where (u_i, v_i) is a weak white noise and the initial conditions are $(z_0, y_0) = (0, 0)$. Then y_i and z_i are nonstationary. We verify that $x_i = (y_i, z_i)'$ is $I(1)$:

$$y_i - y_{i-1} = \alpha(z_{i-1} - z_{i-2}) + u_i - u_{i-1}$$

$$= \alpha v_{i-1} + u_i - u_{i-1}$$

and

$$z_i - z_{i-1} = v_i;$$

$u_i - u_{i-1}$ *and* v_i *are stationary, which means that* Δy_i *et* Δz_i *are stationary and satisfy the conditions of Definition 13.1. Moreover*

$$y_i - \alpha z_i = u_i - \alpha v_i$$

is also stationary and a cointegrating vector is $c = \binom{1}{-\alpha}$. Note that $\alpha z_i \neq E(y_i \mid z_i)$, it is not a regression. □

More generally, if $c_1, \dots, c_r$ are linearly independent cointegrating vectors, then $C'x_i$ is stationary where $C = (c_1, \dots, c_r)$ is of dimension $m \times r$ and x_i is of dimension $m \times 1$.

Note that since we restrict ourselves to full rank matrices C, we can not have $r = m$, because the stationarity of $C'x_i$ would be equivalent to that of x_i, which is excluded by assumption. Moreover, note that C is not unique. If C is a cointegrating matrix, so is CF (where F is a $r \times r$ invertible matrix) because $F'C'x_i$ is stationary. If we wish to uniquely identify C, we can always write

$$C = \begin{pmatrix} I_r \\ -\Gamma \end{pmatrix}.$$

This representation will be discussed later. It is not necessary for the developments that follow.

13.3.1   Cointegration and MA Representation

Let (x_i) be the process satisfying

$$\Delta x_i - \mu \sim I(0) \text{ with } \mu = E(\Delta x_i)$$

and

$$\Delta x_i - \mu = u_i = B(L)\varepsilon_i.$$

Then, we have the following proposition.

Theorem 13.1   *C is a cointegrating matrix if and only if $C'\mu = 0$ and $C'B(1) = 0$.*   ∎

Proof: Beveridge-Nelson decomposition implies that

$$x_i = \mu i + B(1) \sum_{j=1}^{i} \varepsilon_j + B^*(L)\varepsilon_i + \tilde{u}_0$$

and

$$C'x_i = C'\mu i + C'B(1) \sum_{j=1}^{i} \varepsilon_j + C'B^*(L)\varepsilon_i + C'\tilde{u}_0.$$

The last two terms of this decomposition are stationary and $C'x_i$ is stationary if and only if the first two terms vanish, i.e. if $C'\mu = 0$ and $C'B(1) = 0$.   ∎

Hence, the multiplication by C' eliminates the deterministic trend μi and the stochastic trend $B(1) \sum_{j=1}^{i} \varepsilon_j$.

Remark.   If there exists a (full rank) cointegrating matrix C then the determinant of $B(1)$ equals zero and hence $B(L)$ is noninvertible, which prevents the existence of an AR representation in differences (because $B(L)^{-1}u_i = \varepsilon_i$ does not make sense).   □

The previous remark does not prevent x_i from admitting a *VAR* representation in levels; cointegration is investigated very often in this setting.

13.3.2 Cointegration in a *VAR* Model in Levels

Suppose that x_i still satisfies

$$\Delta x_i - \mu = u_i = B(L)\varepsilon_i \qquad (13.3)$$

and moreover that x_i admits a *VAR* representation in levels of the form

$$A(L)x_i = v + \eta_i \qquad (13.4)$$

where v is a constant and η_i is a weak white noise that is the innovation of the process. We first investigate the relationship between (13.3) and (13.4). Note that the noises η_i and ε_i are necessarily equal to each other. Indeed, from the definition of *VAR* in levels, we have

$$\eta_i = x_i - EL(x_i \mid past)$$

and from the Wold representation of u_i in $B(L)\varepsilon_i$:

$$\varepsilon_i = \Delta x_i - EL(\Delta x_i \mid past).$$

Now we note that

$$\varepsilon_i = x_i - x_{i-1} - EL(x_i - x_{i-1} \mid past)$$
$$= x_i - x_{i-1} - EL(x_i \mid past) + x_{i-1} = \eta_i.$$

Moreover

$$(1 - L)x_i = \mu + B(L)\varepsilon_i$$
$$(1 - L)A(L)x_i = A(1)\mu + A(L)B(L)\varepsilon_i$$
$$(1 - L)(v + \varepsilon_i) = A(1)\mu + A(L)B(L)\varepsilon_i$$
$$(1 - L)\varepsilon_i = A(1)\mu + A(L)B(L)\varepsilon_i,$$

which implies, by taking the expectation on both sides, that

$$A(1)\mu = 0.$$

Moreover,

$$(1 - L) = A(L)B(L)$$

and hence

$$A(1)B(1) = 0.$$

Theorem 13.2   *C is the cointegrating matrix of the process x_i that admits the VAR representation (13.3) and (13.4) if and only if $A(1) = DC'$ where D is a full rank $m \times r$ matrix.*   ∎

Proof: Assume first that $A(1) = DC'$. Then, we have $DC'\mu = 0$ and $DC'B(1) = 0$, which implies $C'\mu = 0$ and $C'B(1) = 0$ and hence the fact that C is a cointegrating matrix (Theorem 13.1).

Conversely, we go back to the double representation

$$A(L)x_i = v + \varepsilon_i$$

$$(1 - L)x_i = \mu + B(L)\varepsilon_i.$$

Using the same argument as in Beveridge and Nelson, we have

$$A(L) = A(1) + A^*(L)(1 - L).$$

Hence

$$A(1)x_i + A^*(L)(1 - L)x_i = v + \varepsilon_i$$

$$A(1)x_i = -A^*(1)\mu - A^*(L)B(L)\varepsilon_i + v + \varepsilon_i.$$

A^* is a polynomial matrix (and not an infinite series) and hence $A^*(L)B(L)\varepsilon_i$ is a stationary process for all $A(L)$; therefore, $A(1)x_i$ is stationary. The rank of $A(1)$ is consequently equal to the maximum number of cointegrating relations (that is r) and $A(1)$ can be written as $A(1) = D_* C'_*$ (where D_* is of dimension $m \times r$ and C_* of dimension $r \times m$), with C_* cointegrating matrix.   ∎

Remark.   The fact that D is full rank means that we consider the maximum number of cointegrating relations.   □

Remark.   This decomposition is not valid if we consider only matrices not including all of cointegrating vectors.   □

Return to the *VAR* representation:

$$A(L)x_i = v + \varepsilon_i.$$

Note that

$$A(L) = A_0 + \overline{A}(L)L.$$

Using Beveridge-Nelson decomposition, we can write

$$\overline{A}(L) = \overline{A}(1) + \overline{A}^*(L)(1 - L).$$

Then x_i satisfies

$$A_0 x_i + \overline{A}(1)x_{i-1} + \overline{A}^*(L)\Delta x_{i-1} = v + \varepsilon_i.$$

This representation is that of an *error correction model*. Subtracting and adding $A_0 x_{i-1}$ in the left-hand side of this equation yields

$$A_0 \Delta x_i + \overline{A}(1) \Delta x_{i-1} + \left(\overline{A}(1) + A_0\right) x_{l-1} = v + \varepsilon_i.$$

By setting

$$A_0 \Delta x_i + \overline{A}(1) \Delta x_{i-1} = \widetilde{A}(L) \Delta x_i$$

and noticing that $\overline{A}(1) + A_0 = A(1)$ and $\widetilde{A}(L) = A_0 + \overline{A}^*(L)L$, we infer

$$\widetilde{A}(L) \Delta x_i + A(1) x_{i-1} = v + \varepsilon_i.$$

Under the assumption of cointegration, $A(1) = DC'$ and

$$\widetilde{A}(L) \Delta x_i + D z_{i-1} = v + \varepsilon_i$$

$$C' x_i = z_i.$$

Hence, we decomposed the dynamics of x_i into a long-run equation $C' x_i = z_l$ where the residuals z_i are stationary, and a short-run relationship that associates the variations of x_i with the lagged residuals of the long-run equation and an innovation.

13.3.3 Triangular Representation

Let x_i be the process satisfying

$$\Delta x_i = \mu + u_i$$

($x_i \in \mathbb{R}^m$, u_i is a centered stationary process) and admitting a $m \times r$ cointegrating matrix C. We partition x_i as (x_{i1}, x_{i2}) (where $x_{i1} \in \mathbb{R}^r$ and $x_{i2} \in \mathbb{R}^{m-r}$) and use the notation

$$C' x_i = C_1' x_{i1} + C_2' x_{i2}$$

with

$$C = \begin{pmatrix} C_1 : r \times r \\ C_2 : m - r \times m - r \end{pmatrix}.$$

Then, we have

$$\begin{cases} C_1' x_{i1} + C_2' x_{i2} = z_i \\ \Delta x_{i2} = \mu_2 + u_{i_2} \end{cases} \tag{13.5}$$

with $\mu = \begin{pmatrix} \mu_1 \\ \mu_2 \end{pmatrix}$ and $u_i = \begin{pmatrix} u_{i1} \\ u_{i2} \end{pmatrix}$. The process $\begin{pmatrix} z_i \\ u_{i_1} \end{pmatrix}$ is centered and stationary. In particular, if $C = \begin{pmatrix} I \\ -\Gamma \end{pmatrix}$, we obtain a triangular representation

$$\begin{cases} x_{i1} = \Gamma' x_{i2} + z_i \\ \Delta x_{i2} = \mu_2 + u_{i_2} \end{cases} \tag{13.6}$$

Conversely, if the process x_i is characterized by (13.6), it is easy to show that $x_i \sim I(1)$ (with drift). Indeed

$$\Delta x_{i1} = -C_1' C_2' \mu_2 - C_1^{-1'} u_{i2} + \Delta z_i = \mu_1 + u_{i1}$$

$$\Delta x_{i2} = \mu_2 + u_{i_2}$$

with

$$\mu_1 = -C_1' C_2' \mu_2 \text{ and } u_{i1} = -C_1^{-1'} u_{i2} + \Delta z_i.$$

Moreover, C is a cointegrating matrix by definition. Hence, any $I(1)$ process, characterized by r cointegrating relations, admits a representation (13.6). This writing should not lead to a wrong interpretation. The relation

$$\Delta x_{i2} = \mu_2 + u_{i2}$$

is the description of the marginal process that generates x_{i_2}, but the relation

$$C_1' x_{i1} + C_2' x_{i2} = z_i$$

(where $x_{i1} = \Gamma' x_{i2} + z_i$) is not a representation of the process that generates x_{i1} conditionally on x_{i2}.

13.3.4   Estimation of a Cointegrating Vector

First, we analyze the problem of estimating a unique cointegrating vector of a model in its triangular form. We choose the normalization $C = \begin{pmatrix} 1 \\ -\gamma \end{pmatrix}$. Consider

$$x_{i1} = \alpha + \gamma' x_{i2} + z_i$$

$$\Delta x_{i2} = \mu_2 + u_{i2},$$

where $x_{i1} \in \mathbb{R}$ and $x_{i2} \in \mathbb{R}^q$. Note that we relax here the mean zero condition of the cointegrated vector by including a constant α in the cointegrating relation. In the general case, $\begin{pmatrix} z_i \\ u_{i2} \end{pmatrix}$ is stationary and z_i and u_{i2} are correlated. To underline the different problems, we examine our model step by step. We assume first that z_i and u_{i2} are uncorrelated white noise, second that z_i and u_{i2} are arbitrary stationary but still not correlated. Finally, we examine the general case.

1.   Suppose that $\begin{pmatrix} z_i \\ u_{i2} \end{pmatrix}$ is a white noise with

$$Var(z_i) = \sigma^2 \text{ and } Var(u_i) = \Omega.$$

The OLS estimators are given by

$$
\begin{pmatrix} \widehat{\alpha}_n \\ \widehat{\gamma}_n \end{pmatrix} = \begin{bmatrix} n & \sum x'_{i2} \\ \sum x_{i2} & \sum x_{i2}x'_{i2} \end{bmatrix}^{-1} \begin{pmatrix} \sum x_{i1} \\ \sum x_{i1}x_{i2} \end{pmatrix},
$$

which implies that

$$
\begin{pmatrix} \widehat{\alpha}_n - \alpha \\ \widehat{\gamma}_n - \gamma \end{pmatrix} = \begin{bmatrix} n & \sum x'_{i2} \\ \sum x_{i2} & \sum x_{i2}x'_{i2} \end{bmatrix}^{-1} \begin{pmatrix} \sum z_i \\ \sum x_{i2}z_i \end{pmatrix}.
$$

Does

$$
\begin{pmatrix} \sqrt{n}\,(\widehat{\alpha}_n - \alpha) \\ n\,(\widehat{\gamma}_n - \gamma) \end{pmatrix}
$$

converge to a limiting distribution? Consider m independent Brownian motions grouped into

$$
\begin{pmatrix} W_1 \\ W_2 \end{pmatrix}, \quad W_1 \in \mathbb{R}, \ W_2 \in \mathbb{R}^q.
$$

We have

$$
n^{-\frac{1}{2}} \sum z_i \to N\left(0, \sigma^2\right) = \sigma W_1(1).
$$

As $\Omega = PP'$, we have

$$
n^{-2} \sum x_{i2}x'_{i2} \to P \int W_2(s)W'_2(s)ds\,P',
$$

$$
n^{-\frac{3}{2}} \sum x_{i2} \to P \int W_2(s)ds
$$

and

$$
n^{-1} \sum x_{i2}z_i \to \sigma P \int W_2 dW_1.
$$

Since $u_i \perp z_i$, we obtain

$$
\begin{pmatrix} \sqrt{n}\,(\widehat{\alpha}_n - \alpha) \\ n\,(\widehat{\gamma}_n - \gamma) \end{pmatrix} \to \begin{bmatrix} 1 & \int W'_2 P' \\ P \int W_2 & P \int W_2 W'_2 P' \end{bmatrix}^{-1} \begin{pmatrix} \sigma W_1(1) \\ \sigma P \int W_2 dW_1 \end{pmatrix}.
$$

This distribution has mean zero.

2. $\begin{pmatrix} z_i \\ u_{i2} \end{pmatrix} = B(L)\eta_i$ is a centered stationary process where η_i is a white noise. The z_i and u_{i2} are mutually independent and

$$
B(L) = \begin{pmatrix} B_{11}(L) & 0 \\ 0 & B_{22}(L) \end{pmatrix}
$$

hence

$$\begin{pmatrix} z_i \\ u_{i2} \end{pmatrix} = \begin{pmatrix} B_{11}(L) & 0 \\ 0 & B_{22}(L) \end{pmatrix} \begin{pmatrix} \eta_{1i} \\ \eta_{2i} \end{pmatrix}.$$

The OLS estimators are

$$\begin{pmatrix} \sqrt{n}\,(\widehat{\alpha}_n - \alpha) \\ n\,(\widehat{\gamma}_n - \gamma) \end{pmatrix} = \begin{bmatrix} 1 & n^{-\frac{3}{2}} \sum x'_{i2} \\ n^{-\frac{3}{2}} \sum x_{i2} & n^{-2} \sum x_{i2} x'_{i2} \end{bmatrix}^{-1} \begin{pmatrix} n^{-\frac{1}{2}} \sum z_i \\ n^{-1} \sum x_{i2} z_i \end{pmatrix}.$$

Setting $Var(u_i) = \Omega = PP'$, we get

$$Var(\eta_i) = \begin{pmatrix} \sigma^2 & 0 \\ 0 & \Omega \end{pmatrix} = \begin{pmatrix} \sigma^2 & 0 \\ 0 & PP' \end{pmatrix}.$$

Let

$$\begin{cases} \lambda = \sigma B_{11}(1) \\ \Lambda = B_{22}(1)P \end{cases}$$

and let W_1 and W_2 be independent Brownian motions belonging to $\mathbb{R}$ and $\mathbb{R}^q$ respectively. Then

$$\begin{pmatrix} \sqrt{n}\,(\widehat{\alpha}_n - \alpha) \\ n\,(\widehat{\gamma}_n - \gamma) \end{pmatrix} \to \begin{bmatrix} 1 & \int W'_2 \Lambda' \\ \Lambda \int W_2 & \Lambda \int W_2 W'_2 \Lambda' \end{bmatrix}^{-1} \begin{pmatrix} \lambda W_1(1) \\ \lambda \Lambda \int W_2 dW_1 \end{pmatrix}.$$

This distribution has mean zero. Let us verify this for α:

$$\frac{\sqrt{n}}{n} \sum z_i \to N\left[0, \sum_{j=-\infty}^{\infty} cov\left(\varepsilon_i, \varepsilon_{i+j}\right)\right]$$

$$\sum_{j=-\infty}^{\infty} E\left(\varepsilon_i \varepsilon_{i+j}\right) = \sum_{j=-\infty}^{\infty} \sum_{l=0}^{\infty} \sum_{k=0}^{\infty} b_l b_k E\left[\eta_{i-l} \eta_{i+j-k}\right].$$

Now

$$E\left[\eta_{i-l} \eta_{i+j-k}\right] = \begin{vmatrix} \sigma^2 & \text{if } i-l = i+j-k \text{ or } k = j+l \\ 0 & \text{otherwise.} \end{vmatrix}$$

Hence

$$\sum_{j=-\infty}^{\infty} E\left(\varepsilon_i \varepsilon_{i+j}\right) = \sigma^2 \sum_{l,k} b_l b_k = \sigma^2 \left(\sum b_l\right)^2 = \sigma^2 \left(B_{11}(1)\right)^2.$$

The result follows.

3. Let $\left(\begin{smallmatrix} z_i \\ u_{i2} \end{smallmatrix}\right) = B(L)\eta_i$ be an arbitrary centered stationary process with z_i and u_{i2} not mutually independent. We have

$$
\begin{pmatrix} \sqrt{n}\,(\widehat{\alpha}_n - \alpha) \\ n\,(\widehat{\gamma}_n - \gamma) \end{pmatrix} = \begin{bmatrix} 1 & n^{-\frac{3}{2}} \sum x_{i2}' \\ n^{-\frac{3}{2}} \sum x_{i2} & n^{-2} \sum x_{i2} x_{i2}' \end{bmatrix}^{-1} \begin{pmatrix} n^{-\frac{1}{2}} \sum z_i \\ n^{-1} \sum x_{i2} z_i \end{pmatrix}.
$$

There exist $(W_1, W_2) \in \mathbb{R} \times \mathbb{R}^q$, standard Brownian motions (independent, with unit variance) and such that

$$
\begin{bmatrix} 1 & n^{-\frac{3}{2}} \sum x_{i2}' \\ n^{-\frac{3}{2}} \sum x_{i2} & n^{-2} \sum x_{i2} x_{i2}' \end{bmatrix} \rightarrow \begin{pmatrix} 1 & \int W_2' P' \lambda \\ \lambda \int W_2 P & \Lambda \int W_2 W_2' \Lambda' \end{pmatrix}
$$

with

$$
\frac{1}{\sqrt{n}} \sum z_i \rightarrow N(0, b(1)^2).
$$

(by the central limit theorem) and

$$
\frac{1}{n} \sum x_{i2} z_i \rightarrow \frac{1}{n} \sum \Delta x_{i2} z_i + \frac{1}{n} \sum x_{i2-1} z_i
$$

$$
\begin{pmatrix} \frac{1}{\sqrt{n}} \sum z_i \\ n^{-1} \sum x_{i2} z_i \end{pmatrix} \rightarrow \begin{pmatrix} \lambda_1 W_1(1) \\ \lambda \Lambda \int W_2 dW_1 + \sum_{v=0}^{\infty} cov(u_{i2}, z_{i+v}) \end{pmatrix}.
$$

As a consequence

$$
\begin{pmatrix} \widehat{\alpha}_n \\ \widehat{\gamma}_n \end{pmatrix} \rightarrow \begin{pmatrix} \alpha \\ \gamma \end{pmatrix} \text{ in probability,}
$$

which implies that the OLS estimators are consistent in spite of the lack of exogeneity. But there is an asymptotic bias because $\left(\begin{smallmatrix} \sqrt{n}(\widehat{\alpha}_n - \alpha) \\ n(\widehat{\gamma}_n - \gamma) \end{smallmatrix}\right)$ converges to a distribution whose mean is nonzero. It is possible to correct for this bias but we prefer other estimators in order to avoid this bias problem.

Consider the system

$$
\begin{cases} y_i = \alpha + \gamma' z_i + \varepsilon_i \\ \Delta z_i = u_i \end{cases}
$$

with $\left(\begin{smallmatrix} \varepsilon_i \\ u_i \end{smallmatrix}\right)$ stationary and centered, where $E\left(\varepsilon_i \mid z_i, u_i\right)$ is a linear function of u_i; hence

$$
E(y_i \mid z_i, u_i) = \alpha + \gamma' z_i + E\left(\varepsilon_i \mid z_i, u_i\right) = \alpha + \gamma' z_i + \pi u_i.
$$

The system becomes

$$
\begin{cases}
y_i = \alpha + \gamma' z_i + \pi u_i + \bar{\varepsilon}_i \\
\varepsilon_i = \pi u_i + \bar{\varepsilon}_i \\
\Delta z_i = u_i
\end{cases}
$$

with $\left(\begin{smallmatrix} \bar{\varepsilon}_i \\ u_i \end{smallmatrix}\right)$ centered stationary. The correlation between $\bar{\varepsilon}_i$ and u_i is of course zero by definition. The model becomes

$$
y_i = \alpha + \gamma' z_i + \pi \Delta z_i + \bar{\varepsilon}_i.
$$

The OLS estimators of this model

$$
\begin{pmatrix}
\sqrt{n}\,(\widehat{\alpha}_n - \alpha) \\
n\,(\widehat{\gamma}_n - \gamma) \\
\sqrt{n}\,(\widehat{\pi}_n - \pi)
\end{pmatrix}
$$

converge to a distribution that we can derive in a similar fashion as before.

Example 13.8 *Consider the system*

$$
\begin{cases}
y_i = \alpha + \gamma' z_i + \varepsilon_i \\
\Delta z_i = u_i
\end{cases}
$$

with $\left(\begin{smallmatrix} \varepsilon_i \\ u_i \end{smallmatrix}\right)$ centered stationary. If

$$
\varepsilon_i = \widehat{\varepsilon}_i + \bar{\varepsilon}_i,
$$

where $\widehat{\varepsilon}_i$ is the projection of ε_i on the trajectory of u, then

$$
y_i = \alpha + \gamma' z_i + \widehat{\varepsilon}_i + \bar{\varepsilon}_i.
$$

We impose the extra assumption that the projection of ε_i on the trajectory of $u \in u_{i-p}, \ldots, u_{i+p}$ is linear. Then

$$
\widehat{\varepsilon}_i = \sum_{l=-p}^{p} \pi_l u_{i-l},
$$

and

$$
y_i = \alpha + \gamma' z_i + \sum_{l=-p}^{p} \pi_l u_{i-l} + \bar{\varepsilon}_i.
$$

The OLS estimators are

$$
\begin{pmatrix}
\sqrt{n}\,(\widehat{\alpha}_n - \alpha) \\
\sqrt{n}\,(\widehat{\pi}_n - \pi) \\
n\,(\widehat{\gamma}_n - \gamma)
\end{pmatrix}
=
\begin{bmatrix}
1 & n^{-1}\sum w_i' & n^{-\frac{3}{2}}\sum z_i' \\
n^{-1}\sum w_i & n^{-1}\sum w_i w_i' & n^{-\frac{3}{2}}\sum w_i z_i' \\
n^{-\frac{3}{2}}\sum z_i & n^{-\frac{3}{2}}\sum z_i w_i' & n^{-2}\sum z_i z_i'
\end{bmatrix}^{-1}
\begin{pmatrix}
n^{-\frac{1}{2}}\sum \bar{\varepsilon}_i \\
n^{-\frac{1}{2}}\sum w_i \bar{\varepsilon}_i \\
n^{-1}\sum z_i \bar{\varepsilon}_i
\end{pmatrix}
$$

in the equation

$$y_i = \alpha + \pi' w_i + \gamma' z_i + \bar{\varepsilon}_i$$

where

$$w_i = \begin{bmatrix} u_{i-p} \\ \vdots \\ u_{i+p} \end{bmatrix}, \quad \pi = \begin{bmatrix} \pi_{-p} \\ \vdots \\ \pi_{+p} \end{bmatrix};$$

$u_{i-p}, \ldots, u_{i+p}$ *have dimension* $q \times 1$ *and* w_i *and* π *have dimension* $2pq \times 1$. *We can show that*

$$\begin{pmatrix} \sqrt{n}\,(\hat{\alpha}_n - \alpha) \\ \sqrt{n}\,(\hat{\pi}_n - \pi) \\ n\,(\hat{\gamma}_n - \gamma) \end{pmatrix} \rightarrow \begin{pmatrix} 1 & 0 & \int W_2' \Lambda' \\ 0 & \Sigma & 0 \\ \Lambda \int W_2 & 0 & \Lambda \int W_2 W_2' \Lambda' \end{pmatrix}^{-1} \begin{pmatrix} \sigma W_1(1) \\ \sigma \Sigma^{-\frac{1}{2}} W_1(1) \\ \frac{1}{2}\sigma[\Lambda \int W_2 dW_1] \end{pmatrix}.$$

with $\sum = Var(w_i)$ *and* $(W_1, W_2) \in \mathbb{R} \times \mathbb{R}^q$ *are independent standard Brownian motions.* □

13.3.5 Maximum Likelihood Estimation of an Error Correction Model Admitting a Cointegrating Relation

Let x_i be a $I(1)$ vector of $\mathbb{R}^m$ admitting a *VAR* representation in levels

$$A(L)x_i = v + \varepsilon_i, \quad \varepsilon_i \text{ is a white noise.}$$

We saw that this model can be rewritten as

$$\tilde{A}(L)\Delta x_i + A(1)x_{i-1} = v + \varepsilon_i$$

and assuming that C is a cointegrating matrix is equivalent to imposing the restriction $A(1) = DC'$. Under this condition, we have

$$\Delta x_i = -DC'x_{i-1} - \tilde{A}_1 \Delta x_{i-1} - \cdots - \tilde{A}_{p-1}\Delta x_{i-p+1} + v + \varepsilon_i. \tag{13.7}$$

We assume that the ε_i are independent normal with variance Σ. We wish to estimate D, C, $\tilde{A}_1, \ldots, \tilde{A}_{p-1}$, and v by maximum likelihood. The previous equation can be written as

$$Y = ZCD' + W\Pi + E \tag{13.8}$$

with

$$Y = \left(y_{ij}\right)_{i,j}, \ y_{ij} = x_{ij} - x_{i-1j}, \ x_i = \begin{pmatrix} x_{i1} \\ \vdots \\ x_{im} \end{pmatrix},$$

$$Z = \left(z_{ij}\right)_{i,j}, \ z_{ij} = -x_{i-1,j},$$

$$W = \begin{pmatrix} \vdots & & \vdots & & \vdots \\ -\Delta x'_{i-1} & \cdots & -\Delta x'_{i-p+1} & \cdots & 1 \\ \vdots & & \vdots & & \vdots \end{pmatrix},$$

and

$$\Pi = \begin{pmatrix} \widetilde{A}'_1 \\ \vdots \\ \widetilde{A}'_p \\ v' \end{pmatrix}, \tag{13.9}$$

where Y, Z, W, and Π have dimensions $n \times m$, $n \times m$, $n \times (pm + 1)$, and $(pm + 1) \times m$ respectively.

Remarks.

1. The model (13.8) is a restricted multivariate normal regression model.
2. We impose no restrictions on the $\widetilde{A}_j$ and v.
3. The matrix D is not constrained.
4. The matrix W may possibly contain a trend (which changes the asymptotic properties but not the calculation of the estimators).   □

The density of the observations (conditional on $x_{-p-1}, \ldots, x_0$) takes the form

$$|\Sigma|^{-\frac{n}{2}} \exp -\frac{1}{2} tr \, \Sigma^{-1} \left(Y - ZCD' - W\Pi\right)' \left(Y - ZCD' - W\Pi\right) \tag{13.10}$$

Using the usual least squares formulas, we can verify that the maximum with respect to Π is reached for

$$\widehat{\Pi} = \left(W'W\right)^{-1} W' \left(Y - ZCD'\right).$$

Replacing Π by $\widehat{\Pi}$ in (13.10), we obtain

$$|\Sigma|^{-\frac{n}{2}} \exp -\frac{1}{2} tr \Sigma^{-1} \left(Y - ZCD'\right)' M_W \left(Y - ZCD'\right)$$

with

$$M_W = I - W(W'W)^{-1}W'.$$

Similarly, the maximization of this expression with respect to D' leads to

$$\widehat{D'} = \left(C'Z'M_W ZC\right)^{-1} C'Z'M_W Y.$$

After substituting $\widehat{D'}$ for D', the likelihood becomes

$$|\Sigma|^{-\frac{n}{2}} \exp -\frac{1}{2} tr \Sigma^{-1} Y' \left(M_W - M_W ZC \left(C'Z'M_W ZC\right)^{-1} C'Z'M_W\right) Y.$$

The estimator of Σ is equal to

$$\widehat{\Sigma} = \frac{1}{n} \left[Y' \left(M_W - M_W ZC \left(C'Z'M_W ZC\right)^{-1} C'Z'M_W\right) Y \right].$$

Replacing Σ by $\widehat{\Sigma}$, we see that the maximization of the likelihood is equivalent to the minimization of

$$\left| Y'M_W Y - Y'M_W ZC \left(C'Z'M_W ZC\right)^{-1} C'Z'M_W Y \right|.$$

Using the formula

$$\begin{vmatrix} A_{11} & A_{12} \\ A_{21} & A_{22} \end{vmatrix} = |A_{11}| \left| A_{22} - A_{21} A_{11}^{-1} A_{12} \right| = |A_{22}| \left| A_{11} - A_{12} A_{22}^{-1} A_{21} \right|,$$

we get

$$\left| Y'M_W Y - Y'M_W ZC \left(C'Z'M_W ZC\right)^{-1} C'Z'M_W Y \right|$$

$$= \frac{\left| Y'M_W Y \right| \left| C'Z'M_W ZC - C'Z'M_W Y \left(Y'M_W Y\right)^{-1} Y'M_W ZC \right|}{|C'Z'M_W ZC|}.$$

Hence, C is obtained by minimizing

$$\frac{|C'QC|}{|C'RC|}$$

with

$$Q = Z'M_W Z$$

and

$$R = Z'M_W Z - Z'M_W Y \left(Y'M_W Y\right) Y'M_W Z.$$

This is identical to finding the r largest roots of the determinant equation

$$\left| Z'M_W \left(Y'M_W Y\right)^{-1} Y'M_W Z - \lambda Z'M_W Z \right| = 0$$

or finding the r largest eigenvalues that are the solutions of

$$\left| \left(Z'M_W Z\right)^{-1} Z'M_W Y \left(Y'M_W Y\right)^{-1} Y'M_W Z - \lambda I \right| = 0. \qquad (13.11)$$

If the λ_i are the canonical correlations obtained by solving the equation (13.11), then $(1 - \lambda_i)$ are the eigenvalues of

$$\left(I - \left(Z'M_W Z\right)^{-1} Z'M_W Y \left(Y'M_W Y\right)^{-1} Y'M_W Z \right).$$

As the determinant of a matrix is equal to the product of its eigenvalues, we have

$$\prod_{i=1}^{r} (1 - \lambda_i) = \left| I - \left(Z'M_W Z\right)^{-1} Z'M_W Y \left(Y'M_W Y\right)^{-1} Y'M_W Z \right|$$

$$= \frac{\left| Z'M_W Z - Z'M_W Y \left(Y'M_W Y\right)^{-1} \right|}{|Z'M_W Z|}$$

$$= \frac{\left| Y'M_W Y - Z'M_W Y \left(Z'M_W Z\right)^{-1} Y'M_W Z \right|}{|Y'M_W Y|},$$

hence, the likelihood is proportional to

$$L(.) = |Y'M_W Y| \prod_{i=1}^{r} (1 - \lambda_i) \qquad (13.12)$$

and

$$\log L(.) = -\frac{nm}{2} \log 2\pi - \frac{nm}{2} - \frac{n}{2} \log |Y'M_W Y| - \frac{n}{2} \sum_{i=1}^{r} \log (1 - \lambda_i),$$

where the λ_i are the roots of Equation (13.11).

13.3.6 Cointegration Test Based on the Canonical Correlations: Johansen's Test

To determine the number of cointegrating vectors, Johansen suggests two tests: the trace test and the maximum eigenvalue test. The number r of cointegrating relations in the system is determined from the likelihood ratio (LR) test. The trace test tests the null hypothesis that there are at most r cointegrating vectors. The maximum eigenvalue test tests the hypothesis that there are r cointegrating vectors against the alternative that there are $r + 1$ of them. We use the fact that, if there exist r cointegrating vectors, then the $m - r$ smallest eigenvalues of Equation (13.11) are zero. The r vectors corresponding to the nonzero eigenvalues are chosen as cointegrating vectors. This way of imposing $m - r$ restrictions yields an optimal and asymptotically efficient estimator of the cointegrating vectors.

Trace Test

Result (13.12) shows that the maximum likelihood is given by

$$-2 \ln L_{\max} \propto n \sum_{i=1}^{m} \ln(1 - \lambda_i)$$

where the λ_i are the solutions of (13.11). The LR test of the null hypothesis \at most r cointegrating vectors" is

$$\lambda_{trace} = -n \sum_{i=1}^{m-r} \ln\left(1 - \widehat{\lambda}_i\right)$$

where $\widehat{\lambda}_1, \ldots, \widehat{\lambda}_{m-r}$ are the $m - r$ smallest eigenvalues of Equation (13.11). The asymptotic distribution is given by the trace of the stochastic matrix

$$\int_0^1 (dW) W' \left(\int_0^1 WW'dr\right)^{-1} \int_0^1 W(dW)' \tag{13.13}$$

where W is a Brownian motion of dimension $m - r$. In the case where there is a constant or a trend in the VAR model, we use, instead of (13.13),

$$\int_0^1 (dW) \widetilde{W}' \left(\int_0^1 \widetilde{W}\widetilde{W}'dr\right)^{-1} \int_0^1 \widetilde{W}(dW)' \tag{13.14}$$

where $\widetilde{W}$ is the demeaned or detrended Brownian motion.

Maximum Eigenvalue Test

To test the null hypothesis of r cointegrating vectors against the alternative hypothesis that there exist $r + 1$ cointegrating vectors, the LR test statistic is:

$$\lambda_{\max} = -n \ln\left(1 - \widehat{\lambda}_{r+1}\right).$$

The asymptotic distribution of this statistic is given by the largest eigenvalue of the stochastic matrix (13.13) or (13.14), according to the different specifications of the VAR model.

Detailed tables for the critical values are given by Osterwald and Lenum (1992).

Notes

The literature concerning unit root tests and cointegration models is large. Let us recall the synthesis by Phillips and Xiao (1998), the books by Hamilton (1994) and by Johansen (1995). White (1958) stressed that the convergence criteria for the estimators of $I(1)$ processes were special. Donsker's theorem, the functional central limit theorem, and the invariance principal can be found in Billingsley (1968).

A large number of tests have been developed in the literature. We cite in particular Choi (1999), Ahn and Choi (1999), Elliott, Rothenberg, and Stock (1992), Schmidt and Phillips (1992), Kiatkowsky, Phillips, Schmidt, and Shen (1992), who develop a Lagrange multiplier test, and Ahn (1993) in the deterministic cases. Levin, Lin, and Chu (2002), Quah (1994), Breitung (2002), Pesaran and Shin (1996) consider panel data, Toda and McKenzie (1999) take into account missing data.

We did not discuss long-memory processes. For this, we refer to the seminal paper by Granger and Joyeux (1980) and to the books by Beran (1994) and by Samorodnisky and Taqqu (1995) for α-stable processes. Important developments of cointegrated models are made in the context of panel data and models with structural breaks. Regarding panel data, we refer to the synthesis by Baltagi (2001) and for models with breaks to Johansen, Mosconi, and Nielsen (2000). For nonparametric and nonlinear cointegration models, we refer to the work of Bierens (1997).

14. Models for Conditional Variance

14.1 Introduction

For a long time, heteroskedasticity rested on a specification of the variance as a function of observable exogenous variables. But this formulation appeared to be too restrictive, especially for financial problems, and it became necessary to introduce an endogenous dynamics in the determination of the variance.

Hence, this chapter will address the *AutoRegressive Conditional Heteroskedastic* (ARCH) models that have experienced an important development over the past 20 years after the original article by Engle in 1982. We will not provide a complete theoretical exposition of these models, but often proceed with examples to point out their fundamental characteristics.

After a review of different types of ARCH models, we will tackle their estimation by the generalized method of moments. Then, we will see some applications of Rao procedure to testing for the null hypothesis of homoskedasticity. We will finish with a few specific aspects of this type of modeling.

14.2 Various Types of ARCH Models

First, we introduce a simplified notation for the conditional mean and conditional variance

$$\begin{cases} E^{\theta}(y_i|\eta_{i-1}) \equiv E^{\theta}_{i-1}(y_i) \\ Var^{\theta}(y_i|\eta_{i-1}) \equiv Var^{\theta}_{i-1}(y_i) \end{cases} \tag{14.1}$$

where θ represents the vector of all unknown parameters. The conditioning is done with respect to η_{i-1} which includes simultaneously the past of the variable y_i (this past may have a finite or infinite horizon) and the past, present, and future path of a vector z_i of explanatory variables:

$$\eta_{i-1} = \left\{ y_{i-1}, y_{i-2}, \ldots, z^{+\infty}_{-\infty} \right\}. \tag{14.2}$$

We study processes for which the conditional moments take the form

$$\begin{cases} E^\theta_{i-1}(y_i) \equiv m_i(\eta_{i-1}, \lambda) \\ Var^\theta_{i-1}(y_i) \equiv h_i(\eta_{i-1}, \lambda) \end{cases} \quad (14.3)$$

where m_i and h_i are arbitrary functions of unknown parameters and of η_{i-1}, that may be linear, piecewise linear, or nonlinear. For the sake of simplicity, these functions are sometimes denoted $m_i(\lambda)$ and $h_i(\lambda)$ or simply m_i and h_i. We exit the framework of the linear space $H(y)$, the subspace of L^2 generated by y_τ, $\tau \le i$, and we consider the space L^2 of all measurable functions of η_i.

The following representation is sometimes used that strengthens the preceding assumptions

$$y_i = m_i + \sqrt{h_i} u_i \quad (14.4)$$

where the u_i are i.i.d. with mean zero and variance 1, not necessarily normal. Assumptions (14.1) define the errors u_i as the innovations of a model of the following type

$$\begin{cases} u_i = y_i - m_i \\ E^\theta_{i-1}(u_i) = 0 \\ Var^\theta_{i-1}(u_i) = h_i. \end{cases} \quad (14.5)$$

We provide examples that illustrate some of the adopted specifications for ARCH-type models where the conditional variance, also called volatility in the financial literature, may take various forms.

Example 14.1   *Consider one of the simplest models, namely the AR(1) model with ARCH(1) errors:*

$$E^\theta_{i-1}(y_i) = m_i = \beta_1 + \beta_2 y_{i-1}$$

and

$$Var^\theta_{i-1}(y_i) = \alpha_0 + \alpha_1 [y_{i-1} - m_{i-1}]^2$$
$$= \alpha_0 + \alpha_1 [y_{i-1} - (\beta_1 + \beta_2 y_{i-2})]^2$$

with $\alpha_0 > 0$ and $\alpha_1 \ge 0$ to insure the positivity of the conditional variance, and $|\beta_2| < 1$ using the canonical representation of the $AR(1)$ process. Expanding the expression of the conditional variance yields a quadratic form that depends on the lags of the endogenous variable

$$Var^\theta_{i-1}(y_i) = \xi_1 y^2_{i-1} + \xi_2 y^2_{i-2} + \xi_3 y_{i-1} y_{i-2} + \xi_4 y_{i-1} + \xi_5 y_{i-2} + \xi_6$$

with the following restrictions

$$\xi_2 = \xi_1\beta_2^2,$$

$$\xi_3 = -2\xi_1\beta_2,$$

$$\xi_4 = -2\xi_1\beta_1,$$

$$\xi_5 = 2\xi_1\beta_1\beta_2,$$

the other parameters, i.e., β_1, β_2, ξ_1, and ξ_6, being not restricted. This can be rewritten as

$$Var^\theta_{i-1}(y_i) = \begin{bmatrix} y_{i-1} \\ y_{i-2} \end{bmatrix}' A \begin{bmatrix} y_{i-1} \\ y_{i-2} \end{bmatrix} + B' \begin{bmatrix} y_{i-1} \\ y_{i-2} \end{bmatrix} + \xi_6$$

with

$$A = \xi_1 \begin{bmatrix} 1 & -\beta_2 \\ -\beta_2 & \beta_2^2 \end{bmatrix} \quad and \quad B = 2\xi_1\beta_1 \begin{bmatrix} -1 \\ \beta_2 \end{bmatrix}.$$

Note here that a popular way to write this model is

$$\begin{cases} u_i = y_i - \beta_1 - \beta_2 y_{i-1} \\ E^\theta_{i-1}(u_i) = 0 \\ Var^\theta_{i-1}(u_i) = \alpha_0 + \alpha_1 u_{i-1}^2. \end{cases} \qquad \square$$

The endogenous dynamics that determine the variance in this AR(1)-ARCH(1) model involve some restrictions on the parameters. This generalizes to higher-order model, as the following example shows.

Example 14.2 *Consider the ARCH(q) model with an even simpler specification of the conditional expectation*

$$E^\theta_{i-1}(y_i) = m_i = 0$$

and

$$Var^\theta_{i-1}(y_i) = \alpha_0 + \sum_{r=1}^q \alpha_r (y_{i-r} - m_{i-r})^2 = \alpha_0 + \sum_{r=1}^q \alpha_r y_{i-r}^2.$$

This model has a simple dynamic based on the squared lags of the endogenous variable where the only restriction on the parameters is the nonnegativity of the coefficients ($\alpha_0 > 0$ and $\alpha_r \geq 0$, for all $r \geq 1$). If we introduce a more complex specification of the conditional expectation in the form of an AR(m)

$$\begin{aligned} E^\theta_{i-1}(y_i) &= \beta_0 + \beta_1 y_{i-1} + \cdots + \beta_m y_{i-m} \\ &= \beta_0 + (\beta_1 L + \cdots + \beta_m L^m) y_i \\ &= \beta_0 + \Phi(L) y_i \end{aligned}$$

then the conditional variance can be expressed as

$$Var_{i-1}^{\theta}(y_i) = \sum_{k=1}^{q+m} \xi_k y_{i-k}^2 + \sum_{k=1}^{q+m} \sum_{r=1,r\neq k}^{q+m} \gamma_{kr} y_{i-k} y_{i-r} + \sum_{k=1}^{q+m} \delta_k y_{i-k} + v_0$$

with restrictions on the coefficients ξ_k, γ_{kr}, and δ_k for $k, r = 1, \ldots, q + m$. Indeed, there are $(q + m)(q + m + 1)$ coefficients in this last equation, that depend on $q + m + 2$ coefficients α_i and β_j for $i = 0, \ldots, q$ and $j = 0, \ldots, m$. □

Example 14.3 *In order to have a more flexible structure of the lags and fewer parameters than in ARCH(q) model, an autoregressive moving average dynamics of the variance has been introduced which gave rise to the Generalized ARCH or GARCH(p,q) model of the form*

$$E_{i-1}^{\theta}(y_i) = m_i = \beta' z_i$$

and

$$Var_{i-1}^{\theta}(y_i) = h_i$$
$$= \alpha_0 + \sum_{r=1}^{q} \alpha_r \left[y_{i-r} - \beta' z_{i-r} \right]^2 + \sum_{k=1}^{p} \delta_k h_{i-k}$$

with $p \geq 0$, $q > 0$, $\alpha_0 > 0$, $\alpha_r \geq 0$ for $r = 1, \ldots, q$, and $\delta_k \geq 0$ for $k = 1, \ldots, p$. We took here a very general form for the conditional expectation where z_i is a $l \times 1$ vector that may contain lags of the endogenous variable and β is a $l \times 1$ vector of parameters. □

Example 14.4 *The ARCH in mean (ARCH-M) models allow the conditional expectation to depend on the conditional variance:*

$$E_{i-1}^{\theta}(y_i) = m_i = \beta' z_i + \delta Var_{i-1}^{\theta}(y_i)$$

and

$$Var_{i-1}^{\theta}(y_i) = \alpha_0 + \sum_{r=1}^{q} \alpha_r \left[y_{i-r} - m_{i-r} \right]^2$$

or, by setting $Var_{i-1}^{\theta}(y_i) = h_i$,

$$E_{i-1}^{\theta}(y_i) = \beta' z_i + \delta h_i$$

and

$$Var_{i-1}^{\theta}(y_i) = \alpha_0 + \sum_{r=1}^{q} \alpha_r \left[y_{i-i} - \beta' z_{i-r} - \delta h_{i-r} \right]^2.$$ □

Example 14.5 *In the Exponential GARCH model, also called EGARCH(p,q), the conditional variance responds in an asymmetric manner to the residuals depending on their signs:*

$$\ln h_i = \alpha_0 + \sum_{r=1}^{q} \alpha_r g(\zeta_{i-r}) + \sum_{j=1}^{p} \delta_j \ln h_{i-j}$$

with

$$g(\zeta_i) = \rho\zeta_i + \gamma \left(|\zeta_i| - E\,|\zeta_i|\right)$$

and

$$\zeta_i = \frac{y_i - m_i}{\sqrt{h_i}}.$$

Hence ζ_i is conditionally standardized, i.e., $E^\theta_{i-1}(\zeta_i) = 0$ and $V^\theta_{i-1}(\zeta_i) = 1$. $g(\zeta_i)$ is an i.i.d. sequence of random variables with mean zero and finite constant variance. The asymmetric effect is obvious: if $\zeta_i > 0$, $g(\zeta_i)$ has a slope $\rho + \gamma$, and if $\zeta_i < 0$, the slope is $\rho - \gamma$. □

Example 14.6 *The Nonlinear ARCH or NARCH(q) is characterized by a general functional form of the conditional variance:*

$$Var^\theta_{i-1}(y_i) = h_i = \left[\alpha_0 \left(\sigma^2\right)^\delta + \sum_{r=1}^{q} \alpha_r \left(y_{i-r} - m_{i-r}\right)^\delta \right]^{1/\delta}$$

with $\sigma^2 > 0$, $\alpha_0 > 0$, $\alpha_i \geq 0$ for $i = 1, \ldots, q$, $\delta > 0$, and $\sum_{r=0}^{q} \alpha_r = 1$. The interest of this specification is that it allows us to test the null hypothesis of linearity against a variety of nonlinear alternatives. The estimate of δ gives an idea of the degree of nonlinearity. Hence, if $\delta = 1$, we get back the ARCH(q) model. If $\delta = 0$, we get a logarithmic form that is used by some authors

$$\ln h_i = \alpha_0 \ln \sigma^2 + \sum_{r=1}^{q} \alpha_r \ln \left(y_{i-r} - m_{i-r}\right)^2.$$ □

ARCH models can be extended to the multivariate case. The large number of parameters they contain, coming partly from the conditional variance matrix, requires the introduction of some restrictions. We exhibit two of these models in the following examples.

Example 14.7 *The multivariate GARCH model with constant conditional correlations can be written as*

$$\begin{cases} E^\theta_{i-1}(y_i) = m_i \\ Var^\theta_{i-1}(u_i) = H_i \end{cases}$$

where y_i is a $N \times 1$ vector with $N \times 1$ expectation m_i and $N \times N$ conditional variance-covariance matrix H_i that is almost surely positive definite for all i. The fundamental assumption in this type of model is that the conditional correlations ρ_{kji}, given by $\rho_{kji} = h_{kji}/\sqrt{h_{kki}h_{jji}}$, are constant over time and equal to ρ_{kj}, for $j = 1, \ldots, N$ and $k = j + 1, \ldots, N$. Hence, the elements of H_i are:

$$\begin{cases} h_{kki} = \omega_k + \sum_{r=1}^{q} \alpha_{kr} u_{k,i-r}^2 + \sum_{r=1}^{p} \delta_{kj} h_{kk,i-r} & k = 1, \ldots, N \\ h_{kji} = \rho_{kj} \left(h_{kki} h_{jji} \right)^{1/2} & k, j = 1, \ldots, N, \text{ and } k \neq j. \end{cases}$$

with $u_i = y_i - m_i$. Thus, the conditional variances and covariances of the bivariate GARCH(1,1) model are

$$\begin{cases} h_{11i} = \omega_1 + \alpha_{11} u_{1,i-1}^2 + \delta_{11} h_{11,i-1} \\ h_{22i} = \omega_2 + \alpha_{22} u_{2,i-1}^2 + \delta_{22} h_{22,i-1} \\ h_{12i} = \rho \sqrt{h_{11i} h_{22i}} \end{cases}$$
□

Example 14.8   *The diagonal ARCH model permits to simplify the multivariate case by assuming that some matrices are diagonal. Thus, the bivariate diagonal GARCH(1,1) model with variance-covariance matrix H_i is characterized by*

$$\text{vech} H_i = \begin{bmatrix} h_{11i} \\ h_{12i} \\ h_{22i} \end{bmatrix} = \begin{bmatrix} \gamma_{11} \\ \gamma_{12} \\ \gamma_{22} \end{bmatrix} + \begin{bmatrix} \alpha_{11} & 0 & 0 \\ 0 & \alpha_{22} & 0 \\ 0 & 0 & \alpha_{33} \end{bmatrix} \begin{bmatrix} u_{1,i-1}^2 \\ u_{1,i-1} u_{2,i-1} \\ u_{2,i-1}^2 \end{bmatrix}$$
$$+ \begin{bmatrix} \xi_{11} & 0 & 0 \\ 0 & \xi_{22} & 0 \\ 0 & 0 & \xi_{33} \end{bmatrix} \begin{bmatrix} h_{11i-1} \\ h_{12i-1} \\ h_{22i-1} \end{bmatrix}$$

where vech is the operator that stacks the columns of the lower part of a symmetric matrix. Each element of H_i (variance or covariance) depends only on its past values and cross products of the innovations that correspond to it.
□

14.3   Estimation Method

We study in detail the application of GMM to ARCH-type models. The quasi-maximum likelihood method appears only as an example.

First, we introduce some notation. In what follows, the data-generating process is assumed to be strongly stationary and the moments computed with respect to the true distribution are still indexed by θ. To simplify, we set:

$$\begin{cases} E_{i-1}^{\theta}(y_i) = m_i(\lambda) \\ Var_{i-1}^{\theta}(y_i) = h_i(\lambda) \end{cases} \tag{14.6}$$

where θ is the vector of all parameters, including those of the distribution of y_i, and λ is the vector of the parameters of interest, those that appear in the conditional mean and variance.

Example 14.9 *For an ARCH(1) model defined by*

$$\begin{cases} E_{i-1}^{\theta}(y_i) = \beta' z_i \\ Var_{i-1}^{\theta}(y_i) = \alpha_0 + \alpha_1 \left(y_{i-1} - E_{i-1}^{\theta}(y_i) \right)^2, \end{cases}$$

the vector of the parameters of interest is $\lambda = (\beta', \alpha_0, \alpha_1)'$. □

In this chapter, we sometimes consider the process

$$u_i(\lambda) = y_i - m_i(\lambda) \tag{14.7}$$

which is such that

$$E_{i-1}^{\theta}(u_i(\lambda)) = 0 \quad \text{and} \quad Var_{i-1}^{\theta}(u_i(\lambda)) = h_i(\lambda).$$

To simplify the formulas, we do not always specify the arguments in the various functions.

Here, it is assumed that the process is mixing and ergodic, which has been proven for ARCH and GARCH models. Consider the general specification of ARCH models represented by the conditional moments (14.6). From these two moments, we infer orthogonality conditions that are the basis for the use of GMM. From (14.6) and

$$Var_{i-1}^{\theta}(y_i) = E_{i-1}^{\theta}(y_i^2) - \left[E_{i-1}^{\theta}(y_i) \right]^2 = E_{i-1}^{\theta}(y_i^2) - m_i(\lambda)^2,$$

we have

$$\begin{cases} E_{i-1}^{\theta}(y_i) = m_i(\lambda) \\ E_{i-1}^{\theta}(y_i^2) = h_i(\lambda) + m_i(\lambda)^2. \end{cases} \tag{14.8}$$

We apply here the method for transforming conditional moments into unconditional moments that has been studied in Chapter 3 and that is also used in other chapters. Let w_i be a $r \times 2$ matrix of functions of η_{i-1}; assume that $r \geq k$, where k is the dimension of the vector λ, which insures that there are sufficiently many moment equations.

Set

$$\rho(y_i, \lambda) = \begin{bmatrix} y_i - m_i(\lambda) \\ y_i^2 - h_i(\lambda) - m_i(\lambda)^2 \end{bmatrix}. \tag{14.9}$$

The orthogonality conditions can be written as

$$E^\theta \left(w_i \rho(y_i, \lambda) \right) = 0 \tag{14.10}$$

or to return to the notation of Chapter 3, as

$$E^\theta \left(\psi(y_i, \lambda) \right) = 0 \tag{14.11}$$

with

$$\psi(y_i, \lambda) = w_i \rho(y_i, \lambda);$$

hence $\psi(y_i, \lambda)$ is of dimension $r \times 1$. The GMM estimator of λ, denoted $\widehat{\lambda}_n$, is given by

$$\widehat{\lambda}_n = \arg\min_\lambda \left(\frac{1}{n} \sum_{i=1}^n \psi(y_i, \lambda) \right)' H_n \left(\frac{1}{n} \sum_{i=1}^n \psi(y_i, \lambda) \right) \tag{14.12}$$

where the $r \times r$ matrix H_n may depend on the sample and is supposed to satisfy $H_n \to H \ P^\theta$−a.s.

It follows from Theorem 3.4 in Chapter 3 about the asymptotic properties of GMM estimator that $\widehat{\lambda}_n \to \lambda \quad P^\theta$−a.s. (where λ is the solution to (14.10)) and that

$$\sqrt{n} \left(\widehat{\lambda}_n - \lambda \right) \to N\left(0, \Sigma_\theta\right) \quad \text{in } P^\theta \text{ distribution,}$$

with

$$\Sigma_\theta = \left[E^\theta \left(\frac{\partial \psi'}{\partial \lambda} \right) H E^\theta \left(\frac{\partial \psi}{\partial \lambda'} \right) \right]^{-1} E^\theta \left(\frac{\partial \psi'}{\partial \lambda} \right) H V_\theta H$$
$$\times E^\theta \left(\frac{\partial \psi}{\partial \lambda'} \right) \left[E^\theta \left(\frac{\partial \psi'}{\partial \lambda} \right) H E^\theta \left(\frac{\partial \psi}{\partial \lambda'} \right) \right]^{-1}, \tag{14.13}$$

(the various expressions are calculated at λ) and V_θ is given by (3.31). Note that V_θ simplifies to $V_\theta = Var^\theta \left(w_i \rho_i \right)$ since $Cov^\theta \left(w_i \rho_i, w_{i+j} \rho_{i+j} \right) = 0, \ \forall j \neq 0$ (see above Formula (14.20)).

Using the fact that

$$\frac{\partial \psi}{\partial \lambda'} = w_i \frac{\partial \rho}{\partial \lambda'},$$

we can write Σ_θ in the form

$$\Sigma_\theta = \left[E^\theta \left(\frac{\partial \rho'}{\partial \lambda} w_i' \right) H E^\theta \left(w_i \frac{\partial \rho}{\partial \lambda'} \right) \right]^{-1} E^\theta \left(\frac{\partial \rho'}{\partial \lambda} w_i' \right) H V_\theta H$$

$$\times E^\theta \left(w_i \frac{\partial \rho}{\partial \lambda'} \right) \left[E^\theta \left(\frac{\partial \rho'}{\partial \lambda} w_i' \right) H E^\theta \left(w_i \frac{\partial \rho}{\partial \lambda'} \right) \right]^{-1}. \tag{14.14}$$

Hence, when $r > k$, the expression of Σ_θ is complicated because $E^\theta(w_i \frac{\partial \rho}{\partial \lambda'})$ is of dimension $r \times k$ and hence is not square. We consider two cases.

The first one is where $H = V_\theta^{-1}$. This corresponds to the optimal choice of H_n. Then, we can apply the result of Theorem 3.5 in Chapter 3 to obtain

$$\Sigma_\theta = \left[E^\theta \left(\frac{\partial \rho'}{\partial \lambda} w_i' \right) V_\theta^{-1} E^\theta \left(w_i \frac{\partial \rho}{\partial \lambda'} \right) \right]^{-1}. \tag{14.15}$$

The second case is where $r = k$. $E^\theta(w_i \frac{\partial \rho}{\partial \lambda'})$ is here square and invertible. We use the results of Theorem 3.3 in Chapter 3, corresponding to a simple system of moment equations (the matrix H disappears by simplification) and we obtain

$$\Sigma_\theta = \left[E^\theta \left(w_i \frac{\partial \rho}{\partial \lambda'} \right) \right]^{-1} V_\theta \left[E^\theta \left(\frac{\partial \rho'}{\partial \lambda} w_i' \right) \right]^{-1}. \tag{14.16}$$

Note that this formula is equivalent to (14.14) when $H = V_\theta^{-1}$ and the restriction $r = k$ holds.

These results can be summarized in the following theorem, which follows from Theorems 3.3, 3.4, and 3.5 in Chapter 3, assuming their general assumptions are satisfied. The process is assumed to be stationary and ergodic, and to satisfy the conditions for the application of the central limit theorem.

Theorem 14.1 *Under general assumptions and assuming that $H_n \to H$ P^θ − a.s., the GMM estimator $\widehat{\lambda}_n$ of λ, the solution to the minimization of*

$$\left(\frac{1}{n} \sum_{i=1}^n w_i \rho(y_i, \lambda) \right)' H_n \left(\frac{1}{n} \sum_{i=1}^n w_i \rho(y_i, \lambda) \right),$$

satisfies the following asymptotic properties:

1) $\widehat{\lambda}_n \to \lambda$ P^θ − a.s. *(where λ is the solution to (14.10)),*
2) $\sqrt{n} (\widehat{\lambda}_n - \lambda) \to N(0, \Sigma_\theta)$ *in P^θ-distribution with*

a) *in the general case*

$$\Sigma_\theta = \left[E^\theta \left(\frac{\partial \rho'}{\partial \lambda} w_i' \right) H E^\theta \left(w_i \frac{\partial \rho}{\partial \lambda'} \right) \right]^{-1} E^\theta \left(\frac{\partial \rho'}{\partial \lambda} w_i' \right) H V_\theta H$$

$$\times E^\theta \left(w_i \frac{\partial \rho}{\partial \lambda'} \right) \left[E^\theta \left(\frac{\partial \rho'}{\partial \lambda} w_i' \right) H E^\theta \left(w_i \frac{\partial \rho}{\partial \lambda'} \right) \right]^{-1}, \tag{14.17}$$

b)   *if* $H = V_\theta^{-1}$,

$$\Sigma_\theta = \left[E^\theta \left(\frac{\partial \rho'}{\partial \lambda} w_i' \right) V_\theta^{-1} E^\theta \left(w_i \frac{\partial \rho}{\partial \lambda'} \right) \right]^{-1} \qquad (14.18)$$

($\widehat{\lambda}_n$ *is then the optimal GMM estimator*),
c)   *if* $r = k$,

$$\Sigma_\theta = \left[E^\theta \left(w_i \frac{\partial \rho}{\partial \lambda'} \right) \right]^{-1} V_\theta \left[E^\theta \left(\frac{\partial \rho'}{\partial \lambda} w_i' \right) \right]^{-1} \qquad (14.19)$$

($\widehat{\lambda}_n$ *is then an estimator of the simple method of moments*).   ∎

Now, we study in more detail the case where $r = k$. Formula (14.19) shows that the asymptotic variance Σ_θ depends on the variables w_i. We look for the optimal variable, also referred to as *optimal instrument*, w_i^* that minimizes Σ_θ. We know that

$$E^\theta \left(w_i \frac{\partial \rho}{\partial \lambda'} \right) = E^\theta \left[E_{i-1}^\theta \left(w_i \frac{\partial \rho}{\partial \lambda'} \right) \right] = E^\theta \left[w_i E_{i-1}^\theta \left(\frac{\partial \rho}{\partial \lambda'} \right) \right].$$

In addition,

$$\begin{aligned}
V_\theta &= Var^\theta (\psi) \\
&= Var^\theta (w_i \rho(y_i, \lambda)) \\
&= E^\theta \left(w_i \rho(y_i, \lambda) \rho(y_i, \lambda)' w_i' \right) - E^\theta (w_i \rho(y_i, \lambda)) E^\theta \left(\rho(y_i, \lambda)' w_i' \right) \\
&= E^\theta \left(w_i \rho(y_i, \lambda) \rho(y_i, \lambda)' w_i' \right)
\end{aligned}$$

in consequence of the moment conditions (14.10). Hence

$$\begin{aligned}
V_\theta &= E^\theta \left(w_i \rho \rho' w_i' \right) = E^\theta \left[w_i E_{i-1}^\theta \left(\rho \rho' \right) w_i' \right] \\
&= E^\theta \left[w_i \left(Var_{i-1}^\theta (\rho) \right) w_i' \right]
\end{aligned} \qquad (14.20)$$

since $E_{i-1}^\theta (\rho) = 0$. Σ_θ can be rewritten as

$$\Sigma_\theta = \left[E^\theta \left[w_i E_{i-1}^\theta \left(\frac{\partial \rho}{\partial \lambda'} \right) \right] \right]^{-1}$$
$$\times E^\theta \left[w_i \left(Var_{i-1}^\theta (\rho) \right) w_i' \right] \left[E^\theta \left[E_{i-1}^\theta \left(\frac{\partial \rho'}{\partial \lambda} \right) w_i' \right] \right]^{-1}. \qquad (14.21)$$

Let us set

$$w_i^* = \left(E_{i-1}^\theta \left(\frac{\partial \rho'}{\partial \lambda} \right) \right) \left(Var_{i-1}^\theta (\rho) \right)^{-1}. \qquad (14.22)$$

For this particular value of w_i, Σ_θ takes the form

$$\Sigma_\theta^* = \left[E^\theta \left[\left(E_{i-1}^\theta \left(\frac{\partial \rho'}{\partial \lambda} \right) \right) \left(Var_{i-1}^\theta (\rho) \right)^{-1} \left(E_{i-1}^\theta \left(\frac{\partial \rho}{\partial \lambda'} \right) \right) \right] \right]^{-1}.$$

(14.23)

The optimality of this choice for w_i^* follows from the results seen in Chapter 3, namely that the difference $\Sigma_\theta - \Sigma_\theta^*$ (where Σ_θ is given by (14.19)) is a positive semidefinite matrix and hence w_i^* is asymptotically optimal.

Let us examine more precisely the terms that compose w_i^* in (14.22). The first term is the transpose of

$$E_{i-1}^\theta \left(\frac{\partial \rho}{\partial \lambda'} \right) = \left[\begin{array}{c} -\frac{\partial m_i(\lambda)}{\partial \lambda'} \\ -\frac{\partial h_i(\lambda)}{\partial \lambda'} - 2m_i(\lambda) \frac{\partial m_i(\lambda)}{\partial \lambda'} \end{array} \right].$$

(14.24)

The second term of (14.22) is the inverse of

$$Var_{i-1}^\theta (\rho) = \left[\begin{array}{cc} Var_{i-1}^\theta (y_i) & Cov_{i-1}^\theta \left(y_i, y_i^2 \right) \\ Cov_{i-1}^\theta \left(y_i, y_i^2 \right) & Var_{i-1}^\theta \left(y_i^2 \right) \end{array} \right].$$

(14.25)

Consider the elements of this matrix. Given the general specification of the conditional moments given in (14.6), the first term is

$$Var_{i-1}^\theta (y_i) = h_i(\lambda).$$

(14.26)

According to (14.8), the second diagonal element can be rewritten as

$$Var_{i-1}^\theta \left(y_i^2 \right) = E_{i-1}^\theta \left(y_i^4 \right) - \left[E_{i-1}^\theta \left(y_i^2 \right) \right]^2 = E_{i-1}^\theta \left(y_i^4 \right) - \left(h_i + m_i^2 \right)^2.$$

(14.27)

From the definition of the conditionally standardized process, ζ_i, we can write

$$y_i = h_i^{1/2} \zeta_i + m_i,$$

we have

$$E_{i-1}^\theta \left(y_i^4 \right) = E_{i-1}^\theta \left(h_i^2 \zeta_i^4 + 4 h_i^{3/2} \zeta_i^3 m_i + 6 h_i \zeta_i^2 m_i^2 + 4 h_i^{1/2} \zeta_i m_i^3 + m_i^4 \right)$$

$$= h_i^2 M_{4i} + 4 h_i^{3/2} m_i M_{3i} + 6 h_i m_i^2 + m_i^4,$$

where M_{3i} and M_{4i} are given by

$$\begin{cases} M_{3i} = E_{i-1}^\theta \left(\zeta_i^3 \right) \\ M_{4i} = E_{i-1}^\theta \left(\zeta_i^4 \right), \end{cases}$$

hence

$$Var_{i-1}^\theta \left(y_i^2 \right) = h_i^2 M_{4i} + 4 h_i^{3/2} m_i M_{3i} + 4 h_i m_i^2 - h_i^2.$$

(14.28)

Finally, regarding the off-diagonal terms, we have

$$Cov^{\theta}_{i-1}\left(y_i, y_i^2\right) = Cov^{\theta}_{i-1}\left(h_i^{1/2}\zeta_i + m_i, h_i\zeta_i^2 + 2h_i^{1/2}\zeta_i m_i + m_i^2\right)$$

$$= h_i^{3/2} Cov^{\theta}_{i-1}\left(\zeta_i, \zeta_i^2\right) + 2h_i m_i Var^{\theta}_{i-1}\left(\zeta_i\right)$$

$$= h_i^{3/2} M_{3i} + 2h_i m_i$$

since $Var^{\theta}_{i-1}\left(\zeta_i\right) = 1$ and $Cov^{\theta}_{i-1}\left(\zeta_i, \zeta_i^2\right) = E^{\theta}_{i-1}\left(\zeta_i^3\right) = M_{3i}$. Then, the matrix $Var^{\theta}_{i-1}\left(\rho\right)$ can be written as

$$Var^{\theta}_{i-1}\left(\rho\right) = \begin{bmatrix} h_i & h_i^{3/2} M_{3i} + 2h_i m_i \\ h_i^{3/2} M_{3i} + 2h_i m_i & h_i^2 M_{4i} + 4h_i^{3/2} m_i M_{3i} + 4h_i m_i^2 - h_i^2 \end{bmatrix}.$$

$$\tag{14.29}$$

In empirical applications, one needs to replace the terms in the definition of w_i^* in (14.22) with consistent estimators.

In the following example, we detail the method based on the maximization of the log likelihood assuming conditional normality. Thus, we do as if the conditionally standardized process ζ_i follows a normal distribution. Using the results of Chapter 3, we will show that, even if the normality assumption does not hold (i.e., the true distribution is not conditionally normal), the estimator – then called *quasi-maximum likelihood* estimator – is consistent and asymptotically normal.

Example 14.10   *Consider the log-likelihood*

$$\ln l(y|\lambda) = \frac{1}{n}\sum_{i=1}^{n}\ln f(y_i|\lambda) \tag{14.30}$$

with

$$\ln f(y_i|\lambda) = -\tfrac{1}{2}\ln h_i(\lambda) - \tfrac{1}{2}\zeta_i(\lambda)^2$$

$$= -\tfrac{1}{2}\ln 2\pi - \tfrac{1}{2}\ln h_i(\lambda) - \tfrac{1}{2}\frac{(y_i - m_i(\lambda))^2}{h_i(\lambda)}. \tag{14.31}$$

The quasi-maximum likelihood estimator of λ, *denoted* $\widehat{\lambda}_n$, *is defined as*

$$\widehat{\lambda}_n = \arg\max_{\lambda}\frac{1}{n}\sum_{i=1}^{n}\ln f(y_i|\lambda).$$

To return to the notation of Chapter 3, we set

$$\phi(y_i, \lambda) = \ln f(y_i|\lambda)$$

and

$$\psi(y_i, \lambda) = \frac{\partial \phi(y_i, \lambda)}{\partial \lambda} = \frac{\partial \ln f(y_i|\lambda)}{\partial \lambda}.$$

The theoretical moment condition is written as

$$E^\theta \left(\psi(y_i, \lambda) \right) = E^\theta \left(\frac{\partial \ln f(y_i|\lambda)}{\partial \lambda} \right) = 0. \tag{14.32}$$

This is a moment condition corresponding to a misspecified model with normal distribution, and we assume that (14.32) has as unique solution the vector λ *which we wish to estimate. The estimator* $\widehat{\lambda}_n$ *is hence the solution to*

$$\frac{1}{n} \sum_{i=1}^{n} \psi(y_i, \lambda) = \frac{1}{n} \sum_{i=1}^{n} \frac{\partial \phi(y_i, \lambda)}{\partial \lambda} = \frac{1}{n} \sum_{i=1}^{n} \frac{\partial \ln f(y_i|\lambda)}{\partial \lambda} = 0.$$

From Theorem 3.3 in Chapter 3, $\widehat{\lambda}_n$ *has the following properties:*

$$\widehat{\lambda}_n \to \lambda \quad P^\theta - a.s.$$

(where λ *is the solution to (14.32)) and*

$$\sqrt{n} \left(\widehat{\lambda}_n - \lambda \right) \to N(0, \Sigma_\theta) \quad \text{in } P^\theta\text{-distribution}$$

with

$$\begin{cases} \Sigma_\theta = J_\theta^{-1} I_\theta J_\theta^{-1} \\ I_\theta = Var^\theta \left(\frac{\partial \ln f(y_i|\lambda)}{\partial \lambda} \right) \\ J_\theta = E^\theta \left(\frac{\partial^2 \ln f(y_i|\lambda)}{\partial \lambda \partial \lambda'} \right). \end{cases}$$

I_θ *can be rewritten as*

$$I_\theta = E^\theta \left(\frac{\partial \ln f(y_i|\lambda)}{\partial \lambda} \frac{\partial \ln f(y_i|\lambda)}{\partial \lambda'} \right) - \left[E^\theta \left(\frac{\partial \ln f(y_i|\lambda)}{\partial \lambda} \right) \right]^2$$

$$= E^\theta \left(\frac{\partial \ln f(y_i|\lambda)}{\partial \lambda} \frac{\partial \ln f(y_i|\lambda)}{\partial \lambda'} \right)$$

given the moment condition (14.32). It follows from (14.31) that

$$\frac{\partial \ln f(y_i|\lambda)}{\partial \lambda} = -\frac{1}{2h_i} \frac{\partial h_i}{\partial \lambda} + \frac{(y_i - m_i)}{h_i} \frac{\partial m_i}{\partial \lambda} + \frac{1}{2} \frac{(y_i - m_i)^2}{h_i^2} \frac{\partial h_i}{\partial \lambda}$$

and

$$\frac{\partial^2 \ln f(y_i|\lambda)}{\partial\lambda\partial\lambda'} = \frac{1}{2h_i^2}\frac{\partial h_i}{\partial\lambda}\frac{\partial h_i}{\partial\lambda'} - \frac{1}{2h_i}\frac{\partial^2 h_i}{\partial\lambda\partial\lambda'} - \frac{1}{h_i}\frac{\partial m_i}{\partial\lambda}\frac{\partial m_i}{\partial\lambda'}$$

$$- \frac{(y_i - m_i)}{h_i^2}\frac{\partial m_i}{\partial\lambda}\frac{\partial h_i}{\partial\lambda'} + \frac{(y_i - m_i)}{h_i}\frac{\partial^2 m_i}{\partial\lambda\partial\lambda'} - \frac{(y_i - m_i)}{h_i^2}\frac{\partial h_i}{\partial\lambda}\frac{\partial m_i}{\partial\lambda'}$$

$$- \frac{(y_i - m_i)^2}{h_i^3}\frac{\partial h_i}{\partial\lambda}\frac{\partial h_i}{\partial\lambda'} + \frac{(y_i - m_i)^2}{2h_i^2}\frac{\partial^2 h_i}{\partial\lambda\partial\lambda'}.$$

In these expressions, we use the term

$$\zeta_i = (y_i - m_i)/h_i^{1/2}$$

whose moments are

$$E_{i-1}^\theta(\zeta_i) = 0,\ E_{i-1}^\theta(\zeta_i^2) = 1,\ E_{i-1}^\theta(\zeta_i^3) = M_{3i}\ \text{and}\ E_{i-1}^\theta(\zeta_i^4) = M_{4i}.$$

Then, we can write

$$\frac{\partial \ln f(y_i|\lambda)}{\partial\lambda} = -\frac{1}{2h_i}\frac{\partial h_i}{\partial\lambda} + \frac{1}{h_i^{1/2}}\zeta_i\frac{\partial m_i}{\partial\lambda} + \frac{1}{2h_i}\zeta_i^2\frac{\partial h_i}{\partial\lambda}$$

and

$$\frac{\partial^2 \ln f(y_i|\lambda)}{\partial\lambda\partial\lambda'} = \frac{1}{2h_i^2}\frac{\partial h_i}{\partial\lambda}\frac{\partial h_i}{\partial\lambda'} - \frac{1}{2h_i}\frac{\partial^2 h_i}{\partial\lambda\partial\lambda'} - \frac{1}{h_i}\frac{\partial m_i}{\partial\lambda}\frac{\partial m_i}{\partial\lambda'}$$

$$- \frac{\zeta_i}{h_i^{3/2}}\frac{\partial m_i}{\partial\lambda}\frac{\partial h_i}{\partial\lambda'} + \frac{\zeta_i}{h_i^{1/2}}\frac{\partial^2 m_i}{\partial\lambda\partial\lambda'} - \frac{\zeta_i}{h_i^{3/2}}\frac{\partial h_i}{\partial\lambda}\frac{\partial m_i}{\partial\lambda'}$$

$$- \frac{\zeta_i^2}{h_i^2}\frac{\partial h_i}{\partial\lambda}\frac{\partial h_i}{\partial\lambda'} + \frac{\zeta_i^2}{2h_i}\frac{\partial^2 h_i}{\partial\lambda\partial\lambda'}.$$

Consequently, using the expressions of the conditional moments of ζ_i, we can write I_θ and J_θ as

$$I_\theta = E^\theta\left[\frac{1}{4h_i^2}\frac{\partial h_i}{\partial\lambda}\frac{\partial h_i}{\partial\lambda'}(M_{4i} - 1) + \frac{1}{h_i}\frac{\partial m_i}{\partial\lambda}\frac{\partial m_i}{\partial\lambda'}\right.$$

$$\left. + \frac{1}{2h_i^{3/2}}\left(\frac{\partial h_i}{\partial\lambda}\frac{\partial m_i}{\partial\lambda'} + \frac{\partial m_i}{\partial\lambda}\frac{\partial h_i}{\partial\lambda'}\right)M_{3i}\right]$$

and

$$J_\theta = E^\theta\left[-\frac{1}{2h_i^2}\frac{\partial h_i}{\partial\lambda}\frac{\partial h_i}{\partial\lambda'} - \frac{1}{h_i}\frac{\partial m_i}{\partial\lambda}\frac{\partial m_i}{\partial\lambda'}\right].$$

In the empirical applications, I_θ and J_θ need to be approximated by replacing λ by $\widehat{\lambda}_n$ and the expectations by their sample counterparts.

An important case is that of the conditional normality. Indeed, when the model is actually conditionally normal, then $M_{3i} = 0$ and $M_{4i} = 3$, which implies that $J_\theta = -I_\theta$, hence

$$\sqrt{n}\left(\hat{\lambda}_n - \lambda\right) \longrightarrow N\left(0, I_\theta^{-1}\right) \quad \text{in } P^\theta\text{-distribution}$$

with

$$I_\theta = E^\theta \left[\frac{1}{2h_i^2} \frac{\partial h_i}{\partial \lambda} \frac{\partial h_i}{\partial \lambda'} + \frac{1}{h_i} \frac{\partial m_i}{\partial \lambda} \frac{\partial m_i}{\partial \lambda'} \right]. \tag{14.33}$$

□

The example below shows that the estimators of the mean and the variance are asymptotically independent from each other, which justifies a two-stage estimation method that we will outline later.

Example 14.11 *Consider an ARCH(q) model given by*

$$\begin{cases} E_{i-1}^\theta(y_i) = \beta' z_i = m_i(\beta) \\ Var_{i-1}^0(y_i) = \alpha_0 + \alpha_1(y_{i-1} - \beta' z_{i-1})^2 + \cdots + \alpha_q(y_{i-q} - \beta' z_{i-q})^2 = h_i(\beta, \alpha) \end{cases}$$

where z_i and β are $l \times 1$ vectors. Assume that $u_i = y_i - \beta' z_i$ is conditionally distributed as a $N(0, h_i)$. Thus, there are two types of parameters: β that appears in both the mean and variance and α that appears only in the variance. The derivatives of m_i and h_i with respect to β and α are

$$\frac{\partial m_i}{\partial \beta} = z_i \quad \text{and} \quad \frac{\partial m_i}{\partial \alpha} = 0,$$

$$\frac{\partial h_i}{\partial \beta} = -2\sum_{j=1}^q \alpha_j z_{i-j} u_{i-j} \quad \text{and} \quad \frac{\partial h_i}{\partial \alpha} = \begin{pmatrix} 1 \\ u_{i-1}^2 \\ \vdots \\ u_{i-q}^2 \end{pmatrix}.$$

The asymptotic covariance matrix of the vector $\hat{\lambda}_n = (\hat{\beta}_n', \hat{\alpha}_n')'$ is given, under the conditional normality assumption (see preceding example), by

$$\Sigma_\theta = I_\theta^{-1}$$

with

$$I_\theta = \begin{bmatrix} I_\theta^{\beta\beta} & I_\theta^{\beta\alpha} \\ I_\theta^{\alpha\beta} & I_\theta^{\alpha\alpha} \end{bmatrix}$$

$$= E^\theta \left[\frac{1}{2h_i^2} \begin{pmatrix} \frac{\partial h_i}{\partial \beta} \\ \frac{\partial h_i}{\partial \alpha} \end{pmatrix} \begin{pmatrix} \frac{\partial h_i}{\partial \beta} \\ \frac{\partial h_i}{\partial \alpha} \end{pmatrix}' + \frac{1}{h_i} \begin{pmatrix} \frac{\partial m_i}{\partial \beta} \\ 0 \end{pmatrix} \begin{pmatrix} \frac{\partial m_i}{\partial \beta} \\ 0 \end{pmatrix}' \right].$$

Now, we consider successively the submatrices that make up I_θ. First,

$$I_\theta^{\beta\beta} = E^\theta \left[\frac{1}{2h_i^2} \frac{\partial h_i}{\partial \beta} \frac{\partial h_i}{\partial \beta'} + \frac{1}{h_i} \frac{\partial m_i}{\partial \beta} \frac{\partial m_i}{\partial \beta'} \right]$$

$$= E^\theta \left[\frac{2}{h_i^2} \left(\sum_{j=1}^q \alpha_j z_{i-j} u_{i-j} \right) \left(\sum_{j=1}^q \alpha_j z'_{i-j} u_{i-j} \right) + \frac{1}{h_i} z_i z'_i \right],$$

then

$$I_\theta^{\alpha\alpha} = E^\theta \left[\frac{1}{2h_i^2} \frac{\partial h_i}{\partial \alpha} \frac{\partial h_i}{\partial \alpha'} \right]$$

$$= E^\theta \left[\frac{1}{2h_i^2} \begin{pmatrix} 1 \\ u_{i-1}^2 \\ \vdots \\ u_{i-q}^2 \end{pmatrix} \left(1, u_{i-1}^2, \ldots, u_{i-q}^2 \right) \right],$$

and finally

$$I_\theta^{\beta\alpha} = E^\theta \left[\frac{1}{2h_i^2} \frac{\partial h_i}{\partial \beta} \frac{\partial h_i}{\partial \alpha'} \right]$$

$$= E^\theta \left[-\frac{1}{h_i^2} \left(\sum_{j=1}^q \alpha_j z_{i-j} u_{i-j} \right) \left(1, u_{i-1}^2, \ldots, u_{i-q}^2 \right) \right]$$

$$= 0$$

because the third moments are zero. Hence, the estimators $\widehat{\beta}_n$ and $\widehat{\alpha}_n$ are asymptotically uncorrelated when u admits a conditionally normal ARCH representation (i.e., the true underlying distribution is normal). However, they are correlated in the general case. In practice, the asymptotic covariances are calculated by replacing E^θ by a sample mean and the parameters α_j and β by their estimators. □

In the case of a regression model with ARCH error, since the information matrix is block diagonal, β and α can be separately estimated and one of them can be replaced by its estimator in order to estimate the other parameter. This takes us to the two-stage method presented in the following example of a ARCH(q) model.

Example 14.12 *Return to the notation of the preceding example. The two-stage procedure is the following:*
    * *The OLS estimation of the model*

$$y_i = \beta' z_i + u_i$$

allows us to obtain a consistent estimator of β, denoted $\widetilde{\beta}_n$. From this, we can extract the estimated residuals $\widetilde{u}_i$.

* Consider the model associated with the conditional second moment where the u_i are replaced by $\widetilde{u}_i$:*

$$\widetilde{u}_i^2 = \alpha_0 + \alpha_1 \widetilde{u}_{i-1}^2 + \cdots + \alpha_q \widetilde{u}_{i-q}^2 + \eta_i.$$

The OLS estimators, denoted $\widetilde{\alpha}_{0n}, \widetilde{\alpha}_{1n}, \ldots, \widetilde{\alpha}_{qn}$, are consistent estimators of the corresponding parameters.

* We now take the heteroskedasticity into account. We approximate the volatility h_i by*

$$\widetilde{h}_i = \widetilde{\alpha}_{0n} + \widetilde{\alpha}_{1n} \widetilde{u}_{i-1}^2 + \cdots + \widetilde{\alpha}_{qn} \widetilde{u}_{i-q}^2.$$

Then, we estimate the regression model

$$\frac{y_i}{\sqrt{\widetilde{h}_i}} = \beta_1 \frac{z_{i1}}{\sqrt{\widetilde{h}_i}} + \cdots + \beta_l \frac{z_{il}}{\sqrt{\widetilde{h}_i}} + \frac{u_i}{\sqrt{\widetilde{h}_i}}.$$

We obtain GLS-type estimators β_n^*.

* Under the assumption of conditional normality, the term η_i is conditionally heteroskedastic with conditional variance*

$$Var_{i-1}^\theta(\eta_i) = 2h_i^2.$$

Then, we estimate by OLS the model

$$\frac{\widetilde{u}_i^2}{\widetilde{h}_i} = \alpha_0 \frac{1}{\widetilde{h}_i} + \alpha_1 \frac{\widetilde{u}_{i-1}^2}{\widetilde{h}_i} + \cdots + \alpha_q \frac{\widetilde{u}_{i-q}^2}{\widetilde{h}_i} + \frac{\eta_i}{\widetilde{h}_i},$$

and call $\alpha_{0n}^*, \alpha_{1n}^*, \ldots, \alpha_{qn}^*$ the resulting GLS estimators. □

This approach is simpler (there is no problem of numerical maximization) but less efficient than the maximization of the likelihood function. To finish, it is worth noting that a two-stage procedure can also be used in the normal GARCH model because the asymptotic variance-covariance matrix is also diagonal.

14.4 Tests for Conditional Homoskedasticity

We present two tests for conditional homoskedasticity that both derive from the Rao procedure. The application of the Rao procedure to test for homoskedasticity in a ARCH(q) model leads to the so-called *Engle test*. The theoretical presentation of this test is provided in Example 14.14 that deals with the general case. The first example describes its practical implementation. It is based on the idea that the autocorrelation of the squared residuals estimated by OLS indicates the presence of an ARCH effect.

Example 14.13   *We return to the notation of the preceding example. The homoskedasticity assumption can be expressed as*

$$H_0: \quad \alpha_1 = \cdots = \alpha_q = 0 .$$

The steps of the Engle test are the following. First, regress y_i on z_i: $y_i = \beta' z_i + u_i$, calculate the estimated residuals $\widehat{u}_i$, then estimate the following regression

$$\widehat{u}_i^2 = \alpha_0 + \alpha_1 \widehat{u}_{i-1}^2 + \cdots + \alpha_q \widehat{u}_{i-q}^2 + \eta_i.$$

and calculate

$$n_0 R^2$$

(R^2 is the centered coefficient of determination and n_0 the number of observations in this auxiliary regression). This statistic follows asymptotically a chi-squared distribution with q degrees of freedom under the null hypothesis.   □

This test is the locally asymptotically most powerful test, as are the Wald and Likelihood ratio tests. A more general exposition of the application of the Rao test is given in the example that follows.

Example 14.14   *We start from a more general representation of a conditionally heteroskedastic model where the conditional mean and variance are given by*

$$\begin{cases} E^\theta_{i-1}(y_i) = m_i(\beta) \\ Var^\theta_{i-1}(y_i) = h_i(\beta, \alpha_0, \alpha^1) \end{cases}$$

and we assume that

$$h_i(\beta, \alpha_0, 0) = h(\alpha_0)$$

where $\lambda = (\beta', \alpha_0, \alpha^{1'})'$, α_0 is scalar and α^1 is a $r \times 1$ vector. This immediately applies to ARCH(q) models. For a GARCH model, α^1 contains the parameters associated with the squared lagged residuals and lagged conditional variances. Assume moreover that y_i follows conditionally a normal distribution. We use the results of Chapter 4 on the asymptotic tests and more particularly the part devoted to the tests based on the maximum likelihood estimation. The null hypothesis of homoskedasticity is written as $H_0 : \alpha^1 = 0$. We partition the vector λ as

$$\lambda = (\lambda_1', \lambda_2')' \quad with \quad \lambda_1 = (\beta', \alpha_0)' \quad and \quad \lambda_2 = \alpha^1;$$

and partition the information matrix I_θ (drawn from (14.33)) in the corresponding way:

$$I_\theta = E^\theta \left(\frac{1}{2h_i^2} \frac{\partial h_i}{\partial \lambda} \frac{\partial h_i}{\partial \lambda'} + \frac{1}{h_i} \frac{\partial m_i}{\partial \lambda} \frac{\partial m_i}{\partial \lambda'} \right) = \begin{pmatrix} I_\theta^{11} & I_\theta^{12} \\ I_\theta^{21} & I_\theta^{22} \end{pmatrix} .$$

The restricted MLE of λ under the null hypothesis is $\widehat{\lambda}_n = (\widehat{\lambda}'_{1n}, \widehat{\lambda}'_{2n})' = (\widehat{\beta}'_n, \widehat{\alpha}_{0n}, 0)'$. Then, the Rao statistic is given by

$$RAO_n = n \left(\frac{1}{n} \sum_{i=1}^{n} \frac{\partial \ln f(y_i | \widehat{\beta}_n, \widehat{\alpha}_{0n}, 0)}{\partial \alpha^1} \right)' \left(\widehat{I}_\theta^{22} - \widehat{I}_\theta^{21} (\widehat{I}_\theta^{11})^{-1} \widehat{I}_\theta^{12} \right)^{-1}$$

$$\times \left(\frac{1}{n} d \sum_{i=1}^{n} \frac{\partial \ln f(y_i | \widehat{\beta}_n, \widehat{\alpha}_{0n}, 0)}{\partial \alpha^1} \right)$$

where the submatrices $\widehat{I}_\theta^{11}$, $\widehat{I}_\theta^{12}$, $\widehat{I}_\theta^{21}$, and $\widehat{I}_\theta^{22}$ are evaluated at $\widehat{\lambda}_n$. Under H_0, this statistic follows asymptotically a chi-squared distribution with degrees of freedom equal to the dimension of α^1. Given that at the point $(\beta, \alpha_0, 0)$, we have

$$\frac{\partial h_i}{\partial \beta} = 0,$$

and

$$\frac{\partial m_i}{\partial \alpha_0} = 0 \quad \text{and} \quad \frac{\partial m_i}{\partial \alpha^1} = 0,$$

I_θ takes the form

$$I_\theta = E^\theta \left[\frac{1}{2h_i^2} \begin{pmatrix} 0 \\ \frac{\partial h_i}{\partial \alpha_0} \\ \frac{\partial h_i}{\partial \alpha^1} \end{pmatrix} \begin{pmatrix} 0 \\ \frac{\partial h_i}{\partial \alpha_0} \\ \frac{\partial h_i}{\partial \alpha^1} \end{pmatrix}' + \frac{1}{h_i} \begin{pmatrix} \frac{\partial m_i}{\partial \beta} \\ 0 \\ 0 \end{pmatrix} \begin{pmatrix} \frac{\partial m_i}{\partial \beta} \\ 0 \\ 0 \end{pmatrix}' \right]$$

at $(\beta, \alpha_0, 0)$. Hence, the submatrices can be written as

$$I_\theta^{11} = E^\theta \begin{pmatrix} \frac{1}{h_i} \frac{\partial m_i}{\partial \beta} \frac{\partial m_i}{\partial \beta'} & 0 \\ 0 & \frac{1}{2h_i^2} \left(\frac{\partial h_i}{\partial \alpha_0} \right)^2 \end{pmatrix},$$

$$I_\theta^{12} = I_\theta^{21'} = E^\theta \begin{pmatrix} 0 \\ \frac{1}{2h_i^2} \frac{\partial h_i}{\partial \alpha_0} \frac{\partial h_i}{\partial \alpha^{1'}} \end{pmatrix},$$

$$I_\theta^{22} = E^\theta \left(\frac{1}{2h_i^2} \frac{\partial h_i}{\partial \alpha^1} \frac{\partial h_i}{\partial \alpha^{1'}} \right).$$

Thus, at $(\beta, \alpha_0, 0)$, we have

$$I_\theta^{22} - I_\theta^{21} (I_\theta^{11})^{-1} I_\theta^{12}$$

$$= E^\theta \left(\frac{1}{2h_i^2} \frac{\partial h_i}{\partial \alpha^1} \frac{\partial h_i}{\partial \alpha^{1'}} \right) - E^\theta \left(\frac{1}{2h_i^2} \frac{\partial h_i}{\partial \alpha^1} \frac{\partial h_i}{\partial \alpha_0} \right)$$

$$\times \left[E^\theta \left(\frac{1}{2h_i^2} \left(\frac{\partial h_i}{\partial \alpha_0} \right)^2 \right) \right]^{-1} E^\theta \left(\frac{1}{2h_i^2} \frac{\partial h_i}{\partial \alpha_0} \frac{\partial h_i}{\partial \alpha^{1'}} \right).$$

Setting

$$h_i(\widehat{\beta}_n, \widehat{\alpha}_{0n}, 0) = \widehat{h}_0 \quad and \quad \frac{\partial h_i(\widehat{\beta}_n, \widehat{\alpha}_{0n}, 0)}{\partial \alpha^1} = l_i,$$

we can write the matrix that appears in the Rao statistic as

$$\widehat{I}_\theta^{22} - \widehat{I}_\theta^{21} \left(\widehat{I}_\theta^{11}\right)^{-1} \widehat{I}_\theta^{12} = \frac{1}{2n} \frac{1}{\widehat{h}_0^2} \left[\sum_{i=1}^n l_i l_i' - \frac{1}{n} \left(\sum_{i=1}^n l_i\right) \left(\sum_{i=1}^n l_i\right)' \right].$$

In addition, since

$$\ln f(y_i|\lambda) = -\frac{1}{2} \ln 2\pi - \frac{1}{2} \ln h_i - \frac{1}{2} \frac{(y_i - m_i)^2}{h_i},$$

we can write

$$\frac{1}{n} \sum_{i=1}^n \frac{\partial \ln f(y_i|\lambda)}{\partial \alpha^1} = \frac{1}{n} \sum_{i=1}^n \left(-\frac{1}{2h_i} + \frac{1}{2} \frac{(y_i - m_i)^2}{h_i^2} \right) \frac{\partial h_i}{\partial \alpha^1},$$

hence

$$\frac{1}{n} \sum_{i=1}^n \frac{\partial \ln f(y_i|\widehat{\beta}_n, \widehat{\alpha}_{0n}, 0)}{\partial \alpha^1} = \frac{1}{2n} \frac{1}{\widehat{h}_0^2} \sum_{i=1}^n \left((y_i - m_i(\widehat{\beta}_n))^2 - \widehat{h}_0 \right) l_i.$$

Setting $\widehat{u}_i^0 = y_i - m_i(\widehat{\beta}_n)$, the Rao statistic is then written as

$$RAO_n = \frac{1}{2\widehat{h}_0^2} \left(\sum_{i=1}^n \left[\widehat{u}_i^{02} - \widehat{h}_0\right] l_i \right)' \left(\sum_{i=1}^n l_i l_i' - \frac{1}{n} \left(\sum_{i=1}^n l_i\right) \left(\sum_{i=1}^n l_i\right)' \right)^{-1}$$

$$\times \left(\sum_{i=1}^n \left[\widehat{u}_i^{02} - \widehat{h}_0\right] l_i \right).$$

This Rao test can be computed using the following simple approach. Consider an approximated model obtained from an expansion where the unknown parameters are replaced by the restricted estimators

$$\widehat{u}_i^2 \simeq h(\widehat{\alpha}_0) + \frac{\partial h_i}{\partial \alpha^1}(\widehat{\beta}, \widehat{\alpha}_0, 0)\alpha^1 + \eta_i$$

with $E_{i-1}^\theta(\eta_i) = 0$, $Var_{i-1}^\theta(\eta_i) = 2h^2(\widehat{\alpha}_0)$. The Rao statistic of $H_0 : \alpha^1 = 0$, the null hypothesis of conditional homoskedasticity, is then

$$RAO_n = n_0 R^2$$

where R^2 is the coefficient of multiple correlation in the approximated homoskedastic model and n_0 the number of observations. Under H_0, this statistic follows asymptotically a chi-squared with degrees of freedom equal to the dimension of the vector α^1.   □

The simple Engle test for an ARCH(q) model immediately follows from this more general presentation.

Other methods are sometimes used to identify q in the equation of the conditional variance in a ARCH(q) model, such as the likelihood ratio test or an information criterion like that of Akaike or that of Schwarz. The drawback of these methods is that they require a large number of maximizations of the likelihood function, corresponding to different values of q.

Once the presence of conditional heteroskedasticity has been established, it is natural to search for the specification of the functional form. For example, one may wonder whether the simplest ARCH specification is sufficient or whether it is better to look for a broader formulation. The Rao procedure can also be used to test specific forms of the heteroskedasticity against each other, for instance to test an ARCH model against a NARCH alternative.

14.5 Some Specificities of ARCH-Type Models

14.5.1 Stationarity

It is important to note that the statistical theory that we presented above requires the process to be strongly stationary, ergodic, and mixing. In the literature, the study of the conditions for weak and strong (also called strict) stationarity have traditionally focused on GARCH models. We know that strong stationarity implies weak stationarity provided the second moments exist, which is not always the case for GARCH models. We simply provide the main results regarding the weak stationarity of GARCH(p,q) models and the strong stationarity of GARCH(1,1).

In a conditionally normal GARCH(p,q) model with conditional variance

$$Var_{i-1}^{\theta}(y_i) = h_i = \alpha_0 + \sum_{j=1}^{q} \alpha_j u_{i-j}^2 + \sum_{r=1}^{p} \xi_r h_{i-r},$$

with $u_i = y_i - E_{i-1}^{\theta}(y_i)$, $\alpha_q \neq 0$ and $\xi_p \neq 0$, we have the following result: the process u_i is weakly stationary as long as the roots of the characteristic polynomial

$$1 - \sum_{r=1}^{\max\{p,q\}} (\alpha_r + \xi_r) z^r$$

are outside the unit circle, which is equivalent to

$$\sum_{r=1}^{\max\{p,q\}} (\alpha_r + \xi_r) < 1.$$

For some values of the parameters, strong stationarity does not imply weak stationarity because the second moments do not exist. This has been shown in the case of a conditionally normal GARCH(1,1) of the form

$$\begin{cases} E_{i-1}^{\theta}(y_i) = 0 \\ Var_{i-1}^{\theta}(y_i) = \alpha_0 + \alpha_1 u_{i-1}^2 + \xi h_{i-1} \end{cases}$$

where $\alpha_0 > 0$, $\alpha_1 \geq 0$, $\xi \geq 0$, and α_1 and ξ may take any values including those for which $\alpha_1 + \xi \geq 1$. Let ζ_i be the standardized normal process defined by $\zeta_i h_i^{1/2} = y_i$. It can be shown that the parameter space can be partitioned in three regions:

- Region 1 $((\alpha_1 + \xi) < 1)$: y_i is strongly stationary and its second moment exists,
- Region 2 $(1 \leq (\alpha_1 + \xi)$ and $E \log(\alpha_1 \zeta^2 + \xi) < 0)$: y_i is strongly but not weakly stationary because its second moment does not exist,
- Region 3 $(E \log(\alpha_1 \zeta^2 + \xi) \geq 0)$: this is an explosive region (not strongly stationary and the second moment does not exist).

The IGARCH(1,1) process, characterized by $\alpha_1 + \xi = 1$, corresponds to the border between regions 1 and 2 and hence are strongly stationary with marginal distributions that have thick tails.

Hence, one of the noteworthy properties of GARCH processes is that they may be strongly stationary without being weakly stationary, given that the weak stationary demands that the mean, variance, and autocovariances be finite and time invariant, while the strong stationarity does not require finite moments.

14.5.2 Leptokurticity

Recall that for an arbitrary series u_i, the kurtosis is defined by

$$K = \frac{E^{\theta}(u_i^4)}{\left[E^{\theta}(u_i^2)\right]^2}$$

and measures the thickness of the tails of the distribution. For a normal distribution, $K = 3$. It has been established that the marginal distributions of ARCH and GARCH processes with conditionally normal errors are leptokurtic (i.e., $K > 3$) and hence have thicker tails than the normal distribution.

Example 14.15 *Consider a ARCH-type process that is conditionally normal. The conditional kurtosis is equal to 3:*

$$K_i = \frac{E_{i-1}^{\theta}(u_i^4)}{\left[E_{i-1}^{\theta}(u_i^2)\right]^2} = 3.$$

The second and forth moments, $E_{i-1}^{\theta}(u_i^2)$ and $E_{i-1}^{\theta}(u_i^4)$, are linked by

$$E_{i-1}^{\theta}(u_i^4) = 3\left[E_{i-1}^{\theta}(u_i^2)\right]^2.$$

Let us write the kurtosis of the unconditional distribution using the law of iterated expectations:

$$K = \frac{E^{\theta}(u_i^4)}{\left[E^{\theta}(u_i^2)\right]^2} = \frac{E^{\theta}\left(3E_{i-1}^{\theta}(u_i^2)\right)^2}{\left[E^{\theta}\left(E_{i-1}^{\theta}(u_i^2)\right)\right]^2} = \frac{3E^{\theta}\left[\left(E_{i-1}^{\theta}(u_i^2)\right)^2\right]}{\left[E^{\theta}\left(E_{i-1}^{\theta}(u_i^2)\right)\right]^2} \geq 3$$

since

$$E^{\theta}\left(\left[E_{i-1}^{\theta}(u_i^2)\right]^2\right) \geq \left[E^{\theta}\left(E_{i-1}^{\theta}(u_i^2)\right)\right]^2.$$

Hence, the marginal distribution of u_i has thicker tails than the normal distribution. It can also be shown that

$$K = 3 + 3\frac{Var^{\theta}(h_i)}{\left[E^{\theta}(u_i^2)\right]^2}.$$

Thus, the kurtosis depends on the conditional heteroskedasticity represented by h_i. In particular, if $Var^{\theta}(h_i) = 0$, i.e., the conditional variance is constant (case of conditional homoskedasticity), we have $K = 3$. ☐

In the case of a conditional distribution that is a Student's t distribution with v degrees of freedom, $v > 4$, the kurtosis is equal to

$$K = 3(v-2)(v-4)^{-1} = 3 + \frac{6}{v-4} \geq 3.$$

This is an example of leptokurtic conditional distribution.

14.5.3   Various Conditional Distributions

Notice that, besides the normal, other distributions have been used, such as the Student's t distribution and the Generalized Error Distribution (GED) which we see in the two examples that follow.

Example 14.16   *Consider the model*

$$\begin{cases} E_{i-1}^{\theta}(y_i) = m_i \\ Var_{i-1}^{\theta}(y_i) = h_i \end{cases}$$

where $u_i = y_i - m_i$ follows conditionally a Student's t distribution. Its density is of the form:

$$f(u_i, \lambda) = \frac{1}{\sqrt{\pi}} \Gamma \left(\frac{\nu + 1}{2} \right) \Gamma \left(\frac{\nu}{2} \right)^{-1} ((\nu - 2) h_i)^{-1/2} \left(1 + u_i^2 h_i^{-1} (\nu - 2)^{-1} \right)^{-\frac{\nu+1}{2}}$$

with $\nu > 2$ (Γ represents the usual gamma function). Recall that if $1/\nu \longrightarrow 0$, then the t distribution converges to a normal distribution with variance h_i, and if $1/\nu > 0$, the t distribution has thicker tails than the corresponding normal distribution. To estimate this model, it suffices to write the log-likelihood function and to maximize it by numerical procedures such as that of Berndt, Hall, Hall, and Hausman.   □

Example 14.17 *The density of a GED random variable, normalized to have mean zero and unit variance is*

$$f(\zeta) = \frac{\nu \exp \left(-\frac{1}{2} |\zeta/\lambda|^\nu \right)}{\lambda 2^{(1+1/\nu)} \Gamma(1/\nu)} , \quad -\infty < \zeta < \infty , \quad 0 < \nu \le \infty$$

where $\Gamma(.)$ is the gamma function and

$$\lambda = \left[2^{-2/\nu} \Gamma(1/\nu) / \Gamma(3/\nu) \right]^{1/2} .$$

This distribution is symmetric around zero. The parameter ν determines the thickness of the tails:

* *If $\nu = 2$, ζ has a standard normal distribution. To show this, we recall a few properties of the gamma function: $\Gamma(\alpha + 1) = \alpha \Gamma(\alpha)$, $\Gamma(1) = 1$, and $\Gamma(1/2) = \sqrt{\pi}$. Hence, $\Gamma(3/2) = \frac{1}{2}\sqrt{\pi}$ and $\lambda = 1$. Then, we can write the density of ζ as*

$$f(\zeta) = \frac{2 \exp \left(-\frac{1}{2}\zeta^2 \right)}{2^{(1+1/2)} \sqrt{\pi}} = \frac{1}{\sqrt{2\pi}} \exp \left(-\frac{1}{2}\zeta^2 \right),$$

from which it follows that $\zeta \sim N(0, 1)$.
* *If $\nu < 2$, the distribution of ζ has thicker tails than the normal, i.e., is leptokurtic.*
* *If $\nu > 2$, the distribution has thinner tails than the normal, i.e., is platikurtic.*

Moreover, if $\nu = 1$, ζ follows a double exponential distribution. The log-likelihood is given by

$$\ln l(y|\lambda) = \sum_{i=1}^{n} \ln \left[\frac{\nu \exp \left(-\frac{1}{2} |\zeta_i/\lambda|^\nu \right)}{\lambda 2^{(1+1/\nu)} \Gamma(1/\nu)} \right]$$

$$= n \log \frac{\nu}{\lambda} - n(1 + 1/\nu) \ln 2 - n \ln \Gamma(1/\nu) - \frac{1}{2} \sum_{i=1}^{n} |\zeta_i/\lambda|^\nu.$$

□

Notes

For a general study of ARCH models, refer to the book by Gourieroux and Jasiak (2001) and to various articles, among them those of Bera and Higgins (1993), of Bollerslev, Chou, and Kroner (1992) and of Bollerslev, Engle, and Nelson (1994); see also Pagan (1996). Regarding the models presented in the examples, see in particular Engle (1982 and 1983) for the ARCH model, Bollerslev (1986) and Engle and Bollerslev (1986) for the GARCH model (refer to Nelson and Cao (1992) for the positivity restrictions), Engle, Lilien, and Robins (1987) for the ARCH-M model, Nelson (1991) for the EGARCH model, Bera and Higgins (1992) for the NARCH model (for other types of models, see for example Dufrenot, Marimoutou, and Péguin-Feissolle (2004)). As for the multivariate models presented in the examples, the multivariate GARCH model with constant conditional correlations is studied by Bollerslev (1990), Baillie and Bollerslev (1990), Bera and Higgins (1993), Baillie and Myers (1991), Bera, Garcia, and Roh (1997), Kroner and Claessens (1991), Kroner and Sultan (1991). On the other hand, the diagonal ARCH model has been presented by Bollerslev, Engle, and Wooldridge (1988), Bera and Higgins (1993).

Regarding the estimation methods, the mixing and ergodicity properties have been proven in the context of some ARCH and GARCH models, see for instance Carrasco and Chen (2002) for GARCH(p,q) models. The quasi-maximum likelihood and maximum likelihood methods are described in Engle (1982), Bollerslev (1986), Engle and Bollerlev (1986), and Hamilton (1994). The two-stage approach has been initiated by the article of Engle (1982). In addition, Bollerslev (1986) proved that the information matrix is block-diagonal in a normal GARCH model. To simplify some positivity and stationarity conditions, some reparametrizations have been considered, see Engle (1982), Hsieh (1989a), and Diebold and Pauly (1988). In the empirical applications, the optimization method usually employed is that of Berndt, Hall, Hall, and Hausman (1974).

Regarding the application of the Rao test, Engle (1982) presents the test for homoskedasticity in an ARCH model (see Péguin-Feissolle (1999) and Caulet and Péguin-Feissolle (2000) for a test based on artificial neural-networks). One can also read Engle, Hendry, and Trumble (1985). Bera and Higgins (1993) make some remarks on the Rao test (see also Demos and Sentana (1998), Lee and King (1991), Engle and Gonzales-Rivera (1991), Bera and Ng (1991), Gallant, Hsieh, and Tauchen (1991), Higgins and Bera (1992)).

Hsieh (1989a) is a good reference for the use of the likelihood ratio test and the Akaike and Schwarz information criteria to determine the order q in ARCH-type models. The test of an ARCH model against a NARCH model is described in Higgins and Bera (1992).

Now, we turn to the specificities of ARCH models. For more details on the stationarity, read Nelson (1990 and 1991), Bougerol and Picard (1992). About the kurtosis, see Engle and Bollerslev (1986)), Hsieh (1989a). Regarding the various conditional distributions used in ARCH models besides the normal, we mention: the Student t distribution which is the most popular (Engle and Bollerslev (1986), Bollerslev (1987), Baillie and Bollerslev (1989), Baillie and Osterberg (1993), to cite only a few), the GED (Nelson (1991)), a normal-Poisson mixture (Jorion (1988)), a normal-log-normal mixture (Hsieh (1989a), Tauchen and Pitts (1983)), or the Gram-Charlier distribution (Lee and Tse (1991)).

15. Nonlinear Dynamic Models

15.1 Introduction

The past 15 years have witnessed important developments in the modelling of nonlinear time series. This modelling opens the path to a variety of different models. It poses multiple difficulties, both from a theoretical point of view relative to the basic properties of the models and the estimators, and from an empirical point of view, for instance in the choice of the specification of nonlinearity.

The theoretical basis that is necessary to prove consistency and asymptotic normality of the moment estimators has been treated in Chapter 2, including for the non i.i.d. case. Indeed, Chapter 2 introduced tools that allow us to apply the law of large numbers and the central limit theorem to dynamic models. In particular, we have seen the concept of statistical models that are uniformly mixing stationary and the concept of near epoch dependence (NED). This enabled us to state Theorem 2.6 in Chapter 2, which is nothing but a central limit theorem for stationary mixing processes. We will return to some of these concepts again in this chapter.

Here, we are not attempting to provide a general and comprehensive presentation of nonlinear dynamic models because each model has characteristics and properties that result in complexity and difficulties that are specific to those. Moreover, the study of these models is expanding fast. Therefore, we will settle for the presentation of some examples only. In particular, we will not introduce bilinear models, which nevertheless constitute an important class of nonlinear dynamic models. We divide models into two groups, each corresponding to a specific section of this chapter:

- the first group (Section 2) contains models where the conditional expectation of y_i can be written as a continuously differentiable function g of endogenous lagged variables and a set of exogenous variables;
- the second group (Section 3) corresponds to the case where the function g is not smooth. We will provide some examples.

Section 4 describes the problems relating to the testing in nonlinear dynamic models. We will discuss the case in which some parameters are not identified under the null hypothesis, as happens sometimes in this type of model.

15.2 Case Where the Conditional Expectation Is Continuously Differentiable

15.2.1 Definitions

In this section, we consider nonlinear dynamic models, for which the conditional expectation takes the following form:

$$E^{\theta}\left(y_i \,\middle|\, y_{-\infty}^{i-1}, z_{-\infty}^{+\infty}\right) = g\left(y_{-\infty}^{i-1}, z_{-\infty}^{+\infty}, \lambda(\theta)\right) \tag{15.1}$$

with

$$z_{-\infty}^{+\infty} = (\dots, z_{i+1}, z_i, z_{i-1}, \dots) \quad \text{and} \quad y_{-\infty}^{i-1} = (y_{i-1}, y_{i-2}, \dots),$$

or alternatively, using the notation $w_i = (y_{-\infty}^{i-1}, z_{-\infty}^{+\infty})$,

$$E^{\theta}\left(y_i \,\middle|\, w_i\right) = g\left(w_i, \lambda(\theta)\right); \tag{15.2}$$

$\lambda(\theta)$ is a mapping from Θ to $\Lambda \subset \mathbb{R}^k$ and g is a function, which is assumed to be continuously differentiable with respect to w_i and λ, and is identified in the following sense:

$$\forall w_i \quad g(w_i, \lambda_1) = g(w_i, \lambda_2) \Rightarrow \lambda_1 = \lambda_2.$$

Assumption (15.1) means that the model is correctly specified and that the inference problem we are interested in is indeed a parametric problem, i.e., g is known and belongs to a parametric family of functions. In practice, g will depend only on a finite number of elements of the past ys and of the zs.

Moreover, we assume that

$$E^{\theta}\left(\frac{\partial g(w_i, \lambda)}{\partial \lambda} \frac{\partial g(w_i, \lambda)}{\partial \lambda'}\right)$$

is nonsingular. In this chapter, we restrict ourselves to univariate models, that is $y_i \in \mathbb{R}$.

These models generalize the stationary nonlinear regression models of Chapter 8. We will also treat the optimality of the instruments and take into account the central limit theorems in a dynamic setting.

15.2.2 Conditional Moments and Marginal Moments in the Homoskedastic Case: Optimal Instruments

The results of this section specialize the content of the final remark of Section 3.5 to the regression model, while extending it to the dynamic case.

Consider ψ, a mapping from $X \times \Lambda$ to $\mathbb{R}^r$, such that

$$\psi(y_i, w_i, \lambda(\theta)) = (y_i - g(w_i, \lambda(\theta))) h(w_i) \tag{15.3}$$

where h denotes a $r \times 1$ vector of instruments with $r \geq k$, k is the dimension of λ. We are interested in a system of moment equations:

$$E^\theta(\psi(y_i, w_i, \lambda)) = 0, \tag{15.4}$$

which is a set of r equations relating θ and λ; λ is the solution of (15.4). Indeed, since $\lambda(\theta)$ satisfies (15.2) and thus

$$E^\theta(u_i|w_i) = 0 \quad \text{with} \quad u_i = y_i - g(w_i, \lambda(\theta)),$$

we have

$$\begin{aligned} E^\theta(\psi(y_i, w_i, \lambda(\theta))) &= E^\theta\left(E^\theta(\psi(y_i, w_i, \lambda(\theta))|w_i)\right) \\ &= E^\theta\left(E^\theta((y_i - g(w_i, \lambda(\theta))|w_i) h(w_i)\right) \\ &= E^\theta\left(E^\theta(u_i|w_i) h(w_i)\right) \\ &= 0. \end{aligned}$$

The instrumental variable h must be chosen so that the solution is unique in order to make (15.1) equivalent to (15.4).

Recall that if $r = k$, we have a simple system of moment equations, whereas we have a generalized system if the number of moment conditions is greater than k. We are going to show that

$$h(w_i) = \frac{\partial g(w_i, \lambda)}{\partial \lambda} \tag{15.5}$$

is the optimal function of w_i, which transforms the conditional moment condition into a marginal moment condition. In part of the econometrics literature, this function is called the optimal instrument by analogy to the theory of instrumental variables developed in the simultaneous equations models (see Chapter 17). This optimality result has been mentioned in Section 3.5, but we are going to prove it here for a special case.

First, we show that the solution to Equation (15.4) is unique. The uniqueness of $\lambda(\theta)$ comes from the nonsingularity of

$$E^\theta\left(\frac{\partial \psi(y_i, w_i, \lambda(\theta))}{\partial \lambda'}\right)$$

(see Chapter 16 for more details about local identification) because

$$E^\theta \left(\frac{\partial \psi(y_i, w_i, \lambda(\theta))}{\partial \lambda'} \right) = E^\theta \left(u_i \frac{\partial^2 g}{\partial \lambda \partial \lambda'} - \frac{\partial g}{\partial \lambda} \frac{\partial g}{\partial \lambda'} \right)$$

$$= E^\theta \left(E^\theta (u_i | w_i) \frac{\partial^2 g}{\partial \lambda \partial \lambda'} \right) - E^\theta \left(\frac{\partial g}{\partial \lambda} \frac{\partial g}{\partial \lambda'} \right)$$

$$= -E^\theta \left(\frac{\partial g}{\partial \lambda} \frac{\partial g}{\partial \lambda'} \right),$$

and this last matrix is invertible by assumption.

To prove that (15.5) is the optimal instrument, consider first the case where $h(w_i)$ is an arbitrary instrumental function of dimension $r \geq k$. The estimator obtained by the generalized method of moments, denoted $\widehat{\lambda}_n$, satisfies

$$\widehat{\lambda}_n = \arg\min_{\lambda \in \Lambda} \left(\frac{1}{n} \sum_{i=1}^n \psi(y_i, w_i, \lambda) \right)' H_n \left(\frac{1}{n} \sum_{i=1}^n \psi(y_i, w_i, \lambda) \right)$$

$$(15.6)$$

where $H_n \to H$ $P^\theta - a.s.$, H_n and H are symmetric, positive definite matrices. We assume that x_i is stationary, ergodic, and mixing so that the central limit theorem holds (provided the process satisfies near epoch dependence (NED)) and that we can use the results of Chapter 3. Hence, Theorem 3.4 in Chapter 3 implies, assuming all its conditions are satisfied, that $\widehat{\lambda}_n$ satisfies the following two properties:

$$\widehat{\lambda}_n \to \lambda(\theta) \quad P^\theta - a.s.$$

and

$$\sqrt{n} \left(\widehat{\lambda}_n - \lambda(\theta) \right) \to N(0, \Sigma_\theta) \text{ in } P^\theta\text{-distribution} \qquad (15.7)$$

with

$$\Sigma_\theta = \left[E^\theta \left(\frac{\partial \psi'}{\partial \lambda} \right) H E^\theta \left(\frac{\partial \psi}{\partial \lambda'} \right) \right]^{-1} E^\theta \left(\frac{\partial \psi'}{\partial \lambda} \right) H V_\theta$$

$$\times H E^\theta \left(\frac{\partial \psi}{\partial \lambda'} \right) \left[E^\theta \left(\frac{\partial \psi'}{\partial \lambda} \right) H E^\theta \left(\frac{\partial \psi}{\partial \lambda'} \right) \right]^{-1}$$

where V_θ is the asymptotic variance matrix of

$$\sqrt{n} \left(\frac{1}{n} \sum_{i=1}^n \psi(y_i, w_i, \lambda) \right).$$

The optimal choice of H consists in taking

$$H = V_\theta^{-1},$$

as shown in Theorem 3.5 in Chapter 3. Therefore, the asymptotic variance of the optimal estimator of λ is:

$$\Sigma_\theta = \left[E^\theta \left(\frac{\partial \psi'}{\partial \lambda} \right) V_\theta^{-1} E^\theta \left(\frac{\partial \psi}{\partial \lambda'} \right) \right]^{-1}. \tag{15.8}$$

From (15.3), we have

$$\frac{\partial \psi'}{\partial \lambda} = -\frac{\partial g}{\partial \lambda} h'(w_i). \tag{15.9}$$

Moreover, as we are in a dynamic setting, the matrix V_θ takes the form:

$$V_\theta = \sum_{j=-\infty}^{+\infty} Cov^\theta \left(\psi(y_i, w_i, \lambda), \psi(y_{i+j}, w_{i+j}, \lambda) \right)$$

$$= \sum_{j=-\infty}^{+\infty} Cov^\theta \left(u_i h(w_i), u_{i+j} h(w_{i+j}) \right)$$

with $u_i = y_i - g(w_i, \lambda)$. From (15.4), it follows that for each i

$$E^\theta \left(\psi(y_i, w_i, \lambda(\theta)) \right) = E^\theta \left(u_i h(w_i) \right) = 0,$$

and V_θ can be rewritten as

$$V_\theta = \sum_{j=-\infty}^{+\infty} E^\theta \left(h(w_i) h(w_{i+j})' u_i u_{i+j} \right).$$

When j is positive, we obtain

$$E^\theta \left[h(w_i) h(w_{i+j})' u_i u_{i+j} \right] = E^\theta \left[h(w_i) h(w_{i+j})' u_i E^\theta \left(u_{i+j} \mid w_{i+j} \right) \right]$$

$$= 0.$$

Indeed, we can take the product $h(w_i) h(w_{i+j})' u_i$ out of the conditional expectation because, as

$$w_{i+j} = \left(y_{-\infty}^{i+j-1}, z_{-\infty}^{+\infty} \right),$$

this product belongs to the space spanned by w_{i+j}. Moreover, we use the fact that

$$E^\theta \left(u_{i+j} \mid w_{i+j} \right) = 0.$$

When j is negative, it suffices to permute the roles of i and j to obtain the same result.

Therefore,

$$V_\theta = E^\theta \left(h(w_i) h(w_i)' u_i^2 \right)$$

$$= E^\theta \left(h(w_i) h(w_i)' E^\theta \left(u_i^2 \mid w_i \right) \right), \tag{15.10}$$

hence, using the homoskedasticity assumption $E^\theta(u_i^2|w_i) = \sigma^2$,

$$V_\theta = \sigma^2 E^\theta \left(h(w_i)h(w_i)' \right).$$ (15.11)

It follows from (15.8), (15.9), and (15.11) that

$$\Sigma_\theta = \sigma^2 \left[E^\theta \left(\frac{\partial g}{\partial \lambda} h'(w_i) \right) \left[E^\theta \left(h(w_i)h(w_i)' \right) \right]^{-1} \right.$$

$$\left. \times F^\theta \left(h(w_l) \frac{\partial g}{\partial \lambda'} \right)^{-1} \right].$$ (15.12)

Now consider the case where

$$h(w_i) = \frac{\partial g(w_i, \lambda)}{\partial \lambda},$$

for which $r = k$. Here, we can use the simple method of moments where the estimator is defined as the solution to the system of equations

$$\frac{1}{n} \sum_{i=1}^n \psi(y_i, w_i, \lambda) = 0.$$ (15.13)

For this choice of instruments, V_θ becomes

$$V_\theta = \sigma^2 E^\theta \left(\frac{\partial g(w_i, \lambda)}{\partial \lambda} \frac{\partial g(w_i, \lambda)}{\partial \lambda'} \right)$$ (15.14)

and from Theorem 3.5 in Chapter 3, we obtain the following expression of the variance matrix of the estimator of λ:

$$\Sigma_\theta^* = \left[E^\theta \left(\frac{\partial \psi}{\partial \lambda'} \right) \right]^{-1} V_\theta \left[E^\theta \left(\frac{\partial \psi'}{\partial \lambda} \right) \right]^{-1},$$ (15.15)

and therefore

$$\Sigma_\theta^* = \sigma^2 \left[E^\theta \left(\frac{\partial g(w_i, \lambda)}{\partial \lambda} \frac{\partial g(w_i, \lambda)}{\partial \lambda'} \right) \right]^{-1}$$ (15.16)

because

$$E^\theta \left(\frac{\partial \psi'}{\partial \lambda} \right) = -E^\theta \left(\frac{\partial g(w_i, \lambda)}{\partial \lambda} \frac{\partial g(w_i, \lambda)}{\partial \lambda'} \right).$$

To show that

$$h(w_i) = \frac{\partial g(w_i, \lambda)}{\partial \lambda}$$

is the optimal instrument, it suffices to prove that $\Sigma_\theta \geq \Sigma_\theta^*$, or alternatively $\Sigma_\theta^{*-1} \geq \Sigma_\theta^{-1}$, where Σ_θ and Σ_θ^* are respectively defined in (15.12) and (15.16). To prove this, let us define

$$A = \frac{\partial g(w_i, \lambda)}{\partial \lambda}, \quad B = h(w_i)$$

and

$$R = A - E^\theta(AB')E^\theta(BB')^{-1}B. \tag{15.17}$$

Then, the difference $\Sigma_\theta^{*-1} - \Sigma_\theta^{-1}$ can be rewritten as

$$\Sigma_\theta^{*-1} - \Sigma_\theta^{-1} = E^\theta(AA') - E^\theta(AB')E^\theta(BB')^{-1}E^\theta(BA') = E^\theta(RR').$$

As the matrix $E^\theta(RR')$ is symmetric and positive semidefinite, we deduce that $\Sigma_\theta^{*-1} \geq \Sigma_\theta^{-1}$.

It is worth noting that the fact that $\lambda(\theta)$ is the solution of (15.4) is equivalent to

$$\lambda(\theta) = \arg\min_\lambda E^\theta\left((y_i - g(w_i, \lambda))^2\right). \tag{15.18}$$

The estimation method used here, is the simple method of moments or the least-squares method, the estimator $\widehat{\lambda}_n$ is defined as the solution of the system

$$\frac{1}{n}\sum_{i=1}^n \psi(y_i, w_i, \lambda(\theta)) = \frac{1}{n}\sum_{i=1}^n (y_i - g(w_i, \lambda(\theta))) \frac{\partial g(w_i, \lambda)}{\partial \lambda} = 0, \tag{15.19}$$

and has the following asymptotic distribution

$$\sqrt{n}\left(\widehat{\lambda}_n - \lambda\right) \to N\left(0, \sigma^2\left[E^\theta\left(\frac{\partial g(w_i, \lambda)}{\partial \lambda}\frac{\partial g(w_i, \lambda)}{\partial \lambda'}\right)\right]^{-1}\right) \text{ in } P^\theta\text{-distribution.}$$

It is noticeable in dynamic models that the asymptotic results are of the same nature as those obtained in the i.i.d. setting.

15.2.3   Heteroskedasticity

This section provides the dynamic generalization of Chapter 9. If the model is heteroskedastic, that is $E^\theta(u_i^2|w_i)$ is not equal to a constant σ^2, then it is possible to show that the optimal instrument consists of

$$h(w_i) = \frac{1}{E^\theta\left(u_i^2\mid w_i\right)}\frac{\partial g(w_i, \lambda)}{\partial \lambda}; \tag{15.20}$$

indeed, V_θ is in this case

$$V_\theta = E^\theta \left[h(w_i) h(w_i)' u_i^2 \right]$$
$$= E^\theta \left[h(w_i) h(w_i)' E^\theta \left(u_i^2 \,|\, w_i \right) \right].$$

We have, for an arbitrary instrument $h(w_i)$ of dimension $r \times 1$ and from (15.8), (15.9), and (15.10), the following expression of the asymptotic variance of the estimator:

$$\Sigma_\theta = \left[E^\theta \left(\frac{\partial g}{\partial \lambda} h'(w_i) \right) \left[E^\theta \left(h(w_i) h(w_i)' E^\theta \left(u_i^2 \,|\, w_i \right) \right) \right]^{-1} E^\theta \left(h(w_i) \frac{\partial g}{\partial \lambda'} \right) \right]^{1}.$$

When h is given by (15.20), this asymptotic variance becomes

$$\Sigma_\theta^* = \left[E^\theta \left(\frac{1}{E^\theta \left(u_i^2 \,|\, w_i \right)} \frac{\partial g(w_i, \lambda)}{\partial \lambda} \frac{\partial g(w_i, \lambda)}{\partial \lambda'} \right) \right]^{-1}.$$

We can show again that $\Sigma_\theta \geq \Sigma_\theta^*$. The proof is identical to that used in the homoskedastic case, letting

$$A = \frac{1}{\sqrt{E^\theta \left(u_i^2 \,|\, w_i \right)}} \frac{\partial g(w_i, \lambda)}{\partial \lambda} \quad \text{and} \quad B = \sqrt{E^\theta \left(u_i^2 \,|\, w_i \right)} h(w_i),$$

and taking for R the same matrix as before (that is the matrix (15.17)).

15.2.4 Modifying of the Set of Conditioning Variables: Kernel Estimation of the Asymptotic Variance

An alternative way to define a nonlinear dynamic model would be to write the conditional expectation in the form

$$E^\theta \left(y_i \,|\, y_{i-1}, \dots, y_{i-\tau}, z_{i+s}, \dots, z_{i-t} \right)$$
$$= g \left(y_{i-1}, \dots, y_{i-\tau}, z_{i+s}, \dots, z_{i-t}, \lambda(\theta) \right) \qquad (15.21)$$

instead of using (15.1), or alternatively, denoting $w_i^* = (y_{i-1}, \dots, y_{i-\tau}, z_{i+s}, \dots, z_{i-t})$, a vector of $\mathbb{R}^{r^*}$, with $r^* = \tau + s + t + 1$,

$$E^\theta \left(y_i \,|\, w_i^* \right) = g \left(w_i^*, \lambda(\theta) \right).$$

We do not assume that

$$E^\theta \left(y_i \,|\, y_{i-1}, \dots, y_{i-\tau}, z_{i+s}, \dots, z_{i-t} \right)$$

in (15.21) is equal to

$$E^\theta \left(y_i \,|\, y_{-\infty}^{i-1}, z_{-\infty}^{+\infty} \right)$$

in (15.1). Apart from this important exception, the assumptions are the same as before, that is, we maintain identification, correct specification, homoskedasticity, differentiability of g, and also invertibility of

$$E^\theta \left(\frac{\partial g(w_i, \lambda)}{\partial \lambda} \frac{\partial g(w_i, \lambda)}{\partial \lambda'} \right).$$

The results regarding consistency and asymptotic normality are the same as before, the only difference stems from the calculation of the matrix V_θ, for which we can no longer do the simplifications leading to formula (15.10). This matrix V_θ is

$$V_\theta = \sum_{j=-\infty}^{+\infty} E^\theta \left(\psi(y_i, w_i^*, \lambda) \psi(y_{i+j}, w_{i+j}^*, \lambda) \right)'. \tag{15.22}$$

As this is an infinite sum and the available sample is finite, we need to use some approximation: the idea consists in estimating the expectation by the weighted sample mean and in truncating the infinite sum. There are several methods based on this principle, which allow us to obtain a consistent estimator of V_θ, denoted $\widehat{V}_n$. They usually consist in setting

$$\widehat{V}_n = \sum_{m=-l(n)}^{l(n)} \omega_m \widehat{V}_{nm}^* = \omega_0 \widehat{V}_{n0}^* + \sum_{m=1}^{l(n)} \omega_m \left(\widehat{V}_{nm}^* + \widehat{V}_{nm}^{*\prime} \right)$$

with, for $m = 0, 1, \dots, l(n)$ (where $l(n)$ depends on n),

$$\widehat{V}_{nm}^* = \frac{1}{n} \sum_{i=m+1}^{n} \psi(y_i, w_i, \widehat{\lambda}_n) \psi(y_{i-m}, w_{i-m}, \widehat{\lambda}_n)'. \tag{15.23}$$

Regarding the weights or *kernels* ω_m, it is possible to choose

$$\omega_m = \begin{vmatrix} 1 - 6m^2 + 6|m|^3 & \text{if } 0 \le m \le 0.5l(n) \\ 2(1 - |m|)^3 & \text{if } 0.5l(n) \le m \le 1 \end{vmatrix}$$

and

$$l(n) = O(n^{1/5})$$

(that is $l(n)$ is selected to be the closest integer to $n^{1/5}$); ω_m is called Parzen kernel. Another possibility consists in defining ω_m as

$$\omega_m = 1 - \frac{m}{l(n) + 1},$$

then ω_m is called Bartlett kernel (the number of autocovariances $l(n)$ is again determined as a function of n).

With regard to the estimation, the partial derivatives of g do not constitute the optimal instruments any more.

Now, we consider an example of a nonlinear dynamic model where the conditional expectation is continuously differentiable and where we use the preceding results. This is the Smooth Threshold Autoregressive (STAR) model, which has the property that the transition between two distinct regimes is smooth.

Example 15.1 *A quite general form of the STAR models corresponds to*

$$E^\theta\left(y_i \left| y_{-\infty}^{i-1}\right.\right) = E^\theta\left(y_i \left| y_{i-1}, \ldots, y_{i-p}\right.\right) = E^\theta\left(y_i \left| w_i\right.\right) = g(w_i, \lambda) \tag{15.24}$$

where

$$g(w_i, \lambda) = \alpha_0 + \alpha' w_i + (\beta_0 + \beta' w_i)F\left(y_{i-d}\right), \tag{15.25}$$

with $w_i = (y_{i-1}, \ldots, y_{i-p})'$, $\alpha = (\alpha_1, \ldots, \alpha_p)'$ *and* $\beta = (\beta_1, \ldots, \beta_p)'$; α_0 *and* β_0 *are scalar parameters. F is a continuous function, which is either even or odd. Indeed it may be odd and monotone increasing with* $F(-\infty) = 0$ *and* $F(+\infty) = 1$, *such as the cumulative distribution function of a* $N(\mu, \sigma^2)$ *variable. Likewise, F may be even with* $F(\pm\infty) = 0$ *and* $F(0) = 1$, *as the probability density function of a* $N(\mu, \sigma^2)$ *variable. The parameter d is a positive integer. Exogenous variables may also appear in* w_i.

Two special types of STAR models are frequently encountered in the literature: the Logistic STAR (LSTAR) where the transition function F is logistic

$$F(y_{i-d}) = [1 + \exp\{-\gamma(y_{i-d} - c)\}]^{-1} \qquad (\gamma > 0), \tag{15.26}$$

and the Exponential STAR (ESTAR) where the function F is exponential, that is

$$F(y_{i-d}) = 1 - \exp\left[-\gamma(y_{i-d} - c)^2\right] \qquad (\gamma > 0). \tag{15.27}$$

γ *is called transition parameter and c threshold parameter.*

We know a number of results about STAR models. In particular, when the following condition holds

$$\sup_{0 \le \theta \le 1}\left(\sum_{j=1}^p |\alpha_j + \theta\beta_j|\right) < 1$$

(or, in the special case where $p = d = 1$, *if* $\alpha_1 < 1$, $\alpha_1 + \beta_1 < 1$ *and* $\alpha_1(\alpha_1 + \beta_1) < 1$), *one can show that the process* $\{y_i\}$ *is stationary ergodic and that its distribution admits a finite moment of order k if the following extra condition is satisfied:* $E^\theta(|u_i|^k) < \infty$ *with* $u_i = y_i - g(w_i, \lambda)$.

Regarding the estimation, suppose the process y_i, *whose conditional expectation is defined by*

$$E^\theta\left(y_i \left| w_i\right.\right) = g(w_i, \lambda)$$

where g is given by (15.25), is stationary and mixing such that we can use the results of Chapter 3 mentioned above. The moment estimator $\widehat{\lambda}_n$ is obtained by the simple method of moments as the solution of (15.13) with

$$\psi(y_i, w_i, \lambda) = (y_i - g(w_i, \lambda)) \frac{\partial g(w_i, \lambda)}{\partial \lambda}. \tag{15.28}$$

Therefore, it satisfies consistency and asymptotic normality and the variance matrix in the optimal case is given by Σ_θ^* (see (15.15)) with

$$V_\theta = \sum_{j=-\infty}^{+\infty} E^\theta \left(\psi(y_i, w_i, \lambda)\psi(y_{i+j}, w_{i+j}, \lambda)' \right).$$

Notice that the terms of this infinite sum equal zero for $j \neq 0$. Indeed, in the case where $j > 0$, we have

$$E^\theta \left(\psi(y_i, w_i, \lambda)\psi(y_{i+j}, w_{i+j}, \lambda)' \right)$$

$$= E^\theta \left(u_i \frac{\partial g(w_i, \lambda)}{\partial \lambda} \frac{\partial g(w_{i+j}, \lambda)}{\partial \lambda'} u_{i+j} \right)$$

$$= E^\theta \left(u_i \frac{\partial g}{\partial \lambda} \frac{\partial g}{\partial \lambda'} E^\theta \left(u_{i+j} \big| w_{i+j} \right) \right)$$

$$= 0,$$

because, given that u_{i+j} is the innovation of y_{i+j}, the conditional expectation $E^\theta(u_{i+j}|w_{i+j})$ is zero. The same is true for $j < 0$. Consequently, V_θ becomes

$$V_\theta = Var^\theta \left(\psi(y_i, w_i, \lambda) \right),$$

hence,

$$V_\theta = \sigma^2 E^\theta \left(\frac{\partial g(w_i, \lambda)}{\partial \lambda} \frac{\partial g(w_i, \lambda)}{\partial \lambda'} \right),$$

assuming here, for simplicity, that the distribution of $y_i|w_i$ is homoskedastic, with constant variance σ^2. Therefore, the variance matrix of the optimal estimator of λ is given by

$$\Sigma_\theta^* = \sigma^2 \left[E^\theta \left(\frac{\partial g(w_i, \lambda)}{\partial \lambda} \frac{\partial g(w_i, \lambda)}{\partial \lambda'} \right) \right]^{-1}$$

and can be estimated consistently. $\square$

15.3   Case Where the Conditional Expectation Is Not Continuously Differentiable: Regime-Switching Models

Another large category of nonlinear dynamic models is represented by models where the function g is not continuously differentiable. The basic idea behind these regime-switching models is that there exist different regimes, such that the transition from one regime to the next depends on time, on an endogenous variable, or occurs with some probability.

The probabilistic and statistical properties of some models, where the function g is not continuously differentiable, have been studied in the literature, such as ergodicity and existence of moments. Numerous questions remain open and depend on the class of models under consideration, the study of stationarity is one of them.

When the switching parameters are known, the function g is differentiable in the parameters and we can return to the models studied in the previous paragraph. In the case where they are unknown, the difficulty of these models stems from the estimation of the break parameters. First, we provide a few examples of these models, setting aside the estimation problems for the next subsection.

15.3.1 Presentation of a Few Examples

The first example looks at a *structural change model*.

Example 15.2 *Consider the following model:*

$$y_i = \lambda_0 + \lambda_1 \mathbf{1}_{i \geq n\pi} + u_i \tag{15.29}$$

where u_i is i.i.$N(0, \sigma^2)$ and n is the size of the sample; $n\pi$ is the timing of the break ($\pi \in (0, 1)$). It is implicitly assumed that there exists a continuous time process between 0 and 1, which is observed at a countable number of points, so that the numbers of points before and after the breakpoint increase in the same manner. Hence, we observe $n\pi$ points before and $n - n\pi$ points after the breakpoint. □

The second example is that of a *threshold model*.

Example 15.3 *Consider the following model:*

$$y_i = \lambda_0 + \lambda_1 \mathbf{1}_{y_{i-d} \leq c} + u_i \tag{15.30}$$

where u_i is i.i.$N(0, \sigma^2)$; d and σ are given, and the threshold c is unknown. The conditional distribution of y_0 given y_{-d} is

$$N(\lambda_0 + \lambda_1 \mathbf{1}_{y_{-d} \leq c}, \sigma^2).$$

We denote the corresponding conditional density by $f_c(y_0 | y_{-d})$. We are looking for the marginal density f_m such that

$$f_m(y_0) = \int f_m(y_{-d}) f_c(y_0 | y_{-d}) dy_{-d}.$$

Thus,

$$f_m(y_0) = \int\limits_{y_{i-d} \leq c} f_m(y_{-d}) f_c(y_0 \,|\, y_{-d}) dy_{-d}$$

$$+ \int\limits_{y_{i-d} > c} f_m(y_{-d}) f_c(y_0 \,|\, y_{-d}) dy_{-d}.$$

We derive the stationary density

$$f_m(y_i) = \frac{\Phi\left(\frac{c-\lambda_0}{\sigma}\right)}{1 - \Phi\left(\frac{c-\lambda_0-\lambda_1}{\sigma}\right) + \Phi\left(\frac{c-\lambda_0}{\sigma}\right)} \frac{1}{\sigma\sqrt{2\pi}} \exp{-\frac{(y_i - \lambda_0 - \lambda_1)^2}{2\sigma^2}}$$

$$+ \frac{1 - \Phi\left(\frac{c-\lambda_0-\lambda_1}{\sigma}\right)}{1 - \Phi\left(\frac{c-\lambda_0-\lambda_1}{\sigma}\right) + \Phi\left(\frac{c-\lambda_0}{\sigma}\right)} \frac{1}{\sigma\sqrt{2\pi}} \exp{-\frac{(y_i - \lambda_0)^2}{2\sigma^2}}$$

where Φ is the cumulative distribution function of the standard normal. The expectation and the variance of y_i are given by

$$E^\theta(y_i) = \lambda_0 + \delta\lambda_1$$

and

$$Var^\theta(y_i) = \sigma^2 + \delta(1 - \delta)\lambda_1^2$$

with

$$\delta = \Pr(y_i \leq c) = \frac{\Phi\left(\frac{c-\lambda_0}{\sigma}\right)}{1 - \Phi\left(\frac{c-\lambda_0-\lambda_1}{\sigma}\right) + \Phi\left(\frac{c-\lambda_0}{\sigma}\right)}. \tag{15.31}$$

One can also show that, when the parameter d is equal to 1, $\{\mathbf{1}_{y_{i-d} \leq c}\}$ is a Markov chain and when d is greater than 1, $\{\mathbf{y}_i\}$ is ϕ-mixing because the data is generated by independent series, which are specific Markov processes. $\qquad\square$

We finish by providing a general example of threshold model.

Example 15.4   *A general form of threshold model corresponds to*

$$g(w_i, \lambda) = \sum_{j=1}^{l} \left[\left(\lambda_0^{(j)} + \lambda_1^{(j)} y_{i-1} + \cdots + \lambda_p^{(j)} y_{i-p} \right) I_{w_i \in R^{(j)}} \right],$$

where $w_i = (y_{i-1}, \ldots, y_{i-p})$ and $R^{(j)}$, for $j = 1, \ldots, l$, are specific subsets that define a partition of $\mathbb{R}^p$ in disjoint sets. This model, which in the literature, is called the Threshold Autoregressive (TAR) model, can be considered as a \piecewise" linear approximation of a more general nonlinear model. When $R^{(j)}$ depends on lagged values of the endogenous variable y_i, then we have

Self-Exciting Threshold Autoregressive (SETAR) models. A simple example corresponding to the case where $p = 1$ and $l = 2$ is

$$y_i = \begin{vmatrix} \lambda_0^{(1)} + \lambda_1^{(1)} y_{i-1} + u_i^{(1)} & \text{if } y_{i-1} < c \\ \lambda_0^{(2)} + \lambda_1^{(2)} y_{i-1} + u_i^{(2)} & \text{if } y_{i-1} \geq c \end{vmatrix}$$

where the constant c is called the threshold, $\{u_i^{(1)}\}$ and $\{u_i^{(2)}\}$ are white noise processes. A somewhat more general case takes $p = 1$ and l as arbitrary:

$$y_i = \lambda_0^{(j)} + \lambda_1^{(j)} y_{i-1} + u_i^{(j)} \quad \text{if } y_{i-1} \in R^{(j)} \quad j = 1, \dots, l$$

where $R^{(j)}$ define a partition of the real line: $(-\infty, r_1]$, $(r_1, r_2], \dots,$ $(r_{l-1}, +\infty)$, with $R^{(1)} = (-\infty, r_1]$, $R^{(j)} = (r_{j-1}, r_j]$ for $j = 2, \dots, l-1$ and $R^{(l)} = (r_{l-1}, +\infty)$. Lagged exogenous variables can be included among the regressors, the resulting model is called Open-Loop Self-Exciting Threshold Autoregressive (SETARSO) model:

$$y_i = \alpha_o^{(j)} + \sum_{k=1}^{p} \alpha_k^{(j)} y_{i-k} + \sum_{k=1}^{m} \beta_k^{(j)} z_{i-k}^{(j)} + u_i^{(j)}$$

$$\text{if } y_{i-d} \in R^{(j)}, \, j = 1, \dots, l. \qquad \square$$

15.3.2 Problem of Estimation

When the break parameters are known, the estimation of regime-switching models by the method of moments proceeds as outlined in the previous subsection. In the opposite case, the complexity of the estimation comes from the various switching and delay parameters, which have to be estimated. Let us examine now the two possible cases.

First, consider two examples where the switching parameters are known.

Example 15.5 *Consider the previously introduced Example 15.2, namely the structural change model described by (15.29), and suppose that the timing of the break $n\pi$ is known. The maximum likelihood estimators of λ_0 and λ_1 are:*

$$\widehat{\lambda}_{0n} = \frac{1}{n\pi} \sum_{i < n\pi} y_i$$

and

$$\widehat{\lambda}_{1n} = \frac{1}{n(1 - \pi)} \sum_{i \geq n\pi} y_i - \frac{1}{n\pi} \sum_{i < n\pi} y_i \qquad (15.32)$$

and have the asymptotic distribution:

$$\sqrt{n}\begin{pmatrix}\widehat{\lambda}_{0n}-\lambda_0\\\widehat{\lambda}_{1n}-\lambda_1\end{pmatrix}\to N\left(\begin{pmatrix}0\\0\end{pmatrix},\ \sigma^2\begin{pmatrix}1/\pi & -1/\pi\\-1/\pi & 1/(\pi(1-\pi))\end{pmatrix}\right).$$

(15.33)

This last result can be easily proven. It suffices to apply the least squares method to this model. The explanatory variable matrix is given by

$$Z=\begin{pmatrix}Z_1\\Z_2\end{pmatrix}\quad\text{with}\quad Z_1=\begin{pmatrix}1\cdots 1\\0\cdots 0\end{pmatrix}'\quad\text{and}\quad Z_2=\begin{pmatrix}1\cdots 1\\1\cdots 1\end{pmatrix}',$$

where Z_1 and Z_2 have respectively the dimensions $n\pi\times 2$ and $(n-n\pi)\times 2$; then, the asymptotic variance of

$$\sqrt{n}\begin{pmatrix}\widehat{\lambda}_{0n}-\lambda_0\\\widehat{\lambda}_{1n}-\lambda_1\end{pmatrix}$$

takes the form

$$n\sigma^2\left(Z'Z\right)^{-1}=n\sigma^2\begin{pmatrix}n & n(1-\pi)\\n(1-\pi) & n(1-\pi)\end{pmatrix}^{-1},$$

and the result follows. □

Consider the threshold model introduced in Example 15.3.

Example 15.6 *Let us resume model (15.30) and suppose that the threshold parameter c is known. The maximum likelihood parameters of λ_0 and λ_1 are*

$$\widehat{\lambda}_{0n}=\frac{\sum_{i=1}^{n}y_i\mathbf{1}_{y_{i-d}>c}}{\sum_{i=1}^{n}\mathbf{1}_{y_{i-d}>c}}$$

and

$$\widehat{\lambda}_{1n}=\frac{\sum_{i=1}^{n}y_i\mathbf{1}_{y_{i-d}\le c}}{\sum_{i=1}^{n}\mathbf{1}_{y_{i-d}\le c}}-\frac{\sum_{i=1}^{n}y_i\mathbf{1}_{y_{i-d}>c}}{\sum_{i=1}^{n}\mathbf{1}_{y_{i-d}>c}}$$

and have the asymptotic distribution

$$\sqrt{n}\begin{pmatrix}\widehat{\lambda}_{0n}-\lambda_0\\\widehat{\lambda}_{1n}-\lambda_1\end{pmatrix}\to N\left(\begin{pmatrix}0\\0\end{pmatrix},\ \sigma^2\begin{pmatrix}1/(1-\delta) & -1/(1-\delta)\\-1/(1-\delta) & 1/(\delta(1-\delta))\end{pmatrix}\right).$$

where δ is given by (15.31). □

Let us examine now an example where the switching parameters are unknown. In this case, we usually obtain nonstandard distributions as in the next example.

Example 15.7 *Consider the following example:*

$$Y_t = \lambda(t - \pi)\mathbf{1}_{t \geq \pi} + \sigma W(t) \qquad t \in [0, 1]$$

where $W(t)$ is a Brownian motion, σ a positive scalar and π the break parameter. Using the mapping that associates with each t the element $i = nt$ (so that $i \in [0, n]$) and the fact that

$$W\left(\frac{i+1}{n}\right) - W\left(\frac{i}{n}\right) \sim i.i.N\left(0, \frac{1}{n}\right),$$

one can write

$$Y_{\frac{i+1}{n}} - Y_{\frac{i}{n}} = \lambda\left(\frac{i+1}{n} - \pi\right)\mathbf{1}_{\frac{i+1}{n} \geq \pi} - \lambda\left(\frac{i}{n} - \pi\right)\mathbf{1}_{\frac{i}{n} \geq \pi} + \frac{\sigma}{\sqrt{n}}u_i$$

with $u_i \sim i.i.N(0, 1)$. Disregarding the intermediate case where $\frac{i}{n} < \pi < \frac{i+1}{n}$, two cases are possible

$$\begin{cases} Y_{\frac{i+1}{n}} - Y_{\frac{i}{n}} = \frac{\lambda}{n} + \frac{\sigma}{\sqrt{n}}u_i & \text{if } \frac{i}{n} \geq \pi \\ Y_{\frac{i+1}{n}} - Y_{\frac{i}{n}} = \frac{\sigma}{\sqrt{n}}u_i & \text{otherwise.} \end{cases}$$

Let

$$y_i = \sqrt{n}\left(y_{\frac{i+1}{n}} - Y_{\frac{i}{n}}\right),$$

so that we consider the following model:

$$y_i = \frac{\lambda}{\sqrt{n}}\mathbf{1}_{\frac{i}{n} \geq \pi} + \sigma u_i. \tag{15.34}$$

Now, suppose that λ is known and focus on the estimation of π. Let $\widehat{\pi}_n$ be the least squares estimator of π. We can write

$$\widehat{\pi}_n = \arg\min_{\pi} \sum_{i=1}^{n}\left(y_i - \frac{\lambda}{\sqrt{n}}\mathbf{1}_{\frac{i}{n} \geq \pi}\right)^2.$$

Denote π_0 the true value of the break parameter π. Replacing y_i by

$$\frac{\lambda}{\sqrt{n}}\mathbf{1}_{\frac{i}{n} \geq \pi_0} + \sigma u_i,$$

we obtain

$$\widehat{\pi}_n = \arg\min_{\pi} \sum_{i=1}^{n}\left(\frac{\lambda}{\sqrt{n}}\mathbf{1}_{\frac{i}{n} \geq \pi_0} + \sigma u_i - \frac{\lambda}{\sqrt{n}}\mathbf{1}_{\frac{i}{n} \geq \pi}\right)^2,$$

hence, ignoring the terms independent of π,

$$\widehat{\pi}_n = \arg\min_{\pi} \left[-2\frac{\lambda\sigma}{\sqrt{n}} \sum_{i=1}^n u_i \mathbf{1}_{\frac{i}{n} \geq \pi} + \frac{\lambda^2}{n} \sum_{i=1}^n \left(\mathbf{1}_{\frac{i}{n} \geq \pi} - 2\mathbf{1}_{\frac{i}{n} \geq \pi} \mathbf{1}_{\frac{i}{n} \geq \pi_0} \right) \right].$$

$$(15.35)$$

Because

$$u_i = \sqrt{n} \left(W\left(\frac{i+1}{n} \right) - W\left(\frac{i}{n} \right) \right),$$

the first term in bracket can be rewritten as

$$-2\frac{\lambda\sigma}{\sqrt{n}} \sum_{i=1}^n u_i \mathbf{1}_{\frac{i}{n} \geq \pi} = -2\lambda\sigma \sum_{i \geq n\pi} \left(W\left(\frac{i+1}{n} \right) - W\left(\frac{i}{n} \right) \right)$$

$$= -2\lambda\sigma \left(W(1) - W(\pi) \right).$$

The second term is equal to

$$\frac{\lambda^2}{n} \sum_{i=1}^n \left(\mathbf{1}_{\frac{i}{n} \geq \pi} - 2\mathbf{1}_{\frac{i}{n} \geq \pi} \mathbf{1}_{\frac{i}{n} \geq \pi_0} \right) = \begin{vmatrix} \lambda^2 (-1 + \pi) & \text{if } \pi \geq \pi_0 \\ \lambda^2 (-1 - \pi + 2\pi_0) & \text{otherwise} \end{vmatrix}.$$

Expression (15.35) becomes, ignoring the terms independent of π,

$$\widehat{\pi}_n = \arg\min_{\pi} \left[-2\lambda\sigma \left(W(1) - W(\pi) \right) + \lambda^2 \left(\pi \mathbf{1}_{\pi \geq \pi_0} - \pi \mathbf{1}_{\pi < \pi_0} \right) \right]$$

or alternatively, changing the signs, adding terms in π_0, and replacing $W(1)$ by $W(\pi_0)$, which does not alter the optimization result with respect to π,

$$\widehat{\pi}_n = \arg\max_{\pi} \left[\lambda\sigma \left(W(\pi_0) - W(\pi) \right) - \frac{1}{2}\lambda^2 |\pi - \pi_0| \right]. \qquad (15.36)$$

Now, let $v = \lambda^2 (\pi - \pi_0)$, hence the estimator of v is

$$\widehat{v}_n = \lambda^2 (\widehat{\pi}_n - \pi_0).$$

We can replace (15.36) by an equivalent expression in v

$$\widehat{v}_n = \arg\max_{v} \left[\lambda\sigma \left(W(\pi_0) - W\left(\frac{v}{\lambda^2} + \pi_0 \right) \right) - \frac{1}{2} |v| \right], \qquad (15.37)$$

which becomes

$$\widehat{v}_n = \arg\max_{v} \left[\lambda\sigma W^s \left(\frac{v}{\lambda^2} \right) - \frac{1}{2} |v| \right] \qquad (15.38)$$

where W^s is the symmetric Brownian motion on $\mathbb{R}$ such that

$$W^s(-u) = W^s(u)$$

for all $u > 0$. Hence, the least squares estimator of v follows the distribution (conditional on π_0):

$$\widehat{v}_n = \arg\max_v \left[\sigma W^s(v) - \frac{1}{2}|v| \right]. \tag{15.39}$$

Note that, because $\pi \in [0, 1]$, the maximization space for v is precisely

$$\left[-\lambda^2 \pi_0, \lambda^2(1 - \pi_0) \right].$$

Note also that the distribution is exact in the case of normal residuals. □

15.4 Linearity Test

Before studying a nonlinear model, which is in general complex to estimate and to analyze, it is necessary to perform linearity tests. In a large number of cases, the problem of nonidentification of some parameters under the null hypothesis arises.

15.4.1 All Parameters Are Identified Under H_0

Before addressing the problem of nonidentification of a subset of parameters under the null hypothesis, we start by presenting an example of a nonlinear model in which this type of problem does not arise.

Example 15.8 *Consider the following model*

$$E^\theta(y_i | w_i) = \phi' w_i + b(\pi, w_i)$$

where $w_i = (1, y_{i-1}, \ldots, y_{i-p})'$, $\phi = (\phi_0, \phi_1, \ldots, \phi_l)'$ with $l = p + k$, and $\pi = (\pi_1, \ldots, \pi_m)'$. Some exogenous variables may be included in w_i. The function b is twice continuously differentiable with respect to π, and such that

$$b(0, w_i) = 0.$$

The null hypothesis that we are testing is the linearity hypothesis $H_0 : \pi = 0$. The most popular test is that of Rao because it does not require the estimation of the model under the alternative.

To simplify the calculations, we suppose that the innovations are normally distributed and homoskedastic of variance σ^2, such that the log-density function of each y_i takes the following form

$$\ln f(y_i | \theta) = -\frac{1}{2}\ln 2\pi - \ln \sigma - \frac{1}{2\sigma^2}\left(y_i - \phi' w_i - b(\pi, w_i) \right)^2.$$

where $\theta' = (\phi', \sigma, \pi')$. The first derivatives are given by

$$\frac{\partial \ln f}{\partial \phi} = \frac{1}{\sigma^2} \left(y_i - \phi' w_i - b(\pi, w_i) \right) w_i,$$

$$\frac{\partial \ln f}{\partial \sigma} = -\frac{1}{\sigma} + \frac{1}{\sigma^3} \left(y_i - \phi' w_i - h(\pi, w_i) \right)^2,$$

$$\frac{\partial \ln f}{\partial \pi} = \frac{1}{\sigma^2} \left(y_i - \phi' w_i - b(\pi, w_i) \right) \frac{\partial b(\pi, w_i)}{\partial \pi}.$$

The second derivatives are the following

$$\frac{\partial^2 \ln f}{\partial \phi \partial \phi'} = -\frac{1}{\sigma^2} w_i w_i',$$

$$\frac{\partial^2 \ln f}{\partial \phi \partial \sigma} = -\frac{2}{\sigma^3} \left(y_i - \phi' w_i - b(\pi, w_i) \right) w_i,$$

$$\frac{\partial^2 \ln f}{\partial \phi \partial \pi'} = -\frac{1}{\sigma^2} w_i \frac{\partial b(\pi, w_i)}{\partial \pi'},$$

$$\frac{\partial^2 \ln f}{\partial \sigma^2} = \frac{1}{\sigma^2} - \frac{3}{\sigma^4} \left(y_i - \phi' w_i - b(\pi, w_i) \right)^2,$$

$$\frac{\partial^2 \ln f}{\partial \sigma \partial \pi'} = -\frac{2}{\sigma^3} \left(y_i - \phi' w_i - b(\pi, w_i) \right) \frac{\partial b(\pi, w_i)}{\partial \pi'},$$

$$\frac{\partial^2 \ln f}{\partial \pi \partial \pi'} = \frac{1}{\sigma^2} \left[-\frac{\partial b(\pi, w_i)}{\partial \pi} \frac{\partial b(\pi, w_i)}{\partial \pi'} \right.$$
$$\left. + \left(y_i - \phi' w_i - b(\pi, w_i) \right) \frac{\partial^2 b(\pi, w_i)}{\partial \pi \partial \pi'} \right].$$

From Section 4.4 in Chapter 4, the Rao statistic is

$$RAO_n = n \left(\frac{1}{n} \sum_i \frac{\partial \ln f(y_i | \tilde{\theta}(\widehat{\mu}_n))}{\partial \theta} \right)' \left(J_{\tilde{\theta}(\widehat{\mu}_n)}^{-1} - \frac{\partial \tilde{\theta}(\widehat{\mu}_n)}{\partial \mu'} J_{\widehat{\mu}_n}^{-1} \frac{\partial \tilde{\theta}(\widehat{\mu}_n)'}{\partial \mu} \right)$$
$$\times \left(\frac{1}{n} \sum_i \frac{\partial \ln f(y_i | \tilde{\theta}(\widehat{\mu}_n))}{\partial \theta} \right)$$

where $\mu' = (\phi', \sigma)$ and $\tilde{\theta}(\mu) = (\phi', \sigma, 0)$, J_θ and J_μ are the information matrices of the unrestricted and restricted models, respectively. $\widehat{\mu}_n = (\widehat{\phi}'_n, \widehat{\sigma}_n)$ is *the maximum likelihood estimator of μ of the restricted model. This leads to*

$$\frac{1}{n} \sum_i \frac{\partial \ln f(y_i | \widetilde{\theta}(\widehat{\mu}_n))}{\partial \theta}$$

$$= \begin{bmatrix} 0 \\ 0 \\ \frac{1}{n} \sum_i \frac{\partial \ln f(y_i | \widetilde{\theta}(\widehat{\mu}_n))}{\partial \pi} \end{bmatrix} = \begin{bmatrix} 0 \\ 0 \\ \frac{1}{n \widehat{\sigma}_n^2} \sum_i \left(y_i - \widehat{\phi}_n' w_i \right) \widehat{\frac{\partial b}{\partial \pi}} \end{bmatrix}$$

where $\widehat{\frac{\partial b}{\partial \pi}}$ is the vector $\frac{\partial b(\pi, w_i)}{\partial \pi}$ valued at $\widetilde{\theta}(\widehat{\mu}_n)$ and $\widehat{\sigma}_n^2$ is the maximum likelihood estimator of σ^2.

From (15.4) and (15.28), we have

$$E^{\theta} \left(\left(y_i - \phi' w_i - b(\pi, w_i) \right) w_i \right) = 0,$$

$$E^{\theta} \left(\left(y_i - \phi' w_i - b(\pi, w_i) \right) \frac{\partial b(\pi, w_i)}{\partial \pi} \right) = 0.$$

Moreover,

$$E^{\theta} \left(\frac{\partial^2 \ln f}{\partial \pi \, \partial \pi'} \right) = -\frac{1}{\sigma^2} E^{\theta} \left(\frac{\partial b(\pi, w_i)}{\partial \pi} \frac{\partial b(\pi, w_i)}{\partial \pi'} \right)$$

and

$$E^{\theta} \left(\frac{\partial^2 \ln f}{\partial \sigma^2} \right) = -\frac{2}{\sigma^2}$$

since

$$E^{\theta} \left(\left(y_i - \phi' w_i - b(\pi, w_i) \right)^2 \right) = \sigma^2.$$

From this, we can infer J_θ and similarly, J_μ:

$$J_\theta = \frac{1}{\sigma^2} \begin{bmatrix} E^{\theta} \left(w_i w_i' \right) & 0 & E^{\theta} \left(w_i \frac{\partial b(\pi, w_i)}{\partial \pi'} \right) \\ 0 & 2 & 0 \\ E^{\theta} \left(\frac{\partial b(\pi, w_i)}{\partial \pi} w_i' \right) & 0 & E^{\theta} \left(\frac{\partial b(\pi, w_i)}{\partial \pi} \frac{\partial b(\pi, w_i)}{\partial \pi'} \right) \end{bmatrix},$$

$$J_\mu = \frac{1}{\sigma^2} \begin{bmatrix} E^{\theta} \left(w_i w_i' \right) & 0 \\ 0 & 2 \end{bmatrix}.$$

Given that $\frac{\partial \widetilde{\theta}(\mu)}{\partial \mu'} = \begin{bmatrix} 1 & 0 \\ 0 & 1 \\ 0 & 0 \end{bmatrix}$, we have

$$J_\theta^{-1} - \frac{\partial \widetilde{\theta}(\mu)}{\partial \mu'} J_\mu^{-1} \frac{\partial \widetilde{\theta}(\mu)'}{\partial \mu}$$

$$= \sigma^2 \left(\begin{bmatrix} E^\theta \left(w_i w_i' \right) & 0 & E^\theta \left(w_i \frac{\partial b(\pi, w_i)}{\partial \pi'} \right) \\ 0 & 2 & 0 \\ E^\theta \left(\frac{\partial b(\pi, w_i)}{\partial \pi} w_i' \right) & 0 & E^\theta \left(\frac{\partial b(\pi, w_i)}{\partial \pi} \frac{\partial b(\pi, w_i)}{\partial \pi'} \right) \end{bmatrix}^{-1} \right.$$

$$\left. - \begin{bmatrix} \left[E^\theta \left(w_i w_i' \right) \right]^{-1} & 0 & 0 \\ 0 & 1/2 & 0 \\ 0 & 0 & 0 \end{bmatrix} \right).$$

Hence,

$$RAO_n = n \left(\frac{1}{n\widehat{\sigma}_n^2} \sum_i (y_i - \widehat{\phi}_n' w_i) \frac{\widehat{\partial b}}{\partial \pi} \right)' \left(\sigma^2 \left[E^\theta \left(\frac{\partial b(\pi, w_i)}{\partial \pi} \frac{\partial b(\pi, w_i)}{\partial \pi'} \right) \right.\right.$$

$$\left.\left. - E^\theta \left(\frac{\partial b(\pi, w_i)}{\partial \pi} w_i' \right) \left[E^\theta \left(w_i w_i' \right) \right]^{-1} E^\theta \left(w_i \frac{\partial b(\pi, w_i)}{\partial \pi'} \right) \right]^{-1} \right)$$

$$\times \left(\frac{1}{n\widehat{\sigma}_n^2} \sum_i (y_i - \widehat{\phi}_n' w_i) \frac{\widehat{\partial b}}{\partial \pi} \right)$$

where the middle term is the (3,3) element of the inverse of the partitioned matrix

$$J_\theta^{-1} - \frac{\partial \widetilde{\theta}(\mu)}{\partial \mu'} J_\mu^{-1} \frac{\partial \widetilde{\theta}(\mu)'}{\partial \mu}$$

valued at $\widehat{\mu}_n$. This statistic is asymptotically distributed according to a χ_m^2 where m is the dimension of the vector π. It is estimated by $\widehat{RAO}_n$ where all the parameters come from the restricted model:

$$\widehat{RAO}_n = \frac{1}{\widehat{\sigma}_n^2} \left(\sum_i (y_i - \widehat{\phi}_n' w_i) \frac{\widehat{\partial b}}{\partial \pi} \right)' \left[\sum_i \frac{\widehat{\partial b}}{\partial \pi} \frac{\widehat{\partial b}}{\partial \pi'} - \left(\sum_i \frac{\widehat{\partial b}}{\partial \pi} w_i' \right) \right.$$

$$\left. \times \left[\sum_i w_i w_i' \right]^{-1} \left(\sum_i w_i \frac{\widehat{\partial b}}{\partial \pi'} \right) \right]^{-1} \left(\sum_i (y_i - \widehat{\phi}_n' w_i) \frac{\widehat{\partial b}}{\partial \pi} \right).$$

The test can be obtained in three steps:
1. Estimate ϕ by $\widehat{\phi}_n$ in the regression

$$y_i = \phi' w_i + \varepsilon_i, \ i = 1, \dots, n,$$

and compute the residual sum of squares

$$\sum_i \widehat{\varepsilon}_i^2 = \sum_i \left(y_i - \widehat{\phi}_n' w_i \right)^2.$$

2. Estimate the model

$$\widehat{\varepsilon}_i = \delta' z_i + \eta_i, \ i = 1, \dots, n,$$

with $z_i' = (w_i', \frac{\widehat{\partial b}}{\partial \pi'})$ and compute

$$\sum_i \widehat{\eta}_i^2 = \sum_i \left(\widehat{\varepsilon}_i - \widehat{\delta}_n' z_i \right)^2.$$

Note here that

$$\sum_i \widehat{\eta}_i^2 = \sum_i \widehat{\varepsilon}_i^2 - \left(\sum_i \widehat{\varepsilon}_i z_i \right)' \left[\sum_i z_i z_i' \right]^{-1} \left(\sum_i \widehat{\varepsilon}_i z_i \right)$$

$$= \sum_i \widehat{\varepsilon}_i^2 - \begin{pmatrix} 0 \\ \sum_i \widehat{\varepsilon}_i \frac{\widehat{\partial b}}{\partial \pi} \end{pmatrix}' \begin{bmatrix} \sum_i w_i w_i' & \sum_i w_i \frac{\widehat{\partial b}}{\partial \pi}' \\ \sum_i \frac{\widehat{\partial b}}{\partial \pi} w_i' & \sum_i \frac{\widehat{\partial b}}{\partial \pi} \frac{\widehat{\partial b}}{\partial \pi}' \end{bmatrix}^{-1} \begin{pmatrix} 0 \\ \sum_i \widehat{\varepsilon}_i \frac{\widehat{\partial b}}{\partial \pi} \end{pmatrix}$$

$$= \sum_i \widehat{\varepsilon}_i^2 - \left(\sum_i \widehat{\varepsilon}_i \frac{\widehat{\partial b}}{\partial \pi} \right)' \left(\sum_i \frac{\widehat{\partial b}}{\partial \pi} \frac{\widehat{\partial b}}{\partial \pi'} - \left(\sum_i \frac{\widehat{\partial b}}{\partial \pi} w_i' \right) \left[\sum_i w_i w_i' \right]^{-1} \right.$$

$$\left. \times \left(\sum_i w_i \frac{\widehat{\partial b}}{\partial \pi'} \right) \right)^{-1} \left(\sum_i \widehat{\varepsilon}_i \frac{\widehat{\partial b}}{\partial \pi} \right)$$

since $\sum_i \widehat{\varepsilon}_i w_i = 0$.
3. Finally, compute

$$\widehat{RAO}_n = \frac{\sum_i \widehat{\varepsilon}_i^2 - \sum_i \widehat{\eta}_i^2}{\sum_i \widehat{\varepsilon}_i^2 / n}$$

(recall that $\widehat{\sigma}_n^2 = \sum_i \widehat{\varepsilon}_i^2 / n$). $\qquad\square$

15.4.2 The Problem of the Nonidentification of Some Parameters Under H_0

In the following section, we consider examples in which some parameters are not identified under the null hypothesis. This implies in particular that the information matrix calculated under H_0 is singular. The procedure usually used, namely the Davies procedure, consists in letting the test statistic depend on the nonidentified parameters and in using the maximum of this function to construct the critical region of the test. The asymptotic distribution is usually not a χ^2 (since the maximum of a set of dependent χ^2 is not itself a χ^2), but must be determined on a case-by-case basis, as we will see below.

Example 15.9   *We return to the previous example where*

$$E^\theta(y_i \mid w_i) = \phi'w_i + b(\pi, w_i)$$

with the same notation and assumptions, except that here the function b can be written as a product

$$b(\pi, w_i) = b_1(\pi_1, w_i)\pi_2'w_i$$

with

$$b_1(0, w_i) = 0 \quad and \quad \pi' = (\pi_1', \pi_2').$$

The linearity hypothesis can be written as $H_0 : \pi_1 = 0$; under this hypothesis, π_2 is not identified in the sense that its elements can take any values. Another linearity hypothesis that can be considered is $H_0 : \pi_2 = 0$, but it leads again to a problem of nonidentification, here of the vector π_1. STAR type models enter in this framework, because, from (15.24) and (15.25), they satisfy:

$$E^\theta(y_i \mid w_i) = \alpha_0 + \alpha'w_i + (\beta_0 + \beta'w_i)F(y_{i-d})$$

where F is very often a logistic or exponential function (see (15.26) or (15.27)).

   The Davies procedure consists in considering the test statistic for the null hypothesis $H_0 : \pi_1 = 0$ assuming π_2 fixed, namely $RAO_n(\pi_2)$, and in studying finally $\sup_{\pi_2} RAO_n(\pi_2)$. In other words, the critical region, to which this procedure leads, is simply the union of the critical regions corresponding to the possible values of π_2:

$$R = \left\{ x \,\middle|\, \sup_{\pi_2} RAO_n(\pi_2) > \alpha \right\}$$

$$= \{x \mid \exists \pi_2 \quad RAO_n(\pi_2) > \alpha\}$$

$$= \bigcup_{\pi_2} R(\pi_2)$$

where

$$R(\pi_2) = \{x / RAO_n(\pi_2) > \alpha\}$$

is the critical region for a given π_2. In this general example, the statistic $RAO_n(\pi_2)$ has the advantage of following asymptotically a χ^2 with degree of freedom the dimension of π_1.

It is worth noting that in STAR type models, most of the frequently used linearity tests rely on a Taylor expansion of the nonlinear function and a reparametrization, and not on Davies procedure. ☐

Now, we study two examples where the Davies procedure leads to statistics that follow nonstandard distributions. These are two examples that we have seen in Section 3, the structural change model and the threshold model.

Example 15.10 *Consider the structural change model presented in Example 15.2 and continued in Example 15.5*

$$y_i = \lambda_0 + \lambda_1 I_{i>n\pi} + u_i$$

where u_i is i.i.$N(0, \sigma^2)$ and n is the sample size. For a breakpoint π, there are $n\pi$ observed points before and $n - n\pi$ observed points after. When $n\pi$ is unknown, the tests of the null hypothesis $H_0 : \lambda_1 = 0$ and their asymptotic distributions are the following

$$\sup_{\pi \in \Pi} WALD_n(\pi), \quad \sup_{\pi \in \Pi} RAO_n(\pi), \quad \sup_{\pi \in \Pi} COMP_n(\pi)$$

$$\to \sup_{\pi \in \Pi} \frac{BB_\pi^2}{\pi(1-\pi)} \tag{15.40}$$

where $WALD_n$, RAO_n, and $COMP_n$ correspond respectively to the Wald, Rao, and Likelihood ratio test. Π is a subset of $(0, 1)$ (it is sometimes recommended to take it equal to $[0.15, 0.85]$), $BB_\pi = W(\pi) - \pi W(1)$ is a Brownian bridge and $W(.)$ is a Brownian motion on $[0, 1]$, restricted to Π. We are going to sketch the proof, which leads to result (15.40) in the case of the Wald test. From (15.32) and (15.33), it follows that

$$WALD_n(\pi) = n \frac{\pi(1-\pi)}{\sigma^2} \widehat{\lambda}_{1n}^2$$

$$= n \frac{\pi(1-\pi)}{\sigma^2} \left[\frac{1}{n(1-\pi)} \sum_{i>n\pi} y_i - \frac{1}{n\pi} \sum_{i<n\pi} y_i \right]^2 .$$

Using the fact that $\lambda_1 = 0$ under the null hypothesis, we have

$$\sum_{i>n\pi} y_i = \sum_{i>n\pi} (\lambda_0 + u_i) = n(1-\pi)\lambda_0 + \sum_{i>n\pi} u_i$$

and

$$\sum_{i<n\pi} y_i = \sum_{i<n\pi} (\lambda_0 + u_i) = n\pi\lambda_0 + \sum_{i<n\pi} u_i = n\pi\lambda_0 + \sum_i u_i - \sum_{i>n\pi} u_i .$$

The statistic can be rewritten as

$$WALD_n(\pi) = \frac{\pi(1-\pi)}{n\sigma^2} \left[\left(\frac{1}{(1-\pi)} + \frac{1}{\pi} \right) \sum_{i>n\pi} u_i - \frac{1}{\pi} \sum_i u_i \right]^2$$

$$= \frac{1}{n\pi(1-\pi)\sigma^2} \left[\sum_{i>n\pi} u_i - (1-\pi) \sum_i u_i \right]^2$$

$$= \frac{1}{n\pi(1-\pi)} \left[\sum_{i>n\pi} \varepsilon_i - (1-\pi) \sum_i \varepsilon_i \right]^2$$

with $\varepsilon_i = \frac{u_i}{\sigma} \sim N(0,1)$. After expansion, we obtain

$$WALD_n(\pi) = \frac{1}{n\pi(1-\pi)} \left[\left(\sum_{i>n\pi} \varepsilon_i \right)^2 - 2(1-\pi) \sum_{i>n\pi} \varepsilon_i \sum_i \varepsilon_i \right.$$

$$\left. + (1-\pi)^2 \left(\sum_i \varepsilon_i \right)^2 \right]$$

or, furthermore,

$$WALD_n(\pi) = \frac{1}{\pi(1-\pi)} \left[\left(\frac{\sqrt{n}}{n} \sum_{i>n\pi} \varepsilon_i \right)^2 - 2(1-\pi) \left(\frac{\sqrt{n}}{n} \sum_{i>n\pi} \varepsilon_i \right) \left(\frac{\sqrt{n}}{n} \sum_i \varepsilon_i \right) \right.$$

$$\left. + (1-\pi)^2 \left(\frac{\sqrt{n}}{n} \sum_i \varepsilon_i \right)^2 \right].$$

Next we will use two convergence results, that we state here without proof. The first is the following weak convergence of a process

$$\frac{\sqrt{n}}{n} \sum_{i>n\pi} \varepsilon_i \to W(1) - W(\pi)$$

and the second is the convergence

$$\sup_{\pi} h_n(\pi) \to \sup_{\pi} h(\pi)$$

when the functional convergence $h_n \to h$ holds. These results hold under some assumptions, which we assume to be satisfied. We have

$$WALD_n(\pi) \to \frac{1}{\pi(1-\pi)} \left[(W(1) - W(\pi))^2 - 2(1-\pi)(W(1) \right.$$

$$\left. - W(\pi))W(1) + (1-\pi)^2 W(1)^2 \right]$$

$$\to \frac{1}{\pi(1-\pi)} \left[(W(\pi) - \pi W(1))^2 \right],$$

hence it follows

$$\sup_{\pi} WALD_n(\pi) \to \sup_{\pi} \frac{(W(\pi) - \pi W(1))^2}{\pi(1 - \pi)},$$

which leads to expression (15.40). ☐

Example 15.11 *In the threshold model of Example 15.3, the parameter c is not identified under the null hypothesis* $H_0 : \lambda_1 = 0$. *One can show that*

$$\sup_{c \in R} WALD_n(c), \quad \sup_{c \in R} RAO_n(c), \quad \sup_{c \in R} COMP_n(c)$$

$$\to \sup_{\delta \in \Delta} \frac{BB_\delta^2}{\delta(1-\delta)}$$

where

$$\delta(c) = E^\theta(\mathbf{1}_{y_{i-d} \leq c})$$

and $\Delta \subset (0, 1)$ *is the image of R by* δ. *It is sometimes suggested to take* $R = [c_1, c_2]$ *where* c_1 *and* c_2 *are respectively the 15th and 85th percentiles of the empirical distribution of* $\{y_i\}$. ☐

Notes

Some authors have investigated the theoretical problems that arise in nonlinear dynamic models, such as Gallant (1987, Chapter 7), Gallant and White (1988), Hall (1993), Priestley (1991), and Tong (1990).

In Section 2, regarding the estimation of nonlinear dynamic models by generalized method of moments, we named two possible choices for estimating the asymptotic covariance matrix, the first based on Parzen weights is given in Gallant (1987), and the second can be found in Newey and West (1987a and 1987b); see also Ogaki (1993). The example is taken from Tauchen (1986), see also for instance Hansen and Singleton (1982), Hansen (1982), and Hall (1993).

The LSTAR and ESTAR models are studied in Luukkonen (1990), Luukkonen, Saikkonen, and Teräsvirta (1988a and 1988b), Luukkonen and Teräsvirta (1991), Teräsvirta (1994), Teräsvirta and Anderson (1992). For their asymptotic properties, see Chan and Tong (1986) (for a Bayesian analysis of these models, see Péguin-Feissolle (1994) and for multiple regimes, see Dufrenot, Mignon, and Péguin-Feissolle (2004)).

Threshold models have been introduced by Tong (see for instance Tong (1990)). Regarding more specifically EAR models, see Laurance and Lewis (1980 and 1985). The examples relating to the models where the function g is not smooth, namely the structural change model, and the threshold model are taken from Carrasco (1995 and 2002).

Regarding linearity tests, we refer to Granger and Teräsvirta (1993) and numerous articles by Teräsvirta (especially Teräsvirta (1994)) for everything about this type of tests in the class of STR model. Davies procedure was treated in Davies (1977 and 1987). The examples of specific nonsmooth models are again borrowed from Carrasco (1995) (see also Andrews (1993), Garcia (1998), and Chan (1990)).

Part IV

Structural Modeling

16. Identification and Overidentification in Structural Modeling

16.1 Introduction

In the previous chapters, we presented a set of statistical methods that were initially general and then specific to particular classes of statistical models. These methods and models have been chosen because they were suited to treat economic data but they belonged essentially to mathematical statistics. It is sufficient to look at some textbooks for the application of statistics in scientific areas other than economics (physics, biology, sociology, psychology and so on) to find an important part of the tools presented here, sometimes with a different relative importance or a different terminology, but fundamentally similar regarding the modes of thought and the results. The recent development in econometrics attests of the increasing diversity of the methods it uses. Formerly centered around a small number of models, econometrics has seized more and more statistical techniques; there are few statistical methods that have not found a use in the treatment of economic data.

Does the econometric method coincide with statistics? Most econometricians would answer no to this question. Most likely, the econometricians would consider that the autonomy of their field results from the approach of *structural modeling*. In broad outline, we mean by structural modeling a specification of the statistical model starting from theoretical relations that describe the phenomenon under study. These relations result from the "micro" or "macro" economic analysis and are essentially the mathematical expression of behavioral rules of agents or groups of agents involved in the examined phenomenon. Structural modeling associates a statistical model with the economic model that it describes, and it allows us to validate or reject the economic model or some of the theoretical assumptions embedded in it.

The relationship between theoretical model and statistical model is obviously not specific to econometrics, it can be found in all scientific approaches in any field. It presents some characteristics specific to econometrics, whose main features we consider in the last chapters of this book.

16.2 Structural Model and Reduced Form

It is extremely difficult to provide a general mathematical definition of *structural models*. We describe their main elements. The models are about observed units denoted i, that may be as before individuals (households, firms, . . .), periods (months, quarters, days), or an intersection of the two.

For each i, a vector of variables denoted x_i^* is defined. These variables are of a diverse nature: they represent measures relevant in economics (individual consumption of a good, price of a production factor, willingness to pay for a phone connection, gross domestic product) or error variables that reflect the inexactness of the model (residuals). The variables may be directly observable (from surveys, national income accounting, . . .), partially observed (the willingness to pay for an apartment is greater than the actual price paid by a household, but is not directly observable), or completely unobservable (residuals, unobserved heterogeneity such as the ability to perform a job, the efficiency of a company).

These various variables are related through equations. The first group of equations reflect the behavior of economic agents and are most often based on an optimization criterion (utility maximization, cost minimization). In general, optimization is represented by the first order conditions and a set of restrictions. Besides these autonomous behavioral equations of each actor of an economic phenomenon, there are equations that make all the different behaviors compatible (equilibrium condition, rationality condition). These equations explain the essence of the nature of the economic analysis that deals with rational behaviors and their interdependence.

This system of structural equations is built in order to be solved. The variables are split into two categories, the endogenous variables on one hand and the exogenous variables and residuals on the other hand. The aim of the structural model is to explain the interaction between the variables, and the determination of the endogenous variables by the exogenous variables and the residuals. We met this terminology before, but here we will try to make it more precise.

The structural equations are related to the economic choices of the agents. In practice, a structural model cannot analyze all the decisions of an economic agent (for the obvious reason of dimension) but considers some of them as given (the decision to work by a woman is in some models analyzed taking the matrimonial status and the number of children as given, but other models choose to explain simultaneously the fertility decision and the search for a job).

Therefore, a structural model is always partially reduced; progress has been made in econometrics in *endogenizing* variables (i.e., in explaining their generation) that were previously exogenous (i.e., considered as given).

Finally, a structural model contains *parameters* that may be vectors (elasticities for instance) or functions (the probability distribution of residuals or of heterogeneity). The econometricians does not know the values of these parameters. The goal is to estimate them or to test some hypotheses about them.

It is usually assumed that the parameters are known by the economic agents who are able (at least implicitly) to calculate the solution to the optimization problems. Other models assume that the economic agents accumulate information on the parameters over time; hence, there is a learning process by the economic agents and the econometrician observes this (with sometimes a relationship between these two mechanisms).

The parameters that we consider here are also structural, in the sense that they are "independent." This intuitively means that a change in one of them occurs without affecting the set of parameters, e.g., the price elasticity of the supply of the firms can stay constant while the elasticity of household demand varies, which obviously affects the market equilibrium.

The parameters are by definition fixed in the model. Some authors use the term "random parameters," but we will treat these "random parameters" as unobservable variables whose distributions themselves depend on fixed parameters. We find another confusion among authors who compute a sequence of successive estimates of the parameters that grows with the sample size and interpret them as random parameters. Of course, the estimates vary but the underlying parameters themselves are constant.

The fact that the model depends only on parameters (possibly functionals) that are fixed across individuals or periods is a necessary restriction of the statistical method and is its limitation. For example, an econometric model may be used for forecasting only if its parameters are constant. However, those obviously vary in particular under the effect of economic policies, which make it difficult to use econometric models to forecast their effect. This argument returned often in the econometrics literature – mainly Anglo-Saxon – under the name of *Lucas critique*. We do not discuss its relevance here, but we note that the more structural a model is, the more accurately we can simulate the impact of an economic policy by modifying (arbitrarily, i.e., by using a non-statistical argument) one or several of the parameters. The structural form is useful for manipulations of some parameters, because these parameters are easily interpretable as behavioral parameters and they may change independently from each other. However, structural modeling with parameters kept constant is useless for forecasting.

Computing a *reduced form* of a structural model consists in performing two types of tasks:

- Solve a part or all of the equations of the model to express a subset of variables as functions of the others. The second subset contains the residuals that are by nature random. This way, we construct a conditional probability of the endogenous variables (those that were unknown and with respect to which the model has been solved) given the other (exogenous or conditioning) variables. Thus, we obtain a usual conditional statistical model. Various ways to solve the model may reflect diverse interests: in a dynamic model, we solve the endogenous variables at time t as a function of past variables and exogenous variables, or we can express the endogenous variable as a function of the path of the exogenous variables only. This latter form of the model is sometimes called *final form* while the previous one is called reduced form.

- Use marginalization to determine the probability distribution of the observable endogenous variables conditional on the observable exogenous variables. For instance, we can first calculate the reduced form conditional on the observable and unobservable exogenous variables, then eliminate the latter ones by integration, and thus obtain what is called the *solved form*. Integrating out the unobservables allows us to take the partial observation scheme of the endogenous variables (censoring, truncation, selection of observed individuals, and so on) into account.

We provide some notation to formalize the previous concepts: the variables x_i^* are partitioned into $\left(y_i^*, z_i^*, u_i \right)$ where y_i^* is the vector of endogenous variables, z_i^* is the vector of the exogenous variables and u_i the vector of the residuals. In turn, y_i^* is partitioned into (y_i, η_i) and z_i^* into (z_i, ζ_i), respectively representing the observable and unobservable elements of these vectors. The system of structural equations must allow us to calculate y_i^* as a function of (z_i, ζ_i) and u_i, and the model must specify the probability distribution of u_i in order to infer the conditional distribution of y_i^* as a function of z_i^*. To eliminate ζ_i, we need to know additionally its probability distribution (conditional on the z_i). In contrast, the distribution of z_i does not play a central role in the model and is in general little constrained.

The parameters of the structural model (possibly including functional parameters) are denoted by θ. The various conditional models that we consider depend on different functions of θ.

16.3   Identification: The Example of Simultaneous Equations

16.3.1   General Definitions

In the presentation of general statistical methods and in the analysis of the estimation of specific econometric models, the identification assumption has been introduced, more or less explicitly. This assumption may have appeared as a technical regularity condition, only necessary for the mathematical rigor of the exposition. In the context of structural modeling, that is when the econometric model formalizes an economic phenomenon, the identification condition is more than a simple technical assumption, but covers a more fundamental aspect that is intuitively the adequacy of a theoretical model for an observed process. The economic theory of the phenomenon under study defines the relevant parameters, whereas the observation scheme characterizes the data generating process (DGP). Hence, it is important that these relevant parameters are correctly determined by the DGP, i.e., that they are an injective function of the

DGP. In the statistical analysis, we learn only about the DGP and we can recover the parameters of the theoretical model only if they are uniquely determined by the DGP. Our viewpoint is the viewpoint of the "classical" statistician, in the sense that only the observed data brings information. The Bayesian analysis, in which the observations are complemented by a prior information, would of course be different.

In this section, we consider only the distributions of observable variables, possibly conditional on other observable variables. Indeed, these are the distributions that the observations will allow us to learn about. On the other hand, the parameters θ may be defined in a system containing unobservable variables that are eliminated by integration.

We recall the notions of identification that we previously introduced, but our goal in this chapter is mainly to illustrate them using examples of models.

1. In Chapter 1 (Definition 1.2), we introduced the notion of identification of a model $\{X_n, \Theta, P_n^\theta\}$ as the property:

    $$P_n^{\theta_1} = P_n^{\theta_2} \Rightarrow \theta_1 = \theta_2.$$

2. In Chapter 3, we introduced the notion of identification of a function $\lambda(\theta)$ of parameters defined by a moment condition (3.5): $\lambda(\theta)$ is identified if the solution of the equation

    $$E^\theta(\psi(x_i, \lambda)) = 0$$

    is unique (when it exists).
3. A special case of the second definition meets the first definition. If the model (which we assume to be i.i.d. to simplify) is dominated and correctly specified, we can use as moment condition the equation that sets the expectation of the score equal to zero:

    $$E^\theta\left(\frac{\partial}{\partial \lambda'} \ln f(x_i|\lambda)\right) = 0,$$

    which admits $\lambda(\theta) = \theta$ as a solution. The uniqueness of this solution is then equivalent to the property: the probability distributions with densities $f(.|\theta_1)$ and $f(.|\theta_2)$ are identical (which is equivalent to $P_n^{\theta_1} = P_n^{\theta_2}$) if and only if $\theta_1 = \theta_2$.

We focus on the second point whose generality we have just demonstrated and provide the following definition.

Definition 16.1 *Let $\{X_n, \Theta, P_n^\theta\}$ be a statistical model and consider a set of moment conditions:*

$$E^\theta(\psi(x_i, \lambda)) = 0. \tag{16.1}$$

1. *Two functions $\lambda_1(\theta)$ and $\lambda_2(\theta)$ are equivalent if they both satisfy Equation (16.1).*

2. *The function* $\lambda(\theta)$ *is identified if all functions equivalent to* $\lambda(\theta)$ *are equal to* $\lambda(\theta)$. *Otherwise, the function is underidentified.*
3. *The function* $\lambda(\theta)$ *is locally identified at* θ_0 *if all functions equivalent to* $\lambda(\theta)$ *coincide with* $\lambda(\theta)$ *in a neighborhood of* θ_0. *The function* $\lambda(\theta)$ *is locally identified if it is locally identified for all values of* θ_0.   □

To simplify this presentation, we defined only a concept of unconditional identification. Generally, we could examine a condition

$$E^\theta\left(\widetilde{\psi}(x_i, \lambda) | z_i\right) = 0.$$

In this case, λ_1 and λ_2 are equivalent if these two functions of parameters satisfy this equation for all values of z_i. However, we decided to examine here only cases where the conditional moment conditions can be transformed into joint conditions (see Chapter 3) and the useful concepts are then those defined in Section 3.5.

The concept of local identification is of interest for two reasons.

1. Local identification is sufficient to ensure the asymptotic properties of the estimator $\hat{\lambda}_n$. We do not develop here the argument that is a bit technical. We simply note that if the sample size is sufficiently large, we can limit the parametric space to a neighborhood of the true value and settle for local identification.
2. The second argument in favor of a local study of identification rests on the possibility to transform the uniqueness condition of the solution to the equation $E^\theta(\psi(x_i, \lambda)) = 0$ into a rank condition of a matrix. Here again, passing rapidly over the regularity conditions (differentiability, permutation of the expectation, and differentiation), we can state the following sufficient condition for local identification. Let $\theta_0 \in \Theta$ and $\lambda(\theta_0)$ be the solution to

    $$E^{\theta_0}(\psi(x_i, \lambda(\theta_0))) = 0.$$

    If the matrix

    $$E^\theta\left(\frac{\partial}{\partial\lambda'}\psi(x_i, \lambda)\right)$$

    evaluated at the point $(\theta_0, \lambda(\theta_0))$ has rank k (where k is the dimension of λ), then there exists a function $\lambda(\theta)$ satisfying

    $$E^\theta(\psi(x_i, \lambda(\theta))) = 0$$

    in a neighborhood of θ_0 and this function is unique. This theorem follows from the implicit function theorem (see for instance Schwartz (1992), Chapter 4, Section 8). The implicit function theorem applies strictly speaking to the case when r (the dimension of ψ) is equal to k, and in this case implies both existence and local uniqueness. Only uniqueness is obtained if $r \geq k$.

To conclude these general considerations on identification, let us examine the relationship between the asymptotic rank condition and the finite sample rank condition.

Suppose

$$E^\theta \left(\frac{\partial}{\partial \lambda'} \psi \left(x_i, \lambda \left(\theta \right) \right) \right) \tag{16.2}$$

has rank k for all θ. As the set of full rank matrices is open, we infer that

$$\frac{1}{n} \sum_{i=1}^{n} \frac{\partial}{\partial \lambda'} \psi \left(x_i, \lambda \left(\theta \right) \right),$$

which converges almost surely to (16.2), has also rank k for n sufficiently large. For example, if $r = k$, the estimator $\hat{\lambda}_n$, which is the solution to

$$\frac{1}{n} \sum_{i=1}^{n} \psi \left(x_i, \lambda \right) = 0,$$

is therefore locally unique; in this case, note that the invertibility of (16.2) and that of its estimator

$$\frac{1}{n} \sum_{i=1}^{n} \frac{\partial}{\partial \lambda'} \psi \left(x_i, \hat{\lambda}_n \right)$$

are used in the study of the asymptotic properties.

This result is useful mostly for its opposite implication. In practice, it is sometimes difficult to verify the assumptions that imply identification because they often involve conditions on the DGP (for example, rank conditions on the moment matrix, or as we will see in the next section, conditions that some of (obviously unknown) parameters are equal to zero). Hence, it is common to use a numerical procedure to solve the equation

$$\frac{1}{n} \sum_{i=1}^{n} \psi \left(x_i, \lambda \right) = 0$$

without being positive on identification. The fact that some numerical difficulties arise when solving, indicative of the multiplicity of solutions, allows us to question the identification of the function $\lambda \left(\theta \right)$. The existence of numerical problems is more often caused by a modeling and identification problem than by a failure of the algorithm or of the computer.

16.3.2   Linear i.i.d. Simultaneous Equations Models

The simultaneous equations models have constituted the heart of econometrics from the 1950s to the 1970s. They define a class of problems that are specific to econometrics and apparently do not have an equivalent in other domains of statistics. They result from the structural approach of modeling and illustrate perfectly the essential questions raised by this approach. The simplest case is that of a linear i.i.d. model for which we summarize here the identification conditions. Another specific problem of these models, namely endogeneity, will be examined in the following chapter. The linear i.i.d. simultaneous equation models can obviously be generalized in two directions, nonlinear models and dynamic models. The latter ones are considered in the next section.

The role of simultaneous equation models in theoretical research in econometrics has declined considerably, as can be seen from the importance of this topic in recent books and scientific conferences. However, it remains true that many applied econometrics problems must be modeled by simultaneous equations systems. Hence, their empirical and pedagogical importance remains.

The traditional construction of linear i.i.d. simultaneous equations models is the following. The observations $x_i \in \mathbb{R}^m$ are split into y_i, z_i with dimensions p and q. The goal of the model is to build the conditional distribution of y_i given z_i or, at least, to characterize some moment conditions. We assume that we can write

$$By_i + Cz_i = u_i \qquad i = 1, \ldots, n \tag{16.3}$$

where B is an invertible $p \times p$ matrix, C is a $p \times q$ matrix and u_i is a random vector with dimension p. We also specify a distribution of u_i conditional on z_i or assumptions regarding some conditional moments of u_i given z_i. It is also necessary to complete these assumptions with some minimal characterization of the distribution of z_i.

For instance, we can assume:

Assumption A1   *The joint process (z_i, u_i) is i.i.d. conditionally on the parameters θ, with square integrable components, and satisfies*

$$E^\theta (u_i|z_i) = 0. \tag{16.4}$$

$\square$

Then, Equation (16.3) implies that

$$y_i = \Pi z_i + v_i \qquad i = 1, \ldots, n \tag{16.5}$$

with

$$\Pi = -B^{-1}C \quad \text{and} \quad v_i = B^{-1}u_i$$

and it follows from A1 and (16.5) that the $x_i = (y_i, z_i)$ are i.i.d. and satisfy

$$E^\theta (y_i|z_i) = \Pi z_i. \tag{16.6}$$

This equation defines the reduced form of the model.

Assumption A1 can be strengthened by a homoskedasticity assumption:

Assumption A2

$$Var^{\theta}\left(u_i|z_i\right) = \Sigma$$

       □

or by a distributional assumption:

Assumption A3

$$u_i|z_i \sim N_p\left(0, \Sigma\right).$$

(16.7)

□

Actually, the matrices B and C in Equation (16.3) have a specific structure, some of their elements are assumed to be zero, other equal to 1, or more generally their elements are linked by relations. We express these restrictions by assuming that B and C can be written as some functions of a vector λ of $\mathbb{R}^k$. Then, Equation (16.3) is rewritten as

$$B_\lambda y_i + C_\lambda z_i = u_i.$$

(16.8)

Equation (16.8) is called structural form of the simultaneous equations model. It is i.i.d. because the distribution of (z_i, u_i) (and hence that of x_i) is i.i.d., it is linear because the equation system is linear in y_i. The usual terminology refers to z_i as exogenous variables and to y_i as endogenous variables. The vector u_i is the vector of *structural residuals*. This terminology (in particular the distinction between endogenous and exogenous) is a special case of the more general terminology studied in the first part.

Example 16.1 *A special case of (16.8) is the following*

$$\begin{cases} y_{i1} + \lambda_1 y_{i2} + \lambda_2 z_{i1} + \lambda_3 = u_{i1} \\ y_{i1} + \lambda_4 y_{i2} + \lambda_5 z_{i2} + \lambda_6 = u_{i2}. \end{cases}$$

(16.9)

Hence, $\lambda \in \mathbb{R}^6$ and

$$B = \begin{pmatrix} 1 & \lambda_1 \\ 1 & \lambda_4 \end{pmatrix}, \quad C = \begin{pmatrix} \lambda_2 & 0 & \lambda_3 \\ 0 & \lambda_5 & \lambda_6 \end{pmatrix},$$

$y_i = (y_{i1}, y_{i2})'$ and $z_i = (z_{i1}, z_{i2}, 1)'$.

The study of a market in equilibrium provides an illustration for this system. y_{i1} and y_{i2} are the equilibrium prices and quantities in this market for observation i, z_{i1} and z_{i2} are two exogenous variables that respectively characterize the *supply and demand equations. Hence, the two equations are behavioral equations of economic agents and can describe individual behavior, the behavior of the representative agent or of an aggregation of agents. These relationships are structural, but include already a preliminary phase of computation: utility maximization under budget constraints by the consumers and, for example, profit maximization under technological constraints by the producers. The solving of these optimization problems does not mix both sides of the market (supply and demand) while the reduced form*

$$
\begin{cases}
y_{i1} = -\dfrac{\lambda_2\lambda_4}{\lambda_4 - \lambda_1}z_{i1} + \dfrac{\lambda_5}{\lambda_4 - \lambda_1}z_{i2} + \dfrac{\lambda_6 - \lambda_3\lambda_4}{\lambda_4 - \lambda_1} + \dfrac{\lambda_4 u_{i1} - u_{i2}}{\lambda_4 - \lambda_1} \\[3mm]
y_{i2} = \dfrac{\lambda_1\lambda_2}{\lambda_4 - \lambda_1}z_{i1} + \dfrac{\lambda_5}{\lambda_4 - \lambda_1}z_{i2} + \dfrac{\lambda_3\lambda_4 - \lambda_6}{\lambda_4 - \lambda_1} + \dfrac{u_{i2} - \lambda_4 u_{i1}}{\lambda_4 - \lambda_1}
\end{cases}
$$

shows how the two behavioral equations determine the equilibrium. Note that the coefficients of the exogenous variables in the reduced form combine the supply and demand parameters. □

Now, we study the identification of the unknown elements of matrices B and C, i.e., the functions $\lambda\,(\theta)$ on which they depend. The model we consider is defined by Assumption A1 and by the structural equation (16.3). The parameter θ, on which the generating process of u_i and z_i depends, actually plays no role in our presentation: we could adopt a semiparametric viewpoint and assume that (z_i, u_i) is generated by some totally unconstrained distribution Q, except for the existence of moments and Assumption A1. Indeed, our interest focuses on the function $\lambda\,(\theta)$ defined by the relation

$$
E^\theta\left((B_\lambda y_i + C_\lambda z_i)\,z_i'\right) = 0 \tag{16.10}
$$

that follows from (16.4) (we examined in other chapters in more detail the passage from conditional moment conditions to unconditional equations).

We examine here only the uniqueness of the solution of this system of equations (and not the existence problems). Let us introduce the following assumption that eliminates a possible collinearity between explanatory variables.

Assumption A4   *The rank of $E^\theta\left(z_i z_i'\right)$ is equal to q.*   □

Then, the following is true.

Theorem 16.1 *Under A1 and A4, $\lambda_1\,(\theta)$ and $\lambda_2\,(\theta)$ are equivalent if and only if*

$$
\Pi_{\lambda_1(\theta)} = \Pi_{\lambda_2(\theta)}.
$$

In other words, two structural parameters are equivalent if they determine the same coefficients for the explanatory variables in the reduced form model. ∎

This result is immediate by noticing that, under the invertibility conditions of B_λ and $E^\theta(z_i z_i')$, Equation (16.10) is equivalent to

$$E^\theta\left(y_i z_i'\right) E^\theta\left(z_i z_i'\right)^{-1} = \Pi_{\lambda(\theta)}. \tag{16.11}$$

We complete this result with three comments. First, we note that the observations identify the reduced form of the model, i.e., the relationship between explained and explanatory variables. The statistical learning occurs only with this relationship, while getting back to the structural parameters requires specific assumptions on the matrices B and C. Second, Equation (16.11) underlines the nature of simultaneous equations model: it is just a linear regression model for which the regression coefficient matrix

$$E^\theta\left(y_i z_{i'}\right) E^\theta\left(z_i z_i'\right)^{-1}$$

is constrained by the structural form to depend on the function $\lambda(\theta)$ of the parameters. Finally, it follows from the identification condition that some assumptions restricting the matrices B and C are necessary for this condition to be satisfied.

The econometrics literature provides a set of results that allow us to verify the identification condition in cases with specific matrices B_λ and C_λ. We do not provide a comprehensive list of these theorems, but we show two cases.

Example 16.2 *Consider the system*

$$\begin{cases} y_{i1} + \alpha' y_{i2} + \beta' z_{i1} = u_{i1} \\ \quad y_{i2} \quad - \Pi_2 z_i = u_{i2} \\ \quad y_{i3} \quad - \Pi_3 z_i = u_{i3} \end{cases} \tag{16.12}$$

with

$$y_i = (y_{i1}, y_{i2}, y_{i3})', \quad y_{i1} \in \mathbb{R}, \quad y_{i2} \in \mathbb{R}^{p_2}, \quad y_{i3} \in \mathbb{R}^{p_3},$$
$$u_i = (u_{i1}, u_{i2}, u_{i3})', \quad u_{i1} \in \mathbb{R}, \quad u_{i2} \in \mathbb{R}^{p_2}, \quad u_{i3} \in \mathbb{R}^{p_3}$$

and

$$z_i = (z_{i1}, z_{i2})' \in \mathbb{R}^q \quad and \quad z_{i2} \in \mathbb{R}^{q_2}$$

(where $1 + p_2 + p_3 = p$ and $q_1 + q_2 = q$). The parameters are $\lambda = (\alpha, \beta, \Pi_2, \Pi_3)$ where α and β are vectors with dimensions p_2 and q_1 respectively and Π_2 and Π_3 are matrices with dimensions $p_2 \times q$ and $p_3 \times q$.

This model is special in the sense that only one equation mixes the explained variables. The only assumption implied by the two other relations is the linearity *of the conditional expectations of y_{i2} and y_{i3} given z_i. It can be built starting from a more general simultaneous equations model by solving $p - 1$ equations and keeping only one structural equation. Moreover, we assume that the matrices Π_2 and Π_3 are not constrained. This model can also be obtained directly by specifying a structural equation and adding to it some relations between explained and explanatory variables.*

We maintain the general assumptions A1 and A4 but we need to introduce an additional assumption to guarantee identification. Consider the coefficients of the linear regression of y_{i2} on z_i:

$$\Pi_2 = E^\theta \left(y_{i2} z_i' \right) E^\theta \left(z_i z_i' \right)^{-1}. \tag{16.13}$$

We split Π_2 into (Π_{21}, Π_{22}) of dimensions $p_2 \times q_1$ and $p_2 \times q_2$. Then, we have the following result: the parameters of Model (16.12) are identified if and only if the rank of Π_{22} is equal to p_2.

Indeed, the matrix Π of the reduced form of (16.12) takes the form:

$$\Pi = \begin{pmatrix} -\alpha'\Pi_{21} - \beta' & -\alpha'\Pi_{22} \\ \Pi_{21} & \Pi_{22} \\ \Pi_{31} & \Pi_{32} \end{pmatrix};$$

and here

$$\lambda = (\alpha, \beta, \Pi_{21}, \Pi_{22}, \Pi_{31}, \Pi_{32}).$$

Consider two values λ^1 and λ^2 of λ such that $\Pi_{\lambda^1} = \Pi_{\lambda^2}$; hence we have

$$\Pi_{21}^1 = \Pi_{21}^2, \ \Pi_{22}^1 = \Pi_{22}^2, \ \Pi_{31}^1 = \Pi_{31}^2, \ \Pi_{32}^1 = \Pi_{32}^2,$$

$$\alpha^{1'}\Pi_{21}^1 + \beta^{1'} = \alpha^{2'}\Pi_{21}^2 + \beta^{2'} \text{ and } \alpha^{1'}\Pi_{22}^1 = \alpha^{2'}\Pi_{22}^2.$$

The rank condition of $\Pi_{22}^1 \ (= \Pi_{22}^2)$ implies that

$$\alpha^1 = \alpha^2 \text{ and hence } \beta^1 = \beta^2.$$

This condition is called the "rank condition" for identification. Note that this condition requires in particular $q_2 \geq p_2$. This condition, necessary only, is called order condition for identification. In many cases, it is easy to verify that this condition does not hold and hence the model is not identified. The proof of this result is left to the reader whom we refer to the literature summarized at the end of this chapter. Note also that the third equation plays no role in identification. □

The following classical example in the literature on simultaneous equations models leaves the framework of Theorem 16.1, but shows how identification can result from an additional moment equation introducing an assumption on the conditional variance.

Example 16.3 *Consider the system*

$$\begin{cases} y_{i1} + \lambda_1 y_{i2} + \lambda_2 z_i = u_{i1} \\ y_{i1} + \lambda_3 y_{i2} = u_{i2} \end{cases}$$

where $y_i = (y_{i1}, y_{i2}) \in \mathbb{R}^2$ and $z_i \in \mathbb{R}$. Assumptions A1 and A4 are not enough to conclude that the vector $\lambda = (\lambda_1, \lambda_2, \lambda_3)'$ is identified. We add the condition:

$$Var^\theta (u_i | z_i) = \begin{pmatrix} \sigma_1^2 & 0 \\ 0 & \sigma_2^2 \end{pmatrix}. \tag{16.14}$$

Condition (16.14) contains at the same time a homoskedasticity assumption and an assumption of non correlation of the structural residuals. We can verify that the five conditions:

$$\begin{cases} E^\theta ((y_{i1} + \lambda_1 y_{i2} + \lambda_2 z_i) z_i) = 0 \\ E^\theta ((y_{i1} + \lambda_3 y_{i2}) z_i) = 0 \\ E^\theta ((y_{i1} + \lambda_1 y_{i2} + \lambda_2 z_i)(y_{i1} + \lambda_3 y_{i2})) = 0 \\ E^\theta ((y_{i1} + \lambda_1 y_{i2} + \lambda_2 z_i)^2) = \sigma_1^2 \\ E^\theta ((y_{i1} + \lambda_3 y_{i2})^2) = \sigma_2^2 \end{cases}$$

define a system whose solution is unique. It is clear that the third condition is implied by the zero conditional covariance and zero conditional expectation of u_i.

Note that here the parameters of interest include the coefficients of the equations of interest as well as the variances of the residuals. We leave again to the care of the reader to verify identification in this example. □

16.3.3 Linear Dynamic Simultaneous Equations Models

We extend the previous models to the dynamic case and link it to the models presented in Chapters 12 and 13.

Let $(x_i)_{i=1,\dots,n}$ with $x_i \in \mathbb{R}^m$ be a sequence of observations generated by a stochastic process. We maintain the decomposition of x_i as (y_i, z_i). The model specifies a set of equations:

$$B_0 y_i + B_1 y_{i-1} + \cdots + B_r y_{i-r} + C_0 z_i + \cdots + C_r z_{i-r} = u_i \tag{16.15}$$

where the B_j are invertible $p \times p$ matrices and the C_j are $p \times q$. We can also write

$$B(L) y_i + C(L) z_i = u_i$$

with

$$\begin{cases} B(L) = B_0 + B_1 L + \cdots + B_r L^r \\ C(L) = C_0 + C_1 L + \cdots + C_r L^r. \end{cases}$$

Note that these equations contain only a finite number of lags. This simplifying assumption limits our approach to vector autoregressive (VAR) models, which is the most common case in applied econometrics. The matrices $B(L)$ and $C(L)$ are not completely unknown and depend on parameters λ.

These equations differ from the usual VAR model by the fact that B_0 is in general different from the identity matrix. We do not list as many equations as variables but only as *endogenous* variables y_i.

Equation (16.15) is well defined only if the process of the residuals is restricted, which is obtained by the following assumption.

Assumption A1   *Conditionally on the parameters θ of the model, the components of the observations are square integrable and satisfy*

$$E^\theta \left(u_i \left| y_{-\infty}^{i-1}, z_{-\infty}^i \right. \right) = 0 \tag{16.16}$$

where $y_{-\infty}^{i-1}$ represents the observations $y_{i-1}, y_{i-2}, \ldots$ (back to 0 or $-\infty$ depending on the type of process) and $z_{-\infty}^i$ is the path of the process z up to i.   □

Condition (16.16) is necessary to build the sequential distribution of y_i conditionally on the realization of z_i using some assumptions on the distribution of u_i. This is an exogeneity assumption that corresponds to the concept of sequential cut developed in Chapter 2.

We generalize Assumptions A2 and A3 of the preceding section.

Assumption A2

$$Var^\theta \left(u_i \left| y_{-\infty}^{i-1}, z_{-\infty}^i \right. \right) = \Sigma.$$ □

Assumption A3

$$u_i \left| y_{-\infty}^{i-1}, z_{-\infty}^i \right. \sim N(0, \Sigma).$$ □

Note that the condition on the numbers of lags being identical for y and z is not restrictive because some matrices may be zero.

Equations (16.15) represent behavioral equations of economic agents and define (under A1) the structural form of the model.

The reduced form of the model can be written as:

$$y_i = -B_0^{-1} B_1 y_{i-1} - \cdots - B_0^{-1} B_r y_{i-r}$$
$$- B_0^{-1} C_0 z_i - \cdots - B_0^{-1} C_r z_{i-r} + B_0^{-1} u_i$$

hence,

$$y_i = \Lambda_1 y_{i-1} + \cdots + \Lambda_r y_{i-r} + \Pi_0 z_i + \cdots + \Pi_r z_{i-r} + v_i,$$

or

$$(I - \Lambda_1 L - \cdots - \Lambda_r L^r) y_i = (\Pi_0 + \Pi_1 L + \cdots + \Pi_r L^r) z_i + v_i.$$

This model can be considered as a VAR on y_i whose instantaneous matrix is I and contains explanatory variables.

This model allows us, under A3, to derive the distribution of y_i conditionally on the past of y and z and on z_i:

$$y_i \,\big|\, y_{-\infty}^{i-1}, z_{-\infty}^i \sim N \left(\sum_{j=1}^r \Lambda_j y_{i-j} + \sum_{j=0}^r \Pi_j z_{i-j}, \Sigma \right).$$

It is also possible to express the distribution of y_i as a function of the past of z and the residuals by eliminating the lagged ys. In a stationary model, this operation comes to calculate the $MA(\infty)$ form of the model:

$$y_i = -B(L)^{-1} C(L) z_i + B(L)^{-1} u_i$$

which supposes the usual conditions on the roots of $|B(z)| = 0$.

In a nonstationary model, solving in the lagged ys can not be done all the way back to $-\infty$ and must stop at the initial conditions.

The identification of a dynamic simultaneous equations model can be examined as in the i.i.d. case by treating the lagged endogenous variables as if they were exogenous variables. Indeed, if w_i is the vector of $y_{i-1}, \ldots, y_{i-r}, z_i, \ldots, z_{i-r}$, we infer from (16.16) the moment equation:

$$E^\theta \left([B_\lambda(L) y_i + C_\lambda(L) z_i] \, w_i' \right) = 0$$

which is analogous to Formula (16.10). Thus, we can verify that two functions $\lambda_1(\theta)$ and $\lambda_2(\theta)$ are equivalent if

$$\forall j = 1, \ldots, r \qquad B_{0,\lambda_1(\theta)}^{-1} B_{j,\lambda_1(\theta)} = B_{0,\lambda_2(\theta)}^{-1} B_{j,\lambda_2(\theta)}$$

and

$$\forall j = 0, \ldots, r \qquad B_{0,\lambda_1(\theta)}^{-1} C_{j,\lambda_1(\theta)} = B_{0,\lambda_2(\theta)}^{-1} C_{j,\lambda_2(\theta)}.$$

We stress that this analysis can be realized even if the model does not include z_i, which then allows us to examine a structural VAR (i.e., VAR for which the matrix of instantaneous variables is not equal to I). These models are not necessarily identified and require some restrictions on the lag structure to guarantee identification.

Remarks.   Cointegration analysis has replaced in the mind of many econometricians the modeling by dynamic simultaneous equations model. Both approaches treat the nonstationarity of economic series in different ways. Although this is not strictly necessary, the simultaneous models are conditional models in which implicitly the nonstationarity is limited to the marginal distribution of exogenous variables. In addition, the model is usually assumed to be conditionally stationary. In contrast, the cointegration analysis concerns the joint distribution of all variables and searches for transformations that are marginally stationary. We could imagine an intermediate case where we would condition on nonstationary exogenous variables while maintaining the nonstationarity of the vector of the y_i in the model conditional on exogenous variables. Then, we could search for conditional cointegrating vectors. In general, these would not be marginal cointegrating vectors as the following example shows.   □

Example 16.4   *Suppose that z_i follows a random walk*

$$z_i - z_{i-1} \sim N\left(0, \sigma^2\right)$$

and that the process y_i conditional on the path of the $(z_i)_i$ satisfies

$$y_i \left| y_{-\infty}^{i-1}, z_{-\infty}^{+\infty} \sim N\left(\beta z_i, \gamma z_i^2\right) \right. \qquad \text{(with } \gamma > 0\text{)}.$$

Without making this concept very precise, we state that the distribution of y_i is conditionally stationary given the process z in the sense that

$$\forall n, s \quad y_1, \dots, y_n \, | z_1 = \zeta_1, \dots, z_n = \zeta_n$$

$$\sim y_{1+s}, \dots, y_{n+s} | z_{1+s} = \zeta_1, \dots, z_{n+s} = \zeta_n.$$

The transformation $y_i - \beta z_i$ defines a cointegrating vector conditionally on z, but its marginal distribution is not stationary since

$$Var\left(y_i - \beta z_i\right) = E\left(Var\left(y_i - \beta z_i | z_{-\infty}^{+\infty}\right)\right) = \gamma E\left(z_i^2\right) = \gamma\left(t\sigma^2\right). \quad □$$

16.4   Models from Game Theory

A good example of structural modeling and of the resulting identification problem is provided by the econometric formalization of individual behaviors in the setting of a game. We know the importance that game theory has taken in microeconomic theory, in industrial organization, in contract theory, and so on and it is natural that this modeling gives rise to econometric models to confront the theory with the observations.

We simplify our presentation by limiting ourselves to the following model. We observe L matches between N opposing players. Player j during match l receives the signal ξ_{jl} and transforms this signal to an action x_{jl} using a strategy function φ_θ, that depends on parameters θ; all agents have the same strategy function. This function, as a function of ξ_{jl} and of θ, is also known by the econometrician. We focus on a parametric specification for which $\theta \in \Theta \subset \mathbb{R}^k$ and the signals ξ_{il} are i.i.d. with density $f(.|\theta)$. We do not discuss of the choice of the function φ that follows from an equilibrium condition, for example the Nash equilibrium. This equilibrium condition makes φ depend on the signal but also on the distribution that generated the signal.

An example of this structure is given by a first price auction model with private values. An object is auctioned and each player attributes a value ξ_{jl} to this object. Then, he proposes a price x_{jl}. The object is assigned to the player who bids the highest price. A player will bid a price lower than his private value and the difference between bid and value depends on the number of players and the position of ξ_{jl} in the support of the distribution with density $f(.|\theta)$ (a player with a "high" value bids a price that is further away from his value than a player with a "low" value). This game admits a symmetric Nash equilibrium described by the function

$$x = \xi - \frac{\int_{\underline{\xi}}^{\xi} F(u|\theta)^{N-1} \, du}{F(\xi|\theta)^{N-1}} = \varphi_0(\xi)$$

where $\underline{\xi}$ is the lower bound of the domain of values and F is the distribution function associated with the density f. We see in particular that this function is complicated and nonlinear. This model could of course be generalized by considering very different objects for each auction, a varying number of participants, and so on.

The density of the signals is simple to calculate. If $i = (l, j)$ and $n = LN$, it is written as

$$\prod_{i=1}^{n} f(\xi_i|\theta).$$

Moreover, we assume that the parameters θ would be identified if the ξ_i were observed, which implies the invertibility of the matrix

$$E^\theta \left[\frac{\partial^2}{\partial\theta\partial\theta'} \ln f(\xi_i|\theta) \right].$$

The likelihood function differs from the above expression and is

$$\prod_{i=1}^{n} g(x_i|\theta) = \prod_{i=1}^{n} \frac{d\varphi_\theta^{-1}}{dx}(x_i) \, f\left(\varphi_\theta^{-1}(x_i)|\theta\right) \tag{16.17}$$

if φ_θ is invertible and smooth.

In this writing, we ignore the difficulties that would arise if the distribution of ξ had a compact support, which would imply that the distribution of x had a support dependent on the parameters.

The first order condition associated with the maximization of the likelihood is given by

$$E^\theta \left[\frac{\partial}{\partial \theta} \ln \left[g(x_i | \theta) \right] \right] = 0. \tag{16.18}$$

The local identification condition of the model becomes the invertibility of the matrix

$$E^\theta \left[\frac{\partial^2}{\partial \theta \partial \theta'} \ln g(x_i | \theta) \right]$$

in a neighborhood of the true value of the parameters. Notice that this invertibility is not at all implied by that of

$$E^\theta \left[\frac{\partial^2}{\partial \theta \partial \theta'} \ln f(\xi_i | \theta) \right],$$

as illustrated on the following example.

Example 16.5   *Let $\xi_i \in \mathbb{R}$, i.i.d. $N(\theta, 1)$, and $\varphi_\theta(\xi_i) = \xi_i - \theta$. It follows that x_i is i.i.d. $N(0, 1)$ and θ is not identified in the observable model. The function g does not depend on θ any longer and the expectation of the second derivative is zero and hence singular.* $\square$

Computing the maximum likelihood estimator of this model is delicate because of the presence of the Jacobian of the transformation and possibly support conditions. It is simpler to estimate using the method of moments in the following manner. Set

$$h(\xi_i, \theta) = \frac{\partial}{\partial \theta} \ln f(\xi_i | \theta).$$

The true value θ is the unique solution to

$$E^\theta(h(\xi_i, \lambda)) = 0 \qquad \left(\lambda \in \Theta \subset \mathbb{R}^k \right).$$

We can note that

$$E^\theta \left(h \left(\varphi_\lambda^{-1}(x_i), \lambda \right) \right) = 0,$$

which suggests a moment condition that is easy to compute. From an initial value of θ, denoted $\theta^{(0)}$, we calculate

$$\xi_i^{(0)} = \varphi_{\theta^{(0)}}^{-1}(x_i)$$

and we estimate θ by $\theta^{(1)}$ the solution to

$$\sum_{i=1}^{n} h\left(\xi_i^{(0)}, \lambda\right) = 0.$$

This value of $\theta^{(1)}$ allows us to revise the ξ_i as

$$\xi_i^{(1)} = \varphi_{\theta^{(1)}}^{-1}(x_i)$$

and we iterate this procedure until it converges, which yields an estimator that is the solution of

$$\sum_{i=1}^{n} h\left(\varphi_\lambda^{-1}(x_i), \lambda\right) = 0. \tag{16.19}$$

The problem is then to verify the identification condition, i.e., the uniqueness of the solution to (16.19). Using the implicit function theorem, the local identification condition can be written as

$$E^\theta \frac{\partial}{\partial \lambda'} \left(h\left(\varphi_\lambda^{-1}(x_i), \lambda\right)\right)|_{\lambda=\theta} \text{ invertible.}$$

Using the chain rule for the differentiation of composite functions, this matrix becomes

$$E^\theta \left(\frac{\partial h}{\partial \xi}\left(\varphi_\lambda^{-1}(x_i), \lambda\right) \frac{\partial \varphi_\lambda^{-1}(x_i)}{\partial \lambda'} + \frac{\partial h}{\partial \lambda'}\left(\varphi_\lambda^{-1}(x_i), \lambda\right)\right).$$

Noticing that the differentiation of the identity

$$\varphi_\lambda\left(\varphi_\lambda^{-1}(x_i)\right) = x_i$$

with respect to λ gives

$$\left[\frac{\partial \varphi_\lambda}{\partial \xi}\left(\varphi_\lambda^{-1}(x_i)\right) \frac{\partial \varphi_\lambda^{-1}}{\partial \lambda} \right] + \frac{\partial \varphi_\lambda}{\partial \lambda} = 0,$$

we infer the local identification condition: the parameters are identified if the matrix

$$E^\theta \left[\frac{\partial h}{\partial \lambda}(\xi_i, \lambda) \right]_{\lambda=\theta} - E^\theta \left[\frac{\partial h}{\partial \xi}(\xi, \lambda) \left(\frac{\partial \varphi_\lambda}{\partial \xi}(\xi, \lambda) \right)^{-1} \frac{\partial \varphi_\lambda}{\partial \lambda} \right]_{\lambda=0}$$

is invertible. We leave to the reader to verify this condition in a first price auction model with private values for usual parametric distributions. The interest of this expression is that it depends on the given initial elements of the problem (h and φ_θ) and does not require the derivation of the distribution of x_i or of φ_θ^{-1}.

This analysis can be extended to the case where φ is not completely known but depends on extra parameters and exogenous variables.

16.5   Overidentification

The term overidentification has appeared several times in previous chapters and here again, we return to this notion in the context of our discussion on structural modeling.

The term *overidentification* is ill-chosen. If one defines it precisely, one actually obtains the notion of hypothesis, in the sense of a restriction to a parameter space. This identity between overidentification and hypothesis explains why the term overidentification is associated with the idea of a test of overidentification.

Intuitively, the notion of overidentification appears in econometrics in the following manner. We consider a structural model from which we infer the reduced form, i.e., the class of distributions of the observable explained variables conditionally on the observable explanatory variables. In many cases, the reduced form can be nested within a different, more general, conditional statistical model and the family of sampling distributions of the reduced form is a subfamily of the class of sampling distributions in this other model. This other model is often simple and easy to estimate, whereas the reduced form has a much more complex structure. It is said then that the structural model overidentifies the reduced form by restricting its family of sampling distributions.

Example 16.6   *The estimation of the cost function provides a good example of overidentification without needing to specify completely the structural model. In such a model, the explained variables are the total cost C_i of firm i and the quantities of production factors, $Q_{1i}, \ldots, Q_{pi}$ if the model analyzes p inputs. The explanatory variables are the vector of production quantities Y_i and the vector of the prices of the production factors $P_{1i}, \ldots, P_{pi}$. A "natural" model consists of a multivariate regression model:*

$$\begin{pmatrix} C_i \\ Q_i \end{pmatrix} = g \begin{pmatrix} Y_i \\ P_i \end{pmatrix} + u_i = \begin{pmatrix} g_C(Y_i, P_i) \\ g_Q(Y_i, P_i) \end{pmatrix} + \begin{pmatrix} u_{Ci} \\ u_{Qi} \end{pmatrix}$$

where g is the conditional expectation function. We can also limit ourselves to a parametric specification by assuming that g is indexed by a vector β of unknown parameters. We could choose for instance a quadratic form, after transforming the variables in logarithm, which defines a functional form commonly called translog model.

Note that this model has a redundancy, in the sense that an accounting equation links the explained variables ($C_i = \sum_{j=1}^{p} P_{ji} Q_{ji}$), therefore the variance matrix of u_i is necessarily singular. In general, this problem is eliminated by suppressing the equation of one input quantity.

The structural modeling of the firm involves a production function that relates Y_i and Q_i and supposes that for given Y_i and P_i, the firm chooses the combination of inputs Q_i minimizing total cost. This assumption (combined *with an appropriate specification of the stochastic components of the model) implies that the function g_Q is equal to the vector of partial derivatives of g_C with respect to P_i (Shepard's lemma). This constraint gives rise to restrictions on β which can be interpreted as the overidentification hypothesis. Consider the simple case with two factors and without production level. For instance, the unrestricted model may be written as*

$$\begin{cases} C_i = \beta_1 + \beta_2 P_i + \beta_3 P_i^2 + u_{Ci} \\ Q_i = \beta_4 + \beta_5 P_i + \beta_6 P_i^2 + u_{Qi} \end{cases}$$

and the overidentification hypothesis is expressed by the restrictions $\beta_6 = 0$, $\beta_5 = 2\beta_3$, and $\beta_4 = \beta_2$. Hence, the economic hypotheses regarding the firm behavior are tested by jointly testing these three equalities. □

The previous example shows that the overidentifying restrictions are part of the reduced form, which itself is further constrained by the "maintained" assumptions, i.e., not reconsidered. In the model, the quadratic form of regressions constitutes a maintained assumption.

In Chapters 5 and 10, we saw some overidentified semiparametric cases of the simple i.i.d. model with unknown distribution. We provide an additional example of nonparametric overidentification.

Example 16.7   *For a set of households constituted only by couples, we observe for $i = 1, \ldots, n$, the vector $(y_i, Z_i^M, Z_i^F)_{i=1,\ldots,n}$ where y_i is the total consumption by the household of a given good (for example a food product such as sugar or meat) and Z_i^M and Z_i^F are the characteristics of the man and the woman (age, diploma, social demographic category, . . .). The consumed quantities by each partner are not observed but they are assumed to satisfy the following relations:*

$$\begin{cases} y_i^M = m\left(Z_i^M\right) + u_i^M \\ y_i^F = m\left(Z_i^F\right) + u_i^F \end{cases}$$

with

$$E\left(u_i^M | Z_i^M\right) = E\left(u_i^M | Z_i^M, Z_i^F\right)$$
$$= E\left(u_i^F | Z_i^F\right) = E\left(u_i^F | Z_i^M, Z_i^F\right) = 0.$$

The essential assumption is that the consumed quantities do not depend on the sex of the consumer except through the individual characteristics.

Thus, we obtain a model of the household

$$y_i = m\left(Z_i^M\right) + m\left(Z_i^F\right) + u_i$$

with

$$y_i = y_i^M + y_i^F \quad and \quad u_i = u_i^M + u_i^F,$$

which can also be expressed by the relation:

$$E\left(y_i | Z_i^M, Z_i^F\right) = m\left(Z_i^M\right) + m\left(Z_i^F\right).$$

The model defined by this equation is therefore a model of conditional expectation for which the structural assumptions restrict

$$E\left(y_i | Z_i^M, Z_i^F\right)$$

to take a specific form. Instead of being an arbitrary function of Z_i^H and Z_i^F, this conditional expectation is defined as the sum of the same function m evaluated at Z_i^H and Z_i^F.   □

As we remarked before, it is difficult to formally define overidentification. This property is defined with respect to a "simple" reference model $P^\theta, \theta \in \Theta$, which can be for example, a linear regression model or a general nonparametric model. This model is simple in the sense that there exists a "natural" estimator such as the least squares estimator, the empirical distribution or a kernel smoothing. On the other hand, the structural model leads to a reduced form characterized by the same family P^θ, but with a restriction $\theta \in \Theta^*$ where Θ^* is a subset of Θ. In general, the "natural" estimator does not belong to Θ^* and hence cannot be used to estimate the structural form. We need to rely on a more complex estimation procedure to satisfy the restrictions of the structural form.

However, the interest of an overidentified model is that it allows us to test the structural form by testing the hypothesis $\theta \in \Theta^*$, for example by comparing the "natural" estimator and the restricted estimator.

Remarks.   The overidentifying restriction plays an important role only if Θ^* has an empty interior in the sense of a topology for which the natural estimator converges to the true value. Suppose for instance that the reference model is an i.i.d. model with $x_i \in \mathbb{R}$ and that the overidentifying restriction is expressed by $\mu = E^\theta(x_i) > 0$. The natural estimator $\bar{x}_n$ of μ is not necessarily positive but if the true value μ_0 is positive, the almost sure convergence of $\bar{x}_n$ to μ_0 guarantees that any sequence $\bar{x}_n$ becomes positive for a finite sample size with probability 1; the size of the finite sample depends generally on the data sequence. In contrast, if the model is i.i.d. with

$$x_i = (x_{i1}, x_{i2}) \in \mathbb{R}^2$$

and

$$\mu = (\mu_1, \mu_2) = E^\theta(x_i),$$

an overidentifying restriction such that $\mu_1 = \mu_2$ is never satisfied by $\bar{x}_{1n}$ and $\bar{x}_{2n}$ for all n even if $\bar{x}_{1n}$ and $\bar{x}_{2n}$ converge to equal values.   □

16.5.1 Overidentification in Simultaneous Equations Models

Consider a static simultaneous equations model for which the reduced form is the multivariate regression equation (16.5). The model is overidentified with respect to the regression model if the set of matrices $\Pi_\lambda = -B_\lambda^{-1} C_\lambda$ is a strict subset of the set of $p \times q$ matrices. The following example illustrates this situation.

Example 16.8 *Return to Example 16.2. Let Π_0 be an arbitrary $p \times q$ matrix. The question of overidentification is that of the existence of α such that*

$$
\begin{pmatrix}
-\alpha'\Pi_{21} - \beta' & -\alpha'\Pi_{22} \\
\Pi_{21} & \Pi_{22} \\
\Pi_{31} & \Pi_{32}
\end{pmatrix}
= \Pi^0.
$$

This equality holds if there exists α such that

$$
-\alpha'\Pi_{22}^0 = \Pi_{12}^0,
$$

which is always satisfied only if Π_{22}^0 is invertible. If $q_2 > p_2$, there are more equations than unknowns and an α satisfying this relation does not always exist. Thus in this case, the model is in general overidentified. □

Example 16.9 *Consider the system*

$$
\begin{cases}
y_{i1} + \lambda_1 y_{i2} + \lambda_2 z_{i1} + \lambda_3 z_{i2} + \lambda_4 = u_{i1} \\
y_{i1} + \lambda_5 y_{i2} + \lambda_6 z_{i1} + \lambda_7 = u_{i2}.
\end{cases}
$$

The matrix Π_λ of the reduced form is written as

$$
\Pi_\lambda = -\frac{1}{\lambda_5 - \lambda_1}
\begin{pmatrix}
\lambda_2\lambda_5 - \lambda_6 & \lambda_3\lambda_5 & \lambda_4\lambda_5 - \lambda_7 \\
-\lambda_1\lambda_2 + \lambda_6 & -\lambda_1\lambda_3 & -\lambda_1\lambda_4 + \lambda_7
\end{pmatrix}
$$

and this matrix is restricted by a proportionality relation. □

Example 16.10 *The assumption of the existence of cointegration introduces overidentifying restrictions that appear in the error correction model. Let x_i be a $I(1)$ process that satisfies a VAR(p) in levels $A(L)x_i = \varepsilon_i$. We verified in Chapter 13 that this assumption implies the relation*

$$
A^*(L)\Delta x_i + A(1)x_{i-1} = \varepsilon_i
$$

where $A^*(L)$ is a matrix of degree $p - 1$. This model is a multivariate dynamic linear regression model. Assuming the existence of cointegration leads to

$$
A(1) = DC'
$$

and hence to an overidentifying restriction. □

16.5.2   Overidentification and Moment Conditions

The problem of overidentification has already been mentioned in Chapter 3 and we recall it here in a slightly special case.

Let $x_1, \ldots, x_n$ be an i.i.d. sample. θ is here the probability distribution Q of each observation. We consider the moment condition

$$E^Q \left(\psi \left(x_i, \lambda \right) \right) = 0. \tag{16.20}$$

The dimension r of ψ is strictly greater than k, the dimension of λ; the model is in general overidentified in the sense that the set of Q such that a solution to (16.20) exists is a strict subset of the set of probability distributions of x_i. This overidentification prevents us from replacing Q with its natural estimator, namely the empirical distribution

$$\widehat{Q}_n = \frac{1}{n} \sum_{i=1}^{n} \delta_{x_i}$$

because

$$E^{\widehat{Q}_n} \left(\psi \left(x_i, \lambda \right) \right) = \frac{1}{n} \sum_{i=1}^{n} \left(\psi \left(x_i, \lambda \right) \right) = 0$$

has in general no solution.

Then, there are three possible solutions to handle this problem.

- The usual statistical approach would eliminate some moment conditions and keep only the necessary number to estimate λ. This is not the adopted approach in structural econometrics because the economic theory of the phenomenon under study is useful only beyond this minimal number of conditions. Moreover, we wish to test these economic hypotheses, which necessitate treating an overidentified model.
- The approach of the generalized method of moments consists of eliminating the overidentification by modifying the definition of the parameter λ. As we saw in Chapter 3, this parameter is defined as the value of λ that minimizes

$$E^Q \left(\psi \left(x_i, \lambda \right) \right)' H E^Q \left(\psi \left(x_i, \lambda \right) \right).$$

This new function $\lambda(Q)$ coincides with the solution to (16.20) if Q belongs to the family of probability distributions such that (16.20) admits a solution. But $\lambda(Q)$ is defined for a much larger family that comprises in particular the empirical distribution. Hansen's test for overidentifying restrictions, introduced in the Example 4.4 in Chapter 4, provides a test of overidentification.
- A third approach that is closer to that of the usual parametric econometrics consists in keeping the overidentifying restriction and to estimate Q by an estimator Q_n^* satisfying the existence of a solution to the equation

$$E^{Q_n^*} \left(\psi \left(x_i, \lambda \right) \right) = 0.$$

The solution to this problem can be found by estimating Q by a weighted sum $\sum_{i=1}^{n} \alpha_i \delta_{x_i}$ with weights that are different from $\frac{1}{n}$. We do not develop this approach here (see for instance Kitamura and Stutzer (1997)).

16.5.3 Overidentification and Nonparametric Models

In a general manner, a nonparametric structural model is characterized by an i.i.d. sample whose observations are generated by a distribution Q and whose parameter of interest is a function associated with Q. Overidentification follows from the fact that this function does not exist for some distributions Q. Consider the example of an additive regression model. Using the notation of Chapter 10 (section 10.4.2), this model is characterized by

$$E^Q (y|\widetilde{z}_1 = z_1, \widetilde{z}_2 = z_2) = \psi_1 (z_1) + \psi_2 (z_2). \tag{16.21}$$

We wish to estimate the pair of functions ψ_1 and ψ_2. The overidentifying restriction comes from the fact that if Q is arbitrary, then the expectation of y given $\widetilde{z}_1$ and $\widetilde{z}_2$ does not take an additive form. In Chapter 10, we adopted an approach of overidentification that is of the same type as that adopted by GMM, i.e., we extend the definition of ψ_1 and ψ_2 for a much larger class of distributions Q. We extend the definition of ψ_1 and ψ_2 by considering the solution to

$$\min_{\psi_1, \psi_2} E^Q (y - \psi_1 (z_1) - \psi_2 (z_2))^2 .$$

This minimization yields a conditional expectation if the overidentifying restriction is satisfied, but allows us to define ψ_1 and ψ_2 even outside this restriction (see Subsection 10.4.2).

The same approach can be adopted regarding index models for which the overidentifying restriction

$$E^Q (y |z) = \psi \left(\lambda' z\right)$$

is satisfied only for a subfamily of distributions. However, we extend the definition of ψ and of λ to a set of distributions (with very weak restrictions on the existence of moments) by defining ψ and λ as the arguments of the minimization of $E^Q (y - \psi (\lambda' z))^2$.

The question raised by the elimination of the overidentifying restriction by extending the definition of parameters is that of the nonuniqueness of such extension and hence the choice of the optimal extension. This question, which has been solved in the case of GMM for minimizations of quadratic forms, remains largely open in nonparametric problems.

Notes

The questions of identification in simultaneous equations models were addressed in the founding work by the Cowles Commission. Preliminary contributions quoted by Malinvaud (1980) are those of Working (1925) and Working (1927) that solve a paradox raised by Moore (1914). The essential findings on simultaneous equations are due to Koopmans (1949) and were later extended by Fisher (1959, 1961a, and 1961b). The study of identification and overidentification in the method of moments is presented in the seminal paper by Hansen (1982). Game theoretic models are studied in the articles by Paarsch (1992), Laffont and Vuong (1993), Laffont, Ossard, and Vuong (1995), Florens, Protopopescu, and Richard (2002), and Sbai (2003). Identification and overidentification in nonparametric econometrics are examined in various papers, of which Florens (2003) provides a synthesis.

17. Simultaneity

17.1 Introduction

The notion of simultaneity is essential in econometrics and although familiar to every econometrician it is not easy to give it a simple mathematical definition. In a very stylized way, simultaneity between two variables, x_1 and x_2, exists if we cannot recursively decompose the features represented by them into the features represented by x_1 and the features represented by x_2 given x_1. This might seem surprising since we can always decompose the joint distribution of x_1 and x_2 into its marginal and its conditional distribution. To say there exists simultaneity or that x_1 is not exogenous means the conditional model does not allow us to identify and thus to estimate the parameters of interest. The notion of simultaneity thus comes back to the question of parameterization, i.e., of structural modeling of the features we are interested in. The notion of exogeneity defined by a cut as it was presented in Chapter 1 contains another element, namely that there is no loss of information in considering only the conditional model. In summary, a cut means that the conditional model identifies and efficiently estimates the parameters of interest. We note that the essential element in this concept is identification rather than efficiency. The most classical example of simultaneity is the study of a market in equilibrium. The structural model specifies a supply function

$$Q_s = \varphi_s(P, z_s) + u_s$$

where Q_s is the quantity supplied, P is the price, z_s is a vector of explanatory variables, φ_s is the supply function, and u_s is a residual. In the same way, the demand function is

$$Q_d = \varphi_d(P, z_d) + u_d.$$

The equilibrium condition is $Q_s = Q_d (= Q)$, which reduces the model to two explained variables, quantity and price. The functions φ_s and φ_d or their parameters are the objects of interest in the system. We already examined the identification of such a system that requires, for example in the linear case, that the explanatory variables in the two equations satisfy some conditions.

The problem of simultaneity between P and Q is of a different nature. We can obviously decompose the joint probability distribution of P and Q into the marginal distribution of P and the distribution of Q given P, but this conditional distribution is neither the distribution of the supply nor the one of the demand, and although this decomposition is well defined from a probabilistic view point and can be estimated, it does not have any economic content.

This inadequacy between conditional distribution and economic meaning characterizes the situation when simultaneity is present.

17.2   Simultaneity and Simultaneous Equations

We will concentrate in our discussion to the following example, which is in fact a special case of the model that we examined in the previous chapter (Equation (16.12)). Let the model be given by

$$\begin{cases} y_{i1} + \alpha y_{i2} + \beta' z_{i1} = u_{i1} \\ \qquad\quad y_{i2} + \gamma' z_i = u_{i2}. \end{cases} \tag{17.1}$$

The two explained variables are

$$(y_{i1}, y_{i2}) \in \mathbb{R}^2$$

and the explanatory variables are

$$z_i = (z_{i1}, z_{i2}) \in \mathbb{R}^{q_1+q_2} = \mathbb{R}^q.$$

This example can be examined without distributional assumptions under assumptions A1, A2, and A4 of Section 16.3.2 or with the assumption of normality A3. The rank identification condition given in Example 16.2 is in the current case not very restrictive: the coefficient of one of the variables in the vector z_{i2} in the second equation has to be non zero, or equivalently, the second equation has to contain one variable that is not present in the first equation.

The concept of simultaneity or of endogeneity can be explained intuitively for this example by the following remark: a quick analysis of these equations might lead us to consider them as one equation (the second) that explains y_{i2} by z_i and one equation (the first) that explains y_{i1} by y_{i2} and z_{i1}. One would treat these two equations separately and estimate them by least squares method. However, because of the dependence between u_{i1} and u_{i2}, this approach leads to a transformation of the first equation, which is reflected in particular in the inconsistency of the least squares estimators of α and β. The variable y_{i2} is *endogenous* in the first equation, and neglecting this property introduces a *simultaneity bias*. We will clarify this intuition by examining this problem under different but essentially equivalent angles.

First, it is easy to show that the least squares estimators are not consistent. We can verify this directly by simplifying the problem to the case when $\beta = 0$ and when z_{i2}, now denoted z_i, is scalar. The model becomes

$$\begin{cases} y_{i1} + \alpha y_{i2} = u_{i1} \\ y_{i2} + \gamma' z_i = u_{i2}. \end{cases} \tag{17.2}$$

In this case the estimator of α satisfies

$$\hat{\alpha}_n = -\frac{\frac{1}{n}\sum_{i=1}^{n} y_{i1}y_{i2}}{\frac{1}{n}\sum_{i=1}^{n} y_{i2}^2}. \tag{17.3}$$

The denominator is equal to

$$\frac{1}{n}\sum_{i=1}^{n}(-\gamma' z_i + u_{i2})^2 = \gamma^2 \frac{1}{n}\sum_{i=1}^{n} z_i^2 - \frac{2\gamma}{n}\sum_{i=1}^{n} z_i u_{i2} + \frac{1}{n}\sum_{i=1}^{n} u_{i2}^2$$

which converges almost surely to

$$\gamma^2 E^\theta\left(z_i^2\right) + \sigma_{22},$$

where $\sigma_{22} = Var^\theta(u_{i2})$. The covariance between z_i and u_{i2} is indeed zero because of A1 (Equation (16.4)). The numerator is equal to

$$\frac{1}{n}\sum_{i=1}^{n}(-\gamma z_i + u_{i2})(\alpha\gamma z_i - \alpha u_{i2} + u_{i1})$$

which converges almost surely to

$$-\alpha\gamma^2 E^\theta\left(z_i^2\right) - \alpha\sigma_{22} + \sigma_{12}$$

and thus

$$\hat{\alpha}_n \to \alpha - \frac{\sigma_{12}}{\gamma^2 E^\theta\left(z_i^2\right) + \sigma_{22}} \tag{17.4}$$

with $\sigma_{12} = Cov^\theta(u_{i1}, u_{i2})$. Thus, the estimator converges to a value different from α except in the case when the structural residuals are independent.

This result generalizes to a system of simultaneous equations. If we consider a system of equations of the type (16.8), then the least squares estimators do not converge in general to the corresponding values in the matrices B_λ and C_λ.

Second, a different perspective of the endogeneity bias is obtained when considering the moment equations. In the preceding special case, the estimation of the system by least squares leads us back to the empirical moment equations

$$
\begin{cases}
\dfrac{1}{n} \displaystyle\sum_{i=1}^{n} (y_{i1} + a y_{i2}) y_{i2} = 0 \\[2mm]
\dfrac{1}{n} \displaystyle\sum_{i=1}^{n} (y_{i1} + c y_{i2}) z_i = 0
\end{cases}
\tag{17.5}
$$

for which the solution converges to the solution of the asymptotic problem

$$
\begin{cases}
E^\theta (u_{i1} y_{i2}) = E^\theta [(y_{i1} + a y_{i2}) y_{i2}] = 0 \\
E^\theta (u_{i2} z_i) = E^\theta [(y_{i1} + c z_i) z_i] = 0.
\end{cases}
\tag{17.6}
$$

System (17.6) has a solution

$$
a = \alpha - \frac{\sigma_{12}}{\gamma^2 E^\theta (z_i) + \sigma_{22}} \quad \text{and} \quad c = \gamma
$$

which is different from the moment conditions given in A1 that defines the simultaneous equations model, i.e.,

$$
E^\theta (u_i | z_i) = 0.
\tag{17.7}
$$

Multiplying this by z_i and taking expectations with respect to z_i, it follows that

$$
E^\theta (u_i z_i) = 0
\tag{17.8}
$$

or equivalently

$$
\begin{cases}
E^\theta [(y_{i1} + \alpha y_{i2}) z_i] = 0 \\
E^\theta [(y_{i2} + \gamma z_i) z_i] = 0.
\end{cases}
\tag{17.9}
$$

We need to emphasize that the moment conditions that specify the orthogonality of the structural residuals and the exogenous variables do not define the same parameters as the moment equations that define the regression equations in the least square estimation (of y_{i2} on z_i and of y_{i1} on y_{i2}).

What Model (17.7) tells us is that the relation between y_{i1} and y_{i2} which interests the econometrician is not the regression line but a different line characterized by (17.9).

Note that the system (17.9) determines a consistent estimator of α. Replacing the theoretical expectation by the sample means, we obtain the estimator

$$
\hat{\alpha}_n = - \frac{\sum y_{i1} z_i}{\sum y_{i2} z_i}
$$

for which we can easily verify that it converges almost surely to α. This estimator is a special case of *instrumental variables estimators* which we study more extensively later in this chapter.

A third perspective on the endogeneity bias can be obtained by means of the concept of exogeneity as introduced in Chapter 2. To simplify the presentation, we assume that assumption A3 holds, that means we consider a parametric model under normality.

Model (17.2) admits a reduced form

$$\begin{cases} y_{i1} = \alpha\gamma z_i + u_{i1} \quad \alpha u_{i2} \\ y_{i2} = -\gamma z_i + u_{i2} \end{cases} \tag{17.10}$$

from which we derive the sampling probabilities of an observation

$$\begin{pmatrix} y_{i1} \\ y_{i2} \end{pmatrix} \Big|_{z_i} \sim N\left(\begin{pmatrix} \alpha\gamma z_i \\ -\gamma z_i \end{pmatrix}, \begin{pmatrix} \sigma_{11} - 2\alpha\sigma_{12} + \alpha^2\sigma_{22} & \sigma_{12} - \alpha\sigma_{22} \\ \sigma_{12} - \alpha\sigma_{22} & \sigma_{22} \end{pmatrix} \right).$$

The y_i are independent conditionally on the z_i. This distribution can be decomposed into a marginal distribution of y_{i2} and the conditional distribution of y_{i1} given y_{i2}, both distributions remain conditional on z_i:

$$y_{i2}|z_i \sim N\left(-\gamma z_i, \sigma_{22}\right)$$

$$y_{i1}|y_{i2}, z_i \sim N\left(\rho y_{i2} + \gamma\left(\alpha + \rho\right) z_i, \tau^2\right)$$

with

$$\rho = \frac{\sigma_{12} - \alpha\sigma_{22}}{\sigma_{22}} \quad \text{and} \quad \tau^2 = \sigma_{11} - \frac{\sigma_{12}^2}{\sigma_{22}}.$$

Considering the parameter vector $(\alpha, \gamma, \sigma_{11}, \sigma_{12}, \sigma_{22})$, we can verify that the functions of these parameters that enter the marginal and the conditional model are *variation free*. The problem appears in the fact that the parameter of interest α is not identified by the conditional model (which only identifies ρ, $\gamma(\alpha + \rho)$ and τ^2 and from which we cannot recover α). This shows that for the parameterization of interest, y_{i2} is not an exogenous variable. Evidently, the exogeneity condition holds if $\sigma_{12} = 0$ since then $-\alpha = \rho$ and the conditional model becomes

$$y_{i1}|y_{i2}, z_i \sim N\left(-\alpha y_{i2}, \tau^2\right) \tag{17.11}$$

which shows in particular that $-\alpha$ is the coefficient of the regression line.

17.3 Endogeneity, Exogeneity, and Dynamic Models

Exogeneity presents itself in a different way in a nonstationary process with one or more cointegrating relationships. This cointegration introduces overidentifying restrictions which modify the exogeneity conditions. We make this point using the following example.

Consider a vector x_i that is partitioned into y_i, z_i and w_i, which, for simplicity, are assumed to be scalars. Suppose that x_i is specified as a $VAR(1)$ in levels:

$$\begin{pmatrix} y_i \\ z_i \\ w_i \end{pmatrix} = \begin{pmatrix} a_1 & a_2 & a_3 \\ b_1 & b_2 & b_3 \\ c_1 & c_2 & c_3 \end{pmatrix} \begin{pmatrix} y_{i-1} \\ z_{i-1} \\ w_{i-1} \end{pmatrix} + \begin{pmatrix} \varepsilon_{1i} \\ \varepsilon_{2i} \\ \varepsilon_{3i} \end{pmatrix}. \tag{17.12}$$

Suppose ε_i is an innovation of the process and that $\varepsilon_i \sim N(0, \Sigma)$ with

$$\Sigma = \begin{pmatrix} \sigma_{yy} & \sigma_{yz} & \sigma_{yw} \\ \sigma_{yz} & \sigma_{zz} & \sigma_{zw} \\ \sigma_{yw} & \sigma_{zw} & \sigma_{ww} \end{pmatrix}. \tag{17.13}$$

The vector x_i is nonstationary, integrated of order 1 and admits by assumption a cointegrating relation

$$y_i + \beta z_i + \gamma w_i = u_i \tag{17.14}$$

where u_i is a stationary process. Thus we can equivalently express this process as

$$\begin{pmatrix} \Delta y_i \\ \Delta z_i \\ \Delta w_i \end{pmatrix} = \begin{pmatrix} \alpha_1 \\ \alpha_2 \\ \alpha_3 \end{pmatrix} \begin{pmatrix} 1 & \beta & \gamma \end{pmatrix} \begin{pmatrix} y_{i-1} \\ z_{i-1} \\ w_{i-1} \end{pmatrix} + \begin{pmatrix} \varepsilon_{1i} \\ \varepsilon_{2i} \\ \varepsilon_{3i} \end{pmatrix}. \tag{17.15}$$

We study the weak exogeneity of Δw_i, which essentially means to study the decomposition of the above process into the marginal distribution of Δw_i conditional on the past and the conditional distribution of Δy_i and Δz_i conditional on Δw_i and on the past. Since the process (17.12) is Markov of order 1, the past enters here only through x_{i-1}.

We have

$$\Delta w_i \,|\, x_{i-1} \sim N\left(\alpha_3\left(y_{i-1} + \beta z_{i-1} + \gamma w_{i-1}\right), \sigma_{ww}\right) \tag{17.16}$$

and

$$\begin{pmatrix} \Delta y_i \\ \Delta z_i \end{pmatrix}\bigg|\, \Delta w_i, x_{i-1} \sim N\left(\begin{pmatrix} \pi_0 \Delta w_i + \pi_1 y_{i-1} + \pi_2 z_{i-1} + \pi_3 w_{i-1} \\ \lambda_0 \Delta w_i + \lambda_1 y_{i-1} + \lambda_2 z_{i-1} + \lambda_3 w_{i-1} \end{pmatrix}, \Omega\right)$$

$$\tag{17.17}$$

with

$$\pi_0 = \sigma_{yw}/\sigma_{ww} \qquad\qquad \lambda_0 = \sigma_{zw}/\sigma_{ww}$$

$$\pi_1 = \alpha_1 - \alpha_3\pi_0 \qquad\qquad \lambda_1 = \alpha_2 - \alpha_3\lambda_0$$

$$\pi_2 = \alpha_1\beta - \alpha_3\beta\pi_0 \qquad\qquad \lambda_2 = \alpha_2\beta - \alpha_3\beta\lambda_0$$

$$\pi_3 = \alpha_1\gamma - \alpha_3\gamma\pi_0 \qquad\qquad \lambda_3 = \alpha_2\gamma - \alpha_3\gamma\lambda_0$$

and Ω is the usual conditional variance-covariance matrix.

Recall that the concept of exogeneity rests on two considerations: can we identify (and estimate) the parameters of interest in the conditional model? If we can, do we lose information if we consider only the marginal model? Also recall that the answer to the last question is negative if the parameters of the conditional and of the marginal models are variation free.

It is clear in this example that the parameters of (17.16) and of (17.17) are not variation free, however, in contrast to the static model of the preceding section, the conditional model (17.17) identifies the parameters of the cointegrating relationship. Indeed, we have

$$\beta = \frac{\pi_2}{\pi_1} = \frac{\lambda_2}{\lambda_1} \quad \text{and} \quad \gamma = \frac{\pi_3}{\pi_1} = \frac{\lambda_3}{\lambda_1},$$

which moreover introduce overidentifying restrictions on the conditional model. Therefore, from the point of view of inference about the cointegrating vector, conditioning on Δw_i does not prevent the estimation. However, the parameters α_1, α_2, and α_3 are not identified by the conditional model and the relationship between the parameters of (17.16) and (17.17) implies that in general the estimation of β and γ is less efficient if only (17.17) is used than if the full system is used. We emphasize that the identification of β and γ using the conditional model (which can be generalized by conditioning on Δw_i and on Δz_i) does not come from the nonstationarity but from the restrictions that are imposed by equation (17.15).

The restriction $\alpha_3 = 0$ eliminates the parameters from the marginal model and implies the identification of α_1 and α_2 in the conditional model. Strictly speaking, it assures the weak exogeneity of Δw_i. In our case, this condition is the same as a non-causality condition as far as it eliminates the past of the process of y and z from the process w.

The question of exogeneity can here be posed also in other terms. The general principle in the analysis in terms of cointegration is in considering all variables as endogenous and thereby eliminating all assumptions of exogeneity. This principle is sometimes difficult to apply either because of the dimensionality of the vector of variables or because we are interested for example in a "small" sector of the economy for which the macroeconomic variables are "exogenous."

The general principle is then the following: we regress the relevant variables on the exogenous variables and analyze cointegration for the residuals (see Johansen (1995)). The question arises under which assumptions this approach is legitimate. Under the condition

$$\gamma = -\frac{\sigma_{yw}}{\sigma_{ww}} - \beta\frac{\sigma_{zw}}{\sigma_{ww}}, \tag{17.18}$$

the model conditional on w can be rewritten in the following way

$$\begin{pmatrix} \Delta y_i - \frac{\sigma_{yw}}{\sigma_{ww}}\Delta w_i \\ \Delta z_i - \frac{\sigma_{zw}}{\sigma_{ww}}\Delta w_i \end{pmatrix} = \begin{pmatrix} \alpha_1 - \alpha_3\frac{\sigma_{yw}}{\sigma_{ww}} \\ \alpha_2 - \alpha_3\frac{\sigma_{zw}}{\sigma_{ww}} \end{pmatrix} \left[\left(y_{i-1} - \frac{\sigma_{yw}}{\sigma_{ww}}w_{i-1} \right) \right.$$

$$\left. + \beta\left(z_{i-1} - \frac{\sigma_{zw}}{\sigma_{ww}}w_{i-1} \right) \right] + \begin{pmatrix} \eta_{1i} \\ \eta_{2i} \end{pmatrix}$$

where

$$\begin{pmatrix} \eta_{1i} \\ \eta_{2i} \end{pmatrix} \sim N(0, \Omega).$$

Thus we see that the residuals

$$y_i - \frac{\sigma_{yw}}{\sigma_{ww}}w_i \quad \text{and} \quad z_i - \frac{\sigma_{zw}}{\sigma_{ww}}w_i$$

form a cointegrating relation that identifies the same coefficients β and γ as in the preceding model

Condition (17.18) is rewritten as

$$\sigma_{yw} + \beta\sigma_{zw} + \gamma\sigma_{ww} = 0$$

and is interpreted as orthogonality between u_i (the structural residual of the cointegration equation) and w_i. This condition is identical to the classical condition of exogeneity. If, moreover, $\alpha_3 = 0$, then the conditional model contains all information about β and γ and identifies α_1 and α_2.

17.4   Simultaneity and Selection Bias

Another example is provided by the problem of selection bias or, equivalently, the endogenous selection of observations. We limit our presentation to a simplistic example in order to focus the discussion on the essential aspects.

Consider a sample of individuals indexed by $i = 1, \dots, n$. Each individual has a characteristic x_i, and we assume that the x_i are independently drawn from the same distribution and has expectation μ. This expectation is the parameter of interest to the statistician. However, not all individuals are observed, which is expressed by the variable d_i with value equal to 1 if individual i is observed and 0 otherwise. This Bernoulli random variable is not necessarily independent of the value of x_i, which implies in particular that the probability of the event $d_i = 1$ (i is observed) conditionally on x_i effectively depends on x_i. For example in the case of an income survey, we can assume that the probability of obtaining a response from an individual depends on his income level. As in the previous example, we illustrate the role that the dependence between d_i and x_i plays by considering the consistency of the parameters, the different moment equations and the absence of exogeneity of d_i in a parametric specification.

Thus, we assume that the (d_i, x_i) are i.i.d. and that

$$\Pr(d_i = 1 | x_i) = p(x_i)$$

and $E(x_i) = \mu$.

1. Again, it is trivial but important to note that the natural estimator of μ which neglects the selection mechanism is not consistent. This estimator is equal to the sample mean of the x_i for the individuals that are observed and can be written as

$$\hat{\mu}_n = \frac{\sum\limits_{i=1}^{n} d_i x_i}{\sum\limits_{i=1}^{n} d_i}. \tag{17.19}$$

Dividing both the numerator and the denominator by n and using the strong law of large numbers, we obtain

$$\hat{\mu}_n \to \frac{E^\theta(d_i x_i)}{E^\theta(d_i)} = \frac{E^\theta\left(x_i E^\theta(d_i | x_i)\right)}{E^\theta\left(E^\theta(d_i | x_i)\right)} = \frac{E^\theta(p(x_i) x_i)}{E^\theta(p(x_i))}. \tag{17.20}$$

This limit is in general different from μ. It is however equal to μ if $p(x_i)$ is constant, which means that the distribution of d_i (fully characterized by $p(x_i)$) conditional on x_i does not depend on x_i and that therefore d_i and x_i are independent.

2. The underlying moment conditions of the estimator (17.19) can be written as

$$E^\theta(x_i | d_i = 1) = \nu \tag{17.21}$$

and defines the parameter ν. Indeed, the basic definition of conditional probabilities implies

$$E^\theta(x_i | d_i = 1) = \frac{E^\theta(x_i d_i)}{E^\theta(d_i)}$$

which yields the estimator $\hat{\mu}_n$ after replacing the theoretical expectations by their sample counterparts. Thus, $\hat{\mu}_n$ is an estimator of ν and not of μ.

Not taking the selection mechanism into account essentially means that we are conditioning on $d_i = 1$ (or that we are using the moment condition $E^\theta (x_i d_i - v d_i) = 0$) which does not define the same parameter as the original moment condition $E^\theta (x_i - \mu) = 0$.

3. To show the absence of exogeneity of d_i in the sense of the definition in Chapter 1, we use a particular case of the preceding approach by introducing a parametric specification.

Consider the i.i.d. vector (x_i, ξ_i) with distribution

$$\begin{pmatrix} x_i \\ \xi_i \end{pmatrix} \sim N \left(\begin{pmatrix} \mu \\ \alpha \end{pmatrix}, \begin{pmatrix} \sigma_{xx} & \sigma_{x\xi} \\ \sigma_{x\xi} & \sigma_{\xi\xi} \end{pmatrix} \right) \tag{17.22}$$

and set $d_i = I(\xi_i \geq 0)$. This model assigns to each i two variables x_i and ξ_i which in general are not independent. The variable ξ_i is not observable, or only its sign is observable; additionally, x_i is only observed if ξ_i is positive.

As an example, we can define ξ_i to be the willingness to pay for a phone connection (net of the connection cost). If ξ_i is positive then the individual will be connected, and not otherwise. The variable x_i is then the spending on telephone communications. Thus we only observe whether an individual is connected, and if yes, the phone expenses. The parameter of interest is then the expectation of the expenses μ, evaluated with respect to the marginal distribution, i.e., not conditional on being connected. This measures a "latent" average expense of an individual whether she is connected or not. This choice of the parameter of interest might seem strange since it appears more natural to estimate the mean expense only of those individuals who are connected, i.e., v in our Equation (17.21). The two parameters μ and v describe different aspects of the data generating process, for each we can justify our interest in it. We can verify in particular that if the model of the demand is derived from utility maximization by the consumer, then it is easier to map the parameter μ to the parameters of the utility function than it is for the parameter v.

From Model (17.22), we can derive the following marginal and conditional probabilities

$$d_i \sim \text{Bernoulli} \left(\Phi \left(\frac{\alpha}{\sigma_{\xi\xi}} \right) \right),$$

and

$$x_i | d_i = 1 \sim x_i | \xi_i \geq 0,$$

which is i.i.d. with density g,

$$g(u|\theta) = \frac{1}{\Phi\left(\dfrac{\alpha}{\sigma_{\xi\xi}}\right)} \int_{\xi \geq 0} (2\pi)^{-1} |\Sigma|^{-1/2}$$

$$\times \exp\left[-\left(\begin{matrix} u - \mu \\ \xi - \alpha \end{matrix}\right)' \Sigma^{-1} \left(\begin{matrix} u - \mu \\ \xi - \alpha \end{matrix}\right)\right] d\xi$$

where Φ denotes the standard normal distribution function.

The marginal model is parameterized by $\frac{\alpha}{\sigma_{\xi\xi}}$. To show that exogeneity is not satisfied for the parameter μ, we have to show that μ is not identified by the conditional model. Here, we do not provide a proof, but instead only verify that μ is not identified by the first two moments of the conditional distribution. Indeed, we have

$$E[x_i|\xi_i \geq 0] = \mu + \frac{\sigma_{x\xi}}{\sigma_{\xi\xi}} \frac{\varphi\left(\dfrac{\alpha}{\sigma_{\xi\xi}}\right)}{\Phi\left(\dfrac{\alpha}{\sigma_{\xi\xi}}\right)} \quad \text{and} \quad V(x_i|\xi_i \geq 0) = \sigma$$

where φ is the density of a standard normal distribution. From the marginal model we can learn the value of $\frac{\alpha}{\sigma_{\xi\xi}}$, but the expectation and the variance of x_i conditional on $\xi_i \geq 0$ does not enable us to recover μ even if we know $\frac{\alpha}{\sigma_{\xi\xi}}$.

17.5 Instrumental Variables Estimation

17.5.1 Introduction

We extensively studied conditional expectation and statistical regression models in the Part II of this book. The conditional expectation is a function associated with the probability distribution of a vector: if $\tilde{x} = (\tilde{y}, \tilde{z}) \in \mathbb{R} \times \mathbb{R}^q$ is a random vector, then the conditional expectation of $\tilde{y}$ given $\tilde{z}$ is the function $g(\tilde{z})$ introduced in Definition 7.1. This function satisfies the equation

$$E^\theta((\tilde{y} - g(\tilde{z}))|\tilde{z}) = 0. \tag{17.23}$$

The concept of instrumental variable can be introduced in a very general way as follows. We suppose that the random vector $\tilde{x}$ can be partitioned into $(\tilde{y}, \tilde{z}, \tilde{w}) \in \mathbb{R} \times \mathbb{R}^k \times \mathbb{R}^r$, and we are interested in the function $g_{\tilde{w}}(\tilde{z})$ of $\tilde{z}$, called instrumental variables regression of $\tilde{y}$ on $\tilde{z}$ given $\tilde{w}$, which satisfies

$$E^\theta((\tilde{y} - g_{\tilde{w}}(\tilde{z}))|\tilde{w}) = 0. \tag{17.24}$$

Then $\widetilde{w}$ is called *instrumental variable*. We see that this concept extends (17.23), since $g_{\widetilde{w}}(\widetilde{z}) = g(\widetilde{z})$ if $\widetilde{w} = \widetilde{z}$.

Remarks.   The notion of instrument is used here in its original historical meaning and not as a means to transform conditional moment equations into marginals (function h in Section 3.3).

Equation (17.24) is an integral equation of the function $g_{\widetilde{w}}$ and we do not discuss here the existence and uniqueness of a solution to it. It is necessary to study this for the non-parametric estimation of $g_{\widetilde{w}}(\widetilde{z})$, but we first confine ourselves to the parametric case. Suppose we search for $g_{\widetilde{w}}$ in the family of $g_{\widetilde{w}}(\widetilde{z}|\lambda)$ $(\lambda \in \Lambda \subset \mathbb{R}^k)$. In this case, Equation (17.24) becomes a conditional moment equation we can easily transform into a usual moment equation by writing

$$E^\theta\left(\widetilde{w}\left(\widetilde{y} - g_{\widetilde{w}}(\widetilde{z}|\lambda)\right)\right) = 0. \tag{17.25}$$

We attached an index w to the function g_w to emphasize that its definition depends on the choice of the instruments $\widetilde{w}$ and evidently changes if $\widetilde{w}$ is modified. More generally, $\widetilde{w}$ can be replaced by a vector of function of $\widetilde{w}$, this poses a problem of optimality which we will discuss later.

Equation (17.25) is implied by (17.24). Thus we face a problem that appears as a special case of the general methodology presented in the first part. Note, that the vectors $\widetilde{z}$ and $\widetilde{w}$ can have, in general, common elements.

Equation (17.25) introduces an overidentifying assumption as soon as $r > k$, unless some moment conditions are redundant. We have to assume that λ is identified, i.e., that the solution $\widetilde{\lambda}(\theta)$ to Equation (17.25) is unique.

Example 17.1   *We examine the case where $g_w(\widetilde{z}|\lambda)$ is linear and thus can be written as $\widetilde{z}'\lambda$ $(k = q)$.*
– If $r = k$ and if $E^\theta(\widetilde{w}\widetilde{z}')$ has full rank, then the solution to (17.25) is

$$\widetilde{\lambda}(\theta) = E^\theta\left(\widetilde{w}\widetilde{z}'\right)^{-1} E^\theta\left(\widetilde{w}\widetilde{y}\right).$$

– If $\widetilde{w} = \widetilde{z}$, then we recover the coefficients of the linear regression of $\widetilde{y}$ on $\widetilde{z}$.
– If $\widetilde{w}$ is arbitrary, then $\widetilde{\lambda}(\theta)$ is the solution to

$$E^\theta\left(\widetilde{w}\widetilde{y}\right) = E^\theta\left(\widetilde{w}\widetilde{z}'\right)\lambda.$$

Uniqueness of the solution requires $k \geq r$ (and rank$[E^\theta(\widetilde{w}\widetilde{z}')] = k$) and, if $k > r$, this equation restricts the DGP to satisfy that the vector of cross-moments of $\widetilde{w}$ and $\widetilde{y}$ lies in the space spanned by the columns of the cross-moments of $\widetilde{w}$ and $\widetilde{z}$. $\square$

Example 17.2 *Consider the case where $\widetilde{z}$ is included in $\widetilde{w}$, which we then write as $\widetilde{w} = (\widetilde{z}, \widetilde{z}^*)$. Condition (17.24) implies that*

$$g_w\left(\widetilde{z} | \lambda\left(\theta\right)\right) = E^\theta\left(\widetilde{y} | \widetilde{z}, \widetilde{z}^*\right).$$

The function g_w is the conditional expectation but it is subject to an overidentifying restriction: the expectation of $\widetilde{y}$ conditional on $\widetilde{z}$ and $\widetilde{z}^*$ only depends on $\widetilde{z}$. □

Example 17.3 *Given a linear simultaneous equations model as defined in Chapter 16, consider one particular equation of this model written as*

$$y_1 + \alpha'y_2 + \beta'z_1 = u_1$$

(see Example 16.2). The set of exogenous variables in the model forms the vector $z = (z_1, z_2)$. We saw that the simultaneous equations model is defined by the property $E^\theta\left(u|z\right) = 0$, and thus our structural equation satisfies

$$E^\theta\left[z\left(y_1 + \alpha'y_2 + \beta'z_1\right)\right] = 0.$$

Therefore, we are in the setting of linear instrumental variables where, in this case, z becomes $(y_2, z_2) \in \mathbb{R}^{p_2+q_2}$. The identification condition $r \geq q$ is $q_1 + q_2 \geq p_2 + q_1$, i.e. $q_2 \geq p_2$, which is the rank condition for identification that we examined in Example 16.2. □

Example 17.4 *Consider a linear dynamic equation of the form*

$$y_{2i} + \alpha y_{1i} + \beta y_{2,i-1} + \gamma y_{1,i-1} + \delta z_i + \mu z_{i-1} = u_i$$

which is taken from a dynamic simultaneous equations model. The model is completed with two assumptions:

- *the process z is exogenous and thus*

$$E^\theta\left(u_i z_i\right) = 0,$$

- *the residuals u_i are innovations with respect to the set of variables, i.e.,*

$$E^\theta\left(u_i y_{1,i-j}\right) = E^\theta\left(u_i y_{2,i-j}\right) = E^\theta\left(u_i z_{i-j}\right) = 0 \qquad \forall j \geq 1.$$

Thus, we can define a vector $\widetilde{w}$ of instruments consisting of the variables (y_1, y_2, z) lagged up to an arbitrary order k and the current value of z_i. □

17.5.2 Estimation

We analyze the estimation problem in a general manner (with nonlinear functions and dynamic observations), but we show that, with an appropriate assumption on the residuals, we are able to obtain simple results in spite of this generality

Suppose the observations $x_i = (y_i, z_i, w_i)$, $i = 1, \ldots, n$, are generated by a stationary ergodic process and satisfy the central limit theorem for all $\theta \in \Theta$ which indexes the sampling probability. The parameter of interest $\widetilde{\lambda}(\theta)$ is the unique solution to the equation

$$E^{\theta}[w_i(y_i - g_w(z_i|\lambda))] = 0. \tag{17.26}$$

Note that w_i and z_i, which are vectors of dimension r and q respectively, may contain the same variable with various lags. For example, $g_w(z_i|\lambda)$ can be of the form $\alpha p_i + \beta p_{i-1} + \gamma R_{i-1} + \delta$ where p_i and p_{i-1} are two observations of a price at i and $i-1$ and R_{i-1} is the income at $i-1$. In this case, $z_i = (p_i, p_{i-1}, R_{i-1})$.

Similarly, w_i may contain one or several variables and their lagged values. In contrast, y_i remains scalar in our analysis.

By assumption, the solution $\widetilde{\lambda}(\theta)$ to (17.26) is unique. A local condition for uniqueness is given by

$$rank\left[E^{\theta}\left(w_i \frac{\partial}{\partial \lambda'} g_w(z_i|\lambda)\Big|_{\lambda=\widetilde{\lambda}(\theta)}\right)\right] = k$$

which, for a linear model $\left(g_w(z_i|\lambda) = z_i'\lambda\right)$, becomes

$$rank\left[E^{\theta}\left(w_i z_i'\right)\right] = k.$$

Furthermore, we assume that θ belongs to Θ_*, the set of values of θ such that (17.26) admits a solution.

We proceed to the estimation by GMM using immediately the context of an optimal weighting matrix. To determine the latter, we consider the variance of the limiting distribution of

$$\frac{\sqrt{n}}{n} \sum_{i=1}^{n} w_i u_i$$

(with $u_i = y - g_w(z_i|\lambda)$), which is equal to

$$V^{\theta} = \sum_{j=-\infty}^{+\infty} Cov^{\theta}(w_i u_i, w_{i-j} u_{i-j}) = \sum_{j=-\infty}^{+\infty} E^{\theta}(w_i w_{i-j}' u_i u_{i-j}).$$

We make the following assumptions

$$E^{\theta}\left(u_i u_{i-j} | (w_l)_{l\in\mathbb{N}}\right) = \begin{vmatrix} \sigma^2 & \text{if } j = 0 \\ 0 & \text{otherwise.} \end{vmatrix} \tag{17.27}$$

This assumption requires homoskedasticity if $j = 0$ and no correlation if $j \neq 0$. It is conditional on the entire path of the instrumental variables. In particular, if the u_i are a difference martingale conditional on w_l, then the following orthogonality property holds

$$E^\theta \left(u_i u_{i-j} | (w_l)_{l \in \mathbb{N}} \right)$$
$$= E^\theta \left[E^\theta \left(u_{i-j} E^\theta \left(u_i | u_{i-1}, u_{i-2}, \ldots, (w_l)_{l \in \mathbb{N}} \right) | (w_l)_{l \in \mathbb{N}} \right) \right] = 0$$

since

$$E^\theta \left(u_i | u_{i-1}, u_{i-2}, \ldots, (w_l)_{l \in \mathbb{N}} \right) = 0.$$

It is then clear that the asymptotic variance of

$$\frac{\sqrt{n}}{n} \sum_{i=1}^n w_i u_i$$

is equal to

$$\sigma^2 E^\theta \left(w_i w_i' \right).$$

As the weighting matrix is defined only up to a multiplicative constant, we can use, in a finite sample,

$$\Pi_n = \left[\sum_{i=1}^n w_i w_i' \right]^{-1}$$

as weighting matrix which, after multiplying it by n, converges to

$$\left[E^\theta \left(w_i w_i' \right) \right]^{-1}.$$

This matrix is assumed to be invertible.

The estimation then solves

$$\min_{\lambda \in \Lambda} (y - g_w (z|\lambda))' W' (W'W)^{-1} W (y - g_w (z|\lambda))$$

with

$$y = \begin{pmatrix} y_1 \\ \vdots \\ y_n \end{pmatrix}, \quad g_w (z|\lambda) = \begin{pmatrix} g(z_i|\lambda) \\ \vdots \\ g(z_n|\lambda) \end{pmatrix}, \quad W = \begin{pmatrix} w_1' \\ \vdots \\ w_n' \end{pmatrix}$$

where W has dimension $n \times r$.

Thus, the estimator $\hat{\lambda}_n$ has to satisfy the first order conditions

$$\frac{\partial}{\partial \lambda} g_w (z|\lambda)' W' (W'W)^{-1} W (y - g_w (z|\lambda)) = 0. \tag{17.28}$$

In a linear context, $g_w(z|\lambda) = Z\lambda$, with

$$Z = \begin{pmatrix} z_1' \\ \vdots \\ z_n' \end{pmatrix},$$

the estimator is equal to

$$\hat{\lambda}_n = \left(Z'W \left(W'W \right)^{-1} W'Z \right)^{-1} Z'W \left(W'W \right)^{-1} W'y. \qquad (17.29)$$

Remarks.   This estimator is called the two-stage least squares estimator. It can be obtained in three equivalent ways:

1.   By the method we just described.
2.   By regressing y on $\widehat{Z}$ where

$$\widehat{Z} = W(W'W)^{-1}W'y$$

is the matrix that is computed in the regression of Z on W. This decomposition justifies the name two-stage least squares.

3.   By regressing y on Z and on

$$\widehat{V} = Z - \widehat{Z} = \left[I - W(W'W)^{-1}W' \right] Z$$

and keeping only the coefficients of Z. The intuition behind this result is the following. In the setting with normal distributions, using an argument in terms of linear conditional expectations, we can write in matrix form

$$\begin{cases} y = Z\lambda + u \\ Z = W\pi + V \end{cases} \qquad (17.30)$$

and u is factorized as

$$u = V\mu + \epsilon$$

where ϵ is independent of V (conditional on W). The first equation then becomes

$$y = Z\lambda + V\mu + \epsilon$$

and thus $Z\lambda + V\mu$ is the regression of y on Z and V. So, we first estimate V (by $Z - \widehat{Z} = Z - W\widehat{\pi}$) and then regress linearly y on Z and $\widehat{V}$. It can be easily verified that this procedure leads once again to (17.29). This method illustrates the so-called *control function approach* which we will present more generally later on. Its equivalence to the instrumental variable method is only true in a linear setting. $\qquad\Box$

We can apply the following general results to the generalized moment condition defined in (17.26). $\hat{\lambda}_n$ converges almost surely to $\tilde{\lambda}(\theta)$, i.e., is consistent, and we have

$$\sqrt{n}\left(\hat{\lambda}_n - \tilde{\lambda}(\theta)\right) \to N(0, \Sigma_\theta) \tag{17.31}$$

with

$$\Sigma_\theta = \sigma^2 \left[E^\theta \left(\frac{\partial}{\partial \lambda} g_w\left(z_i | \tilde{\lambda}(\theta)\right) w_i' \right) \left[E^\theta \left(w_i w_i' \right) \right]^{-1} \right.$$
$$\left. \times E^\theta \left(w_i \frac{\partial}{\partial \lambda'} g_w(z_i) \tilde{\lambda}(\theta) \right) \right]. \tag{17.32}$$

In the linear case, this matrix simplifies to

$$\Sigma_\theta = \sigma^2 \left[E^\theta \left(z_i w_i' \right) \left[E^\theta \left(w_i w_i' \right) \right]^{-1} E^\theta \left(w_i z_i' \right) \right]^{-1}. \tag{17.33}$$

This matrix is estimated by replacing the expectations by the corresponding sample means, $\tilde{\lambda}(\theta)$ by $\hat{\lambda}_n$ and σ^2 by the following consistent estimator

$$\hat{\sigma}_n^2 = \frac{1}{n} \sum_{i=1}^n \left(y_i - g_w\left(z_i | \hat{\lambda}_n \right) \right)^2. \tag{17.34}$$

If Assumption (17.27) does not hold, then we first need to estimate V, which requires:

- to first calculate a consistent estimator of λ in $g_w(z_i | \lambda)$ in order to derive a first estimator of the u_i,
- to estimate $E^\theta(w_i w_{i-j}' u_i u_{i-j})$ for some j by their empirical averages,
- to estimate the sum by using truncation and possibly a regularization procedure through filtering (see Section 15.2.4).

Thus, λ is estimated by minimizing

$$(y - g_w(z|\lambda))' W \widehat{V}^{-1} W (y - g_w(z|\lambda))$$

where $\widehat{V}$ is the estimator V that we previously obtained. The asymptotic properties remain the same as those studied in Chapter 3.

17.5.3 Optimal Instruments

The expression for the optimal instruments follows from the remark in Section 3.5 and its dynamic extension analyzed in Chapter 15 (see 15.2.2 and 15.2.3). The condition

$$E^\theta \left[(y_i - g_w(z_i|\lambda)) | w_i \right] = 0$$

implies

$$E^\theta \left[(y_i - g_w (z_i | \lambda)) h(w_i) \right] = 0$$

for every function h. In the static case, we can conclude from Chapter 3 that the optimal choice of h is

$$h(w_i) = E^\theta \left[\frac{\partial}{\partial \lambda} (y_i - g_w (z_i | \lambda)) | w_i \right] Var (u_i | w_i)^{-1}$$

where $u_i = y_i - g_w (z_i | \lambda)$. Thus, we have

$$h(w_i) = E^\theta \left[\frac{\partial}{\partial \lambda} g_w (z_i | \lambda) | w_i \right] Var (u_i | w_i)^{-1}.$$

If the model is homoskedastic ($Var (u_i | w_i) = \sigma^2$), then we can choose

$$h(w_i) = E^\theta \left[\frac{\partial}{\partial \lambda} g_w (z_i | \lambda) | w_i \right],$$

since h is defined only up to a multiplicative constant.

If, additionally, g_w is linear, then the choice of h simplifies to

$$h(w_i) = E^\theta \left[z_i | w_i \right].$$

Even in this simple case with homoskedastic residuals and linearity, the optimal moments require either the specification of $E^\theta [z_i | w_i]$ or a nonparametric estimation (which can be performed by kernel estimation). The system simplifies even more if $E^\theta [z_i | w_i]$ is assumed to be linear. Then we have

$$E^\theta [z_i | w_i] = E^\theta \left[w_i w_i' \right]^{-1} E^\theta \left[w_i z_i' \right] z_i$$

and we can easily verify that the optimal choice of h leads to two-stage least squares.

The argument in the dynamic case is identical. The only change consists in replacing the variance of u_i by

$$\sum_{j=-\infty}^{+\infty} E \left(u_i u_{i+j} | w_i \right),$$

which only reduces to $E(u_i^2 | w_i) = V(u_i | w_i)$ if the sequence of u_i is a martingale difference conditional on w_i (see Chapter 15).

In practice, the optimal instruments can only be calculated in two-stages. For example, if g_w is not linear, then a preliminary estimate of λ is necessary in order to calculate $E^\theta [g_w(z_i | \lambda) | w_i]$, and it is the same for estimating the conditional variance of the residuals in the heteroskedastic case.

17.5.4 Nonparametric Approach and Endogenous Variables

We briefly explain two nonparametric approaches for simultaneity, the general-ization of the instrumental variables method and the control function method. In the following, $\tilde{x} = (\tilde{y}, \tilde{z}, \tilde{w})$ and the sample is i.i.d. with distribution Q.

Nonparametric Instrumental Variables

For simplicity, we assume that $\tilde{z}$ and $\tilde{w}$ do not have any elements in common. We are looking for a function $g_w(z)$ that satisfies

$$\tilde{y} = g_w(\tilde{z}) + \tilde{u} \quad \text{with} \quad E^Q(\tilde{u} \,|\, \tilde{w}) = 0 \tag{17.35}$$

(here we generalize Equation (17.24)), which comes down to finding the func-tion g_w that solves

$$\int g_w(z) f(z \,|\, w)\, dz = \int y f(y \,|\, w)\, dy, \tag{17.36}$$

where f denotes the marginal or conditional densities of $(\tilde{y}, \tilde{z}, \tilde{w})$. For the solution to this equation to be unique, and thus for g_w to be identified by (17.35), we need to assume that the joint distribution of $\tilde{z}$ and $\tilde{w}$ satisfies

$$\forall \text{ integrable } \phi, \ E^Q(\phi(\tilde{z}) \,|\, \tilde{w}) = 0 \Rightarrow \phi = 0. \tag{17.37}$$

Indeed, two solutions g_w^1 and g_w^2 of (17.36) satisfy necessarily

$$E^Q\left[g_w^1(\tilde{z}) - g_w^2(\tilde{z}) \,|\, \tilde{w}\right] = 0$$

which implies $g_w^1 = g_w^2$ under (17.37).

Condition (17.37) is a condition of "strong" dependence between $\tilde{z}$ and $\tilde{w}$ which generalizes the condition of linear dependence previously introduced ($E^Q(\tilde{w}\tilde{z}')$ has rank equal to the dimension of $\tilde{z}$). We can show that, if $\tilde{z}$ and $\tilde{w}$ are jointly normal, then Assumption (17.37) is equivalent to the fact that the rank of the covariance matrix between $\tilde{z}$ and $\tilde{w}$ is equal to the dimension of $\tilde{z}$.

Furthermore, Equation (17.36) does not always admit a solution. Assuming that (17.36) holds restricts the class of distributions Q (or of densities f) and imposes an overidentifying restriction on the model. To solve this problem, we look for the g_w that minimizes

$$E^Q\left[\left(E^Q(g_w(\tilde{z}) \,|\, \tilde{w}) - E^Q(\tilde{y} \,|\, \tilde{w})\right)^2\right]. \tag{17.38}$$

This problem admits a solution under weaker conditions than (17.36). We can moreover show that the minimization of (17.38) leads to the search for a g_w that satisfies

$$E^Q\left[E^Q(g_w(\tilde{z}) \,|\, \tilde{w}) \,|\, \tilde{z}\right] = E^Q\left[E^Q(\tilde{y} \,|\, \tilde{w}) \,|\, \tilde{z}\right]. \tag{17.39}$$

Then we look for $\widetilde{g}$ by solving (17.39) after we have replaced the conditional expectations by their kernel estimators, which yields

$$
\frac{1}{\sum_{j=1}^n K_n(z-z_j)} \sum_{j=1}^n \frac{\sum_{i=1}^n g_w(z_i)K_n(w_j-w_i)}{\sum_{i=1}^n K_n(w_j-w_i)} K_n(z-z_j)
$$

$$
= \frac{1}{\sum_{j=1}^n K_n(z-z_j)} \sum_{j=1}^n \frac{\sum_{i=1}^n y_i K_n(w_j-w_i)}{\sum_{i=1}^n K_n(w_j-w_i)} K_n(z-z_j) \tag{17.40}
$$

Equation (17.40) has as solution $g_w(z_i) = y_i$ and $g_w(z)$ is indeterminate for $z \notin \{z_1, \ldots, z_n\}$. This solution is not a consistent estimator of g_w and we have to "regularize" the problem. We present here a classical solution to this type of problem, namely the Tikhonov regularization or the nonparametric extension of *ridge regression* method.

Equation (17.40) is replaced by

$$
\alpha_n g_w(z) + \frac{1}{\sum_{j=1}^n K_n(z-z_j)} \sum_{j=1}^n \frac{\sum_{i=1}^n g_w(z_i)K_n(w_j-w_i)}{\sum_{i=1}^n K_n(w_j-w_i)} K_n(z-z_j)
$$

$$
= \frac{1}{\sum_{j=1}^n K_n(z-z_j)} \sum_{j=1}^n \frac{\sum_{i=1}^n y_i K_n(w_j-w_i)}{\sum_{i=1}^n K_n(w_j-w_i)} K_n(z-z_j) \tag{17.41}
$$

where α_n is a positive scalar that depends on n and goes to 0 as $n \to \infty$. Then, Equation (17.41) is solved in two steps. First, we replace z by $z_1, \ldots, z_n$ and obtain a linear system of n equations in n unknown $g_w(z_i)$ which we solve. Then, we use (17.41) to calculate $g_w(z)$ for each point.

This method yields a consistent estimator of g_w if α_n goes to 0 at an appropriate rate. Establishing asymptotic normality is a complex problem.

Control Function Method

Another approach can be used to nonparametrically treat a structural relation. Consider the following generalization of (17.1)

$$
\begin{cases} \widetilde{y} = h_w(\widetilde{z}) + \widetilde{u} \\ \widetilde{z} = m(\widetilde{w}) + \widetilde{v} \end{cases} \tag{17.42}
$$

where

$$
E(\widetilde{v}|\widetilde{w}) = 0, \quad m(w) = E(\widetilde{z}|\widetilde{w} = w)
$$

and $\widetilde{u}$ and $\widetilde{v}$ are not mutually independent. Instead of assuming as previously that

$$
E^Q(\widetilde{u}|\widetilde{w}) = 0,
$$

we now assume that

$$E^Q(\tilde{u} \,|\, \tilde{w}, \tilde{v}) = E^Q(\tilde{u} \,|\, \tilde{v}).$$ (17.43)

This assumption is not equivalent to Assumption (17.35), and in general g_w and h_w are not identical. We can nevertheless note that, if $\tilde{w}$ is independent of the pair $(\tilde{u}, \tilde{v})$, then Equations (17.35) and (17.43) hold and thus $g_w = h_w$.

The estimation of h_w is based on the following calculation:

$$E^Q(\tilde{y} \,|\, \tilde{z}, \tilde{w}) = h_w(\tilde{z}) + E^Q(\tilde{u} \,|\, \tilde{z}, \tilde{w}).$$ (17.44)

However, the information contained in $\tilde{z}$ and $\tilde{w}$ is the same as the one contained in $\tilde{v}$ and $\tilde{w}$, consequently

$$E^Q(\tilde{y} \,|\, \tilde{z}, \tilde{w}) = h_w(\tilde{z}) + E^Q(\tilde{u} \,|\, \tilde{v}, \tilde{w})$$

or

$$E^Q(\tilde{y} \,|\, \tilde{z}, \tilde{w}) - h_w(\tilde{z}) + E^Q(\tilde{u} \,|\, \tilde{v}).$$ (17.45)

Denote

$$r(v) = E^Q(\tilde{u} \,|\, \tilde{v} = v).$$

Then we have

$$E^Q(\tilde{y} \,|\, \tilde{z}, \tilde{w}) = h_w(\tilde{z}) + r(\tilde{v}),$$ (17.46)

the function $r(\tilde{v})$ is called the *control function*.

We then proceed to a generalization of the least squares estimation:

- First, we estimate $m(w)$, for example by kernel smoothing, and the residuals v_i by $\widehat{v}_i$;
- Then, we nonparametrically regress $\tilde{y}$ on $\tilde{z}$ and $\tilde{v}$, imposing an additive structure (17.46), and thus we use the method of Chapter 10.

In this approach, r is normalized by $E^Q(r(\tilde{v})) = 0$ assuming that $E^Q(\tilde{u}) = 0$. This approach itself also poses an identification problem which we can explain in the following way. Let (h_w^1, r^1) and (h_w^2, r^2) be two solutions to (17.46). By setting

$$h_w = h_w^1 - h_w^2 \quad \text{and} \quad r = r^1 - r^2,$$

we obtain the following equality

$$h_w(z) + r(z - m(w)) = 0. \tag{17.47}$$

The function m is perfectly identified since it is defined as a conditional expectation.

To establish identification, we need to show that (17.47) implies $h_w = 0$. Taking the derivative of (17.47) with respect to w, we obtain

$$\frac{\partial m'}{\partial w} \frac{\partial r}{\partial v} (r - m(w)) = 0. \tag{17.48}$$

Thus, it is necessary that the rank of $\frac{\partial m'}{\partial w}$ is equal to the dimension of z for it to be true that (17.48) implies $\frac{\partial r}{\partial v} = 0$, i.e., r is constant. Furthermore, $E^Q(r) = 0$ then implies that r and, therefore, h_w are zero.

The identification condition is here weaker than in the instrumental variables approach since it only affects the dependence between w and the conditional expectation of z given w and not the entire conditional distribution.

17.5.5   Test of Exogeneity

The study of the tests of exogeneity provides a more precise meaning to this notion than we discussed several times so far. Recall that a variable is exogenous if the model conditional on this variable allows us to identify and estimate the parameter of interest. We are here more specifically interested in the relation between two variables (or vectors) $\tilde{y}$ and $\tilde{z}$. We say that $\tilde{z}$ is exogenous if the structural relation of interest between $\tilde{y}$ and $\tilde{z}$ is the conditional expectation of $\tilde{y}$ given $\tilde{z}$. Given that the conditional expectation is an element of the conditional distribution, this definition does not contradict the general notion.

The question then is to define the relation of interest. This definition, at least in a parametric setting, is in general incorporated in a moment equation. Here, we are essentially interested in a definition of the structural relation through instrumental variables.

Consider the linear homoskedastic case with independent sampling. Let $\tilde{x} = (\tilde{y}, \tilde{z}, \tilde{w})$ be a random vector in $\mathbb{R} \times \mathbb{R}^p \times \mathbb{R}^k$ and consider the linear equation

$$\tilde{y} = \lambda' \tilde{z} + \tilde{u}. \tag{17.49}$$

To take account of the overidentification, we characterize $\tilde{\lambda}(\theta)$ by

$$\tilde{\lambda}(\theta) = \arg\min E\left(\tilde{w}\left(\tilde{y} - \lambda'\tilde{z}\right)\right)' E\left(\tilde{w}\tilde{w}'\right)^{-1} E\left(\tilde{w}\left(\tilde{y} - \lambda'\tilde{z}\right)\right). \tag{17.50}$$

This definition of $\tilde{\lambda}(\theta)$ immediately leads to the two-stage least squares estimator given in (17.29) in the case of i.i.d. sampling.

Suppose furthermore that the regression of $\tilde{y}$ on $\tilde{z}$ is linear and thus define a parameter

$$\lambda^*(\theta) = E\left(\tilde{z}\tilde{z}'\right)^{-1} E\left(\tilde{z}\tilde{y}\right). \tag{17.51}$$

The hypothesis of exogeneity is then the equality

$$\tilde{\lambda}(\theta) = \lambda^*(\theta). \tag{17.52}$$

This hypothesis can be immediately tested by the Hausman test procedure. Indeed, we have two estimators of λ available, the one derived from Definition (17.50), denoted by $\tilde{\lambda}_n$ (see (17.29)), and the OLS estimator

$$\hat{\hat{\lambda}}_n = (Z'Z)^{-1}Z'y.$$

We know that under the null hypothesis (17.52), $\hat{\hat{\lambda}}_n$ is the best consistent and asymptotically normal estimator, and that $\hat{\lambda}_n$ is a consistent and asymptotically normal estimator of $\tilde{\lambda}(\theta)$.

We can without difficulty show the joint normality of these two estimators and we conclude that

$$\sqrt{n}\left(\hat{\hat{\lambda}}_n - \hat{\lambda}_n\right) \tag{17.53}$$

$$\to N\left(0, \sigma^2\left\{\left(E\left(\tilde{z}\tilde{w}'\right)E\left(\tilde{w}\tilde{w}'\right)^{-1}E\left(\tilde{w}\tilde{z}'\right)\right)^{-1} - E\left(\tilde{z}\tilde{z}'\right)^{-1}\right\}\right).$$

Denote the above variance by Ω. Then, this implies that

$$\sqrt{n}\left(\hat{\hat{\lambda}}_n - \hat{\lambda}_n\right)' \Omega^+ \left(\hat{\hat{\lambda}}_n - \hat{\lambda}_n\right)$$

is distributed according to a χ^2 with the degrees of freedom equal to the rank of V. One can verify that this rank is equal to the number of components of $\tilde{z}$ which are not in $\tilde{w}$. Intuitively, we can note that $\tilde{\lambda}(\theta) = \lambda^*(\theta)$ if and only if

$$E\left(\tilde{z}\left(\tilde{y} - \tilde{\lambda}(\theta)'\tilde{z}\right)\right) = 0,$$

i.e., if $\tilde{z}$ is orthogonal to the structural residuals $\tilde{u}$. This condition is true for the $\tilde{z}$ that belong to $\tilde{w}$ but it constitutes a hypothesis for the other components of $\tilde{z}$ that can be tested. The problem is thus to test that a number of moments is equal to zero, where the number of moments is equal to the number of components of $\tilde{z}$ that do not belong to $\tilde{w}$, which forms the dimension of the null hypothesis.

In the linear case, in practice, the Hausman test is identical to a usual test (the Student t test) whether the coefficients of $\hat{V}$ (defined by the estimation of V in the model (17.30)) in the regression of y on z and $\hat{V}$ are zero (see the previous remark).

This approach generalizes to the nonlinear case (still maintaining homoskedasticity). By comparing the instrumental variable estimate of λ defined by (17.25) and the least squares estimate of λ (arg min $\sum_{i=1}^{n}(y_i - g(z_i, \lambda))^2$), we test the equality of the structural parameters $\widetilde{\lambda}(\theta)$ and the approximation of the regression of $\widetilde{y}$ on $\widetilde{z}$ within the family $g(\cdot, \lambda)$.

Finally, we can construct a nonparametric test of exogeneity for which we provide the principle without giving details on the procedure nor on the properties. The idea still is to test

$$g_w(z) = E(\widetilde{y} \,|\, \widetilde{z} = z) \tag{17.54}$$

where g_w is defined by

$$E(\widetilde{y} - g_w(\widetilde{z}) \,|\, \widetilde{w}) = 0$$

(see Section 17.5.4). Assuming the above equation defines a unique g_w, the Equality (17.54) is equivalent to

$$E(\widetilde{y} - E(\widetilde{y} \,|\, \widetilde{z}) \,|\, \widetilde{w}) = 0. \tag{17.55}$$

Thus, it suffices to verify that the regression residuals (reduced form residuals) satisfy the condition on the structural residuals,

$$\widetilde{u} = \widetilde{y} - g_w(\widetilde{z}).$$

In practice, the properties of the test are improved by testing the following equation which is implied by (17.55)

$$E[E(\widetilde{y} - E(\widetilde{y} \,|\, \widetilde{z}) \,|\, \widetilde{w}) \,|\, \widetilde{z}] = 0. \tag{17.56}$$

We test this by comparing the value of

$$\int E[E(\widetilde{y} - E(\widetilde{y} \,|\, \widetilde{z}) \,|\, \widetilde{w}) \,|\, \widetilde{z}]^2 \, \pi(z) dz$$

to zero, where π is a weighting function. The conditional expectations are then replaced by their estimates, for example using kernel smoothing (see Chapter 10).

Notes

The nonconvergence of the least squares estimators to the structural parameters of a model with endogenous variables has been remarked upon since the beginning of econometrics. The use of instrumental variables is due to Frisch (1934 and 1938) and continued by Riersol (1941 and 1945) within the Cowles Commission. The instrumental variables approach has been developed by Sargan (1958), while Basmann (1957) and Theil (1953) constructed independently the two-stage least squares estimation. The theory of optimal instruments was initiated by Amemiya (1974b), Berndt, Hall, Hall, and Hausman (1974), and generalized by Hansen (1985). The nonparametric approach to endogeneity is recent and has been developed in connection to the theory of inverse problems. The instrumental variable approach is presented by Florens (2003), Darolles, Florens, and

Renault (2002), and Newey and Powell (2003) (see also Carrasco, Florens, and Renault (2003)). The control function approach is put forward by Newey, Powell, and Vella (1999). The test of exogeneity is a particular case of the Hausmann test (see the bibliographical notes in Chapter 4). The study of selection bias is linked to the work of Heckman (see Heckman (1979) and Heckman and Robb (1985)) among a long series of contributions. The use of instrumental variables in this context is in particular treated in Heckman (1997).

18.   Models with Unobservable Variables

18.1   Introduction

The structural modeling in econometrics leads often to specify a model that is relevant in terms of economic theory but includes one or several variables for which no observation is available. This nonobservability may come from the specific data bases used by the econometrician. In a model of individual job search, the job offers received by the individual are often not observed although some data bases record them. Other variables are unobservable by nature (such as ability, taste, risk aversion) and at best we have some variables available that are related or are close to the relevant unobservable value.

The unobservable variable may be either an explained or an explanatory variable. This distinction is actually not that important because, in all cases, the model will have to specify the distribution of the unobservable variable which hence becomes explained if it originally were explanatory. Therefore, we focus our presentation on the case of unobservable conditioning variables in the structural model.

A structural econometric model with unobservable variables is in general built in the following manner. The relevant variables for the ith observation are grouped in x_i^*, itself partitioned into observables x_i and unobservables ζ_i. The structural model specifies a set of assumptions on the distribution of x_i conditional on ζ_i (conditional distribution or conditional moments). More generally, x_i can itself be partitioned into the explained variables y_i and the explanatory variables z_i. The modeling is formalized by the specification of the conditional distribution of $(y_i)_i$ given $(z_i)_i$ and $(\zeta_i)_i$, or by a set of assumptions regarding the conditional moments of $(y_i)_i$ given $(z_i)_i$ and $(\zeta_i)_i$. The structural model needs always to be completed by assumptions on the distribution of ζ_i (or ζ_i given $(z_i)_i$, in the case of a specification conditional on z_i).

The reduced form is obtained by eliminating the unobservable variables in this model and by calculating the marginal distribution of x_i or some of its moments, or by calculating the conditional distribution of y_i given z_i or some of its moments.

446

For simplicity, consider the case in which x_i^* is assumed to be i.i.d. and the conditional model of y_i given z_i and ζ_i is described by a density with parameter β denoted $\bar{f}(y_i|z_i, \zeta_i, \beta)$. The density of ζ_i given z_i is of the form $g(\zeta_i|z_i, \gamma)$. Then, the generating process of (y_i, z_i) is necessarily i.i.d. and the conditional distribution of y_i given z_i and the parameters $\lambda = (\beta, \gamma)$ has the density

$$\int \bar{f}(y_i|z_i, \zeta_i, \beta) g(\zeta_i|z_i, \gamma) d\zeta_i. \tag{18.1}$$

If the structural model consists just in specifying the condition

$$E^\theta \left(\bar{\psi}\left(y_i, z_i, \zeta_i, \beta\right) | z_i, \zeta_i \right) = 0 \tag{18.2}$$

and if ζ_i remains i.i.d. with density $g(\zeta_i, |z_i, \gamma)$, then the model is in its reduced form characterized by the conditions

$$E^\theta \left(\psi\left(y_i, z_i, \beta, \gamma\right) | z_i \right) = 0 \tag{18.3}$$

with

$$\psi\left(y_i, z_i, \beta, \gamma\right) = \int \bar{\psi}\left(y_i, z_i, \zeta_i, \beta\right) g\left(\zeta_i|z_i, \gamma\right) d\zeta_i, \tag{18.4}$$

which is a classical moment condition that combines the parameters of the moment condition (18.2) and the parameters of the distribution of the unobservable variables.

We notice that, except under very special conditions on $\bar{\psi}$ (linearity in ζ_i for example), the specification of g is necessary to calculate ψ.

The models with unobservable variables are very diverse in the literature but all raise essentially the following three questions:

1. The first type of problem consists in comparing the structural and the reduced model. The motivation for this comparison is essentially to examine the distortion between the "naive" message of the data expressed by the reduced form and the contributions of observations toward the validation of economic theory which is made possible by the structural form.
2. The second problem is an identification problem. In general, the structural model is identified in the sense that its parameters would be identified if the $(\zeta_i)_i$ were observed. But their unobservability may destroy this identification. Another identification problem arises regarding the distribution of ζ_i or some of its characteristics.
3. The third problem concerns estimation. It does not pose theoretical difficulties but often requires complicated numerical computations. Thus, econometricians proposed methods that were simpler to implement but specific to particular models.

Our goal is not to provide the most general presentation; instead, we focus on examples of classes of models with unobservable variables. These examples are presented in Section 2, whereas the following three sections examine successively the three problems we just mentioned.

Remarks

In practice, the distribution of ζ_i given z_i and γ is often specified as independent of z_i. This assumption is quite natural to the extent that ζ_i represents all what describes the heterogeneity of the individuals and is not included in z_i. Imagine for example that the complete description of the characteristics of an individual constitutes a normal vector (z_i, z_i^*) where only z_i is observed; it is then possible to transform this vector into a normal vector (z_i, ζ_i) where z_i and ζ_i are independent.

Various distributions of the heterogeneity are of interest. The density $g(\zeta_i|z_i, \gamma)$ can be considered as a prior distribution of the heterogeneity given the exogenous variables and the parameters. The observation of y_i for individual i allows us to calculate the posterior distribution (conditional on the parameters)

$$g(\zeta_i|y_i, z_i, \beta, \gamma) = \frac{g(\zeta_i|z_i, \gamma)\overline{f}(y_i|z_i, \zeta_i, \beta)}{\int g(\zeta_i|z_i, \gamma)\overline{f}(y_i|z_i, \zeta_i, \beta)d\zeta_i}$$

using Bayes theorem. Conditionally on β and γ, the i.i.d. property implies that the posterior distribution of the individual heterogeneity depends only on the observables of this individual. However, the parameters are usually estimated by $\widehat{\beta}$ and $\widehat{\gamma}$, and the econometrician uses

$$g(\zeta_i|y_i, z_i, \widehat{\beta}, \widehat{\gamma})$$

which depends on all observations through $\widehat{\beta}$ and $\widehat{\gamma}$. This expression should be considered as an estimator of the density.   □

18.2   Examples of Models with Unobservable Variables

We illustrate the importance of econometric models containing unobservable variables by presenting four classes of models.

18.2.1   Random-Effects Models and Random-Coefficient Models

The two classes of models we are going to present in this example are mainly used to model *panel data*. By panel data, we mean an observation scheme that generates data with a double index representing an individual dimension and a temporal dimension. For each individual $i = 1, \ldots, n$ and each period $t = 1, \ldots, T$, we observe a vector x_{it}. However, modeling deals with a larger vector $x_{it}^* = (x_{it}, \zeta_i)$, where ζ_i is an unobservable component of individual i that is different across individuals by constant over time. We limit ourselves to this case which could be generalized by introducing also an unobservable temporal component η_t, identical across individuals but varying over time.

We partition x_{it} into $y_{it} \in \mathbb{R}^p$ and $z_{it} \in \mathbb{R}^q$. The models we examine are about the conditional expectation of y_{it} given z_{it} and ζ_i, and we focus on two specifications:

$$E^\theta(y_{it}|z_{it}, \zeta_i) = z_{it}'\beta + \zeta_i \tag{18.5}$$

and

$$E^\theta(y_{it}|z_{it}, \zeta_i) = z_{it}'\beta\,(\zeta_i). \tag{18.6}$$

Assumption (18.5) introduces a vector of parameters β and an error term ζ_i of dimension p. This defines a *random-effects model* (ζ_i is an individual effect which, in this case, is considered as the realization of a random phenomenon), in contrast to a *fixed-effects model* for which individuals differ from one another by an individual specific constant term in the affine regression of y_{it} on z_{it}. In the random-effects model, we can define u_{it} by the relation

$$y_{it} = z_{it}'\beta + \zeta_i + u_{it}, \tag{18.7}$$

which we can interpret by saying that y_{it} differs from a linear combination of the z_{it} by two errors ζ_i and u_{it}, the first one being independent of time.

The second model (18.6) is referred to as *random-coefficient model*. It specifies that the regression of y_{it} on z_{it} and ζ_i is not linear and that the relationship between y_{it} and z_{it} involves parameters which are specific to each individual and are functions of an unobservable variable ζ_i. A special case of Model (18.6) is that where ζ_i has the same dimension as z_{it} so that

$$E^\theta(y_{it}|z_{it}, \zeta_i) = z_{it}\zeta_i. \tag{18.8}$$

If the distribution of ζ_i is such that the expectation of ζ_i is independent of i and equal to a vector β, we can write

$$E^\theta(y_{it}|z_{it}, \zeta_i) = z_{it}\beta + z_{it}\varepsilon_i \tag{18.9}$$

where $\varepsilon_i = \zeta_i - \beta$, which underlines the difference between specifications (18.5) and (18.6).

In a random-effects model, specification (18.5) is completed by some assumptions on ζ_i. They are usually assumed to be i.i.d. with mean zero (conditionally on z_{it}), in which case the conditional moment condition (18.5) becomes

$$E^\theta(y_{it}|z_{it}) = z_{it}'\beta \tag{18.10}$$

and we are back to a model with linear conditional expectation which is a function of observables.

The relevance of the random-effects model is not limited to the specification of the conditional expectation but follows from the decomposition of the conditional variance. Consider the vector y_i of the scalar y_{it} ($t = 1, \ldots, T$) and the matrix z_i ($T \times q$) of the z_{it}. Assume that y_i is homoskedastic conditionally on z_i and ζ_i:

$$Var^\theta (y_i | z_i, \zeta_i) = \sigma^2 I_T. \tag{18.11}$$

Moreover, assume that conditionally on z_{it}, ζ_i has mean zero and variance τ^2. Then, we can show that

$$Var^\theta (y_i | z_i) = \sigma^2 I_T + \tau^2 \mathbf{1}_T \mathbf{1}_T'$$

$$= \begin{pmatrix} \sigma^2 + \tau^2 & & \tau^2 & \tau^2 \\ \tau^2 & \ddots & & \vdots \\ \vdots & & \ddots & \ddots & \tau^2 \\ \tau^2 & & \cdots & \tau^2 & \sigma^2 + \tau^2 \end{pmatrix}. \tag{18.12}$$

This result follows from

$$Var^\theta (y_i | z_i) = Var^\theta \left(E^\theta (y_i | z_i, \zeta_i) | z_i \right) + E^\theta \left(Var^\theta (y_i | z_i, \zeta_i) | z_i \right) \tag{18.13}$$

$$= Var^\theta (z_i \beta + \zeta_i \mathbf{1}_T | z_i) + \sigma^2 I_T.$$

The random-coefficient model presents the same characteristics. Consider specification (18.6) complemented by the assumption

$$Var^\theta (y_i | z_i, \zeta_i) = \sigma^2 I_T, \tag{18.14}$$

from which we infer

$$Var^\theta (y_i | z_i) = \sigma^2 I_T + z_i \Sigma z_i', \tag{18.15}$$

provided ζ_i has a variance matrix Σ conditional on z_i.

18.2.2   Duration Models with Unobserved Heterogeneity

A *duration model* is a statistical model in which the explained variable represents the duration of stay in a state. In demography, the most important duration is the human life duration, but we can also analyze the duration separating the birth of two children, the age of getting married (seen as the time spent since birth) or multiple durations separating the main events that structure a biography. In the reliability theory, analysts are interested in the duration between the commissioning of equipment and the first breakdown of the equipment or the duration necessary for the repair. Insurance companies model the time separating two disasters of the same nature. In finance, one may examine the time between two transactions on the same asset. Labor econometrics has popularized the use of duration models among economists by analyzing the unemployment duration, the duration of work periods or the retirement age. Duration models are the simpler versions of more complex models, such as queueing models or transition models with multiple states. These specifications use counting or point processes and go beyond the scope of our presentation.

The simplest duration model is (as usual) an i.i.d. model where the observations are given by the series $(\tau_i)_{i=1,\dots,n}$ of nonnegative numbers generated by the same probability distribution Q with support in $\mathbb{R}^+ = [0, +\infty)$. Our usual notation x_i is hence replaced by τ_i to underline the nature of the observations. We denote by F the distribution function of Q, and we assume that F is differentiable with derivative f, the density of Q.

In duration analysis, it is customary to characterize Q by its *survival function*

$$S(t) = 1 - F(t) = Q(\tau_i \geq t)$$

and its *hazard function* h defined by

$$h(t) = \frac{f(t)}{S(t)} = \lim_{\delta \downarrow 0} \frac{1}{\delta} Q(\tau_i \in [t, t + \delta] \mid \tau_i \geq t). \tag{18.16}$$

The hazard function is the derivative with respect to δ evaluated at $\delta = 0$ of the probability that the duration lies between t and $t + \delta$, given that it is greater than t.

The term

$$H(t) = \int_0^t h(u)\, du, \tag{18.17}$$

is called *cumulative or integrated hazard*. It is easy to verify that

$$H(t) = -\ln S(t) \tag{18.18}$$

with

$$S(t) = e^{-H(t)} \quad \text{and} \quad f(t) = h(t) e^{-H(t)}. \tag{18.19}$$

The simplest duration model is an exponential model characterized by a constant hazard function $h(t) = \lambda$, and thus satisfies

$$H(t) = \lambda t, \quad S(t) = e^{-\lambda t} \quad \text{and} \quad f(t) = \lambda e^{-\lambda t}. \tag{18.20}$$

In general, a duration model involves explanatory variables that capture the difference among individuals. In unemployment duration models, these are for example gender, the age at the beginning of the period, skills, existence and level of unemployment benefits, matrimonial status, and so on. Some variables are fixed during the period of stay in the state while others vary. To simplify, we neglect this second type of variables that depend on time (in practice, we often convert these variables to fixed variables by retaining only their values at the end of the period of which we study the duration, but this simplification actually results from a complex study and is subject to some specific assumptions).

We denote by z_i the explanatory variables observed for individual i. We need to model the distribution of τ_i given z_i while keeping the independence across individuals. We already mentioned (Example 5.2 in Chapter 5) *proportional hazard models* for which the conditional survival function takes the form

$$S(t|\alpha)^{r(\beta,z_i)},$$

where S is the baseline survival function depending on α (α is one or several parameters, but in a semiparametric approach, S could be itself the parameter) and r is a positive function depending on an unknown β. A simple calculation shows that the conditional hazard function can be written as

$$r(\beta, z_i) h(t|\alpha)$$

where

$$h(t|\alpha) = \frac{f(t|\alpha)}{S(t|\alpha)}$$

is the *baseline hazard function*, which justifies the term *proportional hazard*.

We denote by $f(\tau_i|z_i, \lambda)$ the density of observation τ_i conditional on z_i and some possibly functional parameters λ. The survival function is $S(.|z_i, \lambda)$ and the hazard function $h(.|z_i, \lambda)$.

No matter how large the vector of explanatory variables z_i is, it can not include all individual characteristics.

Some of them are unobservable by nature, such as the intensity of the job search, the skills in passing selection tests or more generally the so-called employability, in the unemployment duration model. We show below how the conditional model is modified if a relevant variable has not been included. Hence, we replace in the previous specification z_i by the pair (z_i, ζ_i), where z_i remains the vector of observable explanatory variables and ζ_i is a real variable representing unobservable heterogeneity.

We complete the model by specifying the generating mechanism of the ζ_i. To maintain the independence across individuals, we assume that the ζ_i are independently distributed with density $g(\zeta_i|z_i, \gamma)$ depending on z_i and a parameter γ of finite or infinite dimension. The joint density of τ_i and ζ_i given z_i and (γ, λ) is equal to

$$g(\zeta_i|z_i, \gamma) \overline{f}(\tau_i|z_i, \zeta_i, \lambda)$$

and the density of τ_i given only the observable variables z_i is written as

$$f(\tau_i|z_i, \gamma, \lambda) = \int \overline{f}(\tau_i|z_i, \zeta_i, \lambda) g(\zeta_i|z_i, \gamma) d\zeta_i. \tag{18.21}$$

Then, the conditional likelihood of the observables is

$$\prod_{i=1}^{n} f(\tau_i | z_i, \gamma, \lambda).$$

This construction can be simplified by assuming that ζ_i and z_i are mutually independent, which eliminates z_i in the density g.

18.2.3 Errors-in-Variables Models

Several justifications lead to the statistic structure referred to as *errors-in-variables models*.

Under its simplest form, this model is written as

$$\begin{pmatrix} y_{i1} \\ y_{i2} \end{pmatrix} | z_i, \zeta_i \sim IN \left(\begin{pmatrix} \beta' z_i + \gamma \zeta_i \\ \zeta_i \end{pmatrix}, \Sigma \right), \tag{18.22}$$

with unobservable ζ_i, or equivalently

$$\begin{cases} y_{i1} = \beta' z_i + \gamma \zeta_i + u_{i1} \\ y_{i2} = \zeta_i + u_{i2} \end{cases} \quad \text{and} \quad \begin{pmatrix} u_{i1} \\ u_{i2} \end{pmatrix} | z_i, \zeta_i \sim IN(0, \Sigma). \tag{18.23}$$

Hence, this bivariate model is conditional on observable explanatory variables z_i and an unobservable variable ζ_i.

We can consider that y_{i2} is an observation of ζ_i with "error" u_{i2}. This model can then be interpreted as a linear regression model made of the first equation in which the explanatory variable ζ_i is measured up to an additive error.

We can also consider this model as a special case of the more general class described by

$$y_i = B_\lambda z_i + C_\lambda \zeta_i + u_i \qquad u_i | z_i, \zeta_i \sim i.i.N.(0, \Sigma) \tag{18.24}$$

where y_i is a vector of $\mathbb{R}^p$, z_i of $\mathbb{R}^q$ and ζ_i of $\mathbb{R}^l$; B_λ and C_λ are matrices that depend on λ. In this representation, y_i appears as a vector whose expectation depends linearly on observables and a vector of unobservable components (sometimes called factors).

Here, we limit ourselves to conditionally independent models (the vector u_i has no dynamic behavior) but an extension of this model to time series is possible.

Specification (18.24) allows us to write the conditional likelihood function:

$$\bar{l}(y|z, \zeta, \lambda, \Sigma) = (2\pi)^{-\frac{n}{2}} |\Sigma|^{-\frac{n}{2}}$$

$$\times \exp{-\frac{1}{2} \sum_{i=1}^{n} (y_i - B_\lambda z_i - C_\lambda \zeta_i)' \Sigma^{-1} (y_i - B_\lambda z_i - C_\lambda \zeta_i)}.$$

Here again, we need to complete the model by a distribution of $\zeta = (\zeta_i)_{i=1,\dots,n}$ conditional on the z. The independence of the observations is preserved if the ζ_i are themselves conditionally independent vectors. For instance, we can assume that ζ_i are independently normally distributed with mean Πw_i and variance Ω, where w_i is a vector of observable explanatory variables and Π and Ω are two matrices of parameters. To make the construction consistent, we need to assume that the joint vector (y_i, ζ_i) is conditioned on z_i and w_i (possibly having common elements) even if only z_i appears in the distribution of y_i and only w_i appears in that of ζ_i. More formally, the joint model of observables and unobservables is

$$\begin{cases} \zeta_i|w_i, z_i \sim i.i.N. \left(\Pi w_i, \Omega\right) \\ y_i|\zeta_i, w_i, z_i \sim i.i.N. \left(B_\lambda z_i + C_\lambda \zeta_i, \Sigma\right), \end{cases} \tag{18.25}$$

from which we infer the marginal model of observable explanatory variables

$$y_i|w_i, z_i \sim i.i.N. \left(B_\lambda z_i + C_\lambda \Pi w_i, \Sigma + C_\lambda \Omega C_\lambda'\right). \tag{18.26}$$

The specification of the distribution of the ζ_i may be used to introduce temporal dependence. Consider Model (18.22) and suppose ζ_i is first order Markov

$$\zeta_i|\zeta_1, \dots, \zeta_{i-1}, w_i, z_i \sim N \left(\rho \zeta_{i-1}, \tau^2\right). \tag{18.27}$$

By completing this specification by a distribution for ζ_1, we obtain the distribution for the vector $(\zeta_i)_{i=1,\dots,n}$ conditional on z_i. If the process generating ζ_i is stationary, the joint process (y_i, ζ_i) is also stationary and thus also the marginal process y_i remains stationary. In Example (18.22), y_i is moreover normally distributed, and the only problem is to compute its first and second moments. A general method to perform this evaluation rests on the Kalman filter.

18.2.4 Partially Observed Markov Models and State Space Models

A motivation to construct models that contain an unobservable (hidden) Markov component is the study of regime changes in dynamic models. Suppose the observations are indexed by the time period $i = 1, \dots, n$ and we are interested in a linear relation of the type

$$y_i = \alpha + \beta z_i + u_i,$$

but in which we wish to build in the variability of one of the parameters, β for example. Several specifications are possible.

- The *structural change models* suppose that β is constant only within groups of successive observations. To simplify, we assume that only two groups of data can be distinguished corresponding to $i \leq i_0$ and $i > i_0$. Then, we have the model

$$y_i = \alpha + \beta z_i + \gamma z_i \mathbb{I}(i > i_0) + u_i \tag{18.28}$$

where the coefficient of z_i is β for the first group of observations and $\beta + \gamma$ for the second group. The estimation of this model does not pose any specific problem if i_0 is known. In this case, α, β, and γ can be estimated by least squares. As we saw in Chapter 15, the asymptotic theory when i_0 is estimated is more delicate because one needs to assume that the numbers of observations before and after i_0 go to infinity.

- The *threshold models* assume that β varies according to the previous value of y. For example, we have

$$y_i = \alpha + \beta z_i + \gamma z_i \mathbb{I}(|y_{i-1} - y_0| > \varepsilon) + u_i. \tag{18.29}$$

Hence, the coefficient of z_i is β if y_{i-1} does not deviate too much from the level y_0, but is equal to $\beta + \gamma$ if y_{i-1} deviates from y_0 by more than ε. Even if u_i is a white noise, this model generates a nonlinear dynamic of y_i.

- We focus on a third type of model with multiple regimes defined by a dynamic latent variable:

$$y_i = \alpha + \beta z_i + \gamma z_i \zeta_i + u_i \tag{18.30}$$

where ζ_i is a Markov chain with two states 0 and 1 and transition probabilities defined by

$$\begin{cases} \text{Prob}\,(\zeta_i = 1 | \zeta_{i-1} = 1) = p \\ \text{Prob}\,(\zeta_i = 0 | \zeta_{i-1} = 0) = q. \end{cases}$$

Hence, the coefficient of z_i is β for the observations corresponding to zero ζ_i and $\beta + \gamma$ otherwise. This model is an example of the so-called *Markov-switching model* or *hidden Markov model*.

The variable ζ_i is not observable and our goal is to describe the distribution of $(y_1, \ldots, y_n)$ given $(z_1, \ldots, z_n)$. This model resembles a random-coefficient model but here the coefficients may take only two values and the regime change is dynamic by nature.

More generally, a model is said to be a hidden Markov model if it contains an unobservable Markov variable that, most often, drives the dynamic of the phenomenon. The previous errors-in-variables model is a special case of the hidden Markov model.

- An important class of partially observed Markov models is constituted by the *linear state space model* that can be described in the following manner.

We have an *observation equation* characterizing the relationship between y_i, z_i, and ζ_i that takes the form

$$y_i = Bz_i + C\zeta_i + u_i \tag{18.31}$$

with $y_i \in \mathbb{R}^p$, $z_i \in \mathbb{R}^q$, $\zeta_i \in \mathbb{R}^l$, $B : p \times q$, $C : p \times l$ and $E(u_i|z_i, \zeta_i) = 0$. In addition, the *state equation* describes the Markov dynamic of ζ_i:

$$\zeta_i = F\zeta_{i-1} + \varepsilon_i \tag{18.32}$$

where ε_i is independent of $\zeta_{i-1}, \zeta_{i-2} \ldots$ We often assume the normality and homoskedasticity of u_i and ζ_i as well as their independence.

This model is the simple version of the state space model that has experienced numerous generalizations (seasonality, nonlinearity, dependence, and so on).

18.3   Comparison Between Structural Model and Reduced Form

As previously defined, a structural model describes the generation of the observations $(y_i)_i$ conditionally on observations $(z_i)_i$ and a vector of unobservable variables $(\zeta_i)_i$. The structural feature means that the parameters are directly interpretable based on the economic theory that the statistical model formalizes. The reduced form associated with this model is obtained by integration with respect to the probability distribution of the unobservable variables and then becomes a model of the $(y_i)_i$ conditional on the $(z_i)_i$.

This model no longer reflects the underlying economic theory and its parameters mix the elements of the initial structural model and the generating process of ζ_i. However, it presents an interest to perform predictions. Indeed, knowing the distribution of the $(y_i)_i$ conditional on the $(z_i)_i$ and (ζ_i) is useless for prediction, because ζ_i is unknown and the aim of prediction is to determine y_i using only z_i. This remark is relevant if we are concerned with the prediction of new units (out-of-sample forecast). However, consider an observed individual i for which we wish to predict the endogenous variable y_i^* conditional on a change of z_i into z_i^* (in-sample prediction); then, the observed y_i becomes y_i^* that we predict. This prediction is done using the distribution of y_i^* given z_i^*, y_i and z_i and their parameters. Hence, we need to calculate

$$f\left(y_i^*|z_i^*, y_i, z_i\right) = \int \bar{f}\left(y_i^*|z_i^*, \zeta_i, \gamma, \beta\right) g\left(\zeta_i|y_i, z_i, \beta, \gamma\right) d\zeta_i$$

(see the remark at the end of the introduction of this chapter) and thus we use the structural specification.

However, the relevant features of the structural model can be fundamentally modified as a result of integrating the unobservables. An econometrician that would model directly the distribution of the (y_i) conditional on the (z_i) could exhibit phenomena that only result from the omission of the variables $(\zeta_i)_i$.

We talk then of *heterogeneity bias* or of *spurious* properties. An important theoretical and applied literature focuses on the study of these phenomena. To take a naive example, we can observe a correlation between variables (and hence conclude that there is causality between them) while this correlation comes from the fact that both variables are related to a third variable and that conditionally on this third variable, the two observed variables are independent from each other.

We can provide a different (but not contradictory) interpretation of the relevance of modeling with unobservable variables. The econometrician can analyze the relationship between the $(y_i)_i$ and the $(z_i)_i$ and provide a complex conditional model. Then, one tries to represent this complex model as the marginal model of a simpler model that includes more variables, some of them unobservable. The unobservable variable is then an artificial object built by the statistician and allowing an easy description of the model. If the observations are given by the grades of a student in diverse subjects, it is interesting to show that their correlations can be completely explained by the fact that they all depend on the same variable: conditionally to this variable, the grades become uncorrelated. This approach is obviously very popular in statistics (for example, all methods of factor analysis) but the "structural" interpretation essentially dominates econometrics.

We do not attempt a general theory of the relationships between the structural model and its reduced form, but illustrate the difference between their properties using three examples taken from those presented in the preceding section.

18.3.1 Duration Models with Heterogeneity and Spurious Dependence on the Duration

The main difference between a duration model with unobservable variables and its reduced form lies in the hazard function. More precisely, integrating out heterogeneity leads to the modification of the relationship between the hazard and the time spent in the state. In order to emphasize this change, we recall the relationship between the density in a structural model and the density of τ_i conditional on z_i

$$\bar{f}(t|z_i) = \int f(t|z_i, \zeta) g(\zeta|z_i) d\zeta \tag{18.33}$$

(to simplify the notation, we do not display the parameters). In an identical manner, the survival functions in both models satisfy

$$\bar{S}(\tau_i|z_i) = \int S(\tau_i|z_i, \zeta) g(\zeta|z_i) d\zeta. \tag{18.34}$$

The relationship between hazard functions is not as simple:

$$\bar{h}(t|z_i) = \frac{f(t|z_i)}{\bar{S}(t|z_i)} = \int \frac{f(t|z_i, \zeta)}{S(t|z_i, \zeta)} \frac{S(t|z_i, \zeta)}{\bar{S}(t|z_i)} g(\zeta|z_i) d\zeta$$

$$= \int h(t|z_i, \zeta) g(\zeta|\tau_i \geq t, z_i) d\zeta \qquad (18.35)$$

where, using Bayes theorem,

$$g(\zeta|\tau_i \geq t, z_i) = \frac{g(\zeta|z_i) S(t|\zeta, z_i)}{\bar{S}(t|z_i)}. \qquad (18.36)$$

We examine the difference between the functions $h(t|z_i, \zeta_i)$ and $\bar{h}(t|z_i)$. Recall that the hazard function describes the "probability" that the duration is in the interval $[t, t + dt]$ given that it is greater than t. The dependence of the function h on t then represents "wear" and "aging" phenomena. In the models regarding the unemployment duration, a decreasing h means that the probability to find a job diminishes with the length of the unemployment period.

The main result claims, intuitively speaking, that going from h to $\bar{h}$ "pulls" the function toward the horizontal axis. This phenomenon is illustrated in the following case. Suppose that $h(t|z_i, \zeta_i)$ is constant in t and equal to $h_0(z_i, \zeta_i)$. In other words, if we know all the characteristics of individual i, observable or not, the distribution of the duration is exponential. Of course, different individuals have different hazard rates h_0. Calculate the hazard conditional on the observable variables

$$\bar{h}(t|z_i) = \int h_0(z_i, \zeta) g(\zeta|\tau_i \geq t, z_i) d\zeta.$$

Then, we can show that

$$\frac{d}{dt}\bar{h}(t|z_i) \leq 0.$$

To simplify the calculation, we suppress the exogenous variables and assume that $h_0(z_i, \zeta) = \zeta > 0$. Then, we have $\tau|\zeta \sim Exp(\zeta)$, or

$$h(t) = \frac{\int \zeta e^{-\zeta t} g(\zeta) d\zeta}{\int e^{-\zeta t} g(\zeta) d\zeta}.$$

The condition $\frac{d}{dt}\bar{h}(t) \leq 0$ is equivalent to

$$-\left[\int \zeta^2 e^{-\zeta t} g(\zeta) d\zeta\right]\left[\int e^{-\zeta t} g(\zeta) d\zeta\right] + \left[\int \zeta e^{-\zeta t} g(\zeta) d\zeta\right]^2 \leq 0.$$

Setting

$$\bar{g}(\zeta) = \frac{e^{-\zeta t} g(\zeta)}{\int e^{-\zeta t} g(\zeta) d\zeta},$$

notice that $\bar{g}$ is a density and that the above expression becomes

$$\left[\int \varsigma^2 \bar{g}(\varsigma)\,d\varsigma\right] + \left[\int \varsigma g(\varsigma)\,d\varsigma\right]^2 \le 0,$$

which is always satisfied by Jensen's inequality.

This result can be intuitively interpreted in the following manner: the individuals for which $h_0(z_i, \varsigma_i)$ is the highest have the shortest duration of stay in the state and hence exit first. If we ignore the conditioning characteristics ς_i, we get the impression of observing a decreasing hazard function. Hence, a statistician, who neglects heterogeneity, would conclude that there is a negative dependence between the hazard and the duration, whereas he observes individuals with constant but different hazards.

18.3.2 Errors-in-Variables Model and Transformation of the Coefficients of the Linear Regression

Consider the errors-in-variables model in the form given in (18.22) or in (18.23). To simplify the argument, we limit our presentation to models without observable conditioning variable z_i, i.e., we set $\beta = 0$. The model takes the form

$$\binom{y_{i1}}{y_{i2}} \mid \varsigma_i \sim N\left[\binom{\gamma \varsigma_i}{\varsigma_i}, \Sigma\right] \quad \text{with} \quad \Sigma = \binom{\sigma_{11} \quad \sigma_{12}}{\sigma_{12} \quad \sigma_{22}}.$$

Assume that ς_i is i.i.d. $N(0, v)$. Then, the reduced form satisfies:

$$\binom{y_{i1}}{y_{i2}} \sim N\left[\binom{0}{0}, \binom{\sigma_{11} + \gamma^2 v \quad \sigma_{12} + \gamma v}{\sigma_{12} + \gamma v \quad \sigma_{22} + v}\right]. \tag{18.37}$$

To obtain this result, it suffices to note that the integration of ς_i preserves the normality and to calculate the moments.

The econometrician, who neglects the observation error in the variable y_{i2}, will then confuse y_{i2} for ς_i, and will think that he is estimating γ when calculating the coefficient of the linear regression of y_{i1} with respect to y_{i2}. From (18.37), we easily verify that this coefficient is actually equal to

$$\frac{\sigma_{12} + \gamma v}{\sigma_{22} + v},$$

which differs from γ, even if $\sigma_{12} = 0$.

Hence, not taking the unobservable variable into account modifies the coefficients of the linear regression which then lose their structural meaning.

18.3.3   Markov Models with Unobservable Variables and Spurious Dynamics of the Model

The hidden Markov model is often Markov conditionally on an unobservable component but its dynamics is more complex after integrating out this component. In particular, the Markov property disappears in general. To illustrate the transformation of the dynamics, consider the state space model characterized by (18.31) and (18.32). It follows from the first equation that

$$y_i - Fy_{i-1} = Bz_i - FBz_{i-1} + C\zeta_i - FC\zeta_{i-1} + u_i - Fu_{i-1}.$$

$$(18.38)$$

Suppose that F and C are such that $FC = CF$ (which is true, for example, in the scalar case or if $C = I$). Using the second equation, we infer that

$$y_i - Fy_{i-1} = Bz_i - FBz_{i-1} + C\varepsilon_i + u_i - Fu_{i-1}. \qquad (18.39)$$

The noise $C\varepsilon_i + u_i - Fu_{i-1}$ follows an $MA(1)$, as we can show by calculating its second moments. It admits a representation $\varepsilon_i - \Lambda\varepsilon_i$. Hence, we have

$$(1 - FL)y_i = Bz_i - FBz_{i-1} + (1 - \Lambda)\varepsilon_i, \qquad (18.40)$$

which characterizes a vector $ARMA(1, 1)$ conditional on the path of z_i. This process is not Markov and its dynamics is complex. However, the permutation assumption makes it relatively tractable.

In general, the process after integrating out ζ_i possesses a longer dynamics than conditional on the ζ_i. Another example of this situation is provided by the *stochastic volatility models* that are models where the variance is random and unobservable. For example, consider the equation

$$x_i = \sigma_i \varepsilon_i \qquad (18.41)$$

where ε_i is i.i.d. $N(0, 1)$. Conditional on $\sigma_i > 0$, x_i is therefore i.i.d. $N(0, \sigma_i^2)$. Assume now that $\ln \sigma_i$ is random and generated by an AR(1)

$$\ln \sigma_i = \rho \ln \sigma_{i-1} + \omega_i. \qquad (18.42)$$

Hence, the joint process (x_i, σ_i) is jointly Markov, but the marginal process of the x_i is no longer Markov. Indeed, we can verify that

$$E\left(x_i^2 x_{i-k}^2\right) \neq 0 \qquad \forall k.$$

Notice that in this special case, it is necessary to consider cross-moments of the squared of x_i since

$$E\left(x_i x_{i-k}\right) = 0 \qquad \forall k.$$

These examples illustrate one of the advantages of using unobservable variables. Indeed, they allow us to model long dynamics of the observable variables in a simpler way and in particular using only a small number of parameters.

18.4   Identification Problems

An important identification problem raised by the presence of unobservable variables is the following. From the parameters (possibly functionals) of the reduced model that described the generation of $y = (y_i)_i$ given $z = (z_i)_i$ we wish to determine the parameters of the structural model characterized by the distribution of the $(y_i)_i$ conditional on the $(z_i, \zeta_i)_i$ and the parameters of the distribution of $(\zeta_i)_i$. This problem is known in statistics as the *mixture* identification.

We limit ourselves to a structural model with likelihood function

$$\overline{f}(y_i | z_i, \zeta_i, \beta).$$

The density of the unobservables is denoted by $g(\zeta_i | z_i, \gamma)$ and hence depends on unknown elements γ (if ζ_i is i.i.d., γ could be the distribution of ζ_i). Then, the conditional distribution of y given z is given by

$$f(y_i | z_i, \beta, \gamma) = \int \overline{f}(y_i | z_i, \zeta_i, \beta) g(\zeta_i | z_i, \gamma) d\zeta_i. \tag{18.43}$$

To establish the identification of the model, one needs to verify that two different pairs (β, γ) and (β^*, γ^*) define two different conditional distributions.

There is no general answer to this question and it is easy to construct models that are not identified. The errors-in-variables model (18.37) is obviously not identified, because two vectors of parameters

$$(\sigma_{11}, \sigma_{22}, \sigma_{12}, \gamma, v) \quad \text{and} \quad (\sigma_{12}^*, \sigma_{22}^*, \sigma_{12}^*, \gamma^*, v^*)$$

are equivalent if

$$\begin{cases} \sigma_{11} + \gamma^2 v = \sigma_{11}^* + \gamma^{*2} v^* \\ \sigma_{12} + \gamma v = \sigma_{12}^* + \gamma^* v^* \\ \sigma_{22} + v = \sigma_{22}^* + v^*, \end{cases}$$

which does not imply their equality.

Another example of nonidentification is the following. Consider a duration τ generated by an exponential distribution of parameter $\lambda \zeta$ where ζ is an unobservable heterogeneity, itself exponential with parameter γ. We have

$$\overline{f}(t | \zeta, \lambda) = \lambda \zeta e^{-\lambda \zeta t} \, I\!\!I(t \geq 0)$$

and

$$g(\zeta | \gamma) = \gamma e^{-\gamma \zeta} \, I\!\!I(\zeta \geq 0).$$

Therefore,

$$f(t|\lambda, \gamma) = \left\{ \int_0^\infty \lambda \gamma \zeta e^{-(\lambda t + \gamma)\zeta} d\zeta \right\} \, \mathbb{I}(t \geq 0)$$

$$= \frac{\lambda \gamma}{(\lambda t + \gamma)^2} \, \mathbb{I}(t \geq 0),$$

thus, only the ratio λ/γ is identified. Identification can be obtained by setting $\gamma = 1$ or by introducing exogenous variables in the model. We can also use this example to illustrate the point made in Section 18.3.1. Indeed, it is easy to verify that the hazard function associated with the density $f(t|\lambda, \gamma)$ is equal to

$$h(t|\lambda, \gamma) = \frac{\lambda}{\lambda t + \gamma}$$

which is decreasing in t, while the hazard conditional on the unobservables is constant.

18.5   Estimation of Models with Unobservable Variables

There are many methods for estimating models with unobservable variables, usually built to deal with a specific model. Hence, it would be difficult and simplistic to summarize them all. In broad outline, we can group these methods into two categories.

1. In a set of models, it is possible to isolate a statistic $t(y)$ such that the distribution of $t(y)$ given z and the unobservables ζ does not depend on ζ but allows us to identify the parameters of interest to the model. The two elements are obviously contradictory: the "simpler" $t(y)$ is, the less likely it is to depend on ζ and to identify the parameters of interest.
2. A second class of methods considers the set of observations y and estimates the parameters from the likelihood or moment conditions that then take the form of integrals. The evaluation of these integrals raises two problems: first the dependence on the parameters, problem that can be simplified by using recursive methods (EM algorithm, Kalman filter) and second the actual computation of the integral that can be treated using simulation techniques.

We illustrate these different approaches by examples.

18.5.1   Estimation Using a Statistic Independent of the Unobservables

The general principle of these methods is to estimate the parameters of interest without integrating out the unobservable variables. The advantage is to avoid complicated calculations and to allow us to be robust with respect to the distribution of the unobservables. These methods are not always applicable and are in general only possible if several observations related to the same realization of the unobservable variable are available. This is the case in the linear panel model with random individual effect defined by Model (18.5), i.e.,

$$y_{it} = z'_{it}\beta + \zeta_i + u_{it}. \tag{18.44}$$

One can estimate β (except for the constant term if the model contains one) by replacing the variables by their difference with their time average. Indeed, Equation (18.44) implies

$$y_{it} - \overline{y}_i = (z_{it} - \overline{z}_i)' \beta + u_{it} - \overline{u}_i \tag{18.45}$$

where

$$\overline{y}_i = \frac{1}{T}\sum_{t-1}^{T} y_{it}, \quad \overline{z}_i = \frac{1}{T}\sum_{t=1}^{T} z_{it}, \quad \overline{u}_i = \frac{1}{T}\sum_{t=1}^{T} u_{it}.$$

Equation (18.45) identifies the elements of the vector β except for the constant that vanishes. Then, Equation (18.45) is estimated by generalized least-squares. We note that for $v_{it} = u_{it} - \overline{u}_i$, we have

$$\begin{pmatrix} v_{11} \\ \vdots \\ v_{1T} \\ \vdots \\ v_{n1} \\ \vdots \\ v_{nT} \end{pmatrix} = \left[I_N \otimes \left(I_T - \frac{J_T}{T} \right) \right] \begin{pmatrix} u_{11} \\ \vdots \\ u_{1T} \\ \vdots \\ u_{n1} \\ \vdots \\ u_{nT} \end{pmatrix}$$

where J_T is the $T \times T$ matrix of ones and $I_T - \frac{J_T}{T}$ transforms a vector of T components into their demeaned counterparts. Denote

$$W = I_N \otimes \left(I_T - \frac{J_T}{T} \right)$$

and let v and u be the vectors of the v_{it} and the u_{it}, then it follows that

$$Var(v) = W (Var(u)) W' = \sigma^2 W W' = \sigma^2 W,$$

assuming that the u_{it} are homoskedastic and independent (i.e., the error term is not dynamic). Moreover, W is idempotent and symmetric ($W = WW = WW'$). The matrix W is not invertible and we denote by W^+ its generalized inverse.

Denoting by y the vector of the y_{it} and by Z the matrix whose columns are the explanatory variables, the GLS estimator of β is

$$\hat{\beta} = \left(Z'W^+Z\right)^{-1}Z'W^+y. \tag{18.46}$$

This estimator is called *within* estimator.

18.5.2   Maximum Likelihood Estimation: EM Algorithm and Kalman Filter

The objective function to maximize is

$$\ln l\,(y|z, \beta, \gamma) = \ln \int \bar{l}\,(y|z, \varsigma, \beta)g\,(\varsigma|z, \gamma)\,d\varsigma \tag{18.47}$$

where g is the density of the unobservables conditional on the exogenous variables.

1. A first method consists in numerically evaluating the integral. For this, we refer to Section 6.3.
2. A second method called EM algorithm (E for expectation and M for maximization) rests on the following calculations. Define $\bar{g}$ by

$$\bar{l}\,(y|z, \varsigma, \beta)g\,(\varsigma|z, \gamma) = l\,(y|z, \beta, \gamma)\bar{g}\,(\varsigma|y, z, \beta, \gamma). \tag{18.48}$$

Hence, $\bar{g}$ is the joint posterior distribution of the unobservables, i.e., after observing the y and conditional on the exogenous variables and the parameters. We see that if $\theta = (\beta, \gamma)$,

$$\frac{\partial}{\partial\theta}\ln l\,(y|z, \theta) = 0$$

$$\Leftrightarrow \int \left[\frac{\partial}{\partial\theta}\ln\{\bar{l}\,(y|z, \varsigma, \beta)g\,(\varsigma|z, \gamma)\}\right]\bar{g}\,(\varsigma|y, z, \beta, \gamma)\,d\varsigma = 0. \tag{18.49}$$

Indeed

$$\frac{\partial}{\partial\theta}\ln\{\bar{l}\,(y|z, \varsigma, \beta)g\,(\varsigma|z, \gamma)\}$$

$$= \frac{\partial}{\partial\theta}\ln l\,(y|z, \varsigma, \beta) + \frac{\partial}{\partial\theta}\ln\bar{g}\,(\varsigma|y, z, \beta, \gamma)$$

and hence

$$\int \left[\frac{\partial}{\partial\theta}\ln\{\bar{l}\,(y|z, \varsigma, \beta)g\,(\varsigma|z, \gamma)\}\right]\bar{g}\,(\varsigma|y, z, \beta, \gamma)\,d\varsigma$$

$$= \frac{\partial}{\partial\theta}\ln l\,(y|z, \varsigma, \beta)\int \bar{g}\,(\varsigma|y, z, \beta, \gamma)\,d\varsigma$$

$$+ \int \frac{\partial}{\partial\theta}\ln\bar{g}\,(\varsigma|y, z, \beta, \gamma)\bar{g}\,(\varsigma|y, z, \beta, \gamma)\,d\varsigma$$

and

$$\int \overline{g}(\zeta|y, z, \beta, \gamma) d\zeta = 1$$

and

$$\int \frac{\partial}{\partial \theta} \ln \overline{g}(\zeta|y, z, \beta, \gamma) \overline{g}(\zeta|y, z, \beta, \gamma) d\zeta$$

$$= \frac{\partial}{\partial \theta} \int \overline{g}(\zeta|y, z, \beta, \gamma) d\zeta = 0.$$

Condition (18.49) can be implemented as the limit of an algorithm that alternates the following steps:

- Fixing β and γ equal to some values β_0 and γ_0, we maximize

$$\int \{\ln \overline{l}(y|z, \zeta, \beta) g(\zeta|z, \gamma)\} \overline{g}(\zeta|y, z, \beta_0, \gamma_0) d\zeta,$$

which is equivalent to maximizing

$$\int \{\ln \overline{l}(y|z, \zeta, \beta)\} \overline{g}(\zeta|y, z, \beta_0, \gamma_0) d\zeta$$

in β and

$$\int \{\ln g(\zeta|z, \gamma)\} \overline{g}(\zeta|y, z, \beta_0, \gamma_0) d\zeta$$

in γ.
- We replace β_0 and γ_0 by the values that we previously obtained.

Under appropriate regularity assumptions, this algorithm converges to the MLE based on the observable data.

3. A third method for computing the likelihood of observable variables adapted to dynamic models is the Kalman filter. Consider the model defined by Equations (18.31) and (18.32) where we assume that the vectors are normally distributed and the two residuals are innovations. Our goal is to maximize the likelihood of y_i factorized as the product of the conditional likelihood given the past (18.47). The distribution of y_i conditional on $H_i = (y_{i-1}, y_{i-2}, \dots, z_i, z_{i-1}, \dots)$ is normal with expectation and variance respectively equal to

$$Bz_i + CE(\zeta_i|H_i) \quad \text{and} \quad \Sigma + CVar(\zeta_i|H_i)C'.$$

For a fixed value of the parameters, the Kalman filter provides a sequential algorithm to compute $E(\zeta_i|H_i)$ and $Var(\zeta_i|H_i)$. We proceed in the following manner. Given that the joint distribution of the set of variables is normal, we use the general formula

$$E(a|b, c) = E(a|c) + Cov(a, b|c) Var(b|c)^{-1}(b - E(b|c)).$$

Here, $a = \zeta_i$, $b = y_{i-1}$, $c = H_{i-1}$ (hence $(b, c) = H_i$). Thus,

$$E(\zeta_i|H_i) = E(\zeta_i|H_{i-1}) + Cov(\zeta_i, y_{i-1}|H_{i-1})$$
$$\times Var(y_{i-1}|H_{i-1})^{-1}(y_{i-1} - E(y_{i-1}|H_{i-1})).$$

For simplicity, the exogenous variables have been eliminated from the calculation, the path of the z is included in H_i and y_{i-1} is replaced by

$$y_{i-1} - Bz_{i-1}.$$

Moreover, we have

$$E(\zeta_i|H_{i-1}) = FE(\zeta_{i-1}|H_{i-1}),$$

$$E(y_{i-1}|H_{i-1}) = CE(\zeta_{i-1}|H_{i-1}),$$

$$Var(y_{i-1}|H_{i-1}) = CVar(\zeta_{i-1}|H_{i-1})C' + \Sigma$$

and

$$Cov(\zeta_i, y_{i-1}|H_{i-1}) = FVar(\zeta_{i-1}|H_{i-1})C'.$$

These results obviously use the properties of the residuals of Equations (18.31) and (18.32). Hence

$$E(\zeta_i|H_i) = FE(\zeta_{i-1}|H_{i-1}) + FVar(\zeta_{i-1}|H_{i-1})C'$$
$$\times \left[CVar(\zeta_{i-1}|H_{i-1})C' + \Sigma\right]^{-1} \qquad (18.50)$$
$$\times (y_{i-1} - CE(\zeta_{i-1}|H_{i-1})).$$

In addition, we know that

$$Var(a|b, c) = Var(a|c) - Cov(a, b|c)Var(b|c)^{-1}Cov(b, a|c),$$

and hence

$$Var(\zeta_i|H_i) = Var(\zeta_i|H_{i-1}) - Cov(\zeta_i, y_{i-1}|H_{i-1})$$
$$\times Var(y_{i-1}|H_{i-1})^{-1}Cov(y_{i-1}, \zeta_i|H_{i-1}).$$

Moreover

$$Var(\zeta_i|H_{i-1}) = FVar(\zeta_{i-1}|H_{i-1})F' + Q$$

where $Q = Var(\varepsilon_i)$, hence

$$Var(y_{i-1}|H_{i-1}) = Var(C\zeta_{i-1} + u_{i-1}|H_{i-1})$$
$$= CVar(\zeta_{i-1}|H_{i-1})C' + \Sigma$$

and

$$Cov\,(\zeta_i, y_{i-1}|H_{i-1}) = Cov\,(F\zeta_{i-1} + \varepsilon_i, C\zeta_{i-1} + u_{i-1}|H_{i-1})$$
$$= F\,Var\,(\zeta_{i-1}|H_{i-1})\,C'.$$

Thus

$$Var\,(\zeta_i|H_i) = F\,Var\,(\zeta_{i-1}|H_{i-1})\,F' + Q - F\,Var\,(\zeta_{i-1}|H_{i-1})\,C'$$
$$\times \left[C\,Var\,(\zeta_{i-1}|H_{i-1})\,C' + \Sigma\right]^{-1} C\,Var\,(\zeta_{i-1}|H_{i-1})\,F'.$$
$$(18.51)$$

Formulas (18.50) and (18.51) provide a recursive algorithm to compute $E\,(\zeta_i|H_i)$ and $Var\,(\zeta_i|H_i)$. This algorithm is initialized by

$$E\,(\zeta_1|H_1) = E\,(\zeta_1) \quad \text{and} \quad Var\,(\zeta_1|H_1) = Var\,(\zeta_1).$$

These initial conditions may be considered to be known or generated by the stationary distribution of ζ_i if this assumption is acceptable.

This calculation method also applies to nonlinear models. Consider, for example, the Markov-switching model described by (18.30). Our goal is to maximize

$$E\,(\ln l\,(y|z, \beta, \gamma)).$$

Using the argument of the EM algorithm, we know that this objective is attained by solving

$$E\left[\frac{\partial}{\partial \theta}\,\{\ln \bar{l}\,(y|z, \zeta, \beta)\,g\,(\zeta|z, \gamma)\}\,|y, z, \beta, \gamma\right] = 0.$$

For a given initial value of β and γ $(\beta^0$ and $\gamma^0)$, we estimate β by maximizing

$$E\left[\ln \bar{l}\,(y|z, \zeta, \beta)\,|y, z, \beta^0, \gamma^0\right]$$

and γ by maximizing

$$E\left[\ln g\,(\zeta|z, \gamma)\,|y, z, \beta^0, \gamma^0\right]$$

which yields a value (β^1, γ^1). This algorithm is iterated until it converges.

Consider the first maximization. If y_i is normal with variance σ^2 conditional on z_i and ζ_i, then we have

$$\ln \bar{l}\,(y|z, \zeta, \beta) = \sum_{i=1}^{n} (y_i - (\alpha + \beta z_i + \gamma z_i \zeta_i))^2$$

(assuming, for simplicity, that σ^2 is known), and thus

$$E\left[\ln \bar{l}\left(y|z, \zeta, \beta\right)|y, z, \beta^0, \gamma^0\right]$$

$$= \sum_{\zeta}\left\{\sum_{i=1}^{n}\left(y_i - (\alpha + \beta z_i + \gamma z_i \zeta_i)\right)^2\right\} g\left(\zeta|y, z, \gamma^0, \beta^0\right).$$

In our case, $g\left(\zeta|z, \gamma\right)$ represents the joint probability of a sequence $\zeta_1, \ldots, \zeta_n$ given the complete path $y_1, \ldots, y_n, z_1, \ldots, z_n$ for the parameter values β^0 and γ^0. The first order condition is

$$\sum_{\zeta}\left\{\sum_{i=1}^{n}\left(y_i - (\alpha + \beta z_i + \gamma z_i \zeta_i)\right)\begin{pmatrix} 1 \\ z_i \\ z_i \zeta_i \end{pmatrix}\right\} g\left(\zeta|y, z, \gamma^0, \beta^0\right) = 0.$$

We can factorize $g(\zeta|y, z, \gamma^0, \beta^0)$ into

$$g\left(\zeta_i|y, z, \gamma^0, \beta^0\right) g\left(\zeta_{-i}|\zeta_i, y, z, \gamma^0, \beta^0\right)$$

where ζ_{-i} represents the components of the vector ζ different from i. We know that

$$\sum_{\zeta_{-i}} g\left(\zeta_{-i}|\zeta_i, y, z, \gamma^0, \beta^0\right) = 1$$

and, thus, the first order condition leads back to

$$\sum_{i=1}^{n}\left(y_i - (\alpha + \beta z_i)\right)\begin{pmatrix} 1 \\ z_i \\ 0 \end{pmatrix} g\left(\zeta_i = 0|y, z, \gamma^0, \beta^0\right)$$

$$+ \sum_{i=1}^{n}\left(y_i - (\alpha + (\beta + \gamma) z_i)\right)\begin{pmatrix} 1 \\ z_i \\ z_i \end{pmatrix} g\left(\zeta_i = 1|y, z, \gamma^0, \beta^0\right) = 0$$

with

$$g\left(\zeta_i = 0|y, z, \gamma^0, \beta^0\right) + g\left(\zeta_i = 1|y, z, \gamma^0, \beta^0\right) = 1.$$

If $\alpha = 0$ and $\delta = \beta + \gamma$, we can show that β and δ are solutions of

$$\begin{cases} \sum_{i=1}^{n}\left(y_i - \beta z_i\right) z_i g_0 = 0 \\ \sum_{i=1}^{n}\left(y_i - \delta z_i\right) z_i g_1 = 0. \end{cases}$$

To implement this method, we have to be able to calculate

$$g(\zeta_i = 1|y, z, \gamma, \beta) = E(\zeta_i|y, z, \gamma, \beta)$$

for all parameter values. To do this, an algorithm of the Kalman filter type is used.

18.5.3 Estimation by Integrated Moments

Consider the i.i.d. model presented in the introduction that satisfies the moment condition (18.2). We transform it into a marginal moment condition:

$$E^\theta(\rho(y_i, z_i, \zeta_i, \lambda)) = 0, \tag{18.52}$$

where $\lambda = (\beta, \gamma)$ and θ is the true value of these parameters. Condition (18.52) is derived from (18.2) by multiplying $\bar{\psi}$ by an appropriately chosen function of z_i and ζ_i, and possibly of the parameters.

Condition (18.52) can be rewritten as

$$E^\theta\left(\int \rho(y_i, z_i, \zeta_i, \lambda) g(\zeta_i|y_i, z_i, \lambda) d\zeta_i\right) = 0, \tag{18.53}$$

which immediately gives rise to a generalization of the EM algorithm. Suppose the number of moment conditions is equal to the dimension of λ. Fixing λ at λ_0, we solve

$$\sum_{i=1}^n \int \rho(y_i, z_i, \zeta_i, \lambda) g(\zeta_i|y_i, z_i, \lambda_0) d\zeta_i = 0 \tag{18.54}$$

and we replace λ_0 by the value just obtained until the procedure converges. If the number of moment conditions is larger than the dimension of λ, then solving (18.54) is replaced by minimizing the usual quadratic form in λ and the iterative procedure between λ and λ_0 remains the same.

This procedure assumes that it is feasible to analytically calculate the integral of the form (18.53). If this is not possible, then the integral can be replaced by a Monte-Carlo approximation analogous to that presented in Section 6.3.1 of Chapter 6. If it is easy to simulate data from the density $g(\zeta_i|y_i, z_i, \lambda)$, then we can use this distribution as *importance function* and solve the following expression for λ:

$$\frac{1}{n}\sum_{i=1}^n \frac{1}{N}\sum_{e=1}^N \rho(y_i, z_i, \zeta_{ie}, \lambda) = 0, \tag{18.55}$$

where the ζ_{ie} are i.i.d. with density $g(\zeta_i|y_i, z_i, \lambda_0)$. Even though it is natural, the choice of g as importance function is not necessary, we can choose other distributions in order to simplify the simulation. In this case, we solve

$$\frac{1}{n}\sum_{i=1}^n \frac{1}{N}\sum_{e=1}^N \frac{\rho(y_i, z_i, \zeta_{ie}, \lambda) g(\zeta_{ie}|y_i, z_i, \lambda_0)}{f_{y_i, z_i, \lambda_0}(\zeta_{ie})} = 0 \tag{18.56}$$

where the ζ_{ie} are an i.i.d. sample of f_{y_i,z_i,λ_0} (see Section 6.3.2 for a discussion of the choice of the importance function). In the case where the number of moment conditions is larger than the dimension of λ, Equations (18.55) or (18.56) are replaced by minimizations. In both cases of the procedure, λ_0 is replaced by the computed value of λ.

18.6   Counterfactuals and Treatment Effects

The econometrics literature has recently been enriched by the inclusion of models with treatment effects coming from medical experiments. These models found a natural application in the empirical analysis of the effectiveness of public policies. The central idea of these models is the description of the effects on an individual of all possible levels of a treatment, even if, for each individual, only one particular treatment level is observed. The important part of the effect is therefore unobservable (the counterfactuals), which justifies the inclusion of these models in this chapter, even if a first presentation appeared in Chapter 11.

The models with treatment effects have a range that is much larger than the analysis of public policies. They allow us to better understand the structural approach, in particular a discussion of causality that is more satisfying than the viewpoint adopted in time-series analysis.

We define a model with treatment effect by the following three steps.

1.   The distribution of the counterfactuals. We consider three variables (for simplicity, we suppress the index i for an individual):
  - $d \in D$, a nonrandom index describing the level of the treatment. In a simple case, $d \in \{0, 1\}$ (nontreated, treated (see 11.2.5)), but d can also describe the dosage of the treatment, the number of years of schooling, and so on.
  - a random vector $\tilde{z}$ representing the observable characteristics of the individual,
  - a sequence $(\tilde{y}_d)_{d \in D}$ of random variables representing the outcome of the treatment ($=$ counterfactual) for all values of d; indeed, if d is a continuous index, then $(\tilde{y}_d)_{d \in D}$ is a random process indexed by d, the random variable $\tilde{y}_d$ may be discrete (finding an employment or not) or continuous (the level of the salary).

  The model of counterfactuals specify the distribution of the process $(\tilde{y}_d)_d$ given $\tilde{z}$, as a function of (possibly functional) parameters. Thus it specifies for example the distribution of the salary levels for all levels of education. This concerns the joint distribution of the $(\tilde{y}_d)_d$ and not the distribution conditional on d. Thus in the case where $d \in \{0, 1\}$, we specify the joint distribution of $(\tilde{y}_0, \tilde{y}_1)$ conditional on $\tilde{z}$.

  In many models, we are principally only interested in the expectation

$$E(\tilde{y}_d | \tilde{z} = z) = \varphi_d(z)$$

which is then the average level of the effect of treatment d for an individual with characteristics z. The parameter of interest is in the discrete case

$$\varphi_1(z) - \varphi_0(z)$$

and in the continuous case

$$\frac{\partial}{\partial d}\varphi_d(z).$$

This parameter is called the *Average Treatment Effect* (ATE). It obviously poses identification problems, but it exactly measures the treatment effect independently of all selection problems.

2. The second element of the model is the mechanism that assigns the treatment level. We define a random variable $\tilde{d}$ which is generated conditionally on z. In fact, the model specifies the joint distribution of $\left((\tilde{y}_d)_d, \tilde{d}\right)$ given $\tilde{z}$. We will see that, in practice, identification requires exclusion restrictions on the exogenous variables.

If $D = \{0, 1\}$, and thus $\tilde{d}$ is a binary random variable, then the distribution is characterized by

$$\Pr\left(\tilde{d} = 1|z\right) = p(z).$$

This value is called the *propensity score*. More generally, we denote by $p(z)$ the conditional expectation of $\tilde{d}$ given z. The model of the counterfactuals and the assignment (or selection) model can be jointly written as

$$\begin{cases} \tilde{y}_d = \varphi_d(z) + \tilde{u}_d \\ \tilde{d} = p(z) + \tilde{v}. \end{cases}$$

In this new model, we can consider expressions such as

$$E\left(\tilde{y}_{d_1}|\tilde{d} = d_2, \tilde{z} = z\right)$$

from which we derive in particular, if d is continuous:

$$\frac{\partial}{\partial d_1}E\left(\tilde{y}_{d_1}|\tilde{d} = d_2, \tilde{z} = z\right)_{d_1=d_2=d},$$

which is called the marginal effect of the *treatment on the treated* (TT). In the discrete case, we consider

$$E\left(\tilde{y}_1 - \tilde{y}_0|\tilde{d} = 0, \tilde{z} = z\right)$$

and

$$E\left(\tilde{y}_1 - \tilde{y}_0|\tilde{d} = 1, \tilde{z} = z\right).$$

The dependence of the process of the counterfactuals $\tilde{y}_d$ and the assignment of the treatment $\tilde{d}$ is the source of the selection bias (if the treatment is allocated to the individuals for which one thinks it will be the most effective). An assignment is a randomization if

$$(\tilde{y}_d)_d \perp\!\!\!\perp \tilde{d} | \tilde{z},$$

i.e., the choice of the treatment is independent of the latent results (conditionally on $\tilde{z}$). This property is realized in particular if $\tilde{d}$ is generated by a random draw of the treated and the nontreated groups in the case where $D = \{0, 1\}$. In practice, this assumption rarely holds in econometrics, it is rarely true even in clinical trials because it assumes that the patient ignores whether he is treated or not, which is impossible in cases with serious illnesses.

3. The third level of the model is made up of the observation equations. For an individual, we observe $\tilde{y}_d$ only at the level $\tilde{d} = d$, i.e., $\tilde{y}_{\tilde{d}}$. This approach is identical to the one where a random process is observed only at a random time. Denoting the random variable $\tilde{y}_{\tilde{d}}$ by $\tilde{y}$, we then have the model

$$\begin{cases} \tilde{y} = \varphi_{\tilde{d}}(z) + \tilde{u}_d \\ \tilde{d} = p(z) + \tilde{v} \end{cases}$$

for the realization $\tilde{z} = z$.

This model poses problems of identification and of estimation. It is clearly not identified (the parameter of interest $\frac{\partial \varphi}{\partial d}$ is not identified by the observation model) without specific assumptions, notably the exclusion restrictions on the exogenous variables in the equation of the counterfactuals and the assignment equation.

The simple case that eliminates the selection bias is the case of randomization. In this case, we can show that

$$\varphi_d(z) = E\left(\tilde{y}_{\tilde{d}} | \tilde{d} = d, \tilde{z} = z\right).$$

In the discrete case, $\varphi_1(z)$ is the expectation for the treated individuals conditional on z and $\varphi_0(z)$ is the conditional expectation for the nontreated individuals given z. These two functions can be estimated nonparametrically, and we are interested in

$$\varphi_1(z) - \varphi_0(z)$$

obtained by imposing the same value of z in both functions. This technique is called *matching*. The usual practice of matching consists of comparing the observed result y_{1i} of a treated ($\tilde{d} = 1$) individual i with a nonparametric estimate $\varphi_0(z_i)$ of the regression of the nontreated on z evaluated at the point z_i which describes the characteristics of individual i.

A classical problem is the one of the dimensionality of z. In order to treat this difficulty, we construct models where the dependence of the outcome on z is entirely described by the probability $p(z)$ of being treated:

$$E\left(y_{\tilde{d}}|z\right) = E\left(y_{\tilde{d}}|p(z)\right).$$

Thus, we first estimate (parametrically) $p(z)$ and then regress (nonparametrically) y_0 and y_1 on $p(z)$.

Even though often employed, this method of matching is not satisfactory in the presence of a selection bias, in this case the model has an identification problem. Consider the discrete example $d \in \{0, 1\}$, the observed model is the following, after replacing the random variables by their realizations and setting $\varepsilon_0 = u_0$ and $\varepsilon_1 = u_1 - u_0$:

$$d = p(z) + v$$

$$y = (1 - d)\varphi_0(z) + d\varphi_1(z) + d\varepsilon_1 + \varepsilon_0.$$

Indeed, the model of the counterfactuals can be written as

$$y_0 = \varphi_0(z) + u_0 \quad \text{and} \quad y_1 = \varphi_1(z) + u_1.$$

If y is the observed value ($y - y_0$ if $d = 0$ and $y = y_1$ if $d = 1$), then

$$y = (1 - d)y_0 + dy_1$$

$$= (1 - d)\varphi_0 + d\varphi_1 + d(u_1 - u_0) + u_0.$$

The model generating d is identified ($p(z)$ is identified). The data identifies

$$E(y|d, z) = (1 - d)\varphi_0(z) + d\varphi_1(z) + dr_1(d, z) + r_0(d, z)$$

where $r_1(d, z) = E(\varepsilon_1|d, z)$ and $r_0(d, z) = E(\varepsilon_0|d, z)$. Knowing $E(y|d, z)$ does not allow us to identify for example $\varphi_1(z) - \varphi_0(z)$, even with exclusion restrictions in φ_0 and φ_1. Several assumptions can be made that imply identification.

An extension of the assumption of instrumental variables. Suppose $z = (z^*, w)$ such that

$$\varphi_0(z) = \varphi_0(z^*) \quad \text{and} \quad \varphi_1(z) = \varphi_1(z^*);$$

suppose moreover that

$$E(\varepsilon_0|z) = 0 \quad \text{and} \quad E(d\varepsilon_1|z) = 0.$$

Then

$$E(y|z) = \left[\varphi_0(z^*) - \varphi_1(z^*)\right] E(d|z) + \varphi_0(z). \tag{18.57}$$

Under regularity conditions of the same nature as those considered in 18.5.4, this equation has at least one solution in $\varphi_0(z^*)$ and $\varphi_1(z^*)$. We consider an example for identification: if w_1 is a continuous component of w, and let (φ_0, φ_1) and (ψ_0, ψ_1) be two parameter values, then

$$\left\{\left[\varphi_0(z^*) - \psi_0(z^*)\right] - \left[\varphi_1(z^*) - \psi_1(z^*)\right]\right\} E(d|z)$$
$$+ \left[\varphi_0(z^*) - \psi_0(z^*)\right] = 0.$$

Taking derivatives with respect to w and assuming

$$\frac{\partial}{\partial w} E(d|z) \neq 0,$$

then we obtain the equality

$$[\varphi_0 - \psi_0] - [\varphi_1 - \psi_1] = 0,$$

where $\varphi_0 - \psi_0 = \varphi_1 - \psi_1$ and thus, it follows from (18.57) that $\varphi_0 = \psi_0$ and $\varphi_1 = \psi_1$. This approach allows us to nonparametrically estimate φ_0 and φ_1 replacing $E(y|z)$ and $E(d|z)$ in (18.57) by their kernel estimates and by solving the equation thus obtained. To get around the overidentification problem, we derive from (18.57) the equation

$$E(E(y|z)|d, z^*) = \left\{\varphi_0(z^*) - \varphi_1(z^*)\right\} E(E(d|z)|d, z^*) + \varphi_1(z^*),$$

which admits a unique solution in φ_0 and φ_1 after replacing the conditional expectations by their kernel estimates. In practice, setting $d = 0$ and $d = 1$ yields two equations that we solve in φ_0 and φ_1 (see Florens and Malavolti (2003) for the properties).

A different approach rests on the assumption of control functions. Suppose

$$\begin{cases} r_1(d, z) = r_1^*(d - p(z), z^*) \\ r_0(d, z) = r_0^*(d - p(z), z^*); \end{cases}$$

then we can show that, under quite general regularity conditions, the equation

$$E(y|d, z) = (1 - d)\varphi_0(z^*) + d\varphi_1(z^*) + dr_1^*(d - p(z), z^*)$$
$$+ r_0^*(d - p(z), z^*)$$

admits at most one solution, up to normalization. The model that generates y given d and z is thus an extension of the additive model for which the estimation is treated in Florens et al. (2003). This approach generalizes to the case where d is continuous (see Florens et al. (2003)).

We emphasize again the relevance of the treatment effects models to the model builder by raising two important questions.

We say that d does not cause the outcome variable (in expectation) if

$$\frac{\partial \varphi}{\partial d}(z) = 0.$$

This definition makes sense since d is not a random variable but deterministic and can be controlled by the experimenter. The definition of noncausality in terms of control (see Pearl (2000)) can thus also be used in an econometric context.

Macroeconomic modeling regularly runs up against the status of political and economic variables for which one would like to assume exogeneity, to the extent that they are deterministic, but that are endogenous because they depend on the view of the economy that the decision makers have. In the context of the treatment effects models, the political and economic variables are naturally the (deterministic) treatment index for which only one particular realization is observed. This viewpoint requires a dynamic extension of the models of treatment effects (see Florens and Heckman (2001)). This extension provides specifically a relation between Granger causality and the one previously defined.

Notes

The modeling of unobservable variables, that are intended to describe individual unobserved heterogeneity in microeconometrics or latent dynamics in macroeconometrics and finance, is a major element of modern econometrics. An exhaustive bibliography is therefore impossible to achieve. Nevertheless, we provide some references on some of the topics of this chapter:

- the analysis of panel data is presented in a detailed manner in the collective book edited by Matyas and Sevestre (2004) and in Sevestre (2002),
- heterogeneity in duration models is presented for example in Lancaster (1990) and Heckman and Singer (1984), for identification see in particular Elbers and Ridder (1982),
- the presentation of the errors-in-variables models is very complete in Malinvaud (1980), one important reference concerning the identification is Reiersol (1950a and 1950b),
- for hidden Markov models, see Hamilton (1989),
- the EM algorithm has been introduced by Dempster, Laird, and Rubin (1977) and has been the subject of many articles since then,
- the model of treatment effects (counterfactuals) generalizes the analysis of the Roy model presented by Heckman and Honoré (1990), the study of noncausality in these models is inspired by the recent work in Florens and Heckman (2001).

Bibliography

[1] AAKVIK H., HECKMAN J.J., VYTLACIL E.J. (1998). Local instrumental variables and latent variable models for estimating treatment effects. Working paper, University of Chicago.

[2] AI C. (1997). A semiparametric likelihood estimator. *Econometrica*, 65, 933–963.

[3] AHN S.K. (1993). Some tests for unit root in autoregressive-integrated-moving average model with deterministic trends. *Biometrika*, 80, 855–868.

[4] AHN B. C., CHOI I. (1999). Testing the null of stationarity for multiple time series. *Journal of Econometrics*, 88, 41–77.

[5] AKAIKE H. (1970). Statistical predictor identification. *Annals of the Institute of Statistical Mathematics*, 22, 203–217.

[6] AKAIKE H. (1973) *Information theory and an extension of the maximum likelihood principle*. In PETROV B.N. and CSAKI F. (Eds.). Second international symposium on information theory, Budapest (pp. 267–281), Akademia Kiado.

[7] AKAIKE H. (1974). A new look at the statistical model identification. *IEEE Transactions on Automatic Control*, AC-19, 716–723.

[8] AMEMIYA T. (1974a). A note on a Fair and Jaffee model. *Econometrica*, 42, 759–762.

[9] AMEMIYA T. (1974b). The non-linear two-stage least squares estimator. *Journal of Econometrics*, 2, 105–110.

[10] ANDERSON S.A., BRONS H.K., JENSEN S.T. (1983). Distributions of eigenvalues in multivariate statistical analysis. *Annals of Statistics*, 11, 392–415.

[11] ANDREWS D.W.K. (1993). Tests for parameter instability and structural change point. *Econometrica*, 61, 821–856.

[12] ANDREWS D.W.K. (1994). Empirical process methods in econometrics. In ENGLE R.F. and MCFADDEN D.L. (Eds.). *Handbook of Econometrics*, Vol. 4 (pp. 2247–2294), North Holland, Amsterdam.

[13] BAILLIE R.T., BOLLERSLEV T. (1989). The message in daily exchange rates: a conditional variance tale. *Journal of Business and Economic Statistics*, 7, 297–305.

[14] BAILLIE R.T., BOLLERSLEV T. (1990). A multivariate generalized ARCH approach to modeling risk premia in forward foreign exchange rate markets. *Journal of International Money and Finance*, 9, 309–324.

[15] BAILLIE R.T., MYERS R.T. (1991). Bivariate GARCH estimation of optimal commodity future hedge. *Journal of Applied Econometrics*, 16, 109–124.

[16] BAILLIE R.T., OSTERBERG W.P. (1993). Central bank intervention and risk in the forward premium. *Econometrics and Economic Theory Papers* 9109, Department of Economics, Michigan State University, East Lansing.

[17] BALTAGI B.H. (2001). *Econometrics analysis of panel data*. John Wiley & Sons, Chichester.

[18] BALTAGI B.H., KAO C. (2000). Non stationary panels, cointegration in panels and dynamic panels: a survey. In B.H. BALTAGI, T.B. FOMBY and R.C. HILLS (Eds.). *Nonstationary panels, panel cointegration and dynamics panels, Advances in econometrics*, Vol. 15, Elsevier.

[19] BANERJEE A. (1999). Panel data unit roots and cointegration: an overview. *Oxford Bulletin of Economics and Statistics*, 61, 607–629.

[20] BARBE P., BERTAIL P. (1994). *The weighted bootstrap*. Lectures Notes in Statistics, 98, Springer-Verlag, New York.

[21] BARRA J.R. (1981). *Mathematical basis of statistics*. Academic Press, New York.

[22] BASMANN R.L. (1957). A classical method of linear estimation of coefficients in a structural equation. *Econometrica*, 25, 77–83.

[23] BAUWENS L., LUBRANO M., RICHARD J.F. (1999). *Bayesian inference in dynamic econometric models*. Oxford University Press, New York.

[24] BERA A.K., GARCIA P., ROH J.S. (1997). Estimation of time-varying hedge ratios for corn and soybeans: BGARCH and random coefficient approaches. *The Indian Journal of Statistics*, Series B, 59, 346–368.

[25] BERA A.K., HIGGINS M.L. (1992). A test for conditional heteroskedasticity in time series models. *Journal of Time Series Analysis*, 13, 6, 501–519.

[26] BERA A.K., HIGGINS M.L. (1993). ARCH models: properties, estimation and testing. *Journal of Economic Surveys*, 7, 305–366.

[27] BERA A.K., NG P.T. (1991). Robust test for heteroskedasticity and autocorrelation using score function. Mimeo, Department of Economics, University of Illinois at Urbana-Champaign.

[28] BERAN J. (1994). *Statistics for long memory process*. Chapman and Hall, New York.

[29] BERNDT E.R., HALL B.H., HALL R.E., HAUSMAN J.A. (1974). Estimation and inference in nonlinear structural models. *Annals of Economic and Social Measurement*, 3, 653–665.

[30] BEVERIDGE S., NELSON C.R. (1981). A new approach to decomposition of economic time series into permanent and transitory components with particular attention to measurement of the business cycle. *Journal of Monetary Economics*, 7, 151–174.

[31] BIERENS H.J. (1993). Higher order autocorrelations and the unit root hypothesis. *Journal of Econometrics*, 57, 137–160.

[32] BIERENS H.J. (1994). *Topics in advanced econometrics – Estimation, testing and specification of cross-section and time series models*. Cambridge University Press, New York.

[33] BIERENS H.J. (1997). Testing the unit root hypothesis against non linear trend stationary, with an application to the price level and interest rate in the US. *Journal of Econometrics*, 81, 29–64.

[34] BIERENS H.J. (1997). Non parametric cointegration analysis. *Journal of Econometrics, 77,* 379–404.

[35] BIERENS H.J., GUO S. (1993). Testing stationarity and trend stationarity against the unit root hypothesis. *Econometric Reviews, 12,* 1–32.

[36] BILLINGSLEY P. (1968). *Convergence of probability measures.* John Wiley & Sons, New York.

[37] BOLLERSLEV T. (1986). Generalized autoregressive heteroscedasticity. *Journal of Econometrics,* 31, 307–327.

[38] BOLLERSLEV T. (1987). A conditionnally heteroskedastic time series model for speculative prices and rates of return. *Review of Economics and Statistics,* 69, 542–547.

[39] BOLLERSLEV T. (1990). Modelling the coherence in short run nominal exchange rates: a multivariate generalized ARCH model. *Review of Economics and Statistics,* 72, 498–505.

[40] BOLLERSLEV T., CHOU R.Y., KRONER K.F. (1992). ARCH modeling in finance: a review of the theory and empirical evidence. *Journal of Econometrics,* 52, 5–59.

[41] BOLLERSLEV T., ENGLE R.F., NELSON D.B. (1994). ARCH models. In ENGLE R.F. and MCFADDEN D.L. (Eds.). *Handbook of Econometrics,* Volume IV (pp. 2959–3037), Elsevier Science, New York.

[42] BOLLERSLEV T., ENGLE R.F., WOOLDRIDGE J.M. (1988). A capital asset pricing model with time varying covariances. *Journal of Political Economy,* 96, 116–131.

[43] BOSQ D. (1996). *Nonparametric statistics for stochastic processes.* Springer-Verlag, New York.

[44] BOSQ D., LECOUTRE J.P. (1992). *Analyse et prévision des séries chronologiques, Méthodes paramétriques et non paramétriques.* Masson.

[45] BOSWIJK H.P. (1994). Testing for an unstable root in conditional and structural error correction models. *Journal of Econometrics, 63,* 37–60.

[46] BOSWIJK H.P. (1995). Efficient inference on cointegrating parameters in structural error correction models. *Journal of Econometrics, 69,* 133–158.

[47] BOUGEROL P., PICARD N. (1992). Stationarity of GARCH processes and of some non-negative time series. *Journal of Econometrics,* 52, 115–128.

[48] BOX G.E.P., JENKINS G.M. (1976). *Time series analysis: forecasting and control.* Holden-Day, San Francisco.

[49] BREITUNG J. (2002). Non parametric tests for unit roots and cointegration. *Journal of Econometrics,* 108, 343–364.

[50] BREUSCH T., PAGAN A. (1979). A simple test for heteroscedasticity and random coefficient variation. *Econometrica,* 47, 1287–1294.

[51] BROCKWELL P.J., DAVIS R.A. (1987). *Time series theory and methods.* Springer-Verlag, New York.

[52] CARRASCO M. (1995). Économétrie des modèles dynamiques avec ruptures. PhD thesis in applied mathematics, Université des Sciences Sociales de Toulouse.

[53] CARRASCO M. (2002). Misspecified Structural Change, Threshold, and Markov-Switching Models. *Journal of Econometrics,* 109, 2, 239–273.

[54] CARRASCO M., CHEN X. (2002). Mixing and Moment Properties of Various GARCH and Stochastic Volatility Models. *Econometric Theory,* 18, 1, 17–39.

[55] CARRASCO M., FLORENS J.P. (2000). Generalization of GMM to a continuum of moment conditions. *Econometric Theory,* 16, 797–834.

[56] CARRASCO M., FLORENS J.P. (2002). Simulation based method of moments and efficiency. *Journal of Business and Economic Statistics*, 20, 482–492.

[57] CARRASCO M., FLORENS J.P., RENAULT E. (2004). Linear inverse problems in structural econometrics: estimation based on spatial decomposition and regularization. Working paper, GREMAQ, University of Toulouse. Forthcoming in HECKMAN J.J. and LEAMER E.E. (Eds.). *Handbook of Econometrics*, Vol. 6.

[58] CAULET R., PEGUIN-FEISSOLLE A. (2000). Un test d'hétéroscédasticité conditionnelle inspiré de la modélisation en termes de réseaux neuronaux artificiels. *Annales d'économie et de statistique*, 59, 177–197.

[59] CHAN K.S. (1990). Testing for Threshold autoregression. *The Annals of Statistics*, 18, 1886–1894.

[60] CHAN W.S., TONG H. (1986). On tests for nonlinearity in a time series analysis. *Journal of Forecasting*, 5, 217–228.

[61] CHOI I. (1999). Testing the random walk hypothesis for real exchange rates. *Journal of Applied Econometrics*, 14, 293–308.

[62] COX D.R. (1961). Tests of separate families of hypothesis. Proceedings of the Fourth Berkeley Symposium on Mathematical Statistics and Probability 1, The University of California Press, Berkeley.

[63] COX D.R. (1962). Further results on tests of separate families of hypotheses. *Journal of the Royal Statistical Society*, Series B, 24, 406–424.

[64] COX D.R., OAKES D. (1984). *Analysis of survival data*. London, Chapman and Hall.

[65] COX D.R., MILLER H.D. (1965). *The theory of stochastic processes*. Methuen & Co Ltd, London.

[66] DACUNHA-CASTELLE D., DUFLO M. (1982). *Probabilités et statistiques 1: Problèmes à temps fixe*. Masson.

[67] DACUNHA-CASTELLE D., DUFLO M. (1983). *Probabilités et statistiques 2: Problèmes à temps mobile*. Masson.

[68] DANIELSON J., RICHARD J.F. (1993). Accelerated gaussian importance sampler with application to dynamic latent variable models. *Journal of Applied Econometrics*, 8, S153–S173.

[69] DAROLLES S., FLORENS J.P., RENAULT E. (2002). Nonparametric instrumental regression. Working paper, GREMAQ, University of Toulouse.

[70] DAVIDSON J.E.H. (1994). *Stochastic limit theory*. Oxford University Press, New York.

[71] DAVIDSON R., MACKINNON J.G. (1987). Implicit alternatives and the local power of test statistics. *Econometrica*, 55, 1305–13329.

[72] DAVIDSON R., MACKINNON J.G. (1993). *Estimation and inference in econometrics*. Oxford University Press, New York.

[73] DAVIDSON R., MACKINNON J.G. (1999a). Bootstrap testing in nonlinear models. *International Economic Review*, 40, 487–508.

[74] DAVIDSON R., MACKINNON J.G. (1999b). The size distortion of bootstrap tests. *Econometric Theory*, 15, 361–376.

[75] DAVIDSON R., MACKINNON J.G. (2002a). Bootstrap J tests of nonnested linear regression models. *Journal of Econometrics*, 109, 167–193.

[76] DAVIDSON R., MACKINNON J.G. (2002b). Fast double bootstrap tests of nonnested linear regression models. *Econometric Reviews*, 21, 417–427.

[77] DAVIDSON R., MACKINNON J.G. (2004). *Econometric theory and methods*. Oxford University Press, New York.

[78] DAVIES R.B. (1977). Hypothesis testing when a nuisance parameter is present only under the alternative. *Biometrika*, 64, 247–254.

[79] DAVIES R.B. (1987). Hypothesis testing when a nuisance parameter is present only under the alternative. *Biometrika*, 74, 33–44.

[80] DE GROOT M.H. (2004). *Optimal statistical decisions*. John Wiley & Sons, New York.

[81] DELLACHERIE C., MEYER P.A. (1978). *Probabilities and potential*. North Holland, Amsterdam.

[82] DELLACHERIE C., MEYER P.A. (1982). *Probabilities and potentials B*. North Holland, Amsterdam.

[83] DEMOS A., SENTANA E. (1998). Testing for GARCH effects: a one-sided approach. *Journal of Econometrics*, 86, 97–127.

[84] DEMPSTER A.P., LAIRD N.M., RUBIN D.B. (1977). Maximum likelihood from incomplete data via the EM algorithm. *Journal of the Royal Statistical Society* Series B, 39, 1–38.

[85] DEVROYE L. (1985). *Non-uniform random variate generation*. Springer-Verlag, New York.

[86] DICKEY D.A., FULLER W.A. (1979). Distribution of the estimators for autoregressive time series with a unit root. *Journal of the American Statistical Association*, 74, 427–431.

[87] DICKEY D.A., FULLER W.A. (1981). Likelihood ratio statistics for autoregressive time series with a unit root. *Econometrica*, 49, 4, 1057 1072.

[88] DIEBOLD F.X., PAULY P. (1988). Endogeneous risk in portfolio-balance rational expectations model of the Deutschmark-Dollar rate. *European Economic Review*, 32, 27–53.

[89] DONSKER M.D. (1951). An invariance principle for certain probability limit theorems. *Memoirs of the American Mathematical Society*, 6, 1–12.

[90] DOOB J. (1953). *Stochastic processes*. John Wiley & Sons, New York.

[91] DOUKHAN P., OPPENHEIM G., TAQQU M. (2003). *Memory and applications of long range dependence*. Birkhaüser, Boston.

[92] DUFFIE D., SINGLETON K. (1993). Simulated moments estimation of Markov models of asset prices. *Econometrica*, 61, 929–952.

[93] DUFOUR J.M. (1997). Some impossibility theorems in econometrics with applications to structural and dynamic models. *Econometrica*, 65, 6, 1365–1388.

[94] DUFRENOT G., MARIMOUTOU V., PEGUIN-FEISSOLLE A. (2004). Modeling the volatility of the US S&P500 index using an LSTGARCH model. *Revue d'économie politique*, 114, 4, 453–465.

[95] DUFRENOT G., MIGNON V., PEGUIN-FEISSOLLE A. (2004). Business cycles asymmetry and monetary policy: a further investigation using MRSTAR models. *Economic Modelling*, 21, 1, 37–71.

[96] DURBIN J. (1954). Errors in variables. *Review of the International Statistical Institute*, 22, 23–32.

[97] ELBERS C., RIDDER G. (1982). True and spurious duration dependence: the identifiability of the proportional hazard model. *Review of Economic Studies*, 49, 403–440.

[98] ELIOT G., ROTHENBERG T.J., Stock J.H. (1992). Efficient tests of an autoregressive unit root. NBER Technical Paper 130.

[99] ENGLE R.F. (1982). Autoregressive conditional heteroskedasticity with estimates of the variance of United Kingdom inflation. *Econometrica*, 50, 987–1007.

[100] ENGLE R.F. (1983). Estimates of the variance of US inflation based on the ARCH model. *Journal of Money, Credit and Banking*, 15, 3, 286–301.

[101] ENGLE R.F., BOLLERSLEV T. (1986). Modeling the persistence of conditional variances (with comments and response). *Econometric Reviews*, 5, 1–87.

[102] ENGLE R.F., GONZALES-RIVERA G. (1991). Semiparametric ARCH models. *Journal of Business and Economic Statistics*, 9, 345–3589.

[103] ENGLE R.F., GRANGER C.W.J. (1987). Cointegration and error cointegration. Representation, estimation and testing. *Econometrica*, 55, 251–276.

[104] ENGLE R.F., HENDRY D.F., RICHARD J.F. (1983). Exogeneity. *Econometrica*, 51, 277–304.

[105] ENGLE R.F., HENDRY D.F., TRUMBLE D. (1985). Small-sample properties of ARCH estimators and tests. *Canadian Journal of Economics*, 18, 66–93.

[106] ENGLE R.F., LILIEN D.M., ROBINS R.P. (1987). Estimating time varying risk premia in the term structure: the ARCH-M model. *Econometrica*, 55, 391–407.

[107] FAIR R.C., JAFFEE D.M. (1972). Methods of estimation for markets in disequilibrium: a further study. *Econometrica*, 42, 497–514.

[108] FAN J., GIJBELS I. (1992). Variable bandwidth and local linear regression smoothers. *Annals of Statistics*, 20, 2008–2036.

[109] FAN J., GIJBELS I. (1996). *Local polynomial modeling and applications*. Chapman and Hall, London.

[110] FISHER F.M. (1959). Generalization of the rank and order conditions for identifiability. *Econometrica*, 27, 3 431–447.

[111] FISHER F.M. (1961a). On the cost of approximate specification in simultaneous equation estimation. *Econometrica*, 29, 2, 139–170.

[112] FISHER F.M. (1961b). Identifiability criteria in nonlinear systems. *Econometrica*, 29, 4, 574–590

[113] FLORENS J.P. (2003). Inverse problem and structural econometrics: the example of instrumental variables. In DEWATRIPONT M., HANSEN L.P. and TURNOVSKY S.J. (Eds.). *Advances in economics and econometrics, theory and applications, Eight World Congress*, Vol. II (p. 284–310).

[114] FLORENS J.P., FOUGERE D. (1996). Noncausality in continuous time. *Econometrica*, 64, 5, 1195–1212.

[115] FLORENS J.P., HECKMAN J.J. (2001). Econometrics, counterfactuals and causal models. Invited lecture at the 12th EC^2 conference, Louvain-la-Neuve.

[116] FLORENS J.P., HECKMAN J.J., MEGHIR C., VYTLACIL E.J. (2003). Instrumental variables, local instrumental variables and control functions. Working paper, GREMAQ, Université des Sciences Sociales, Toulouse.

[117] FLORENS J.F., HENDRY D., RICHARD J.F. (1996). Encompassing and specificity. *Econometric Theory*, 12, 620–656.

[118] FLORENS J.P., IVALDI M., LARRIBEAU S. (1996). Sobolev estimation of approximate regressions. *Econometric Theory*, 12, 753–772.

[119] FLORENS J.P., LARRIBEAU S. (1996). Derivative consistent estimation of a misspecified regression. Working paper, GREMAQ, Université des Sciences Sociales, Toulouse.

[120] FLORENS J.P., MALAVOLTI L. (2003). Instrumental regression with discrete endogeneous variables. Working paper, GREMAQ, Université des Sciences Sociales, Toulouse.

[121] FLORENS J.P., MOUCHART M. (1982). A note on noncausality. *Econometrica*, 50, 583–592.

[122] FLORENS J.P., MOUCHART M. (1985a). A linear theory for non causality. *Econometrica*, 53, 1, 157–176.

[123] FLORENS J.P., MOUCHART M. (1985b). Conditioning in dynamic models. *Journal of Time Series*, 6, 1, 15–35.

[124] FLORENS J.P., MOUCHART M. (1993). Bayesian testing and testing bayesian. In MADDALA G.S., RAO C.R. and VINOD H.D. (Eds.). *Handbook of Statistics*, Vol. 11 (pp. 303–334), Elsevier Science, New York.

[125] FLORENS J.P., MOUCHART M., RICHARD J.F. (1979). Specification and inference in linear models. CORE Discussion Paper 7943, Université Catholique de Louvain, Belgique.

[126] FLORENS J.P., MOUCHART M., ROLIN J.M. (1990). *Elements of bayesian statistics*. Marcel Dekker, New York.

[127] FLORENS J.P., PROTOPOPESCU C., RICHARD J.F. (2002). Identification and estimation of a class of game theory models. Working paper, GREMAQ, Université des Sciences Sociales, Toulouse.

[128] FLORENS J.F., ROLIN J.M. (1996). Bayes, bootstrap moments. Working paper, GREMAQ, Université des Sciences Sociales, Toulouse.

[129] FOATA D., FUCHS A. (1996). *Calcul des probabilités*. Masson, Paris.

[130] FOMBY T.B., HILL R.C., JOHNSON S.R. (1984). *Advanced econometric methods*. Springer-Verlag, New York.

[131] FRISCH R. (1934). Statistical confluence analysis by means of complete regression systems. Working paper, Universitets Økonomiske Institutt, Oslo.

[132] FRISCH R. (1938). Statistical versus theoretical relations in economic macrodynamics. Working paper, Cambridge University.

[133] FULLER,W.A. (1996). *Introduction to statistical time series*. 2nd edition, John Wiley & Sons, New York.

[134] GALLANT A.R. (1987). *Nonlinear statistical model*. John Wiley & Sons, New York.

[135] GALLANT A.R., HSIEH D., TAUCHEN G. (1991). On fitting a recalcitrant series: the Pound/Dollar exchange rate. In BARNETT W., POWELL J., TAUCHEN G. (Eds.). *Nonparametric and semiparametric methods in econometrics and statistics*, Cambridge University Press, New York.

[136] GALLANT A.R., NYCHKA R. (1987). Semi-nonparametric maximum likelihood estimation. *Econometrica*, 55, 363–390.

[137] GALLANT A.R., TAUCHEN G. (2003). Efficient methods of moments. Working paper, Duke University.

[138] GALLANT A.R., WHITE H. (1988). *A unified theory of estimation and inference for nonlinear dynamic models*. Oxford, Basil Blackwell.

[139] GARCIA R. (1998). Asymptotic null distribution of the likelihood ratio test in markov switching models. *International Economic Review*, 39, 3, 763–788.

[140] GOLDFELD S.M., QUANDT R.E. (1965). Some tests for homoskedasticity. *Journal of the American Statistical Association*, 60, 539–547.

[141] GOURIEROUX C. (1989). *Économétrie des variables qualitatives*. Economica.

[142] GOURIEROUX C., JASIAK J. (2001). *Financial econometrics: problems, models and methods*. Princeton University Press, Princeton.

[143] GOURIEROUX C., LAFFONT J.J., MONFORT A. (1980). Disequilibrium econometrics in simultaneous equations systems. *Econometrica*, 48, 75–96.

[144] GOURIEROUX C., MONFORT A. (1996a). *Statistics and econometric models* (2 volumes). Cambridge University Press, New York.

[145] GOURIEROUX C., MONFORT A.(1996b). *Simulation-based econometric method*. CORE Lectures, Oxford University Press.

[146] GOURIEROUX C., MONFORT A., TROGNON A. (1983). Testing nested or non-nested hypotheses. *Journal of Econometrics*, 21, 83–115.

[147] GOURIEROUX C., MONFORT A., RENAULT E. (1993). Indirect inference. *Journal of Applied Econometrics*, 8, 85–118.

[148] GRANGER C.W.J. (1969). Investigating causal relations by econometric models and cross-spectral methods. *Econometrica*, 37, 424–438.

[149] GRANGER C.W.J. (1980). Long memory relationships and the agregation of dynamics models. *Journal of Econometrics*, 14, 227–238.

[150] GRANGER C.W.J., JOYEUX R. (1980). An introduction to long memory times series. *Journal of Times Series Analysis*, 15–30.

[151] GRANGER C.W.J., TERASVIRTA T. (1993). *Modelling nonlinear economic relationships*. Oxford University Press.

[152] GREENE W.H. (1999). *Econometric analysis*. MacMillan, New York.

[153] HALL P. (1992). *The bootstrap and Edgeworth expansions*. Springer-Verlag, New York.

[154] HALL A. (1993). Some aspects of Generalized Method of Moments estimation. In MADDALA G.S., RAO C.R. and VINOD H.D. (Eds.). *Handbook of statistics*, Vol. 11, Elsevier Science Publishers.

[155] HAMILTON J.D. (1989). A new approach to the econometric analysis of nonstationary time series and the business cycle. *Econometrica*, 57, 2, 357–384.

[156] HAMILTON J.D. (1990). Analysis of times series subject to changes in regime. *Journal of Econometrics*, 45, 39–70.

[157] HAMILTON J.D. (1993). Estimation inference, and forecasting of time series subject to changes in regime. In MADDALA G.S., RAO C.R., and VINOD H.D. (Eds.). *Handbook of Statistics*, Vol 11, North Holland.

[158] HAMILTON J.D. (1994). *Time series analysis*. Princeton University Press, New York.

[159] HANNAN E.J. (1970). *Multiple time series*. John Wiley & Sons, New York.

[160] HANSEN B.E. (1992). Tests for parameter instability in regression with I(1) processes. *Journal of Business and Economic Statistics*, 10, 321–335.

[161] HANSEN L.P. (1982). Large sample properties of Generalized Method of Moments estimators. *Econometrica*, 50, 1029–1054.

[162] HANSEN L.P. (1985). A method of calculating bounds on the asymptotic covariance matrices of generalized method of moments estimators. *Journal of Econometrics*, 30, 203–238.

[163] HANSEN L.P., Singleton K.J. (1982). Generalized instrumental variables estimators of nonlinear rational expectations models. *Econometrica*, 50, 1269–1286.

[164] HARDLE W. (1990). *Applied nonparametric regression*. Cambridge University Press, New York.

[165] HAUSMAN J.A. (1978). Specification tests in econometrics. *Econometrica*, 46, 1251–1272.

[166] HECKMAN J.J. (1979). Sample selection bias as a specification error. *Econometrica*, 47, 5, 153–161.

[167] HECKMAN J.J. (1997). Instrumental variables: a study of implicit behavioral assumptions in one widely used estimator. *Journal of Human Ressources*, 33, 3, 447–463.

[168] HECKMAN J.J., HONORE B. (1990). The empirical content of the Roy model. *Econometrica*, 58, 5, 1121–1149.

[169] HECKMAN J.J., ICHIMURA H., SMITH J., TODD P. (1998). Characterizing selection bias using experimental data. *Econometrica*, 66, 5, 1017–1098.

[170] HECKMAN J.J., ROBB R. (1985). Alternative methods for evaluating the impact of interventions. In HECKMAN J.J. and SINGER B. (Éds.). *Longitudinal analysis of labor market data* (pp. 156–245), John Wiley & Sons, New York.

[171] HECKMAN J.J., SINGER B. (1984). Econometric duration analysis. *Journal of Econometrics*, 24, 1–2, 63–132.

[172] HECKMAN J.J., VYTLACIL E. (2005). Structural equations, treatment effects, and econometric policy evaluation. *Econometrica*, 73, 3, 669–738.

[173] HENDRY D.F. (1984) Monte-Carlo experimentations in econometrics. In GRILICHES Z. and INTRILIGATOR M.D., *Handbook of Econometrics*, Vol. II (pp. 937–976), North Holland, Amsterdam.

[174] HENDRY D.F. (1995). *Dynamic econometrics*. Oxford University Press, Oxford.

[175] HIGGINS M.L., BERA A.K. (1992). A class of nonlinear ARCH models. *International Economic Review*, 33, 137–158.

[176] HOLLY A. (1982). A remark on Hausman's specification test. *Econometrica*, 50, 749–759.

[177] HOLLY A., MONFORT A. (1986). Some useful equivalence properties of Hausman's test. *Economics Letters*, 20, 39–43.

[178] HOROWITZ J.L. (1998). *Semiparametric methods in econometrics*. Springer-Verlag, New York.

[179] HSIEH D.A. (1989a). Modeling heteroscedasticity in daily foreign-exchange rates. *Journal of Business and Economic Statistics*, 7, 307–317.

[180] HSIEH D.A. (1989b). Testing for nonlinear dependence in daily foreign exchange rate changes. *Journal of Business*, 62, 339–368.

[181] HUBER P. (1967). The behavior of the maximum likelihood estimation under non-standard conditions. *Proceedings of the 5th Berkeley Symposium*, 221–234.

[182] JOHANSEN S. (1988). Statistical analysis of cointegrated vectors. *Journal of Economic Dynamics and Control*, 12, 231–254.

486   **Bibliography**

[183] JOHANSEN S. (1991). Estimation and hypothesis testing and cointegrating vectors in gaussian vector autoregressive model. *Econometrica*, 59, 1551–1580.

[184] JOHANSEN S. (1994). The role of the constant and linear terms in cointegration analysis of non stationary variables. *Econometric Reviews*, 13, 205–229.

[185] JOHANSEN S. (1995). *Likelihood-based inference in cointegrated vector auto-regression models*. Oxford University Press, Oxford.

[186] JOHANSEN S., JUSELIUS K. (1990). Maximum likelihood estimation and inference on cointegration: with applications to the demand for money. *Oxford Bulletin of Economics and Statistics*, 52, 169–210.

[187] JOHANSEN S., MOSCONI R., NIELSEN B. (2000). Cointegration analysis in the presence of structural breaks in the deterministic trends. *Econometrics Journal*, 3, 216–249.

[188] JOHNSON N.L., KOTZ S. (1970). *Continuous univariate distributions*. Vol. 1 and 2, Houghton-Mifflin, Boston.

[189] JORION P. (1988). On jump processes in the foreign exchange and stock markets. *Review of Financial Studies*, 1, 427–445.

[190] JUDGE G.G., GRIFFITHS W.E., HILL R.C., LUTKEPOHL H., LEE T.C (1985). *The theory and practice of Econometrics*. John Wiley & Sons, New York.

[191] JUDGE G.G., HILL R.C., GRIFFITHS W.E., LUTKEPOHL H., LEE T.C. (1988). *Introduction to the theory and practice of econometrics*. John Wiley & Sons, New York.

[192] KARLIN S. (1950). Operator treatment of minimax principle. In KUHN H.W. and TUCKER A.W. (Eds.). *Contributions to the theory of games* (pp. 133–154), Princeton University Press, Princeton.

[193] KITAMURA Y., STUTZER M. (1997). An information-theoretic alternative to generalized method of moments estimation. *Econometrica*, 65, 4, 861–874.

[194] KLEIN R.W., SPADY R.H. (1993). An efficient semiparametric estimator for binary response models. *Econometrica*, 61, 387–421.

[195] KLOEK T., VAN DIJK H.K. (1978). Bayesian estimates of equation system parameters: an application of integration by Monte-Carlo. *Econometrica*, 46, 1–19.

[196] KOOPMANS T.C. (1949). Identification problems in economic model construction. *Econometrica*, April 1949.

[197] KOOPMANS T.C. (Ed.) (1950). *Statistical inference in dynamic economic models*. Cowles Commission Monograph 10, John Wiley & Sons, New York.

[198] KRONER K.F., CLAESSENS S. (1991). Optimal dynamic hedging portfolios and the currency composition of external debt. *Journal of International Money and Finance*, 10, 131–148.

[199] KRONER K.F., SULTAN J. (1991). Exchange rate volatility and time varying hedge ratios. In RHEE S.G. and CHANG R.P. (Eds.). *Pacific-basin capital markets research*, Volume 11, North Holland, Amsterdam.

[200] KWIATKOWSKY D., PHILLIPS P.C.B., SCHMIDT P., SHIN Y. (1992). Testing the null hypothesis of stationnarity against the alternative of a unit root: how sure we are that economic time series have a unit root. *Journal of Econometrics*, 54, 159–178.

[201] LAFFONT J.J., GARCIA R. (1977). Disequilibrium econometrics for business loans. *Econometrica*, 45, 1187–1204.

[202] LAFFONT J.J., OSSARD H., VUONG Q. (1995). Econometrics of first price auctions. *Econometrica*, 63, 953–980.

[203] LAFFONT J.J., VUONG Q. (1993). Structural econometric analysis of decending auctions. *European Economic Review*, 37, 329–341.

[204] LANCASTER T. (1990). *The econometric analysis of transition data*. Cambridge University Press, New York.

[205] LAURANCE A.J., LEWIS P.A.W. (1980). The exponential autoregressive moving average EARMA(p,q) process. *Journal of the Royal Statistical Society*, B, 42, 150–161.

[206] LAURANCE A.J., LEWIS P.A.W. (1985). Modelling and residual analysis of nonlinear autoregressive time series in exponential variables (avec discussions). *Journal of the Royal Statistical Society*, B, 47, 165–202.

[207] LEE J.H., KING M.L. (1991). A locally most mean powerful based score test for ARCH and GARCH regressions disturbances. *Journal of Business and Economic Statistics*, 11, 17–27.

[208] LEE T.K.Y., TSE Y.K. (1991). Term strucure of interest rate in the Singapore Asian Dollar market. *Journal of Applied Econometrics*, 6, 143–152.

[209] LEVIN A., LIN C.F., CHU C.-S. (2002). Unit root tests in panel data: asymptotic and finite sample properties. *Journal of Econometrics*, 108, 1–24.

[210] LUBRANO M., MARIMOUTOU V. (1988). Bayesian specification searches. *Les cahiers du CERO*, 30, 4, 201–223.

[211] LUTKEPOHL H. (1993). *Introduction to multiple time series analysis*. 2nd edition, Springer-Verlag, New York.

[212] LUUKKONEN R. (1990). Estimating smooth transition autoregressive models by conditional least squares. In LUUKKONEN R. (Ed.). *On linearity testing and model estimation in non-linear time series analysis*, Helsinki, Finnish Statistical Society.

[213] LUUKKONEN R., SAIKKONEN P., TERASVIRTA T. (1988a). Testing linearity in univariate time series models. *Scandinavian Journal of Statistics*, 15, 161–175.

[214] LUUKKONEN R., SAIKKONEN P., TERASVIRTA T. (1988b). Testing linearity against smooth transition autoregressive models. *Biometrika*, 75, 3, 491–499.

[215] LUUKKONEN R., TERASVIRTA T. (1991). Testing linearity of economic time series against cyclical asymmetry. *Annales d'économie et de statistique*, 20/21, 125–142.

[216] MALINVAUD E. (1980). *Statistical methods of econometrics*. North Holland, Amsterdam.

[217] MATYAS L., SEVESTRE P. (Eds.) (2004). *The econometrics of panel data*. 3rd edition. Kluwer Academic Publishers, Dordrecht.

[218] McFADDEN D. (1989). A method of simulated moments for estimation of discrete response models without numerical integration. *Econometrica*, 57, 995–1026.

[219] METIVIER M. (1972). *Notions fondamentales de la théorie des probabilités*. Dunod.

[220] MIZON G.E., RICHARD J.F. (1986). The encompassing principle and its application to testing non-nested hypotheses. *Econometrica*, 54, 6567–6678.

[221] MONFORT A. (1980). *Cours de probabilités*. Economica.

[222] MONFORT A. (1982). *Cours de statistiques mathématiques*. Economica.

[223] MOOD A.M., GRAYBILL F.A. (1963). *Introduction to the theory of statistics*. McGraw-Hill, New York.

[224] MOORE H.L. (1914). *Economic cycles: their law and cause*. MacMillan, New York.

[225] NAKAMURA M., NAKAMURA A. (1981). On the relationships among several specification error tests presented by Durbin, Wu and Hausman, *Econometrica*, 49, 1583–1588.

[226] NELSON D.B. (1990). Stationnarity and persistence in the GARCH(1,1) model. *Econometric Theory*, 6, 318–334.

[227] NELSON D.B. (1991). Conditional heteroscedasticity in asset returns: a new approach. *Econometrica*, 59, 347–370.

[228] NELSON D.B., Cao C.Q. (1992). Inequality constraints in the univariate GARCH model. *Journal of Business and Economic Statistics*, 10, 229–235.

[229] NEVEU J. (1965). *Mathematical foundations of the calculus of probability*. Holden-Day.

[230] NEVEU J. (1975). *Discrete-parameter martingales*. North Holland, Amsterdam.

[231] NEWEY W.K. (1993). Efficient estimation of models with conditional moment restrictions. In G.S. MADDALA, C.R. RAO and H.D. VINOD (Eds.). *Handbook of Statistics*, Vol. 11, Elsevier Science Publishers, Amsterdam.

[232] NEWEY W.K., McFADDEN D. (1994). Large sample estimation and hypothesis testing. In R.F. ENGLE and D.L. McFADDEN (Eds.). *Handbook of Econometrics*, Vol. 4 (pp. 2111–2245), North Holland, Amsterdam.

[233] NEWEY W.K., POWELL J. (2003). Instrumental variables for nonparametric models. *Econometrica*, 71, 1565–1578.

[234] NEWEY W.K., POWELL J., VELLA F. (1999). Nonparametric estimation of triangular simultaneous equations models. *Econometrica*, 67, 565–604.

[235] NEWEY W.K., WEST K.D. (1987a). A simple, positive semi-definite, heteroskedasticity and autocorrelation consistent covariance matrix. *Econometrica*, 55, 703–708.

[236] NEWEY W.K., WEST K.D. (1987b). Hypothesis testing with efficient method of moments estimators. *International Economic Review*, 28, 777–787.

[237] NEYMAN J., PEARSON E.S. (1928). On the use and interpretation of certain test criteria for purposes of statistical inference. *Biometrika*, 20A, 175–240, 263–2954.

[238] NICHOLLS D. (1976). The efficient estimation of vector linear time series models. *Biometrika*, 63, 381–390.

[239] OGAKI M. (1993). Generalized method of moments: econometric applications. In G.S. MADDALA, C.R. RAO and H.D. VINOD (Eds.). *Handbook of Statistics*, Vol. 11, Elsevier Science, Amsterdam.

[240] OSTERWALD-LENUM M. (1992). A note on quantiles of the asymptotic distribution of the maximum likelihood cointegration rank test statistics. *Oxford Bulletin of Economics and Statistics*, 54, 461–472.

[241] PAARSCH H.J. (1992). Deciding between the common and private value paradigms in empirical models of auctions. *Journal of Econometrics*, 51, 191–215.

[242] PAGAN A. (1996). The econometrics of financial markets. *Journal of Empirical Finance*, 3, 15–102.

[243] PAGAN A., ULLAH A. (1999). *Nonparametric econometrics*. Cambridge University Press, New York.

[244] PAKES A., POLLARD D. (1989). Simulation and the asymptotics of optimization estimators. *Econometrica*, 57, 1027–1058.

[245] PEARL J. (2000). *Causality: models, reasoning, and inference*. Cambridge University Press, New York.

[246] PEGUIN-FEISSOLLE A. (1994). Bayesian estimation and forecasting in nonlinear models: application to an LSTAR model. *Economics Letters*, 46, 187–194.

[247] PEGUIN-FEISSOLLE A. (1999). A comparison of the power of some tests for conditional heteroscedasticity. *Economics Letters*, 63, 1, 5–17.

[248] PERRON P. (1988). Trends and random walks in macroeconomic time series: further evidence from a new approach. *Journal of Economics Dynamics and Control*, 12, 297–332.

[249] PERRON P. (1989). The great crash, the oil price and the unit root hypothesis. *Econometrica*, 57, 1361–1402.

[250] PERRON P. (1990). Testing the unit root in a time series with a changing mean. *Journal of Business and Economics Statistics*. Vol. 8(2), 153–162.

[251] PESARAN M.H., SMITH R. (1995). Estimating long run relationships from dynamic heterogeneous panels. *Journal of Econometrics*, 68, 79–113.

[252] PESARAN M.H., SHIN Y., SMITH R. (1999). Pooled mean group estimation of dynamic heterogeneous panels. *Journal of American Statistical Association*, 94, 621–634.

[253] PHAM-DINH T. (1975). *Estimation et tests dans les modèles paramétriques des processus stationnaires*. PhD thesis, The University of Grenoble, France.

[254] PHILLIPS P.C.B. (1987). Time series regression with a unit root. *Econometrica*, 55, 277–301.

[255] PHILLIPS P.C.B. (1991). Optimal inference in cointegrated system. *Econometrica*, 59, 283–306.

[256] PHILLIPS P.C.B. (2001). Descriptive econometrics for non stationary time series with empirical application. *Journal of Applied Econometrics*, 389–413.

[257] PHILLIPS P.C.B., HANSEN B. (1990). Statistical inference in instrumental variables regression with I(1) processes. *Review of Economic Studies*, 57, 99–125.

[258] PHILLIPS P.C.B., MOON H.R. (1999). Linear regression limit theory for non stationary panel data. *Econometrica*, 67, 1057–1111.

[259] PHILLIPS P.C.B., MOON H.R. (2000). Non stationary panel data analysis: an overview and some recents developments. *Econometric Reviews*, 263–286.

[260] PHILLIPS P.C.B., PARK J. (2000). Non stationary binary choices. *Econometrica*, 68, 1249–1280.

[261] PHILLIPS P.C.B., PARK J. (2001). Non linear regressions with integrated time series. *Econometrica*, 69, 21–27.

[262] PHILLIPS P.C.B., PERRON P. (1988). Testing for a unit root in time series regression. *Biometrika*, 75, 335–346.

[263] PHILLIPS P.C.B., SUL D. (2003). Dynamic panel estimation and homogeneity testing under cross section dependance. *Econometrics Journal*, 6, 217–259.

[264] PHILLIPS P.C.B., XIAO Z. (1998). A primer on unit root testing. *Journal of Economics Survey*, 612, 5, 423–469.

[265] PITMAN E.J.G. (1949). Notes on non-parametric statistical inference. Miméo, Columbia University, New York.

[266] PRIESTLEY M.B. (1991). *Non-linear and non-stationary time series analysis*. Academic Press.

[267] QUAH D. (1994). Exploiting cross section variation for unit root inference in dynamic data. *Economics Letters*, 44, 9–19.

[268] RAO C.R. (1948). Large sample tests of statistical hypotheses concerning several parameters with applications to problems of estimation. *Proceedings of the Cambridge Philosophical Society*, 44, 50–57.

[269] RAOULT J.P. (1975). *Structures statistiques*. PUF, Paris.

[270] REIERSOL O. (1941). Confluence analysis of lag moments and other methods of confluence analysis, *Econometrica*, 9, 1–24.

[271] REIERSOL O. (1945). Confluence analysis by means of instrumental sets of variables. *Arkiv for Mathematik, Astronomie och Fysik*, 32.

[272] REIERSOL O. (1950a). Identifiability of a linear relation between variables which are subject to error. *Econometrica*, 18, 4, 375–389.

[273] REIERSOL O. (1950b). On the identifiability of parameters in Thurstone's multiple factor analysis. *Psychometrika*, 15, 121–149.

[274] REINSEL G.C. (1993). *Elements of multivariate analysis*. Springer Series in Statistics, Springer-Verlag, New York.

[275] RICHARD J.F. (1996). Simulation techniques in the econometrics of panel data. In MATYAS L. and SEVESTRE P. (Eds.). *The econometrics of panel data*, 3rd edition. Kluwer Academic Publishers, Dordrecht.

[276] RICHARD J.F., ZHANG W. (1996). Econometric modelling of UK house prices using accelerated importance sampling. *The Oxford Bulletin of Economics and Statistics*, 58, 601–613.

[277] RICHARD J.F., ZHANG W. (2000). Accelerated Monte-Carlo integration: an application to dynamic latent variable models. In MARIANO R., SCHUERMANN T. and WEEKS M.J. (Eds.). *Simulation-based inference in econometrics*, Cambridge University Press, New York.

[278] RIEDER H. (1994). *Robust asymptotic statistics*. Springer-Verlag, New York.

[279] SAID S.E, DICKEY D.A. (1984). Testing for unit roots in autoregressive moving average of unknown order. *Biometrika,* 71, 599–607.

[280] SAID S.E. (1991). Unit root test for time series data with a linear trend. *Journal of Econometrics,* 47, 285–303.

[281] SAMORODNITSKY G., TAQQU M. (1995). *Stable non gaussian random processes stochastic models with infinite variance*. Chapman and Hall, New York.

[282] SARGAN J.D. (1958). The estimation of economic relationships using instrumental variables. *Econometrica*, 26, 393–415.

[283] SCHMIDT P., PHILLIPS P.C.B. (1992). LM tests for a unit root in the presence of deterministic trends. *Oxford Bulletin of Economics and Statistics*, 54, 257–287.

[284] SCHWARZ G. (1978). Estimating the dimension of a model. *Annals of Statistics*, 6, 461–464

[285] SCHWARTZ L. (1992). *Analyse. Calcul différentiel et équations différentielles*. Hermann, Paris.

[286] SERFLING R.J. (1980). *Approximation theorems of mathematical statistics*. John Wiley & Sons, New York.

[287] SEVESTRE P. (2002). *Économétrie des données de panel*. Dunod, Paris.

[288] SILVERMAN B.W. (1986). *Density estimation for statistics and data analysis*. Chapman and Hall, London.

[289] SIMS C.A. (1972). Money, income and causality. *American Economic Review*, 62, 540–552.

[290] SIMS C.A. (1980). Macroeconomics and reality. *Econometrica*, 48, 1–48.

[291] SIMS C.A., STOCK J.H., WATSON M.W. (1990). Inference in linear time series models with some unit roots. *Econometrica*, 58, 113–144.

[292] SPANOS A. (1986). *Statistical foundations of econometric modelling*. Cambridge University Press, Cambridge.

[293] STOCK J.H., WATSON M.W. (1988) Testing for common trends. *Journal of the American Statistical Association*, 83, 1097–1107.

[294] STOCKER T.M. (1991). *Lectures on semiparametric econometrics*. Core Lecture Series, Oxford University Press, Oxford.

[295] TAUCHEN G.E. (1986). Statistical properties of generalized method of moments estimators of structural parameters obtained from financial market data (with discussion and response). *Journal of Business and Economic Statistics*, 4, 397–424.

[296] TAUCHEN G.E., PITTS M. (1983). The price variability-volume relationship on speculative markets. *Econometrica*, 51, 485–505.

[297] TERASVIRTA T. (1994). Specification, estimation and evaluation of smooth transition autoregressive models. *Journal of the American Statistical Association*, 89, 208–218.

[298] TERASVIRTA T., ANDERSON H.M. (1992). Characterizing nonlinearities in business cycles using smooth transition autoregressive models. *Journal of Applied Econometrics*, 7, S119–S136.

[299] THEIL H. (1953). Repeated least squares applied to complete equations systems; Central Planning Bureau (mimeo), The Hague.

[300] TODA H.Y., McKENZIE C.R. (1999). LM tests for unit roots in the presence of missing observations: small sample evidence. *Mathematics and Computers in Simulation*, 48, 4–6, 457–468.

[301] TONG H. (1990). *Nonlinear time series. A dynamical system approach*. Clarendon Press, Oxford.

[302] TSYBAKOV A.B. (2004). *Introduction à l'estimation non paramétrique*. Springer-Verlag, New York.

[303] VAN DER VAART A.W., WELLNER J.A. (1996). *Weak convergence of the empirical processes with application to statistics*. Springer-Verlag, New York.

[304] WALD A. (1943). Tests of statistical hypothesis concerning several parameters when the number of observations is large. *Transactions of the American Mathematical Society*, 54, 426–482.

[305] WAND M.P., JONES M.C. (1995). *Kernel smoothing*. Chapman and Hall, London.

[306] WHITE J.S. (1958). The limiting distribution of the serial correlation coefficient in the explosive case. *Annals of Mathematical Statistics*, 29, 1188–1197.

[307] WHITE H. (1980). A heteroskedasticity-consistent covariance matrix estimator and a direct test for heteroskedasticity. *Econometrica*, 48, 817–838.

[308] WHITE H. (1982). Maximum likelihood estimation of misspecified models. *Econometrica*, 50, 1–26.

[309] WHITE H. (1994). *Estimation, inference and specification analysis*. Cambridge University Press, New York.

[310] WORKING H. (1925). The statistical determination of demand curves. *The Quarterly Journal of Economics*, Vol 39, N.4., 503–543.

[311] WORKING E.J. (1927). What do statistical demand curves show? *The Quarterly Journal of Economics*, Vol 41, N. 2, 212–235.

[312] WU D.M. (1973). Alternative tests of independence between stochastic regressors and disturbances. *Econometrica*, 41, 733–750.

[313] ZELLNER A. (1962). An efficient method of estimating seemingly unrelated regressions, and tests for aggregation bias. *Journal of the American Statistical Association*, 57, 348–368.

[314] ZELLNER A., PALM F. (1974). Time series analysis and simultaneous equation econometric models. *Journal of Econometrics*, 2, 17–54.

Index